A Documentary History of Communism

A Documentary History of Communism

edited, with introduction,
notes and new translations,
by ROBERT V. DANIELS

RANDOM HOUSE · NEW YORK

First Printing

 Published in New York by Random House, Inc., and simultaneously in Toronto, Canada, by Random House of Canada, Limited.

Library of Congress Catalog Card Number: 60-6380

Manufactured in the United States of America by the Colonial Press, Inc.

Preface

It would naturally be impossible in one volume of documentary materials to cover a subject as broad and complex as communism from every point of view. The careful description of political institutions, events and everyday life as they have proceeded over the years under communism would require whole shelves of source materials. The present work has been deliberately focused on the subject of Communist thought and doctrine, for reason of its commanding importance, its relative uniformity within the Communist scheme of things, and the appropriateness of the documentary approach to its elucidation. We will be primarily concerned with the evolution of top-level guiding ideas, policies and intentions among the Communists. Statements of deviators of all sorts are included along with the official line of those in power—we may regard anyone who claims descent from Lenin as equally meriting the label "Communist." Through the pronouncements of its leading figures, both those who have ruled and those who have fallen from grace, we may arrive at a reasonably approximate picture of what communism actually is, historically considered.

The problems of selecting materials for a purpose such as this never permit a fully satisfactory solution. I have attempted a fair digest and representative choice of statements expressing all the main concepts and currents in communism. Many readers, however, will find that their areas of interest are under-represented. This failing is the price that must be paid in an effort to survey the entire Communist movement in one documentary volume, and meet the needs of the student, the general reader, and the scholar who is not a specialist in this field.

The present work would never have materialized without

the assistance of the many people who helped in its preparation or who paved the way with their own studies. I am indebted to the many publishers who kindly permitted me to reprint selections of previously translated material (individually acknowledged under each item). Certain documentary collections which have been particularly helpful deserve special mention—the pioneering *Documentary History of Chinese Communism,* by Conrad Brandt, Benjamin Schwartz and John K. Fairbank (Harvard University Press, 1952); the *Materials for the Study of the Soviet System,* by James H. Meisel and Edward S. Kozera (The George Wahr Publishing Co., Ann Arbor, Michigan, 1950), which brings together a wide selection of previously translated Soviet documents; the documentary compilations prepared by the Legislative Reference Service of the Library of Congress; the various collections of Soviet documents published by the Stanford University Press; and the English editions of the selected works of Lenin and Stalin, published by the Foreign Languages Publishing House in Moscow. The Harvard University Library has kindly permitted me to include my translations from a number of hitherto unpublished documents in the Trotsky Archive. For their suggestions regarding documents on Far Eastern communism I am indebted to Professors Justus M. van der Kroef and George T. Little, and to Professor Little and Professor Lewis S. Feuer I am grateful for many helpful criticisms. To Mr. Nathan Glazer I wish to express my appreciation for initially encouraging me to undertake this project, and for his editorial assistance since that time. Mrs. Joyce McLaughlin of the Inter-Library Loan Department of the University of Vermont Library rendered me invaluable service in locating and obtaining many scarce but important publications. The vast work of transcribing and assembling the documentary materials was ably done by Mrs. Madeline Chaplin, Mrs. Jean Falls, Mrs. Phyllis Reservitz, Mrs. Roberta Stetson, and my wife, Alice Daniels.

Contents

Introduction: The Evolution of the Communist Mind

The subject of this work is the world-wide movement which was initially brought into being by Vladimir Ilich Lenin when he organized his Bolshevik faction of Russian revolutionaries in the years 1902-1904. Earlier doctrines and movements going under the name "communism" are not of concern except as they were relevant to the thinking of the specific contemporary Communist movement founded by Lenin and developed in Russia after the revolution of 1917. This applies particularly to the philosophy of Marx and Engels, of which Russian communism was by no means a simple, uncomplicated application (nor the only school of followers, for that matter). Marxism is of interest here insofar as, and only so far as, it contributed to Communist thought, policies and problems. By itself, Marxism is wholly inadequate either to define or explain the Communist movement.

The Communist Movement and Communist Doctrine

There is one essential point on which the whole matter of the correct understanding of communism rests. Contrary to every assertion, the Communist movement is not truly described by its doctrine. Broadly speaking, the doctrine is a picture of history, past, present and future, which gives the present movement that definite place which was forecast by the original authors of the picture a century ago. Very strong doubts can be cast upon the present validity of the picture as a whole. But it can be shown beyond any reasonable question that within the terms of the Marxist picture itself, the present Communist movement does not occupy the place which its official spokesmen ascribe to it. As a picture of Communist society and a map of its intentions, Communist doctrine is not a free and honest approach to the apprehension of reality, but a forced political imposition.

It is accordingly necessary for anyone who wants to understand communism to look beneath the doctrine and to question all the assumptions which it casts in the way of a clear view. The lack of correspondence between theory and reality will then become readily apparent. This divergence of statement and fact is actually one of the basic features of the Communist movement as it now exists, and it dictates in turn another prime Communist characteristic—the institution of complete control of communication and expression, in order to sustain the irrelevant theoretical picture which it is in the nature of communism to demand. The Communist mentality can be described in essence as a compulsively self-justifying opportunism, where the leaders assume full freedom of action but insist on squaring every step with the holy verities of Marxism-Leninism.

Since Communist doctrine has been so far abstracted from reality, it can well be asked why the doctrinal statements of the movement are worth studying. What, indeed, can be the value of putting forth a collection of Communist ideological pronouncements like the present one, if the real nature of the movement is neither expressed nor governed by its doctrine? Taken at their face value these doctrinal statements can be quite misleading; the reader must bear in mind the context and learn the habit—essential to every student of communism—of reading between the lines. Doctrine has always been extremely important to the Communist movement, though for a long time not in its literal sense. An awareness of the evolving use and reinterpretation of doctrine is basic in appreciating how the movement has developed. The documents are thus primarily useful for the pursuit of historical understanding, which is the only way to comprehend how the movement acquired the paradoxical characteristics which it now displays.

Marx and the Russians

Communist thought cannot be understood apart from Marx, but neither can it be understood on a simple, unqualified

Marxist basis. The intellectual origins of the movement must be approached as an interaction of Marx's ideas and the political and intellectual setting of pre-revolutionary Russia in which they took root. The circumstances in which Marxism became popular in Russia in the 1890's belie the expectations of the theory itself. Russia was not a capitalistic country with a proletariat ripe for revolution; it was just beginning to experience the change and dislocation which accompany the initial stages of industrialization. For decades, however, Russia had possessed a class of energetic and articulate intellectuals who devotedly embraced each new radical or utopian idea that came to them from Europe. Marx himself recognized this fashion among the Russians, and commented sardonically that they "always run after the most extreme that the West can offer. . . . This does not prevent the same Russians, once they enter State service, from becoming rascals." * Revolutionary elements among the Russian intelligentsia were primed to respond to any revolutionary doctrine from the West. When Marxism became known to them, they devotedly embraced it in large numbers.

The intellectual success of Marxism had nothing to do with its logical applicability to Russia. It was difficult to apply it at all, as Marx realized: "The 'historical necessity' of . . . capitalist production . . . is explicitly restricted to the *countries of Western Europe.*" ** Rigorously construed —as Marx's Russian disciples construed it—Marxism could give scant hope for an early proletarian revolution in Russia. The expectation for a country at the Russian stage of development was a "bourgeois-democratic revolution" and an extended period of capitalistic industrial development, before Russia would follow the socialist course that her West-European neighbors were supposed to initiate. For the immediate future Marxism would serve more appropriately as an ideological justification of capitalism, and in fact the

* Marx to Kugelman, October 1, 1868, in *Letters to Dr. Kugelman* (New York, International Publishers, 1934), pp. 77-78.

** Marx to Vera Zasulich, March 8, 1881, in Blackstock and Hoselitz, eds., *The Russian Menace to Europe* (Glencoe, Illinois, The Free Press, 1952), p. 278.

theory did have considerable appeal in Russia on just this basis, among the so-called "legal Marxists."

Among the revolutionaries in Russia, Marxism could not appeal on logical grounds. People did not become revolutionary after an intellectual conversion to the Marxian historical analysis. They became Marxists—in Russia as everywhere else—because they were revolutionary for prior emotional reasons and because Marxism appealed to them on emotional grounds as a pseudo-scientific rationale for revolution. Logical inconsistency was no obstacle. Marxism in Russia has from the very beginning neatly fit Marx's own definition of ideology as "false consciousness"—a set of ideas used without concern for truth or consistency to rationalize the interests and aims of a particular social group. Marxism became the "ideology" of a large part of the revolutionary Russian intelligentsia. Since the revolution it has fulfilled the same function for the ruling Communist Party.

Lenin, in this context, represents simply the clearest and most extreme example of emotional commitment to Marxism in disregard of its incongruence in Russia. Lenin had grown up with the burning revolutionary ardor so familiar among the scions of the educated gentry. He embraced Marxism with religious devotion, as the ultimate word in human affairs, almost as a supernatural prophecy which no mortal could dare question or modify without committing the sin of blasphemy. Despite this dogmatism, however, Lenin was quite capable of ignoring or violating Marxian principles when it came to the actual formulation of revolutionary programs and tactics. Lenin's program and tactics did not come from Marx at all, but from his own emotional make-up as a member of the Russian revolutionary intelligentsia, and from the previous traditions of the revolutionary movement in Russia. Lenin's Marxism was superimposed upon his Russianism, to supply the terminology and conviction of righteous inevitability.

While we cannot understand Lenin as a Marxist, the study of his theoretical pronouncements and his tactical statements does contribute basic understanding about the Communist movement. What we have to deal with is in reality a new doctrine—Leninism—which, while observing the Marxian language and professing spiritual continuity from Marx, actually contradicted him in many vital respects. Leninism as a system of belief has had a very profound effect in shaping the Communist movement, and so it is the natural starting point for any analysis of modern communism.

The Premises of Leninism

Lenin's political thinking rested on two cardinal assumptions, neither of which bore any logical relation to Marxism. One of these implicit beliefs was his conception of the overall nature of the historical process: that history is made in the last analysis not by classes or the forces of production, but by willful individual leaders and by ideas. This was an outlook he shared with practically all pre-Marxist Russian social thinkers. Lenin had assimilated it so deeply that he was scarcely conscious of its import, so that he could go right on resting his thought on such an assumption while he imagined himself to be a perfectly orthodox Marxist. Time and again Lenin railed against "spontaneity" and proclaimed the vital role of "consciousness." He made it abundantly clear that he never expected the working class to carry out a revolution by itself. Only the deliberate leadership of dedicated "professional revolutionaries" like himself could bring the event about.

In his emotional orientation toward revolution Lenin shared a trait with the unscientific aspect of Marx's outlook which did not follow logically from his theoretical system. This was what might be called the moral imperative of revolution. Lenin, like Marx, was dedicated to the anticipated revolution as a moral absolute, as a sort of purgative judgment day which would extirpate all the evil in the old way of life, and usher in the millenium. For both Marx and Lenin, all questions of good and evil hinged on the ultimate question of revolution. They differed, however, in the manner in which they sustained their hopes about revolution. Marx's solution was that of pseudo-scientific inevitability; having committed himself to the moral necessity for the revolutionary reconstruction of society, he proceeded to work out an elaborate, sweeping, in many respects brilliant system of social analysis which purported to prove the inevitability of that prospective upheaval: the relentless dialectic of historical materialism would sooner or later raise the chosen class of proletarians to the seats of power.

Lenin followed all this verbally, but the actual foundation which he established for his revolutionary goal was in fact diametrically opposed to Marx's. For Lenin the revolution was not inevitable at all; it had to be brought about by the deliberate action of conscious revolutionaries, *against* the natural flow of history. If the spontaneous forces of history were not interfered with, Lenin implied, the moral imperative of revolution would never become a reality. Hence it was on willful revolutionaries, sustained by a sense of moral duty, that Lenin had to rest his hopes. How guarantee, however, that the revolutionaries would keep striving in the right direction against the frustrating spontaneity of the passive herd? Lenin's answer was the same on which any religious movement relies to assure individual rectitude: the proper doctrine, the true faith.

The proper doctrine was Marxism as read by Lenin. Any questioning of the doctrine or of Lenin's own interpretation of it—in fact, any independence of mind at all—not only disqualified a member of the revolutionary movement but classified him irretrievably with the enemies of the revolution, as far as Lenin was concerned. Lenin and his followers were sustained by an absolute faith in Marx's revolutionary prophecy, with all its pseudo-science of dialetical inevitability. It mattered not that the doctrine of inevitability contradicted the philosophy of will and idea which all of Lenin's political practice implied, for the Bolsheviks were revolutionaries before they were Marxists. They displayed the Calvinistic paradox of people who believed in a foreordained future but who, thanks to this belief, were all the more vigorously determined on individual action to make that future come true. The psychological truth here is that people with a strong emotional impulse toward a given goal are irrationally inclined to embrace a doctrine that says that that goal is inevitably going to be realized.

The emotional commitment to strive mightily for a revolution that was regarded as inevitable had significant moral implications for the Bolsheviks: it allowed them to conclude without qualms that the end justifies any means. Like the Russian extremists who preceded them, the Bolsheviks regarded the revolution as the all-decisive event, the leap from the kingdom of Evil to the kingdom of Good. Nothing had any value or made any sense except in relation to the revolution. But the revolution could not be passively awaited, according to the Bolshevik philosophy; it required a total commitment and the utmost exertion by those morally committed to it to make it a reality. Therefore, it was morally binding upon the adherents of revolution to employ every expedient means, not excepting violence, falsehood, robbery and treachery, to prepare and consummate the revolutionary victory. All such questionable tactics could be utilized with equanimity because the expected revolution would be all-decisive in governing the high moral level of the new society; it would wipe away any evil effects of evil means presently used.

The grave defect in this reasoning was the lack of assurance that the revolution—i.e., the right kind of revolution, the real revolution—would actually follow from the revolutionaries' action and offset the expedient evils employed by them. How know that the present evil means would assuredly procure the future good? For this foundation to their righteousness the Bolsheviks had to depend on the Marxian inevitability of the proletarian revolution and the classless society. However, it was precisely the lack of real conviction about such inevitability that required them to adopt evil expedients in the first place. Far from being corrected in the revolution which actually took place, the Bolsheviks' system of violent, authoritarian and deceitful expedients rapidly became an end in itself; it is now the basis of the Communist social order.

The Party as the Instrument of Revolution

The major contribution which Lenin made to the theory and practice of communism was by way of implementing his belief in the moral imperative of a historically uncertain revolution. He had to have reliable means for accomplishing a problematical political goal, and he found them in a feature which had been a distinguishing trait of the earlier Russian revolutionary movements—the stress on conspiratorial organization, the revolutionary party. The party represents the essence of Leninism.

The function of the party, as Lenin conceived it, was to force the revolution to occur, against all the resistance of the old order. The party would overcome the impracticality of the intellectuals and the formless spontaneity of the masses, and drive for a victory which otherwise would never materialize. For this instrument of revolution Lenin had in mind forms of organization, dictated both by the circumstances of the political underground and by his own proclivities, from which he never deviated. First of all, the party was to be a narrow organization, not the mass of like-minded sympathizers, but the active and conscious minority, the professional revolutionaries. This was the specific issue over which the factional split of the Russian Social Democrats into Bolsheviks and Mensheviks began in 1903. For the accomplishment of its revolutionary objective Lenin required that this minority organization be constituted on military lines, with a hierarchy of command and binding discipline upon its members. The formula which he proposed to guide the party organization was "democratic centralism," meaning the democratic determination of policy and the centralized execution of it. In practice, however, Lenin could brook no expression of policy contrary to his own thinking; any one who differed with Lenin found himself attacked as "opportunist" or "petty bourgeois," an unreliable element if not a potential traitor to the revolutionary cause. Lenin recognized none as genuine proletarian Marxists save those who unreservedly followed his own leadership. Thus, while the notion of a one-party dictatorship was never explicitly formulated before the Bolsheviks came to power, the exclusion of all who differed had already been long implicit in the monopoly of revolutionary morality which in practice Lenin ascribed to himself.

There is irony in the fact that when the Bolsheviks took power in October, 1917, the Leninist rigor of their organization was at its lowest point, the party having been diluted with hundreds of thousands of new members and many new leaders like Trotsky who had never committed themselves to the principles of Bolshevik discipline. A spontaneous mass upheaval and the enthusiasm of the party members—forces which Lenin had distrusted or discounted—were responsible much more than organization and narrow discipline for the Bolshevik success. It was only through a step-by-step process in the years following the revolution that the organization of the party was tightened up to approximate Lenin's old ideal, with the major imposition of discipline coming in 1921, after the crisis of civil war had been weathered. The great difference now was in the function which the party had to play—not the underground conspiracy aiming to get the revolution started, but the exclusive association of people engaged in ruling the state. Never anticipated, this new role for the disciplined party was to constitute the backbone of Communist totalitarianism.

Whose Revolution?

After Lenin had worked out his plan for the "proletarian" party as the instrument of revolution, he had to find a place for it to operate in the Marxian scheme of things as applied to Russia. The dilemma, as we have seen, was how to hold strictly to the Marxian prognosis of bourgeois revolution and still envision an opportunity to lead an anticapitalist mass revolutionary movement. Among most of Lenin's rivals in the Menshevik faction of the Social Democrats, a weaker emotional attachment to revolution was attested by their acceptance of the prospect of a "bourgeois-democratic" revolution and of a long period of capitalism after that, during which the workers' party could be nothing more than a legal opposition. Lenin, however, took the bull very boldly by the horns at the time of the revolutionary ferment of 1905, to declare that the bourgeois revolution could be carried through to its conclusion only by the party of the proletariat, because the bourgeoisie was not revolutionary enough. It did not occur to Lenin that this made mincemeat of the basic Marxian propositions governing the relationships of economic stages, class forces, and political movements. He blithely called for a "democratic dictatorship of the proletariat and peasantry," which would hold power until the capitalists prepared the industrial conditions for their own demise, after which the real dictatorship of the proletariat would confiscate the means of production and effectuate the transition to the socialist society.

There was another approach to the dilemma of Marxist revolution in Russia which avoided Lenin's violence to the doctrine and at the same time preserved the prospect of immediate revolutionary action by the workers and their leaders. This was the "theory of permanent revolution" expounded by Trotsky, a set of ideas which proved to be very important later on—in 1917 as the rationale for the Bolshevik seizure of power, and during the 1920's as a major subject of factional controversy among the Communists. Trotsky's view proceeded from the observation that Russia's economic development had been uneven, with some modern industry and a politically conscious working class surrounded by a vast majority of impoverished peasants mainly interested in owning more land. It would be natural, he suggested, for the bourgeois revolution to swing without any break in continuity (hence "permanent") into a proletarian phase where the workers as an energetic minority could temporarily take power. They would soon be in danger of falling before the "petty-bourgeois" (mainly peasant) majority, were it not for the international repercussions which Trotsky expected their momentary success to have. Supposedly the exploits of the revolutionary workers in Russia would provide the stimulus for the ripening forces of proletarian revolution elsewhere in the world, and the socialist upheaval would therefore proceed without interruption (again "permanent") on the international plane. Brotherly socialist states would hasten to succor the embattled proletarians of Muscovy and help raise the whole population of Russia to the industrial level where the advantages of socialism would be apparent to all.

Trotsky's theory gradually gained adherents in the years before 1917, and then, after the fall of the Czar in February, 1917, was startlingly borne out by events. "Bourgeois" revolution did indeed open the way for the proletarians and the party they supported to surge toward power; recognizing this, Lenin and most of the other Bolshevik leaders accepted Trotsky's reasoning in all but name. The Bolsheviks prepared to seize power in the fall of 1917, assuming that their social backing as well as the underdeveloped economy in Russia were not sufficient to sustain their program of socialist revolution, but with the conviction that their success of the moment would evoke the instantaneous response of international revolution. Some Bolsheviks (led by Zinoviev and Kamenev) were skeptical about the latter, and on this ground opposed the October coup d'état as an irresponsible gamble. Lenin, in contrast, demanded insurrection as a Russian duty to give the European workers the signal they needed. Implicit in all this was the irrational faith, inherited from mid-nineteenth-century Russian thinkers, in the efficacy of Russia's revolutionary mission to the world. The fact remains, however, that the Bolsheviks took power with a theoretical outlook which told them that their aims could not possibly be achieved in Russia without the assistance of like-minded revolutionary regimes in those advanced countries where socialism, according to Marxism, was supposed to begin first. Such help never came, and in its absence a drastic reconstruction of theory was required if the most embarrassing implications were to be evaded.

The Paradox of Marxian Socialism in Russia

It has sometimes been suggested that the successful proletarian revolution in Russia proved Marx wrong by showing that socialism could win without previous industrial development under capitalism. But if Marx's predictions cannot be relied upon, with what assurance can the revolution be described as "proletarian"? Actually the Soviet system has developed in an entirely different direction. The Marxist labels of proletarian socialism and the "workers' state" have been kept only for the sake of self-righteousness and propaganda—the "ideology" or "false consciousness" of the new post-revolutionary regime.

The step-by-step adaptations of Marxist theory after the establishment of the Soviet regime illustrate very clearly the impact of circumstances which forced the Communists to revamp their program. Within a matter of months after the October Revolution basic decisions had been made which fatally compromised the Marxian logic of the Communists' position. They kept power, but only by shifts of policy which changed the whole direction of their revolution and brought it into line with what Russian conditions permitted.

The first of these major policy changes was the decision in February, 1918, to make peace with Germany instead of proclaiming an international civil war against all the capitalist powers. The Bolsheviks' seizure of power had been predicated on the imminence of proletarian revolution in the West, which the Russian assault on the "imperialist" Provisional Government was supposed to evoke, and which in turn was presumably indispensable to sustain socialist hopes in Russia. Once in power, however, Lenin declined to gamble his position in the interests of world revolution; over the anguished protests of the left-wing utopians, he decided to make peace and buy time rather than risk losing power in Russia while attempting to set a fighting example for the European workers. In other words, his estimate of the revolutionary potential outside Russia had now dropped—but that estimate had been the only Marxist way of justifying his seizure of power in the first place. Lenin rejected the alleged possibility of immediately evoking international revolution, in the interest of holding power which could have no Marxian socialist meaning in the absence of that international revolution. This is how the Communists came to rule in a country where Marxism ruled out the success of the proletariat.

Following the peace of Brest Litovsk, during the period of civil strife and economic disruption which goes by the term "War Communism," the ranks of the Communist Party were torn repeatedly with dissension over the implications of holding power where conditions made the realization of the program of proletarian socialism, as theretofore conceived, entirely chimerical. Lenin had espoused the utopian program as firmly as anyone in the programmatic tract, "State and Revolution," which he wrote while hiding in Finland in 1917. The workers would seize power, subject the whole economy to their control, destroy the existing state machinery, and install new officials of their own choosing whose pay would be no higher than "workman's wages." The resistance of the former exploiting classes would be crushed, and the state—i.e., the organs of law-enforcement and repression—would commence to "wither away." The annihilation of authority and the apotheosis of equality were visions animating vast numbers of Russians, not excepting the Communists, during the revolutionary years.

By the spring of 1918, Lenin had turned emphatically against these attitudes on the ground of total impracticability for the foreseeable future (though the evidence of most of his career strongly suggests that he was emotionally set against anarchy and equality in any event). In the government, the army, the factories, the Communist Party, Lenin (joined by Trotsky) demanded an end to equalitarianism and collective decision-making, and called instead for the establishment of firm hierarchies of individual authority and responsibility with clear differentials of individual reward. Step by step the institutions of the new Soviet society were recast in the old mold. By 1921, with the elimination of the trade unions from industrial management, the abolition of factions within the Communist Party, and the enunciation of the "New Economic Policy" (NEP) with its concessions to the individual profit motive, the Communist leaders had completed their adaptation of a late-industrial program to early-industrial conditions.

The occasion for the introduction of the New Economic Policy was a growing state of economic crisis and mass dissatisfaction, coming to a head in armed rebellion against the Soviet regime. In the perspective of past revolutions this marked the point where the national convulsion of revolutionary emotion was subsiding in favor of growing demands for normal living. Revolutionary emotion among large numbers of people in Russia had sustained for a time the illusion that the immediate socialistic transformation of the country was still possible, whether or not strong authority and stringent controls were necessary to accomplish this. By early 1921, however, it was clear to Lenin and the more practical-minded Communists that power and program could not both be held to at the same time; again, as with the world revolution in 1918, one of these desiderata would have to be sacrificed, and again it was the program. Lenin, thanks to his compelling leadership and the strength of the party organization, was able to command the Communists to go into retreat, postpone their socialistic objectives, and come to terms with the realities of an underdeveloped country. In effect, he carried out his own "Thermidorean reaction" (by analogy with the fall of the Jacobins in France in 1794), and by adapting his party's policies from the stage of violent revolutionary emotion to the stage of post-revolutionary convalescence he was able to keep power.

This change was not effected, however, without serious difficulties within the ranks of the Communist Party. The utopians demanded that the party hew to the strictly idealist course, and began to attack Lenin for betraying the workers. Lenin, for his part, was determined to claim full Marxist justification for his compromising policy, and as was his custom, to condemn as un-Marxist anyone who took issue with him. At the Tenth Party Congress in March, 1921, Lenin used his control of the party organization to have the leftists condemned as a "petty-bourgeois" deviation, and to ban any recurrence of factional criticism.

It is interesting to note that the political and social situation in Russia after the introduction of the NEP in 1921 comes remarkably close to Lenin's old notion of the "democratic dictatorship of the proletariat and peasantry," with a self-styled party of the workers holding power but adapting its policies to the capitalistic necessities of industrial development. This arrangement, as we have seen, contradicts the basic Marxian proposition regarding the dependence of the political "superstructure" on the economic "base." The only way to salvage the Marxian analysis is to dismiss the "proletarian" label and regard the Communist politico-economic structure as an expression of industrialism in its developmental phase—not the successor of capitalism but a parallel alternative.

The transition to the New Economic Policy meant a major change as regards the vitality of Marxist theory among the Communists. Prior to this time they could still imagine that a lucky conjunction of circumstances in Russia was enabling them to proceed with the Marxian plan of proletarian dictatorship. After the "Thermidor" of 1921, when revolutionary hopes had to be suspended, the basic perspective was one of adaptation to the wrong conditions. The function of Marxist doctrine then had to shift from direct inspiration to the justification of a regime which no longer fit the requirements of the theory. In the language of Karl Mannheim, Marxism was changed from a "utopia" to an "ideology," from an inspirational illusion to a rationalization of actuality.* The defense of the "ideology" demanded stringent suppression of anyone who would again take the doctrine seriously as a "utopia" and hold it up as a challenge to the status quo; hence the necessity of rooting out the left-wing Communists and making the party line—the official interpretation of doctrine—an obligatory canon of faith. We have here, in the picture of the revolutionary party trying to explain away its conversion to a post-revolutionary role, the key to the mentality of total thought-control which was soon to become a permanent feature of the Communist system.

Although the Communist Party leaders claimed exclusive doctrinal sanction for their compromises of 1921, they remained for the time being aware that their policies were indeed expedients that did not point directly toward the ultimate socialistic goal. Concessions in the capitalistic or bureaucratic direction were recognized as such; they were simply regarded as practical necessities for the preservation of the power of the Communist Party until the industrial development of the country had proceeded to the point

* See Karl Mannheim, *Ideology and Utopia* (New York, Harcourt, Brace, n.d.), pp. 192 ff.

where the fully socialist ideal could be put into effect. The real fallacy here from the Marxist standpoint lay in the notion that there was value in the retention of power *per se* regardless of the social base with which the authorities had to operate. The concessions which the Communists had to make at the expense of their program bear out clearly the conditions which social circumstances can impose on a government. Furthermore, thanks to their habit of justifying each practical expedient in terms of basic Marxist doctrine, the Communists began to lose any clear notion of what the ultimate goal was, as opposed to the pattern of immediate expedients. As is so often the case in human affairs, it was the practical steps rather than the original intention or blueprint that determined the outcome: the means became ends in themselves.

Socialism in One Country

During the factional controversies in the Communist Party after Lenin's demise the most bitter debate raged around the theoretical implications of the anomaly of the self-styled proletarian socialist state in Russia. The Trotskyists, who had been forced out of their positions of influence in 1921-23, sought arguments to use against Stalin and the other more direct followers of Lenin who were endeavoring to follow the NEP compromise of economic leniency plus firm party control. It was easy for Trotsky and the Left Opposition to find lapses by the leadership from the strict proletarian path, and they stressed these with warnings that the isolation of the revolution in a backward country made it very difficult to sustain a socialist policy without great care and effort. They began to suggest that Stalin's leadership was the embodiment of a "Thermidorean reaction," yielding to the desires of the petty-bourgeois majority of the country.

Stalin's defense against this line of reasoning represents a major change in the intellectual status and political function of Communist doctrine, though its meaning has usually been misunderstood. To meet the challenge of the opposition Stalin looked to the scriptures for assurance that he could not possibly be in error and particularly that national backwardness was not a crippling embarrassment. He found what he sought in a statement made by Lenin in 1915, to the effect that the country first going over to socialism would stand alone and fight the others until the revolution spread. Taking this remark out of context, Stalin applied it to Russia and appealed to it as the authority for his contention that the socialist regime could stand alone in Russia whether or not it was sustained by international revolution. At the same time the party propaganda machine whipped up a storm over Trotsky's theory of permanent revolution, on the grounds of its pessimistic "lack of faith" in Russia's own revolutionary potential. Neither faction, it must be understood, rejected the world revolution as a Communist desideratum, while on the other hand neither was prepared to take great risks to bring it about. The issue in this respect was only over the implications for Russia of a delay in the world revolution: Trotsky said they were dangerous and required careful scrutiny of the existing leadership, and Stalin denied this.

The major significance of "socialism in one country" lay not with the Communist International, for which it made no difference, nor with the factional struggle among the Russian Communists, which was decided by organizational pressure, but with the meaning and role of Communist ideology as a whole. While it is pointless to debate whether Marxian socialism was really feasible in Russia (the whole experience of modern industrialism makes it appear more and more utopian), Stalin's manner of asserting the possibility of socialism is highly significant. He did not inquire empirically as to how the conditions of Russian life might be shaped in order to promote the ideal. (Bukharin did attempt this in some of his statements about the anticapitalist bent of the peasantry around the world.) Stalin preferred the scholastic method of turning to the scriptures for an authoritative statement that would give doctrinal sanction for what he was determined to do anyway. He did not base his action on an honest effort to understand and follow the doctrine as such; as his opposition critics irrefutably pointed out, he had distorted Lenin's meaning completely. Lenin had in mind the most advanced country, and had no intention of asserting the immediate possibility of socialism in an underdeveloped country. Stalin's maneuver was a purely casuistical trick, indicative of the determination which he and his like-minded associates felt to maintain absolute doctrinal justification of their rule. The new theory was a major step in the manipulation of doctrine to make it accord with action that was decided on pragmatically.

The immediate consequence of the doctrinal twisting represented by "socialism in one country" was the suppression of all criticism, political or otherwise, aimed at the leadership or its rationalizations. From the standpoint of any serious regard for the doctrine itself it was easy to expose the maneuvers of the party leadership, as the Trotskyist opposition clearly demonstrated. In fact the ideological embarrassment which the Trotskyists posed was a major reason why Stalin and Bukharin were led to the decision to expel them from the party and silence them altogether. Thenceforth, to uphold their suppression of criticism, the Soviet leaders had to assert the absolute right of the party to pass definitive judgment on any question whatsoever. In this manner the compulsive pursuit of self-justification led to the establishment of totalitarian thought-control soon after Stalin achieved personal rule in 1929.

The Industrialization Program and the Easternization of Communism

Simultaneously with the Stalin-Trotsky political struggle and the development of Communist dogmatism, the Russian leaders were beginning to face the implications of the actual conditions under which they ruled, i.e., the economic problems of an underdeveloped country. The problems were serious and acute, and the differences of opinion which they evoked added fuel to the flames of factional controversy. As it happened, however, it was the accidents of factional politics rather than any particularly convincing analysis that governed the response to the industrialization problem which Russia made under Stalin's direction.

After the introduction of the NEP, as we have seen, both the Stalin-Bukharin faction and the Trotsky faction were nervously concerned about the weakness of Russian society as the base for the dictatorship of the proletariat. The dominant group took the position of caution, relying on tight party controls together with a conciliatory policy toward the peasants to keep the Communists in power during the expected long period of gradual development of state-owned industry. This was the program for which "socialism in one country" was required as the doctrinal justification. On the other hand, Trotsky and his supporters, much less patient, were calling by 1923 for concerted economic planning and industrial development by the state, in order to rectify as quickly as possible the economic backwardness which, according to the earlier orthodoxy, made socialism in Russia a very insecure proposition. The Trotskyist position, however, made no more sense from the strictly Marxian point of view than did "socialism in one country"; in suggesting that the "workers' state" could rapidly create its own economic base of large-scale industry the Trotskyists turned Marx's conception of the relation of economics and politics completely upside down.

While the Trotskyist demand for deliberate, intensive industrialization defied the traditional preconceptions of Marxism, it was nonetheless of major significance for the future development of the Communist movement. Implied in the Trotsky approach was a fundamentally new conception of the historical role of the socialist organization of society. From the beginning of the socialist movement in the early nineteenth century socialist thinkers and parties had been almost exclusively concerned with the redistribution of existing wealth, the reapportionment on some more equitable basis of the proceeds from society's productive capacity. The productive capacity itself was taken for granted, either as a static quantity or (as Marx approached it) as the creature of capitalism prior to the establishment of socialism. The Trotskyists' great innovation was to apply the socialist system of a state-operated economy to the task of developing productive capacity. All previous schools of socialist thought, including Marx and Lenin, represented forms of what we might call "distributive" socialism. Trotsky's was the first school of "productive" socialism—the essentially un-Marxist idea that the socialist state could and should be used to promote industrialization and overcome the poverty of low productivity.

Ironically, the actual shift in the Communist movement from the distributive to the productive orientation was not accomplished by Trotsky but by his principal enemy. Until 1927, the party leadership headed by Stalin and Bukharin had steadfastly resisted Trotsky's demand for rapid, planned, tax-supported industrial development, in favor of gradual development financed mainly out of the profits made by Soviet industry while catering to the needs of the consuming public. By the end of 1927, however, when the factional struggle within the Communist Party had reached its climax with the expulsion of Trotsky and Zinoviev and their followers from the party's ranks, the party leadership had itself begun to move toward a somewhat more aggressive economic policy. Then, rapidly playing his hand with remarkable political finesse, Stalin commenced in 1928 to maneuver against his erstwhile colleagues in the party leadership, Bukharin, Rykov and Tomsky. Knowing that these men were committed to economic caution, Stalin abruptly took over the Trotskyist approach to industrialization and with it the plan of wholesale collectivization of the peasants (a step necessary to squeeze from them the unrecompensed surplus necessary to support the industrialization effort). Carefully representing his ideas as the continuation of established party policies, Stalin was able to take the protests made by Bukharin, Rykov and Tomsky as the pretext for having them condemned as a "right deviation" secretly favoring capitalism. With this Right Opposition group out of the way in 1929, Stalin found himself all-powerful but also all-responsible, and committed to an irrationally extreme program of intensive industrial development. He apparently saw no alternative except to forge ahead under the scarcely Marxian slogan, "There are no fortresses which Bolsheviks cannot storm."

With the industrialization program launched by Stalin, paid for by national belt-tightening and enforced by totalitarian police controls, Soviet Russia had entered into the new productive form of socialism. This was socialism not of the overripe industrial society but of a partially backward and preindustrial country, not the successor to capitalism but the alternative to it for accumulating the industrial plant to bring the country to a modern level of economic development. Soviet socialism served not to solve the problems of industrial life, but to accentuate them and to carry them afield into virgin territory.

The Soviet economic example has proved highly infectious, because it is such a logical and effective approach to the problem of developing a backward country. Even among non-Communist circles in Asia and Africa the notion of using the authority of the state to accelerate economic development has proved to one degree or another irresistible since World War II. Under Stalin's leadership, communism was converted from an essentially Western response to Western problems of industrial life under capitalism, to an essentially Eastern response of applying despotic state authority to the pursuit of rapid industrial development and equality with the West. By viewing Russia in the early part of this century as a hybrid society, part Western and part Eastern, partially industrialized yet substantially backward, we may understand why this transitional role of converting a Western revolutionary movement into an Eastern one fell to her. The product of this Russian alchemy was a unique system of oriental state capitalism.

Stalin and the Virtue of Necessity

The new productive emphasis on economic development had profound implications for other aspects of the Communist movement in Russia. It became necessary to make a wide variety of policy adjustments, converting the Western postcapitalist socialist ideal to the Eastern state-capitalist pattern. The many such adjustments already made, ostensibly as temporary concessions, had to be accepted as permanent.

Under Stalin's leadership the Communist Party adapted itself to the harsh realities of industrialization and of the industrial way of life—realities which made the social ideals professed by every Marxist up to 1917 completely utopian.

Contrary to Marx's egalitarian, anarchistic expectations, industrial society does not permit a diminution of hierarchical authority to the advantage of the democratic collective—it puts all the greater premium on the hierarchical division of labor and responsibility and on maintaining complex organizations in which everyone observes instructions with unflagging discipline. It was apparent by the 1930's that the real task for Russia was not the introduction of collectivist equality but the training of responsible leaders and responsible subordinates, to convert lackadaisical peasants into disciplined troops in an industrial army. The real Russian innovation was a new organizational basis for industrial development—the postcapitalistic institutions of the "managerial" society.

Discipline and authority in political and economic life, hateful as they had been from the standpoint of the Russian revolutionaries of 1917, had been substantially restored by the end of the Civil War period. Stalin's innovation was to declare them to be in effect on a practically permanent basis as positive aspects of the socialist ideal, and he further laid it down as the official line that socialism had never meant anything else. Similarly with the ideal of equality, which to some extent had continued to be observed up until 1929, Stalin declared it to be un-Marxist and un-Leninist, and justified inequality of economic rewards as a natural aspect of Soviet socialism. Between 1931 and 1937, for reasons of political practicality or personal preference, Stalin proceeded to reverse the party line on a wide range of policy matters, ranging from education and art to religion and the family. In every case the earlier revolutionary attitude was condemned as a "petty-bourgeois" deviation from Marxism, and what the outside world regarded as the conservative norm became the standard of official Communist belief and practice (except for religion, which enjoys toleration but is still officially disparaged). Together with these adjustments Stalin overhauled the basic political theory of Marxism by asserting the long-term positive role of the state in overcoming economic obstacles and developing the socialist society, instead of withering away. Stalin simply made his theory conform to what he had actually been doing, with the characteristic twist that the new version was alleged to have been the only correct interpretation of Marxism all along.

Stalin's transformation of the aims and practices of communism, was directly responsible for fundamental changes in the realm of Communist thinking, not only with respect to what was thought but with respect to the basic function of doctrine in the Communist system. The Communists faced circumstances where either the theoretical prerequisites of the old ideal were lacking (the weakness of the Russian industrial base), or where it became evident that those presumed preconditions were themselves not conducive to the ideal (the bureaucratic requirements of industry itself). Under Lenin the party made expedient adaptations to these circumstances, while still imagining that these were temporary maneuvers. Machinery of control was meanwhile set up over the channels of thought and communication, and was used to justify the necessity of the expedients. Stalin's changes were to pursue such expedients more freely, intensify the controls over public communication, and then to proclaim that his policies were not temporarily necessary deviations but the direct implementation of the revolutionary program. Instead of guiding Soviet practice, the goals of communism were redefined to conform with the trend that expedient practice had taken.

Paradoxically, as doctrine ceased to operate as a basic motive and guide, the stress laid by the Soviet regime on rigorous orthodoxy became all the greater. This has made it difficult for outside observers to appreciate how little Marxist theory really shapes Communist behavior. Its function is to provide the sense of revolutionary legitimacy which the Communist leaders since Lenin have always insisted on maintaining, and also to serve as the vehicle for party control over every aspect of life. The thoroughgoing control which requires this orthodoxy is in turn necessitated by the difficulty of bridging the vast gulf between theory and practice and suppressing the innumerable opportunities for criticizing the doctrinal manipulations in which the Communist regime has indulged. The Soviet leaders have long been committed to a self-enforcing false image of their system. In all probability they believe in this image, in a narrow-minded and defensive way, and will endeavor to sustain it at any cost, even though the real standards in their action are those of free-wheeling practicality rather than loyalty to the spirit of any theory. Communism has become wedded to a psychology of compulsively self-justifying opportunism, so dogmatically unscrupulous that it is not even faithful to its own principles.

The real meaning of communism is to be found in the pattern of evolution through expedients, in the course of which the movement was changed to deal with its circumstances. During the first two decades of the Soviet regime communism was systematically Easternized. It was converted into a system for solving the Eastern problems of rapid modernization and national self-assertion against the West, through the method of terror and compulsion wielded by an autocratic government. Subsequent replacement of leading personalities has made no fundamental difference in the system.

World Revolution or Imperialist Expansion

The commanding importance of the subject of communism is due to the international character of the movement. Up to this point we have dealt with the movement entirely as a Russian phenomenon, because its actual origins were Russian and the critical stages of its evolution were intimately shaped by Russian circumstances. From the time of its initial success in Russia, however, the movement has had an increasingly important impact on the rest of the world, in two principal ways: the power exercised by communism in Russia as the ruling movement in a large country, and the doctrinally-inspired, Russia-oriented Communist revolutionary movements which have appeared almost everywhere else in the world.

These two lines of influence suggest the basic duality which has characterized international communism. In part it is an international revolutionary movement ostensibly animated by Marx's vision of the world dictatorship of the proletariat. On the other hand, most of the time and in most places it has been firmly under the control of the rulers of Soviet Russia, who have not hesitated to employ the movement, in the short run at least, as an instrument for promoting the power and security of that particular state. There has been a definite trend from the first of these aspects to the second—from primitive revolutionary enthusiasm to calculated manipulation, with the power of the Russian state as a primary criterion. However, the old doctrine still contributes the basic sense of hostility toward the non-Communist world, which sometimes approaches the intensity of religious war.

World revolution, according to Marxism, was not a deliberate policy or duty (as many anxious opponents of the Communists imagine it to be), but merely a prediction of what the development of international capitalism supposedly made inevitable. For a person who does not accept the Marxian philosophy of history there is no particular reason for regarding the world-wide success of communism as inevitable or even possible. For one brief moment—the time of the controversy in 1918 over peace with Germany or revolutionary war—the Russian Communists were at the point of direct action to help the inevitable along, but Lenin's cautious counsel of preserving power in one country prevailed. Had the Trotskyists been victorious in the 1920's, with their stress on the importance of world revolution for the realization of the socialist plan in Russia, it is conceivable that the issue could have arisen again, but Stalin's ideological tour de force of "socialism in one country" eliminated all theoretical grounds for risking the security of the regime in Russia in order to advance the fortunes of the revolution abroad.

From 1918 to 1935, insofar as Russian national security was not risked, the Soviet leaders encouraged and assisted various Communist revolutionary movements abroad—notably in Germany and China—without questioning the identity of interest between Soviet Russia and the foreign revolutionaries. However, with the change of line to collective security and the "popular front" in 1935, the Soviet leadership temporarily suspended the revolutionary drive in international communism. From 1935 to 1939 and from 1941 to 1946 or

1947 the Communists in most places coöperated with liberal and socialist groups, and made a highly successful appeal as a party aiming at democratic reform and resistance to fascism, rather than the one-party proletarian dictatorship. During this period the Communists were distinguished only by the typical Leninist party organization and the unquestioning subservience to Russia which had been implanted in the international movement during the 1920's. A particularly dramatic demonstration of Communist preoccupation with the security of the Soviet state came with the Nazi-Soviet pact in 1939, which was concluded at the cost of a severe shock to Communist loyalties the world over.

The history of international communism since World War II has been governed by a complicated interaction between Communist-oriented revolutionary emotion in many countries and the aggressive and unscrupulous pursuit of power politics and national security by the Soviet Union, which has used the non-Russian Communist movements as much as possible as an instrument of this policy. Where communism has come to power outside Russia it has been through direct Russian imposition (as in most of Eastern Europe) or through guerilla warfare conducted by the Communists against both enemy occupation forces and domestic rivals (as in Yugoslavia and China). No purely internal and independent Communist revolution has ever been accomplished since the short-lived Hungarian Soviet Republic of 1919.

The vague Marxist conviction survives that eventually the Communist movement will inevitably triumph everywhere. Khrushchev plays this theme with great pride, but the very notion of inevitability absolves the Soviet leaders from the obligation to take any risks to which they do not feel emotionally inclined. The main theoretical source of their anxiety is the fear that the capitalist powers, seeing the ground slipping from under their feet, might resort to force in order to check the presumed historical trend toward communism. Non-Communists who do not believe this is the trend need have little to fear unless the Russians are provoked or tempted into preventive war by threats or weakness on the part of the anti-Communist powers.

The Export of Communism—Eastern Europe

The establishment of Communist governments in the Soviet Union's satellite states of Eastern Europe represents the outstanding Russian success in the employment of communism as an instrument of power politics. Everywhere that Soviet occupation regimes were in control—Poland, Rumania, Bulgaria, Hungary, East Germany—Communist Party dictatorships were installed in power with direct Russian backing and pressure, under the cover of the ostensibly democratic coalition governments established in the region when the Nazis collapsed in 1944-45. In these cases there was no significant popular revolutionary movement, and the Communists did not use a revolutionary appeal in driving for power; they preferred to work behind the scenes, penetrating (with the aid of Soviet leverage) the police and military organizations of the respective countries, and gradually constricting the opportunity for genuine legal opposition to their rule. By the end of 1947 the process was complete, though the dummy forms of multi-party coalition have survived to the present.

In marked contrast to this pattern in East Central Europe, the Communists came to power in Yugoslavia and Albania and scored their near-victory in Greece as active revolutionaries, waging guerrilla war simultaneously against the German and Italian occupying forces and against the native representatives of the status quo. When World War II ended, Communist Party rule was firmly established in Yugoslavia and Albania, without any appreciable Russian help.

Czechoslovakia stands somewhat apart, as the case where the Communist assumption of power most nearly resembled the original Bolshevik revolution in Russia. A large popular minority, animated not so much by revolutionary feeling as by reform aims and pro-Russian, anti-Nazi sentiment, had backed the Communists since the end of World War II; the Communist leader Gottwald was prime minister of a democratically functioning government. At the opportune moment, in February, 1948, the Communists precipitated a cabinet crisis; wielding the revolutionary force of a workers' militia and the threat of Russian intervention, they secured the support necessary for a parliamentary majority and overawed the opposition into nonresistance. Once they were in undisputed control of the government, it was an easy matter for the Communists to suppress the opposition altogether and proceed with the establishment of totalitarian controls.

The experience of communism in Eastern Europe has been particularly stressful because of the telescoped imposition of Soviet political development, under close Russian control and strictly subordinated to considerations of Russian national power. Within the short span of years from 1945 to 1950, Eastern Europe experienced military defeat or occupation, Communist maneuvering for power, the distribution of estates to the peasants, the nationalization of industry, the establishment of one-party dictatorship, the creation of totalitarian police controls and censorship, the beginnings of collectivization of the peasants, the establishment of Communist industrial discipline, the pursuit of heavy-industry construction programs at the expense of national belt-tightening, and purge trials within the Communist parties themselves—developments which were spread over two decades in Russia. These rapid changes were brought about mainly at Russian behest, to cement Communist control over the satellite countries and to facilitate Soviet economic exploitation of the region.

Despite the traditional Communist antagonism toward imperialism, Soviet Russia suffered neither moral nor economic impediments to the exploitation of regions under its control. Under the state capitalism of the USSR such exploitation of the "colonies" eased the problem of capital accumulation without constituting the threat to the level of employment which it would mean in an ordinary capitalist economy. The terms of "international proletarian solidarity" in which the Russians cloaked their operations might be regarded as a rationalization on a par with the "white man's burden."

The main problem in Eastern Europe, from the Russian standpoint, was to maintain control over the local Communists in the face of increasingly apparent divergence between Communist aims in each country and the economic and strategic interests of the Russians. All of the Communist leaders in Eastern Europe had risen in the movement by accepting Russian authority and the disciplined duty of supporting the interests of the Soviet state. Most of them, moreover, owed their acquisition and tenure of political power to the backing which the Russians gave the Communist Party in each country. Yugoslavia is the outstanding exception, where Tito assumed power independently as the leader of a successful revolutionary and resistance movement. Outside of Yugoslavia it is certain that no Communist government could survive in Eastern Europe without Russian backing.

Despite their obligations to the Russians, most East-European Communist leaders found themselves in conflict between what their own ambitions or the interests of their respective countries called for, and the requirements of the Russians. The Russians, declining to rely solely on the doctrinal loyalty of their East-European comrades, moved swiftly to establish more reliable controls over the satellites by infiltrating Russian agents directly into their police and military organizations. With all the lines of influence at the Russians' disposal it was easy in most cases for them to shake up any satellite leadership which was too independent-minded, and assure an unquestioning response to Moscow's demands.

Under these circumstances of Russian control there could be no independent development of doctrine or policy by the East European Communists. They were compelled to conform to the Soviet model of forced industrialization and total organizational control, although in the more developed and sophisticated countries like Czechoslovakia and Poland less utility and more discontent were inherent in these steps. Communist doctrine in its finished Soviet form as an elaborately fraudulent but rigorously enforced rationalization of the modernizing dictatorship was made the rule. It remained only for Soviet propagandists to demonstrate scholastically how Eastern Europe remained at a lower level of the dictatorship of the proletariat than the Soviet Union, in the form of the so-called "People's Democracies."

All of the most important events in Eastern Europe since 1948 have centered around the understandable tendency of local Communist leaders to resist Russian domination—i.e., the movement of "national communism." The basic consideration in national communism is simply the distribution of power within the Communist movement—shall the national regimes dictate in their own right or serve merely as agents of Moscow? The basic features of communism as developed in Russia—the party dictatorship, the quasi-capitalist economic function, and the rigid rationalizing doctrine—are for the most part carried over into national communism. However, the national Communists have characteristically tried to alleviate popular discontent by asserting national independence, suspending collectivization of the peasants, and scaling down industrial ambitions to permit a somewhat freer and more abundant economic life to the citizenry. In the economic caution which they combine with the party dictatorship the national Communist tendency in Eastern Europe is comparable to the Russian right-wing Communist faction led by Bukharin in the late 1920's. Beyond this, save for a modicum of uneasy cultural freedom, national communism has not yielded.

The initial success of national communism in Yugoslavia is easily understandable in terms of geography and the historical background. This was the satellite most defensible and most accessible to the non-Communist world, and at the same time one where the Communists had come to power without decisive Russian assistance. By inclination Tito was a thoroughly orthodox Communist, Stalin's most successful pupil in Eastern Europe, but his emulation of Stalin proceeded so far that he would brook no challenge to his own authority, not even from Stalin himself. When Russian efforts to penetrate the Yugoslav army and police assumed dangerous proportions by 1948, Tito undertook both protests and counter-measures. The Soviet reply was to expel Yugoslavia from the community of Communist states. This showed that in Stalin's eyes genuine communism could not exist without unquestioning subordination to Soviet Russia. Here was the final step in the identification of the Communist movement and Russian national power.

The essence of Yugoslav communism since the break in 1948 has been the effort to justify national independence from Moscow while at the same time maintaining firm Communist rule at home. The direct justification for independence has been sought by asserting the necessity for every country to approach socialism in its own way and at its own time. In effect, the revolution is not regarded as an international process at all, but a strictly national one (the logical extension of "socialism in one country"). The Yugoslavs have also sought to defend themselves against Russian denunciations by pointing to the internal imperfections of communism in Russia, and correcting such defects in their own regime. The Soviet Union was especially criticized for allowing bureaucratic distortions of socialism, while the Yugoslavs, looking back in the Soviet past, rediscovered the old revolutionary ideal of decentralized administration carried out by the populace. This theory was then actually put into practice in Yugoslavia through administrative decentralization and workers' councils, although Tito and the Communist Party leaders keep firm political supervision over the country as a whole.

The Yugoslav antibureaucratic line has not been without danger to its users. Anyone following the argument consistently would find that in large measure the Yugoslav system conformed to the basically bureaucratic transformation of the Communist movement which had come about in the Soviet Union. One leading Yugoslav Communist—Milovan Djilas—actually did pursue this argument, which brought him to the rejection of the Communist dictatorship altogether (and to his prosecution and conviction by the Yugoslav government for treasonable activities).

Immediately after Tito's break with Moscow, signs of the national-Communist tendency appeared almost everywhere in Eastern Europe. It was a natural reaction against foreign domination and the rigors of the economic policies demanded by Soviet interests. Severe shake-ups were undertaken in

1948 and 1949 to eliminate national-Communist sentiment: in Poland, the Communist secretary-general Gomulka was ousted and then jailed, while in Hungary and Bulgaria deputy premiers Rajk and Kostov, respectively, were executed after show trials were staged. Similar purges characterized the other satellites, and the intensive development of heavy industry and agricultural collectivization were then pushed throughout the entire Soviet-dominated region.

The death of Stalin in 1953 opened the way for gestures of leniency in East European communism. By 1956 the East Europeans were pressing their opportunity ambitiously, and one of the most severe crises in the history of communism was the result. The Polish Communists brought Gomulka back to power despite Soviet threats, and under Gomulka's leadership the worst excesses of satellite economic policy and police controls were checked. The clock in Poland was turned back to a compromise similar to Russia's NEP, with the abandonment of collective farms, the restoration of considerable intellectual freedom outside the political sphere, and the end of arbitrary police terror, though the characteristic discipline of the Communist Party and its dominant position in the state were emphatically retained, together with subservience to Russia in matters of foreign policy. Poland has become the least totalitarian of any Communist country.

For a brief moment Hungary promised to outdo the Poles by far in the revision of communism. Popular agitation for reform in October, 1956, developed into a nation-wide insurrectionary movement so powerful that the Communist government saw its only course of survival in endorsing the revolution and acceding to its demands. The moderate-minded Communist ex-premier Imre Nagy was recalled to his post. In a rapid series of decrees Nagy in effect proclaimed the end of the Communist system in Hungary, abolishing its police controls and economic rigors, ending the political monopoly of the Communist Party, and renouncing ties with the Soviet bloc.The Nagy government was thus returning to the form of coalition regime which had prevailed in Eastern Europe between the end of World War II and the establishment of the Communist dictatorships. This course was rudely interrupted, however, by the intervention of Soviet troops (who were already present in Hungary under the terms of the Communist alliance and who had briefly fought the revolution in its initial stages). Early in November, 1956, Soviet forces overthrew the Nagy government and installed a new regime, headed by Janos Kadar, made up of those Hungarian Communists who preferred to serve as Soviet puppets and maintain the Communist Party dictatorship. Hungary was thus brought forcibly back into line with the majority of the satellites, though all of them henceforth enjoyed considerably more lenient economic conditions without any more direct Soviet exploitation.

National communism is now a reality, in different forms, in two countries (Poland with more internal freedom and Yugoslavia with unimpaired national sovereignty), while it is an ever-present potential in the rest of Eastern Europe. Discipline over the Communist bloc (not counting Yugoslavia) is still maintained by the Soviet Union under the theoretical guise of "proletarian internationalism." The Western threat to Communist rule as such is made the most of to keep the European Communists firmly committed to the Soviet alliance, whatever propensity for independent action they might have.

China and Asian Communism

In contrast to Eastern Europe, communism in Asia is to a far lesser degree a direct Russian imposition. The movement in China grew independently and came to power basically under its own power. Moreover, communism has proved to be more appropriate to the problems of the East; it conforms to conditions and traditions rather than defying them.

The Communist appeal in the East has nothing to do with the Marxian analysis of history or the dictatorship of the proletariat. Whereas communism has had its main appeal in the West under its old proletarian guise, the East has responded to the more straightforward attraction of actual Soviet aims and methods. Communism captures the imagination of many Eastern intellectuals and semi-intellectuals and appeals to them as a new way of life, a new discipline, that will enable their country to pursue the goals of industrialization and national power, and thus to compete with the hitherto dominant West on equal terms. Communism comes to the East as the ideology, program and instrument of anti-Western westernization.

One of the distinctive characteristics of communism in China was its complete divorce from the industrial working class during most of the years before its assumption of power. While the movement did have some worker participation just after its establishment in the early 1920's, it was primarily the expression of radically-minded intellectuals, and in alliance with Chiang Kai-shek helped bring the Nationalist Party to power. Then, hard-pressed by their erstwhile ally, the Communists at the initiative of Mao Tse-tung shifted the focus of their operations to the peasantry. The Communist Party became a major political force in China as a disciplined party of intellectuals mobilizing the peasants in order to wage war and revolution.

With respect to the strongly centralized party and its leading role in the revolution the Chinese Communists were following closely in the footsteps of Lenin. In their dogmatic adherence to Marxist doctrine and the rigorous enforcement of the official doctrinal justification of each policy measure, the Chinese were quick pupils of Stalin. But where the Russian Revolution could at least in part be described as a working-class affair, this presumed foundation of the Marxist dictatorship was quite lacking in China. The Chinese Communist revolution actually proceeded much more in conformity with the pre-Marxist doctrines of the Russian "populists," who called for a peasant revolution led by a determined party of intellectuals. Maoism, coming to terms with these circumstances, is the ultimate extension of the philosophical changes which Lenin had begun to introduce in Marx.

In the absence of working-class participation, the Chinese Communists could claim Marxist legitimacy only by insisting that the party was proletarian in "spirit," i.e., in its discipline and revolutionary single-mindedness. Implicitly this reasoning transferred the essence of revolution from the realm of social classes to the realm of thought. In actuality, apart from the liquidation of landlords, there has been comparatively little clear-cut class struggle in the Chinese revolution. The choice was rather one between systems of moral authority; anyone accepting Communist authority and discipline could be absorbed into the movement, and from the very beginning of their rule the Communists have readily taken middle-class elements into collaboration with them if these conditions were met. The tasks of maintaining doctrinal discipline on the basis of Marxist orthodoxy, however, were all the more demanding—hence the unique Chinese development of indoctrination and "brain washing."

In the nature of its policies once power was consolidated, Chinese communism represents the logical extension of Leninism-Stalinism in yet another respect—the use of totalitarian political controls to effect a cultural transformation and carry out the industrial revolution with the utmost rapidity. With the exception of a few areas developed by foreign capital, Chinese communism began with no industrial base at all, whereas Russia was appreciably industrialized at the time of the revolution (though very unevenly and to a low per capita degree). With the adoption of the military commune system China is striving toward the ultimate in the bureaucratic direction of individual energy toward the compelling national goal of industrial power.

Communism as both the goal and the instrument of building national power through industrialization naturally exercises a powerful fascination for the self-conscious minority of would-be revolutionary nationalist leaders throughout Asia and the underdeveloped regions of the world generally. As such it is the end-product of centuries of European political, economic and cultural domination of the world. Long stagnant or subservient peoples have been discovering new energies, thanks to the impact of Western influence upon them. Their emotional reaction is to bite the hand that has culturally fed them, and turn to a movement which emulates Western ways at the same time that it expresses the anti-Western resentment of the former underdog. Communism is admirably suited to satisfy these desires, and its potential for expansion in this part of the world is by no means exhausted.

An alternative to communism can be observed in the one-party nationalist reform movements which have appeared at various times in China, the Near East, and at present in West Africa. These movements have the same political and emotional function as communism in such regions, though they have not ordinarily displayed the requisite drive and discipline. The main difference is that they are free of communism's two great burdens of irrelevance—doctrinaire commitment to Marxist ideology, and the obligations of loyalty to Moscow.

The Meaning of Communism

There are two important characteristics of the Communist movement which are rarely understood and are responsible for most of the widespread confusion on the subject (among both opponents and sympathizers). One of these is the relation between theory and practice. The other is the course of evolution which the practice itself has followed.

It is rare indeed that a doctrinaire movement, whether of religion or politics or whatever, has kept strictly to the literal dictates of its principles. Life never turns out as the founder of a doctrine expects. Historically speaking, the function of a doctrine is to give reinforcement and cohesiveness to a social emotion, which emotion may or may not be logically consistent with the doctrine to which it becomes attached. The outcome of the movement is the result of interaction between its central emotion and the circumstances of life in which it finds itself, with all the innumerable complications of chance. Such an interaction, as we have noted, underlay the basic changes which have taken place in communism over the years. This is natural, and it would be readily intelligible were it not for the unnatural stance which communism maintains toward its original doctrine. The doctrine is still invested with absolute validity, and made to square with the actual flow of life by a clumsy process of scholastic reinterpretation. The truth of the doctrine as officially interpreted is then enjoined upon the faithful with all the force at the command of the Communist state. Thus refashioned according to the needs or preferences of the leader, the doctrine loses all long-term guiding significance. It serves two purposes only: to maintain mental discipline in the totalitarian state, and to perpetuate the sense of basic enmity between people and countries who subscribe to the doctrine, and those who do not.

In the evolving policies and institutions of Communism which the doctrine is made to justify there is much more than the chaos of zigs and zags which some observers see. To be sure, Communist decision-making is highly pragmatic—tactical rather than philosophical—but the contours of social reality confer a definite shape upon the movement as it maneuvers from one turning point to the next. Essentially the history of the Communist movement has been one of progressive adaptation to the problems of modernization and national regeneration of underdeveloped countries whose traditional cultural equilibrium was upset by European influence. By the time the movement crystallized firmly, its essential meaning had changed so much that the propositions of its prophets had become quite irrelevant. The Western, international, post-industrial, anarchistic, proletarian revolution had become the Eastern, national, industrializing, totalitarian, middle-class-intellectual revolution. Two movements could scarcely be less similar, yet this is the situation in which the Communist faithful feel compelled to maintain the complete Marxist orthodoxy of their ideas and their system. The madness of this dogmatism is death to the free individual or the creative mind.

There are four basic attributes which define the Communist movement as it exists today. Its structural core is the Leninist concept of the party, a disciplined, hierarchical organization serving either to spearhead a revolutionary movement or to rule the Communist state. Its dynamic urge is the drive to industrialize, to overcome backwardness and fashion the sinews of national power by systematic exhortation and compulsion imposed on the population through the party. Its mentality is the ideology of Marxism as officially interpreted

—the obligatory rationalization of the party's policies enforced by totalitarian thought controls. Its international orientation is unquestioning loyalty to Soviet Russia as the initiator, sustainer, and doctrinal authority of the movement, together with uncompromising hostility toward the liberalism and capitalism associated with the "imperialism" of the major Western powers. (In the one case—Yugoslavia—where this no longer holds, it was nonetheless true at the time the Communist system took shape there.) Taken together, these four features necessarily indicate the Communist movement and nothing but the Communist movement. They are the necessary and sufficient counts in a definition of communism.

The Communist movement, thus defined, did not come into being because of some law of historical inevitability. It is the product of a complicated interaction of circumstances, human intentions and historical accidents (particularly the events of the Russian Revolution). It has spread and gained strength because it has adapted itself to the resolution of widespread and serious social problems and weaknesses. If it is not the only solution to these ills, it has often been the most vigorous alternative. It enjoys today the prospect of gaining still more ground, on more than one continent. One might wonder, however, about the implications which success itself might have for the communist movement. Will the solution of those problems which have contributed to the growth of the movement deprive it of any reason for further existence, and thus require it to change or collapse? Does communism, as it were, contain the seeds of its own destruction? Or will the strength of the totalitarian system enable it to outlive indefinitely the circumstances which called it into being, as so many despotic systems have in the past? Only the future can yield the answers to such questions.

Volume I

Chapter One: Leninism and the Bolshevik Party, to 1917

The pre-1917 background of the Communist movement is dominated by one powerful figure, that of Lenin. The Bolshevik Party was largely his personal creation, and its distinctive doctrines were his also. The disciplined organization, the revolutionary mission of the party, and the stern enforcement of Lenin's version of doctrinal orthodoxy, were all firmly established in the Bolshevik faction of the Russian Social-Democratic Party long before 1917. The reactions of other Marxists testify eloquently to the unique impress which Lenin's personality made in the movement. When revolution came in 1917, Lenin was prepared to strike for power, not only in Russia but internationally, with the aid of the foreign socialist sympathizers whom he had gathered.

Lenin as a Marxist

As early as 1894, when he was twenty-four, Lenin (born Vladimir Ilich Ulyanov) had become a revolutionary agitator and a convinced Marxist. He exhibited his new faith and his polemical talents in a diatribe of that year against the peasant-oriented socialism of the Populists led by N. K. Mikhailovsky.

. . . Now—since the appearance of *Capital*—the materialist conception of history is no longer a hypothesis, but a scientifically demonstrated proposition. And until some other attempt is made to give a scientific explanation of the functioning and development of any form of society—form of

FROM: Lenin, "What the 'Friends of the People' Are and How They Fight the Social-Democrats" (April, 1894; in V. I. Lenin, *Selected Works*, Moscow, Foreign Languages Publishing House, 1950-52, Vol. I, book 1, pp. 110, 165-66).

society, mind you, and not the mode of life of any country or people, or even class, etc.—another attempt which would be just as capable as materialism of introducing order into the "pertinent facts" and of presenting a living picture of a definite formation and at the same time of explaining it in a strictly scientific way, until then the materialist conception of history will be synonymous with social science. Materialism is not "primarily a scientific conception of history," as Mr. Mikhailovsky thinks, but the only scientific conception of history. . . .

. . . Russian Marxists . . . began precisely with a criticism of the subjective methods of earlier Socialists. Not satisfied with merely stating the fact that exploitation exists and condemning it, they desired to *explain* it. Realizing that the whole post-Reform* history of Russia consisted in the impoverishment of the mass and the enrichment of a minority, observing the colossal expropriation of the small producers side by side with universal technical progress, noting that these opposite tendencies arose and became intensified wherever, and to the extent that, commodity production developed and became consolidated, they could not but conclude that they were confronted with a bourgeois (capitalist) organization of social economy, which *necessarily* gave rise to the expropriation and oppression of the masses. Their practical program was quite directly determined by this conviction; this program was, to join the struggle of the proletariat against the bourgeoisie, the struggle of the propertyless classes against the propertied, which constitutes the principal content of economic reality in Russia, from the most out-of-the-way village to the most up-to-date and perfected factory. How were they to join it? The answer was again suggested by real life. Capitalism had brought the principal branches of industry to the stage of large-scale machine industry; by thus socializing production, it had created the material conditions for a new system and had at the same time created a new social force—the class of factory workers, the urban proletariat. Subjected to the same bourgeois exploitation—for such, in its economic essence, is the exploitation to which the whole toiling popula-

* I.e., since the emancipation of the serfs in 1861—Ed.

tion of Russia is subjected—this class, however, has been placed in a special, favourable position as far as its emancipation is concerned: it has no longer any ties with the old society, which is wholly based on exploitation; the very conditions of its labour and circumstances of life organize it, compel it to think and enable it to step into the arena of the political struggle. It was only natural that the Social-Democrats should direct all their attention to, and base all their hopes on, this class, that they should make the development of its class consciousness their program, that they should direct all their activities towards helping it to rise and wage a direct political struggle against the present regime and towards drawing the whole Russian proletariat into this struggle. . . .

The Foundation of the Russian Marxist Party

While Marxism had been winning adherents among the Russian revolutionary intelligentsia for more than a decade previously, an avowedly Marxist party was not organized until 1898. In that year a "congress" of nine men met at Minsk to proclaim the establishment of the Russian Social-Democratic Workers' Party. The manifesto issued in the name of the congress after the police broke it up was drawn up by the economist Peter Struve, a member of the moderate "legal Marxist" group who soon afterward left the Marxist movement altogether. The manifesto is indicative of the way Marxism was applied to Russian conditions, and of the special role for the proletariat which the Russian Marxists envisaged.

. . . Fifty years ago the invigorating storm of the Revolution of 1848 burst over Europe.

For the first time the modern working class appeared on the scene as a major historical force. With its forces the

FROM: Manifesto of the Russian Social-Democratic Workers' Party, issued by the First Congress of the party, Minsk, March, 1898 (in *The Communist Party of the Soviet Union in the Resolutions and Decisions of its Congresses, Conferences, and Plenums of the Central Committee* [hereafter referred to as "CPSU in Resolutions"], 7th ed., Moscow, 1954, Vol. I, pp. 11-14; editor's translation).

bourgeoisie succeeded in removing many antiquated feudal-monarchial systems. But the bourgeoisie quickly perceived in its new ally its most hostile foe, and betrayed both it and itself and the cause of freedom into the hands of reaction. However, it was already late: the working class, pacified for the time being, after ten or fifteen years appeared again on the stage of history with redoubled force, with matured consciousness, as a full-grown fighter for its own liberation.

All this time Russia apparently remained aside from the main road of the historical movement. The class struggle was not apparent there, but it was there, and the main thing was that it was steadily growing and maturing. The Russian government, with laudable zeal, itself planted the seeds of class struggle by cheating the peasants, patronizing the landlords, fattening up the big capitalists at the expense of the toiling population. But the bourgeois-capitalist order is unthinkable without a proletariat or working class. The latter is born together with capitalism, grows together with it, gets stronger, and in proportion to its growth is thrown more and more into conflict with the bourgeoisie.

The Russian factory worker, serf or free, has always carried on a hidden or open struggle with his exploiters. In proportion to the development of capitalism, the proportions of this struggle have grown, they have embraced more and more layers of the working class population. The awakening of the class self-consciousness of the Russian proletariat and the growth of the spontaneous workers' movement have coincided with the conclusive development of international Social Democracy as the bearer of the class struggle and the class ideal of the conscious workers of the whole world. . . . Vainly the government imagines that by concessions it can calm the workers. Everywhere the working class is becoming more demanding, the more they give it. It will be the same with the Russian proletariat. They have given in to it up to now only when it *demands,* and in the future will give it only what it *demands.*

And what does the Russian working class not need? It is completely deprived of what its foreign comrades freely and quietly enjoy: participation in the administration of the state, freedom of speech and of the press, freedom of organization and assembly—in a word, all those instruments and means with which the West-European and American proletariat improves its position and at the same time struggles for its final liberation, against private property and capitalism—for socialism. Political freedom is necessary for the Russian proletariat like fresh air is necessary for healthy breathing. It is the basic condition for its free development and the successful struggle for partial improvements and final liberation.

But the Russian proletariat can only win the political freedom which it needs *by itself*.

The farther east one goes in Europe, the more the bourgeoisie becomes in the political respect weaker, more cowardly, and meaner, and the larger are the cultural and political tasks which fall to the share of the proletariat. On its broad shoulders the Russian working class must bear and will bear the cause of the fight for political freedom. This is essential, but it is only the first step toward the realization of the great historical mission of the proletariat—towards the creation of that social order in which the exploitation of man by man will have no place. The Russian proletariat will throw off its burden of autocracy so that with all the more energy it will continue the struggle against capitalism and the bourgeoisie until the complete victory of socialism. . . .

As a socialist movement and inclination, the Russian Social-Democratic Party continues the cause and the traditions of all the preceding revolutionary movements in Russia; taking as the principal immediate task of the party the goal of conquering political freedom, Social Democracy moves toward the goal which has already been marked out by the glorious activists of the old "People's Will." But the means and the path which Social Democracy chooses are different. The choice of them is determined by its conscious desire to be and remain a class movement of the organized working masses. It is firmly convinced that "the liberation of the working class can only be its own business," and it will undeviatingly make all its action conform to this fundamental basis of international Social Democracy.

Long live Russia, long live international Social Democracy!

Lenin on the Workers' Party

While exiled to Siberia from 1897 to 1900 for his revolutionary activity, Lenin wrote optimistically of the growing political weight of the working class and of the role of the Marxists as its leaders.

. . . The socialist activities of Russian Social-Democrats consist in conducting *propaganda* in favour of the doctrines of scientific Socialism, of spreading among the workers a proper understanding of the present social and economic system, its foundations and its development, an understanding of the various *classes* in Russian society, of their mutual relations, of the struggle between these classes, of the role of the working class in this struggle, of the attitude of this class towards the declining and the developing classes, towards the past and the future of capitalism, of the historical task of international Social-Democracy and of the Russian working class. Inseparably connected with propaganda is *agitation* among the workers, which naturally comes to the forefront in the present political conditions in Russia and level of development of the masses of workers. Agitation among the workers consists in the Social-Democrats taking part in all the spontaneous manifestations of the struggle of the working class, in all the conflicts between the workers and the capitalists over the working day, wages, conditions of labour, etc., etc. Our task is to merge our activities with the practical, everyday questions of working-class life, to help the workers to understand these questions, to draw the attention of the workers to the most important abuses, to help them to formulate their demands to the employers more precisely and practically, to develop among the workers the consciousness of their solidarity, consciousness of the common interests and common cause of all the Russian workers as a

FROM: Lenin, "The Tasks of the Russian Social-Democrats" (1898; *Selected Works*, Vol. I, book 1, pp. 179-80, 198-99).

united working class that constitutes a part of the international army of the proletariat. . . .

Our work is primarily and mainly concentrated on the factory, the urban workers. Russian Social-Democracy must not dissipate its forces; it must concentrate its activities on the industrial proletariat, which is most susceptible to Social-Democratic ideas, most developed intellectually and politically, and most important from the point of view of numbers and concentration in the large political centres of the country. The creation of a durable revolutionary organization among the factory, the urban workers, is, therefore, the first and most urgent task that confronts Social-Democracy, and it would be very unwise indeed to allow ourselves to be diverted from this task at the present time. But, while recognizing the necessity of concentrating our forces on the factory worker and decrying the dissipation of forces, we do not in the least wish to suggest that the Russian Social-Democrats should ignore other strata of the Russian proletariat and working class. . . .

Russian Social-Democracy has still an enormous, almost untouched field of work open before it. The awakening of the Russian working class, its spontaneous striving after knowledge, unity, Socialism, for the struggle against its exploiters and oppressors is manifesting itself more strikingly and widely every day. The enormous success which Russian capitalism has achieved in recent times serves as a guarantee that the working-class movement will grow uninterruptedly in breadth and depth. Apparently, we are now passing through the period in the capitalist cycle when industry is "flourishing," when business is brisk, when the factories are working at full capacity and when countless new factories, new enterprises, joint-stock companies, railway enterprises, etc., etc., are springing up like mushrooms. But one need not be a prophet to foretell the inevitable crash (more or less abrupt) that must succeed this period of industrial "prosperity." This crash will cause the ruin of masses of small masters, will throw masses of workers into the ranks of the unemployed, and will thus confront all the masses of the workers in an acute form with the questions of Socialism and democracy which have already confronted every class-conscious and thinking worker long ago. Russian Social-Democrats must see to it that when this crash comes the Russian proletariat will be more class-conscious, more united, able to understand the tasks of the Russian working class, capable of putting up resistance to the capitalist class—which is now reaping huge profits and always strives to throw the burden of the losses upon the workers—and capable of taking the lead of Russian democracy in the resolute struggle against the police despotism which binds and fetters the Russian workers and the whole of the Russian people.

And so, to work, comrades! Let us not lose precious time! Russian Social-Democrats have much to do to meet the requirements of the awakening proletariat, to organize the working-class movement, to strengthen the revolutionary groups and their contacts with each other, to supply the workers with propaganda and agitational literature, and to unite the workers' circles and Social-Democratic groups scattered all over Russia into a single *Social-Democratic Labour Party!*

Lenin's Theory of the Party

Leaving Russia in 1900, Lenin went to Geneva to join Plekhanov's circle of older Russian Marxists in publishing a paper for the new Social-Democratic party—*Iskra,* "The Spark." In the course of this work he turned his attention to the organizational problems of the movement, and formulated what in retrospect have proven to be the fundamental ideas underlying the Communist movement—his theory of the tightly organized and disciplined party of "professional revolutionaries." This idea Lenin first developed in "What Is to Be Done?," a lengthy polemic against the "Economists" —those Marxists who preferred to stress the economic struggle of the workers rather than a separate revolutionary movement. The publication of "What Is to Be Done?" in 1902 marks the true beginning of Leninism as a distinctive political current.

. . . It is no secret that two trends have taken shape in the present-day international Social-Democracy. The fight between these trends now flares up in a bright flame, and now dies down and smoulders under the ashes of imposing "truce resolutions." What this "new" trend, which adopts a "critical" attitude towards "obsolete dogmatic" Marxism, represents has with sufficient precision been *stated* by Bernstein, and *demonstrated* by Millerand.*

Social-Democracy must change from a party of the social revolution into a democratic party of social reforms. Bernstein has surrounded this political demand with a whole battery of symmetrically arranged "new" arguments and reasonings. The possibility of putting Socialism on a scientific basis and of proving from the point of view of the materialist conception of history that it is necessary and inevitable was denied, as was also the growing impoverishment, proletarianization and the intensification of capitalist contradictions. The very conception, "*ultimate aim*," was declared to be unsound, and the idea of the dictatorship of the proletariat was absolutely rejected. It was denied that there is any counterdistinction in principle between liberalism and Socialism. *The theory of the class struggle* was rejected on the grounds that it could not be applied to a strictly democratic society, governed according to the will of the majority, etc.

Thus, the demand for a resolute turn from revolutionary Social-Democracy to bourgeois Social-reformism was accompanied by a no less resolute turn towards bourgeois criticism of all the fundamental ideas of Marxism. . . .

He who does not deliberately close his eyes cannot fail to see that the new "critical" trend in Socialism is nothing more nor less than a new variety of *opportunism*. And if we judge people not by the brilliant uniforms they don, not by the high-sounding appellations they give themselves, but by their actions, and by what they actually advocate, it will be clear that "freedom of criticism" means freedom for an

FROM: Lenin, "What Is to Be Done?" (1902, *Selected Works,* Vol. I, book 1, pp. 207-8, 210, 227-28, 233-34, 242-44, 286-88, 322-25, 330, 336, 338-39, 347-48).

* Eduard Bernstein: leader of the "revisionist" or avowedly nonrevolutionary tendency in the German Social-Democratic Party; Alexandre Millerand: French socialist leader, the first to join a "bourgeois" cabinet (later President of France)—Ed.

opportunistic trend in Social-Democracy, the freedom to convert Social-Democracy into a democratic party of reform, the freedom to introduce bourgeois ideas and bourgeois elements into Socialism. . . .

Without a revolutionary theory there can be no revolutionary movement. This thought cannot be insisted upon too strongly at a time when the fashionable preaching of opportunism goes hand in hand with an infatuation for the narrowest forms of practical activity. . . . Our Party is only in process of formation, its features are only just becoming outlined, and it is yet far from having settled accounts with other trends of revolutionary thought, which threaten to divert the movement from the correct path. . . . The national tasks of Russian Social-Democracy are such as have never confronted any other socialist party in the world. . . . The *role of vanguard fighter can be fulfilled only by a party that is guided by the most advanced theory.* . . .

. . . The strikes of the nineties represented the class struggle in embryo, but only in embryo. Taken by themselves, these strikes were simply trade union struggles, but not yet Social-Democratic struggles. They testified to the awakening antagonisms between workers and employers, but the workers were not, and could not be, conscious of the irreconcilable antagonism of their interests to the whole of the modern political and social system, i.e., theirs was not yet Social-Democratic consciousness. In this sense, the strikes of the nineties, in spite of the enormous progress they represented as compared with the "riots," remained a purely spontaneous movement.

We have said that *there could not yet be* Social-Democratic consciousness among the workers. It could only be brought to them from without. The history of all countries shows that the working class, exclusively by its own effort, is able to develop only trade union consciousness, i.e., the conviction that it is necessary to combine in unions, fight the employers and strive to compel the government to pass necessary labour legislation, etc. The theory of Socialism, however, grew out of the philosophic, historical and economic theories that were elaborated by the educated representatives of the propertied classes, the intellectuals. According to their social status, the founders of modern scientific Socialism, Marx and Engels, themselves belonged to the bourgeois intelligentsia. In the very same way, in Russia, the theoretical doctrine of Social-Democracy arose quite independently of the spontaneous growth of the working-class movement, it arose as a natural and inevitable outcome of the development of ideas among the revolutionary socialist intelligentsia. At the time of which we are speaking, i.e., the middle of the nineties, this doctrine not only represented the completely formulated program of the Emancipation of Labour group, but had already won over to its side the majority of the revolutionary youth in Russia.

Hence, we had both the spontaneous awakening of the masses of the workers, the awakening to conscious life and conscious struggle, and a revolutionary youth, armed with the Social-Democratic theory, eager to come into contact with the workers. In this connection it is particularly important to state the oft-forgotten (and comparatively little-known) fact that the *early* Social-Democrats of that period *zealously carried on economic agitation* (being guided in this by the really useful instructions contained in the pamphlet *On Agitation* that was still in manuscript), but they did not regard this as their sole task. On the contrary, *right from the very beginning* they advanced the widest historical tasks of Russian Social-Democracy in general, and the task of overthrowing the autocracy in particular. . . . The adherents of the "pure" working-class movement, the worshippers of the closest "organic" . . . contacts with the proletarian struggle, the opponents of any non-worker intelligentsia (even if it be a socialist intelligentsia) are compelled, in order to defend their positions, to resort to the arguments of the *bourgeois* "pure" trade unionists. . . . This shows . . . that *all* worship of the spontaneity of the working-class movement, all belittling of the role of "the conscious element," of the role of Social-Democracy, *means, quite irrespective of whether the belittler wants to or not, strengthening the influence of the bourgeois ideology over the workers.* All those who talk about "overrating the importance of ideology," about exaggerating the role of the conscious element, etc., imagine that the pure working-class movement can work out, and will work out, an independent ideology for itself, if only the workers "wrest their fate from the hands of the leaders." But this is a profound mistake. . . .

Since there can be no talk of an independent ideology being developed by the masses of the workers themselves in the process of their movement the *only* choice is: either the bourgeois or the socialist ideology. There is no middle course (for humanity has not created a "third" ideology, and, moreover, in a society torn by class antagonisms there can never be a non-class or above-class ideology). Hence, to belittle the socialist ideology *in any way*, to *turn away from it in the slightest degree* means to strengthen bougeois ideology. There is a lot of talk about spontaneity, but the *spontaneous* development of the working-class movement leads to its becoming subordinated to the bougeois ideology, *leads to its developing according to the program* of the *Credo*,* for the spontaneous working-class movement is trade unionism, and trade unionism means the ideological enslavement of the workers by the bourgeoisie. Hence, our task, the task of Social-Democracy, is to *combat spontaneity*, to *divert* the working-class movement from this spontaneous, trade-unionist striving to come under the wing of the bourgeoisie, and to bring it under the wing of revolutionary Social-Democracy. The phrase employed by the authors of the "economic" letter in the *Iskra*, No. 12, about the efforts of the most inspired ideologists not being able to divert the working-class movement from the path that is determined by the interaction of the material elements and the material environment, *is absolutely tantamount* therefore *to the abandonment of Socialism*. . . .

We have seen that the conduct of the broadest political agitation, and consequently the organization of comprehensive political exposures, is an absolutely necessary, and the *most urgently* necessary, task of activity, that is, if that activity is to be truly Social-Democratic. . . . *However much*

* *The Credo:* a statement of the views of the "Economists," 1899—Ed.

we may try to "lend the economic struggle itself a political character" *we shall never be able* to develop the political consciousness of the workers (to the level of Social-Democratic political consciousness) by keeping within the framework of the economic struggle, for *that framework is too narrow*. . . .

Class political consciousness can be brought to the workers *only from without,* that is, only from outside of the economic struggle, from outside of the sphere of relations between workers and employers. The sphere from which alone it is possible to obtain this knowledge is the sphere of relationships between *all* the classes and strata and the state and the government, the sphere of the interrelations between *all* the classes. For that reason, the reply to the question: what must be done in order to bring political knowledge to the workers? cannot be merely the one which, in the majority of cases, the practical [party] workers, especially those who are inclined towards Economism, mostly content themselves with, i.e., "go among the workers." To bring political knowledge to the *workers* the Social-Democrats must *go among all classes of the population,* must dispatch units of their army *in all directions*. . . .

. . . The political struggle of Social-Democracy is far more extensive and complex than the economic struggle of the workers against the employers and the government. Similarly (and indeed for that reason), the organization of a revolutionary Social-Democratic party must inevitably be of a *different* kind than the organizations of the workers designed for this struggle. A workers' organization must in the first place be a trade organization; secondly, it must be as broad as possible; and thirdly, it must be as little clandestine as possible (here, and further on, of course, I have only autocratic Russia in mind). On the other hand, the organizations of revolutionaries must consist first, foremost and mainly of people who make revolutionary activity their profession (that is why I speak of organizations of *revolutionaries,* meaning revolutionary Social-Democrats). In view of this common feature of the members of such an organization, *all distinctions as between workers and intellectuals,* and certainly distinctions of trade and profession, must be *utterly obliterated.*

Such an organization must of necessity be not too extensive and as secret as possible. . . .

The workers' organizations for the economic struggle should be trade union organizations. Every Social-Democratic worker should as far as possible assist and actively work in these organizations. That is true. But it is not at all to our interest to demand that only Social-Democrats should be eligible for membership in the "trade" unions: that would only narrow down our influence over the masses. Let every worker who understands the need to unite for the struggle against the employers and the government join the trade unions. The very aim of the trade unions would be unattainable if they failed to unite all who have attained at least this elementary degree of understanding, and if they were not very *wide* organizations. And the wider these organizations are, the wider our influence over them will be—an influence due not only to the "spontaneous" development of the economic struggle but also to the direct and conscious effort of the socialist trade union members to influence their comrades. . . .

. . . A small, compact core of the most reliable, experienced and hardened workers, with responsible representatives in the principal districts and connected by all the rules of strict secrecy with the organization of revolutionaries, can, with the widest support of the masses and without any formal organization, perform *all* the functions of a trade union organization, and perform them, moreover, in a manner desirable to Social-Democracy. Only in this way can we secure the *consolidation* and development of a *Social-Democratic* trade union movement, in spite of all the gendarmes.

. . . I assert: 1) that no revolutionary movement can endure without a stable organization of leaders that maintains continuity; 2) that the wider the masses spontaneously drawn into the struggle, forming the basis of the movement and participating in it, the more urgent the need of such an organization, and the more solid this organization must be (for it is much easier for demagogues to sidetrack the more backward sections of the masses); 3) that such an organization must consist chiefly of people professionally engaged in revolutionary activity; 4) that in an autocratic state, the more we *confine* the membership of such an organization to people who are professionally engaged in revolutionary activity and who have been professionally trained in the art of combatting the political police, the more difficult will it be to wipe out such an organization, and 5) the *greater* will be the number of people of the working class and of the other classes of society who will be able to join the movement and perform active work in it.

. . . The centralization of the most secret functions in an organization of revolutionaries will not diminish, but rather increase the extent and quality of the activity of a large number of other organizations which are intended for a broad public and are therefore as loose and as non-secret as possible, such as workers' trade unions, workers' self-education circles and circles for reading illegal literature, socialist and also democratic circles among *all* other sections of the population, etc., etc. We must have such circles, trade unions and organizations everywhere in *as large a number as possible* and with the widest variety of functions; but it would be absurd and dangerous to *confuse* them with the organization of *revolutionaries,* to obliterate the border line between them, to dim still more the masses' already incredibly hazy appreciation of the fact that in order to "serve" the mass movement we must have people who will devote themselves exclusively to Social-Democratic activities, and that such people must *train* themselves patiently and steadfastly to be professional revolutionaries.

Yes, this appreciation has become incredibly dim. Our chief sin with regard to organization is that *by our amateurishness we have lowered the prestige of revolutionaries in Russia.* A person who is flabby and shaky in questions of theory, who has a narrow outlook, who pleads the spontaneity of the masses as an excuse for his own sluggishness, who resembles a trade union secretary more than a people's tribune, who is unable to conceive of a broad and bold plan that would command the respect even of opponents, and who is inexperienced and clumsy in his own professional art—the art of combating the political police—why, such a man is not a revolutionary but a wretched amateur!

Let no active worker take offence at these frank remarks, for as far as insufficient training is concerned, I apply them first and foremost to myself. I used to work in a circle that set itself very wide, all-embracing tasks; and all of us, members of that circle, suffered painfully, acutely from the realization that we were proving ourselves to be amateurs at a moment in history when we might have been able to say, paraphrasing a well-known epigram: "Give us an organization of revolutionaries, and we shall overturn Russia!" And the more I recall the burning sense of shame I then experienced, the more bitter are my feelings towards those pseudo Social-Democrats whose teachings "bring disgrace on the calling of a revolutionary," who fail to understand that our task is not to champion the degrading of the revolutionary to the level of an amateur, but to *raise* the amateurs to the level of revolutionaries. . . .

. . . The history of the revolutionary movement is so little known among us that the name "Narodnaya Volya" * is used to denote any idea of a militant centralized organization which declares determined war upon tsarism. But the magnificent organization that the revolutionaries had in the seventies, and which should serve us as a model, was not established by the Narodnaya Volya-ites, but by the *Zemlya i Volya-ites,* who split up into the Cherny Peredel and Narodnaya Volya. Consequently, to regard a militant revolutionary organization as something specifically Narodnaya Volya-ite is absurd both historically and logically, because *no* revolutionary tendency, if it seriously thinks of fighting, can dispense with such an organization. The mistake the Narodnaya Volya-ites committed was not that they strove

* "Narodnaya Volya": The "People's Will," the terrorist organization which assassinated Tsar Alexander II in 1881. Its ancestor was the "Land and Liberty" party (*Zemlia i Volia*), which split in 1879 into the "People's Will" and the "Black Repartition" (*Cherny Peredel*) party of those who favored mass agitation—Ed.

to enlist in their organization *all* the discontented, and to direct this organization to decisive battle against the autocracy; on the contrary, that was their great historical merit. Their mistake was that they relied on a theory which in substance was not a revolutionary theory at all, and they either did not know how, or were unable, inseparably to link up their movement with the class struggle within developing capitalist society. And only a gross failure to understand Marxism (or an "understanding" of it in the spirit of Struve-ism) could prompt the opinion that the rise of a mass, spontaneous working-class movement *relieves* us of the duty of creating as good an organization of revolutionaries as the *Zemlya i Volya* had, and even an incomparably better one. On the contrary, this movement *imposes* this duty upon us, because the spontaneous struggle of the proletariat will not become its genuine "class struggle" until this struggle is led by a strong organization of revolutionaries. . . .

Lenin on the Party Split

The first true congress of the Russian Social-Democratic Workers' Party was the Second. It convened in Brussels in the summer of 1903, but was forced by the interference of the Belgian authorities to move to London, where the proceedings were concluded. The Second Congress was the occasion for bitter wrangling among the representatives of various Russian Marxist factions, and ended in a deep cleavage that was mainly caused by Lenin—his personality, his drive for power in the movement, and his "hard" philosophy of the disciplined party organization. At the close of the congress Lenin commanded a temporary majority for his faction and seized upon the label "Bolshevik" (from the Russian *bolshinstvo*—majority), while his opponents (led by Y. O. Martov) who inclined to the "soft" or more democratic position became known as the "Mensheviks" or minority. The terms stuck despite the fact that for most of the time between 1903 and 1917 the Bolsheviks were the numerically weaker group.

Following the Second Congress Lenin prepared a polemical account of the issues, in which he argued that the weaknesses shown by the "intellectuals" at the congress proved the need for the kind of organization which he advocated.

. . . It is quite natural . . . that the work of the *Iskra* and the entire work of organizing the Party, the entire work of *actually* restoring the Party, *could not* be regarded as finished until the whole Party had adopted and officially registered certain definite ideas of organization. This task was to be performed by the rules of organization of the Party.

The principal ideas which the *Iskra* strove to make the basis of the Party's organization amounted essentially to the following two: first, the idea of centralism, which defined in principle the method of deciding all particular and detail questions of organization; second, the special function of an organ, a newspaper, for ideological leadership, an idea which took into account the temporary and special requirements of the Russian Social-Democratic working-class movement amidst conditions of political slavery, on the understanding that the *initial* base of operations for the revolutionary assault would be set up abroad. . . .

. . . Martov, as is usually the case, forgot a good deal and, therefore, again muddled things up. . . .

I could not have "liked" the "idea" of paragraph one of Martov's draft, for that draft did not contain a *single idea* that came up at the Congress. His memory played him false. I have been fortunate enough to find Martov's draft among my papers, and in it "*paragraph one is not formulated in the way he proposed it at the Congress*"! So much for the "open vizor"!

§1 of Martov's draft: "A member of the Russian Social-Democratic Labour Party is one who, accepting its program, works actively to carry out its aims under the control and direction of the organs (*sic!*) of the Party."

§1 of my draft: "A Party member is one who accepts its program and who supports the Party both financially and by personal participation in one of the Party organizations."

FROM: Lenin, "One Step Forward, Two Steps Back" (May, 1904; *Selected Works,* Vol. I, book 1, pp. 452, 454-56, 468, 470-72, 609, 613-16, 618-20, 632-34, 644-45).

§1 as formulated by Martov at the Congress and adopted by the Congress: "A member of the Russian Social-Democratic Labour Party is one who accepts its program, supports the Party financially and renders it regular personal assistance under the direction of one of its organizations."

It is clearly evident from this comparison that there is no *idea* in Martov's draft but only *empty phrases*. It goes without saying that Party members must work under the control and direction of the *organs* of the Party; *it cannot be otherwise*, and it is talked about only by those who love to talk in order to say nothing, who love to flood "rules" with huge quantities of verbal water and bureaucratic formulas (i.e., formulas that are useless for the matter in hand and supposed to be useful for display). . . .

. . . Comrade Martov's three years' *Iskra* training has not imbued him with disdain for the anarchist phrasemongering by which the unstable mentality of the intellectual is capable of justifying the violation of rules adopted by common consent. . . . When I say that the Party should be a *sum* (and not a mere arithmetical sum, but a complex) of *organizations*, does that mean that I "confuse" the concepts Party and organization? Of course not. I thereby express clearly and precisely my wish, my demand, that the Party, as the vanguard of the class, should be as *organized* as possible, that the Party should admit to its ranks only such elements *as lend themselves to at least a minimum of organization*. My opponent, on the contrary, wants to *lump together* organized elements and unorganized elements in the Party, those who submit to direction and those who do not, the advanced and the incorrigibly backward—for the corrigibly backward may join the organization. . . .

. . . There can be no talk of throwing anybody overboard, in the sense of preventing them from working, from taking part in the movement. On the contrary, the stronger our Party organizations consisting of *real* Social-Democrats are, and the less wavering and instability there is *within* the Party, the broader, the more varied, the richer and more fertile will be the influence of the Party on the elements of the working-class *masses* surrounding it and guided by it. After all, the Party, as the vanguard of the working class, must not be confused with the entire class. . . . To forget the distinction between the vanguard and the whole of the masses which gravitate towards it, to forget the constant duty of the vanguard to *raise* ever wider strata to this most advanced level, means merely to deceive oneself, to shut one's eyes to the immensity of our tasks, and to narrow down these tasks. And it is just such a shutting of one's eyes, it is just such forgetfulness, to obliterate the difference between those who associate and those who belong, between those who are conscious and active and those who only help. . . .

. . . A Jacobin who maintains an inseparable bond with the *organization* of the proletariat, a proletariat *conscious* of its class interests, is a *revolutionary Social-Democrat.* A Girondist* who yearns for professors and high-school students, who is afraid of the dictatorship of the proletariat and who sighs about the absolute value of democratic demands is an *opportunist.* It is only opportunists who can still detect a danger in conspiratorial organizations today, when the idea of narrowing down the political struggle to a conspiracy has been rejected thousands of times in written publications and has long been rejected and swept aside by the realities of life, and when the cardinal importance of mass political agitation has been elucidated and reiterated to the point of nausea. The real basis of this fear of conspiracy, of Blanquism,** is not any definite feature to be found in the practical movement (as Bernstein and Co. have long, and vainly, been trying to show), but the Girondist timidity of the bourgeois intellectual whose mentality is so often revealed among the Social-Democrats of today. . . .

. . . Unity on questions of program and tactics is an essential but by no means a sufficient condition for Party unity and for the centralization of Party work (good God, what rudimentary things one has to keep repeating nowadays, when all concepts have been confused!). The centralization of Party

* Referring to the moderate group of French revolutionaries, ousted by the Jacobins in 1793—Ed.

** Blanquism: the conspiratorial doctrine of the nineteenth-century French revolutionary L. A. Blanqui—Ed.

work requires, in addition, unity of organization, which, in a party that has grown to be anything more than a mere family circle, is inconceivable without formal rules, without the subordination of the minority to the majority, of the part to the whole. As long as we lack unity on the fundamental questions of program and tactics, we bluntly admitted that we were living in a period of disunity and the circle spirit; we bluntly declared that before we can unite, we must draw lines of demarcation; we did not even talk of the forms of a joint organization, but exclusively discussed the new (at that time they really were new) questions of how to fight opportunism on program and tactics. At present, as we all agree, this fight had already ensured a sufficient degree of unity, as formulated in the Party program and in the Party's resolution on tactics; we had to take the next step, and, by common consent, we did take it, working out the *forms* of a united organization that would merge all the circles together. We have been dragged back and half of these forms have been destroyed, we have been dragged back to anarchist conduct, to anarchist phrasemongering, to the revival of a circle in place of a Party editorial board. . . .

. . . The point at issue is whether our ideological struggle is to have forms *of a higher type* to clothe it, forms of Party organization binding on all, or the forms of the old disunity and the old circles. . . . The proletariat is trained by its whole life for organization far more radically than many an intellectual prig. Having gained some understanding of our program and our tactics, the proletariat will not start justifying backwardness in organization by arguing that the form is less important than the content. It is not the proletariat, but *certain intellectuals* in our Party who lack *self-training* in the spirit of organization and discipline, in the spirit of hostility and contempt for anarchist phrasemongering. . . . The proletarian who has become a conscious Social-Democrat and feels that he is a member of the Party will reject *khvostism* ["tail-endism," i.e., following the masses] in matters of organization with the same contempt as he rejected *khvostism* in matters of tactics.

. . . The factory, which seems only a bogey to some, represents that highest form of capitalist cooperation which has united and disciplined the proletariat, taught it to organize, and placed it at the head of all the other sections of the toiling and exploited population. And it is precisely Marxism, the ideology of the proletariat trained by capitalism, that has taught and is teaching unstable intellectuals to distinguish between the factory as a means of exploitation (discipline based on fear of starvation) and the factory as a means of organization (discipline based on collective work united by the conditions of a technically highly-developed form of production). The discipline and organization which come so hard to the bourgeois intellectual are especially easily acquired by the proletariat just because of this factory "schooling." Mortal fear of this school and utter failure to understand its importance as an organizing factor are characteristic of the ways of thinking which reflect the petty-bourgeois mode of life and which give rise to that species of anarchism which the German Social-Democrats call Edelanarchismus, i.e., the anarchism of the "noble" gentleman, or aristocratic anarchism, as I would call it. This aristocratic anarchism is particularly characteristic of the Russian nihilist. He thinks of the Party organization as a monstrous "factory"; he regards the subordination of the part to the whole and of the minority to the majority as "serfdom" (see Axelrod's* articles); division of labour under the direction of a centre evokes from him a tragicomical outcry against people being transformed into "wheels and cogs" (to turn editors into contributors being considered a particularly atrocious species of such transformation); mention of the organizational rules of the Party calls forth a contemptuous grimace and the disdainful remark (intended for the "formalists") that one could very well dispense with rules altogether. . . .

. . . Aristocratic anarchism cannot understand that formal rules are needed precisely in order to replace the narrow circle ties by the broad Party tie. It was unnecessary and impossible to give formal shape to the internal ties of a circle or the ties between circles, for these ties rested on friendship

* P. B. Axelrod: a Menshevik leader who stressed democratic party organization—Ed.

or on a "confidence" for which no reason or motive had to be given. The Party tie cannot and must not rest on either of these; it must be founded on *formal*, "bureaucratically" worded rules (bureaucratic from the standpoint of the undisciplined intellectual), strict adherence to which can alone safeguard us from the wilfulness and caprices characteristic of the circles, from the circle methods of scrapping that goes by the name of the free "process" of the ideological struggle. . . .

. . . The presence of large numbers of radical intellectuals in the ranks of our Marxists and our Social-Democrats has made, and is making, the existence of opportunism, produced by their mentality, inevitable in the most varied spheres and in the most varied forms. We fought opportunism on the fundamental problems of our world conception, on questions of our program, and a complete divergence of aims inevitably led to an irrevocable division between the liberals who had corrupted our legal Marxism and the Social-Democrats. . . .

When we speak of fighting opportunism, we must never forget a feature that is characteristic of present-day opportunism in every sphere, namely, its vagueness, diffuseness, elusiveness. An opportunist, by his very nature, will always evade formulating an issue clearly and decisively, he will always seek a middle course, he will always wriggle like a snake between two mutually exclusive points of view and try to "agree" with both and to reduce his differences of opinion to petty amendments, doubts, good and pious suggestions, and so on and so forth. . . . Their "principles" of organization therefore display all the colours of the rainbow: the predominant note is innocent and high-sounding declamations against autocracy and bureaucracy, against blind obedience and wheels and cogs—declamations that are so innocent that it is very, very difficult to discern in them what is really concerned with principle and what is really concerned with co-option. But the further you go, the worse it gets: attempts to analyze and precisely define this detestable "bureaucracy" inevitably lead to autonomism; attempts to "deepen" and justify inevitably lead to vindicating backwardness, to *khvostism*, to Girondist phrasemongering. At last there emerges the principle of *anarchism,* as the sole really definite principle, which for that reason stands out in practice in particular relief (practice is always in advance of theory). Sneering at discipline—autonomism—anarchism—there you have the ladder by which our opportunism in the sphere of organization now climbs and now descends, skipping from rung to rung and skilfully evading any definite statement of its principles. Exactly the same stages are displayed by opportunism in questions of program and tactics: sneering at "orthodoxy," narrowness and immobility—revisionist "criticism" and ministerialism*—bourgeois democracy. . . .

One step forward, two steps back — It happens in the lives of individuals, and it happens in the history of nations and in the development of parties. It would be the greatest criminal cowardice to doubt even for a moment the inevitable and complete triumph of the principles of revolutionary Social-Democracy, of proletarian organization and Party discipline. We have already won a great deal, and we must go on fighting, without being discouraged by reverses, fighting steadfastly, scorning the philistine methods of circle scrapping, doing our very utmost to preserve the single Party tie among all the Russian Social-Democrats which has been established at the cost of so much effort, and striving by dint of stubborn and systematic work to make all Party members, and the workers in particular, fully and intelligently acquainted with the duties of Party members, with the struggle at the Second Party Congress, with all the causes and all the stages of our disagreements, and with the utter disastrousness of opportunism, which, in the sphere of organization, as in the sphere of our program and our tactics, helplessly surrenders to the bourgeois psychology, uncritically adopts the point of view of bourgeois democracy, and blunts the weapon of the class struggle of the proletariat.

In its struggle for power the proletariat has no other weapon but organization. Disunited by the rule of anarchic competition in the bourgeois world, ground down by forced labour for capital, constantly thrust back to the "lower

* Ministerialism: participation in a non-socialist government, abjured by extreme leftists—Ed.

depths" of utter destitution, savagery and degeneration, the proletariat can become, and inevitably will become, an invincible force only when its ideological unification by the principles of Marxism is consolidated by the material unity of an organization which will weld millions of toilers into an army of the working class. Neither the decrepit rule of Russian tsardom, nor the senile rule of international capital will be able to withstand this army. Its ranks will become more and more serried, in spite of all zigzags and backward steps, in spite of the opportunist phrasemongering of the Girondists of present-day Social-Democracy, in spite of the smug praise of the antiquated circle spirit, and in spite of the tinsel and fuss of *intellectual* anarchism.

Marxist Reactions to Lenin—Rosa Luxemburg

Rosa Luxemburg, born of a Jewish family in Russian Poland in 1870, became one of the most articulate representatives of idealistic radicalism in the Russian Marxist movement. After 1900, having acquired German nationality through marriage, she exerted her revolutionary efforts primarily in the German Social-Democatic Party, and helped found the Spartacus League which became the nucleus of the German Communist Party in 1919. She did not cease to concern herself with the revolutionary movement in Russia, and published a penetrating attack on Lenin's concept of the centralized party. Her position is significant as a Marxist stand equally as revolutionary as Lenin's, but emphatically repudiating his faith in discipline.

. . . The present book of Comrade Lenin, one of the prominent leaders and debaters of *Iskra* in its campaign preliminary to the Russian Party Congress (N. Lenin: "One Step Forward, Two Steps Backward," Geneva, 1904), is the systematic exposition of the views of the ultra-centralist wing of the party. The conception which has here found expression in penetrating and exhaustive form is that of a thorough-going centralism of which the vital principle is, on

FROM: Luxemburg, *Leninism or Marxism* (1904; English translation, Glasgow, Anti-Parliamentary Communist Federation, 1935, pp. 6-7, 15, 17-20, 22-23).

the one hand, the sharp separation of the organized bodies of outspoken and active revolutionists from the unorganized though revolutionary active masses surrounding them, and on the other hand, strict discipline and direct, decisive and determining intervention of the central authorities in all expressions of life in the party's local organizations. It suffices to note, for example, that the central committee, according to this conception, is authorized to organize all sub-committees of the party, hence also has power to determine the personal composition of every single local organization, from Geneva and Liège to Tomsk and Irkutsk, to give it a set of self-made local statutes, to completely dissolve it by a decree and create it anew, and finally in this manner to influence the composition of the highest party authority, the Party Congress. According to this, the central committee appears as the real active nucleus of the party, and all other organizations merely as its executive organs. . . .

But to desire, as Lenin does, to deck out a party leadership with such absolute powers of a negative character would be only to multiply artificially and in a most dangerous measure the conservatism which is a necessary outgrowth of every such leadership. Just as the Social-Democratic tactic was formed, not by a central committee but by the whole party or, more correctly stated, by the whole movement, so the separate organizations of the party plainly require such elbow-room as alone enables complete utilization of all means offered by the situation of the moment, as well as the unfolding of revolutionary initiative. The ultra-centralism advocated by Lenin, however, appears to us as something which, in its whole essence, is not informed with the positive and creative spirit, but with the sterile spirit of the night-watchman. His thought is patterned mainly upon the *control* of party activity and not upon its promotion, upon narrowing and not upon unfolding, upon the hemming and not upon the drawing together of the movement. . . .

. . . Social-Democratic centralization cannot be based on blind obedience, on mechanical subordination of the party fighters to their central authority; and, furthermore, . . . no absolute partition can be erected between the nucleus of the class-conscious proletariat already organized into fixed party cadres and the surrounding element engaged in the class struggle but still in process of class enlightenment. The setting up of the central organization on these two principles—on the blind subordination of all party organizations, with their activity, down to the least detail, under a central authority which alone thinks, acts and decides for all, and on a sharp separation of the organized nucleus of the party from the surrounding revolutionary milieu, as championed by Lenin—appears to us for that reason as a mechanical carrying-over of the organizational principles of the Blanquist movement of conspiratorial circles onto the social-democratic movement of the working masses. . . .

. . . It is not by adding on to the discipline impressed upon it by the capitalist State—with the mere transfer of the baton from the hand of the bourgeoisie into that of a social-democratic central committee—but by the breaking up and uprooting of this slavish spirit of discipline, that the proletariat can be prepared for the new discipline, the voluntary self-discipline of the Social Democracy. . . .

Even from the standpoint of the fears entertained by Lenin, that is, the dangerous influence of the intellectuals upon the proletarian movement, his own conception of organization constitutes the greatest danger for the Russian Social Democracy.

As a matter of fact, there is nothing which so easily and so surely hands over a still youthful labour movement to the private ambitions of the intellectuals as forcing the movement into the strait jacket of a bureaucratic centralism, which debases the fighting workers into a pliable tool in the hands of a "committee." And, inversely, nothing so surely preserves the labour movement from all opportunistic abuses on the part of an ambitious intelligentsia as the revolutionary self-activation of the working masses, the intensification of their feeling of political responsibility. . . .

In this frightened effort of a part of the Russian Social Democracy to preserve from false steps the aspiring labour movement of Russia, through the guardianship of an omniscient and omnipresent central committee, we seem to see also the same subjectivism involved by which socialist thought in Russia has frequently been imposed upon in the past. . . .

. . . Now, however, the ego of the Russian revolutionary quickly stands on its head and declares itself once more to be an almighty ruler of history—this time, in the direction of the Social-Democratic working masses. In so doing, the bold acrobat overlooks the fact that the only subject to which this role has now fallen is the mass-ego of the working class, which everywhere insists on venturing to make its own mistakes and learning historical dialectic for itself. And by way of conclusion, let us say openly just to ourselves: Mistakes which a truly revolutionary labour movement commits are, in historical perspective, immeasurably more fruitful and valuable than the infallibility of the very best "central committee." . . .

Marxist Reactions to Lenin—Leon Trotsky

Though born only in 1879, Trotsky had gained a leading place among the Russian Social-Democrats by the time of the Second Party Congress in 1903. Like Rosa Luxemburg, he represented ultra-radical sentiment that could not reconcile itself to Lenin's stress on the party organization. Trotsky stayed with the Menshevik faction until he joined Lenin in 1917. From that point on he accommodated himself in large measure to Lenin's philosophy of party dictatorship, but his reservations came to the surface again in the years after his fall from power. His comments on Lenin in 1904 were truly prophetic.

. . . We wish that our comrades would not overlook the difference of principle between the two methods of work. . . . This difference, if we reduce it to its basis of principle, has decisive significance in determining the character of all the work of our party. In the one case we have the contriving of ideas for the proletariat, the political *substitution* for the

FROM: Trotsky, *Our Political Tasks* (Geneva, Russian Social-Democratic Workers' Party, 1904, pp. 50, 52, 54, 73-75, 105; editor's translation).

proletariat; in the other, political *education* of the proletariat, its political *mobilization*. . . .

The system of political substitution, point for point like the "Economists' " system of simplification, proceeds—consciously or unconsciously—from a false "sophisticated" understanding of the relation between the objective interests of the proletariat and its consciousness. . . .

In contrast to the "economists," the "politicians" take as their point of departure the *objective* class interests of the proletariat, established by the method of Marxism. But with the same fear that the "economists" have they turn away from the "distance" which lies between the objective and subjective interests of the class whom in principle they "represent." . . . Thus, if the "economists" do not lead the proletariat because they are dragged *behind it*, the "politicians" do not lead the proletariat because they themselves *carry out its obligations*. If the "economists" have saved themselves from the immensity of the task by assigning themselves a modest role—to march at the tail end of history—the "politicians" resolve the question by trying to transform history *into their own tail*. . . .

Poorly or well (more poorly) we are revolutionizing the masses, arousing in them the simplest political instincts. But to the extent that this involves complicated tasks—the transformation of these "instincts" into the conscious striving for the political self-determination of the working class—we resort in the broadest way to abbreviated and simplified methods of "contriving" and "substitution."

In the internal politics of the party these methods lead, as we shall yet see, to this: the party organization is substituted for the party, the Central Committee is substituted for the party organization, and finally a "dictator" is substituted for the Central Committee. . . .

According to Lenin's new philosophy . . . it is enough for the proletarian to go through the "school of the factory" in order to give lessons in *political discipline* to the intelligentsia, which has meanwhile been playing the leading role in the party. According to this new philosophy, anyone who does not imagine the ideal party "as a vast factory," who thinks on the contrary that such a picture is "monstrous," anyone who does not believe in the unlimited power of a machine for political education, "immediately exhibits the psychology of the bourgeois intellectual." . . .

Without fear of exhibiting the "psychology of the bourgeois intellectual," we assert above all that the conditions which impel the proletariat to collectively agreed-upon methods of struggle lie not in the factory but in the general social conditions of the proletariat's existence. . . .

Of course, "production which is highly developed technologically" creates the material for the political development and political discipline of the proletariat, just as capitalism in general creates the *preconditions* of socialism. But just as it is unfounded to identify socialism with capitalism, so is it wrong to identify the *factory* discipline of the proletariat with *revolutionary-political* discipline.

The task of Social-Democracy consists of setting the proletariat against that discipline which replaces the work of human thought with the rhythm of physical movement, and against this dead, killing discipline to weld the proletariat into one militant army—all in step and shoulder to shoulder—united by a common political consciousness and revolutionary enthusiasm. *Such* discipline the Russian proletariat does not yet have; the factory and the machine do not provide it with this quality as spontaneously as they dispense occupational diseases.

The barrack regime cannot be the regime of our party, as the factory cannot be its model. . . .

The tasks of the new regime are so complicated that they cannot be solved in any way other than by competition between various methods of economic and political construction, by way of long "disputes," by way of systematic struggle—not only of the socialist world against the capitalist one, but also between various tendencies within socialism, tendencies which will inevitably appear as soon as the dictatorship of the proletariat throws up dozens, hundreds of new, hitherto unsolved problems. And no "strong, authoritative organization" can suppress these tendencies and disagreements in order to hasten and simplify the process, for it is all too clear that a proletariat capable of dictatorship over society will not tolerate dictatorship over itself.

Organization of the Bolshevik Faction

In the months following the Second Congress of the Social-Democratic Party Lenin lost his slim majority and proceeded to organize an insurgent group in opposition to the dominant "Menshevik" leadership. A group of twenty-two Bolsheviks (counting Lenin himself) met in Geneva in August, 1904, to endorse the idea of the highly disciplined party and to urge the reorganization of the whole Social-Democratic movement on Leninist lines.

Recently a private meeting was held of twenty-two like-minded members of the RSDWP who take the point of view of the majority at the Second Party Congress; this conference considered the question of our party crisis and the means of emerging from it, and decided to turn to all Russian Social Democrats with the following proclamation:

Comrades! The severe crisis of party life is becoming more and more involved, and its end is not in sight. Confusion is growing, creating still newer conflicts, and the positive work of the party all along the line is strained by it to the utmost. The forces of the party, which is still young and not successfully stiffened, are fruitlessly wasted to a threatening extent.

Meanwhile, the historical moment presents to the party demands which are vaster than ever before. The revolutionary alertness of the working class is growing, the ferment is increasing, and in the other strata of society, war and crisis, hunger and unemployment are with elemental inevitability undermining the roots of the autocracy. The shameful end of a shameful war is already not far off: and it unavoidably multiplies revolutionary alertness ten-fold, unavoidably

FROM: Resolution of the "Twenty-two Like-minded Members of the RSDWP Who Take the Point of View of the Majority at the Second Party Congress" (August, 1904; CPSU in Resolutions, I, pp. 60-63, 65; editor's translation).

drives the working class face to face with its enemies and demands from Social Democracy colossal work, a terrific intensification of effort, in order to organize the final decisive struggle with the autocracy.

Can our party satisfy these demands in the condition in which it now finds itself? Any conscientious man must without hesitation answer no!

The unity of the party has been deeply undermined; the struggle inside has gone beyond the bounds of any party spirit. Organizational discipline has been shaken to its very foundation; the capacity of the party for harmonious unified action has turned into a dream.

Nevertheless, we consider this illness of the party to be an illness of growth. We see the basis of the crisis in the transition from the circle forms of the life of Social Democracy to party forms; the essence of the internal struggle is in the conflict between the circle spirit and party spirit. Therefore, only by putting an end to this illness can our party *really* become a party.

Under the name of the "minority" in the party [the Mensheviks], heterogeneous elements have gathered, which are linked by the conscious or unconscious effort to retain circle relationships, preparty forms of organization. . . . Their allies are all those elements which in theory or practice have fallen away from the principle of strict Social-Democratism, for only the circle spirit could preserve the individuality of ideas and the influence of these elements; while party spirit threatened to dissolve them or deprive them of any influence. . . . However, the chief cadres of the opposition consisted in general of all those elements in our party which by preference belong to the intelligentsia. In comparison with the proletariat, the intelligentsia is always more individualistic, due to the basic conditions of its life and work, which do not directly give it a broad unification of its forces or a direct education in organized joint labor. Therefore, it is more difficult for intellectual elements to adapt to the discipline of party life, and those of them who are not in a position to undertake this task naturally raise the banner of rebellion against the essential organizational limitations, and elevate their elemental anarchy into a principle of struggle, incorrectly designating this anarchy as the striving for "autonomy," as the demand for "tolerance," etc.

The portion of the party which is abroad, where the circles are distinguished by their relative longevity, where theoreticians of various shades form groupings, where the intelligentsia definitely predominates—this portion of the party had to be the most inclined to the point of view of the "minority." Therefore, it quickly became an actual majority there. On the other hand, Russia, where the voice of the organized proletarians is heard more loudly, where in more vital and closer intercourse with them, the party intelligentsia is educated in a more proletarian spirit, where the gravity of the immediate struggle more strongly compels people to feel the necessity of the organized unity of work—Russia has come out determinedly against the circle spirit, against anarchist disorganizing tendencies. She has definitely expressed this attitude toward them in a whole series of manifestations on the part of the committees and the other party organizations. . . .

The majority of the party, striving however it can to preserve its unity and organizational bond, has struggled only by loyal party means and has not once made concessions for the sake of conciliation. The minority, carrying on the anarchistic tendency, has not bothered about party peace and unity. It has made each concession an instrument of further struggle. Of all the demands of the minority only one has up to this time not been satisfied—the introduction of diversity into the Central Committee of the party by way of co-opting members of the minority who are forcibly bound to it—and the attacks by the minority have become more embittered than ever. Having taken control of the Central Organ and the Party Council, the minority now does not desist from exploiting in its circle interests that very discipline against which in essence it struggles. . . .

Coming forth with this program of struggle for the unity of the party, we invite the representatives of all other shadings and all party organizations to express themselves on the question of their programs, in order to make it possible to prepare for a congress, seriously and consistently, consciously and according to a plan. A question of life, a question of honor and worth is being decided for the party: does it exist as an ideological force and real force capable of rationally organizing itself enough to come forth as the actual leader of the revolutionary workers' movement of our country? In all its manner of action the minority abroad says no! And it continues to act surely and determinedly in this sense, relying on the remoteness of Russia, on the frequent replacement of party workers there, on the irreplaceability of its leaders, its literary figures. A party is being born to us, we say, seeing the growth of the political consciousness of the progressive workers, seeing the active initiative of the committees in the general life of the party. A party is being born to us, our young forces are multiplying, and they are able to replace and outlive the old literary collegia which are losing the confidence of the party; we are more and more getting to be revolutionaries who value the sustained direction of party life more than any circle of former leaders. A party is being born to us, and no tricks or delays will hold back its decisive and final judgment.

From these forces of our party we draw the assurance of victory.

Comrades! Print and distribute this proclamation.

Lenin on the Revolution of 1905

During the revolutionary disturbances of 1905 in Russia, Lenin endeavored to justify a major role for the workers' party, despite the Marxist consensus that Russia was ready only for the "bourgeois-democratic" revolution. Lenin solved the problem by denying the revolutionary capabilities of the bourgeoisie and insisting that the workers' party, so-called, would have to push the "bourgeois" revolution through to the end. The party would gather the land-hungry peasants under its wing, establish the "revolutionary democratic dictatorship of the proletariat and peasantry," and hold power until the opportunity arrived to implement the program of socialism.

This type of reasoning has underlain Communist aspirations to power not only in Russia but in the underdeveloped East in general: they insist on a leading role for the "proletarian" party no matter what social conditions must be faced or what strange alliances must be made.

. . . It is entirely absurd to think that a bourgeois revolution does not express the interests of the proletariat at all. This absurd idea boils down either to the hoary Narodnik [Populist] theory that a bourgeois revolution runs counter to the interests of the proletariat, and that therefore we do not need bourgeois political liberty; or to anarchism, which rejects all participation of the proletariat in bourgeois politics, in a bourgeois revolution and in bourgeois parliamentarism. From the standpoint of theory, this idea disregards the elementary propositions of Marxism concerning the inevitability of capitalist development where commodity production exists. Marxism teaches that a society which is based on commodity production, and which has commercial intercourse with civilized capitalist nations, at a certain stage of its development, itself inevitably takes the road of capitalism. Marxism has irrevocably broken with the ravings of the Narodniks and the anarchists to the effect that Russia, for instance, can avoid capitalist development, jump out of capitalism, or skip over it and proceed along some path other than the path of the class struggle on the basis and within the framework of this same capitalism.

All these principles of Marxism have been proved and explained over and over again in minute detail in general and with regard to Russia in particular. And from these principles it follows that the idea of seeking salvation for the working class in anything save the further development of capitalism is *reactionary*. In countries like Russia, the working class suffers not so much from capitalism as from the insufficient development of capitalism. The working class is therefore *decidedly interested* in the broadest, freest and most rapid development of capitalism. The removal of all the remnants of the old order which are hampering the

FROM: Lenin, "Two Tactics of Social Democracy in the Democratic Revolution" (July, 1905; *Selected Works,* Vol. I, book 2, pp. 48-51, 86-90, 104-5, 107, 142).

broad, free and rapid development of capitalism is of decided *advantage* to the working class. The bourgeois revolution is precisely a revolution that most resolutely sweeps away the survivals of the past, the remnants of serfdom (which include not only autocracy but monarchy as well) and most fully guarantees the broadest, freest and most rapid development of capitalism.

That is why a *bourgeois* revolution is *in the highest degree advantageous to the proletariat.* A bourgeois revolution is *absolutely* necessary in the interests of the proletariat. The more complete and determined, the more consistent the bourgeois revolution, the more assured will be the proletarian struggle against the bourgeoisie for Socialism. Only those who are ignorant of the rudiments of scientific Socialism can regard this conclusion as new or strange, paradoxical. . . .

On the other hand, it is more advantageous for the working class if the necessary changes in the direction of bourgeois democracy take place by way of revolution and not by way of reform; for the way of reform is the way of delay, of procrastination, of the painfully slow decomposition of the putrid parts of the national organism. It is the proletariat and the peasantry that suffer first of all and most of all from their putrefaction. The revolutionary way is the way of quick amputation, which is the least painful to the proletariat, the way of the direct removal of the decomposing parts, the way of fewest concessions to and least consideration for the monarchy and the disgusting, vile, rotten and contaminating institutions which go with it. . . .

Marxism teaches the proletarian not to keep aloof from the bourgeois revolution, not to be indifferent to it, not to allow the leadership of the revolution to be assumed by the bourgeoisie but, on the contrary, to take a most energetic part in it, to fight most resolutely for consistent proletarian democracy, for carrying the revolution to its conclusion. We cannot jump out of the bourgeois-democratic boundaries of the Russian revolution, but we can vastly extend these boundaries, and within these boundaries we can and must fight for the interests of the proletariat, for its immediate needs and for the conditions that will make it possible to prepare its forces for the future complete victory. . . .

The basic idea here is the one that the *Vperiod*[*] has repeatedly formulated, stating that we must not be afraid of a complete victory for Social-Democracy in a democratic revolution, i.e., of a revolutionary-democratic dictatorship of the proletariat and the peasantry, for such a victory will enable us to rouse Europe, and the socialist proletariat of Europe, after throwing off the yoke of the bourgeoisie, will in its turn help us to accomplish the socialist revolution. . . .

The *Vperiod* quite definitely stated wherein lies the real "possibility of holding power"—namely, in the revolutionary-democratic dictatorship of the proletariat and the peasantry, in their joint mass strength, which is capable of outweighing all the forces of counterrevolution, in the inevitable concurrence of their interests in *democratic* changes. . . . If in our fight for a republic and democracy we could not rely upon the peasantry as well as on the proletariat, the prospect of our "holding power" would be hopeless. But if it is not hopeless, if a "decisive victory of the revolution over tsarism" opens up such a possibility, then we must point to it, we must actively call for its transformation into reality and issue practical slogans not only *for the contingency* of the revolution being carried into Europe, but also *for the purpose* of carrying it there. . . . Beyond the bounds of democracy there can be no question of the proletariat and the peasant bourgeoisie having a single will. Class struggle between them is inevitable; but it is in a democratic republic that this struggle will be the most thoroughgoing and widespread struggle of the people *for Socialism.* Like everything else in the world, the revolutionary-democratic dictatorship of the proletariat and the peasantry has a past and a future. Its past is autocracy, serfdom, monarchy and privilege. In the struggle against this past, in the struggle against counterrevolution, a "single will" of the proletariat and the peasantry is possible, for here there is unity of interests.

Its future is the struggle against private property, the

[*] "Forward": Lenin's paper, 1904-5—Ed.

struggle of the wage worker against the employer, the struggle for Socialism. Here singleness of will is impossible. Here our path lies not from autocracy to a republic but from a petty-bourgeois democratic republic to Socialism. . . .

A Social-Democrat must never for a moment forget that the proletariat will inevitably have to wage the class struggle for Socialism even against the most democratic and republican bourgeoisie and petty bourgeoisie. This is beyond doubt. Hence the absolute necessity of a separate, independent, strictly class party of Social-Democracy. Hence the temporary nature of our tactics of "striking jointly" with the bourgeoisie and the duty of keeping a strict watch "over our ally, as over an enemy," etc. All this is also beyond the slightest doubt. But it would be ridiculous and reactionary to deduce from this that we must forget, ignore or neglect these tasks which, although transient and temporary, are vital at the present time. The fight against the autocracy is a temporary and transient task of the Socialists, but to ignore or neglect this task in any way would be tantamount to betraying Socialism and rendering a service to reaction. The revolutionary-democratic dictatorship of the proletariat and the peasantry is unquestionably only a transient, temporary aim of the Socialists, but to ignore this aim in the period of a democratic revolution would be downright reactionary. . . .

. . . We Marxists all know . . . that the bourgeoisie is inconsistent, self-seeking and cowardly in its support of the revolution. The bourgeoisie, in the mass, will inevitably turn towards counterrevolution, towards the autocracy, against the revolution and against the people, immediately its narrow, selfish interests are met, immediately it "recoils" from consistent democracy (*and it is already recoiling from it!*). There remains the "people," that is, the proletariat and the peasantry: the proletariat alone can be relied on to march to the end, for it is going far beyond the democratic revolution. That is why the proletariat fights in the front ranks for a republic and contemptuously rejects silly and unworthy advice to take care not to frighten away the bourgeoisie. The peasantry includes a great number of semiproletarian as well as petty-bourgeois elements. This causes it also to be unstable and compels the proletariat to unite in a strictly class party. But the instability of the peasantry differs radically from the instability of the bourgeoisie, for at the present time the peasantry is interested not so much in the absolute preservation of private property as in the confiscation of the landed estates, one of the principal forms of private property. While this does not make the peasantry become socialist or cease to be petty-bourgeois, it is capable of becoming a wholehearted and most radical adherent of the democratic revolution. . . .

. . . The Russian revolution will begin to assume its real sweep, will really assume the widest revolutionary sweep possible in the epoch of bourgeois-democratic revolution, only when the bourgeoisie recoils from it and when the masses of the peasantry come out as active revolutionaries side by side with the proletariat. In order that it may be consistently carried to its conclusion, our democratic revolution must rely on such forces as are capable of paralyzing the inevitable inconsistency of the bourgeoisie (i.e., capable precisely of "causing it to recoil from the revolution," which the Caucasian adherents of *Iskra* fear so much because of their lack of judgment).

The proletariat must carry to completion the democratic revolution, by allying to itself the mass of the peasantry in order to crush by force the resistance of the autocracy and to paralyze the instability of the bourgeoisie. The proletariat must accomplish the socialist revolution, by allying to itself the mass of the semiproletarian elements of the population in order to crush by force the resistance of the bourgeoisie and to paralyze the instability of the peasantry and the petty bourgeoisie. . . .

Major questions in the life of nations are settled only by force. The reactionary classes themselves are usually the first to resort to violence, to civil war; they are the first to "place the bayonet on the agenda," as the Russian autocracy has been doing systematically and undeviatingly everywhere ever since January 9.* And since such a situation has arisen, since the bayonet has really become the main point on the political agenda, since insurrection has proved to be imperative and urgent—constitutional illusions and school exercises in parliamentarism become only a screen for the bourgeois betrayal of the revolution, a screen to conceal the fact that the bourgeoisie is "recoiling" from the revolution. It is therefore the slogan of dictatorship that the genuinely revolutionary class must advance. . . .

Lenin on Insurrection

Following the abortive uprising of the workers in Moscow in December, 1905, Lenin expressed himself on the decisive importance of revolutionary violence.

. . . We must carry on the widest agitation among the masses in favour of an armed uprising and make no attempt to obscure this question by talk about "preliminary stages," or to befog it in any way. We would be deceiving both ourselves and the people if we concealed from them the fact that the impending revolutionary action must take the form of a desperate, bloody war of extermination. . . .

December confirmed another of Marx's profound propositions, which the opportunists have forgotten, namely, that insurrection is an art, and that the principal rule of this art is that a desperately bold and irrevocably determined *offensive* must be waged. We have not sufficiently assimilated this truth. We have not sufficiently learnt ourselves, nor have we taught the masses this art, this rule to attack, come what may. We must make up for this with all our energy. It is not enough to take sides on the question of political slogans; it is also necessary to take sides on the question of armed insurrection. Those who are opposed to it, those who do not prepare for it, must be ruthlessly dis-

FROM: Lenin, "The Lessons of the Moscow Uprising" (September, 1906; *Selected Works*, Vol. I, book 2, pp. 166, 168-69).

* January 9, 1905: "Bloody Sunday," when troops fired on demonstrators in St. Petersburg—Ed.

missed from the ranks of the supporters of the revolution, sent packing to its enemies, to the traitors or cowards; for the day is approaching when the force of events and the conditions of the struggle will compel us to separate enemies from friends according to this principle. We must not preach passivity, not mere "waiting" until the troops "come over." No! We must proclaim from the housetops the need for a bold offensive and armed attack, the necessity at such times of exterminating the persons in command of the enemy, and of a most energetic fight for the wavering troops. . . .

Trotsky on "Permanent Revolution"

Trotsky's response to the revolution of 1905 and the problem of the workers' role in Russia was to predict a new upheaval in which the proletariat would temporarily find itself in power. It would depend on world revolution to sustain them, however, and rescue the Russian socialists from the backwardness of their country. Herein lay Trotsky's notion of continuous or "permanent" revolution, which reconciled the predominantly backward character of Russia with the Marxists' desire to justify a revolutionary role for themselves.

. . . The Russian working class of 1906 differs entirely from the Vienna working class of 1848. The best proof of it is the all-Russian practice of the Councils of Workmen's Deputies (Soviets). Those are no organizations of conspirators prepared beforehand to step forward in times of unrest and to seize command over the working class. They are organs consciously created by the masses themselves to coördinate their revolutionary struggle. The Soviets, elected by and responsible to the masses, are thoroughly democratic institutions following the most determined class policy in the spirit of revolutionary Socialism. . . .

Within the limits of a revolution at the beginning of the twentieth century, which is also a bourgeois revolution in

FROM: Trotsky, *Results and Prospects* (1906; translated as *Our Revolution* by M. J. Olgin, New York, Holt, 1918, pp. 80, 92, 95-96, 100-03, 109-10, 132, 136-37, 142-44; reprinted by permission of the publisher).

its immediate objective aims, there looms up a prospect of an inevitable, or at least possible, supremacy of the working class in the near future. . . .

To imagine a revolutionary democratic government without representatives of labor is to see the absurdity of such a situation. A refusal of labor to participate in a revolutionary government would make the very existence of that government impossible, and would be tantamount to a betrayal of the cause of the revolution. A participation of labor in a revolutionary government, however, is admissible, both from the viewpoint of objective probability and subjective desirability, *only in the role of a leading dominant power.* Of course, you can call such a government "dictatorship of the proletariat and peasantry," "dictatorship of the proletariat, the peasantry, and the intelligentsia," or "a revolutionary government of the workingmen and the lower middle class." This question will still remain: Who has the hegemony in the government and through it in the country? *When we speak of a labor government we mean that the hegemony belongs to the working class.* . . .

Our attitude towards the idea of a "dictatorship of the proletariat and the peasantry" is now quite clear. It is not a question whether we think it "admissible" or not, whether we "wish" or we "do not wish" this form of political coöperation. In our opinion, it simply cannot be realized, at least in its direct meaning. Such a coöperation presupposes that either the peasantry has identified itself with one of the existing bourgeois parties, or it has formed a powerful party of its own. Neither is possible, as we have tried to point out. . . .

The proletariat can get into power only at a moment of national upheaval, of sweeping national enthusiasm. The proletariat assumes power as a revolutionary representative of the people, as a recognized leader in the fight against absolutism and barbaric feudalism. Having assumed power, however, the proletariat will open a new era, an era of positive legislation, of revolutionary politics, and this is the point where its political supremacy as an avowed spokesman of the nation may become endangered.

The first measures of the proletariat—the cleansing of the Augean stables of the old regime and the driving away of their inhabitants—will find active support of the entire nation whatever the liberal castraters may tell us of the power of some prejudices amoung the masses. The work of political cleansing will be accompanied by democratic reorganization of all social and political relations. The labor government, impelled by immediate needs and requirements, will have to look into all kinds of relations and activities among the people. It will have to throw out of the army and the administration all those who had stained their hands with the blood of the people; it will have to disband all the regiments that had polluted themselves with crimes against the people. This work will have to be done immediately, long before the establishment of an elective responsible administration and before the organization of a popular militia. This, however, will be only a beginning. Labor democracy will soon be confronted by the problems of a normal workday, the agrarian relations and unemployment. The legislative solution of those problems will show the *class character* of the labor government. It will tend to weaken the revolutionary bond between the proletariat and the nation; it will give the economic differentiation among the peasants a political expression. Antagonism between the component parts of the nation will grow step by step as the policies of the labor government become more outspoken, lose their general democratic character and become *class policies*. . . .

Social-Democracy can never assume power under a double obligation: to put the *entire* minimum program into operation for the sake of the proletariat, and to keep strictly *within the limits* of this program, for the sake of the bourgeoisie. Such a double obligation could never be fulfilled. Participating in the government, not as powerless hostages, but as a leading force, the representatives of labor *eo ipso* break the line between the minimum and maximum program. *Collectivism becomes the order of the day.* At which point the proletariat will be stopped on its march in this direction, depends upon the constellation of forces, not upon the original purpose of the proletarian party. . . .

Political supremacy of the proletariat is incompatible with its economic slavery. Whatever may be the banner under which the proletariat will find itself in possession of power, it will be compelled to enter the road of Socialism. It is the greatest Utopia to think that the proletariat, brought to the top by the mechanics of a bourgeois revolution, would be able, even if it wanted, to limit its mission by creating a republican democratic environment for the social supremacy of the bourgeoisie. Political dominance of the proletariat, even if it were temporary, would extremely weaken the resistance of capital which is always in need of state aid, and would give momentous opportunities to the economic struggle of the proletariat. . . .

How far, however, can the Socialist policy of the working class advance in the economic environment of Russia? One thing we can say with perfect assurance: it will meet political obstacles long before it will be checked by the technical backwardness of the country. *Without direct political aid from the European proletariat the working class of Russia will not be able to retain its power and to turn its temporary supremacy into a permanent Socialist dictatorship.* We cannot doubt this for a moment. On the other hand, there is no doubt that a *Socialist revolution in the West would allow us to turn the temporary supremacy of the working class directly into a Socialist dictatorship.* . . .

The influence of the Russian revolution on the proletariat of Europe is immense. Not only does it destroy the Petersburg absolutism, that main power of European reaction; it also imbues the minds and the souls of the European proletariat with revolutionary daring. . . .

. . . The colossal influence of the Russian revolution manifests itself in killing party routine, in destroying Socialist conservatism, in making a clean contest of proletarian forces against capitalist reaction a question of the day. . . .

The Russian proletariat in power, even if this were only the result of a passing combination of forces in the Russian bourgeois revolution, would meet organized opposition on the part of the world's reaction, and readiness for organized support on the part of the world's proletariat. Left to its own resources, the Russian working class must necessarily be crushed the moment it loses the aid of the peasants. Nothing remains for it but to link the fate of its political supremacy and the fate of the Russian revolution with the fate of a Socialist revolution in Europe. All that momentous authority and political power which is given to the proletariat by a combination of forces in the Russian bourgeois revolution, it will thrust on the scale of class struggle in the entire capitalistic world. Equipped with governmental power, having a counter-revolution behind his back, having the European reaction in front of him, the Russian workingman will issue to all his brothers the world over his old battle-cry which will now become the call for the last attack: *Proletarians of all the world, unite!*

Lenin on Democratic Centralism

Following the revolution of 1905 repeated attempts were made by the Bolsheviks and Mensheviks to restore the unity of the Social-Democratic Party. Lenin was criticized for indiscipline, and replied with a defense of the rights of minorities within the system of "democratic centralism." This formula became the official doctrine of the Communist organization, though freedom of factions disappeared very quickly.

The authors of the resolution are completely wrong in their understanding of the relation between *free criticism* within the party and the party's *unity of action*. Criticism within the limits of the *foundations* of the party program must be completely free . . . not only at party meetings, but also at broader ones. To suppress such criticism or such "agitation" (for criticism cannot be separated from agitation) is impossible. The political action of the party must be united. No "appeals" are permissible which violate the unity of actions which have already been decided upon, neither at open meetings, nor at party meetings, nor in the party press.

FROM: Lenin, "Freedom of Criticism and Unity of Action" (June, 1906; *Collected Works,* 3rd ed., Moscow, Marx-Engels-Lenin Institute, 1928, Vol. IX, pp. 274-75; editor's translation).

Obviously the Central Committee has defined the freedom of criticism inaccurately and too narrowly, and the unity of action—inaccurately and too broadly. . . .

The Central Committee's resolution is incorrect in substance and *contradicts the statutes of the party.* The principle of democratic centralism and autonomy of local institutions means specifically freedom of criticism, complete and everywhere, as long as this does not disrupt the unity of action already decided upon—and the intolerability of any criticism undermining or obstructing the unity of action decided on by the party.

We consider it a great mistake on the part of the Central Committee to issue a resolution on this important question without any preliminary consideration of it by the party press and the party organizations; such consideration would have helped it avoid the mistakes indicated by us. . . .

Bogdanov's Philosophical Revision of Marxism

Lenin's outstanding lieutenant in the early years of the Bolshevik faction was Alexander A. Bogdanov—physician, economist, philosopher, sociologist, and exponent of romantic revolutionary extremism. After 1905, Bogdanov became the leader of the left-wing purists among the Bolsheviks who refused to make use of the Duma, the parliamentary body of limited power established in 1906. At the same time he attempted an original philosophical extension of Marxism by applying the philosophy of "empirio-criticism" of the Austrian physicist Ernst Mach and the German philosopher Richard Avenarius. This was of immediate significance because it provoked Lenin's ire and a drastic shake-up in the Bolshevik ranks to enforce Lenin's standards of ideological discipline. It also had implications much later, during the second decade of the Soviet regime, because of its suggestion that truth is conditioned by classes and the class struggle.

. . . The task of cognition, according to the views of Mach and Avenarius, consists of systematizing the content

FROM: Bogdanov, *Empiriomonism* (St. Petersburg, Dorovatovsky and Charushnikov, Book I, 2nd ed., 1905, pp. 9, 10, 25, 36, 40-41, and Book III, 1906, pp. iv-v, ix, xxiii-xxv, xxxiii, 83-84, 139-42, 149-50, 152, 159; editor's translation).

of experience, since experience is both the natural basis and the natural boundary of cognition. In its own objective significance this systematization is a powerful living adaptation, an instrument for preserving life and its development. . . .

But cognition in this picture is not merely adaptation in general; it is also *social* adaptation. The social genesis of cognition, its dependence on social experience, the principled difference of value in the thinking of different people, and its constant social interaction, clearly emerge and are consciously underscored by both thinkers. . . .

Where Mach sketches out the connection of cognition with the social process of labor, the correspondence of his views with the ideas of Marx occasionally becomes quite astonishing. . . .

We arrive at this conclusion: the characteristics of "objectivity" in general cannot have as their basis individual experience. . . . The basis of "objectivity" must lie in the sphere of *collective* experience. . . .

The agreement in collective experience which is expressed in this "objectivity" can only appear as the result of the progressive concordance of the experience of different people as they express themselves to each other. The objectivity of the physical bodies which we encounter in our experience is established in the last analysis on the basis of mutual verification and the concordance in what different people express. In general the physical world is this: socially agreed-upon, socially harmonized, in a word, *socially organized* experience. . . .

Laws do not belong at all to the sphere of immediate experience; laws are the result of conscious reworking of experience; they are not facts in themselves, but are created by thought, as a means of organizing experience, of harmoniously bringing it into agreement as an ordered unity. Laws are *abstract cognition,* and physical laws possess physical qualities just as little as psychological laws possess psychic qualities. . . . The antithesis between the physical and psychic aspects of experience reduces to the distinction between socially organized and individually organized experience. . . .

. . . The social materialism of Marx presented demands to my world view which the old materialism could not satisfy. . . . It was necessary *to know one's knowledge,* to explain one's world view, and according to the idea of Marxism this could and had to be done on the basis of research on its social genesis. It was obvious that the basic concepts of the old materialism—both "matter" and "immutable laws"—were worked out in the course of the *social* development of mankind, and inasmuch as they were "ideological forms," it was necessary to find their "material base." But since the "material base" has the property of changing as society develops, it becomes clear that any given ideological form can have only a historically transitory meaning, not an objectively supra-historical meaning, that it can be a "truth of the time" ("*objective*" truth, but only within the limits of a given epoch)—but in no case can it be a "truth for all time" ("objective" in the absolute meaning of the word). . . . For me Marxism includes the denial of the unconditional objectivity of any truth whatsoever, the denial of every eternal truth. . . .

Truth is an ideological form—the organizing form of human experience; and if we know this without doubt, and know that the material basis of ideology changes, that the content of experience expands—do we have any right whatsoever to assert that this given ideological form will never be transformed by the development of its social basis, that this given form of experience will not be burst apart by its growing contents? Consistent Marxism does not allow such dogmatic and static notions. . . .

Marxist philosophy must above all be one of natural science. Of course, natural science is the *ideology of the productive forces of society,* because it serves as the basis for technical experience and the technical sciences; in concordance with the basic idea of historical materialism, the productive forces of society represent the base of its development in general. But it is also clear that Marxist philosophy must reflect the *social form* of the productive forces, relying obviously on the "social" sciences proper. . . .

Ideological forms are the *organizational adaptation of*

social life, and in the last analysis (directly or indirectly), of the *technical process.* Therefore the development of ideology is determined by *necessities* in the organizational adaptations of the social process and by the *material present* for them. The viability of ideological forms depends, consequently, on the harmony and order with which they really organize the social content of labor. . . .

The world of experience has been crystallized and continues to be crystallized out of chaos. The force which determines the forms of this crystallization is the intercourse of people. Outside of these forms there is really no *experience,* because a disorganized mass of occurrences is not experience. Thus, experience is social in its very basis, and its progress is the *social-psychological process of organizing it.* The individual psychical organizing process is completely adapted to this. If, for the empiriocriticist, the experience of all humans is of equal value, which I have earlier designated as the familiar cognitive "democracy," then for the empiriomonist this experience is rather the result of the collective organizing work of all people—a sort of cognitive "socialism." . . .

Summarizing the connection and dependence between "ideology" and "technology" in the process of social development, we arrive at the following formulations:

1. The technical process is the area of the direct struggle of society with nature; ideology is the area of the organizing forms of social life. In the last analysis the technical process represents just that content which is organized by the ideological forms.

2. Corresponding to this relationship, the technical process represents the basic and ideology the derivative area of social life and social development. From the standpoint of energetics, ideology is conditioned by the technical process in the sense that it arises and develops according to that preponderance of assimilation over disassimilation which is characteristic of it. On the qualitative side the material of ideological forms also has its beginning in the technical area.

3. The development of technical forms is accomplished under the direct action of both "extra-social" selection (influences on the part of external nature) and social selection.

The development of ideology is directly subordinated to social selection alone.

4. The point of departure of any social development lies in the technical process. The basic line of development goes from the technical forms through the lower organizing forms of ideology to the higher. Corresponding to this, there proceeds in the same direction an increase in the conservatism of social forms.

5. The derivative line of social development, directed from the higher organizing forms toward the lower and from ideology toward technology, is always just the continuation and reflection of the basic line. Not only does it never change the relatively greater magnitude of the conservatism of the higher forms of ideology; it actually rests on this conservatism as its necessary condition.

6. Thus the dynamic conditions of social development and degradation, the motive forces of these processes, lie in the technical process; in ideology lie the static conditions, the limiting, regulating, and form-giving forces. . . .

We summarize the main conclusions concerning the group and class differentiation of society:

1. Both group and class divisions in society are the result of the quantitative and qualitative progress of technology. "Social groups" arise on the basis of specialization; classes, on the basis of the progressive isolation of the organizer and executive functions in society. Group and class dissociation essentially amounts to vitally important distinctions in the direction of social selection.

2. Social groups and classes acquire the definite and firm qualities of social complexes when they are provided with definitely distinct ideologies, which condition the firmly distinct direction of social selection within these collectivities. . . .

5. The ideology worked out by the organizer part of society retains full vital significance for both parts of society as long as the content which it organizes remains really common to them. When this condition is violated . . . the ideological dissociation of classes begins; the ideology of the upper class comes into contradiction with the actual experience and

urges of the lower, and this contradiction is then further intensified.

6. The organizer function of the "upper" class allows it to organize the life of the "lower" class by means of norms which do not correspond with the conditions of life of the latter. For the class subordinated to them, such norms acquire the significance of external forces, like the forces of extra-social nature—hostile forces to which one has to adapt. Such a primary and basic class contradiction is the starting point for the development of any class struggle. . . .

8. . . . The organizer class, progressively removing itself from the technical-production process, in the course of time loses its real organizer function, changes into a parasite class, inevitably degenerates, and at the same time loses its social strength. . . .

10. The capitalistic type of class development . . . leads to the progressive transformation of the mass of individual working operatives into a solid collectivity, adapted to the organizer role on a scale which expands without limit. The rapid technical progress which is characteristic of this type of development stimulates the rapid development of opposed class ideologies and the class struggle. This culminates in the downfall of the former organizer class and society's transition from class development through contradictions, to integral-harmonious development. Extrasocial and social spontaneity are both overcome by the planfully organized force of humanity, and its power over nature grows without limit. . . .

In a class society any world view is either the ideology of one definite class or a definite combination of different class ideologies. Even the most individual of them can only be a particular combination of elements of collective, class thinking. For the individual is created and defined by the social milieu—in a class society, by the class milieu.

Such being the case, the ideology of the technical process is inevitably the ideology of the class which stands in the closest relationship to the technical process, i.e., the class of "producers" in the *broad* sense of the word. . . . In the social-labor experience of the worker in machine production there exists material with basic vital significance both for the recognition in principle of the homogeneity of the "psychic" and the "physical," and for the tendency cognitively to subordinate the "psychic" to the collectively elaborated forms of the cognition of the "physical." The philosophy which organizes this material into pure finished forms and makes these forms general must be regarded as the ideology of a given class—of course, just to the extent that it really accomplishes this and does not add alien tendencies which contradict the tendencies of the proletariat. . . .

We have arrived at this characterization of the philosophical world view we are considering: the cognitive ideology of the technical process, proletarian in its tendencies, which in its general scheme reproduces the basic features of the structure of contemporary society. . . .

Lenin's Philosophical Orthodoxy

Lenin wrote his main philosophical work, *Materialism and Empiriocriticism,* as a polemical reply to Bogdanov. Here Lenin revealed his intolerance of any critical attitude toward what he regarded as the absolute truth laid down by Marx and Engels. His dogmatic assertion of an oversimplified nineteenth-century materialism remains the official philosophy for the entire Communist movement.

A number of writers, would-be Marxists, have this year undertaken a veritable campaign against the philosophy of Marxism. . . .

All these people could not have been ignorant of the fact that Marx and Engels scores of times termed their philosophical views dialectical materialism. Yet all these people, who, despite the sharp divergence of their political views, are united in their hostility toward dialectical materialism, at the same time claim to be Marxists in philosophy! Engels'

FROM: Lenin, *Materialism and Empirio-Criticism—Critical Comments on a Reactionary Philosophy* (1908; English translation, New York, International Publishers, 1927, pp. 9-10, 38, 121, 127-29, 335-38, 370-71; reprinted by permission of the publisher).

dialectics is "mysticism," says Berman. Engels' views have become "antiquated," remarks Bazarov casually, as though it were a self-evident fact. Materialism thus appears to be refuted by our bold warriors, who proudly allude to the "modern theory of knowledge," "recent philosophy" (or "recent positivism"), the "philosophy of modern natural science," or even the "philosophy of natural science of the twentieth century." Supported by all these supposedly recent doctrines, our destroyers of dialectical materialism proceed fearlessly to downright fideism (in the case of Lunacharsky it is most evident, but by no means in his case alone!). Yet when it comes to an explicit definition of their attitude towards Marx and Engels, all their courage and all their respect for their own convictions at once disappear. In deed—a complete renunciation of dialectical materialism, i.e., of Marxism; in word—endless subterfuges, attempts to evade the essence of the question, to cover their retreat, to put some materialist or other in place of materialism in general, and a determined refusal to make a direct analysis of the innumerable materialist declarations of Marx and Engels. . . .

Materialism, in full agreement with natural science, takes matter as primary and regards consciousness, thought and sensation as secondary, because in its well-defined form sensation is associated only with the higher forms of matter (organic matter), while "in the foundation of the structure of matter" one can only surmise the existence of a faculty akin to sensation. Such, for example, is the supposition of the well-known German scientist Ernst Haeckel, the English biologist Lloyd Morgan and others. . . . Machism holds to the opposite, the idealist point of view, and at once lands into an absurdity: since, in the first place, sensation is taken as primary, in spite of the fact that it is associated only with definite processes in matter organised in a definite way; and, since, in the second place, the basic premise that bodies are complexes of sensations is violated by the assumption of the existence of other living beings in general, of other "complexes" beside the given great I. . . .

Bogdanov's denial of objective truth is agnosticism and subjectivism. . . . Natural science leaves no room for doubt that its assertion that the earth existed prior to man is a truth. This is entirely compatible with the materialist theory of knowledge: the existence of the thing reflected independent of the reflector (the independence of the external world from the mind) is a fundamental tenet of materialism. The assertion made by science that the earth existed prior to man is an objective truth. This proposition of natural science is incompatible with the philosophy of the Machians and with their doctrine of truth: if truth is an organising form of human experience, then the assertion of the earth's existence *outside* human experience cannot be true. . . .

. . . The Machians are subjectivists and agnostics, for they *do not sufficiently* trust the evidence of our sense-organs and are inconsistent in their sensationalism. They do not recognise objective reality, independent of man, as the source of our sensations. They do not regard sensations as the true copy of this objective reality, thereby directly conflicting with natural science and throwing the door open for fideism. On the contrary, for the materialist the world is richer, livelier, more varied than it actually seems, for with each step in the development of science new aspects are discovered. For the materialist, sensations are images of the ultimate and sole objective reality, ultimate not in the sense that it has already been explored to the end, but in the sense that there is not and cannot be any other. This view irrevocably closes the door not only to every species of fideism, but also to that professorial scholasticism which, while not regarding objective reality as the source of our sensations, "deduces" the concept of the objective by means of such artificial verbal constructions as universal significance, socially-organised, and so on and so forth, and which is unable, and frequently unwilling, to separate objective truth from belief in sprites and hobgoblins. . . .

Matter is a philosophical category designating the objective reality which is given to man by his sensations, and which is copied, photographed and reflected by our sensations, while existing independently of them. Therefore, to say that such a concept can become "antiquated" is *childish talk*, a senseless repetition of the arguments of fashionable *reactionary* philosophy. . . .

Bogdanov's attempt imperceptibly to correct and develop Marx in the "spirit of his principles" is an obvious distortion of these materialist principles in the spirit of *idealism*. It would be ludicrous to deny it. . . . The immanentists, the empirio-criticists and the empiriomonists all argue over particulars, over details, over the formulation of *idealism*, whereas we *from the very outset* reject all the principles of their philosophy common to this trinity. Let Bogdanov, accepting in the best sense and with the best of intentions *all the conclusions* of Marx, preach the "identity" of social being and social consciousness; we shall say: Bogdanov *minus* "empirio-monism" (or rather, *minus* Machism) is a Marxist. For this theory of the identity of social being and social consciousness is *sheer nonsense* and an *absolutely reactionary* theory. If certain people reconcile it with Marxism, with Marxist behaviour, we must admit that these people are better than their theory, but we cannot justify outrageous theoretical distortions of Marxism. . . .

Materialism in general recognises objectively real being (matter) as independent of the consciousness, sensation, experience, etc., of humanity. Historical materialism recognises social being as independent of the social consciousness of humanity. In both cases consciousness is only the reflection of being, at best an approximately true (adequate, perfectly exact) reflection of it. From this Marxian philosophy, which is cast from a single piece of steel, you cannot eliminate one basic premise, one essential part, without departing from objective truth, without falling a prey to a bourgeois-reactionary falsehood. . . .

First and foremost, the theoretical foundations of this philosophy [empirio-criticism] must be compared with those of dialectical materialism. Such a comparison . . . reveals, *along the whole line* of epistemological problems, the *thoroughly reactionary* character of empirio-criticism, which uses new artifices, terms and subtleties to disguise the old errors of *idealism and agnosticism*. Only utter ignorance of the nature of philosophical materialism generally and of the nature of Marx's and Engels' dialectical method can lead one to speak of a "union" of empirio-criticism and Marxism.

Secondly, the place of empirio-criticism, as one very small school of specialists in philosophy, in relation to the other modern schools of philosophy, must be determined. Both Mach and Avenarius started with Kant and, leaving him, proceeded not towards materialism, but in the opposite direction, towards Hume and Berkeley. Imagining that he was "purifying experience" generally, Avenarius was in fact only purifying agnosticism of Kantianism. The whole school of Mach and Avenarius is more and more definitely moving towards idealism, hand in hand with one of the most reactionary of the idealist schools, viz., the so-called immanentists.

Thirdly, the indubitable connection between Machism and one school in one branch of modern science must be borne in mind. The vast majority of scientists, both generally and in this special branch of science in question, viz., physics, are invariably on the side of materialism. A minority of new theories brought about by the great discoveries of recent years, influenced by the crisis in the new physics, which has very clearly revealed the relativity of our knowledge, have, owing to their ignorance of dialectics, slipped into idealism by way of relativism. The physical idealism in vogue today is as reactionary and transitory an infatuation as the fashionably physiological idealism of the recent past.

Fourthly, behind the epistemological scholasticism of empirio-criticism it is impossible not to see the struggle of parties in philosophy, a struggle which in the last analysis reflects the tendencies and ideology of the antagonistic classes in modern society. Recent philosophy is as partisan as was philosophy two thousand years ago. The contending parties are essentially, although it is concealed by a pseudo-erudite quackery of new terms or by a feeble-minded non-partisanship, materialism and idealism. The latter is merely a subtle, refined form of fideism, which stands fully armed, commands vast organisations and steadily continues to exercise influence on the masses, turning the slightest vacillation in philosophical thought to its own advantage. The objective, class role played by empirio-criticism entirely consists in rendering faithful service to the fideists in their struggle against materialism in general and historical materialism in particular. . . .

The 1909 Purge of the Bolshevik Left Wing

The differences between Lenin and the Bogdanov group of revolutionary romantics came to a head in 1909. Lenin condemned the latter—the "otzovists" [Russian for "recallists"] who wanted to recall the Bolshevik deputies in the Duma, and the "ultimatists" who demanded that the deputies take a more radical stand—both for their philosophical vagaries which he rejected as "idealism," and for the utopian purism of their refusal to take tactical advantage of the Duma. The real issue was Lenin's control of the faction and the enforcement of his brand of Marxist orthodoxy. Lenin demonstrated his grip on the Bolshevik faction at a meeting in Paris of the editors of the Bolsheviks' factional paper, which had become the headquarters of the faction. Bogdanov and his followers were expelled from the Bolshevik faction, though they remained within the Social-Democratic fold.

a) Communiqué on the Conference

. . . The Conference declared in its resolutions that in the Bolshevik faction a tendency has been observed which in its definite tactical physiognomy contradicts Bolshevism. Bolshevism is represented for us by the Bolshevik *faction* of the party. A faction is not a party. A party can include a whole scale of shadings, in which the extremes may even sharply contradict each other. In the German party, together with the clearly revolutionary wing of Kautsky,* we see the arch-revisionist wing of Bernstein. This is not a faction.

FROM: The Conference of the Expanded Editorial Board of *The Proletarian*, Paris, June 21-30, 1909 (CPSU in Resolutions, I, 214-15, 220-21; editor's translation).

* Karl Kautsky: leading theorist in the German Social-Democratic Party; later drew Lenin's ire when he opposed violent means of revolution and criticized the Soviet dictatorship—Ed.

Within a party a faction is a group of *like-minded people* formed above all for the purpose of influencing the party in a definite direction, for the purpose of introducing its principles in as clear a form as possible into the party. For this real *unity of thought* is essential. . . .

b) Resolution on Otzovism and Ultimatism

. . . In the course of the bourgeois-democratic revolution our party has been joined by a series of elements which were not purely attracted by its proletarian program, but which preferred its clear and energetic struggle for democracy and which adopted the revolutionary-democratic slogans of the proletarian party apart from its connection with the objective of the struggle of the socialist proletariat.

Such elements, insufficiently permeated with the proletarian point of view, appeared even in the ranks of our Bolshevik faction. Hard times cause these elements to reveal more and more their inadequate Social-Democratic endurance, and coming into sharper and sharper contradiction with the foundations of revolutionary Social-Democratic tactics, they have created in the past year a tendency to try to form a theory of otzovism and ultimatism, which actually has led in principle only to an increasingly false picture of Social-Democratic parliamentarianism and Social-Democratic work in the Duma.

These attempts to create from the otzovist inclination a whole system of otzovist policy lead to a theory which essentially reflects the ideology of political indifferentism on the one hand and anarchistic roaming on the other. With all its revolutionary phraseology the theory of otzovism and ultimatism is in fact to a significant degree the reverse side of constitutional illusions which are connected with hopes that the State Duma itself can satisfy this or that substantial demand of the people, and in essence this replaces the proletarian ideology with petty-bourgeois tendencies. . . .

By their attempts to convert individual applications of the boycott of representative institutions at this or that moment of the revolution, into the line that the boycott is the distinguishing sign of the tactics of Bolshevism even in the period of counter-revolution, ultimatism and otzovism show that these tendencies are in essence the reverse side of Menshevism, which undertakes wholesale participation in all representative institutions, independently of the given stage of development of the revolution, independently of the presence or absence of a revolutionary upsurge.

All the attempts made by otzovism and ultimatism up to now to give theory a foundation of principle inevitably lead them to the denial of the foundations of revolutionary Marxism. The tactics which they have in mind lead to a complete break with the tactics of the left wing of international Social Democracy as applied to contemporary Russian conditions; they lead to anarchist deviations.

Otzovist-ultimatist agitation has already begun to cause undoubted harm to the workers' movement and to Social-Democratic work. If continued further it can become a threat to the unity of the party, for this agitation has already led to such monstrous phenomena as the combination of otzovists and SR's* (in St. Petersburg) to carry out their refusal to help our party's representatives in the Duma, and also to certain public appearances before workers, jointly with confirmed syndicalists.

In view of all this the expanded editorial board of *The Proletarian* declares that Bolshevism as a definite tendency within the RSDWP has nothing in common with otzovism and ultimatism, and that the Bolshevik faction must conduct the most determined struggle against these deviations from the path of revolutionary Marxism.

The Ultra-Left on Lenin's Compromises

After the split of 1909 Lenin's left-wing Bolshevik opponents organized a new Social-Democratic faction, known as the "Forward" group from the name of their newspaper. These extremists denounced Lenin for opportunism in much the same terms that he applied to the Mensheviks, but also attacked his organizational centralism. The group never at-

* SR's: Socialist Revolutionary Party which stressed peasant revolution—Ed.

tracted much rank-and-file support, and most of them found their way back to the Bolshevik ranks after the revolution.

a) Bogdanov, "Letter to All Comrades"

Where are we going? What is the historical fate of our generation—a new revolutionary wave or an organic development? . . .

If we are holding a course toward 'organic development,' then revolutionary-military questions and tasks simply do not exist for our generation, and the tradition connected with them is a harmful survival from the past. . . . But we assert that the long 'organic development' of Russia is only an Octobrist* dream. . . .

[We must consider] sustaining the remaining militant elements in their party spirit and discipline, and accordingly educating those working-class youths who manifest an attraction in this direction; strengthening propaganda among the troops, and, if possible, re-creating the military organizations which have fallen apart. . . .

Some people among your representatives in the executive collegium—the Bolshevik Center—who live abroad, have come to the conclusion that we must radically change the previous Bolshevik evaluation of the present historical moment and hold a course not toward a new revolutionary wave, but toward a long period of peaceful, constitutional development. This brings them close to the right wing of our party, the Menshevik comrades who always, independently of any evaluation of the political situation, pull toward legal and constitutional forms of activity, toward 'organic work' and 'organic development.' But this is what has led to disagreements with those Bolsheviks who do not see in the reaction which they observe sufficient grounds for such a change of front. . . .

FROM: Declarations of the "Vperiod" ("Forward") Group, 1910 (excerpts quoted in K. Ostroukhova, "The 'Vperiod' Group," *Proletarian Revolution,* No. 1, 1925, pp. 200-01; editor's translation).

* Octobrists: conservative party standing by the constitutional concessions of October, 1905—Ed.

Bolshevism continues to exist as before. It lives not in the circles abroad, not among politically sick people who are repressed and beaten by the harsh reaction; it lives in the steadfast and healthy proletarian movement, which organizes itself instead of splitting itself up. . . .

Comrades, a glorious cause—political, cultural, social—stands before us. It would be shameful for us if leaders who have outlived their times, overcome by adversity, should prevent us from fulfilling it. But this is an impossible, absurd suggestion. We will proceed on our way according to the old slogan—with our leaders, if they wish; without them, if they do not wish; against them, if they oppose us. Our cause is the cause of the collective, not of individual personalities. . . .

b) *"Letter to Our Bolshevik Comrades"*

. . . The Bolshevik Center has surrendered every Bolshevik position, one after another. . . . Accountable management by material means has changed into the uncontrolled freewheeling of irresponsible people; this group of people (the Bolshevik Center), which had already become ideologically Menshevik, has assumed the right of disbanding the Bolshevik faction. . . .

The Bolshevik Center, now altered in its composition—the majority were able to get rid of the "inconvenient" members who refused to abandon the position of Bolshevism—is completely cut off from Russia, has essentially become a private circle of former Bolsheviks, and has finally ceased to take account of the opinions and inclinations of the organizations in Russia. . . .

Only the organizations themselves have the right to decide their fate. Only the Russian Bolshevik comrades themselves, those worker socialists who struggle face to face with the enemy, can and must tell the party whether its revolutionary current has really died or whether in this period of blind reaction which is preparing a new outburst of the popular struggle, it has become more essential for the proletarian cause than ever before. . . .

We, the "Forward" group, suggest that the Russian Bolshevik comrades organize in the immediate future Bolshevik conferences on as large a scale as possible, and at them consider the questions of the fundamental vital interests of Bolshevism. As opponents of the old factional forms, we will insist at these conferences on the reconstruction of the Bolshevik faction on new foundations so that its ideological solidarity will be achieved not through formal centralization, but through the living ideological link, and so that these *ideological* centers which are created for this will be under real control by the local organizations. This will prevent the possibility of such a political degeneration of the "higher-ups," of such abuses and corruption as we have witnessed. The ideological current must direct its leaders and representatives. Only the decision of the local Bolshevik organizations can be considered the real decision of a question. . . .

Lenin on Factionalism

In 1912 Lenin held a meeting of the Bolshevik faction which he represented as a congress for the whole party. He had the "liquidator" tendency, among Mensheviks who wished to de-emphasize the revolutionary underground, condemned as un-Marxist. This marked the complete split of Bolsheviks and Mensheviks into separate parties.

Meanwhile, Lenin and Trotsky had been exchanging polemics on the organizational issue. In 1914 Lenin expressed himself against Trotsky in particularly strong terms for defying the decisions of the "congress" and trying to stir up factionalism.

. . . Since 1912, for over two years, there has been *no* factionalism among the organized Marxists in Russia, no controversies over tactics in *united* organizations, at united *conferences* and congresses. There is a *complete* breach between the Party, which in January 1912 formally announced that the Liquidators *do not* belong to it, and the Liquidators.

FROM: Lenin, "Disruption of Unity under Cover of Outcries for Unity" (May, 1914; *Selected Works,* Vol. I, book 2, pp. 249, 251, 255-56).

Trotsky often calls this state of affairs a "split," and with this appellation we will deal separately later on. But it remains an undoubted fact that the term "factionalism" is *misleading*. . . .

Although he claims to be non-factional, Trotsky is known to everybody who is in the least familiar with the working-class movement in Russia as the representative of "Trotsky's *faction*." Here there is factionalism, for we see the two essential symptoms of it: (1) nominal recognition of unity and (2) group segregation in fact. Here there are remnants of factionalism, for there is no evidence whatever of any real connection with the mass working-class movement in Russia. . . .

The Party submitted the question of Liquidatorism, and of condemning it, to the "advanced workers" as far back as 1908, and the question of "splitting" from a very definite group of Liquidators, . . . i.e., that the only way to build up the Party was *without* this group and in opposition to it—this question it submitted in January 1912, over two years ago. The overwhelming majority of the advanced workers expressed themselves *in favour of* supporting the "January (1912) line." Trotsky himself admits this fact when he talks about "victories" and about "numerous advanced workers." But Trotsky wriggles out of this simply by hurling *abuse* at these advanced workers and calling them "schismatists" and "politically bewildered"!

Sane people will draw a different conclusion from these facts. Where the *majority* of the class-conscious workers have rallied around precise and definite decisions there is *unity* of opinion and action, there is the Party spirit, and the Party.

Where we see Liquidators who have been "dismissed from their posts" by the workers, or a half a dozen émigré groups who for two years have produced *no proof whatever* that they are connected with the mass working-class movement in Russia, there, indeed, bewilderment and *schism* reign. In trying, now, to persuade the workers *not to carry out the decisions* of that "body" which the Marxist *Pravda*-

ists [followers of the Bolshevik paper *Pravda*—"Truth"—1912-14] recognize, Trotsky is *trying* to disorganize the movement and to cause a split.

These efforts are vain, but we must expose the arrogantly conceited leaders of coteries of intellectuals who, while causing splits, are shouting about others causing splits, who, after suffering *utter defeat* at the hands of the "advanced workers" for the past two years or more, are with incredible insolence *spurning* the decisions and the will of these advanced workers and saying that *they* are "politically bewildered." . . .

Lenin on National Self-Determination

Early in 1914 Lenin turned his attention to the problem of the national minorities in Russia. His answer to "Great-Russian chauvinism" was the unconditional right of any minority to independent statehood, while those who remained would accept a thoroughly centralized revolutionary party and government. The actual Soviet solution was in form quite different, with the elaborate federal structure of republics embodied first in the Russian Republic in 1918 and then in the Union of Soviet Socialist Republics in 1922. Centralism has of course been maintained in practice by virtue of the power of the highly centralized Communist Party.

. . . From the point of view of the theory of Marxism in general the question of the right of self-determination presents no difficulties. No one can seriously dispute the London resolution [of the Socialist International] of 1896, or the fact that self-determination implies only the right to secession, or the fact that the formation of independent national states is the tendency of all bourgeois-democratic revolutions.

The difficulty is created to a certain extent by the fact that in Russia the proletariat of both oppressed and oppressing nations are fighting and must fight side by side. The task is to preserve the unity of the class struggle of the pro-

FROM: Lenin, "The Right of Nations to Self-Determination (1914; *Selected Works*, Vol. I, book 2, pp. 382-86).

letariat for Socialism, to resist all the bourgeois and Black-Hundred* nationalist influences. Among the oppressed nations the separate organization of the proletariat as an independent party sometimes leads to such a bitter struggle against the nationalism of the respective nation that the perspective becomes distorted and the nationalism of the oppressing nation is forgotten.

But this distortion of the perspective cannot last long. The experience of the joint struggle of the proletarians of various nations has demonstrated only too plainly that we must formulate political questions not from the "Cracow," but from the all-Russian point of view. And in all-Russian politics it is the Purishkeviches and the Kokoshkins who rule.** Their ideas are predominant, their persecution of alien races for "separatism," for *thinking* about secession, are being preached and practiced in the Duma, in the schools, in the churches, in the barracks, and in hundreds and thousands of newspapers. It is this Great-Russian poison of nationalism that is contaminating the entire all-Russian political atmosphere. The misfortune of a nation, which, in subjugating other nations, is strengthening reaction throughout Russia. The memories of 1849 and 1863 form a living political tradition, which, unless great storms sweep the country, threatens to hamper every democratic and *especially* every Social-Democratic movement for many decades.

There can be no doubt that, however natural the point of view of certain Marxists of the oppressed nations (whose "misfortune" is sometimes that the masses of the population are blinded by the idea of "their" national liberation) may appear at times, *in reality* the objective alignment of class forces in Russia makes refusal to advocate the right of self-determination tantamount to the worst opportunism, to the contamination of the proletariat with the ideas of the Kokoshkins. And in substance, these ideas are the ideas and the policy of the Purishkeviches. . . .

* "Black Hundreds": armed bands of ultra-rightists—Ed.

** Purishkevich: an extreme right-wing leader in the Duma; Kokoshkin: a representative of the Constitutional Democratic Party in the Duma—Ed.

Even now, and probably for a fairly long time to come, proletarian democracy must reckon with the nationalism of the Great-Russian peasants (not in the sense of making concessions to it, but in the sense of combating it). The awakening of nationalism among the oppressed nations, which became so pronounced after 1905 (let us recall, say, the group of "Autonomists-Federalists" in the First Duma, the growth of the Ukrainian movement, of the Moslem movement, etc.), will inevitably cause the intensification of nationalism among the Great-Russian petty bourgeoisie in town and country. The slower the democratization of Russia, the more persistent, brutal and bitter will be national persecution and quarrelling among the bourgeoisie of the various nations. The particularly reactionary nature of the Russian Purishkeviches will at the same time engender (and strengthen) "separatist" tendencies among the various oppressed nationalities which sometimes enjoy far greater freedom in the neighbouring states.

This state of affairs confronts the proletariat of Russia with a twofold or, rather, a two-sided task: to combat all nationalism and, above all, Great-Russian nationalism; to recognize not only complete equality of rights for all nations in general but also equality of rights as regards statehood, i.e., the right of nations to self-determination, to secession. And at the same time, precisely in the interest of the successful struggle against the nationalism of all nations in any form, preserving the unity of the proletarian struggle and of the proletarian organizations, amalgamating these organizations into a close-knit international association, in spite of the bourgeois strivings for national segregation.

Complete equality of rights for all nations; the right of nations to self-determination; the amalgamation of the workers of all nations—this is the national program that Marxism, the experience of the whole world, and the experience of Russia, teaches the workers. . . .

Lenin on the "Imperialist War"

The outbreak of a general war in August, 1914, deeply shook the European socialist movement. The moderate wings dominant in most of the socialist parties put national defense ahead of social change, and voted to support their respective governments. The Bolsheviks and many other Russian socialists, together with left-wing splinter groups in the rest of Europe, appealed to the antinationalist tradition of Marxism and tried to make revolutionary capital out of the war. Lenin frankly hoped for the defeat of the czarist government of Russia and urged revolutionaries everywhere to "turn the imperialist war into a civil war."

The European war, for which the governments and the bourgeois parties of all countries have been preparing for decades, has broken out. The growth of armaments, the extreme intensification of the struggle for markets in the epoch of the latest, the imperialist stage of capitalist development in the advanced countries, and the dynastic interests of the most backward East-European monarchies were inevitably bound to lead, and have led, to this war. Seizure of territory and subjugation of foreign nations, ruin of a competing nation and plunder of its wealth, diverting the attention of the working masses from the internal political crises in Russia, Germany, England and other countries, disuniting and nationalist doping of the workers and the extermination of their vanguard with the object of weakening the revolutionary movement of the proletariat—such is the only real meaning, substance and significance of the present war.

On Social-Democracy, primarily, rests the duty of disclosing this true meaning of the war and of ruthlessly exposing the falsehood, sophistry and "patriotic" phrasemongering spread by the ruling classes, the landlords and the bourgeoisie, in defence of the war. . . .

Under present conditions, it is impossible to determine, from the standpoint of the international proletariat, the defeat of which of the two groups of belligerent nations would be the lesser evil for Socialism. But for us, the Russian Social-Democrats, there cannot be the slightest doubt that from the standpoint of the working class and of the labouring masses of all the nations of Russia, the lesser evil would be

FROM: Lenin, "The War and Russian Social-Democracy" (November, 1914; Selected Works, Vol. I, book 2, pp. 397, 404-6).

the defeat of the tsarist monarchy, the most reactionary and barbarous of governments, which is oppressing the greatest number of nations and the largest mass of the population of Europe and Asia.

The immediate political slogan of the Social-Democrats of Europe must be the formation of a republican United States of Europe, but in contrast to the bourgeoisie, which is ready to "promise" anything in order to draw the proletariat into the general current of chauvinism, the Social-Democrats will explain that this slogan is utterly false and senseless without the revolutionary overthrow of the German, Austrian and Russian monarchies.

In Russia, in view of the fact that this country is the most backward and has not yet completed its bourgeois revolution, the task of the Social-Democrats is, as heretofore, to achieve the three fundamental conditions for consistent democratic reform, viz., a democratic republic (with complete equality and self-determination for all nations), confiscation of the landed estates, and an 8-hour day. But in all the advanced countries the war has placed on the order of the day the slogan of socialist revolution, and this slogan becomes the more urgent, the more the burdens of war press upon the shoulders of the proletariat, and the more active its role must become in the restoration of Europe after the horrors of the present "patriotic" barbarism amidst the gigantic technical progress of big capitalism. . . .

The transformation of the present imperialist war into a civil war is the only correct proletarian slogan; it was indicated by the experience of the [Paris] Commune and outlined by the Basle resolution [of the Socialist International] (1912), and it logically follows from all the conditions of an imperialist war among highly developed bourgeois countries. However difficult such a transformation may appear at any given moment, Socialists will never relinquish systematic, persistent and undeviating preparatory work in this direction once war has become a fact.

Only in this way can the proletariat shake off its dependence on the chauvinist bourgeoisie, and, in one form or another, more or less rapidly, take decisive steps towards the real freedom of nations and towards Socialism.

Long live the international fraternity of the workers against the chauvinism and patriotism of the bourgeoisie of all countries!

Long live a proletarian International, freed from opportunism!

Lenin on the Uneven Prospects of Revolution

In reply to some of his radical associates who proposed an international socialist federation, Lenin pointed out the likelihood of the first socialist countries having to fight those which clung to capitalism. This idea was of major significance in the 1920's as the starting point for Stalin's theory of "socialism in one country."

. . . A United States of the World (not of Europe alone) is the state form of the union and freedom of nations which we associate with Socialism—until the complete victory of Communism brings about the total disappearance of the state, including the democratic state. As a separate slogan, however, the slogan of a United States of the World would hardly be a correct one, first, because it merges with Socialism; second, because it may be wrongly interpreted to mean that the victory of Socialism in a single country is impossible, and it may also create misconceptions as to the relations of such a country to the others.

Uneven economic and political development is an absolute law of capitalism. Hence, the victory of Socialism is possible first in several or even in one capitalist country, taken singly. The victorious proletariat of that country, having expropriated the capitalists and organized its own socialist production, would stand up *against* the rest of the world, the capitalist world, attracting to its cause the oppressed classes of other countries, raising revolts in those countries against the capitalists, and in the event of necessity coming out even with

FROM: Lenin, "The United States of Europe Slogan" (August, 1915; *Selected Works,* Vol. I, book 2, pp. 416-17).

armed force against the exploiting classes and their states. The political form of society in which the proletariat is victorious by overthrowing the bourgeoisie, will be a democratic republic, which will more and more centralize the forces of the proletariat of the given nation, or nations, in the struggle against the states that have not yet gone over to Socialism. The abolition of classes is impossible without the dictatorship of the oppressed class, the proletariat. The free union of nations in Socialism is impossible without a more or less prolonged and stubborn struggle of the socialist republics against the backward states.

It is for these reasons and after repeated debates at the conference of the sections of the R.S.D.L.P. abroad, and after the conference, that the editors of the Central Organ have come to the conclusion that the United States of Europe slogan is incorrect.

Karl Liebknecht on International Revolution

Liebknecht was the son of one of the founders of the German Social-Democratic Party and an outstanding figure in the antiwar left wing of the party. Conscripted into the army and in effect a political prisoner, he wrote to express his fervent revolutionary hopes to the conference of antiwar socialists that met in the Swiss village of Zimmerwald (near Berne) in 1915.

Dear Comrades!

Forgive me for writing only a few hurried lines. I am imprisoned and fettered by militarism; therefore, I am unable to come to you. My heart, my head, my entire cause is nevertheless with you.

You have two serious tasks, a hard task of grim duty and a sacred one of enthusiasm and hope.

Settlement of accounts, inexorable settlement of accounts

FROM: Liebknecht, Letter to the Zimmerwald Conference, September, 1915 (English translation in O. H. Gankin and H. H. Fisher, *The Bolsheviks and The World War—The Origin of the Third International,* pp. 326-28; reprinted by permission of the publisher, Stanford University Press. Copyright 1940 by the Board of Trustees of Leland Stanford Junior University.)

with the deserters and turncoats of the International in Germany, England, France, and elsewhere, is imperative.

It is our duty to promote mutual understanding, encouragement, and inspiration among those who remain true to the flag, who are determined not to give way one inch before international imperialism, even if they fall victims to it, and to create order in the ranks of those who are determined to hold out—to hold out and to fight, with their feet firmly planted on the basis of international socialism.

It is necessary to make clear, briefly, the principles of our attitude toward the capitalist order of society. Briefly—so I hope! For in this we are all unanimous and we must be unanimous!

It is above all a matter of drawing tactical consequences from these principles—ruthlessly for all countries!

Civil war, not civil peace! Exercise international solidarity for the proletariat against pseudo-national, pseudo-patriotic class harmony, and for international class war for peace, for the socialist revolution. How the fight is to be fought must be decided. Only in co-operation, in the mutual working of one land with another, by mutually strengthening each other, can the greatest possible forces and thus the attainable results be achieved.

The friends of every country hold in their hands the hopes and prospects of the friends of every other country. You French and you German socialists especially, have one and the same fate. You French friends, I implore you not to allow yourselves to be caught by the phrase of national truce—to this you are really immune—or by the equally dangerous phrase of the party truce! Every protest against this, every manifestation of your rejection of the semi-official government policy, every bold acknowledgment of the class struggle, of solidarity with us and of the proletarian will to peace, strengthens our fighting spirit, increases tenfold our force to work in Germany for the proletariat of the world, for its economic and political emancipation, for its emancipation from the fetters of capitalism, and also from the chains of Tsarism, Kaiserism, Junkerism, and militarism, which is no less international; to fight in Germany for the political and social liberation of the German people against German imperialists' power and lust for territory; to fight for a speedy peace, which would also restore unhappy Belgium to freedom and independence and give back France to the French people.

French brothers, we know the peculiar difficulties of your tragic situation and bleed with you as with the tormented and stoned masses of all peoples! Your misfortune is our misfortune, as we know that our pain is your pain. Let our fight be your fight. Help us, as we swear to help you.

The new International will arise; it can arise on the ruins of the old, on a new and firmer foundation. Today, friends, socialists from all countries, you have to lay the foundation stone for the future structure. Pass irreconcilable judgment upon the false socialists! Ruthlessly urge on those who vacillate or hesitate in all countries, those in Germany as well! The greatness of the aim will raise you above the narrowness and littleness of the day, above the misery of these terrible days!

Long live the people's peace of the future! Long live antimilitarism! Long live international, people-emancipating, revolutionary socialism!

Proletarians of all countries—reunite! . . .

Karl Liebknecht

The "Zimmerwald Left"

Like most revolutionary groups the Zimmerwald conference split into factions, which differed over the revolutionary implications of the war. The left wing, which included Lenin and the Bolshevik representatives, vainly supported the uncompromising resolution written by Karl Radek, a Polish Jew who was high in the councils of the international Communist movement throughout the nineteen-twenties. Although the extremists were rebuffed at Zimmerwald, they had laid the organizational basis for the Third or Communist International which was formally launched in 1919.

The World War, which has been devastating Europe for the last year, is an imperialist war waged for the political and economic exploitation of the world, export markets, sources of raw material, spheres of capital investment, etc. It is a product of capitalist development which connects the entire world in a world economy but at the same time permits the existence of national state capitalist groups with opposing interests.

If the bourgeoisie and the governments seek to conceal this character of the World War by asserting that it is a question of a forced struggle for *national independence,* it is only to mislead the *proletariat,* since the war is being waged for the oppression of foreign peoples and countries. Equally untruthful are the legends concerning the defence of democracy in this war, since imperialism signifies the most unscrupulous domination of big capital and political reaction.

Imperialism can only be overcome by overcoming the contradictions which produced it, that is, by the *Socialist organisation* of the sphere of capitalist civilisation for which the objective conditions are already ripe.

At the outbreak of the war, the majority of the labour leaders had not raised this only possible slogan in opposition to imperialism. Prejudiced by nationalism, rotten with opportunism, *they surrendered the proletariat to imperialism, and gave up the principles of Socialism and thereby the real struggle for the every-day interests of the proletariat.*

Social-patriotism and social-imperialism . . . is a more dangerous enemy to the proletariat than the bourgeois apostles of imperialism, since, misusing the banner of Socialism, it can mislead the unenlightened workers. *The ruthless struggle against social-imperialism constitutes the first condition for the revolutionary mobilisation of the proletariat and the reconstruction of the International.*

It is the task of the Socialist parties, as well as of the Socialist opposition in the now social-imperialist parties, to call and lead the labouring masses to the *revolutionary struggle* against the capitalist governments for the conquest of

FROM: Proposed Resolution of the Zimmerwald Left at the Zimmerwald Conference in September, 1915—"The World War and the Tasks of Social-Democracy" (English translation in *Collected Works of V. I. Lenin,* Vol. XX, book 2, New York, International Publishers, 1929, pp. 386-87; reprinted by permission of the publisher).

political power for the Socialist organisation of society.

Without giving up the struggle for every foot of ground within the framework of capitalism, for every reform strengthening the proletariat, without renouncing any means of organisation and agitation, the revolutionary Social-Democrats, on the contrary, must utilise all the struggles, all the reforms demanded by our minimum programme for the purpose of sharpening this war crisis as well as every social and political crisis of capitalism, of extending them to an attack upon its very foundations. By waging this struggle *under the slogan of Socialism* it will render the labouring masses immune to the slogans of the oppression of one people by another as expressed in the maintenance of the domination of one nation over another, in the cry for new annexations; it will render them deaf to the temptation of national solidarity which has led the proletarians to the battlefields.

The signal for this struggle is the struggle against the World War, for the speedy termination of the slaughter of nations. This struggle demands the refusal of war credits, quitting the cabinets, the denunciation of the capitalist, anti-Socialist character of the war from the tribunes of the parliaments, in the columns of the legal, and where necessary illegal, press, the sharpest struggle caused by the results of the war (misery, great losses, etc.) for the organisation of street demonstrations against the governments, propaganda of international solidarity in the trenches, the encouragement of economic strikes, the effort to transform them into political strikes under favourable conditions. "Civil war, not civil peace"—that is the slogan!

As against all illusions that it is possible to bring about the basis of a lasting peace, the beginning of disarmament, by any decisions of diplomacy and the governments, the revolutionary Social-Democrats must repeatedly tell the masses of the people that only the social revolution can bring about a lasting peace as well as the emancipation of mankind.

Lenin on Imperialism

Like many of his Marxist colleagues, Lenin attempted to bring Marxism up to date to account for the World War and contemporary economic trends. His product was the book, *Imperialism, the Highest Stage of Capitalism,* for which he drew heavily from the work of the English economist J. A. Hobson. The essence of the argument was that the capitalist search for markets and profits made colony-grabbing and imperialist war between capitalist states inevitable. Lenin's presentation remains the basis of the Communist view of the capitalist world.

. . . The principal feature of the latest stage of capitalism is the domination of monopolist combines of the big capitalists. These monopolies are most firmly established when *all* the sources of raw materials are captured by one group, and we have seen with what zeal the international capitalist combines exert every effort to make it impossible for their rivals to compete with them by buying up, for example, iron ore fields, oil fields, etc. Colonial possession alone gives the monopolies complete guarantee against all contingencies in the struggle with competitors, including the contingency that the latter will defend themselves by means of a law establishing a state monopoly. The more capitalism is developed, the more strongly the shortage of raw materials is felt, the more intense the competition and the hunt for sources of raw materials throughout the whole world, the more desperate is the struggle for the acquisition of colonies. . . .

Finance capital is interested not only in the already discovered sources of raw materials but also in potential sources, because present-day technical development is extremely rapid, and land which is useless today may be made fertile tomorrow if new methods are applied (to devise these new methods a big bank can equip a special expedition of engineers, agricultural experts, etc.), and if large amounts of capital are invested. This also applies to prospecting for minerals, to new methods of working up and utilizing raw materials, etc., etc. Hence, the inevitable striving of finance capital to enlarge its economic territory and even its territory in general. In the same way that the trusts capitalize their property at two or three times its

FROM: Lenin, "Imperialism, the Highest Stage of Capitalism" (1916; *Selected Works,* Vol. I, book 2, pp. 517-20, 562-67).

value, taking into account its "potential" (and not present) profits, and the further results of monopoly, so finance capital strives in general to seize the largest possible amount of land of all kinds in all places, and by every means, taking into account potential sources of raw materials and fearing to be left behind in the fierce struggle for the last scraps of undivided territory, or for the repartition of those that have been already divided. . . .

The interests pursued in exporting capital also give an impetus to the conquest of colonies, for in the colonial market it is easier to employ monopolist methods (and sometimes they are the only methods that can be employed) to eliminate competition, to make sure of contracts, to secure the necessary "connections," etc.

The non-economic superstructure which grows up on the basis of finance capital, its politics and its ideology, stimulates the striving for colonial conquest. . . .

We have seen that in its economic essence imperialism is monopoly capitalism. This in itself determines its place in history, for monopoly that grows out of the soil of free competition, and precisely out of free competition, is the transition from the capitalist system to a higher social-economic order. We must take special note of the four principal types of monopoly, or principal manifestations of monopoly capitalism, which are characteristic of the epoch we are examining.

Firstly, monopoly arose out of a very high stage of development of the concentration of production. This refers to the monopolist capitalist combines, cartels, syndicates and trusts. We have seen the important part these play in present-day economic life. At the beginning of the twentieth century, monopolies had acquired complete supremacy in the advanced countries, and although the first steps towards the formation of the cartels were first taken by countries enjoying the protection of high tariffs (Germany, America), Great Britain, with her system of free trade, revealed the same basic phenomenon, only a little later, namely, the birth of monopoly out of the concentration of production.

Secondly, monopolies have stimulated the seizure of the

most important sources of raw materials, especially for the basic and most highly cartelized industries in capitalist society: the coal and iron industries. The monopoly of the most important sources of raw materials has enormously increased the power of big capital, and has sharpened the antagonism between cartelized and non-cartelized industry.

Thirdly, monopoly has sprung from the banks. The banks have developed from humble middlemen enterprises into the monopolists of finance capital. Some three to five of the biggest banks in each of the foremost capitalist countries have achieved the "personal union" of industrial and bank capital, and have concentrated in their hands the control of thousands upon thousands of millions which form the greater part of the capital and income of entire countries. A financial oligarchy, which throws a close network of dependence relationships over all the economic and political institutions of present-day bourgeois society without exception—such is the most striking manifestation of this monopoly.

Fourthly, monopoly has grown out of colonal policy. To the numerous "old" motives of colonial policy, finance capital has added the struggle for the sources of raw materials, for the export of capital, for "spheres of influence," i.e., for spheres for profitable deals, concessions, monopolist profits and so on, and finally, for economic territory in general. When the colonies of the European powers in Africa, for instance, comprised only one-tenth of that territory (as was the case in 1876), colonial policy was able to develop by methods other than those of monopoly —by the "free grabbing" of territories, so to speak. But when nine-tenths of Africa had been seized (by 1900), when the whole world had been divided up, there was inevitably ushered in the era of monopoly ownership of colonies and, consequently, of particularly intense struggle for the division and the redivision of the world.

The extent to which monopolist capital has intensified all the contradictions of capitalism is generally known. It is sufficient to mention the high cost of living and the tyranny of the cartels. This intensification of contradictions constitutes the most powerful driving force of the transitional period of history, which began from the time of the final victory of world finance capital.

Monopolies, oligarchy, the striving for domination instead of striving for liberty, the exploitation of an increasing number of small or weak nations by a handful of the richest or most powerful nations—all these have given birth to those distinctive characteristics of imperialism which compel us to define it as parasitic or decaying capitalism. More and more prominently there emerges, as one of the tendencies of imperialism, the creation of the "rentier state," the usurer state, in which the bourgeoisie to an ever increasing degree lives on the proceeds of capital exports and by "clipping coupons." It would be a mistake to believe that this tendency to decay precludes the rapid growth of capitalism. It does not. In the epoch of imperialism, certain branches of industry, certain strata of the bourgeoisie and certain countries betray, to a greater or lesser degree, now one and now another of these tendencies. On the whole, capitalism is growing far more rapidly than before; but this growth is not only becoming more and more uneven in general, its unevenness also manifests itself, in particular, in the decay of the countries which are richest in capital (England). . . .

The receipt of high monopoly profits by the capitalists in one of the numerous branches of industry, in one of the numerous countries, etc., makes it economically possible for them to bribe certain sections of the workers, and for a time a fairly considerable minority of them, and win them to the side of the bourgeoisie of a given industry or given nation against all the others. The intensification of antagonisms between imperialist nations for the division of the world increases this striving. And so there is created that bond between imperialism and opportunism, which revealed itself first and most clearly in England, owing to the fact that certain features of imperialist development were observable there much earlier than in other countries. . . .

From all that has been said in this book on the economic essence of imperialism, it follows that we must define it as capitalism in transition, or, more precisely, as moribund capitalism. It is very instructive in this respect to note that the bourgeois economists, in describing modern capitalism, frequently employ catchwords and phrases like "interlocking," "absence of isolation," etc.; "in conformity with their functions and course of development," banks are "not purely private business enterprises; they are more and more outgrowing the sphere of purely private business regulation." And this very Riesser,* who uttered the words just quoted, declares with all seriousness that the "prophecy" of the Marxists concerning "socialization" has "not come true"!

What then does this catchword "interlocking" express? It merely expresses the most striking feature of the process going on before our eyes. It shows that the observer counts the separate trees, but cannot see the wood. It slavishly copies the superficial, the fortuitous, the chaotic. It reveals the observer as one who is overwhelmed by the mass of raw material and is utterly incapable of appreciating its meaning and importance. Ownership of shares, the relations between owners of private property "interlock in a haphazard way." But underlying this interlocking, its very base, is the changing social relations of production. When a big enterprise assumes gigantic proportions, and, on the basis of an exact computation of mass data, organizes according to plan the supply of primary raw materials to the extent of two-thirds, or three-fourths of all that is necessary for tens of millions of people; when the raw materials are transported in a systematic and organized manner to the most suitable place of production, sometimes hundreds or thousands of miles, when a single centre directs all the consecutive stages of work right up to the manufacture of numerous varieties of finished articles; when these products are distributed according to a single plan among tens and hundreds of millions of consumers (the distribution of oil in America and Germany by the American "oil trust")—then it becomes evident that we have socialization of production, and not mere "interlocking"; that private economic and private property relations constitute a shell which no longer fits its contents, a shell which must inevitably

* Riesser: author of a study of German banking, cited by Lenin—Ed.

decay if its removal by artificial means be delayed; a shell which may continue in a state of decay for a fairly long period (if, at the worst, the cure of the opportunist abscess is protracted), but which will inevitably be removed. . . .

Bukharin on the Imperialist State

Nikolai Bukharin as a young Bolshevik theorist often criticized Lenin from the left until he became more conservative as a responsible Soviet leader after 1921. During the First World War Bukharin led a "left-Bolshevik" subfaction and wrote of the necessity for the total revolutionary destruction of the existing state. This, he warned, was necessary to forestall the development of a Leviathan of "state capitalism." Without realizing it, Bukharin prophesied the whole modern phenomenon of totalitarianism.

1. The General Theory of the State

. . . From the point of view of Marxism the state is nothing but *the most general organization of the dominant classes, the basic function of which is to maintain and extend the exploitation of the suppressed classes*. . . . Insofar as there is an organization of state power set up according to a plan and consciously regulated (and this appears only at a certain stage in the development of the state), to that extent one can speak of the posing of *goals*, but these goals are defined by the interests of the *dominant* classes and *only by them*. This is not in the least contradicted by the circumstance that the state performs and has performed a whole series of functions for the common good. The latter merely provides the necessary *condition*, the *conditio sine qua non*, for the existence of the state power. The state's "activities for the common good" are thus the *conditions for maximally protracted and maximally successful exploitation of the enslaved classes* in contemporary society, above all the proletariat. . . .

FROM: Bukharin, "On the Theory of the Imperialist State" (1916; published in *The Revolution of Law*, Collection I, Moscow, Communist Academy, 1925, pp. 7-8, 13-16, 21, 23, 26, 27, 29-32; editor's translation).

In this connection it is possible to distinguish two types of relationships: either the state organization is the *direct* organization of exploitation—in which case the state stands forth as the union of the capitalists, having its own enterprises (e.g., railroads, monopoly production of certain products, etc.); or the state organization participates in an *indirect* manner in the process of exploitation, as a service mechanism to sustain and extend the most profitable conditions for the process of exploitation. In the first case—insofar as we are speaking of productive labor—the state absorbs the surplus value which is created in the sphere of its direct activity; in the second—it appropriates part of the surplus value which is produced in the branches of production that lie outside the sphere of direct state control, by means of taxes, etc. Usually the state extracts not only a part of the surplus value, but also a certain part of wages (and where other categories of "labor income" exist, part of the latter as well). In concrete actuality both these types exist simultaneously, although their proportions are subject to change and depend on the stage of historical development which has been attained.

The support and extension of the process of exploitation proceed in two directions: externally, i.e., outside the boundaries of the state's territory, and internally, i.e., within these boundaries. The *foreign* policy of the state organization expresses its struggle to share the surplus value which is produced on a world-wide scale (insofar as there is a non-capitalist world, the struggle for the surplus product), the struggle which is enacted between the various politically organized groups of the dominant classes.

The *internal* policy of the state organization reflects the struggle of the dominant classes for a share of the value (i.e., product) created by way of the systematic suppression of all attempts at liberation on the part of the suppressed classes. . . .

2. The Imperialist State and Finance Capitalism

Even the most superficial glance at social-economic life shows us the colossal growth of the economic significance of the state. This is reflected above all in the growth of the *state budget.* The complicated apparatus of the contemporary state organization requires enormous expenses, which increase with astonishing swiftness. . . .

A vast role in such an increase of the budget is undoubtedly played by militarism, one of the aspects of *imperialist* politics, which in turn stems necessarily from the structure of *finance capitalism.* But not only militarism in the narrow sense of the word. The cause of this is the growing interference of the state power in all branches of social life, beginning with the sphere of production and ending with the higher forms of ideological creation. If the pre-imperialist period—the period of liberalism, which was the political expression of industrial capitalism—was characterized by the noninterference of the state power, and the formula laissez-faire was a symbol of the faith of the ruling circles of the bourgeoisie, who all permitted the "free play of economic forces," our time is characterized by a directly opposite tendency, which has as its logical conclusion *state capitalism,* sucking everything into the area of state regulation. . . .

The *state power thus sucks in almost all branches of production; it not only preserves the general conditions of the process of exploitation; the state becomes more and more a direct exploiter, which organizes and directs production as a collective, composite capitalist.* . . . The anarchistic commodity market is to a significant degree replaced by the organized distribution of the product, in which the supreme authority is again the state power. . . .

. . . In war socialism* class contradictions are not only not eliminated, but are brought to their maximum intensity. In the ideal type of the imperialist state the process of exploitation is not obscured by any secondary forms; the mask of a supraclass institution which treats everyone equally is thrown off from the state. This fact is a basic fact, and it completely refutes the argumentation of the renegades [i.e., the prowar Social Democrats]. For socialism is the regulation of production directed by *society,* not by the state (state socialism is like soft-boiled boots); it is the annihilation of class contra-

* "Kriegssozialismus"—the highly mobilized German economy in World War I—Ed.

dictions, not their intensification. The regulation of production by itself does not mean socialism at all; it exists in any sort of economy, in any slave-owning group with a natural economy. What awaits us in the immediate future is in fact *state capitalism*. . . .

3. The Organizational Process, State Power, and the Working Class . . .

The necessities of imperialist development compel bourgeois society to mobilize all its forces, to become organized on the broadest scale: the state draws into itself the whole series of bourgeois organizations.

Here war gives an enormous impetus. Philosophy and medicine, religion and ethics, chemistry and bacteriology—all are "mobilized" and "militarized" just like industry and finance. The whole grand-scale technical, economic, and ideological machine operates more planfully as soon as the conscious organized adaptation to the "whole" has appeared—i.e., when the state in one way or another has drawn these innumerable groups into its over-all organization. . . .

The general scheme of the state's development is as follows: At first the state is the only organization of the dominant class. Then other organizations arise, whose numbers are especially increased in the epoch of finance capitalism. The state is transformed from the only organization of the dominant class into one of its organizations which exist simultaneously—an organization which is distinguished by its most general character. Finally the third stage arrives, *when the state absorbs these organizations and again becomes the only over-all organization of the dominant class, with a technical division* of labor inside it; the formerly independent organizational groupings are transformed into divisions of a gigantic state mechanism, which descends with crushing force upon the obvious and internal enemy. Thus arises the final type of the contemporary imperialist bandit state, the iron organization which with its grasping, prehensile paws seizes the living body of society. It is a new Leviathan, in the face of which the fantasy of Thomas Hobbes seems like child's play. And all the more "*non est potestas super terram quae* *comparetur ei*" ("there is no power on earth which can compare with it").*

We must now raise the fully natural question of the role of the workers, of proletarian organizations.

Theoretically there can be two possibilities here: *Either the workers' organizations, like all the organizations of the bourgeoisie, will grow into the state-wide organization and be transformed into a simple appendage of the state apparatus, or they will outgrow the framework of the state and burst it from within,* as they organize their own state power (the dictatorship). . . .

The immediate development of state organisms—as long as the socialist overturn does not occur—is possible only in the form of *militaristic state capitalism.* Centralization becomes barrack centralization; the intensification of the most hateful militarism among the upper groups, of bestial drilling of the proletariat, of bloody repressions, is inevitable. On the other hand, as we have already noted above, any move by the proletariat is inevitably transformed under these circumstances into a move against the state power. Hence the definite tactical demand—Social-Democracy must vigorously underscore its hostility in principle to the state power. . . . To support the contemporary state means to support militarism. The historical task of the day is not to worry about the further development of the forces of production (they are quite sufficient for the realization of socialism), but the preparation of a general attack on the ruling bandits. In the growing revolutionary struggle the proletariat destroys the state organization of the bourgeoisie. . . .

* Epigraph to "The Leviathan" [author's note].

Chapter Two: The Bolshevik Revolution, 1917-1921

The Russian Revolution was not a simple matter of the conspiratorial seizure of power, but one of the most complex events in all history. As in the other great revolutions, in England and France, the unexpected collapse of the monarchy's authority initiated a sequence of political convulsions, as power passed through a succession of leading groups, with growing extremism and violence. Stable rule by the Communists (as the Bolsheviks renamed themselves in 1918) was not consolidated until 1921, by which time they had lost much of their revolutionary utopianism.

During the years of the revolution the Communist Party was by no means a single-minded force, though Lenin always exerted commanding influence. At every stage in the revolution deviant groups arose among the Communists to object to Lenin's course of action—some who found it too rash, others who protested its expedient compromises. The revolutionary period reveals the wide range of political and social alternatives which the general standpoint of radical Russian Marxism afforded.

The years 1917-1921, during which the Communists seized power, endured factional controversy, and fought their way to victory in a bitter civil war, were the critical, formative period of the Soviet regime and of the Communist movement as a whole. Communism is specifically the child of the Russian Revolution, and its basic character—the exclusive dictatorship of a bureaucratic party in a bureaucratic state—stems directly from the way in which the conditions of that era selected among the political alternatives offered by the revolutionary movement.

Lenin's Return to Russia

When Czar Nicholas II fell in February, 1917 (March, by the Western Gregorian calendar), Lenin and the Bolsheviks were taken by surprise. The moderate and hopefully democratic Provisional Government which was established under Prince Lvov seemed to refute Lenin's contention that the Russian middle class could not rule. The Bolsheviks in Russia were confused and divided about how to regard the Provisional Government, but most of them, including Stalin, were inclined to accept it for the time being on condition that it work for an end to the war. When Lenin reached Russia in April after his famous "sealed car" trip across Germany, he promptly denounced his Bolshevik colleagues for failing to take a sufficiently revolutionary stand.

1. In our attitude towards the war, which also under the new government of Lvov and Co. unquestionably remains on Russia's part a predatory imperialist war owing to the capitalist nature of that government, not the slightest concession to "revolutionary defencism" is permissible.

The class-conscious proletariat can give its consent to a revolutionary war, which would really justify revolutionary defencism, only on condition: a) that the power pass to the proletariat and the poor sections of the peasantry bordering on the proletariat; b) that all annexations be renounced in actual fact and not in word; c) that a complete break be effected in actual fact with all capitalist interests.

In view of the undoubted honesty of the broad strata of the mass believers in revolutionary defencism, who accept the war as a necessity only, and not as a means of conquest, in view of the fact that they are being deceived by the bourgeoisie, it is necessary with particular thoroughness, persist-

FROM: Lenin, "On the Tasks of the Proletariat in the Present Revolution" (the "April Theses," April 7 [20], 1917;* *Selected Works,* Vol. II, book 2, pp. 13-17).

* Russian dates are old style, with new style in brackets, up to the calendar reform effective February 1[14], 1918; all new style thereafter—Ed.

ence and patience to explain their error to them, to explain the inseparable connection existing between capital and the imperialist war, and to prove that without overthrowing capital *it is impossible* to end the war by a truly democratic peace, a peace not imposed by violence.

The most widespread propaganda of this view in the army on active service must be organized.

Fraternization.

2. The specific feature of the present situation in Russia is that it represents a *transition* from the first stage of the revolution—which, owing to the insufficient class consciousness and organization of the proletariat, placed the power in the hands of the bourgeoisie—*to the second* stage, which must place the power in the hands of the proletariat and the poorest strata of the peasantry.

This transition is characterized, on the one hand, by a maximum of legally recognized rights (Russia is *now* the freest of all the belligerent countries in the world); on the other, by the absence of violence in relation to the masses, and, finally, by the unreasoning confidence of the masses in the government of capitalists, the worst enemies of peace and Socialism.

This peculiar situation demands of us an ability to adapt ourselves to the *special* conditions of Party work among unprecedentedly large masses of proletarians who have just awakened to political life.

3. No support for the Provisional Government; the utter falsity of all its promises should be explained, particularly those relating to the renunciation of annexations. Exposure in place of the impermissible illusion-breeding "demand" that *this* government, a government of capitalists, should *cease* to be an imperialist government.

4. Recognition of the fact that in most of the Soviets of Workers' Deputies our Party is in a minority, and so far in a small minority, as against *a bloc of all* the petty-bourgeois opportunist elements, who have yielded to the influence of the bourgeoisie and convey its influence to the proletariat, from the Popular Socialists and the Socialist-Revolutionaries down

to the Organization Committee (Chkheidze, Tsereteli, etc.), Steklov,* etc., etc.

It must be explained to the masses that the Soviets of Workers' Deputies are the *only possible* form of the revolutionary government, and that therefore our task is, as long as *this* government yields to the influence of the bourgeoisie, to present a patient, systematic, and persistent *explanation* of the errors of their tactics, an explanation especially adapted to the practical needs of the masses.

As long as we are in the minority we carry on the work of criticizing and exposing errors and at the same time we preach the necessity of transferring the entire power of state to the Soviets of Workers' Deputies, so that the masses may by experience overcome their mistakes.

5. Not a parliamentary republic—to return to a parliamentary republic from the Soviets of Workers' Deputies would be a retrograde step—but a republic of Soviets of Workers', Agricultural Labourers' and Peasants' Deputies throughout the country, from top to bottom.

Abolition of the police, the army and the bureaucracy.**

The salaries of all officials, all of whom are to be elected and to be subject to recall at any time, not to exceed the average wage of a competent worker.

6. In the agrarian program the most important part to be assigned to the Soviets of Agricultural Labourers' Deputies.

Confiscation of all landed estates.

Nationalization of *all* lands in the country, the disposal of the land to be put in the charge of the local Soviets of Agricultural Labourers' and Peasants' Deputies. The organization of separate Soviets of Deputies of Poor Peasants. The creation of model farms on each of the large estates (varying from 100 to 300 dessiatins, in accordance with local and other conditions, by decisions of the local institutions) under the control of the Soviets of Agricultural Labourers' Deputies and for the public account.

* Chkheidze, Tsereteli, Steklov: Menshevik leaders in the Petrograd Soviet—Ed.

** I.e., the standing army to be replaced by the arming of the whole people.

7. The immediate amalgamation of all banks in the country into a single national bank, and the institution of control over it by the Soviets of Workers' Deputies.

8. It isn't our *immediate* task to "introduce" Socialism, but only to bring social production and distribution of products at once under the *control* of the Soviets of Workers' Deputies.

9. Party tasks:
   a) Immediate convocation of a Party congress;
   b) Alteration of the Party program, mainly:
      1) On the question of imperialism and the imperialist war;
      2) On our attitude towards the state and *our* demand for a "commune state" (i.e., a state of which the Paris Commune was the prototype);
      3) Amendment of our antiquated minimum program.
   c) Change of the Party's name. Instead of "Social-Democracy," whose official leaders *throughout* the world have betrayed Socialism and deserted to the bourgeoisie (the "defencists" and the vacillating "Kautskyites"), we must call ourselves a *Communist Party*.

10. A new International.

We must take the initiative in creating a revolutionary International, an International against the *social-chauvinists* and against the "Centre". . . .

Lenin on the Soviets

Simultaneously with the establishment of the Provisional Government, the leaders of the Russian socialist parties—Mensheviks, Bolsheviks, and Socialist-Revolutionaries ("SR's")—organized the so-called "soviets (Russian for "councils") of workers' and soldiers' deputies." The soviets, set up in every major city on the model of similar bodies that existed during the Revolution of 1905, began to exert a strong though informal political influence—hence Lenin's expression of "dual power" shared by the more moderate Provisional Government and the more radical soviets. Lenin saw in the soviets the ideal organs of revolution; it remained only for his Bolsheviks to win paramount influence in them, which they did on the eve of their seizure of power.

The basic question in any revolution is that of state power. Unless this question is understood, there can be no conscious participation in the revolution, not to speak of guidance of the revolution.

The highly remarkable specific feature of our revolution is that it has brought about a *dual power.* This fact must be grasped first and foremost: unless it is understood, we cannot advance. We must know how to supplement and amend old "formulas," for example, of Bolshevism, for as it has transpired, they were correct on the whole, but their concrete realization has *turned out to be* different. *Nobody* previously thought, or could have thought, of a dual power.

In what does this dual power consist? In the fact that side by side with the Provisional Government, the government of the *bourgeoisie,* there has arisen *another government,* weak and incipient as yet, but undoubtedly an actually existing and growing government—the Soviets of Workers' and Soldiers' Deputies.

What is the class composition of this other government? It consists of the proletariat and the peasantry (clad in soldier's uniforms). What is the political nature of this government? It is a revolutionary dictatorship, i.e., a power directly based on revolutionary seizure, on the direct initiative of the masses from below, and *not on a law* enacted by a centralized state power. It is a power entirely different from that generally existing in the parliamentary bourgeois-democratic republics of the usual type still prevailing in the advanced countries of Europe and America. This circumstance is often forgotten, often not reflected on, yet it is the crux of the matter. *This* power is of *the same type* as the Paris Commune of 1871. The fundamental characteristics of this type are: 1) the source of power is not a law previously discussed and enacted by parliament, but the direct initiative of the people's masses from below, in their localities—

FROM: Lenin, "On the Dual Power" (April 9 [22], 1917; *Selected Works,* Vol. II, book 1, pp. 20-23).

direct "seizure" to use a current expression; 2) the replacement of the police and the army, which are institutions separated from the people and set against the people, by the direct arming of the whole people; order in the state under such a power is maintained by the armed workers and peasants *themselves,* by the armed people *themselves;* 3) officialdom, the bureaucracy are either similarly replaced by the direct rule of the people themselves or at least placed under special control; they not only become elected officials, but are also *subject to recall* at the first demand of the people; they are reduced to the position of simple agents; from a privileged stratum holding "jobs" remunerated on a high, bourgeois scale, they become workers of a special "branch," whose remuneration *does not exceed* the ordinary pay of a competent worker.

This, and this *alone,* constitutes the *essence* of the Paris Commune as a special type of state. This essence has been forgotten or perverted by the Plekhanovs (out-and-out chauvinists who have betrayed Marxism), the Kautsky's (the men of the "Centre," i.e., those who vacillate between chauvinism and Marxism), and generally by all those Social-Democrats, Socialist-Revolutionaries, etc., etc., who now hold sway.

They are trying to get away with phrases, evasions, subterfuges; they congratulate each other a thousand times upon the revolution, but they refuse to *ponder* over *what* the Soviets of Workers' and Soldiers' Deputies *are.* They refuse to recognize the obvious truth that inasmuch as these Soviets exist, *inasmuch as* they are a power, we have in Russia a state of the *type* of the Paris Commune.

I have underscored the words "inasmuch as," for it is only an incipient power. By direct agreement with the bourgeois Provisional Government and by a series of actual concessions, it has itself *surrendered and is surrendering* its positions to the bourgeoisie.

Why? Is it because Chkheidze, Tsereteli, Steklov, and Co. are making a "mistake"? Nonsense. Only a philistine can think so—not a Marxist. The reason is *insufficient class-consciousness* and organization of the proletarians and peasants. The "mistake" of the leaders I have named lies in their petty-bourgeois position, in the fact that instead of enlightening the minds of the workers, they are *befogging* them; instead of dispersing petty-bourgeois illusions, they are *instilling* them; instead of freeing the masses from bourgeois influence, they are *strengthening* that influence.

It should be clear from this why our comrades too commit so many mistakes when putting the question "simply": should the Provisional Government be overthrown immediately?

My answer is: 1) it should be overthrown, for it is an oligarchic, bourgeois, and not a people's government, and *is unable* to provide peace, or bread, or full freedom; 2) it cannot be overthrown just now, for it is being maintained by a direct and indirect, a formal and actual *agreement* with the Soviets of Workers' Deputies, and primarily with the chief Soviet, the Petrograd Soviet; 3) generally, it cannot be "overthrown" in the ordinary way, for it rests on the "*support*" given to the bourgeoisie by the *second* government—the Soviet of Workers' Deputies, and that government is the only possible revolutionary government, which directly expresses the mind and will of the majority of the workers and peasants. Humanity has not yet evolved and we do not as yet know a type of government superior to and better than the Soviets of Workers', Agricultural Labourers', Peasants' and Soldiers' Deputies.

In order to become a power the class-conscious workers must win the majority to their side. *As long as* no violence is used against the masses there is no other road to power. We are not Blanquists,* we do not stand for the seizure of power by a minority. We are Marxists, we stand for proletarian class struggle against petty-bourgeois intoxication, against chauvinism-defencism, phrasemongering and dependence on the bourgeoisie.

Let us create a proletarian Communist Party; its elements have already been created by the best adherents of Bolshevism; let us rally our ranks for proletarian class work; then, from among the proletarians, from among the *poor*

* Blanquists: adherents of the conspiratorial doctrine of the French Revolutionary L. A. Blanqui—Ed.

peasants, ever greater numbers will range themselves on our side. For *actual experience* will from day to day shatter the petty-bourgeois illusions of the "Social-Democrats"—the Chkheidzes, Tseretelis, Steklovs et al.—of the "Socialist-Revolutionaries," petty bourgeois of a still purer water, and so on and so forth.

The bourgeoisie stands for the undivided power of the bourgeoisie.

The class-conscious workers stand for the undivided power of the Soviets of Workers', Agricultural Labourers', Peasants' and Soldiers' Deputies—for undivided power made possible not by dubious ventures, but by the *enlightenment* of the proletarian minds, by their *emancipation* from the influence of the bourgeoisie.

The petty bourgeoisie—"Social-Democrats," Socialist-Revolutionaries, etc., etc.—vacillates and *hinders* this enlightenment and emancipation.

Such is the actual, the *class* alignment of forces that determines our tasks.

Bukharin and Stalin on the Prospects of International Revolution

In August, 1917, while Lenin was in hiding and the party had been theoretically outlawed by the Provisional Government, the Bolsheviks nonetheless managed to hold their first party congress since 1907. The most significant part of the debate turned on the prospects for immediate revolutionary action in Russia and the relation of this to the anticipated international upheaval. The cleavage between the utopian internationalists and the more practical Russia-oriented people was already apparent.

a) [*Bukharin is reporting on the War and the International Situation*]

. . . History is working for us. History is moving on the path which leads inevitably to the uprising of the proletariat and the triumph of socialism.

FROM: *Protocols,* 6th Congress, Russian Social-Democratic Workers' Party (Bolsheviks), August 1917 (Moscow, Party Press, 1934, pp. 100-01, 192, 233-34; editor's translation).

The continuing progress of the war is sharpening those tendencies which were observed at the very beginning of the war. The intermediate strata and small producers are disappearing. In the first year of the war the petty bourgeoisie decreased 40%. All the means of production are being concentrated in the hands of the capitalist state. State capitalism is growing—rule by a bunch of oligarchs—the last conceivable form of capitalism. On the other hand we see the terrible sharpening of social contradictions. We can speak of the absolute impoverishment of the working class in the economic respect, of their semislave condition thanks to being bound to the factories. Now the worker in Western Europe is a serf in a government factory. And this social antagonism, on the one hand, and on the other the greatest readiness of capitalism for the transition to a socialist economy, tell us that the socialist revolution is being prepared at both ends. . . .

We are going to have a great new upsurge of the revolutionary wave. Then there can be two possibilities: either our peasant-proletarian revolution will be victorious before the revolution breaks out in Western Europe or other countries, or in some one of the West-European countries the revolution will be victorious before it is in ours. In the first case, the next thing for the victorious workers' and peasants' revolution is the declaration of a revolutionary war, i.e., armed help for proletarians who are still not victorious. This war can assume various characters. If we succeed in repairing our disrupted economic organism, we will go over to the offensive. But if we cannot muster the strength to carry on an offensive revolutionary war, then we will conduct a defensive revolutionary war. Then we will have the right to declare to the proletariat of the whole world that we will wage a holy war in the name of the interests of all the proletariat, and this will sound like a comradely appeal. By such a revolutionary war we will light the fire of world socialist revolution. The only really democratic exit from the blind alley into which the West-European and American countries have gone is the international proletarian revolution, however many victims it may cost us. There is no other solution of the problem. . . .

b) [*Bukharin is reading his draft resolution on the Current Moment and the War*]

9. The liquidation of imperialist rule sets before the working class of that country which first realizes the dictatorship of the proletarians and semiproletarians, the task of supporting by any means (even armed force) the struggling proletariat of other countries. In particular such a task stands before Russia, if, as is very probable, the new unavoidable upsurge of the Russian revolution places the workers and poorest peasants in power before an overturn in the capitalist countries of the West.

Preobrazhensky: . . . I am not satisfied with the edited version of the point. I would prefer to restore the original version, which spoke definitely about revolutionary war in the event of a dictatorship of the proletariat.

Bukharin: . . . In the committee on the resolution the question arose realistically—will we have the strength to wage a revolutionary war?—and we adopted a less strong formulation, since we cannot irrevocably assert that we will command the strength to wage a revolutionary war. On the basis of these considerations I am against Comrade Preobrazhensky's amendment.

The amendment is rejected.

c) [*Stalin is reading his draft resolution on the Political Situation*]

9. The task of these revolutionary classes is then to exert every effort to seize governmental power and to direct it, in alliance with the revolutionary proletariat of the progressive countries, toward peace and toward the socialist reconstruction of society.

Preobrazhensky: I propose another version of the end of the resolution: "to direct it toward peace and, in the event of a proletarian revolution in the West, toward socialism."

If we adopt the committee's version, we will have a disagreement with Comrade Bukharin's resolution that we have already adopted.

Stalin: I am against such an ending of the resolution. The possibility is not excluded that Russia itself may be the country which lays down the road to socialism. No country up to now has enjoyed such freedom as there has been in Russia, or has tried to establish workers' control over production. Besides, the base of our revolution is broader than in Western Europe, where the proletariat stands face to face with the bourgeoisie in complete isolation. Here the workers are supported by the poorest strata of the peasantry. Finally, in Germany the apparatus of governmental power works incomparably better than the imperfect apparatus of our bourgeoisie, which itself is a tributary of European capital. We must reject the worn-out assertion that only Europe can show us the way. There exist dogmatic Marxism and creative Marxism. I stand on the basis of the latter.

Chairman: I put Comrade Preobrazhensky's amendment to a vote. It is rejected. . . .

Lenin's Vision of the Revolutionary State

While hiding in Finland in the fall of 1917 Lenin composed what is usually taken to be his main contribution to political theory, a commentary on the political program of Marx and Engels which he published under the title *State and Revolution.* The essence of the argument, in which Lenin was strongly influenced by Bukharin's ideas, was that the "bourgeois" state had to be completely destroyed and replaced by an entirely new revolutionary state on the model of the Paris Commune of 1871 (which the soviets were to provide in Russia). The new state would exclude all bureaucracy and inequality, and eventually "wither away" after the resistance of the old propertied classes was overcome.

Although this view of the revolutionary process has been fully incorporated into official Communist theory, it is obvious that it had very little relationship to Soviet practice after the revolution. How seriously Lenin took the vision when he was writing is difficult to say, but it should be noted that the anti-authoritarian emphasis expressed here offers a sharp contrast to his more characteristic disciplinarian bent both before and after 1917. On the other hand, many of Lenin's supporters, particularly in the left wing of the party, took the anti-authoritarian ideal very seriously indeed; they eventually had to be curbed or purged.

. . . The state is the product and the manifestation of the *irreconcilability* of class antagonisms. The state arises when, where and to the extent that class antagonisms objectively *cannot* be reconciled. And, conversely, the existence of the state proves that the class antagonisms are irreconcilable.

. . . The teaching of Marx and Engels concerning the inevitability of a violent revolution refers to the bourgeois state. The latter *cannot* be superseded by the proletarian state (the dictatorship of the proletariat) through the process of "withering away," but, as a general rule, only through a violent revolution. The panegyric Engels sang in its honour, and which fully corresponds to Marx's repeated declarations (recall the concluding passages of *The Poverty of Philosophy* and the *Communist Manifesto,* with their proud and open proclamation of the inevitability of a violent revolution; recall what Marx wrote nearly thirty years later, in criticizing the Gotha Program of 1875, when he mercilessly castigated the opportunist character of that program)—this panegyric is by no means a mere "impulse," a mere declamation or a polemical sally. The necessity of systematically imbuing the masses with *this* and precisely this view of violent revolution lies at the root of *all* the teachings of Marx and Engels. The betrayal of their teaching by the now predominant social-chauvinist and Kautskyite trends is expressed in striking relief by the neglect of *such* propaganda and agitation by both these trends.

The supersession of the bourgeois state by the proletarian state is impossible without a violent revolution. The abolition of the proletarian state, i.e., of the state in general, is impossible except through the process of "withering away." . . .

The overthrow of bourgeois rule can be accomplished

FROM: Lenin, "The State and Revolution" (August-September, 1917; *Selected Works,* Vol. II, book 1, pp. 204, 219-20, 223-24, 243-44, 291-94, 297-98, 304-06, 313-14).

only by the proletariat, as the particular class whose economic conditions of existence prepare it for this task and provide it with the possibility and the power to perform it. While the bourgeoisie breaks up and disintegrates the peasantry and all the petty-bourgeois strata, it welds together, unites and organizes the proletariat. Only the proletariat—by virtue of the economic role it plays in large-scale production—is capable of being the leader of *all* the toiling and exploited masses, whom the bourgeoisie exploits, oppresses and crushes often not less, but more, than it does the proletarians, but who are incapable of waging an *independent* struggle for their emancipation.

The teaching on the class struggle, when applied by Marx to the question of the state and of the socialist revolution, leads of necessity to the recognition of the *political rule* of the proletariat, of its dictatorship, i.e., of power shared with none and relying directly upon the armed force of the masses. The overthrow of the bourgeoisie can be achieved only by the proletariat becoming transformed into the *ruling class,* capable of crushing the inevitable and desperate resistance of the bourgeoisie, and of organizing *all* the toiling and exploited masses for the new economic order.

The proletariat needs state power, the centralized organization of force, the organization of violence, both to crush the resistance of the exploiters and to *lead* the enormous mass of the population—the peasantry, the petty bourgeoisie, the semiproletarians—in the work of organizing socialist economy.

By educating the workers' party, Marxism educates the vanguard of the proletariat which is capable of assuming power and *of leading the whole people* to Socialism, of directing and organizing the new order, of being the teacher, the guide, the leader of all the toilers and exploited in the task of building up their social life without the bourgeoisie and against the bourgeoisie. . . .

. . . Capitalist culture has *created* large-scale production, factories, railways, the postal service, telephones, etc., and *on this basis* the great majority of the functions of the old "state power" have become so simplified and can be reduced to such exceedingly simple operations of registration, filing and checking that they can be easily performed by every literate person, can quite easily be performed for ordinary "workmen's wages," and that these functions can (and must) be stripped of every shadow of privilege, of every semblance of "official grandeur."

All officials, without exception, elected and subject to recall *at any time*, their salaries reduced to the level of ordinary, "workmen's wages"—these simple and "self-evident" democratic measures, while completely uniting the interests of the workers and the majority of the peasants, at the same time serve as a bridge leading from capitalism to Socialism. These measures concern the reconstruction of the state, the purely political reconstruction of society; but, of course, they acquire their full meaning and significance only in connection with the "expropriation of the expropriators" either being accomplished or in preparation, i.e., with the transformation of capitalist private ownership of the means of production into social ownership. . . .

. . . Forward development, i.e., towards Communism, proceeds through the dictatorship of the proletariat, and cannot do otherwise, for the *resistance* of the capitalist exploiters cannot be *broken* by anyone else or in any other way.

And the dictatorship of the proletariat, i.e., the organization of the vanguard of the oppressed as the ruling class for the purpose of suppressing the oppressors, cannot result merely in an expansion of democracy. *Simultaneously* with an immense expansion of democracy, which *for the first time* becomes democracy for the poor, democracy for the people, and not democracy for the moneybags, the dictatorship of the proletariat imposes a series of restrictions on the freedom of the oppressors, the exploiters, the capitalists. We must suppress them in order to free humanity from wage slavery, their resistance must be crushed by force; it is clear that where there is suppression, where there is violence, there is no freedom and no democracy. . . .

Only in communist society, when the resistance of the capitalists has been completely crushed, when the capitalists have disappeared, when there are no classes (i.e., when there is no difference between the members of society as regards their relation to the social means of production), *only* then "the state . . . ceases to exist," and it "*becomes possible to speak of freedom.*" Only then will there become possible and be realized a truly complete democracy, democracy without any exceptions whatever. And only then will democracy begin to *wither away,* owing to the simple fact that, freed from capitalist slavery, from the untold horrors, savagery, absurdities and infamies of capitalist exploitation, people will gradually *become accustomed* to observing the elementary rules of social intercourse that have been known for centuries and repeated for thousands of years in all copybook maxims; they will become accustomed to observing them without force, without compulsion, without subordination, *without the special apparatus* for compulsion which is called the state. . . .

. . . Only Communism makes the state absolutely unnecessary, for there is *nobody* to be suppressed—"nobody" in the sense of a *class,* in the sense of a systematic struggle against a definite section of the population. We are not utopians, and do not in the least deny the possibility and inevitability of excesses on the part of *individual persons,* or the need to suppress *such* excesses. But, in the first place, no special machine, no special apparatus of suppression is needed for this; this will be done by the armed people itself, as simply and as readily as any crowd of civilized people, even in modern society, interferes to put a stop to a scuffle or to prevent a woman from being assaulted. And, secondly, we know that the fundamental social cause of excesses, which consist in the violation of the rules of social intercourse, is the exploitation of the masses, their want and their poverty. With the removal of this chief cause, excesses will inevitably begin to "*wither away.*" We do not know how quickly and in what succession, but we know that they will wither away. With their withering away the state will also *wither away.* . . .

. . . In the first phase of communist society (usually called Socialism) "bourgeois right" is *not* abolished in its entirety, but only in part, only in proportion to the economic revolution so far attained, i.e., only in respect of the means of production. "Bourgeois right" recognizes them as the private property of individuals. Socialism converts them into *common* property. *To that extent*—and to that extent alone—"bourgeois right" disappears.

However, it continues to exist as far as its other part is concerned; it continues to exist in the capacity of regulator (determining factor) in the distribution of products and the allotment of labour among the members of society. The socialist principle: "He who does not work, neither shall he eat," is *already* realized; the other socialist principle: "An equal amount of products for an equal amount of labour," is also *already* realized. But this is not yet Communism, and it does not yet abolish "bourgeois right," which gives to unequal individuals, in return for unequal (really unequal) amounts of labour, equal amounts of products.

This is a "defect," says Marx, but it is unavoidable in the first phase of Communism; for if we are not to indulge in utopianism, we must not think that having overthrown capitalism people will at once learn to work for society *without any standard of right;* and indeed the abolition of capitalism *does not immediately* create the economic premises for *such* a change.

And there is no other standard than that of "bourgeois right." To this extent, therefore, there still remains the need for a state, which, while safeguarding the public ownership of the means of production, would safeguard equality in labour and equality in the distribution of products.

The state withers away in so far as there are no longer any capitalists, any classes, and, consequently, no *class* can be *suppressed.*

But the state has not yet completely withered away, since there still remains the safeguarding of "bourgeois right," which sanctifies actual inequality. For the state to wither away completely, complete Communism is necessary. . . .

. . . The development of capitalism . . . itself creates the *premises* that *enable* really "all" to take part in the administration of the state. Some of these premises are: universal literacy, which has already been achieved in a number of the most advanced capitalist countries, then the "training and disciplining" of millions of workers by the huge, complex, socialized apparatus of the postal service, railways, big factories, large-scale commerce, banking, etc., etc.

Given these *economic* premises it is quite possible, after the overthrow of the capitalists and the bureaucrats, to proceed immediately, overnight, to supersede them in the *control* of production and distribution, in the work of *keeping account* of labour and products by the armed workers, by the whole of the armed population. (The question of control and accounting should not be confused with the question of the scientifically trained staff of engineers, agronomists and so on. These gentlemen are working today in obedience to the wishes of the capitalists; they will work even better tomorrow in obedience to the wishes of the armed workers.)

Accounting and control—that is the *main* thing required for "arranging" the smooth working, the correct functioning of the *first phase* of communist society. *All* citizens are transformed here into hired employees of the state, which consists of the armed workers. *All* citizens become employees and workers of a *single* nationwide state "syndicate." All that is required is that they should work equally, do their proper share of work, and get equally paid. The accounting and control necessary for this have been *simplified* by capitalism to the extreme and reduced to the extraordinary simple operations—which any literate person can perform—of supervising and recording, knowledge of the four rules of arithmetic, and issuing appropriate receipts.

When the *majority* of the people begin independently and everywhere to keep such accounts and maintain such control over the capitalists (now converted into employees) and over the intellectual gentry who preserve their capitalist habits, this control will really become universal, general, popular; and there will be no way of getting away from it, there will be "nowhere to go."

The whole of society will have become a single office and a single factory, with equality of labour and equality of pay.

But this "factory" discipline, which the proletariat, after defeating the capitalists, after overthrowing the exploiters, will extend to the whole of society is by no means our ideal, or our ultimate goal. It is but a necessary *step* for the purpose of thoroughly purging society of all the infamies and abominations of capitalist exploitation, *and for further* progress.

From the moment all members of society, or even only the vast majority, have learned to administer the state *themselves,* have taken this work into their own hands, have "set going" control over the insignificant minority of capitalists, over the gentry who wish to preserve their capitalist habits and over the workers who have been profoundly corrupted by capitalism—from this moment the need for government of any kind begins to disappear altogether. The more complete the democracy, the nearer the moment approaches when it becomes unnecessary. The more democratic the "state" which consists of the armed workers, and which is "no longer a state in the proper sense of the word," the more rapidly does *every form* of state begin to wither away.

For when *all* have learned to administer and actually do independently administer social production, independently keep accounts and exercise control over the idlers, the gentlefolk, the swindlers and suchlike "guardians of capitalist traditions," the escape from this popular accounting and control will inevitably become so incredibly difficult, such a rare exception, and will probably be accompanied by such swift and severe punishment (for the armed workers are practical men and not sentimental intellectuals, and they will scarcely allow anyone to trifle with them), that the *necessity* of observing the simple, fundamental rules of human intercourse will very soon become a *habit.*

And then the door will be wide open for the transition from the first phase of communist society to its higher phase, and with it to the complete withering away of the state. . . .

As far as the supposedly necessary "bureaucratic" organization is concerned, there is no difference whatever between railways and any other enterprise in large-scale machine industry, any factory, large store, or large-scale capitalist agricultural enterprise. The technique of all such enterprises makes absolutely imperative the strictest discipline, the utmost precision on the part of everyone in carrying out his allotted task, for otherwise the whole enterprise may come to a stop, or machinery or the finished product may be damaged. In all such enterprises the workers will, of course, "elect delegates who will form *a sort of parliament.*"

But the whole point is that this "sort of parliament" will *not* be a parliament in the sense in which we understand bourgeois-parliamentary institutions. The whole point is that this "sort of parliament" will *not* merely "draw up the working regulations and supervise the management of the bureaucratic apparatus," as Kautsky, whose ideas do not go beyond the bounds of bourgeois parliamentarism, imagines. In socialist society the "sort of parliament" consisting of workers' deputies will, of course, "draw up the working regulations and supervise the management" of the "apparatus"—*but* this apparatus will *not* be "bureaucratic." The workers, having conquered political power, will smash the old bureaucratic apparatus, they will shatter it to its very foundations, they will destroy it to the very roots; and they will replace it by a new one, consisting of the very same workers and office employees, *against* whose transformation into bureaucrats the measures will at once be taken which were specified in detail by Marx and Engels: 1) not only election, but also recall at any time; 2) pay not exceeding that of a workman; 3) immediate introduction of control and supervision by *all*, so that *all* shall become "bureaucrats" for a time and that, therefore, *nobody* may be able to become a "bureaucrat". . . .

Lenin's Call for an Uprising

By September, 1917, it was clear that mass sentiment among the workers, soldiers and peasants was shifting to the left. The Bolsheviks won control of the Petrograd and Moscow Soviets. Lenin thereupon called upon the Bolshevik Party to prepare to overthrow the Provisional Government by violence.

. . . Marxists are accused of Blanquism for treating insurrection as an art! Can there be a more flagrant perversion of the truth, when not a single Marxist will deny that it was Marx who expressed himself on this score in the most definite, precise and categorical manner, referring to insurrection precisely as an *art*, and saying that it must be treated as an art, that one must *win* the first success and then proceed from success to success, never ceasing the *offensive* against the enemy, taking advantage of his confusion, etc., etc.?

To be successful, insurrection must rely not upon conspiracy and not upon a party, but upon the advanced class. That is the first point. Insurrection must rely upon a *revolutionary upsurge of the people*. That is the second point. Insurrection must rely upon such a *crucial moment* in the history of the growing revolution when the activity of the advanced ranks of the people is at its height, and when the *vacillations* in the ranks of the enemy and *in the ranks of the weak, halfhearted and irresolute friends of the revolution* are strongest. That is the third point. And these three conditions for raising the question of insurrection distinguish *Marxism from Blanquism.*

But once these conditions are present, to refuse to treat insurrection as an *art* is a betrayal of Marxism and a betrayal of the revolution. . . .

All the objective conditions for a successful insurrection exist. We have the exceptional advantage of a situation in which *only* our victory in the insurrection can put an end to that most painful thing on earth, vacillation, which has worn the people out; a situation in which *only our* victory in the insurrection can *foil* the game of a separate peace directed against the revolution by publicly proposing a fuller, juster and earlier peace, a peace that will *benefit* the revolution. . . .

We must draw up a brief declaration of the Bolsheviks,

FROM: Lenin, "Marxism and Insurrection: A Letter to the Central Committee of the R.S.D.W.P." (Sept. 13-14 [26-27], 1917; *Selected Works,* Vol. II, book 1, 167-68, 170-73).

emphasizing in the most trenchant manner the irrelevance of long speeches and of "speeches" in general, the necessity for immediate action to save the revolution, the absolute necessity for a complete break with the bourgeoisie, for the removal of the whole present government, for a complete rupture with the Anglo-French imperialists, who are preparing a "separate" partition of Russia, and for the immediate transfer of the whole power *to the revolutionary democracy headed by the revolutionary proletariat.*

Our declaration must consist of the briefest and most trenchant formulation of this conclusion in connection with the proposals of the program: peace for the peoples, land for the peasants, confiscation of outrageous profits, and a check on the outrageous sabotage of production by the capitalists.

The briefer and more trenchant the declaration the better. Only two other highly important points must be clearly indicated in it, namely, that the people are worn out by the vacillations, that they are tormented by the irresolution of the Socialist-Revolutionaries and Mensheviks; and that we are definitely breaking with these *parties* because they have betrayed the revolution.

And another thing. By immediately proposing a peace without annexations, by immediately breaking with the Allied imperialists and with all imperialists, either we shall at once obtain an armistice, or the entire revolutionary proletariat will rally to the defence of the country, and a really just, really revolutionary war will then be waged by the revolutionary democracy under the leadership of the proletariat.

Having read this declaration, and having appealed for *decisions* and not talk, for *action* and not resolution-writing, we must *dispatch* our whole group to the *factories and the barracks.* Their place is there, the pulse of life is there, the source of salvation of the revolution is there, and there is the motive force of the Democratic Conference.*

There, in ardent and impassioned speeches, we must

* Democratic Conference: a semi-official meeting of various Russian political leaders, convoked by the Provisional-Government in September, 1917—Ed.

explain our program and put the alternative: either the Conference adopts it *in its entirety,* or else insurrection. There is no middle course. Delay is impossible. The revolution is perishing.

By putting the question thus, by concentrating our entire group in the factories and barracks, *we shall be able to determine the right moment for launching the insurrection.*

And in order to treat insurrection in a Marxist way, i.e., as an art, we must at the same time, without losing a single moment, organize a *headquarter staff* of the insurgent detachments, distribute our forces, move the reliable regiments to the most important points, surround the Alexandrinsky Theatre, occupy the Peter and Paul Fortress, arrest the general staff and the government, and move against the cadets and the Savage Division such detachments as will rather die than allow the enemy to approach the centres of the city; we must mobilize the armed workers and call them to fight the last desperate fight, occupy the telegraph and the telephone exchange at once, place *our* headquarter staff of the insurrection at the central telephone exchange and connect it by telephone with all the factories, all the regiments, all the points of armed fighting, etc.

Of course, this is all by way of example, only to *illustrate* the fact that at the present moment it is impossible to remain loyal to Marxism, to remain loyal to the revolution, *without treating insurrection as an art.*

The Declaration of Revolutionary Intent—Trotsky

The Bolsheviks' hope of seizing power was hardly secret; bold defiance of the Provisional Government was one of their major propaganda appeals. Some three weeks before the insurrection they decided to stage a demonstrative walkout from the advisory assembly (the Council of the Republic or "Pre-Parliament") which the provisional Prime Minister Alexander Kerensky had summoned. When the walkout was staged, Trotsky (a Bolshevik only since August, 1917, but already the party's most articulate spokesman) denounced the

Provisional Government for its alleged counterrevolutionary intentions and called on the masses to support the Bolsheviks.

The officially proclaimed aims of the Democratic Conference summoned by the Central Executive Committee of the Soviets of Workers' and Soldiers' Deputies consisted of the abolition of the irresponsible personal regime that nourished the Kornilov movement and the creation of a responsible power able to liquidate the war and guarantee the convening of the Constituent Assembly after the designated interval.

Meanwhile, behind the back of the Democratic Conference and by means of backstage deals between Kerensky, the Kadets* and the leaders of the S.-R.'s and Mensheviks, results were arrived at which were directly opposed to the officially proclaimed aims.

A power was created in which and around which avowed and secret Kornilovists** play a leading role. The irresponsibility of this power is now confirmed and officially proclaimed. . . .

. . . The bourgeois classes which are directing the policy of the political government have set themselves the goal of *undermining* the Constituent Assembly. This is now the basic task of the privileged elements, to which their whole policy, domestic and foreign, is subordinated.

In the industrial, agrarian, and food-supply fields, the policy of the government and the propertied classes aggravates the natural disruption engendered by the war. The privileged classes, having provoked a peasant uprising, now move to suppress it, and openly hold a course towards the "bony hand of famine," which is to smother the revolution and above all the Constituent Assembly.

FROM: Trotsky, "Declaration of the Bolshevik Fraction to the Council of the Republic" ("Pre-Parliament"), October 7 [20], 1917 (Trotsky, *Works,* Moscow, State Press [1924], Vol. III, book 1, pp. 321-23; editor's translation).

* "Kadets": the Constitutional Democratic Party, from its Russian initials—Ed.

** Kornilovists: followers of General Kornilov, who attempted to overthrow Kerensky in August, 1917—Ed.

No less criminal is the foreign policy of the bourgeoisie and its government.

After forty months of war mortal danger threatens the capital. In answer to this a plan is proposed to transfer the government to Moscow. The idea of surrendering the revolutionary capital to the German troops does not evoke the least indignation among the bourgeois classes; on the contrary, it is accepted by them as a natural link in the general policy, which is to facilitate their counterrevolutionary plot.

Instead of recognizing that the salvation of the country lies in the conclusion of peace; instead of openly throwing out the proposal of immediate peace, over the heads of all the imperialist governments and diplomatic offices, to all the exhausted nations and in this way making further waging of the war actually impossible—the Provisional Government, taking its cue from the Kadet counterrevolutionaries and the Allied imperialists, without meaning, without strength, without a plan, toils along in the murderous harness of war, dooming to pointless destruction ever new hundreds of thousands of soldiers and sailors, and preparing the surrender of Petrograd and the smothering of the revolution. At a time when the soldier and sailor Bolsheviks are perishing together with the other sailors and soldiers as a result of others' mistakes and crimes, the so-called Supreme Commander-in-Chief continues to ruin the Bolshevik press. . . .

The leading parties of the Provisional Council serve as a voluntary cover for this whole policy.

We, the fraction of Bolshevik Social-Democrats, declare: with this government of national betrayal and with this council that tolerates counterrevolution we have nothing in common. We do not wish either directly or obliquely to conceal even for a single day, that work, fatal to the people, which is being accomplished behind the official curtain.

The revolution is in danger! At a time when the troops of [Kaiser] Wilhelm are threatening Petrograd, the government of Kerensky-Konovalov* is preparing to flee from

* Konovalov: a minister in Kerensky's government and acting premier at the time of the Bolshevik revolution—Ed.

Petrograd, in order to transform Moscow into a stronghold of counterrevolution.

We appeal to the vigilance of the Moscow workers and soldiers!

Quitting the Provisional Council, we appeal to the vigilance and courage of the workers, soldiers and peasants of all Russia.

Petrograd is in danger! The revolution is in danger! The nation is in danger!

The government aggravates this danger. The ruling parties help it.

Only the people themselves can save themselves and the country. We turn to the people.

All power to the Soviets!

All the land to the people!

Long live an immediate, honorable, democratic peace!

Long live the Constituent Assembly!

The Decision to Seize Power

On October 10 [23], 1917, Lenin came secretly to Petrograd to overcome hesitancies among the Bolshevik leadership over his demand for armed insurrection. Against the opposition of two of Lenin's long-time lieutenants, Zinoviev and Kamenev, the Central Committee adopted Lenin's resolution which formally instructed the party organizations to prepare for the seizure of power.

The Central Committee recognizes that the international position of the Russian revolution (the revolt in the German navy which is an extreme manifestation of the growth throughout Europe of the world socialist revolution; the threat of peace between the imperialists with the object of strangling the revolution in Russia) as well as the military situation (the indubitable decision of the Russian bourgeoisie and Kerensky and Co. to surrender Petrograd to the Germans), and the fact that the proletarian party

FROM: Lenin, Resolution "On the Armed Uprising," adopted by the Central Committee of the R.S.D.W.P., October 10 [23], 1917 (*Selected Works,* Vol. II, book 1, pp. 189-90).

has gained a majority in the Soviets—all this, taken in conjunction with the peasant revolt and the swing of popular confidence towards our Party (the elections in Moscow), and, finally, the obvious preparations being made for a second Kornilov affair (the withdrawal of troops from Petrograd, the dispatch of Cossacks to Petrograd, the surrounding of Minsk by Cossacks, etc.)—all this places the armed uprising on the order of the day.

Considering therefore that an armed uprising is inevitable, and that the time for it is fully ripe, the Central Committee instructs all Party organizations to be guided accordingly, and to discuss and decide all practical questions (the Congress of Soviets of the Northern Region, the withdrawal of troops from Petrograd, the action of our people in Moscow and Minsk, etc.) from this point of view.

Bolshevik Opposition to the Insurrection

Fearful on Marxist grounds that the Bolsheviks did not have the mass support or the international backing to assure them success, Zinoviev and Kamenev published a statement in which they endeavored to dissuade the party from following Lenin's lead. Lenin denounced them for "strike-breaking," and the uprising went ahead as scheduled.

. . . In labour circles there is developing and growing a current of thought which sees the only outcome in the immediate declaration of an armed uprising. The interaction of all the conditions at present is such that if we are to speak of such an uprising a definite date must be set for it, and that within the next few days. In one or another form this question is already being discussed by the entire press and at workers' meetings, and is occupying the minds of a substantial group of party workers. We on our part consider it our duty and

FROM: Zinoviev and Kamenev, Statement to the Principal Bolshevik Party Organizations, Oct. 11 [24], 1917 (English translation in Lenin, *Collected Works,* New York, International Publishers, 1929, Vol. XXI, book 2, pp. 328-31; reprinted by permission of the publisher).

our right to express ourselves on this question with complete frankness.

We are deeply convinced that to call at present for an armed uprising means to stake on one card not only the fate of our party, but also the fate of the Russian and international revolution.

There is no doubt that there are historical situations when an oppressed class must recognise that it is better to go forward to defeat than to give up without a battle. Does the Russian working class find itself at present in such a situation? *No,* and *a thousand times no!!!!*

As a result of the immense growth of the influence of our party in the cities, and particularly in the army, there has come about at present a situation such that it is becoming more and more impossible for the bourgeoisie to obstruct the Constituent Assembly. Through the army, through the workers, we hold a revolver at the temple of the bourgeoisie: the bourgeoisie is put in such a position that if it should undertake now to attempt to obstruct the Constituent Assembly, it would again push the petty-bourgeois parties to one side, and the revolver would go off.

The chances of our party in the elections to the Constituent Assembly are excellent. The talk that the influence of Bolshevism is beginning to wane, etc., we consider to have absolutely no foundation. In the mouths of our political opponents this assertion is simply a move in the political game, having as its purpose this very thing, to provoke an uprising of the Bolsheviks under conditions favourable to our enemies. The influence of the Bolsheviks is increasing. Whole strata of the labouring population are only now beginning to be drawn in by it. With correct tactics we can get a third and even more of the seats in the Constituent Assembly. The attitude of the petty-bourgeois parties in the Constituent Assembly cannot possibly be the same then as it is now. In the first place their slogan: "For land, for freedom, wait for the Constituent Assembly" will drop out. And aggravation of want, hunger, and the peasant movement, will exert more and more pressure on them and will compel them to seek an alliance with the proletarian party against the landowners and capitalists represented by the Cadet Party.

The Constituent Assembly, by itself, cannot of course abolish the present camouflaging of these interrelations. The Soviets, which have become rooted in life, can not be destroyed. The Constituent Assembly will be able to find support for its revolutionary work only in the Soviets. The Constituent Assembly plus the Soviets—this is that combined type of state institutions towards which we are going. It is on this political basis that our party is acquiring enormous chances for a real victory.

We have never said that the Russian working class *alone*, by its own forces, would be able to bring the present revolution to a victorious conclusion. We have not forgotten, must not forget even now, that between us and the bourgeoisie there stands a huge third camp: the petty bourgeoisie. This camp joined us during the days of the Kornilov affair and gave us victory. It will join us many times more. We must not permit ourselves to be hypnotised by what is the case at the present moment. Undoubtedly, at present this camp is much nearer to the bourgeoisie than to us. But the present situation is not eternal, nor even durable. And only by a careless step, by some hasty action which will make the whole fate of the revolution dependent upon an immediate uprising, will the proletarian party push the petty bourgeoisie into the arms of Milyukov* *for a long time*.

We are told: (1) that the majority of the people of Russia is already with us, and (2) that the majority of the international proletariat is with us. Alas!—neither the one nor the other is true, and this is the crux of the entire situation.

In Russia a majority of the workers and a substantial part of the soldiers are with us. But all the rest is dubious. We are all convinced, for instance, that if elections to the Constituent Assembly were to take place now, a majority of the peasants would vote for the S.-R.'s. What is this, an

* Milyukov: leader of the Constitutional Democratic Party and Foreign Minister in the Provisional Government, March-April, 1917—Ed.

accident? The masses of the soldiers support us not because of the slogan of war, but because of the slogan of peace. This is an extremely important circumstance and unless we take it into consideration we would be risking building on sand. If, having taken power at present by ourselves, we should come to the conclusion (in view of the whole world situation) that it is necessary to wage a revolutionary war, the masses of the soldiers will rush away from us. . . .

Having taken power, the workers' party thereby undoubtedly deals a blow to Wilhelm. It will be harder for him to carry on a war against revolutionary Russia, offering an immediate democratic peace. This is so. But will this blow under present conditions, after [the fall of] Riga, etc., be sufficiently powerful to turn away the hand of German imperialism from Russia? . . . Where then are the data which indicate that the proletarian party alone, and while the petty-bourgeois democracy is resisting, must take the responsibility for such a state of affairs and its inevitable consequences upon itself and upon itself alone?

And here we come to the second assertion—that the majority of the international proletariat allegedly is already with us. Unfortunately this is not so. The mutiny in the German navy has an immense symptomatic significance. There are portents of a serious movement in Italy. But from that to any sort of active support of the proletarian revolution in Russia which is declaring war on the entire bourgeois world is still very far. It is extremely harmful to overestimate forces. Undoubtedly much is given to us and much will be demanded from us. But if we now, having staked the entire game upon one card, suffer defeat, we shall deal a cruel blow to the international proletarian revolution, which is developing extremely slowly, but which is nevertheless developing. Moreover, the development of the revolution in Europe will make it obligatory for us, without any hesitation whatever, immediately to take power into our own hands. This is also the only guarantee of the victory of an uprising of the prolateriat in Russia. It will come, but it is not yet here. . . .

Before history, before the international proletariat, before the Russian Revolution and the Russian working class, we have no right to stake the whole future on the card of an armed uprising. It would be a mistake to think that such action now would, if it were unsuccessful, lead only to such consequences as did July 16-18. Now it is a question of something more. It is a question of decisive battle, and defeat in *that* battle would spell defeat to the revolution. . . .

The Bolshevik Seizure of Power

On October 25 [November 7], 1917, through the agency of the Military-Revolutionary Committee of the Petrograd Soviet—headed by Trotsky—the Bolsheviks and their allies, the Left Socialist-Revolutionaries, forcibly overthrew Kerensky's government and assumed power in the name of the soviets. A new cabinet, designated the "Council of People's Commissars," was set up, with Lenin as chairman and Trotsky as Commissar of Foreign Affairs. Endorsement of the coup was secured from the Second All-Russian Congress of Soviets, which was concurrently in session. This was the "October Revolution."

To the Citizens of Russia!

The Provisional Government has been overthrown. The power of state has passed into the hands of the organ of the Petrograd Soviet of Workers' and Soldiers' Deputies, the Revolutionary Military Committee, which stands at the head of the Petrograd proletariat and garrison.

The cause for which the people have fought—the immediate proposal of a democratic peace, the abolition of landed proprietorship, workers' control over production and the creation of a Soviet government—is assured.

Long live the revolution of the soldiers, workers, and peasants!

Revolutionary Military Committee of Petrograd
Soviet of Workers' and Soldiers' Deputies.

FROM: Proclamation of the Soviet Government, October 25 [November 7], 1917 (English translation in Lenin and Stalin, *The Russian Revolution,* New York, International Publishers, 1938, p. 234; reprinted by permission of the publisher).

Bolshevik Revolutionary Legislation

In a quick series of decrees, the new "soviet" government instituted a number of sweeping reforms, some long overdue and some quite revolutionary. They ranged from "democratic" reforms like the disestablishment of the church and equality for the national minorities, to the recognition of the peasants' land seizures and to openly socialist steps such as the nationalization of the banks. The Provisional Government's commitment to the war effort was repudiated. This was followed by the ominous gesture of suppressing the "bourgeois" press.

a) Decree on Peace

The workers' and peasants' government created by the revolution of October 24-25 and relying on the Soviets of Workers', Soldiers' and Peasants' Deputies calls upon all the belligerent peoples and their governments to start immediate negotiations for a just, democratic peace.

By a just or democratic peace, for which the overwhelming majority of the working and toiling classes of all the belligerent countries, exhausted, tormented and racked by the war, are craving—a peace that has been most definitely and insistently demanded by the Russian workers and peasants ever since the overthrow of the tsarist monarchy—by such a peace the government means an immediate peace without annexations (i.e., without the seizure of foreign lands, without the forcible incorporation of foreign nations) and without indemnities.

This is the kind of peace the government of Russia proposes to all the belligerent nations to conclude immediately, and expresses its readiness to take all the resolute measures immediately, without the least delay, pending the final ratification of all the terms of such a peace by authoritative assemblies of the people's representatives of all countries and all nations.

FROM: Decree on Peace, October 26 [November 8], 1917 (written by Lenin); *Selected Works,* Vol. II, book 1, pp. 328-30, 332-33.

In accordance with the sense of justice of the democracy in general, and of the toiling classes in particular, the government conceives the annexation or seizure of foreign lands to mean every incorporation into a large or powerful state of a small or weak nation without the precisely, clearly and voluntarily expressed consent and wish of that nation, irrespective of the time when such forcible incorporation took place, irrespective also of the degree of development or backwardness of the nation forcibly annexed to, or forcibly retained within, the borders of the given state, and irrespective, finally, of whether this nation resides in Europe or in distant, overseas countries.

If any nation whatsoever is forcibly retained within the borders of a given state, if, in spite of its expressed desire —no matter whether expressed in the press, at public meetings, in the decisions of parties, or in protests and uprisings against national oppression—it is not accorded the right to decide the forms of its state existence by a free vote, taken after the complete evacuation of the troops of the incorporating or, generally, of the stronger nation and without the least pressure being brought to bear, such incorporation is annexation, i.e., seizure and violence.

The government considers it the greatest of crimes against humanity to continue this war over the issue of how to divide among the strong and rich nations the weak nationalities they have conquered, and solemnly announces its determination immediately to sign terms of peace to stop this war on the conditions indicated, which are equally just for all nationalities without exception.

At the same time the government declares that it does not regard the above-mentioned terms of peace as an ultimatum; in other words, it is prepared to consider any other terms of peace, but only insists that they be advanced by any of the belligerent nations as speedily as possible, and that in the proposals of peace there should be absolute clarity and the complete absence of all ambiguity and secrecy.

The government abolishes secret diplomacy, and, for its part, announces its firm intention to conduct all negotiations quite openly under the eyes of the whole people. It will immediately proceed to the full publication of the secret treaties endorsed or concluded by the government of landlords and capitalists from February to October 25, 1917. The government proclaims the absolute and immediate annulment of everything contained in these secret treaties in so far as it is aimed, as is mostly the case, at securing advantages and privileges for the Russian landlords and capitalists and at the retention, or extension, of the annexations made by the Great Russians. . . .

In proposing an immediate armistice, we appeal to the class-conscious workers of the countries that have done so much for the development of the proletarian movement. We appeal to the workers of England, where there was the Chartist movement, to the workers of France, who have in repeated uprisings displayed the strength of their class consciousness, and to the workers of Germany, who waged the fight against the Anti-Socialist Law and have created powerful organizations.

In the manifesto of March 14, we called for the overthrow of the bankers, but, far from overthrowing our own bankers, we entered into an alliance with them. Now we have overthrown the government of the bankers.

That government and the bourgeoisie will make every effort to unite their forces and drown the workers' and peasants' revolution in blood. But the three years of war have been a good lesson to the masses: the Soviet movement in other countries and the mutiny in the German navy, which was crushed by the junkers of Wilhelm the hangman. Finally, we must remember that we are not living in the wilds of Africa, but in Europe, where news can spread quickly.

The workers' movement will triumph and will pave the way to peace and Socialism.

b) Decree on the Land

1. Landlord ownership of land is abolished forthwith without any compensation.

2. The landed estates, as also all crown, monasterial and church lands, with all their livestock, implements, buildings and everything pertaining thereto, shall be placed at the disposal of the volost [township] Land Committees and the uyezd [county] Soviets of Peasants' Deputies pending the convocation of the Constituent Assembly. . . .

4. The following peasant Mandate, compiled by the *Izvestia of the All-Russian Soviet of Peasants' Deputies* from 242 local peasant mandates and published in No. 88 of the *Izvestia* (Petrograd, No. 88, August 19, 1917), shall serve everywhere to guide the implementation of the great land reforms until a final decision on the latter is taken by the Constituent Assembly.

5. The land of ordinary peasants and ordinary Cossacks shall not be confiscated.

PEASANT MANDATE ON THE LAND

"The land question in its full scope can be settled only by the popular Constituent Assembly.

"The most equitable settlement of the land question is to be as follows:

"1) *Private ownership of land shall be abolished forever;* land shall not be sold, purchased, leased, mortgaged, or otherwise alienated.

"All land, whether *state, appanage, crown, monasterial, church, factory, primogenitary, private, public, peasant, etc., shall be alienated without compensation* and become the property of the whole people, and pass into the use of all those who cultivate it.

"Persons who suffer by this property revolution shall be deemed to be entitled to public support only for the period necessary for adaptation to the new conditions of life.

"2) All mineral wealth, e.g., ore, oil, coal, salt, etc., as well as all forests and waters of state importance, shall pass into the exclusive use of the state. All the small streams,

FROM: Decree on the Land, October 26 [November 8], 1917 (written by Lenin); *Selected Works,* Vol. II, book 1, pp. 339-41.

lakes, woods, etc., shall pass into the use of the communities, to be administered by the local self-government bodies.

"3) Lands on which *high-level scientific* farming is practised, e.g., orchards, plantations, seed plots, nurseries, hothouses, etc. *shall not be divided up, but shall be converted into model farms,* to be turned over for exclusive use *to the state or to the communities,* depending on the size and importance of such lands.

"Household land in towns and villages, with orchards and vegetable gardens shall be reserved for the use of their present owners, the size of the holdings, and the size of tax levied for the use thereof, to be determined by law. . . .

"6) The right to use the land shall be accorded to all citizens of the Russian state (without distinction of sex) desiring to cultivate it by their own labour, with the help of their families, or in partnership, but only as long as they are able to cultivate it. The employment of hired labour is not permitted. . . .

"7) Land tenure shall be on an equality basis, i.e., the land shall be distributed among the toilers in conformity with a labour standard or a consumption standard, depending on local conditions.

"There shall be absolutely no restriction on the forms of land tenure: household, farm, communal, or cooperative, as shall be decided in each individual village and settlement.

"8) All land, when alienated, shall become part of the national land fund. Its distribution among the toilers shall be in charge of the local and central self-government bodies, from democratically organized village and city communities, in which there are no distinctions of social rank, to central regional government bodies.

"The land fund shall be subject to periodical redistribution, depending on the growth of population and the increase in the productivity and the scientific level of farming. . . .

c) *Decree on Suppression of Hostile Newspapers*

In the serious decisive hour of the revolution and the days immediately following it the Provisional Revolutionary Committee was compelled to adopt a whole series of measures against the counterrevolutionary press of all shades.

Immediately on all sides cries arose that the new socialistic authority was violating in this way the essential principles of its program by an attempt against the freedom of the press.

The Workers' and Soldiers' Government draws the attention of the population to the fact that in our country behind this liberal shield there is practically hidden the liberty for the richer class to seize into their hands the lion's share of the whole press and by this means to poison the minds and bring confusion into the consciousness of the masses.

Everyone knows that the bourgeois press is one of the most powerful weapons of the bourgeoisie. Especially in this critical moment when the new authority, that of the workers and peasants, is in process of consolidation, it was impossible to leave this weapon in the hands of the enemy at a time when it is not less dangerous than bombs and machine guns. This is why temporary and extraordinary measures have been adopted for the purpose of cutting off the stream of mire and calumny in which the yellow and green press would be glad to drown the young victory of the people.

As soon as the new order will be consolidated, all administrative measures against the press will be suspended; full liberty will be given it within the limits of responsibility before the laws, in accordance with the broadest and most progressive regulations in this respect.

Bearing in mind, however, the fact that any restrictions of the freedom of the press, even in critical moments, are admissible only within the bounds of necessity, the Council of People's Commissaries decrees as follows:

General rules on the press.

1. The following organs of the press shall be subject to

FROM: Decree on Suppression of Hostile Newspapers, October 27 [November 9], 1917 (English translation in *Bolshevik Propaganda:* Hearings before a Subcommittee of the Committee on the Judiciary, U. S. Senate, 65th Congress, 3rd Session, Feb. 11, 1919 to Mar. 10, 1919, Washington, Government Printing Office, p. 1243).

be closed: (a) those inciting to open resistance or disobedience towards the Workers' and Peasants' Government; (b) those sowing confusion by means of an obviously calumniatory perversion of facts; (c) those inciting to acts of a criminal character punishable by the penal laws.

2. The temporary or permanent closing of any organ of the press shall be carried out only by a resolution of the Council of People's Commissaries.

3. The present decree is of a temporary nature and will be revoked by special *ukaz* when the normal conditions of public life will be reestablished.

Chairman of the Council of People's Commissars,
Vladimir Ulianov (Lenin).

d) Declaration of the Rights of the Peoples of Russia

The October revolution of the workmen and peasants began under the common banner of emancipation.

The peasants are being emancipated from the power of the landowners, for there is no longer the landowner's property right in the land—it has been abolished. The soldiers and sailors are being emancipated from the power of autocratic generals, for generals will henceforth be elective and subject to recall. The workingmen are being emancipated from the whims and arbitrary will of the capitalists, for henceforth there will be established the control of the workers over mills and factories. Everything living and capable of life is being emancipated from the hateful shackles.

There remain only the peoples of Russia, who have suffered and are suffering oppression and arbitrariness, and whose emancipation must immediately be begun, whose liberation must be effected resolutely and definitely.

During the period of czarism the peoples of Russia were systematically incited against one another. The results of such a policy are known: massacres and pogroms on the one hand, slavery of peoples on the other.

FROM: Declaration of the Rights of the Peoples of Russia, November 2 [15], 1917 (English translation in *The Nation*, December 28, 1919).

There can be and there must be no return to this disgraceful policy of instigation. Henceforth the policy of a voluntary and honest union of the peoples of Russia must be substituted.

In the period of imperialism, after the February revolution, when the power was transferred to the hands of the Cadet bourgeoisie, the naked policy of instigation gave way to one of cowardly distrust of the peoples of Russia, to a policy of fault-finding and provocation, of "freedom" and "equality" of peoples. The results of such a policy are known: the growth of national enmity, the impairment of mutual trust.

An end must be put to this unworthy policy of falsehood and distrust, of fault-finding and provocation. Henceforth it must be replaced by an open and honest policy which leads to complete mutual trust of the people of Russia. Only as the result of such a trust can there be formed an honest and lasting union of the peoples of Russia. Only as the result of such a union can the workmen and peasants of the peoples of Russia be cemented into one revolutionary force able to resist all attempts on the part of the imperialist-annexationist bourgeoisie.

Starting with these assumptions, the first Congress of Soviets, in June of this year, proclaimed the right of the peoples of Russia to free self-determination.

The second Congress of Soviets, in October of this year, reaffirmed this inalienable right of the peoples of Russia more decisively and definitely.

The united will of these Congresses, the Council of the People's Commissaries, resolved to base their activity upon the question of the nationalities of Russia, as expressed in the following principles:

1. The equality and sovereignty of the peoples of Russia.
2. The right of the peoples of Russia to free self-determination, even to the point of separation and the formation of an independent state.
3. The abolition of any and all national and national-religious privileges and disabilities.

4. The free development of national minorities and ethnographic groups inhabiting the territory of Russia.

The concrete decrees that follow from these principles will be immediately elaborated after the setting up of a Commission on Nationality Affairs. . . .

In the name of the Russian Republic,

Chairman of the Council of People's Commissars,
V. Ulianov (Lenin).

People's Commissar on Nationality Affairs,
Iozef Dzhugashvili (Stalin).

The Issue of a Coalition Government

Immediately after the overthrow of the Provisional Government, many Bolsheviks, together with most members of the other socialist parties, hoped that a multi-party coalition government, based on the soviets, could be agreed upon. The Mensheviks and Right Socialist Revolutionaries, however, would not accept Lenin as head of the government, while Lenin was in no mood to make any concessions at all. Nonetheless, the cautious wing of the Bolshevik leadership—again headed by Zinoviev and Kamenev, together with the future premier Rykov—were so alarmed at the risky prospect of a one-party government that they threatened to resign in protest. Lenin's reply was to have the Central Committee condemn the supporters of the coalition as traitorous deviators, and the latter in turn resigned as they had threatened from the Bolshevik Central Committee and from the Council of People's Commissars. A few weeks later a coalition was actually arrived at between the Bolsheviks and the Left Socialist Revolutionaries, and representatives of the latter party received three posts in the Council of People's Commissars.

By early 1918 the Bolshevik critics individually made their peace with Lenin, and were accepted back into the party and governmental leadership. At the same time, the Left SR's, incensed over the signing of the Treaty of Brest-Litovsk with Germany, resigned from the cabinet in disgust, and the Soviet administration thus acquired the exclusively Communist character which it has had ever since. The Left SR's, like the Right SR's and the Mensheviks, continued to function in the soviets as a more or less legal opposition until the outbreak of large-scale civil war in the middle of 1918. At that point the opposition parties took positions which were either equivocal or openly anti-Bolshevik, and one after another they were suppressed.

a) Resolution of the Central Committee on the Opposition

The Central Committee recognizes that the present session has historic importance and that it is therefore essential to define the two positions which have been revealed here.

1) The Central Committee recognizes that the opposition within the Central Committee who are resigning have completely departed from all the fundamental positions of Bolshevism and the proletarian class struggle in general; they are repeating profoundly un-Marxist remarks about the impossibility of a socialist revolution in Russia, about the necessity of giving in to the ultimatums and threats which come from a conscious minority in the soviet organization; in this manner they are undermining the will and decision of the Second All-Russian Congress of Soviets; in this manner they are sabotaging the dictatorship of the proletariat and the poorest peasantry just after it has begun.

2) The Central Committee charges this opposition with full responsibility for slowing down revolutionary work and for the vacillation which at the present moment is criminal; it invites it to shift its controversy and its skepticism to the press, away from the practical work in which it does not believe. In this opposition there is nothing, except for the fright of the bourgeoisie and the reflection of tendencies of the backward (but nonrevolutionary) part of the population.

3) The Central Committee asserts that it is impossible to refuse a purely Bolshevik government without treason to the slogan of the power of the Soviets, since a majority at the Second All-Russian Congress of Soviets, without excluding

FROM: Resolution of the Central Committee of the RSDWP (Bolsheviks), November 2 [15], 1917, "On the Question of the Opposition within the Central Committee" (CPSU in Resolutions, I, 401-02; editor's translation).

anyone from the congress, handed power over to this government.

4) The Central Committee asserts that it is impossible, without betraying the Soviets of Workers', Soldiers', and Peasants' Deputies, to turn to petty bargaining and join to the Soviets organizations of a nonsoviet type, i.e., organizations which are not voluntary unions of the masses' revolutionary vanguard which is struggling to overthrow the landlords and the capitalists.

5) The Central Committee asserts that concessions in the face of the ultimatums and threats by the minority in the Soviets is equivalent to full renunciation not only of the power of the Soviets, but also of democratism, for such concessions are equivalent to the majority's fear of using its majority, are equivalent to submitting to anarchy and to the repetition of ultimatums on the part of any minority.

6) The Central Committee asserts that without excluding anyone from the Second All-Russian Congress of Soviets, it is now quite ready to restore those who walked out and to accept a coalition with these people within the framework of the Soviets; it is accordingly absolutely false to speak as though the Bolsheviks do not want to share power with anyone. . . .

9) The Central Committee asserts, finally, that the victory of communism both in Russia and in Europe is guaranteed in spite of all difficulties, but only if the policy of the present government is continued undeviatingly. The Central Committee expresses full confidence in the victory of this socialist revolution and calls on all skeptics and vacillators to throw off all their hesitation and support the activity of this government with all their souls and the utmost energy.

b) *Bolshevik Statements of Resignation*

On November 1 the Central Committee of the RSDWP

FROM: Kamenev, Rykov, Miliutin, Zinoviev, and Nogin, Declaration to the Central Committee of the RSDWP (Bolsheviks), November 4 [17], 1917 (*Protocols of the Central Committee of the RSDWP*, 1917-1918, Moscow, State Press, 1929, pp. 167-68; editor's translation).

(Bolsheviks) adopted a resolution which in actuality rejects agreement with the parties making up the Soviet of Workers' and Soldiers' Deputies for the formation of a socialist soviet government.

We consider that only immediate agreement on the conditions indicated by us would make it possible for the proletariat and the revolutionary army to consolidate the conquests of the October Revolution, to consolidate themselves in their new positions and gather their forces for the further struggle for socialism.

We consider that the creation of such a government is essential to avert further bloodshed, the imminent famine, and the destruction of the revolution by the Kaledinites, and also to guarantee the summoning of the Constituent Assembly at the appointed time and the real execution of the program of peace adopted by the All-Russian Congress of Soviets of Workers' and Soldiers' Deputies.

By incredible effort we have succeeded in winning reconsideration of the decision of the Central Committee and of the new resolution, which could become the basis for creating a soviet government.

However, this new decision evoked on the part of the leading group in the Central Committee a series of actions which clearly show that it has firmly decided not to allow the formation of a government of the soviet parties but to fight for a purely Bolshevik government however it can and whatever the sacrifices this costs the workers and soldiers.

We cannot assume responsibility for this ruinous policy of the Central Committee, carried out against the will of a large part of the proletariat and soldiers, who crave the earliest cessation of bloodshed between the separate parts of the democratic forces.

We resign, therefore, from the posts of members of the Central Committee, so that we will have the right to speak our minds openly to the mass of workers and soldiers and to call on them to support our slogan! Long live the Government of the Soviet Parties! Immediate agreement on this condition!

We leave the Central Committee at the moment of victory,

at the moment of our party's domination; we leave because we cannot watch quietly as the policy of the leading group in the Central Committee leads to the workers' parties' losing the fruits of this victory, to the destruction of the proletariat.

Remaining in the ranks of the proletarian party, we hope that the proletariat will overcome all obstacles and will recognize that our step was compelled by our consciousness of our burden of responsibility to the socialist proletariat.

c) *Resignation of the Opposition from the Council of People's Commissars*

We take the point of view of the necessity of forming a socialist government of all the soviet parties. We consider that only the formation of such a government would make it possible to consolidate the fruits of the heroic struggle of the working class and the revolutionary army in the October and November days.

We assert that other than this there is only one path: the preservation of a purely Bolshevik government by means of political terror. We cannot and will not accept this. We see that this will lead to the displacement of mass proletarian organizations from the leadership of political life, to the establishment of an irresponsible regime, and to the ruin of the revolution and the country. We cannot assume responsibility for this policy, and therefore, we renounce before the Central Executive Committee our titles as People's Commissars.

FROM: Declaration of a Group of People's Commissars to the Central Executive Committee of the Soviets, November 5 [18], 1917 (*Protocols of the Central Committee of the RSDWP*, p. 169; editor's translation).

Industrial Democracy

The ideal which commanded the loyalty of most Russian workers at the time of the October Revolution was that of direct administration of industry by elected committees of workers. Such control was often put into effect by direct seizures, just as the peasants were seizing landlords' property.

For the moment, the Bolshevik party acknowledged the practice of workers' control, though Lenin was soon to change his attitude. The ideal continued to animate the ultra-left groups among the Communists, and was revived again in Yugoslavia after Tito's break with Stalin in 1948.

1. In the interests of a systematic regulation of national economy, Workers' Control is introduced in all industrial, commercial, argicultural (and similar) enterprises which are hiring people to work for them in their shops or which are giving them work to take home. This control is to extend over the production, storing, buying and selling of raw materials and finished products as well as over the finances of the enterprise.

2. The workers will exercise this control through their elected organizations, such as factory and shop committees, soviets of elders, etc. The office employees and the technical personnel are also to have representation in these committees.

3. Every large city, province and industrial area is to have its own Soviet of Workers' Control, which, being an organ of the S(oviet) of W(orkers'), S(oldiers'), and P(easants') D(eputies), must be composed of representatives of trade-unions, factory, shop and other workers' committees and workers' co-operatives. . . .

6. The organs of Workers' Control have the right to supervise production, fix the minimum of output, and determine the cost of production.

7. The organs of Workers' Control have the right to control all the business correspondence of an enterprise. Owners of enterprises are legally responsible for all correspondence kept secret. Commercial secrets are abolished. The owners have to show to the organs of Workers' Control all their books and statements for the current year and for the past years.

FROM: Decree on Workers' Control, November 14 [27], 1917 (English translation in James Bunyan and H. H. Fisher, *The Bolshevik Revolution, 1917-1918,* pp. 308-10; this and subsequent selections reprinted by permission of the publisher, Stanford University Press. Copyright 1934 by the Board of Trustees of Leland Stanford Junior University).

8. The rulings of the organs of Workers' Control are binding on the owners of enterprises and can be annulled only by decisions of the higher organs of Workers' Control.

V. Ulianov (Lenin)—President of the Council of People's Commissars
A. Shliapnikov—People's Commissar of Labor.

The Secret Police

Police action by the Bolsheviks to combat political opposition commenced with the creation of the "Cheka" (so called from the Russian initials of the first two terms in its official name, "Extraordinary Commission to Fight Counter-Revolution"). Under the direction of Felix Dzerzhinsky, the Cheka became the prototype of totalitarian secret police systems, enjoying at critical times the right of unlimited arrest and summary execution of suspects and hostages. The principle of such police surveillance over the political leanings of the Soviet population has remained in effect ever since, despite the varying intensity of repression and the organizational metamorphoses of the police—from Cheka to GPU (1922, from the Russian initials for "State Political Administration") to NKVD (1934—the "People's Commissariat of Internal Affairs") to MVD and MGB (after World War II—"Ministry of Internal Affairs" and "Ministry of State Security," respectively) to KGB (since 1953—the "Committee for State Security").

The Commission is to be named the All-Russian Extraordinary Commission and is to be attached to the Council of People's Commissars. [This commission] is to make war on counter-revolution and sabotage. . . .

The duties of the Commission will be:

1. To persecute and break up all acts of counter-revolution and sabotage all over Russia, no matter what their origin.

2. To bring before the Revolutionary Tribunal all counter-

FROM: Decree on Establishment of the Extraordinary Commission to Fight Counter-Revolution [the "Cheka"], December 7 [20], 1917 (English translation in Bunyan and Fisher, pp. 297-98).

revolutionists and saboteurs and to work out a plan for fighting them.

3. To make preliminary investigation only—enough to break up [the counter-revolutionary act]. The Commission is to be divided into sections: (a) the information section, (b) the organization section (in charge of organizing the fight against counter-revolution all over Russia) with branches, and (c) the fighting section.

The Commission will be formed tomorrow (December 21). . . . The Commission is to watch the press, saboteurs, strikers, and the Socialist-Revolutionists of the Right. Measures [to be taken against these counter-revolutionists are] confiscation, confinement, deprivation of [food] cards, publication of the names of the enemies of the people, etc.

Council of People's Commissars.

The Dissolution of the Constituent Assembly

In December, 1917, the Bolsheviks permitted, as they had promised, the election of a Constituent Assembly. This was the only reasonably free and democratic general election which Russia has ever had. The Bolsheviks placed second with some nine million votes, but an overwhelming majority was won by the Right SR's with their peasant backing. Lenin permitted the Assembly to meet for only one day, and then forcibly banned its continuation on the ground that it was a counterrevolutionary threat to the soviets.

. . . The Constituent Assembly, elected on the basis of lists drawn up prior to the October Revolution, was an expression of the old relation of political forces which existed when power was held by the compromisers and the Cadets. When the people at that time voted for the candidates of the Socialist-Revolutionary Party, they were not in a position to choose between the Right Socialist-Revolutionaries, the supporters of the bourgeoisie, and the Left Socialist-Revolutionaries, the supporters of Socialism. Thus the Constituent

FROM: Lenin, Draft Decree on the Dissolution of the Constituent Assembly (January 6 [19], 1918; *Selected Works*, Vol. II, book 1, pp. 382-84).

Assembly, which was to have been the crown of the bourgeois parliamentary republic, could not but become an obstacle in the path of the October Revolution and the Soviet power.

The October Revolution, by giving the power to the Soviets, and through the Soviets to the toiling and exploited classes, aroused the desperate resistance of the exploiters, and in the crushing of this resistance it fully revealed itself as the beginning of the socialist revolution. The toiling classes learnt by experience that the old bourgeois parliamentarism had outlived its purpose and was absolutely incompatible with the aim of achieving Socialism, and that not national institutions, but only class institutions (such as the Soviets), were capable of overcoming the resistance of the propertied classes and of laying the foundations of a socialist society. To relinquish the sovereign power of the Soviets, to relinquish the Soviet republic won by the people, for the sake of bourgeois parliamentarism and the Constituent Assembly, would now be a retrograde step and cause the collapse of the October workers' and peasants' revolution.

Owing to the circumstances mentioned above, the majority in the Constituent Assembly which met on January 5 was secured by the party of the Right Socialist-Revolutionaries, the party of Kerensky, Avksentyev and Chernov. Naturally, this party refused to discuss the absolutely clear, precise and unambiguous proposal of the supreme organ of Soviet power, the Central Executive Committee of the Soviets, to recognize the program of the Soviet power, to recognize the "Declaration of Rights of the Toiling and Exploited People," to recognize the October Revolution and the Soviet power. Thereby the Constituent Assembly severed all ties with the Soviet Republic of Russia. The withdrawal from such a Constituent Assembly of the groups of the Bolsheviks and the Left Socialist-Revolutionaries, who now patently constitute the overwhelming majority in the Soviets and enjoy the confidence of the workers and the majority of the peasants, was inevitable.

The Right Socialist-Revolutionary and Menshevik parties are in fact waging outside the walls of the Constituent Assembly a most desperate struggle against the Soviet power, calling openly in their press for its overthrow and characterizing as arbitrary and unlawful the crushing by force of the resistance of the exploiters by the toiling classes, which is essential in the interests of emancipation from exploitation. They are defending the saboteurs, the servitors of capital, and are going to the length of undisguised calls to terrorism, which certain "unidentified groups" have already begun to practise. It is obvious that under such circumstances the remaining part of the Constituent Assembly could only serve as a screen for the struggle of the counterrevolutionaries to overthrow the Soviet power.

Accordingly, the Central Executive Committee resolves: The Constituent Assembly is hereby dissolved.

Lenin's Call for Peace with Germany

The Eastern Front had been relatively quiet during 1917, and shortly after the Bolshevik Revolution a temporary armistice was agreed upon. Peace negotiations were then begun at the Polish town of Brest-Litovsk, behind the German lines. In conformity with their earlier anti-imperialist line, the Bolshevik negotiators, headed by Trotsky, used the talks as a forum for revolutionary propaganda, while most of the party expected the eventual resumption of war in the name of the revolution.

Lenin startled his followers in January, 1918, by bluntly demanding that the Soviet Republic meet the German conditions and conclude a formal peace in order to win what he regarded as an indispensable "breathing spell," instead of vainly risking the future of the revolution.

1. The position of the Russian revolution at the present moment is that nearly all the workers and the vast majority of the peasants undoubtedly side with the Soviet power and the socialist revolution which it has started. To that extent the socialist revolution in Russia is assured.

2. At the same time, the civil war, provoked by the frantic

FROM: Lenin, "Theses on the Question of Immediate Conclusion of a Separate and Annexationist Peace" (January 7 [20], 1918; *Selected Works*, Vol. II, book 1, pp. 385-87, 390-92).

resistance of the wealthy classes, who perfectly realize that they stand before the last and decisive fight for the preservation of private ownership of the land and means of production, has not yet reached its climax. The victory of the Soviet power in this war is assured, but some time must inevitably elapse, no little exertion of effort will inevitably be required, a certain period of acute economic dislocation and chaos, such as attend all wars, and civil war in particular, is inevitable, before the resistance of the bourgeoisie is crushed.

3. Furthermore, this resistance, in its less active and non-military forms—sabotage, hiring of the declassed elements and of agents of the bourgeoisie, who worm their way into the ranks of the Socialists in order to ruin their cause, and so on and so forth—has proved so stubborn and capable of assuming such diversified forms, that the fight against it will inevitably require some more time, and, in its main forms, is scarcely likely to end before several months. And unless this passive and covert resistance of the bourgeoisie and its supporters is definitely crushed the socialist revolution cannot succeed.

4. Lastly, the organizational problems of the socialist transformation of Russia are so immense and difficult that their solution—in view of the abundance of petty-bourgeois fellow-travellers of the socialist proletariat, and of the latter's low cultural level—will also require a fairly long time.

5. All these circumstances taken together are such as to make it perfectly clear that for the success of Socialism in Russia a certain amount of time, several months at least, will be necessary, during which the hands of the socialist government must be absolutely free for achieving victory over the bourgeoisie in our own country first, and for launching on a wide scale far-reaching mass organizational work.

6. . . . That the socialist revolution in Europe must come, and will come, is beyond doubt. All our hopes for the *final* victory of Socialism are founded on this certainty and on this scientific prognosis. Our propagandist activities in general, and the organization of fraternization in particular, must be intensified and extended. But it would be a

mistake to base the tactics of the Russian socialist government on attempts to determine whether the European, and especially the German, socialist revolution will take place in the next six months (or some such brief period), or not. Inasmuch as it is quite impossible to determine this, all such attempts, objectively speaking, would be nothing but a blind gamble.

7. The peace negotiations in Brest-Litovsk have by this date—January 7, 1918—made it perfectly clear that the upper hand in the German government . . . has undoubtedly been gained by the military party, which has virtually already presented Russia with an ultimatum . . . : either the continuation of the war, or an annexationist peace, i.e., peace on condition that we surrender all the territory we have occupied, while the Germans retain *all* the territory they have occupied and impose upon us an idemnity (outwardly disguised as payment for the maintenance of prisoners)—an indemnity of about three thousand million rubles, payable over a period of several years.

8. The socialist government of Russia is faced with the question—a question which brooks no postponement—of whether to accept this annexationist peace now, or at once to wage a revolutionary war. Actually speaking, no middle course is possible. No further postponement can now be achieved, for we have *already* done everything possible and impossible to protract the negotiations artificially. . . .

12. It is said that in a number of party statements we bluntly "promised" a revolutionary war, and that by concluding a separate peace we would be going back on our word.

That is not true. We said that in the era of imperialism it was *necessary* for a socialist government to "*prepare for and wage*" a revolutionary war; we said this in order to combat abstract pacifism and the theory that "defence of the fatherland" must be completely rejected in the era of imperialism, and, lastly, to combat the purely selfish instincts of a part of the soldiers, but we never gave any pledge to start a revolutionary war without considering how far it is possible to wage it at a given moment. . . .

13. Summing up the arguments in favour of an immediate revolutionary war, we have to conclude that such a policy might perhaps answer the human yearning for the beautiful, dramatic and striking, but that it would totally disregard the objective relation of class forces and material factors at the present stage of the socialist revolution which has begun.

14. There can be no doubt that our army is absolutely in no condition at the present moment, and will not be for the next few weeks (and probably for the next few months), to beat back a German offensive successfully. . . .

17. Consequently, the situation at present in regard to a revolutionary war is as follows:

If the German revolution were to break out and triumph in the coming three or four months, the tactics of an immediate revolutionary war might perhaps not ruin our socialist revolution.

If, however, the German revolution does not eventuate in the next few months, the course of events, if the war is continued, will inevitably be such that grave defeats will compel Russia to conclude a still more disadvantageous separate peace, a peace, moreover, which would be concluded, not by a socialist government, but by some other (for example, a bloc of the bourgeois Rada* and the Chernovites,** or something similar). For the peasant army, which is unbearably exhausted by the war, will after the very first defeats—and very likely within a matter of weeks, and not of months—overthrow the socialist workers' government.

18. Such being the state of affairs, it would be absolutely impermissible tactics to stake the fate of the socialist revolution which has already begun in Russia merely on the chance that the German revolution may begin in the immediate future, within a period measurable in weeks. Such tactics would be a reckless gamble. We have no right to take such risks.

19. And the German revolution will by no means be made

* Rada ["council"]: the Ukrainian nationalist regime in Kiev, 1917-1918—Ed.

** Chernovites: the Right SR's, led by V. M. Chernov—Ed.

more difficult of accomplishment as far as its objective premises are concerned, if we conclude a separate peace. . . .

Lenin's Defense of the Treaty of Brest-Litovsk

The issue of peace split the Bolshevik Party nearly in two, between the doctrinaire adherents of "revolutionary war," led by Bukharin and (somewhat less unequivocally) Trotsky, and the more cautious and practical-minded people like Zinoviev and Stalin who followed Lenin's lead. On February 23, 1918, the Central Committee finally voted to accept the German terms—loss of Poland, the Ukraine, and the Baltic region, and the cessation of all revolutionary propaganda abroad—by a scant five to four margin, with the middle group headed by Trotsky abstaining. The treaty was thereupon signed, on March 3. Ratification depended on approval by the Seventh Party Congress, to which Lenin appealed with the argument that peace was necessary so that the Soviet Republic could hold out until the onset of world revolution.

. . . International imperialism, with the entire might of its capital, with its highly organized military technique, which is a real force, a real fortress of international capital, could not under any circumstances, on any conditions, live side by side with the Soviet Republic, both because of its objective position and because of the economic interests of the capitalist class which are embodied in it—it could not do so because of commercial connections, of international financial relations. In this sphere a conflict is inevitable. Therein lies the greatest difficulty of the Russian revolution, its greatest historical problem: the necessity of solving international problems, the necessity of calling forth an international revolution, of effecting this transition from our strictly national revolution to the world revolution. . . .

. . . History has now placed us in an extraordinarily difficult position; in the midst of organizational work of un-

FROM: Lenin, Report on War and Peace, delivered to the Seventh Congress of the Russian Communist Party (Bolsheviks), March 7, 1918 (*Selected Works,* Vol. II, book 1, pp. 422, 425, 429-30).

paralleled difficulty we shall have to experience a number of painful defeats. If we consider the situation on a world-historical scale, there would doubtlessly be no hope of the ultimate victory of our revolution, if it were to remain alone, if there were no revolutionary movements in other countries. When the Bolshevik Party tackled the job alone, took it entirely into its own hands, we did so being convinced that the revolution was maturing in all countries and that in the end—but not at the very beginning—no matter what difficulties we experienced, no matter what defeats were in store for us, the international socialist revolution would come—because it is coming; would ripen—because it is ripening and will grow ripe. I repeat, our salvation from all these difficulties is an all-European revolution. . . . The German revolution is growing, but not in the way we would like it, not as fast as Russian intellectuals would have it, not at the rate our history developed in October—when we entered any town we liked, proclaimed the Soviet power, and within a few days nine-tenths of the workers came over to our side. The German revolution has the misfortune of not moving so fast. What do you think: must we reckon with the revolution, or must the revolution reckon with us? You wanted the revolution to reckon with you. But history has taught you a lesson. It is a lesson, because it is the absolute truth that without a German revolution we are doomed—perhaps not in Petrograd, not in Moscow, but in Vladivostok, in more remote places to which perhaps we shall have to retreat, and the distance to which is perhaps greater than the distance from Petrograd to Moscow. At all events, under all conceivable vicissitudes, if the German revolution does not come, we are doomed. Nevertheless, this does not in the least shake our conviction that we must be able to bear the most difficult position without blustering.

The revolution will not come as quickly as we expected. History has proved this, and we must be able to take this as a fact, to reckon with the fact that the world socialist revolution cannot begin so easily in the advanced countries as the revolution began in Russia—in the land of Nicholas and Rasputin, the land in which an enormous part of the population was absolutely indifferent as to what peoples were living in the outlying regions, or what was happening there. In such a country it was quite easy to start a revolution, as easy as lifting a feather.

But to start without preparation a revolution in a country in which capitalism is developed, in which it has produced a democratic culture and organization, provided it to everybody, down to the last man—to do so would be wrong, absurd. There we are only just approaching the painful period of the beginning of socialist revolutions. This is a fact. We do not know, no one knows; perhaps—it is quite possible—it will triumph within a few weeks, even within a few days, but we cannot stake everything on that. We must be prepared for extraordinary difficulties, for extraordinarily severe defeats, which are inevitable, because the revolution in Europe has not yet begun, although it may begin tomorrow, and when it does begin then, of course, we shall not be tortured by doubts, there will be no question about a revolutionary war, but just one continuous triumphal march. That will be, it will inevitably be so, but it is not so yet. This is the simple fact that history has taught us, with which she has hit us quite painfully—and a man who has been thrashed is worth two that haven't. That is why I think that after history has given us a very painful thrashing, because of our hope that the Germans cannot attack and that we can get everything by shouting "hurrah!", this lesson, with the help of our Soviet organizations, will be very quickly brought home to the masses all over Soviet Russia. . . .

Bukharin's Attack on the Peace Treaty

Bukharin pleaded at the Seventh Party Congress for the rejection of the Treaty of Brest-Litovsk on the ground that it tarnished the revolutionary appeal of the Soviet Republic at a time when, as he saw it, survival depended on evoking international revolutionary support.

The treaty was nevertheless approved by the party congress and officially ratified by the Congress of Soviets. The Left SR's then quit the cabinet in protest, after some inconsequential negotiations with Bukharin's Left Communists about the idea of forming a new coalition, removing Lenin as head of the government, and resuming the war. This became a count in the indictment of Bukharin when he was tried for treason in 1938.

Meanwhile, the Seventh Congress changed the official name of the party—from "Russian Social-Democratic Party (of Bolsheviks)" to "Russian Communist Party (of Bolsheviks)."

. . . Among the conditions of the peace are . . . points which reduce to nothing the international significance of the Russian revolution. And certainly we have said and say again that in the end the whole business depends on whether the international revolution is victorious or not. In the final reckoning the international revolution—and it alone—is our salvation. Even Comrade Lenin agrees with this. If we refrain from international propaganda, we also give up the sharpest weapon that we have at our disposal. International propaganda is a bell resounding throughout the world; if we refrain from using this bell, we are cutting our tongue off. . . . Up to now all the greatest force of the Russian revolution, all its greatest significance for the international proletarian movement consists in the fact that it has set forth an entirely clear, precise, definite program of action, which it has carried out not only in its newspaper, not only in its press, has carried out not just in words but in deeds. It is precisely the actions of the Soviet Republic, the clarity and definiteness of the program which it is carrying out, that have become its greatest attractive force. But now, when it will be declared to the whole world, when it will be known to all oppressed nations and all the proletariat that it [the Soviet Republic] is refraining from propaganda, that we have taken upon ourselves the holy mission of protecting German interests against English capital in colonial countries [Persia and Afghanistan] whose right to independence we had asserted as a slogan of struggle—excuse me, but I assert that this one point deals us such a blow, so undermines our

FROM: Bukharin's Minority Report to the Seventh Party Congress, March 7, 1918 (*Seventh Congress of the RCP: Stenographic Report,* Moscow, State Press, 1923, pp. 40-44, 50; editor's translation).

Soviet power on all fronts, within and without—that we cannot buy at such a price, such a price, a two-day breathing spell which gives us nothing; it is inexpedient because here we not only make a compromise with capital, here we destroy our own socialist essence. . . .

. . . We do have a way out. This way out, which Lenin rejects but which from our point of view is the only one—this way out is revolutionary war against German imperialism. . . . Opportunists do not take account of the most important fact that the organization of a struggle grows in the very process of struggle. . . .

It is not necessary to point out that it is the greatest illusion to think that we could in the course of a few days utilize a breathing spell to create a formidable army, and fix the railroads, production and provisioning. There is no such prospect; we must reject it. Before us stands the prospect of steadily drawing broad circles of the population into the struggle during the process of this struggle. . . .

Before us we have a very real prospect which we must accept, because it is the only prospect, the only one in the sense of possibility and necessity—the prospect of war against international capital, which will bear the character of a civil war with this capital. . . .

. . . We say now that our task—in this we join you [i.e., Lenin and his supporters]—is for the workers really to dedicate themselves all the time to preparing for the coming inevitable moment, preparing for the terrible clash. On this depends the fate not only of the Russian revolution but of the international revolution as well. . . .

Therefore we propose breaking away from the policy which has been pursued up to now, annulling the peace treaty which gives us nothing and signifies our capitulation, and undertaking the proper preparations, the creation of a combat-ready Red Army. . . .

Trotsky on the Red Army

Trotsky resigned as Foreign Commissar during the Brest-Litovsk crisis, but he was immediately appointed Commissar of Military Affairs and entrusted with the creation of a new Red Army to replace the old Russian army which had dissolved during the revolution. Many Communists wanted the new military force to be built up on strictly revolutionary principles, with guerrilla tactics, the election of officers, and the abolition of traditional discipline. Trotsky set himself emphatically against this attitude and demanded an army organized in the conventional way and employing "military specialists"—experienced officers from the old army.

. . . As regards politics and direct fighting, the October Revolution has come about with unexpected and incomparable successfulness. There has been no case in history of such a powerful offensive of an oppressed class which with such deliberateness and speed overthrew the rule of the propertied ruling classes in all parts of the country and extended its own rule from Petrograd and Moscow to every far-flung corner of Russia.

This successfulness of the October uprising has shown the political weakness of the bourgeois classes, which is rooted in the peculiarities of the development of Russian capitalism. . . .

If, as the working class, following what Marx said, we cannot simply take over mechanically the old apparatus of state power, this does not at all mean that we can do without all of those elements which helped make up the old apparatus of state power.

The misfortune of the working class is that it has always been in the position of an oppressed class. This is reflected in everything: both in its level of education, and in the fact that it does not have those habits of rule which the dominant class has and which it bequeaths to its heirs through its schools, universities, etc. The working class has none of this, but must acquire it.

Having come to power, it has had to view the old state

FROM: Trotsky, "Labor, Discipline, Order" (Speech to a Moscow City Conference of the Russian Communist Party, March 27, 1918; *Works,* Vol. 17, part 1, Moscow, 1926, pp. 157-58, 161-62, 170-71; editor's translation).

apparatus as an apparatus of class oppression. But at the same time it must draw from this apparatus all the worthwhile skilled elements which are technically necessary, put them where they belong, and heighten its proletarian class power by using these elements. This, Comrades, is the task which now stands before us for our overall growth. . . .

Here I turn to a ticklish point which to a familiar degree has now assumed major importance in our party life. This is one of the questions of the organization of the army, specifically the question of recruiting military specialists—i.e., to speak plainly, former officers and generals—to create the army and to run it. All basic, guiding institutions of the army are now set up so that they consist of one military specialist and two political commissars. Such is the present basic type of the leading organs of the army.

I have more than once had to say at open meetings that in the area of command, operations and fighting we will place full responsibility on the military specialists, and therefore will grant them the necessary rights. Many among us are afraid of this, and their misgivings find expression in the resolutions of certain party organizations. . . . Here again the task of the party is to handle such phenomena in our own midst with complete mercilessness, for they ruin the country and disgrace and disrupt our party. . . .

There is still another question in the area of the organization of the army: the so-called elective principle. In general, all it means is to struggle against the old officers' corps, to control the commanding staff.

As long as power was in the hands of a class that was hostile to us, when the commanding staff was an instrument in the hands of this power, we were obliged to strive to smash the class resistance of the commanding personnel by way of the elective principle. But now political power is in the hands of that same working class from whose ranks the army is recruited.

Under the present regime in the army—I tell you this in all frankness—the elective principle is politically pointless and technically inexpedient, and has in fact already been set aside by decree. . . .

The question of creating the army is now a question of life and death for us. You yourselves understand this as well as I. But we cannot create the army only by means of the administrative mechanism which we have as long as it is so very poor. If we have a powerful mechanism, it is an ideological mechanism—this mechanism is our party. It will create the army, Comrades, and do everything to uproot the prejudices of which I spoke; it will help us fill up the cadres of the revolutionary army with militant and devoted workers and peasants, it will apply itself in conducting obligatory military training in the mills, factories and villages, and in this way will create the military apparatus for the defense of the Soviet Republic.

Lenin on Economic Expediency

Once firmly established in power, Lenin began to reconsider the utopianism which characterized the Bolsheviks in 1917 as regards both internal and international revolution. After the conclusion of peace he prepared an extensive statement on the transitional forms which he felt the Soviet economic order would have to adopt, with emphasis on the principal features of large-scale capitalistic industry—individual managerial authority, labor discipline and piecework incentives, and the employment of "bourgeois" managers and technical experts.

Thanks to the peace which has been achieved—notwithstanding its extremely onerous character and extreme instability—the Russian Soviet Republic has received an opportunity for a certain period of time to concentrate its efforts on the most important and most difficult aspect of the socialist revolution, namely, the organizational task. . . .

. . . In every socialist revolution—and consequently in the socialist revolution in Russia which we began on October

FROM: Lenin, "The Immediate Tasks of the Soviet Government: The International Position of the Russian Soviet Republic and the Fundamental Tasks of the Socialist Revolution" (April, 1918; *Selected Works,* Vol. II, book 1, pp. 448, 450, 458-59, 468-71, 475-77, 481-82, 488).

25, 1917—the principal task of the proletariat, and of the poor peasantry which it leads, is the positive or constructive work of setting up an extremely intricate and delicate system of new organizational relationships extending to the planned production and distribution of the goods required for the existence of tens of millions of people. Such a revolution can be successfully carried out only if the majority of the population, and primarily the majority of the toilers, engage in independent creative work as makers of history. Only if the proletariat and the poor peasantry display sufficient class consciousness, devotion to principles, self-sacrifice and perseverance will the victory of the socialist revolution be assured. By creating a new, Soviet type of state, which gives the opportunity to the toiling and oppressed masses to take an active part in the independent building up of a new society, we solved only a small part of this difficult problem. The principal difficulty lies in the economic sphere, viz., the introduction of the strictest and universal accounting and control of the production and distribution of goods, raising the productivity of labour and *socializing* production *in actual practice.* . . .

This is a peculiar epoch, or rather stage of development, and in order to utterly defeat capital, we must be able to adapt the forms of our struggle to the peculiar conditions of this stage.

Without the guidance of specialists in the various fields of knowledge, technology and experience, the transition to Socialism will be impossible, because Socialism calls for a conscious mass advance to greater productivity of labour compared with capitalism, and on the basis achieved by capitalism. Socialism must achieve this advance *in its own way*, by its own methods—or, to put it more concretely, by *Soviet* methods. And the specialists, because of the entire environment of the social life which made them specialists, are, in the main, unavoidably bougeois. Had our proletariat, after capturing power, quickly solved the problem of accounting, control and organization on a national scale (which was impossible owing to the war and the backwardness of Russia), then we, after breaking the sabotage, would have also completely subordinated these bourgeois specialists to ourselves by means of universal accounting and control. . . .

Now we have to resort to the old bourgeois method and to agree to pay a very high price for the "services" of the biggest bourgeois specialists. All those who are familiar with the subject appreciate this, but not all ponder over the significance of this measure being adopted by the proletarian state. Clearly, such a measure is a compromise, a departure from the principles of the Paris Commune and of every proletarian power, which call for the reduction of all salaries to the level of the wages of the average worker, which call for fighting careerism, not with words, but with deeds.

Moreover, it is clear that such a measure not only implies the cessation—in a certain field and to a certain degree—of the offensive against capital (for capital is not a sum of money, but a definite social relation); it is also *a step backward* on the part of our socialist Soviet state power, which from the very outset proclaimed and pursued the policy of reducing high salaries to the level of the wages of the average worker. . . .

. . . It becomes immediately clear that while it is possible to capture the central government in a few days, while it is possible to suppress the military resistance (and sabotage) of the exploiters even in different parts of a great country in a few weeks, the capital solution of the problem of raising the productivity of labour requires, at all events (particularly after a most terrible and devastating war), several years. The protracted nature of the work is certainly dictated by objective circumstances. . . .

. . . We must raise the question of piecework and apply and test it in practice; we must raise the question of applying much of what is scientific and progressive in the Taylor system, we must make wages correspond to the total amount of goods turned out, or to the amount of work done by the railways, the water transport system, etc., etc.

The Russian is a bad worker compared with the advanced peoples. Nor could it be otherwise under the tsarist regime and in view of the tenacity of the remnants of serfdom. The task that the Soviet government must set the people in all its scope is—learn to work. The Taylor system, the last word of capitalism in this respect, like all capitalist progress, is a combination of the refined brutality of bourgeois exploitation and a number of greatest scientific achievements in the field of analyzing mechanical motions during work, the elimination of superfluous and awkward motions, the elaboration of correct methods of work, the introduction of the best system of accounting and control, etc. The Soviet Republic must at all costs adopt all that is valuable in the achievements of science and technology in this field. The possibility of building Socialism is conditioned precisely upon our success in combining the Soviet power and the Soviet organization of administration with the up-to-date achievements of capitalism. We must organize in Russia the study and teaching of the Taylor system and systematically try it out and adapt it to our purposes. . . .

. . . It would be extremely stupid and absurdly utopian to assume that the transition from capitalism to Socialism is possible without coercion and without dictatorship. Marx's theory very definitely opposed this petty-bourgeois-democratic and anarchist absurdity long ago. And Russia of 1917-18 confirms the correctness of Marx's theory in this respect so strikingly, palpably and imposingly that only those who are hopelessly dull or who have obstinately decided to turn their backs on the truth can be under any misapprehension concerning this. Either the dictatorship of Kornilov (if we take him as the Russian type of bourgeois Cavaignac*), or the dictatorship of the proletariat—any other choice is *out of the question* for a country which has gone through an extremely rapid development with extremely sharp turns and amidst desperate ruin created by one of the most horrible wars in history. . . .

. . . Firstly, capitalism cannot be defeated and eradicated without the ruthless suppression of the resistance of the exploiters, who cannot at once be deprived of their wealth, of their advantages of organization and knowledge, and

* Cavaignac: general who put down the uprising of the Paris working class in June, 1848—Ed.

consequently for a fairly long period will inevitably try to overthrow the hated rule of the poor; secondly, every great revolution, and a socialist revolution in particular, even if there were no external war, is inconceivable without internal war, i.e., civil war, which is even more devastating than external war, and involves thousands and millions of cases of wavering and desertion from one side to another, implies a state of extreme indefiniteness, lack of equilibrium and chaos. And of course, all the elements of disintegration of the old society, which are inevitably very numerous and connected mainly with the petty bourgeoisie (because it is the petty bourgeoisie that every war and every crisis ruins and destroys first) cannot but "reveal themselves" during such a profound revolution. And these elements of disintegration *cannot* "reveal themselves" otherwise than in the increase of crime, hooliganism, corruption, profiteering and outrages of every kind. To put these down requires time and *requires an iron hand. . . .*

. . . There is absolutely *no* contradiction in principle between Soviet (*that is,* socialist) democracy and the exercise of dictatorial powers by individuals. The difference between proletarian dictatorship and bourgeois dictatorship is that the former strikes at the exploiting minority in the interests of the exploited majority, and that it is exercised—*also through individuals*—not only by the toiling and exploited masses, but also by organizations which are built in such a way as to rouse these masses to the work of history-making. (The Soviet organizations are organizations of this kind.)

In regard to the second question concerning the significance of precisely individual dictatorial powers from the point of view of the specific tasks of the present moment, it must be said that large-scale machine industry—which is precisely the material source, the productive source, the foundation of Socialism—calls for absolute and strict *unity of will,* which directs the joint labours of hundreds, thousands and tens of thousands of people. The technical, economic and historical necessity of this is obvious, and all those who have thought about Socialism have always regarded it as one of the conditions of Socialism. But how can strict unity of will be ensured?—by thousands subordinating their will to the will of one.

Given ideal class consciousness and discipline on the part of those taking part in the common work, this subordination would rather remind one of the mild leadership of a conductor of an orchestra. It may assume the sharp forms of a dictatorship if ideal discipline and class consciousness are lacking. But be that as it may, *unquestioning subordination* to a single will is absolutely necessary for the success of processes organized on the pattern of large-scale machine industry. On the railways it is twice and three times as necessary. In this transition from one political task to another, which *on the surface* is totally dissimilar to the first, consists the peculiar nature of the present situation. The revolution has only just smashed the oldest, strongest and heaviest fetters to which the masses submitted under duress. That was yesterday. But today the same revolution demands—precisely in the interests of its development and consolidation, precisely in the interests of Socialism—that the masses *unquestioningly obey the single will* of the leaders of the labour process. Of course, such a transition cannot be made at one step. Clearly, it can be achieved only as a result of tremendous jolts, shocks, reversions to old ways, the enormous exertion of effort on the part of the proletarian vanguard, which is leading the people to the new ways. . . .

The fight against the bureaucratic distortion of the Soviet form of organization is assured by the firmness of the connection between the Soviets and the "people," meaning by that the toilers and exploited, and by the flexibility and elasticity of this connection. Even in the most democratic capitalist republics in the world, the poor never regard the bourgeois parliament as "their own" institution. But the Soviets are "their own" and not alien institutions to the masses of workers and peasants. . . .

The Left Communists on a Proletarian Economic Policy

Lenin's espousal of the forms of capitalist industry was a rude shock to the anarchistic hopes of the Communist left wing. The Left Communist opposition which had fought the Treaty of Brest-Litovsk now organized to resist, in the name of the working class, the "petty-bourgeois" policy of "state capitalism" as a menace to the ideals of the revolution.

. . . 8. The economic situation and the grouping of classes in Russia have changed since the conclusion of peace. A situation has arisen which provides the foundation for two opposite tendencies (toward the weakening and toward the growth of revolutionary forces), of which the first was immediately strengthened by the conclusion of the peace and for the time being may prevail. . . .

9. . . . In spite of the temporary weakening of the forces of the revolution, in spite of the serious international position of the Soviet Republic, there is no serious support within the limits of the present Soviet state for the restoration either of the monarchy or of the power of the compromiser parties. . . .

On the contrary, there is a basis for the strengthening and development of the dictatorship of the proletariat and the poorest peasants, and for the socialist reform of society which they have begun. . . . Above all, the preliminary smashing of the bourgeois-compromiser governmental system, of the old relations of production, and of the material class forces of the bourgeoisie and its allies is almost complete. Further, the class education of the proletariat in the course of civil war will give it a great supply of class solidarity, energy and consciousness. Also, the real conquests which it has made have strengthened these revolutionary forces and energy in resisting the enemy who threatens the conquests of the proletariat. The energetic organization of production on socialist lines will on the one hand strengthen the economic base of the proletariat as a revolutionary force, and on the other will be a new school of class organization and activity for it. Finally, the preservation of a link with the international and all-Russian proletarian movement will also increase the

FROM: "Theses on the Present Moment," presented by the faction of Left Communists to a conference of party leaders, April 4, 1918 (*Kommunist*, No. 1, April, 1918; editor's translation).

class activity of the proletariat and protect it from disruption and tiring.

But in connection with the most imminent, immediate consequences of the peace: the reduction of class activeness and the increasing de-classing of the proletariat in the main revolutionary centers, in connection with the increasing class fusion of the proletariat and poorest peasants (which since the signing of the peace must, under the pressure of their demands and influence, become a bulwark of the soviet power), it is quite possible for a tendency to arise toward a deviation by the majority of the Communist Party and the soviet power directed by it into the channel of a petty-bourgeois policy of a new form.

In the event that this tendency becomes a reality, the working class will cease to be the director, the exerciser of hegemony over the socialist revolution, leading the poorest peasantry toward the destruction of the rule of finance capital and the landlords; it will show itself to be a force sprinkled into the ranks of the semiproletarian-petty-bourgeois masses, a force which sets itself the task not of the proletarian struggle in union with the West-European proletariat for the overthrow of the imperialist system, but the defense of the farmers' fatherland from the oppression of imperialism, which is possible to achieve by means of compromise with it. In the event of the rejection of an actively proletarian policy, the conquests of the workers' and peasants' revolution would begin to freeze into a system of state capitalism and petty-bourgeois economic relations.

10. Before the party of the proletariat two paths stand open. One of these paths is to guard and strengthen the intact part of the Soviet state, which now with respect to the economic process—since the revolution is not complete—is only an organization for the transition to socialism (with incomplete nationalization of the banks, with capitalistic forms of financing enterprises, with the partial nationalization of enterprises, with the predominance of small-scale farming and small property-holding in the village, with the effort of the peasants to solve the agrarian question by dividing the land; and in the political respect can be transformed from

the framework of the dictatorship of the proletariat supported by the poorest peasantry, into an instrument for the political domination of the semiproletarian-petty-bourgeois masses, and become merely a transition stage to the full domination of finance capital.

This path can be justified—verbally—as an effort to preserve for the international revolution, in any way at all, the revolutionary forces and soviet power even if in "Great Russia" alone.* In this case every effort will be directed toward the strengthening and development of the forces of the revolution, toward "organic construction," with the rejection of further smashing of capitalistic production relations and even with the partial restoration of them. . . .

11. . . . The economic policy which corresponds to such a course will have to develop in the direction of agreements with capitalistic businessmen, both the "patriotic" ones and the international ones who stand behind them. . . .

With the policy of administering enterprises on the basis of broad participation by capitalists and semibureaucratic centralization it is natural to combine a labor policy directed toward the installation among the workers of discipline under the banner of "self-discipline," toward the introduction of obligatory labor for workers (such a program was proposed by the rightist Bolsheviks), piecework payment, lengthening of the working day, etc.

The form of governmental administration will have to develop in the direction of bureaucratic centralization, the rule of various commissars, the deprivation of local soviets of their independence, and in practice the rejection of the type of "commune state" administered from below. . . .

12. The path described above, taken as a whole, as well as the tendency to deviate along this path, is dangerous in the highest degree to the interests of the Russian and international proletariat. This path strengthens the separation begun by the Brest peace between the "Great-Russian" Soviet Republic and the all-Russian and international revolutonary movement, locking up the Soviet Republic in the frame of a national

* I.e., in Russia minus its non-Russian-speaking western regions —Ed.

state with a transitional economy and a petty-bourgeois political order. . . .

The line of policy sketched above may strengthen the influence of foreign and domestic counterrevolutionary forces in Russia, break down the revolutionary might of the working class, and, by cutting the Russian revolution off from the international revolution, have a ruinous effect on the interests of both.

13. Proletarian Communists consider another course of policy essential: not the course of preserving a soviet oasis in the north of Russia with the help of concessions that transform it into a petty-bourgeois state; not the transition to "organic internal work," fortified by the consideration that the "acute period" of the civil war is over.

The acute period of civil war is over only in the sense of the absence of an objective necessity to apply predominantly the sharpest physical measures of revolutionary violence. Once the bourgeoisie is beaten and is no longer capable of open fighting, "military" methods for the most part subside. But the sharpness of the class contradiction between the proletariat and the bourgeoisie cannot diminish; as before, the position of the proletariat in relation to the bourgeoisie reduces to the complete negation of it, the annihilation of it as a class. The end of the acute period of the civil war cannot signify that deals are possible with the remaining forces of the bourgeoisie, and the "organic construction" of socialism, which is undoubtedly the key task of the moment, can be accomplished only by the efforts of the proletariat itself, with the participation of skilled technicians and adminstrators, and not with some form or other of collaboration with the "privileged elements" as such.

The Russian workers' revolution cannot "save itself" by leaving the international revolutionary path, steadily avoiding a fight, retreating in the face of the pressure of international capital, and making concessions to "patriotic capital." . . .

The administration of enterprises must be placed in the hands of mixed collegia of workers and technical personnel, under the control and direction of the local economic councils. All economic life must be subordinated to the organized influence of these councils, which are chosen by the workers without the participation of the "privileged elements," but with the participation of the unions of the technical and service personnel of the enterprises.

No capitulation to the bourgeoisie and its petty-bourgeois intellectual henchmen, but the finishing off of the bourgeoisie and the final smashing of sabotage. Final liquidation of the counterrevolutionary press and counterrevolutionary bourgeois organizations. Introduction of labor duty for skilled specialists and intellectuals; organization of consumption communes; limitation of consumption by the well-to-do classes and confiscation of their surplus possessions. In the village, organization of pressure by the poorest peasants on the rich ones, the development of large-scale social agriculture, and the support of forms of working the land by the poorest peasants in the transition to social farming . . .

15. The proletarian Communists define their attitude toward the majority of the party as the position of the left wing of the party and the vanguard of the Russian proletariat, which preserves full unity with the party insofar as the policy of the majority does not create an unavoidable split in the ranks of the proletariat itself. They define their attitude toward the Soviet power as the position of unqualified support of this power at a time of necessity, by way of participating in it insofar as the confirmation of the peace has removed from the agenda the question of responsibility for this decision and has created a new objective situation. This participation is possible only on the basis of a definite political program which would prevent the deviation of the Soviet power and the majority of the party on the ruinous path of petty-bourgeois policies. In the event of such a deviation the left wing of the party will have to stand in the position of an effective and responsible proletarian opposition.

One-Party Dictatorship

With the rapid spread of armed resistance to the Communists in the spring of 1918 and the organization of the "White" armies, the relatively moderate phase of Soviet rule came to an end. The anti-Communist socialist parties were ousted from the soviets and in effect outlawed. In July, 1918, the Left SR's abandoned the role of a loyal opposition and tried to overthrow the Communists in the hope of forcing a resumption of the war. With their defeat, the Soviet government became a completely one-party affair. Political terror commenced in the summer of 1918, with widespread summary executions by both "Reds" and "Whites." Revolutionary emotion and violence swelled to a climax as bitter civil war raged from 1918 to 1920. Most Communists were filled with a fanaticism that combined utopian hopes for socialism with dictatorial violence against all who stood in their way.

Taking into consideration that:

1. The Soviet Government is living through its most difficult period, having to withstand at the same time the attacks of international imperialism . . . and those of its allies within the Russian Republic, who spare no means, from the most shameless calumny to conspiracy and armed uprisings, in the struggle against the Workers' and Peasants' Government.

2. The presence in Soviet organizations of representatives of parties which are obviously endeavoring to discredit and overthrow the Soviet Government is absolutely intolerable.

3. From previously published documents, as well as from those cited at the present meeting, it is clear that representatives of the Socialist-Revolutionists (of the Right and Center) and the Russian Social-Democratic Labor Party (Menshevik) . . . are guilty of organizing armed attacks against the workers and peasants, in association with notorious counter-revolutionists. . . .

The All-Russian Central Executive Committee of Soviets

FROM: Decree on the Expulsion of the Right Socialist Parties from the Soviets, June 14, 1918 (English translation in James Bunyan, *Intervention, Civil War, and Communism in Russia, April-December, 1918,* Baltimore, John Hopkins University Press, 1936, p. 191; this and following selection reprinted by permission of the publisher).

resolves: To exclude from its membership the representatives of the Socialist-Revolutionists (of the Right and Center) and the Russian Social-Democratic Labor Party (Menshevik), and to urge all Soviets of Workers', Soldiers', Peasants' and Cossacks' Deputies to remove representatives of these parties from their ranks.

Y. Sverdlov
Chairman of the Central Executive Committee.

War Communism

Upon the outbreak of civil war, radical changes were introduced in Soviet economic policy. Class strife was encouraged among the peasants, and food supplies were forcibly "requisitioned" to keep the cities fed. Industry, up to this point under private ownership with "workers' control," was nationalized without compensation in a series of sweeping decrees, and placed under a highly centralized bureaucratic administration. With the breakdown of transportation and the monetary system, Russia approached a "natural economy" based on the equalization of poverty through rationing.

For the purpose of combating decisively the economic disorganization and the breakdown of the food supply, and of establishing more firmly the dictatorship of the working class and the village poor, the Soviet of People's Commissars has resolved:

1. To declare all of the following industrial and commercial enterprises which are located in the Soviet Republic, with all their capital and property, whatever they may consist of, the property of the Russian Socialist Federated Soviet Republic. [At this point there is given a long list of the most important mines, mills, factories, etc.]

2. The administration of the nationalized industries shall be organized . . . by the different departments of the Supreme Council of National Economy. . . .

FROM: Decree on Nationalization of Large-Scale Industry, June 28, 1918 (English translation in Bunyan, pp. 397-99).

3. Until the Supreme Council of National Economy issues special rulings for each enterprise, the enterprises which have been declared the property of the R.S.F.S.R. by this decree shall be considered as leased rent-free to their former owners; the boards of directors and the former owners shall continue to finance the enterprises . . . and also to receive the income from them. . . .

4. Beginning with the promulgation of this decree, the members of the administration, the directors, and other responsible officers of the nationalized industries will be held responsible to the Soviet Republic both for the intactness and upkeep of the business and for its proper functioning. Those who leave their posts without the permission of the . . . Supreme Council of National Economy, or are found guilty of negligence in the management of the business, are liable both civilly and criminally to the Republic.

5. The entire personnel of every enterprise—technicians, workers, members of the board of directors, and foremen—shall be considered employees of the Russian Socialist Federated Soviet Republic; their wages shall be fixed in accordance with the scales existing at the time of nationalization and shall be paid out of the funds of the respective enterprises. Those who leave their posts . . . are liable to the Revolutionary Tribunal and to the full penalty of the law.

6. All private capital belonging to members of the boards of directors, stockholders, and owners of the nationalized enterprises will be attached pending the determination of the relation of such capital to the turnover capital and resources of the enterprises in question.

7. All boards of directors of the nationalized enterprises must prepare at once a financial statement of their respective businesses as of July 1, 1918.

8. The Supreme Council of National Economy is authorized to formulate at once and send to all nationalized plants detailed instructions on the organization connected with the carrying out of the present decree.

9. Enterprises belonging to consumers' cooperative societies . . . are not to be nationalized.

10. The present decree becomes effective on the day it is signed.

V. Ulianov (Lenin)
Chairman of the Council of People's Commissars
Tsiurupa, Nogin, Rykov
People's Commissars.

Rosa Luxemburg—A Western Radical's Response to the Communists

At the time of the Russian Revolution Rosa Luxemburg was in jail in Germany for her activity in the antiwar wing of the German Social-Democratic Party. She wrote a remarkably objective pamphlet appraising the new Soviet regime and prophetically indicating its fundamental defects.

The Russian Revolution is the mightiest event of the World War. Its outbreak, its unexampled radicalism, its enduring consequences, constitute the clearest condemnation of the lying phrases which official Social-Democracy so zealously supplied at the beginning of the war as an ideological cover for German imperialism's campaign of conquest. . . .

Moreover, for every thinking observer, these developments are a decisive refutation of the doctrinaire theory which Kautsky shared with the Government Social-Democrats,* according to which Russia, as an economically backward and predominantly agrarian land, was supposed not to be ripe for social revolution and proletarian dictatorship. This theory, which regards only a *bourgeois* revolution as feasible in Russia, is also the theory of the opportunist wing of the Russian labor movement, of the so-called Mensheviks. . . .

. . . According to this view, if the revolution has gone beyond that point and has set as its task the dictatorship of

FROM: Luxemburg, *The Russian Revolution* (1918; English translation by Bertram D. Wolfe, New York, Workers Age Publishers, 1940, pp. 1-4, 11-12, 44-48, 53-54, 56).

* I.e., the wing of the German Social-Democratic Party which supported the government's war effort—Ed.

the proletariat, this is simply a mistake of the radical wing of the Russian labor movement, the Bolsheviks. And all difficulties which the revolution has met with in its further course, and all disorders it has suffered, are pictured as purely a result of this fateful error. . . .

The fate of the revolution in Russia depended fully upon international events. That the Bolsheviks have based their policy entirely upon the world proletarian revolution is the clearest proof of their political farsightedness and firmness of principle and of the bold scope of their policies. . . .

The real situation in which the Russian Revolution found itself, narrowed down in a few months to the alternative: victory of the counter-revolution or dictatorship of the proletariat —Kaledin* or Lenin. . . . The Russian Revolution has but confirmed the basic lesson of every great revolution, the law of its being, which decrees: either the revolution must advance at a rapid, stormy and resolute tempo, break down all barriers with an iron hand and place its goals ever farther ahead, or it is quite soon thrown backward behind its feeble point of departure and suppressed by counter-revolution. To stand still, to mark time on one spot, to be contented with the first goal it happens to reach, is never possible in revolution. . . .

Lenin says: the bourgeois state is an instrument of oppression of the working class; the socialist state, of the bourgeoisie. To a certain extent, he says, it is only the capitalist state stood on its head. This simplified view misses the most essential thing: bourgeois class rule has no need of the political training and education of the entire mass of the people, at least not beyond certain narrow limits. But for the proletarian dictatorship that is the life element, the very air without which it is not able to exist. . . .

. . . The very giant tasks which the Bolsheviks have undertaken with courage and determination . . . demand the most intensive political training of the masses and the accumulation of experience.

Freedom only for the supporters of the government, only

* Kaledin: Cossack general who organized the first White resistance to the Bolsheviks—Ed.

for the members of one party—however numerous they may be—is no freedom at all. Freedom is always and exclusively freedom for the one who thinks differently. Not because of any fanatical concept of "justice" but because all that is instructive, wholesome and purifying in political freedom depends on this essential characteristic, and its effectiveness vanishes when "freedom" becomes a special privilege. . . .

The tacit assumption underlying the Lenin-Trotsky theory of the dictatorship is this: that the socialist transformation is something for which a ready-made formula lies completed in the pocket of the revolutionary party, which needs only to be carried out energetically in practice. This is, unfortunately—or perhaps fortunately—not the case. Far from being a sum of ready-made prescriptions which have only to be applied, the practical realization of socialism as an economic, social and juridical system is something which lies completely hidden in the mists of the future. . . .

. . . Socialism by its very nature cannot be decreed or introduced by *ukaz.* It has as its prerequisite a number of measures of force—against property, etc. The negative, the tearing down, can be decreed; the building up, the positive, cannot. New territory. A thousand problems. Only experience is capable of correcting and opening new ways. Only unobstructed, effervescing life falls into a thousand new forms and improvisations, brings to light creative force, itself corrects all mistaken attempts. The public life of countries with limited freedom is so poverty-stricken, so miserable, so rigid, so unfruitful, precisely because, through the exclusion of democracy, it cuts off the living sources of all spiritual riches and progress. . . .

. . . Socialism in life demands a complete spiritual transformation in the masses degraded by centuries of bourgeois class rule. Social instincts in place of egotistical ones, mass initiative in place of inertia, idealism which conquers all suffering, etc., etc. No one knows this better, describes it more penetratingly, repeats it more stubbornly than Lenin. But he is completely mistaken in the means he employs. Decree, dictatorial force of the factory overseer, draconic penalties, rule by terror—all these things are but palliatives. The only way to a rebirth is the school of public life itself, the most unlimited, the broadest democracy and public opinion. It is rule by terror which demoralizes.

When all this is eliminated, what really remains? In place of the representative bodies created by general, popular elections, Lenin and Trotsky have laid down the soviets as the only true representation of the laboring masses. But with the repression of political life in the land as a whole, life in the soviets must also become more and more crippled. Without general elections, without unrestricted freedom of press and assembly, without a free struggle of opinion, life dies out in every public institution, becomes a mere semblance of life, in which only the bureaucracy remains as the active element. Public life gradually falls asleep, a few dozen party leaders of inexhaustible energy and boundless experience direct and rule. Among them, in reality only a dozen outstanding heads do the leading and an elite of the working class is invited from time to time to meetings where they are to applaud the speeches of the leaders, and to approve proposed resolutions unanimously—at bottom, then, a clique affair—a dictatorship, to be sure, not the dictatorship of the proletariat, however, but only the dictatorship of a handful of politicians, that is a dictatorship in the bourgeois sense, in the sense of the rule of the Jacobins. . . . Yes, we can go even further: such conditions must inevitably cause a brutalization of public life: attempted assassinations, shooting of hostages, etc. . . .

"As Marxists," writes Trotsky, "we have never been idol worshippers of formal democracy." . . . All that that really means is: We have always distinguished the social kernel from the political form of *bourgeois* democracy; we have always revealed the hard kernel of social inequality and lack of freedom hidden under the sweet shell of formal equality and freedom—not in order to reject the latter but to spur the working class into not being satisfied with the shell, but rather, by conquering political power, to create a socialist democracy to replace bourgeois democracy—not to eliminate democracy altogether. . . .

Yes, dictatorship! But this dictatorship consists in the

manner of applying democracy, not in its *elimination,* in energetic, resolute attacks upon the well-entrenched rights and economic relationships of bourgeois society, without which a socialist transformation cannot be accomplished. But this dictatorship must be the work of the *class* and not of a little leading minority in the name of the class—that is, it must proceed step by step out of the active participation of the masses; it must be under their direct influence, subjected to the control of complete public activity; it must arise out of the growing political training of the mass of the people. . . .

What is in order is to distinguish the essential from the non-essential, the kernel from the accidental excrescences in the policies of the Bolsheviks. In the present period, when we face decisive final struggles in all the world, the most important problem of socialism was and is the burning question of our time. It is not a matter of this or that secondary question of tactics, but of the capacity for action of the proletariat, the strength to act, the will to power of socialism as such. In this, Lenin and Trotsky and their friends were the *first,* those who went ahead as an example to the proletariat of the world; they are still the *only ones* up to now who can cry with Hutten:* "I have dared!"

This is the essential and *enduring* in Bolshevik policy. In *this* sense theirs is the immortal historical service of having marched at the head of the international proletariat with the conquest of political power and the practical placing of the problem of the realization of socialism, and of having advanced mightily the settlement of the score between capital and labor in the entire world. In Russia the problem could only be posed. It could not be solved in Russia. And in *this* sense, the future everywhere belongs to "Bolshevism."

The Party Program of 1919

An official statement of the aims and principles of the Communist Party was issued by the Eighth Party Congress

* Ulrich von Hutten: German humanist and early follower of Luther—Ed.

in 1919. It is noteworthy for its stress on the superior "democratic" character of the Soviet state, the importance of education and anti-religious propaganda, and the economic role of the trade unions, together with the necessary expedients of economic incentives and "bourgeois" experts.

. . . 2. In contrast to bourgeois democracy, which concealed the class character of the state, the Soviet authority openly acknowledges that every state must inevitably bear a class character until the division of society into classes has been abolished and all government authority disappears. By its very nature, the Soviet state directs itself to the suppression of the resistance of the exploiters, and the Soviet constitution does not stop short of depriving the exploiters of their political rights, bearing in mind that any kind of freedom is a deception if it is opposed to the emancipation of labor from the yoke of capital. The aim of the Party of the proletariat consists in carrying on a determined suppression of the resistance of the exploiters, in struggling against the deeply rooted prejudices concerning the absolute character of bourgeois rights and freedom, and at the same time explaining that deprivation of political rights and any kind of limitation of freedom are necessary as temporary measures in order to defeat the attempts of the exploiters to retain or to reestablish their privileges. With the disappearance of the possibility of the exploitation of one human being by another, the necessity for these measures will also gradually disappear and the Party will aim to reduce and completely abolish them. . . .

8. The proletarian revolution, owing to the Soviet organization of the state, was able at one stroke finally to destroy the old bourgeois, official and judicial state apparatus. The comparatively low standard of culture of the masses, the absence of necessary experience in state administration on the part of responsible workers who are elected by the masses, the pressing necessity, owing to the critical situation of engag-

FROM: *The Program of the All-Russian Communist Party (Bolsheviks)* (1919; English translation, Moscow, Communist Library [1920], reprinted in James H. Meisel and Edward S. Kozera, *Materials for the Study of the Soviet System,* Ann Arbor, Mich., Wahr, 1950, pp. 105, 107-8, 110-15).

ing specialists of the old school, and the calling up to military service of the more advanced section of city workmen, all this led to the partial revival of bureaucratic practices within the Soviet system.

The All-Russian Communist Party, carrying on a resolute struggle with bureaucratism, suggests the following measures for overcoming this evil:

(1) Every member of the Soviet is obliged to perform a certain duty in state administration.

(2) These duties must change in rotation, so as gradually to embrace all the branches of administrative work.

(3) All the working masses without exception must be gradually induced to take part in the work of state administration.

The complete realization of these measures will carry us in advance of the Paris Commune, and the simplification of the work of administration, together with the raising of the level of culture of the masses, will eventually lead to the abolition of state authority. . . .

Jurisprudence

11. Proletarian democracy, taking power into its own hands and finally abolishing the organs of domination of the bourgeoisie—the former courts of justice—has replaced the formula of bourgeois democracy: "judges elected by the people" by the class watchword: "judges elected from the working masses and only by the working masses," and has applied the latter in the organization of law courts, having extended equal rights to both sexes, both in the election of judges and in the exercise of the functions of judges.

In order to induce the broad masses of the proletariat and the poorest peasantry to take part in the administration of justice, a bench of jury-judges sitting in rotation under guidance of a permanent judge is introduced and various labor organizations and trade unions must impanel their delegates. . . .

Public Education

12. The All-Russian Communist Party in the field of education sets itself the task of bringing to fulfillment the work begun by the October Revolution of 1917, of transforming the school from an instrument of class domination of the bourgeoisie into an instrument for the abolition of the class divisions of society, into an instrument for a communist regeneration of society.

In the period of the dictatorship of the proletariat, i.e., in the period of preparation of conditions suitable for the realization of communism, the school must be not only the conductor of communist principles, but it must become the conductor of the intellectual, organizational and educational influences of the proletariat, to the semi-proletariat and non-proletarian sections of the toiling masses, in order to educate a generation capable of establishing communism. . . .

Religion

13. With reference to religion, the All-Russian Communist Party does not content itself with the already decreed separation of church from state, i.e., measures which are one of the items of the programs of bourgeois democracy, which was, however, never fulfilled owing to many and various ties binding capital with religious propaganda.

The All-Russian Communist Party is guided by the conviction that only the realization of conscious and systematic social and economic activity of the masses will lead to the disappearance of religious prejudices. The aim of the Party is finally to destroy the ties between the exploiting classes and the organization of religious propaganda, at the same time helping the toiling masses actually to liberate their minds from religious superstitions, and organizing on a wide scale scientific-educational and anti-religious propaganda. It is, however, necessary carefully to avoid offending the religious susceptibilities of believers, which leads only to the strengthening of religious fanaticism.

Economics

1. Undeviatingly to continue and finally to realize the expropriation of the bourgeoisie which was begun and which has already been largely completed, the transforming of all means of production and exchange into the property of the Soviet republic, i.e., the common property of all toilers.

2. All possible increase of the productive forces of the country must be considered the fundamental and principal point upon which the economic policy of the Soviet Government is based. In view of the disorganization of the country, everything in other spheres of life must be subordinated to the practical aim immediately and at all costs to increase the quantity of products required by the population. The successful functioning of every Soviet institution connected with public economy must be gauged by the practical results in this direction.

At the same time it is necessary in the first place to pay attention to the following:

3. The decaying imperialist system of economy left to the Soviet state a heritage of chaos in the organization and management of production, which hampered it in the first period of construction. The more imperative therefore becomes the fundamental task of concentrating all the economic activity of the country according to a general state plan; the greatest concentration of production for the purpose of amalgamating it into various branches and groups of branches, and centralizing it in the most productive units, and for the purpose of rapidity in carrying out economic achievements; the most efficient arrangement of the productive apparatus and a rational and economical utilization of all material resources of the country. . . .

5. The organizing apparatus of socialized industry must first of all rest upon the trade unions. The latter must free themselves from their narrow guild outlook and transform themselves into large productive combinations which will unite the majority, and finally all the workmen of a given branch of production.

Trade unions, being already, according to the laws of the Soviet Republic and established practice, participants in all local and central organs for managing industry, must actually concentrate in their hands the management of the whole system of public economy as an economic unit. The trade unions, thus securing an indissoluble union between the central state administration, the public system of economy and the masses of toilers must induce the latter to take part in the immediate management of production. The participation of trade unions in the management of production and the attraction by them of the broad masses are, moreover, the principal means to carry on a struggle against bureaucracy in the economic apparatus of the Soviet state, and afford the opportunity of establishing a really democratic control over the results of production.

6. A maximum utilization of all labor power existing in the state, its regular distribution and redistribution among various territorial regions as well as among various branches of production, is necessary for the systematic development of public economy, and must be the immediate aim in the economic policy of the Soviet Government. This aim can be attained in closest co-operation with the trade unions. For the purpose of performing certain social duties, a general mobilization of all capable of work must be carried out by the Soviet Government, aided by the trade unions, on a much wider scale and more systematically than has been done hitherto.

7. In the state of the complete disorganization of the capitalist system of labor, the productive forces of the country can be restored and developed, and a socialist system of production strengthened, only on the basis of the comradely discipline of toilers, maximum activity on their part, responsibility and the strictest mutual control over the productivity of labor.

Persistent systematic effort directed to the re-education of the masses is necessary to attain this aim. This work is now made easier as the masses in reality see the abolition of capitalists, landowners, and merchants, and from their own experience draw the conclusion that the level of their prosperity depends entirely upon the productivity of their own labor.

The trade unions play the principal part in the work of establishing a new socialist discipline. Breaking with old conventions, they must put into practice and try various measures, such as the establishment of control, standards of production, the introduction of responsibility of the workmen before special labor tribunals, etc., for the realization of this aim.

8. Moreover, for the development of the productive forces the immediate, wide and full utilization of all specialists in science and technology left to us by capitalism, is necessary, in spite of the fact that the majority of the latter are inevitably imbued with bourgeois ideas and habits. The Party considers that the period of sharp struggle with this group, owing to organized sabotage on their part, is ended as the sabotage is in the main subdued. The Party, in closest contact with the trade unions, will follow its former line of action, i.e., on the one hand it will make no political concessions to this bourgeois section and mercilessly suppress any counter-revolutionary moves on its part, and on the other hand it will carry on a merciless struggle against the pseudo-radical, but in reality, ignorant and conceited opinion that the working class can overcome capitalism and the bourgeois order without the aid of bourgeois specialists or taking advantage of their knowledge, without passing, together with them, through a thorough schooling of hard work.

While striving toward equal remuneration of labor and to realize communism, the Soviet Government does not regard the immediate realization of such equality possible at the moment, when only the first steps are being taken towards replacing capitalism by communism. It is therefore necessary to maintain a higher remuneration for specialists in order that they should work not worse but better than before, and for that purpose it is not possible to abandon the system of bonuses for the most successful, particularly for work of organization.

To the same degree, it is necessary to place the bourgeois

experts in a setting of comradely common effort, working hand in hand with the mass of average workers, led by class-conscious Communists, and thus to assist the mutual understanding and unity between manual and intellectual workers formerly separated by capitalism. . . .

Centralization of the Communist Party

Under the stress of civil war the Communist leaders had to put a premium on swift decision-making and on the development of a disciplined body of party secretaries to carry out decisions. The Eighth Party Congress accordingly approved the creation of new executive organs for the party—the Politbureau, the Orgbureau, and the Secretariat—and gave these central bodies full authority over the membership (including Communists in nominally separate countries like the Ukraine). With this step the Communist Party began to approximate the organizational ideal laid down by Lenin in 1902.

. . . 1. The Growth of the Party:

The numerical growth of the party is progressive only insofar as healthy proletarian elements of town and country flow into the ranks of the party. The doors of the party should be wide open to workers and to worker and peasant youth. But the party must always follow attentively the progressive changes in its social composition. . . . It is important to handle the admission into the party of non-worker and non-peasant elements by careful selection. . . .

2. The Link with the Masses:

The Russian Communist Party, since it is in power and holds in its hands the whole apparatus of the soviets, has naturally had to turn tens of thousands of its members over to the work of administering the country. One of the party's most important tasks at the present moment is to place new thousands of its best functionaries in the network of the gov-

FROM: Resolution of the Eighth Congress of the Russian Communist Party, March, 1919, "On the Organizational Question," (CPSU in Resolutions, I, 441-44; editor's translation).

ernmental administration (the railroads, provisioning, control, the army, the courts, etc.).

However, in connection with the fulfillment of this substantial task a serious danger has arisen. Many members of the party who have been placed in this governmental work are divorcing themselves from the masses and becoming infected with bureaucratism, which very often applies to many workers who are members of the soviets. It is necessary to begin the most determined struggle against this evil immediately. . . .

4. The Internal Structure of the Central Committee:

The Central Committee has no less than two plenary sessions a month on previously arranged days. All the most important political and organizational questions which do not demand the most hasty decision are considered at these plenary meetings of the Central Committee.

The Central Committee organizes firstly a *Political Bureau*, secondly an *Organizational Bureau*, and thirdly a *Secretariat*.

The Political Bureau consists of five members of the Central Committee. All the other members of the Central Committee who find it possible to participate in one or another of the sessions of the Political Bureau enjoy a consultative voice at the sessions of the Political Bureau. The Political Bureau makes decisions on questions which do not permit delay, and it gives a report on all its work in the two weeks' period to the following meeting of the Central Committee.

The Organizational Bureau consists of five members of the Central Committee. Each of the members of the Organizational Bureau conducts his respective branch of the work. The Organizational Bureau assembles not less than three times a week. The Organizational Bureau directs all the organizational work of the party. The Organizational Bureau reports to the Plenum of the Central Committee every two weeks.

The Secretariat of the Central Committee is composed of one responsible secretary, a member of the Organizational Bureau of the Central Committee, and five technical secretaries from among the experienced party functionaries. The Secretariat organizes a series of departments. The Secretariat reports to the Plenum of the Central Committee every two weeks.

5. Nationality Organizations:

At the present time the Ukraine, Latvia, Lithuania and Byelorussia exist as special Soviet republics. Thus, the question of their forms of *governmental* existence is decided at the present moment.

But this does not at all mean that the Russian Communist Party in its turn should be organized on the basis of a federation of independent Communist parties.

The Eighth Congress of the Russian Communist Party decides that the existence of a *unitary* centralized Communist Party with a unitary Central Committee directing all the work of the party in all parts of the RSFSR is essential. All decisions of the Russian Communist Party and its leading institutions are unconditionally binding on all parts of the party, regardless of their nationality composition. The Central Committees of the Ukrainian, Latvian, and Lithuanian Communists enjoy the rights of regional committees of the party and are wholly subordinated to the Central Committee of the Russian Communist Party. . . .

7. Centralism and Discipline:

The party finds itself in a position where the strictest centralism and the most rigorous discipline are absolute necessities. All decisions of a higher jurisdiction are absolutely binding for lower ones. Each decision must above all be fulfilled, and only after this is an appeal to the respective party organ permissible. In this sense outright military discipline is essential for the party at the present time. . . .

8. The Assignment of Party Forces:

At the present time the correct assignment of party forces is the main guarantee of success and one of the most important tasks. The whole matter of the assignment of party functionaries is in the hands of the Central Committee of the party. Its decision is binding for everyone. In each province the forces are assigned by the provincial committee of the party; in the capitals, by the city committees under the general direction of the Central Committee. The Central Committee is commissioned to wage the most determined struggle against any local privilege or separatism in these questions.

The Central Committee is commissioned to transfer party functionaries systematically from one branch of work to another and from one region to another with the aim of utilizing them the most productively. . . .

The Civil War

Hostilities between the Communists and the Whites reached a decisive climax in 1919. Intervention by the Allied powers on the side of the Whites almost brought them victory. Facing the most serious White threat led by General Denikin in Southern Russia, Lenin appealed to his followers for a supreme effort, and threatened ruthless repression of any opposition behind the lines. By early 1920 the principal White forces were defeated.

Comrades,

This is one of the most critical, probably even the most critical moment for the socialist revolution. The defenders of the exploiters, of the landlords and capitalists, Russian and foreign (and in the first instance the British and French), are making a desperate effort to restore the power of the robbers of the people's labour, the landlords and exploiters, in Russia, in order to bolster up their declining power all over the world. The British and French capitalists have failed in their plan to conquer the Ukraine with their own troops; they have failed in their support of Kolchak* in Siberia; the Red Army, heroically advancing in the Urals with the help of the Urals workers, who are

FROM: Lenin, "All Out for the Fight Against Denikin!" (Letter of the Central Committee of the Russian Communist Party (Bolsheviks) to the Party Organizations, July, 1919; *Selected Works,* Vol. II, book 2, pp. 240-41, 257, 259-60).

* Admiral Kolchak: leader of the White forces in Siberia, and a military dictator, until his capture and execution in 1920—Ed.

rising to a man, is nearing Siberia with the purpose of liberating it from the incredible tyranny and brutality of the overlords there, the capitalists. Lastly, the British and French imperialists have failed in their plan to seize Petrograd by means of a counterrevolutionary conspiracy, in which there took part Russian monarchists, Cadets, Mensheviks and Socialist-Revolutionaries, not even excluding Left Socialist-Revolutionaries.

The foreign capitalists are now making a desperate effort to restore the yoke of capital with the help of an onslaught by Denikin, whom they have helped, as they once had helped Kolchak, with officers, supplies, shells, tanks, etc., etc.

All the forces of the workers and peasants, all the forces of the Soviet Republic, must be harnessed to repulse Denikin's onslaught and to defeat him, without suspending the Red Army's victorious advance into the Urals and Siberia. That is the

Main Task of the Moment

All Communists first and foremost, all sympathizers with them, all honest workers and peasants, all Soviet officials, must *display military efficiency* and concentrate *to the maximum their work,* their efforts and their concern *directly on the tasks of war,* on the speedy repulse of Denikin's onslaught, curtailing and rearranging all their other activities in subordination to this task.

The Soviet Republic is besieged by the enemy. It must becomes *a single military camp,* not in word but in deed.

. . . Counterrevolution is raising its head in our rear, in our midst.

Counterrevolution has been vanquished, but it is far from having been destroyed, and it is naturally taking advantage of Denikin's victories and of the aggravation of the food shortage. And, as always, in the wake of direct and open counterrevolution, in the wake of the Black Hundreds and the Cadets, whose strength lies in their capital, their direct connections with Entente imperialism, and their understanding of the inevitability of dictatorship and their ability to exercise it (on Kolchak lines), follow the wavering, spineless Mensheviks, Right Socialist-Revolutionaries and Left Socialist-Revolutionaries, who embellish their deeds with words. . . .

Our task is to put the question bluntly. What is better? To ferret out, to imprison, sometimes even to shoot hundreds of traitors from among the Cadets, nonparty people, Mensheviks and Socialist-Revolutionaries, who "come out" (some with arms in hand, others with conspiracies, others still with agitation against mobilization, like the Menshevik printers and railwaymen, etc.) *against* the Soviet power, *in other words, in favour of Denikin?* Or to allow matters to reach a pass enabling Kolchak and Denikin to slaughter, shoot and flog to death tens of thousands of workers and peasants? The choice is not difficult to make. . . .

The Soviet Republic is a fortress besieged by world capital. We can concede the right to use it as a refuge from Kolchak, and the right to live in it generally, only to those who take an active part in the war and help us in every way. Hence our right and our duty to mobilize the whole population for the war to a man, some for military duties in the direct meaning of the term, others for subsidiary activities of every kind in aid of the war . . .

Bukharin's Apology for War Communism

Bukharin took it upon himself to justify in Marxist terms the collapse of the Russian economy which occurred during the period of War Communism, and the utilization of the "technical intelligentsia" and the conventional hierarchical organization of industry. The key, for him, was the possession of power by the allegedly "proletarian" state, under which no expedients could possibly harm the interests of the workers.

It is absolutely clear that the disintegration and revolutionary loosening of the links of the system as essential characteristics of the breakdown means a collapse of the "technical

FROM: Bukharin, *The Economics of the Transformation Period* (1920; German edition, Hamburg, Hoym, 1922, pp. 55-56, 71-72, 76, 78-80, 85; editor's translation).

apparatus" of society, insofar as we are considering the technical organization of the people of this society.

But from this it follows that one cannot simply "take possession" of the old economic apparatus. Anarchy in production, or . . . the "revolutionary disintegration of industry" is a historically inevitable stage, which cannot be escaped by lamentations. Certainly, from the absolute standpoint it would be fine if the revolution and the breakdown of the old production relationships were not accompanied by any collapse of the technical relations of production. But the considered judgment of the actual processes, the scientific analysis of them, tells us that the period of this collapse is historically inevitable and historically necessary.

The collapse of the *technical* hierarchy, which appears at a certain stage of the process of broadened negative reproduction,* exerts pressure in turn on the condition of the forces of production. The forces of production are fused with the relationships of production in a definite system of the social organization of labor. Consequently, the collapse of the "apparatus" must inevitably be followed by a further decline in the forces of production. In this way the process of further negative reproduction is extraordinarily accelerated.

From the above analysis it follows that the "restoration of industry" which capitalistic Utopians dream about is impossible on the basis of the old capitalistic relationships, which are flying apart. The only remedy is for the lower links of the system, the basic productive force of capitalist society, the working class, to assume a dominant position in the organization of social labor. In other words, the establishment of communism is the prerequisite for a re-birth of society. . . .

We have seen that that which for society as a whole constitutes a condition of its further existence represents for the proletariat an organizational problem which it must solve in practice. In this period the proletariat must *actively build* socialism and at the same time, in the process of this building, educate itself anew. This task can be met only with

* Reproduction: Marx's concept of the maintenance and expansion of capital; "negative reproduction" would be to allow the industrial plant to wear out—Ed.

the help of specific methods, with methods of *organized* labor. But these methods have already been prepared in the development of capitalism. . . .

Socialism as an organized system must be built by the proletariat as the organized collective subject. Whereas the process of the growth of capitalism was elemental nature, the process of building communism is to a high degree a conscious, i.e., organized process. For communism will be created by a class which in the womb of capitalism has grown up into that "revolutionary association" of which Marx spoke. The epoch of building communism will therefore inevitably be the epoch of planned and organized labor; the proletariat will fulfill its tasks as social-technical tasks of building a new society, tasks which are consciously posed and consciously fulfilled. . . .

In this period the proletariat educates itself, closes ranks, and organizes itself as a class with tremendous intensity and swiftness. The proletariat as the totality of production relations accordingly builds the scaffolding of the whole structure. But the problem of the social organization of production consists of *new combinations of the old elements*. And indeed what elements? . . .

The ex-bourgeois group of organizers and the *technical* intelligentsia which stands beneath it are material which is obviously necessary for the reconstruction period: it is the social deposit of organizational and technical-scientific experience. It is indeed apparent that both these categories must be regrouped. How and under what circumstances is this possible?

We wish to point out above all that this is the decisive—one could say basic—question for our structure. It is no accident that in the mature period of the Russian socialist revolution the problem of the "specialists" played so important a role.

We know that earlier types of social ties survive in the heads of the people in these categories, in the form of an ideological and physiological residue. "Healthy capitalism" hovers before them with the persistency of a fixed idea. The prerequisite for the possibility of a new social combination of production is therefore to dissolve the earlier types of associations in the heads of this technical intelligentsia. . . .

How, in general, is another combination of personal and technical elements of production possible if the logic of the production process itself requires associations of a completely determined kind? Must an engineer or technician indeed give orders to the workers and consequently stand *over* them? In just the same way the former officers in the Red Army must stand over the common soldiers. Here we pose an inner, purely technical, factual logic, which must be observed in any social order whatsoever. How can this contradiction be solved?

Here a whole series of circumstances must be considered, and we will now attack their study.

Above all: Under the proletarian state power and with the proletarian nationalization of production the process of creating surplus value, a specific feature of bourgeois society, ceases. . . . With the dialectical transformation of the bourgeois dictatorship into the proletarian, the technical function of the intelligentsia changes from a capitalistic to a social function of labor, and the creation of surplus value changes (under the conditions of expanded reproduction) into the creation of surplus product, which is applied to the expansion of the reproduction fund. Paralleling this, the *basic type of association* changes, *although in the hierarchical scheme the intelligentsia occupies the same "middle" place.* For the highest authority in the state economy is the concentrated social power of the proletariat. Here the technical intelligentsia on the one hand stands above the great mass of the working class, but on the other is in the last analysis *subordinated* to its collective will, the expression of which is found in the proletariat's organization of the state economy. The transformation of the process of producing surplus value into a process of planned satisfaction of social needs finds expression in the regrouping of production relations, notwithstanding the formal retention of the same place in the hierarchical system of production, which in principle assumes as a whole a different character, the character of the dialectic negation of the structure of capitalism and which, insofar as it destroys the social-caste character of the hierarchy, leads toward the abolition of the hierarchy altogether. . . .

We must now pose the question of the general principle of the system of organization of the proletarian apparatus, i.e., the interrelations between the various forms of proletarian organization. It is indeed clear that formally the same method is necessary for the working class as for the bourgeoisie of the era of state capitalism. This organizational method consists of the coördination of all proletarian organizations by means of the most all-embracing organization possible, i.e., by means of the state organization of the working class, by means of the *proletarian Soviet state*. The "governmentalization" of the trade unions and in practice the governmentalization of all the mass organizations of the proletariat result from the inner logic of the transformation process itself. The smallest germ cell of the labor apparatus must become a support for the general process of organization, which is planfully led and conducted by the collective reason of the working class, which has its material embodiment in the highest, all-embracing organization, its state power. Thus the system of state capitalism is dialectically transformed into its own opposite, into the governmental form of workers' socialism. . . .

Trotsky on Terror and Militarization

During the Civil War years Trotsky was surpassed by none in his advocacy of dictatorial ruthlessness and authoritarianism. He frankly defended every means of violence and intimidation for the compelling end of revolutionary victory, and insisted that tight control and strict discipline of the entire population were essential for the success of the socialist economy. Trotsky was the earliest articulate exponent of the all-embracing totalitarian approach to economic development which Stalin made his own in 1929.

. . . The problem of revolution, as of war, consists in breaking the will of the foe, forcing him to capitulate and to accept the conditions of the conqueror. The will, of course, is a fact of the physical world, but in contradistinction to a meeting, a dispute, or a congress, the revolution carries out its object by means of the employment of material resources —though to a less degree than war. The bourgeoisie itself conquered power by means of revolts, and consolidated it by the civil war. In the peaceful period, it retains power by means of a system of repression. As long as class society, founded on the most deep-rooted antagonisms, continues to exist, repression remains a necessary means of breaking the will of the opposing side.

Even if, in one country or another, the dictatorship of the proletariat grew up within the external framework of democracy, this would by no means avert the civil war. The question as to who is to rule the country, *i.e.*, of the life or death of the bourgeoisie, will be decided on either side, not by references to the paragraphs of the constitution, but by the employment of all forms of violence. . . .

The revolution "logically" does not demand terrorism, just as "logically" it does not demand an armed insurrection. What a profound commonplace! But the revolution does require of the revolutionary class that it should attain its end by all methods at its disposal—if necessary, by an armed rising: if required, by terrorism. A revolutionary class which has conquered power with arms in its hands is bound to, and will, suppress, rifle in hand, all attempts to tear the power out of its hands. Where it has against it a hostile army, it will oppose to it its own army. Where it is confronted with armed conspiracy, attempt at murder, or rising, it will hurl at the heads of its enemies an unsparing penalty. Perhaps Kautsky has invented other methods? Or does he reduce the whole question to the *degree* of repression, and recommend in all circustances imprisonment instead of execution?

The question of the form of repression, or of its degree, of course, is not one of "principle." It is a question of expediency. . . .

. . . Terror can be very efficient against a reactionary class

FROM: Trotsky, *Terrorism and Communism* (1920; English translation, *Dictatorship vs. Democracy: A Reply to Karl Kautsky*, New York, Workers' Party of America, 1922, pp. 54, 57-59, 106-7, 136-37, 141-43).

which does not want to leave the scene of operations. *Intimidation* is a powerful weapon of policy, both internationally and internally. War, like revolution, is founded upon intimidation. A victorious war, generally speaking, destroys only an insignificant part of the conquered army, intimidating the remainder and breaking their will. The revolution works in the same way: it kills individuals, and intimidates thousands. In this sense, the Red Terror is not distinguishable from the armed insurrection, the direct continuation of which it represents. The State terror of a revolutionary class can be condemned "morally" only by a man who, as a principle, rejects (in words) every form of violence whatsoever—consequently, every war and every rising. For this one has to be merely and simply a hypocritical Quaker.

"But, in that case, in what do your tactics differ from the tactics of Tsarism?" we are asked, by the high priests of Liberalism and Kautskianism.

You do not understand this, holy men? We shall explain to you. The terror of Tsarism was directed against the proletariat. The gendarmerie of Tsarism throttled the workers who were fighting for the Socialist order. Our Extraordinary Commissions shoot landlords, capitalists, and generals who are striving to restore the capitalist order. Do you grasp this—distinction? Yes? For us Communists it is quite sufficient. . . .

The Soviets are the organization of the proletarian revolution, and have purpose either as an organ of the struggle for power or as the apparatus of power of the working class. . . .

The very reason why the Soviets are an absolutely irreplaceable apparatus in the proletarian State is that their framework is elastic and yielding, with the result that not only social but political changes in the relationship of classes and sections can immediately find their expression in the Soviet apparatus. Beginning with the largest factories and works, the Soviets then draw into their organization the workers of private workshops and shop-assistants, proceed to enter the village, organize the peasants against the landowners, and finally the lower and middle-class sections of the peasantry against the richest.

The Labor State collects numerous staffs of employees, to a considerable extent from the ranks of the bourgeoisie and the bourgeois educated classes. To the extent that they become disciplined under the Soviet regime, they find representation in the Soviet system. Expanding—and at certain moments contracting—in harmony with the expansion and contraction of the social positions conquered by the proletariat, the Soviet system remains the State apparatus of the social revolution, in its internal dynamics, its ebbs and flows, its mistakes and successes. With the final triumph of the social revolution, the Soviet system will expand and include the whole population, in order thereby to lose the characteristics of a form of State, and melt away into a mighty system of producing and consuming co-operation.

If the party and the trade unions were organizations of preparation for the revolution, the Soviets are the weapon of the revolution itself. After its victory, the Soviets become the organs of power. The role of the party and the unions, without decreasing, is nevertheless essentially altered.

In the hands of the party is concentrated the general control. It does not immediately administer, since its apparatus is not adapted for this purpose. But it has the final word in all fundamental questions. Further, our practice has led to the result that, in all moot questions, generally—conflicts between departments and personal conflicts within departments—the last word belongs to the Central Committee of the party. This affords extreme economy of time and energy, and in the most difficult and complicated circumstances gives a guarantee for the necessary unity of action. Such a regime is possible only in the presence of the unquestioned authority of the party, and the faultlessness of its discipline. Happily for the revolution, our party does possess in an equal measure both of these qualities. Whether in other countries which have not received from their past a strong revolutionary organization, with a great hardening in conflict, there will be created just as authoritative a Communist Party by the time of the proletarian revolution, it is difficult to foretell; but it is quite obvious that on this question, to a very large extent, depends the progress of the Socialist revolution in each country. . . .

If the organization of the new society can be reduced fundamentally to the reorganization of labor, the organization of labor signifies in its turn the correct introduction of general labor service. This problem is in no way met by measures of a purely departmental and administrative character. It touches the very foundations of economic life and the social structure. It finds itself in conflict with the most powerful psychological habits and prejudices. The introduction of compulsory labor service pre-supposes, on the one hand, a colossal work of education, and, on the other, the greatest possible care in the practical method adopted. . . .

The introduction of compulsory labor service is unthinkable without the application, to a greater or less degree, of the methods of militarization of labor. This term at once brings us into the region of the greatest possible superstitions and outcries from the opposition. . . .

The foundations of the militarization of labor are those forms of State compulsion without which the replacement of capitalist economy by the Socialist will forever remain an empty sound. Why do we speak of *militarization?* Of course, this is only an analogy—but an analogy very rich in content. No social organization except the army has ever considered itself justified in subordinating citizens to itself in such a measure, and to control them by its will on all sides to such a degree, as the State of the proletarian dictatorship considers itself justified in doing, and does. Only the army—just because in its way it used to decide questions of the life or death of nations, States, and ruling classes—was endowed with powers of demanding from each and all complete submission to its problems, aims, regulations, and orders. And it achieved this to the greater degree, the more the problems of military organization coincided with the requirements of social development.

The question of the life or death of Soviet Russia is at present being settled on the labor front; our economic, and together with them our professional and productive organizations, have the right to demand from their members all that devotion, discipline, and executive thoroughness, which hitherto only the army required. . . .

. . . We can have no way to Socialism except by the authoritative regulation of the economic forces and resources of the country, and the centralized distribution of labor-power in harmony with the general State plan. The Labor State considers itself empowered to send every worker to the place where his work is necessary. And not one serious Socialist will begin to deny to the Labor State the right to lay its hand upon the worker who refuses to execute his labor duty. But the whole point is that the Menshevik path of transition to "Socialism" is a milky way, without the bread monopoly, without the abolition of the market, without the revolutionary dictatorship, and without the militarization of labor.

Without general labor service, without the right to order and demand fulfilment of orders, the trade unions will be transformed into a mere form without a reality; for the young Socialist State requires trade unions, not for a struggle for better conditions of labor—that is the task of the social and State organizations as a whole—but to organize the working class for the ends of production, to educate, discipline, distribute, group, retain certain categories and certain workers at their posts for fixed periods—in a word, hand in hand with the State to exercise their authority in order to lead the workers into the framework of a single economic plan. To defend, under such conditions, the "freedom" of labor means to defend fruitless, helpless, absolutely unregulated searches for better conditions, unsystematic, chaotic changes from factory to factory, in a hungry country, in conditions of terrible disorganization of the transport and food apparatus. — What except the complete collapse of the working-class and complete economic anarchy could be the result of the stupid attempt to reconcile bourgeois freedom of labor with proletarian socialization of the means of production?

Consequently, comrades, militarization of labor, in the

root sense indicated by me, is not the invention of individual politicians or an invention of our War Department, but represents the inevitable method of organization and disciplining of labor-power during the period of transition from capitalism to Socialism. . . .

The "Democratic Centralists" in Opposition to Centralization

The "Democratic Centralist" group, led by V. V. Osinsky, was an offshoot of the Left Communist movement of early 1918 which held to the original anti-bureaucratic line. They were significant as a group dedicated to the observance of revolutionary principle, in opposition to the expedients promoted by Lenin and Trotsky; they spoke out on many occasions to protest the trend toward centralization and hierarchical authority in the party, the government, the army, and industry. Their ideals were local autonomy and administration of every sort of activity by elected boards or "collegia." At the Ninth Party Congress in 1920, Osinsky spoke against Trotsky's scheme of militarization as a violation of basic revolutionary principles of democracy and collective decision-making.

I propose to make a series of amendments and additions to Comrade Trotsky's theses. . . . First of all I want to give the basis for the amendment which we are introducing on the question of militarization.

What is happening now at the congress is the clash of several cultures, for our setup has given birth to different cultures. We have created a military-Soviet culture, a civil Soviet culture, and, finally, the trade-union movement has created its own sphere of culture. Each of these forms of our movement has its own approach to things, has created its own practices. Comrade Trotsky has posed the question from the point of view of a man coming from the sphere of military culture; we approach it from the point of view of

FROM: Osinsky, Minority Report on Building the Economy, Ninth Party Congress, March, 1920 (*Protocols of the Ninth Congress of the Russian Communist Party* [*of Bolsheviks*], Moscow, Party Press, 1934, pp. 123-26, 128, 130-33; editor's translation).

the civil sphere, and, finally, the trade-union comrades have posed it in their own way. They have posed it the most poorly, insofar as they have for a long time been considering only the need to protect the workers from militarization and to keep labor free, etc.

I want first of all to establish the fact that we approached the question of militarization earlier than the people from the other cultures, and from the other side. . . . I radically reject the proposition that we oppose militarization *per se*. . . . We are against the excessive extension of the concept of militarization, we are against the blind imitation of military models. . . .

The collegium is not the only means for drawing the broad working masses into administration. There are many other ways, such as, for example, the appointment of probationary workers and participation in the Workers' and Peasants' Inspection. But there is no doubt that the collegium is an essential higher-level school of administration, given final preparation and the broadest outlook. The collegium is the proper means to prepare workers for the most responsible work and for completely taking over the state apparatus. . . .

Comrade Lenin reproaches here on the grounds that we approach the question of individual authority vs. the collegial principle not in a practical way but purely "in principle." . . . In the developed socialist system, when the division of labor and skills has been abolished, the collegial principle will be essential for people to be able to replace each other continuously in the organs of administration. . . .

We must not put the question of the collegial principle vs. individual authority on a purely technical plane and seek the absolute technical advantages of one form or another of administration. . . . We must approach the matter from the social-political side. Then we can reach concrete conclusions, including some less favorable to individual authority. . . .

Comrade Lenin has revealed here today a very original understanding of democratic centralism. . . . Comrade Lenin says that all democratic centralism consists of is that the congress elects the Central Committee, and the Central Committee governs. . . . With such an original definition we cannot agree. We consider that democratic centralism—a very old concept, a concept clear to every Bolshevik and fixed in our rules—consists of carrying out the directives of the Central Committee through local organizations; the autonomy of the latter; and their responsibility for individual spheres of work. If party work is broken down into several branches with special departments, and if these departments are under the general direction of the local organization, just as the soviets' departments are under the power and direction of the provincial executive committee—this is democratic centralism, *i.e.*, the execution of the decisions of the center through local organs which are responsible for all the particular spheres of work in the provinces. This is the definition of democratic centralism, a system of administration preserved from bureaucratism and closely connected with the principle of collegia. . . .

If you reduce the collegial principle to nothing in our institutions, bear in mind that this signifies the downfall of the whole system of democratic centralism. I advise careful thought about this, although the speakers following me may try to "smear" this argument. Bearing this in mind, we will conduct an unyielding struggle against the principle of individual authority. . . .

In the unpublished part of his theses Comrade Trotsky raised the question, what to do with democratic centralism in the area of the party, and the answer was—replace the party organizations with political departments, not only on the railroads, but in all the basic branches of industry. Comrade Stalin, whom I deeply respect, but with whom I do not go along on this question, has already surpassed Comrade Trotsky's idea, and has established a political department for coal in the Donets coal industry. In general we need to take all this into account as a manifestation of familiar tendencies. We will also recall how Comrade Lenin, speaking of democratic centralism the first day of the congress, called everyone who spoke of democratic centralism an idiot, and called democratic centralism itself antediluvian and obsolete, etc. If the separate facts are connected, the tendency for me is clear. The ultimate tendency leads to setting up individual administration in every link of the soviet apparatus. We ask ourselves a serious question, what does this mean? This means that once we take this path and go far enough on it, we will collapse under the weight of bureaucracy, which will emasculate all our work, for the basic slogan which we should proclaim at the present time is the unification of military work, military forms of organization and methods of administration, with the creative initiative of the conscious workers. If, under the banner of military work, you in fact begin to implant bureaucratism, we will disperse our own forces and fail to fulfill our tasks.

The unrestrained application of complete formal militarization can also lead to this. To apply it generally is enticing—under the banner of militarization it is all the easier to implant individual bureaucratic authority. Meanwhile, what character does our economic work have to assume? It has to assume a shock-work character, and we can apply complete militarization only in certain branches. Complete militarization is bound up with the limitation of the civil and political rights of man, with his complete bondage in production, etc. Complete militarization means that man is removed to a situation where they tell him: for the moment you are not a citizen, you are only a functionary, you must fulfill your civic duty not at meetings but in the workshop. . . .

Lenin on Revolutionary Purism

Stung by criticisms directed against his policies of centralization and expediency by Communist critics both in Russia and in the newly-founded Communist International, Lenin delivered a diatribe against the "petty-bourgeois childishness" of people who objected to compromises. In his characteristic manner he denounced opponents of party discipline as virtual agents of capitalism.

Certainly, almost everyone now realizes that the Bolsheviks could not have maintained themselves in power for two

FROM: Lenin, "'Left-Wing' Communism: An Infantile Disorder" (April, 1920; *Selected Works,* Vol. II, book 2, pp. 344, 359-60, 366-67).

and a half months, let alone two and a half years, unless the strictest, truly iron discipline had prevailed in our Party, and unless the latter had been rendered the fullest and unreserved support of the whole mass of the working class, that is, of all its thinking, honest, self-sacrificing and influential elements who are capable of leading or of carrying with them the backward strata.

The dictatorship of the proletariat is a most determined and most ruthless war waged by the new class against a *more powerful* enemy, the bourgeoisie, whose resistance is increased *tenfold* by its overthrow (even if only in one country), and whose power lies not only in the strength of international capital, in the strength and durability of the international connections of the bourgeoisie, but also in the *force of habit*, in the strength of *small production*. For, unfortunately, small production is still very, very widespread in the world, and small production *engenders* capitalism and the bourgeoisie continuously, daily, hourly, spontaneously, and on a mass scale. For all these reasons the dictatorship of the proletariat is essential, and victory over the bourgeoisie is impossible, without a long, stubborn and desperate war of life and death, a war demanding perseverance, discipline, firmness, indomitableness and unity of will.

I repeat, the experience of the victorious dictatorship of the proletariat in Russia has clearly shown even to those who are unable to think, or who have not had occasion to ponder over this question, that absolute centralization and the strictest discipline of the proletariat constitute one of the fundamental conditions for victory over the bourgeoisie. . . .

. . . To reject compromises "on principle," to reject the admissibility of compromises in general, no matter of what kind, is childishness, which it is difficult even to take seriously. A political leader who desires to be useful to the revolutionary proletariat must know how to single out *concrete* cases when such compromises are inadmissible, when they are an expression of opportunism and *treachery*, and direct all the force of criticism, the full edge of merciless exposure and relentless war, against *those concrete* compromises. . . .

There are compromises and compromises. One must be able to analyze the situation and the concrete conditions of each compromise, or of each variety of compromise. One must learn to distinguish between a man who gave the bandits money and firearms in order to lessen the damage they can do and facilitate their capture and execution, and a man who gives bandits money and firearms in order to share in the loot. In politics this is by no means always as easy as in this childishly simple example. But anyone who set out to invent a recipe for the workers that would provide in advance ready-made solutions for all cases in life, or who promised that the policy of the revolutionary proletariat would never encounter difficult or intricate situations, would simply be a charlatan. . . .

Repudiation of the party principle and of party discipline . . . is tantamount to completely disarming the proletariat *in the interest of the bourgeoisie*. It is tantamount to that petty-bourgeois diffuseness, instability, incapacity for sustained effort, unity and organized action, which, if indulged in, must inevitably destroy every proletarian revolutionary movement. From the standpoint of Communism, the repudiation of the party principle means trying to leap from the eve of the collapse of capitalism (in Germany), not to the lower, or the intermediate, but to the higher phase of Communism. We in Russia (in the third year since the overthrow of the bourgeoisie) are going through the first steps in the transition from capitalism to Socialism, or the lower stage of Communism. Classes have remained, and will remain everywhere *for years after* the conquest of power by the proletariat. Perhaps in England, where there is no peasantry (but where there are small owners!), this period may be shorter. The abolition of classes means not only driving out the landlords and capitalists—that we accomplished with comparative ease —it also means *abolishing the small commodity producers*, and they *cannot be driven out*, or crushed; we *must live in harmony* with them; they can (and must) be remoulded and re-educated only by very prolonged, slow, cautious organizational work. They encircle the proletariat on every side with a petty-bourgeois atmosphere, which permeates and corrupts the proletariat and causes constant relapses among the proletariat into petty-bourgeois spinelessness, disunity, individualism, and alternate moods of exaltation and dejection. The strictest centralization and discipline are required within the political party of the proletariat in order to counteract this, in order that the *organizational* role of the proletariat (and this is its *principal* role) may be exercised correctly, successfully, victoriously. The dictatorship of the proletariat is a persistent struggle—bloody and bloodless, violent and peaceful, military and economic, educational and administrative—against the forces and traditions of the old society. The force of habit of millions and tens of millions is a most terrible force. Without an iron party tempered in the struggle, without a party enjoying the confidence of all that is honest in the given class, without a party capable of watching and influencing the mood of the masses, it is impossible to conduct such a struggle successfully. It is a thousand times easier to vanquish the centralized big bourgeoisie than to "vanquish" the millions and millions of small owners; yet they, by their ordinary, everyday, imperceptible, elusive, demoralizing activity, achieve the *very* results which the bourgeoisie need and which tend to *restore* the bourgeoisie. Whoever weakens ever so little the iron discipline of the party of the proletariat (especially during the time of its dictatorship), actually aids the bourgeoisie against the proletariat. . . .

The Reaction against Bureaucracy

By the fall of 1920 the Communists had crushed most of the White opposition and the Soviet regime was fairly secure. Within the Communist Party there was an upsurge of feeling against the extremes of hierarchical centralization and discipline which had become the rule for the organization

FROM: Resolution of the Ninth Conference of the Russian Communist Party, September, 1920, "On the Coming Tasks of Building the Party" (CPSU in Resolutions, I, 507, 509, 511-12; editor's translation).

of the party during the Civil War. At the Ninth Party Conference the leadership felt it necessary to acknowledge this sentiment by accepting a resolution on the need for more equality and democracy in the party.

The unprecedentedly difficult position of the Soviet Republic in the first years of its existence, extreme devastation, and the greatest military danger have made it essential to separate "shock" (and therefore actually privileged) offices and groups of functionaries. This was essential, for it was impossible to save the ruined country without concentrating forces and means in such offices and in such groups of functionaries, without which the combined imperialists of the whole world certainly would have crushed us and would not have let our Soviet Republic even begin economic construction. This circumstance, together with the heritage of capitalistic and private-property habits and tendencies which we are enduring with difficulty, explains the necessity of directing the attention of the whole party again and again toward putting more equality into practice, firstly within the party, secondly within the proletariat and among all the toiling masses, and thirdly for the various offices and various groups of functionaries especially the "spetsy" [specialists] and responsible functionaries, in relation to the masses. Distinguishing members of the party only by the degree of their consciousness, devotion, endurance, political vision, revolutionary experience, readiness for self-sacrifice—the party struggles with any attempts to make distinctions among members of the party on any other lines: higher-ups and rank-and-file, intellectuals and workers, on nationality lines, etc. . . .

It is essential to realize in the internal life of the party broader criticism of the central as well as local institutions of the party; to commission the Central Committee to point out by circulars the means for broadening intra-party criticism at general meetings; to create publications which are capable of realizing broader and more systematic criticism of the mistakes of the party and general criticism within the party (discussion sheets, etc.). . . .

Recognizing in principle the necessity of appointment to responsible offices in exceptional cases, it is necessary to propose to the Central Committee that in the assignment of functionaries in general it replace appointment with recommendation.

[It is necessary] to point out that in the mobilization of comrades it is not permissible for party organs and individual comrades to be guided by any considerations except business ones. Any repression whatsoever against comrades because they dissent about some question or another decided by the party is not permissible. . . .

[It is necessary] to work out fully effective practical measures to eliminate inequality (in conditions of life, the wage scale, etc.) between the "spetsy" and the responsible functionaries on the one hand and the toiling masses on the other. . . . This inequality violates democratism and is the source of disruption in the party and of reduction in the authority of Communists. . . .

It is essential to create a Control Commission alongside the Central Committee; this must consist of comrades who have the highest party preparation, who are the most experienced, impartial, and capable of realizing strict party control. The Control Commission, elected by the party congress, must have the right to receive any complaints and examine them. . . .

Bureaucratism, which rules in many of our head offices and centers, often strikes painfully at the entirely legal interests of the mass of the people and serves as one of the most important sources of dissatisfaction within the party, for which the head offices and centers bear the responsibility.

The Central Committee of the party must take the most serious measures against this. The local organizations must help the Central Committee in this struggle, above all by communicating the pertinent facts to it.

The Communist Ideal in Family Life

While the world was shocked by rumors of the "nationalization of women," much Communist thought exhibited a glowing idealism about the future free and equal relationship of the sexes after the abolition of the "slavery" of the "bourgeois" family. The most famous exponent of this ideal—in practice as well as theory—was Alexandra Kollontai, a paragon of revolutionary idealism and the first Commissar of Social Welfare. She was a leader in the ultra-left "Workers' Opposition" movement of 1920-1921, but later made her peace with Stalin and enjoyed a long career as a Soviet diplomat.

. . . There is no escaping the fact: the old type of family has seen its day. It is not the fault of the communist State, it is the result of the changed conditions of life. *The family is ceasing to be a necessity of the State, as it was in the past;* on the contrary, it is worse than useless, since it needlessly holds back the female workers from more productive and far more serious work. Nor is it any longer necessary to the members of the family themselves, since the task of bringing up the children, which was formerly that of the family, is passing more and more into the hands of the collectivity. But on the ruins of the former family we shall soon see a new form rising which will involve altogether different relations between men and women, and which will be *a union of affection and comradeship, a union of two equal members of the communist society, both of them free, both of them independent, both of them workers.* No more domestic "servitude" of women. No more inequality within the family. No more fear on the part of the woman lest she remain without support or aid with little ones in her arms if her husband should desert her. The woman in the communist city no longer depends on her husband but on her work. It is not her husband but her robust arms which will support her. There will be no more anxiety as to the fate of her children. The State of the Workers will assume responsibility for these. Marriage will be purified of all its material elements, of all money calculations, which constitute a hideous blemish on family life in our days. Marriage is henceforth to be transformed into a sublime union of two souls in love with each other, each having faith in the other;

FROM: Kollontai, *Communism and the Family* (1920; excerpts translated in Rudolf Schlesinger, ed., *The Family in the USSR*, London, Routledge and Kegan Paul, 1949, pp. 67-69; reprinted by permission of the publisher).

this union promises to each working man and to each working woman, simultaneously, the most complete happiness, the maximum of satisfaction which can be the lot of creatures who are conscious of themselves and of the life which surrounds them. *This free union,* which is strong in the comradeship with which it is inspired, *instead of the conjugal slavery of the past—that is what the communist society of to-morrow offers to both men and women.* Once the conditions of labour have been transformed, and the material security of working women has been increased, and after marriage such as was performed by the Church—that so-called indissoluble marriage which was at bottom merely a fraud—after this marriage has given place to the free and honest union of men and women who are lovers and comrades, another shameful scourge will also be seen to disappear, another frightful evil which is a stain on humanity and which falls with all its weight on the hungry working woman: prostitution.

This evil we owe to the economic system now in force, to the institution of private property. Once the latter has been abolished, the trade in women will automatically disappear.

Therefore let the women of the working class cease to worry over the fact that the family as at present constituted is doomed to disappear. They will do much better to hail with joy the dawn of a new society which will liberate woman from domestic servitude, which will lighten the burden of motherhood for woman, and in which, finally, we shall see the disappearance of the most terrible of the curses weighing upon women, prostitution.

The woman who is called upon to struggle in the great cause of the liberation of the workers—such a woman should know that in the new State there will be no more room for such petty divisions as were formerly understood: "These are my own children; to them I owe all my maternal solicitude, all my affection; those are your children, my neighbour's children; I am not concerned with them. I have enough to do with my own." Henceforth the worker-mother, who is conscious of her social function, will rise to a point where she no longer differentiates between *yours* and *mine;* she must remember that there are henceforth only *our* children, those of the communist State, the common possession of all the workers.

The Workers' State has need of a new form of relation between the sexes. The narrow and exclusive affection of the mother for her own children must expand until it embraces all the children of the great proletarian family. In place of the indissoluble marriage based on the servitude of woman, we shall see rise the free union, fortified by the love and mutual respect of the two members of the Workers' State, equal in their rights and in their obligations. In place of the individual and egotistic family, there will arise a great universal family of workers, in which all the workers, men and women, will be, above all, workers, comrades. Such will be the relation between men and women in the communist society of to-morrow. This new relation will assure to humanity all the joys of so-called free love ennobled by a true social equality of the mates, joys which were unknown to the commercial society of the capitalist regime.

Make way for healthy blossoming children: make way for a vigorous youth that clings to life and to its joys, which is free in its sentiments and in its affections. Such is the watchword of the communist society. In the name of equality, of liberty, and of love, we call upon the working women and the working men, peasant women and peasants, courageously and with faith to take up the work of the reconstruction of human society with the object of rendering it more perfect, more just, and more capable of assuring to the individual the happiness which he deserves. The red flag of the social revolution which will shelter, after Russia, other countries of the world also, already proclaims to us the approach of the heaven on earth to which humanity has been aspiring for centuries. . . .

The Trade Union Controversy and the Workers' Opposition

In the fall of 1920 sharp controversy broke out in the Communist Party over the role of the trade unions and their relation to the party and the government. Trotsky, with

Bukharin's support, pressed his plan for militarizing or "governmentalizing" the unions as agencies of industrial administration. Lenin and the cautious wing of the party, including Zinoviev, Kamenev, Rykov, and Stalin, decided to eliminate the unions from administration altogether and relegate them to a social-service and educational role. At the other extreme, the left-wing enthusiasts in the trade unions, organized into the "Workers' Opposition," demanded that industrial administration be made the independent responsibility of the unions themselves. One of the most fervent spokesmen for the Workers' Opposition was Alexandra Kollontai, who bewailed the trend to bureaucracy and pleaded for trust in the "class instinct" of the proletariat.

. . . the Workers' Opposition is composed of the most advanced part of our class-organized proletarian-Communists. The opposition consists almost exclusively of members of the trade unions, and this fact is attested by the signatures of those who side with the opposition under the theses on the role of industrial unions. Who are these members of the trade unions? Workers—that part of the advanced guard of the Russian proletariat which has borne on its shoulders all the difficulties of the revolutionary struggle, and did not dissolve itself into the soviet institutions by losing contact with the laboring masses, but on the contrary, remained closely connected with them. . . .

Through their class instinct, these comrades standing at the head of the Workers' Opposition became conscious of the fact that there was something wrong: they understood that even though during these three years we have created the soviet institutions and reaffirmed the principles of the workers' republic, yet the working class, *as a class,* as a self-contained social unit with identical class aspirations, tasks, interests, and, hence, *with a uniform, consistent, clear-cut policy,* becomes an ever less important factor in the affairs of the Soviet republic. . . .

Why was it that none but the unions stubbornly defended

FROM: Kollontai, *The Workers' Opposition* (1921; English translation, Chicago, Industrial Workers of the World, 1921, pp. 3-4, 7, 11, 20, 22-23, 32-33, 37-41, 44).

the principle of collective management, even without being able to adduce scientific arguments in favor of it; and why was it that the specialists' supporters at the same time defended the "one man management"? The reason is that in this controversy, though both sides emphatically denied that there was a question of principle involved, two historically irreconcilable points of view had clashed. The "one-man management" is a product of the individualist conception of the bourgeois class. The "one man management" is in principle an unrestricted, isolated, free will of one man, disconnected from the collective.

This idea finds its reflection in all spheres of human endeavor—beginning with the appointment of a sovereign for the state and ending with a sovereign director of the factory. This is the supreme wisdom of bourgeois thought. The bourgeoisie do not believe in the power of a collective body. They like only to whip the masses into an obedient flock, and drive them wherever their unrestricted will desires. . . .

Rejection of a principle—the principle of collective management in the control of industry—was a tactical compromise on behalf of our party, an act of adaptation; it was, moreover, an act of deviation from that class policy which we so zealously cultivated and defended during the first phase of the revolution.

Why did this happen? How did it happen that our party, matured and tempered in the struggle of the revolution, was permitted to be carried away from the direct road in order to journey along the round-about path of adaptation, formerly condemned severely and branded as "opportunism"? . . .

Beside peasant-owners in the villages and burgher elements in the cities, our party in its soviet state policy is forced to reckon with the influence exerted by the representatives of wealthy bourgeoisie now appearing in the form of specialists, technicians, engineers, and former managers of financial and industrial affairs, who by all their past experience are bound to the capitalist system of production. They can not even imagine any other mode of production but only that one which lies *within the traditional bounds of capitalist economics.*

The more Soviet Russia finds itself in need of specialists in the sphere of technique and management of production, the stronger becomes the influence of these elements, foreign to the working class elements, on the development of our economy. Having been thrown aside during the first period of the revolution, and being compelled to take up an attitude of watchful waiting or sometimes even open hostility toward the soviet authorities, particularly during the most trying months (the historical sabotage by the intellectuals), this social group of brains in capitalist production, of servile, hired, well-paid servants of capital, acquire more and more influence and importance in politics with every day that passes. . . .

The basis of the controversy is namely this: whether we shall realize communism through workers or over their heads, by the hands of soviet officials. And let us, comrades, ponder whether it is possible to attain and build a communist economy by the hands and creative abilities of the scions from the other class, who are imbued with their *routine of the past?* If we begin to think as Marxians, as men of science, we shall answer categorically and explicitly—no. . . .

The solution of this problem as it is proposed by the industrial unions, consists in giving complete freedom to the workers as regards experimenting, class training, adjusting and feeling out the new forms of production, as well as expression and development of their creative abilities, that is, to that class which alone can be the creator of communism. This is the way the Workers' Opposition handles the solution of this difficult problem from which follows the most essential point of their theses. "Organization of control over the social economy is a prerogative of the All-Russian Congress of Producers, who are united in the trade and industrial unions which elect the central body directing the whole economic life of the republic" (Theses of the Workers' Opposition). This point secures freedom for the manifestation of class creative abilities, not restricted and crippled by the bureaucratic machine which is saturated with the spirit of routine of the bourgeois capitalist system of production and control.

The Workers' Opposition relies on the creative powers of its own class—the workers. From this premise is deduced the rest of the program.

But right at this point there begins the deviation of the Workers' Opposition from the line that is followed by the party leaders. Distrust toward the working class (not in the sphere of politics, but in the sphere of economic creative abilities) is the whole essence of the theses signed by our party leaders. They do not believe that by the rough hands of workers, untrained technically, can be created those basic outlines of the economic forms from which in the course of time shall develop a harmonious system of communist production. . . .

The cardinal point of controversy that is taking place between the party leaders and the Workers' Opposition is this: In whom will our party place the trust of building up the communist economy—in the Supreme Council of National Economy with all its bureaucratic branches or in the Industrial Unions? Comrade Trotsky wants "to join" the trade unions to the Supreme Council of National Economy so that with the assistance of the latter it might be possible to swallow the first. Comrades Lenin and Zinoviev, on the other hand, want to "bring up" the masses to such a level of communist understanding that they could be painlessly absorbed into the same soviet institutions. Bukharin and the rest of the factions express essentially the same view, and the variation consists only in the way they put it, the essence is the same. Only the Workers' Opposition expresses something entirely different, defends the class proletarian viewpoint in the very process of creation and realization of its tasks.

The administrative economic body in the labor republic during the present transitory period must be a body directly elected by the producers themselves. All the rest of the administrative economic soviet institutions shall serve only as executive centers of the economic policy of that all-important economic body of the labor republic. All else is a goose-stepping that manifests distrust toward all creative abilities of workers, distrust which is not compatible with the professed ideals of our party whose very strength depends on the perennial revolutionary creative spirit of the proletariat. . . .

There can be no self-activity without freedom of thought and opinion, for self-activity manifests itself not only in initiative, action, and work, but in *independent thought* as well. We are afraid of mass-activity. We are afraid to give freedom to the class activity, we are afraid of criticism, we have ceased to rely on the masses, hence, *we have bureaucracy with us*. That is why the Workers' Opposition considers that bureaucracy is our enemy, our scourge, and the greatest danger for the future existence of the Communist Party itself.

In order to do away with the bureaucracy that is finding its shelter in the soviet institutions, *we must first of all get rid of all bureaucracy in the party itself*. . . .

The Workers' Opposition, together with a group of responsible workers in Moscow, in the name of party regeneration and elimination of bureaucracy from the soviet institutions, demands complete realization of all democratic principles, not only for the present period of respite, but also for times of internal and external tension. This is the first and basic condition of the party regeneration, of its return to the principles of the program, from which in practice it is more and more deviating under the pressure of elements that are foreign to it.

The second condition, fulfillment of which with all determination is insisted upon by the Workers' Opposition, is the *expulsion from the party* of all non-proletarian elements. . . .

The third decisive step toward democratization of the party is the elimination of all non-workers' elements from all the administrative positions; in other words, the central, provincial, and county committees of the party must be composed so that workers closely connected with the working masses would have the preponderant majority therein. . . .

The fourth basic demand of the Workers' Opposition is this: *the party must reverse its policy to the elective principle.*

Appointments must be permissible only as exceptions, but lately they began to prevail as a rule. Appointments are very characteristic of bureaucracy, and yet at present they are a general, legalized and well recognized daily occurrence. The procedure of appointments produces a very unhealthy atmosphere in the party, and disrupts the relationship of equality among the members by rewarding friends and punishing enemies as well as by other no less harmful practices in our party and soviet life. . . .

Wide publicity, freedom of opinion and discussion, right to criticize within the party and among the members of the trade unions—such is the decisive step that can put an end to the prevailing system of bureaucracy. Freedom of criticism, right of different factions to freely present their views at party meetings, freedom of discussion—are no longer the demands of the Workers' Opposition alone. Under the growing pressure from the masses a whole series of measures that were demanded by the rank and file long before the All-Russian conference* was held, are recognized and promulgated officially at present. . . . However, we must not overestimate this "leftism," for it is only a declaration of principles to the congress. It may happen, as it has happened many a time with the decisions of our party leaders during these years, that this radical declaration will be forgotten for, as a rule, they are accepted by our party centres only just as the mass impetus is felt, and as soon as life again swings into normal channels the decisions are forgotten. . . .

The Workers' Opposition has said what has long ago been printed in "The Communist Manifesto" by Marx and Engels, viz.: "Creation of communism can and will be the work of the toiling masses themselves. Creation of communism belongs to the workers." . . .

The Kronstadt Revolt

By early 1921 it was becoming clear to the Communist leaders that the system of "War Communism" had reached an impasse of economic breakdown and mass discontent. The seriousness of the situation was brought home to them by

* The Ninth Party Conference, September, 1920—Ed.

the outbreak of armed defiance of the Soviet government at the Baltic naval base of Kronstadt, a stronghold of anarchistic radicalism. For a few days Kronstadt appealed to the Russian populace to carry out a "third revolution" against the bureaucratic dictatorship of the Communists, in the name of the original ideals of the October Revolution. No effective response was forthcoming, and the rebels were soon overwhelmed by government troops.

After carrying out the October Revolution, the working class hoped to achieve emancipation. The result has been to create even greater enslavement of the individual man.

The power of the police-gendarme monarchy has gone into the hands of the Communist-usurpers, who instead of freedom offer the toilers the constant fear of falling into the torture-chambers of the Cheka, which in their horrors surpass many times the gendarme administration of the czarist regime.

Bayonets, bullets, and the harsh shouts of the *oprichniki** of the Cheka, are what the working man of Soviet Russia has got after a multitude of struggles and sufferings. The glorious arms of labor's state—the sickle and hammer—have actually been replaced by the Communist authorities with the bayonet and the barred window, for the sake of preserving the calm, carefree life of the new bureaucracy of Communist commissars and officials.

But the most hateful and criminal thing which the Communists have created is moral servitude: they laid their hands even on the inner life of the toilers and compelled them to think only in the Communist way.

With the aid of militarized trade unions they have bound the workers to their benches, and have made labor not into a joy but into a new slavery. To the protests of the peasants, expressed in spontaneous uprisings, and of the workers, who

FROM: "What We Are Fighting For," *News* of the Kronstadt Temporary Revolutionary Committee, March 8, 1921 (reprinted in *The Truth about Kronstadt,* Prague, Volia Rossii, 1921, pp. 82-83; editor's translation).

* "Oprichniki": originally, members of the sixteenth-century police force of Czar Ivan the Terrible—Ed.

are compelled to strike by the circumstances of their life, they answer with mass executions and bloodthirstiness, in which they are not surpassed by the czarist generals.

Labor's Russia, the first country to raise the banner of the liberation of labor, has been continuously covered with the blood of the people who have been tortured for the glory of Communist domination. In this sea of blood the Communists are drowning all the great and glowing pledges and slogans of labor's revolution.

It has been sketched out more and more sharply, and now has become obvious, that the Russian Communist Party is not the defender of the toilers which it represents itself to be; the interests of the working nation are alien to it; having attained power, it is afraid only of losing it, and therefore all means are allowed: slander, violence, deceit, murder, vengeance on the families of rebels.

The enduring patience of the toilers has reached its end.

Here and there the glow of insurrection has illuminated the country in its struggle against oppression and violence. Strikes by the workers have flared up, but the Bolshevik *okhrana** has not slept and has taken every measure to forestall and suppress the unavoidable third revolution. . . .

There can be no middle ground. Victory or death!

Red Kronstadt gives this example, threatening the counter-revolutionaries of the right and of the left.

The new revolutionary upheaval has been accomplished here. Here the banner of insurrection has been raised for liberation from the three-year violence and oppression of Communist domination, which has overshadowed the three-century yoke of monarchism. Here at Kronstadt the first stone of the third revolution has been laid, to break off the last fetters on the toiling masses and open a new broad road for socialist creativity.

This new revolution will rouse the laboring masses of the East and of the West, since it shows an example of the new socialist construction as opposed to the Communists' barrack-room "creativity" and directly convinces the laboring masses

* "Okhrana": originally, the Czarist secret police—Ed.

abroad that everything created here up to now by the will of the workers and peasants was not socialism.

The first step has been completed without a single shot, without a drop of blood. The toilers do not need blood. They will shed it only at a moment of self-defense. Firmness is enough for us, in spite of the outrageous actions of the Communists, to confine ourselves to isolating them from social life, so that their evil false agitation will not interfere with revolutionary work.

The workers and peasants unreservedly go forward, abandoning behind them the Constituent Assembly with its bourgeois stratum and the dictatorship of the party of the Communists with its Cheka men, its state capitalism, its hangman's noose encircling the neck of the masses and threatening to strangle them for good.

The present overturn at last makes it possible for the toilers to have their freely elected soviets, working without any violent party pressure, and remake the state trade unions into free associations of workers, peasants and the laboring intelligentsia. At last the policeman's club of the Communist autocracy has been broken.

Institution of the Monolithic Party

Lenin's response to the Kronstadt rebellion was to change his course drastically, in two respects. For the country at large, he ordered a "strategic retreat" to the much more moderate "New Economic Policy." For the Communist Party he demanded a much more rigorous system of discipline, and the Tenth Party Congress in March, 1921, accepted the resolutions which he proposed to this effect—prohibition of organized factions within the party, and condemnation of the ultra-Left Workers' Opposition as an un-Communist deviation. As Alexandra Kollontai had predicted, the democratic concessions of 1920 were abruptly retracted. To enforce the new line of discipline, the personnel of the party Secretariat was shaken up; the old secretaries, who had supported Trotsky, were replaced by a new group including Molotov and influenced by Stalin as the leading figure in the Orgbureau.

a) On Party Unity

1. The Congress calls the attention of all members of the Party to the fact that the unity and solidarity of the ranks of the Party, ensuring complete mutual confidence among Party members and genuine team work, genuinely embodying the unanimity of will of the vanguard of the proletariat, are particularly essential at the present juncture when a number of circumstances are increasing the vacillation among the petty-bourgeois population of the country.

2. Notwithstanding this, even before the general Party discussion on the trade unions, certain signs of factionalism had been apparent in the Party, viz., the formation of groups with separate platforms, striving to a certain degree to segregate and create their own group discipline. Such symptoms of factionalism were manifested, for example, at a Party conference in Moscow (November 1920) and in Kharkov, both by the so-called "Workers' Opposition" group, and partly by the so-called "Democratic-Centralism" group.

All class-conscious workers must clearly realize the perniciousness and impermissibility of factionalism of any kind, for no matter how the representatives of individual groups may desire to safeguard Party unity, in practice factionalism inevitably leads to the weakening of team work and to intensified and repeated attempts by the enemies of the Party, who have fastened themselves onto it because it is the governing Party, to widen the cleavage and to use it for counterrevolutionary purposes.

The way the enemies of the proletariat take advantage of every deviation from the thoroughly consistent Communist line was perhaps most strikingly shown in the case of the Kronstadt mutiny, when the bourgeois counterrevolutionaries and Whiteguards* in all countries of the world immediately expressed their readiness to accept even the slogans

FROM: Resolution of the Tenth Congress of the Russian Communist Party, "On Party Unity," March, 1921 (Lenin, *Selected Works,* Vol. II, book 2, pp. 497-501).

* Whiteguards: anti-Bolshevik units in the Civil War; applied to anti-Communists anywhere—Ed.

of the Soviet system, if only they might thereby secure the overthrow of the dictatorship of the proletariat in Russia, and when the Socialist-Revolutionaries and the bourgeois counterrevolutionaries in general resorted in Kronstadt to slogans calling for an insurrection against the Soviet government of Russia ostensibly in the interest of Soviet power. These facts fully prove that the Whiteguards strive, and are able, to disguise themselves as Communists, and even as the most Left Communists, solely for the purpose of weakening and overthrowing the bulwark of the proletarian revolution in Russia. . . .

4. In the practical struggle against factionalism, every organization of the Party must take strict measures to prevent any factional actions whatsoever. Criticism of the Party's shortcomings, which is absolutely necessary, must be conducted in such a way that every practical proposal shall be submitted immediately, without any delay, in the most precise form possible, for consideration and decision to the leading local and central bodies of the Party. Moreover, everyone who criticizes must see to it that the form of his criticism takes into account the position of the Party, surrounded as it is by a ring of enemies, and that the content of his criticism is such that, by directly participating in Soviet and Party work, he can test the rectification of the errors of the Party or of individual Party members in practice. . . .

5. . . . While ruthlessly rejecting unpractical and factional pseudo-criticisms, the Party will unceasingly continue—trying out new methods—to fight with all the means at its disposal against bureaucracy, for the extension of democracy and initiative, for detecting, exposing and expelling from the Party elements that have wormed their way into its ranks, etc.

6. The Congress therefore hereby declares dissolved and orders the immediate dissolution of all groups without exception that have been formed on the basis of one platform or another (such as the "workers' opposition" group, the "democratic-centralism" group, etc.). Nonobservance of this

decision of the Congress shall involve absolute and immediate expulsion from the Party.

7. In order to ensure strict discipline within the Party and in all Soviet work and to secure the maximum unanimity in removing all factionalism, the Congress authorizes the Central Committee, in cases of breach of discipline or of a revival or toleration of factionalism, to apply all Party penalties, including expulsion, and in regard to members of the Central Committee to reduce them to the status of alternate members and even, as an extreme measure, to expel them from the Party. A necessary condition for the application of such an extreme measure to members of the Central Committee, alternate members of the Central Committee and members of the Control Commission is the convocation of a plenum of the Central Committee, to which all alternate members of the Central Committee and all members of the Control Commission shall be invited. If such a general assembly of the most responsible leaders of the Party, by a two-thirds majority, deems it necessary to reduce a member of the Central Committee to the status of alternate member, or to expel him from the Party, this measure shall be put into effect immediately.

b) On the Syndicalist and Anarchist Deviation in Our Party

1. In the past few months a syndicalist and anarchist deviation has been definitely revealed in our Party, and calls for the most resolute measures of ideological struggle and also for purging and restoring the health of the Party.

2. The said deviation is due partly to the influx into the Party of former Mensheviks and also of workers and peasants who have not yet fully assimilated the Communist world outlook; mainly, however, this deviation is due to the in-

FROM: Resolution of the Tenth Congress of the Russian Communist Party, "On the Syndicalist and Anarchist Deviation in Our Party," March, 1921 (Lenin, *Selected Works,* Vol. II, book 2, pp. 502-06).

fluence exercised upon the proletariat and on the Russian Communist Party by the petty-bourgeois element, which is exceptionally strong in our country, and which inevitably engenders vacillation towards anarchism, particularly at a time when the conditions of the masses have sharply deteriorated as a consequence of the crop failure and the devastating effects of war, and when the demobilization of the army numbering millions releases hundreds and hundreds of thousands of peasants and workers unable immediately to find regular means of livelihood.

3. The most theoretically complete and formulated expression of this deviation (*or:* one of the most complete, etc., expressions of this deviation) are the theses and other literary productions of the so-called "workers' opposition" group. Sufficiently illustrative of this is, for example, the following thesis propounded by this group: "The organization of the administration of the national economy is the function of an All-Russian Producers' Congress organized in industrial trade unions, which elect a central organ for the administration of the entire national economy of the Republic."

The ideas at the bottom of this and numerous analogous statements are radically wrong in theory, and represent a complete rupture with Marxism and Communism as well as with the practical experience of all semiproletarian revolutions and of the present proletarian revolution. . . .

Marxism teaches—and this tenet has not only been formally endorsed by the whole of the Communist International in the decisions of the Second (1920) Congress of the Comintern on the role of the political party of the proletariat, but has also been confirmed in practice by our revolution—that only the political party of the working class, i.e., the Communist Party, is capable of uniting, training and organizing a vanguard of the proletariat and of the whole mass of the working people that alone will be capable of withstanding the inevitable petty-bourgeois vacillations of this mass and the inevitable traditions and relapses of narrow craft unionism or craft prejudices among the proletariat, and of guiding all the united activities of the whole of the proletariat, i.e., of leading it politically, and through it, the whole mass of the working people. Without this the dictatorship of the proletariat is impossible.

The wrong understanding of the role of the Communist Party in relation to the non-Party proletariat, and in the relation of the first and second factor to the whole mass of working people, is a radical theoretical departure from Communism and a deviation towards syndicalism and anarchism, and this deviation permeates all the views of the "workers' opposition" group.

4. The Tenth Congress of the Russian Communist Party declares that it also regards as radically wrong all attempts on the part of the said group and of other persons to defend their fallacious views by referring to point 5 of the economic section of the program of the Russian Communist Party which deals with the role of the trade unions. This point says that "the trade unions must eventually actually concentrate in their hands the entire administration of the whole of national economy as a single economic unit" and that they will "ensure in this way indissoluble ties between the central state administration, the national economy and the broad masses of the working people," "drawing" these masses "into the direct work of managing economy." . . .

Instead of studying the practical experience of participation in administration, and instead of developing this experience further, strictly in conformity with successes achieved and rectified mistakes, the syndicalists and anarchists advance as an immediate slogan "congresses or a Congress of Producers" "which elect" the organs of administration of economy. Thus, the leading, educational and organizing role of the Party in relation to the trade unions of the proletariat, and of the latter to the semi-petty-bourgeois and even wholly petty-bourgeois masses of working people, is utterly evaded and eliminated, and instead of continuing and correcting the practical work of building new forms of economy already begun by the Soviet state, we get petty-bourgeois-anarchist disruption of this work, which can only lead to the triumph of the bourgeois counterrevolution.

5. In addition to theoretical fallacies and a radically wrong attitude towards the practical experience of economic

construction already begun by the Soviet government, the Congress of the Russian Communist Party discerns in the views of these and analogous groups and persons a gross political mistake and a direct political danger to the very existence of the dictatorship of the proletariat.

In a country like Russia, the overwhelming preponderance of the petty-bourgeois element and the devastation, impoverishment, epidemics, crop failures, extreme want and hardship inevitably resulting from the war, engender particularly sharp vacillations in the moods of the petty-bourgeois and semiproletarian masses. At one moment the wavering is in the direction of strengthening the alliance between these masses and the proletariat, and at another moment in the direction of bourgeois restoration. The whole experience of all revolutions in the eighteenth, nineteenth, and twentieth centuries shows with utmost and absolute clarity and conviction that the only possible result of these vacillations—if the unity, strength and influence of the revolutionary vanguard of the proletariat is weakened in the slightest degree—can be the restoration of the power and property of the capitalists and landlords.

Hence, the views of the "workers' opposition" and of like-minded elements are not only wrong in theory, but in practice are an expression of petty-bourgeois and anarchist wavering, in practice weaken the consistency of the leading line of the Communist Party, and in practice help the class enemies of the proletarian revolution.

6. In view of all this, the Congress of the Russian Communist Party, emphatically rejecting the said ideas which express a syndicalist and anarchist deviation, deems it necessary

Firstly, to wage an unswerving and systematic ideological struggle against these ideas;

Secondly, the Congress regards the propaganda of these ideas as being incompatible with membership of the Russian Communist Party.

Instructing the Central Committee of the Party strictly to enforce these decisions, the Congress at the same time points out that space can and should be devoted in special publications, symposiums, etc., for a most comprehensive interchange of opinion among Party members on all the questions herein indicated.

The New Economic Policy

To allay the dangers of popular hostility, particularly among the peasants, Lenin suspended the War Communism policy of requisitioning food, substituted a definite tax system, and began the restoration of a normal money economy qualified only by state ownership of the "commanding heights" of large-scale industry, transportation, communications, etc. He justified the broad use of capitalistic methods—"state capitalism"—as the only way to restore production. Thus, in 1921, the period of utopian revolutionary fervor came to an end.

. . . The most urgent thing at the present time is to take measures that will immediately increase the productive forces of peasant farming. Only in *this way* will it be possible to improve the conditions of the workers and strengthen the alliance between the workers and peasants, to strengthen the dictatorship of the proletariat. The proletarian or representative of the proletariat who *refused* to improve the conditions of the workers in *this way* would *in fact* prove himself to be an accomplice of the Whiteguards and the capitalists; because to refuse to do it in this way would mean putting the craft interests of the workers above their class interests, would mean sacrificing the interests of the whole of the working class, of its dictatorship, its alliance with the peasantry against the landlords and capitalists, its leading role in the struggle for the emancipation of labour from the yoke of capital, for the sake of the immediate, momentary and partial gain of the workers.

Thus, the first thing required is immediate and serious measures to raise the productive forces of the peasantry.

This cannot be done without a serious modification of our food policy. Such a modification was the substitution of the surplus-appropriation system by the tax in kind, which

FROM: Lenin, "The Tax In Kind" (April, 1921; *Selected Works*, Vol. II, book 2, pp. 540-44; 565-66).

implies free trade, at least in local economic exchange, after the tax has been paid.

What, in essence, is the substitution of the surplus-appropriation system by the tax in kind? . . .

The tax in kind is one of the forms of transition from that peculiar "War Communism," which we were forced to resort to by extreme want, ruin and war, to the proper socialist exchange of products. The latter, in its turn, is one of the forms of transition from Socialism, with the peculiar features created by the predominance of the small peasantry among the population, to Communism.

The essence of this peculiar "War Communism" was that we actually took from the peasant all the surplus grain—and sometimes even not only surplus grain, but part of the grain the peasant required for food—to meet the requirements of the army and sustain the workers. . . . We were forced to resort to "War Communism" by war and ruin. It was not, nor could it be, a policy that corresponded to the economic tasks of the proletariat. It was a temporary measure. The correct policy of the proletariat which is exercising its dictatorship in a small-peasant country is to obtain grain in exchange for the manufactured goods the peasant requires. Only such a food policy corresponds to the tasks of the proletariat; only such a policy can strengthen the foundations of Socialism and lead to its complete victory. . . .

The effect will be the revival of the petty bourgeoisie and of capitalism on the basis of a certain amount of free trade (if only local). This is beyond doubt. It would be ridiculous to shut our eyes to it.

The question arises: Is it necessary? Can it be justified? Is it not dangerous? . . .

. . . What is to be done? Either to try to prohibit entirely, to put the lock on, all development of private, nonstate exchange, i.e., trade, i.e., capitalism, which is inevitable amidst millions of small producers. But such a policy would be foolish and suicidal for the party that tried to apply it. It would be foolish because such a policy is economically impossible. It would be suicidal because the party that tried to apply such a policy would meet with inevitable disaster.

We need not conceal from ourselves the fact that some Communists sinned "in thought, word and deed" in this respect and dropped precisely into *such* a policy. We shall try to rectify these mistakes. They must be rectified without fail, otherwise things will come to a very sorry state.

Or (and this is the last *possible* and the only sensible policy) not to try to prohibit, or put the lock on the development of capitalism, but to try to direct it into the channels of *state capitalism*. This is economically possible, for state capitalism—in one form or another, to some degree or other—exists wherever the elements of free trade and capitalism in general exist.

Can the Soviet state, the dictatorship of the proletariat, be combined, united with state capitalism? Are they compatible? Of course they are. . . .

Our Communists still do not sufficiently understand their real duties of administration: they should not strive to do "everything themselves," wearing themselves out and failing to cope with everything, undertaking twenty jobs and finishing none. They should check up on the work of scores and hundreds of assistants, arrange to have their work checked up from below, i.e., by the real masses. They should *direct* the work and *learn* from those who have knowledge (the experts) and experience in organizing large-scale production (the capitalists). A wise Communist will not be afraid of learning from a military expert, although nine-tenths of the military experts are capable of treachery at every opportunity. A wise Communist will not be afraid of learning from a capitalist (no matter whether that capitalist is a big capitalist concessionaire, or a commission agent, or a little capitalist cooperator, etc.), although the capitalist is no better than the military expert. Did we not in the Red Army learn to catch treacherous military experts, to single out the honest and conscientious, and, on the whole, to utilize thousands and tens of thousands of military experts? We are learning to do the same (in an unconventional way) with engineers and teachers, although we are doing it much worse than we did it in the Red Army (there Denikin and Kolchak spurred us on, compelled us to learn more quickly, more diligently and more intelligently). We shall learn to do the same (again in an unconventional way) with the commission agents, with the buyers who are working for the state, with the little cooperator-capitalists, with the entrepreneur concessionaires, etc. . . .

Chapter Three: Soviet Communism: The Era of Controversy, 1922-1929

For nearly a decade after the consolidation of Communist power Soviet Russia was ruled by a collective dictatorship of the top party leaders. At the top level individuals still spoke for themselves, and considerable freedom for factional controversy remained despite the principles of unity laid down in 1921.

The scope of political difference among the Communists was restricted, however, by certain severe limiting conditions. Under the New Economic Policy ("NEP"), the party was in power in a situation of postrevolutionary compromise, where reality made the serious application of its theory very difficult. The party was, however, dogmatically committed to the theoretical premises of the "proletarian revolution" and the "workers' state." Finally, the Civil War had bequeathed a military form of party organization, which put decisive political power in the hands of Stalin's Secretariat. While controversy raged between Right, Center, Left, and Ultra-Left groups about the proper way to advance toward the socialist ideal, the course of events was really dictated by the realities of economic backwardness and organizational power.

The uncertainties of the era of controversy came to an end with the successive victories of Stalin's party machine over Trotsky's Left Opposition and Bukharin's Right Opposition. By this time, the most important enduring features of the Soviet regime were laid down—a new system of personal power resting on total party control; a new use of doctrine as unchallengeable justification for the expediencies of government; and a new attack on the problems of backwardness, to accomplish economic development through dictatorial compulsion and violence.

Protests against the New Economic Policy

The 1921 ban on factions did not immediately check the complaints of leftwing Communists that the NEP was a betrayal of the proletariat. The Workers' Opposition made their last stand in appealing to the Communist International (the "Declaration of the Twenty-Two") against bureaucratic muzzling of working-class sentiment in Russia. Another group, styling itself the "Workers' Truth," formed around Lenin's one-time second-in-command Alexander Bogdanov, and attacked the Communist Party for its "state capitalism" under which the workers were exploited for the benefit of the "organizers." Groups such as the "Workers' Truth," with their tone reminiscent of the old revolutionary protest against czarism, were naturally intolerable to the Soviet leaders and were quickly suppressed by the G.P.U.

a) The Declaration of the Twenty-Two

Dear Comrades:

We have learned from our newspapers that the International Conference of the Communist International is considering the question of the "united Workers' front," and we consider it our Communist duty to make it known to you that in our country things stand unfavorably with the united front, not only in the broad sense of the term, but even in applying it to the ranks of our party.

At a time when the forces of the bourgeois element press on us from all sides, when they even penetrate into our party, whose social content (40% workers and 60% nonproletarians) favors this, our leading centers are conducting an unrelenting, disruptive struggle against all, especially proletarians, who allow themselves to have their own judgment, and against the

FROM: Declaration of Twenty-Two Members of the Russian Communist Party to the International Conference of the Communist International (February, 1922; in the *News of the Central Committee*, March, 1922, pp. 69-70; editor's translation).

expression of this within the party they take all kinds of repressive measures.

The effort to draw the proletarian masses closer to the state is declared to be "anarcho-syndicalism," and its adherents are subjected to persecution and discredit.

In the area of the trade-union movement there is the very same picture of suppression of the workers' independence and initiative, and a struggle using every means against heterodoxy. The combined forces of the party and trade-union bureaucracies, taking advantage of their position and power, are ignoring the decisions of our congresses about carrying out the principles of workers' democracy. Our [Communist] fractions in the unions, even the fractions of entire [trade-union] congresses, are deprived of the right to express their will in the matter of electing their centers. Tutelage and pressure by the bureaucracy lead to the members of the party being constrained by the threat of expulsion and other repressive measures to elect not whom these Communists themselves want, but those whom the higher-ups, ignoring them, want. Such methods of work lead to careerism, intrigue, and toadying, and the workers answer this by quitting the party.

Sharing the idea of a united workers' front . . . we turn to you in the sincere hope of ending all the abnormalities which stand in the way of the unity of this front, above all within our Russian Communist Party. . . .

b) Appeal of the "Workers' Truth" Group

"The liberation of the workers can only be the deed of the working class itself." [Marx]

Message to the Revolutionary Proletariat and to All Revolutionary Elements Who Remain Faithful to the Struggling Working Class:

. . . The working class of Russia, small in numbers, un-

FROM: Appeal of the "Workers' Truth" Group (1922; in *The Socialist Herald*, Berlin, Jan. 31, 1923, pp. 12-14; editor's translation).

prepared, in a peasant country, accomplished in October, 1917, the historically necessary October Revolution. Led by the Russian Communist Party, it has overthrown and destroyed the power of the ruling classes; during long years of revolution and civil war it has firmly contained the pressure of international and Russian reaction.

In spite of the unprecedentedly heavy losses sustained by the working class, the October Revolution remains a decisive and heroic event in the history of the struggle of the Russian proletariat. The Russian October Revolution has given the struggling international proletariat an experience of tremendous value for its struggle against capital.

As a result of the October Revolution all the barriers in the path of the economic development were eliminated; there is no longer any oppression by the landlords, the parasitic czarist bureaucracy, and the bourgeoisie, which relied on reactionary groups of European capitalists. After the successful revolution and civil war, broad perspectives opened before Russia, of rapid transformation into a country of progressive capitalism. In this lies the undoubted and tremendous achievement of the revolution in October.

But what has changed in the position of the working class? The working class of Russia is disorganized; confusion reigns in the minds of the workers: are they in a country of the "dictatorship of the proletariat," as the Communist Party untiringly reiterates by word of mouth and in the press? Or are they in a country of arbitrary rule and exploitation, as life tells them at every step? The working class is leading a miserable existence at a time when the new bourgeoisie (i.e., the responsible functionaries, plant directors, heads of trusts, chairmen of executive committees, etc.) and the Nepmen* live in luxury and recall in our memory the picture of the life of the bourgeoisie of all times. And again long and difficult years of the struggle for existence lie ahead. But the more complicated the circumstances, the more clarity and organization are necessary for the struggling proletariat. To introduce class clarity into the ranks of the

* Nepmen: private traders allowed to operate under the NEP—Ed.

working class of Russia, to aid in every way the organization of the revolutionary powers of the struggling proletariat—this is our task. . . .

The Communist Party, which during the years of the revolution was a party of the working class, has become the ruling party, the party of the organizers and directors of the governmental apparatus and economic life on capitalistic lines, with the general backwardness and lack of organization of the working class. The party has more and more lost its tie and community with the proletariat. The soviet, party, and trade-union bureaucracies and organizers find themselves with material conditions which are sharply distinguished from the conditions of existence of the working class. Their very well-being and the stability of their general position depend on the degree to which the toiling masses are exploited and subordinated to them. All this makes a contradiction between their interests and a break between the Communist Party and the working class inevitable.

The social existence of the Communist Party itself inevitably determines the corresponding social consciousness, interests and ideals, which contradict the interests of the struggling proletariat.

The Russian Communist Party has become the party of the organizer intelligentsia. The abyss between the Russian Communist Party and the working class is getting deeper and deeper, and this fact cannot be glossed over by any resolutions or decisions of the Communist congresses and conferences, etc. . . .

The NEP, i.e., the rebirth of normal capitalistic relations and intensive economic differentiation among the peasantry, intensified by the famine of 1920-21, has contributed to the pronounced growth of the big kulak stratum in the Russian village. The small-scale, unorganized character of peasant farming, together with the disruption of the means of communication, makes it definite that commercial capital will have a dominant role in the immediate future. At the same time the state is growing in influence as the representative of the nation-wide interests of capital and as the mere directing apparatus of political administration and economic regulation by the organizer intelligentsia. The proletariat—broken up in consequence of the destruction of industry; weakened by losses, the detaching (by bourgeois captivation) of part of the most active elements, and ideological confusion; and lacking a proletarian party and revolutionary workers' organizations of its own—is incapable of playing any sort of influential role. . . .

In spite of the catastrophic contraction of industry, the material position of the workers who are working is, although significantly below the subsistence minimum, nevertheless steadily improving. Partly freed from the quest for a piece of bread, the workers are again showing class energy; among the progressive workers a protest is again growing, though still voiceless and confused, against the prospective capitalistic system. The revolutionary element is still small in numbers; its ideology is weakly formed; Communist fetishes are still strong; but the growth of class activity among the progressive nonparty workers and class-minded elements within the Russian Communist Party creates the necessary prerequisite for the creation of a party of the Russian proletariat. . . .

The central "Workers' Truth" group addresses itself to all revolutionary workers and active class-minded elements who have joined the proletariat's struggle, with a burning proletarian appeal to wake up from the class inactivity and confusion produced by Communist illusions, and to begin vigorous work to organize the revolutionary elements and to explain to the working masses the actual threatening state of affairs.

Once a progressive proletarian unit, the Russian Working Class has now been thrown almost a decade back.

Our work will be long and persistent, and first of all ideological. Everywhere in the mills and factories, in the trade-union organizations, the workers' faculties, the Soviet and party schools, the Communist Union of Youth, and the party organizations, propaganda circles must be created in solidarity with the "Workers' Truth."

Organize propaganda circles and do not forget the basic conditions for the development of *Revolutionary* organizations in countries where capital is on the offensive—the careful selection of comrades and strict conspiratorial secrecy.

For our work, Comrades!

Lenin's "Testament"

Lenin began to suffer strokes in May, 1922, and relinquished active leadership of the Soviet state. His lieutenants, particularly Zinoviev, Kamenev and Stalin, banded together to prevent Trotsky from assuming power. Stalin had meanwhile been appointed to the new post of General Secretary of the Communist Party in April, 1922, and was working to get effective control over the party into his own hands. Toward the end of 1922 Lenin recovered sufficiently to make certain acute observations on the Soviet political scene. His comments on the successor leadership were embodied in notes which became known abroad in 1926 as his "testament," and which were finally published in the USSR after Khrushchev's attack on Stalin's record in 1956.

By the stability of the Central Committee of which I spoke before, I mean measures to prevent a split, so far as such measures can be taken. For, of course, the White Guard in *Russkaya Mysl** (I think it was S. E. Oldenburg) was right when, in the first place, in his play against Soviet Russia he banked on the hope of a split in our party, and when, in the second place, he banked for that split on serious disagreements in our party.

Our party rests upon two classes, and for that reason its instability is possible, and if there cannot exist agreement between those classes its fall is inevitable. In such an event it would be useless to take any measures or in general to discuss the stability of our Central Committee. In such an event no measures would prove capable of preventing a split. But I trust that is too remote a future, and too improbable an event, to talk about.

FROM: Lenin, Continuation of Notes, December 24, 1922 (in Lenin, *Letter to the Congress,* Moscow, State Press for Political Literature, 1956; English translation by Max Eastman, *The New York Times,* November 19, 1926).

* "Russian Thought": an emigré journal—Ed.

I have in mind stability as a guarantee against a split in the near future, and I intend to examine here a series of considerations of a purely personal character.

I think that the fundamental factor in the matter of stability—from this point of view—is such members of the Central Committee as Stalin and Trotsky. The relation between them constitutes, in my opinion, a big half of the danger of that split, which might be avoided, and the avoidance of which might be promoted, in my opinion, by raising the number of members of the Central Committee to fifty or one hundred.

Comrade Stalin, having become General Secretary, has concentrated an enormous power in his hand; and I am not sure that he always knows how to use that power with sufficient caution. On the other hand Comrade Trotsky, as was proved by his struggle against the Central Committee in connection with the question of the People's Commissariat of Ways of Communication,* is distinguished not only by his exceptional abilities—personally he is, to be sure, the most able man in the present Central Committee—but also by his too far-reaching self-confidence and a disposition to be too much attracted by the purely administrative side of affairs.

These two qualities of the two most able leaders of the present Central Committee might, quite innocently, lead to a split; if our party does not take measures to prevent it, a split might arise unexpectedly.

I will not further characterize the other members of the Central Committee as to their personal qualities. I will only remind you that the October episode of Zinoviev and Kamenev was not, of course, accidental, but that it ought as little to be used against them personally as the non-bolshevism of Trotsky.

Of the younger members of the Central Committee I want to say a few words about Bukharin and Piatakov. They are, in my opinion, the most able forces (among the youngest), and in regard to them it is necessary to bear in mind the

* Lenin is referring to a controversy of 1920, when Trotsky tried to shake up the administration of transport in a particularly high-handed manner—Ed.

following: Bukharin is not only the most valuable and biggest theoretician of the party, but also may legitimately be considered the favorite of the whole party, but his theoretical views can only with the very greatest doubt be regarded as fully Marxist, for there is something scholastic in him (he never has learned, and I think never has fully understood, the dialectic).

And then Piatakov—a man undoubtedly distinguished in will and ability, but too much given over to administration and the administrative side of things to be relied on in a serious political question.*

Of course, both these remarks are made by me merely with a view in the present time, in the assumption that these two able and loyal workers may not find an occasion to supplement their knowledge and correct their one-sidedness.

Postscript, January 4, 1923:

Stalin is too rude, and this fault, entirely supportable in relations among us Communists, becomes insupportable in the office of General Secretary. Therefore, I propose to the comrades to find a way to remove Stalin from that position and appoint to it another man who in all respects differs from Stalin only in superiority—namely, more patient, more loyal, more polite and more attentive to comrades, less capriciousness, etc. This circumstance may seem an insignificant trifle, but I think that from the point of view of preventing a split and from the point of view of the relation between Stalin and Trotsky which I discussed above, it is not a trifle, or it is such a trifle as may acquire a decisive significance.

Lenin

Lenin on Nationality Policy

The issue which had most to do with turning Lenin against Stalin was the nationality question, particularly as it arose in the Soviet Republic of Georgia. Lenin was extremely cautious about observing the forms of national autonomy; he

* Piatakov sided with Trotsky in the controversies of the twenties, and was tried and shot in 1937—Ed.

reacted against Stalin's excessively centralist handling of the plan for a Union of Soviet Socialist Republics, as the "Great-Russian chauvinism" of the "Russified non-Russian."

. . . We call our own an apparatus which is still completely alien to us and represents a bourgeois and czarist jumble. To overcome this in five years, in the absence of the help of other countries and with the prevalence of military "take-overs" and the struggle with hunger, was in no way possible.

Under such conditions it is quite natural that "the freedom to secede from the Union," by which we justify ourselves, should prove to be an empty scrap of paper, incapable of defending the other nationalities of Russia from the aggression of that truly Russian man, the Great-Russian chauvinist, in reality a scoundrel and man of violence, which the typical Russian bureaucrat reveals himself to be. There is no doubt that an insignificant percentage of Soviet and Sovietized workers will sink in this sea of chauvinistic Great-Russian filth, like flies in milk.

They say in defense of this measure [the formation of the Union] that they have divided up the People's Commissariats which touch immediately on national psychology, national education. But here appears a question: is it possible to divide up these commissariats completely? and a second question: have we taken measures with sufficient care really to defend the other nationalities from the truly Russian Derzhimorda?* I think we have not taken these measures, although they can and must be taken.

I think that here Stalin's haste and administrative enthusiasm have played a fatal role, and also his anger against the notorious "social-nationalism." Anger in general plays the very worst role in politics.

I fear also that Comrade Dzerzhinsky, who went to the

FROM: Lenin, "On the Question of the Nationalities or of 'Autonomization'" (December 30-31, 1922; in Lenin, *Letter to the Congress*, pp. 22-25, 27-28; editor's translation).

* "Derzhimorda": a policeman in Gogol's play, *The Inspector General*—Ed.

Caucasus to investigate the matter of the "crimes" of these "social-nationalists," was also distinguished here only by his truly Russian tendency (it is known, that the russified non-Russian always overdoes things in the truly Russian direction), and that the impartiality of his whole commission is sufficiently illustrated by Ordzhonikidze's resort to force, and that Comrade Dzerzhinsky is unforgivably guilty for approaching this resort to force light-mindedly. . . .

. . . Internationalism on the part of the oppressor or so-called "great" nation (although great only in its violence, great only as the great Derzhimorda) must consist not only in the observance of the formal equality of nations, but also in the inequality which offsets on the part of the oppressor nation, the large nation, that inequality which actually is built up in life. Whoever has not understood this has really not understood the proletarian attitude toward the national question; essentially he retains the petty-bourgeois point of view and therefore cannot but slide continually toward the bourgeois point of view.

What is important for the proletariat? For the proletariat it is not only important, but essentially necessary, to guarantee the maximum confidence in the proletarian class struggle on the part of the other nationalities. What is necessary for this? For this we need not only formal equality. For this it is necessary to compensate, in one way or another by our treatment or concessions in regard to the non-Russian, for that distrust, that suspiciousness, those wrongs, which in the historical past were inflicted upon him by the ruling "great-power" nation.

I think that for the Bolsheviks, for the Communists, it is not necessary to explain this further and in detail. I think that in the present case regarding the Georgian nation we have a typical example of what extreme care, foresight and conciliation are required on our part for a truly proletarian approach to the matter. . . .

We should, of course, make Stalin and Dzerzhinsky politically responsible for this whole truly Great-Russian nationalist campaign. . . .

The harm for our state which can rise from the absence of

national commissariats united with the Russian apparatus is immeasurably less, infinitely less, than the harm which can develop not only for us but for the whole International, for the hundreds of millions of the peoples of Asia, who are ready to make their appearance on the historical stage in the very near future, following us. It would be unforgiveable opportunism if, on the eve of this appearance of the East and at the beginning of its awakening, we undermined our prestige among the peoples of the East by even the slightest rudeness and injustice in regard to our own minorities. The necessity for solidarity of the forces against the imperialists of the West, who defend the capitalist world, is one thing. Here there can be no doubt, and it is superfluous for me to say that I approve of these measures unconditionally. It is another matter when we ourselves fall, even on a small scale, into an imperialistic relationship toward the oppressed nationalities. But tomorrow, in world history, will be the very day when the aroused peoples, oppressed by imperialism, will finally awake, and when the long, severe, decisive battle for their liberation will begin.

Lenin on the Prerequisites for Socialism

Lenin was prepared to admit, as he did in commenting on the memoirs of the Menshevik Sukhanov, that Russia lacked the conditions for socialism, but he saw no reason why the Communist government could not proceed to create them. Here again he revealed his real philosophy, hardly compatible with Marxism, that political power determined all else.

. . . "Russia has not attained the level of development of productive forces that makes Socialism possible." Of this proposition, all the heroes of the Second International, including, of course, Sukhanov, are as proud as a peacock. They keep repeating this incontrovertible proposition over

FROM: Lenin, "Our Revolution: Apropos of the Notes of N. Sukhanov" (January, 1923; *Selected Works,* Vol. II, book 2, pp. 726-27).

and over again in a thousand different keys, and imagine that it is the decisive criterion of our revolution.

But what if peculiar circumstances drew Russia, first, into the world imperialist war in which every more or less influential West-European country was involved, and brought her development to the verge of the revolutions that were maturing and had partly already begun in the East, in conditions which enabled us to achieve precisely that union of a "peasant war" with the working-class movement which no less a "Marxist" than Marx himself had in 1856 suggested as a possible prospect for Prussia?

What if the complete hopelessness of the situation, by stimulating the efforts of the workers and peasants tenfold, offered us the possibility of creating the fundamental requisites of civilization in a different way from that of the West-European countries? Has that altered the general line of development of world history? Has that altered the basic relations between the basic classes of all the countries that are, or have been, drawn into the general course of world history?

If a definite level of culture is required for the building of Socialism (although nobody can say just what that definite "level of culture" is, for it differs in every West-European country), why cannot we begin by first achieving the prerequisites for that definite level of culture in a revolutionary way, and *then,* with the aid of the workers' and peasants' government and the Soviet system, proceed to overtake the other nations?

You say that civilization is necessary for the building of Socialism. Very good. But why could we not first create such prerequisites of civilization in our country as the expulsion of the landlords and the Russian capitalists, and then start moving towards Socialism? Where, in what books, have you read that such variations of the customary historical order of events are impermissible or impossible?

Napoleon, one recalls, wrote: *On s'engage et puis—on voit.* Rendered freely this means: One must first join a serious battle and then see what happens. Well, we did first join serious battle in October 1917, and then we saw such details of development (from the standpoint of world history they were certainly details) as the Brest-Litovsk Peace, the New Economic Policy, and so forth. And now there can be no doubt that in the main we have been victorious. . . .

Lenin on Administrative Reform

In his last articles, early in 1923, Lenin turned his attention to the quality of the Soviet governmental administration, which he found sorely lacking. He proposed various schemes of reform to meet the expectations of the nation and enable the Soviet regime to hold power firmly until the next international revolutionary upsurge. The latter, significantly, Lenin now expected to come from the nations of Asia.

. . . The situation as regards our machinery of state is so deplorable, not to say disgusting, that we must first of all think very carefully how to eliminate its defects, bearing in mind that the roots of these defects lie in the past, which, although it has been overturned, has not yet been overcome, does not yet belong to the culture of the dim and distant past. I say culture deliberately, because in these matters we can regard as achievements only what have become part and parcel of our culture, of our social life, our habits. We can say that what is good in the social system of our country has not been properly studied, understood, felt; it has been hastily grasped at; it has not been tested, tried by experience, made durable, etc. Of course, it could not be otherwise in a revolutionary epoch, when development proceeded at such breakneck speed that we passed from tsarism to the Soviet system in a matter of five years.

We must come to our senses in time. We must be extremely sceptical of too rapid progress, of boastfulness, etc. We must think of testing the steps forward which we proclaim to the world every hour, which we take every minute, and which later on we find, every second, to be flimsy,

FROM: Lenin, "Better Fewer, But Better" (March, 1923; *Selected Works*, Vol. II, book 2, pp. 735-39, 746, 748-51).

superficial and not understood. The most harmful thing here would be haste. The most harmful thing would be to rest on the assumption that we know anything, or on the assumption that we possess to any degree the elements necessary for building a really new state machine that would really deserve to be called socialist, Soviet, etc.

No, the machine of this kind, and even the elements of it that we do possess, are ridiculously small; we must remember that we must not stint time on building this machine, and that it will take many, many years to build.

What elements have we for building this machine? Only two. First, the workers who are absorbed in the struggle for Socialism. These elements are not sufficiently educated. They would like to build a better machine for us, but they do not know how. They cannot build one. They have not yet developed the culture which is required for this; and it is precisely culture that is required. Here nothing will be achieved by doing things in a rush, by assault, by being smart or vigorous, or by any other of the best human qualities in general. Secondly, we have the element of knowledge, education and training, but to a ridiculously low degree compared with all other countries.

Here, too, we must not forget that we are too prone to compensate (or imagine that we can compensate) our lack of knowledge by zeal, haste, etc. . . .

. . . Let us say frankly that the People's Commissariat for Workers' and Peasants' Inspection does not enjoy the slightest prestige at present. Everybody knows that a more badly organized institution than our Workers' and Peasants' Inspection does not exist, and that under present conditions nothing can be expected from this People's Commissariat. We must have this firmly fixed in our minds if we really want to set out to create within a few years an institution that will, firstly, be an exemplary institution, secondly, win everybody's absolute confidence, and, thirdly, prove to all and sundry that we have really justified the work of such a high institution as the Central Control Commission. In my opinion, we must utterly and irrevocably reject all general numerical standards for office staffs. We must make a particularly careful selection of the employees of the Workers' and Peasants' Inspection and put them to the strictest test. Indeed, what is the use of establishing a People's Commissariat which carries on anyhow, which does not enjoy the slightest confidence, and whose word carries scarcely any weight? I think that our main object in launching the work of reconstruction we now have in mind is to change all this. . . .

In all spheres of social, economic and political relationships we are "frightfully" revolutionary. But as regards precedence, the observation of the forms and rites of office routine, our "revolutionariness" often gives way to the mustiest routine. Here, on more than one occasion, we have witnessed the very interesting phenomenon of a great leap forward in social life being accompanied by amazing timidity whenever the slightest changes are proposed.

This is natural, for the boldest steps forward were taken in a field which has long been reserved for theoretical study, which has been cultivated mainly, and even almost exclusively, theoretically. The Russian found solace from the bleak bureaucratic realities at home in unusually bold theoretical constructions, and that is why in our country these unusually bold theoretical constructions assumed an unusually lopsided character. Theoretical audacity in general constructions went hand in hand with amazing timidity as regards certain very minor reforms in office routine. A great universal agrarian revolution was worked out with an audacity unexampled in any other country, and at the same time, the imagination was lacking to work out a tenth-rate reform in office routine; the imagination, or patience, was lacking to apply to this reform the general propositions that produced such "brilliant" results when applied to general problems. . . .

. . . At the present time we are confronted with the question: Shall we be able to hold on with our small and very small peasant production, and in our present state of ruin, while the West-European capitalist countries are consummating their development towards Socialism? But they are consummating it not as we formerly expected. They are not consummating it by the gradual "maturing" of Socialism, but by the exploitation of some countries by others, by the exploitation of the first of the countries to be vanquished in the imperialist war combined with the exploitation of the whole of the East. On the other hand, precisely as a result of the first imperialist war, the East has been definitely drawn into the revolutionary movement, has been definitely drawn into the general maelstrom of the world revolutionary movement.

What tactics does this situation prescribe for our country? Obviously the following: We must display extreme caution so as to preserve our workers' government and enable it to retain its leadership and authority over our small and very small peasantry. We have the advantage in that the whole world is now passing into a movement that must give rise to a world socialist revolution. . . .

. . . The outcome of the struggle as a whole can be foreseen only because we know that in the long run capitalism itself is educating and training the vast majority of the population of the globe for the struggle.

In the last analysis, the outcome of the struggle will be determined by the fact that Russia, India, China, etc., account for the overwhelming majority of the population of the globe. And it is precisely this majority that, during the past few years, has been drawn into the struggle for emancipation with extraordinary rapidity, so that in this respect there cannot be the slightest shadow of doubt what the final outcome of the world struggle will be. In this sense, the complete victory of Socialism is fully and absolutely assured.

But what interests us is not the inevitability of this complete victory of Socialism, but the tactics which we, the Russian Communist Party, we, the Russian Soviet government, should pursue to prevent the West-European counterrevolutionary states from crushing us. To ensure our existence until the next military conflict between the counterrevolutionary imperialist West and the revolutionary and nationalist East, between the most civilized countries of the world and the Orientally backward countries, which, however, account for the majority, this majority must become civilized. We, too, lack sufficient civilization to enable us to pass straight on to Socialism, although we have the political requisites for this. We must adopt the following tactics, or pursue the following policy to save ourselves.

We must strive to build up a state in which the workers retain their leadership in relation to the peasants, in which they retain the confidence of the peasants, and, by exercising the greatest economy, remove every trace of extravagance from our social relations.

We must reduce our state apparatus to the utmost degree of economy. We must remove from it all traces of extravagance, of which so much has been left over from tsarist Russia, from its bureaucratic capitalist apparatus.

Will not this be the reign of peasant narrowness?

No. If we see to it that the working class retains its leadership of the peasantry, we shall be able, by exercising the greatest possible economy in the economic life of our state, to use every kopek we save to develop our large-scale machine industry, to develop electrification, the hydraulic extraction of peat, to finish the construction of Volkhovstroi, etc.

In this, and this alone, lies our hope. Only when we have done this will we, speaking figuratively, be able to change horses, to change from the peasant, muzhik horse of poverty, from the horse of economy fit for a ruined peasant country, to the horse which the proletariat is seeking and cannot but seek—the horse of large-scale machine industry, or electrification, of Volkhovstroi, etc.

That is how I link up in my mind the general plan of our work, of our policy, of our tactics, of our strategy, with the functions of the reorganized Workers' and Peasants' Inspection. . . .

Trotsky on Industrialization

In the early years of the NEP Trotsky devoted himself to problems of economic planning, and urged systematic efforts by the Soviet government to build and improve industry on the basis of a clear hierarchy of authority, ostensibly as the foundation for the "proletarian" dictatorship.

The interrelationship which we have between the working class and the peasantry rests in the last analysis on the interrelationship between industry and agriculture. In the last analysis the working class can maintain and strengthen its guiding position not through the apparatus of government, not through the army, but through industry, which reproduces the proletariat itself. The party, the trade unions, the youth league, our schools, etc., have their tasks of educating and preparing new generations of the working class. But all this work would prove to be built on sand if it did not have a growing industrial base under it. Only the development of industry creates an unshakable foundation for the proletarian dictatorship. . . .

. . . The preparation of our budget, the state's credit policy, the system of measures for the military security of the state, all state activity in general, must give primary concern to the planned development of state industry.

The regeneration of state industry, in the general economic structure of our country, will necessarily be closely dependent on the development of agriculture; the necessary means of exchange must be formed in agriculture, by way of the excess of the agricultural product over the consumption of the village, before industry can take a decisive step forward. But it is just as important for state industry not to lag behind agriculture; otherwise, on the foundation of the latter private industry would be created, which, in the last analysis, would swallow up state industry or suck it dry.

Only such industry can be victorious which gives more than it swallows up. Industry which lives off the budget, i.e., off agriculture,* could not create a firm and lasting support for the proletarian dictatorship. The question of

FROM: Trotsky, "Theses on Industry," March 6, 1923 (editor's translation from copy in the Trotsky Archive, Houghton Library, Harvard University).

* *I.e.,* financed by taxing the peasants—Ed.

creating surplus value within state industry is the question of the fate of the Soviet power, that is, the fate of the proletariat.

The expanded reproduction of state industry, which is unthinkable without the accumulation of surplus value by the state, is in turn the condition for the development of our agriculture in the socialistic rather than the capitalistic direction.

Thus, through state industry lies the road to the socialist social order. . . .

The interrelationship between light and heavy industry cannot be decided through the market alone, for this would actually threaten heavy industry with destruction in the next few years, with the prospect of its restoration afterward on the basis of private property, as a result of the spontaneous work of the market.

Thus, in contrast to capitalist countries, the area of the planning principle is not limited here to the framework of individual trusts or syndicates, but extends to all industry as a whole. Not only that: the state must embrace the interrelationship of industry on the one hand and of agriculture, finance, transport, domestic and foreign trade, on the other.

In other words: Insofar as the state is not only the proprietor but also an economic subject in relation to the majority of productive forces of industry and transport, and in relation to the means of credit, to that extent the planning principle under the NEP is not much different in content from the planning principle in the period of War Communism. But it is most radically different in methods. Arbitrary administration by bureaucratic agencies is replaced by economic maneuvering.

In their administrative application, methods of planning must be extended with extraordinary caution, by way of carefully feeling out the ground. . . .

It is quite obvious that the basic planning of industry cannot be accomplished within industry itself, i.e., by the efforts of its leading administrative organ (the Supreme Economic Council) alone, but must become the task of a special planning organ, standing over the organization of industry and linking the latter with finance, transport, etc. The State Planning Commission, by virtue of its position, appears to be such an organ. However, it is necessary to give the State Planning Commission a more definite position, a firmer organization, clearer and more undisputed rights and (especially) obligations. . . .

The system of actual one-man management must be applied in the organization of industry from top to bottom. For the leading economic organs really to direct industry and to be able to bear responsibility for its fate, it is essential for them to have authority over the selection of functionaries and their transfer and removal. Recommendations and attestations by the trade-union organs must be considered with full attention, but this can in no case remove responsibility from the corresponding economic organs, which in actual practice have full freedom of selection and appointment.

The weak side of state industry and trade is their ponderousness, immobility, lack of enterprise. The cause of this, above all, is still the inadequate selection of business executives, in their lack of experience, in their lack of incentives to succeed in their own work. We need correct systematic measures in all these directions. In particular, the payment of the directors of enterprises must be made to depend on their balance sheets, like wages depend on output. . . .

Formation of the Trotskyist Opposition

In the fall of 1923, after a variety of issues and personal frictions had accumulated, Trotsky launched a behind-the-scenes attack on his colleagues in the party leadership, with particular stress on the abuses being committed by Stalin's Secretariat. This was followed by a collective statement, signed by various former oppositionists, which took the leadership severely to task for their failures in economic policy as well as their violation of party democracy.

a) Trotsky Protests Bureaucratization

One of the proposals of Comrade Dzerzhinsky's commission declares that we must make it obligatory for party members knowing about groupings in the party to communicate the fact to the GPU, the Central Committee and the Central Control Commission. It would seem that to inform the party organizations of the fact that its branches are being used by elements hostile to the party, is an obligation of party members so elementary that it ought not to be necessary to introduce a special resolution to that effect six years after the October Revolution. The very demand for such a resolution is an extremely startling symptom alongside of others no less clear. . . . The demand for such a resolution means: a) that illegal oppositional groups have been formed in the party, which may become dangerous to the revolution; b) that there exist such states of mind in the party as to permit comrades knowing about such groups not to inform the party organizations. Both these facts testify to an extraordinary deterioration of the situation within the party from the time of the Twelfth Congress [April, 1923]. . . .

In the fiercest moment of War Communism, the system of appointment within the party did not have one-tenth of the extent that it has now. Appointment of the secretaries of provincial committees is now the rule. That creates for the secretary a position essentially independent of the local organization. . . .

The Twelfth Congress of the party was conducted under the sign of democracy. Many of the speeches at that time spoken in defense of workers' democracy seemed to me exaggerated, and to a considerable extent demagoguish, in view of the incompatibility of a fully developed workers' democracy with the regime of dictatorship. But it was perfectly clear that the pressure of the period of War Communism ought to give place to a more lively and broader party responsibility. However, this present regime, which began to form itself before the Twelfth Congress, and which subsequently received its final reinforcement and formulation—is much farther from workers' democracy than the regime of the

FROM: Trotsky, Letter to the Central Committee and the Central Control Commission, October 8, 1923 (Excerpts [translated by Max Shachtman] in Trotsky, *The New Course*, New York, New International, 1943, pp. 153-56).

fiercest period of War Communism. The bureaucratization of the party apparatus has developed to unheard-of proportions by means of the method of secretarial selection. There has been created a very broad stratum of party workers, entering into the apparatus of the government of the party, who completely renounce their own party opinion, at least the open expression of it, as though assuming that the secretarial hierarchy is the apparatus which creates party opinion and party decisions. Beneath this stratum, abstaining from their own opinions, there lies the broad mass of the party, before whom every decision stands in the form of a summons or a command. In this foundation-mass of the party there is an unusual amount of dissatisfaction. . . . This dissatisfaction does not dissipate itself by way of influence of the mass upon the party organization (election of party committees, secretaries, etc.), but accumulates in secret and thus leads to interior strains. . . .

It is known to the members of the Central Committee and the Central Control Commission that while fighting with all decisiveness and definiteness within the Central Committee against a false policy, I decisively declined to bring the struggle within the Central Committee to the judgment even of a very narrow circle of comrades, in particular those who in the event of a reasonably proper party course ought to occupy prominent places in the Central Committee. I must state that my efforts of a year and a half have given no results. This threatens us with the danger that the party may be taken unawares by a crisis of exceptional severity. . . . In view of the situation created, I consider it not only my right, but my duty to make known the true state of affairs to every member of the party whom I consider sufficiently prepared, matured and self-restrained, and consequently able to help the party out of this blind alley without factional convulsions. . . .

b) Declaration of the Forty-Six

To the Politbureau of the Central Committee of the Russian Communist Party—Secret:

The extreme seriousness of the situation compels us (in the interests of our party, in the interests of the working class) to tell you openly that the continuation of the policy of the majority of the Politbureau threatens serious harm for the whole party. The economic and financial crisis which began at the end of July of this year, together with all the political (including intra-party) consequences which have stemmed from it, has unmercifully uncovered the unsatisfactoriness of the party leadership, in the area of the economy and especially in the area of intra-party relations.

The casualness, thoughtlessness, lack of system in the decisions of the Central Committee, not making ends meet in the area of the economy, has led to this, that with undoubted large successes in the area of industry, agriculture, finance and transport, successes achieved by the country's economy essentially not thanks to, but in spite of the unsatisfactory leadership, or rather, in the absence of any leadership—we face the prospect not only of the cessation of this success, but of a serious general economic crisis. . . .

If broad, considered, planned and energetic measures are not taken quickly, if the present absence of direction continues, we will face the possibility of an unusually sharp economic shock, unavoidably linked with internal political complications and with complete paralysis of our external activity and strength. And the latter, as anyone understands, we need now more than ever; on it depends the fate of the world revolution and of the working class of all countries.

Similarly, in the area of intraparty relations, we see the incorrectness of direction, paralyzing and disrupting the party, which has appeared with special clarity during the recent crisis.

We explain this not by the political incompetence of the present directors of the party; on the contrary, however we may differ with them in evaluating the situation and in the choice of measures to change it—we consider that the present leadership under any conditions cannot but be kept by the party in the leading posts of the workers' dictatorship. But

FROM: The Declaration of the Forty-Six, October 15, 1923 (editor's translation from copy in the Trotsky Archive).

we explain the crisis thus: that under the external form of official unity we actually have a selection of people and a guiding of action which are one-sided and adapted to the views and sympathies of a narrow circle. As a result of the party leadership being distorted by such narrow considerations, the party is to a significant degree ceasing to be the living, self-acting collective, which really embraces living activity, being linked by thousands of threads with this activity. Instead of this we observe a more and more progressive division of the party, no longer concealed by hardly anyone, into the secretarial hierarchy and the "laymen," into the professional party functionaries, selected from above, and the simple party masses, who do not participate in its group life.

This is a fact which every member of the party knows. Members of the party who are dissatisfied by this or that decision of the Central Committee or even of a provincial committee, who have in mind certain doubts, who have noticed "by themselves" certain mistakes, confusions and disorders, are afraid to speak of these at party meetings; further, they are afraid to converse with each other, unless their conversants appear to be completely reliable men in the sense of keeping quiet. Free discussion within the party has in fact disappeared; the party's social mind has been choked off. In these times the broad masses of the party do not nominate and elect the provincial committees and the Central Committee of the RCP. On the contrary, the secretarial hierarchy of the party to an ever greater degree selects the membership of conferences and congresses, which to an ever greater degree are becoming executive consultations of this hierarchy.

The regime which has been set up within the party is absolutely intolerable; it kills initiative in the party, subjects the party to an apparatus of appointed officials, which undeniably functions in normal times, but which unavoidably misfires in moments of crisis, and which threatens to reveal itself as completely bankrupt in the face of the serious events which are approaching.

The existing situation is explained thus, that the regime of factional dictatorship within the party, which was objectively set up after the Tenth Congress, has outlived its usefulness. Many of us consciously undertook not to resist such a regime. The turn of events of 1921, and later the illness of comrade Lenin demanded, in the opinion of many of us, temporary measures in the nature of a dictatorship within the party. Other comrades from the very beginning reacted to this skeptically or negatively. However that may be, at the Twelfth Congress of the party this regime overdid itself. It began to show its reverse side. Intraparty bonds began to weaken. The party began to sink. Extreme oppositionist tendencies within the party, which were already clearly unhealthy, began to acquire an antiparty character, for there was no intraparty, comradely discussion of painful questions. And such a discussion would with no trouble have revealed the unhealthy character of these tendencies, to the majority of their participants as well as to the party masses. As a result—illegal groupings which are leading members of the party beyond the last limits, and the cutting of the party off from the working masses.

The economic crisis in Soviet Russia and the crisis of the factional dictatorship within the party will, if the existing situation is not radically changed in the very near future, inflict grave blows upon the worker's dictatorship in Russia and the Russian Communist Party. With such a burden on its shoulders, the dictatorship of the proletariat in Russia, and its executive, the RCP, cannot enter the zone of impending new world stresses without the prospect of failure on all fronts of the proletarian struggle. . . .

The impending test demands the single-minded, brotherly, completely conscious, exceptionally active, exceptionally firm action of all members of our party. The factional regime must be eliminated, and this must be done in the first instance with its perpetrators; it must be replaced by a regime of comradely unity and intraparty democracy. . . .

The "New Course" Controversy of December, 1923

The first and most decisive public debate between the Trotskyists and the adherents of the party leadership took place in December, 1923, after some months of behind-the-scenes maneuver. The Politbureau had passed a resolution—largely drafted by Trotsky—promising broad reform in the direction of democracy within the party, and Trotsky then published an open letter warning that the party bureaucracy would try to sabotage the reform. This was the signal for a month-long press and agitational campaign against Trotsky's "factionalism."

The resolution of the Political Bureau on the party organization bears an exceptional significance. It indicates that the party has arrived at an important turning point in its historical road. At turning points, as has been rightly pointed out at many meetings, prudence is required; but firmness and resoluteness are required too. Hesitancy, amorphousness would be the worst forms of imprudence in this case.

Inclined to overestimate the role of the apparatus and to underestimate the initiative of the party, some conservative-minded comrades criticize the resolution of the Political Bureau. The Central Committee, they say, is assuming impossible obligations; the resolution will only engender illusions and produce negative results. It is clear that such an approach reveals a profound bureaucratic distrust of the party. The center of gravity which was mistakenly placed in the apparatus by the old course, has now been transferred by the new course, proclaimed in the resolution of the Central Committee, to the activity, the initiative and the critical spirit of all the party members, as the organized vanguard of the proletariat. The new course does not at all signify that the party apparatus is charged with decreeing, creating, or establishing a democratic regime at such and such a date. No. This regime will be realized by the party itself. To put it briefly: *the party must subordinate to itself its own apparatus* without for a moment ceasing to be a centralized organization.

In the debates and articles of recent times, it has been underlined that "pure," "complete," "ideal" democracy is

FROM: Trotsky, "The New Course" (Open letter to a party meeting, December 8, 1923; English translation by Max Shachtman in Trotsky, *The New Course*, pp. 89-95).

not realizable and that in general for us it is not an end in itself. That is incontestable. But it can be stated with just as much reason that pure, absolute centralism is unrealizable and incompatible with the nature of a mass party, and that it can no more be an end in itself than can the party apparatus. Democracy and centralism are two faces of party organization. The question is to harmonize them in the most correct manner, that is, the manner best corresponding to the situation. During the last period there was no such equilibrium. The center of gravity wrongly centered in the apparatus. The initiative of the party was reduced to the minimum. Thence, the habits and the procedures of leadership, fundamentally contradicting the spirit of revolutionary proletarian organization. The excessive centralization of the apparatus at the expense of initiative engendered a feeling of *uneasiness,* an uneasiness which, at the extremities of the party, assumed an exceedingly morbid form and was translated, among other things, in the appearance of illegal groupings directed by elements indubitably hostile to communism. At the same time, the whole of the party disapproved more and more of apparatus-methods of solving questions. The idea, or at the very least the feeling, that bureaucratism threatened to get the party into a blind alley, had become pretty general. Voices were raised to point out the danger. The resolution on the new course is the first official expression of the change that has taken place in the party. It will be realized to the degree that the party, that is, its four hundred thousand members, will want to realize it and will succeed in doing so. . . .

Bureaucratism kills initiative and thus prevents the elevation of the general level of the party. That is its cardinal defect. As the apparatus is made up inevitably of the most experienced and most meritorious comrades, it is upon the political training of the young Communist generations that bureaucratism has its most grievous repercussions. Also, it is the youth, the most reliable barometer of the party, that reacts most vigorously against party bureaucratism. . . .

. . . We, the "elders," we ought to say to ourselves plainly that our generation, which naturally enjoys the leading role in the party, is not *absolutely* guaranteed against the gradual and imperceptible weakening of the revolutionary and proletarian spirit in its ranks if the party were to tolerate the further growth and stabilization of bureaucratic methods which transform the youth into the passive material of education and inevitably create an estrangement between the apparatus and the mass, the old and the young. The party has no other means to employ against this indubitable danger than a serious, profound, radical change of course toward party democracy and the increasingly large flow into its midst of working-class elements. . . .

Before the publication of the decision of the Central Committee on the "new course," the mere pointing out of the need of modifying the internal party regime was regarded by bureaucratic apparatus functionaries as heresy, as factionalism, as an infraction of discipline. And now the bureaucrats are ready formally to "take note" of the "new course," that is, to *nullify it bureaucratically*. The renovation of the party apparatus— naturally within the clear-cut framework of the statutes—must aim at replacing the mummified bureaucrats with fresh elements closely linked with the life of the collectivity, or capable of assuring such a link. And before anything else, the leading posts must be cleared out of those who, at the first word of criticism, of objection, or of protest, brandish the thunderbolts of penalties before the critic. The "new course" must begin by making everyone feel that from now on nobody will dare terrorize the party.

It is entirely insufficient for our youth to repeat our formulae. It must conquer the revolutionary formulae, it must assimilate them, work out its own opinions, its own physiognomy; it must be capable of fighting for its views with the courage which arises out of the depths of conviction and independence of character. Out of the party with passive obedience, with mechanical levelling by the authorities, with suppression of personality, with servility, with careerism! A Bolshevik is not merely a disciplined man; he is a man who in each case and on each question forges a firm opinion of his own and defends it courageously and independently, not only against his enemies, but inside his own party. Today, perhaps, he will be in the minority in his organization. He will submit, because it is his party. But this does not always signify that he is in the wrong. Perhaps he saw or understood before the others did a new task or the necessity of a turn. He will persistently raise the question a second, a third, a tenth time, if need be. Thereby he will render his party a service, helping it meet the new task fully armed or carry out the necessary turn without organic upheavals, without factional convulsions.

Yes, our party would be unable to discharge its historic mission if it were chopped up into factions. That should not and will not happen. It will not decompose in this way because, autonomous collectivity that it is, its organism resists it. But it will combat successfully the dangers of factionalism only by developing and consolidating the new course toward workers' democracy. *Bureaucratism of the apparatus is precisely one of the principal sources of factionalism.* It ruthlessly represses criticism and drives the discontentment back into the depths of the organiaztion. It tends to put the label of factionalism upon any criticism, any warning. Mechanical centralism is necessarily complemented by factionalism, which is at once a malicious caricature of democracy and a potential political danger. . . .

The Condemnation of the Trotskyist Opposition

By organizational pressure and some rigging of elections the party leadership scored an overwhelming success against the Opposition. At the Thirteenth Party Conference in January, 1924, this was registered in a resolution denouncing the Opposition's defiance of party authority as a Menshevik-like deviation. This was the end of the Trotsky movement as a serious organizational threat to the leadership, though top-level controversy continued.

. . . The opposition, headed by Trotsky, came forth with the slogan of smashing the party apparatus, and tried to shift

FROM: Resolution of the Thirteenth Conference of the Russian Communist Party, January, 1924, "On the Results of the Controversy and on the Petty-Bourgeois Deviation in the Party" (CPSU in Resolutions, I, 780-782; editor's translation).

the center of gravity of the struggle against bureaucratism in the governmental apparatus to "bureaucratism" in the apparatus of the party. Such wholesale criticism and attempts at directly discrediting the party apparatus cannot objectively lead to anything else than the emancipation of the governmental apparatus from influence upon it on the part of the party, to the divorce of the governmental organs from the party. . . .

Trotsky came out with vague insinuations about the degeneration of the basic cadres of our party and thereby tried to undermine the authority of the Central Committee, which between congresses is the only representative of the whole party. Trotsky not only tried to counterpose himself to all the rest of the Central Committee, but also permitted accusations which could not but evoke unrest in broad circles of the working class and a stormy protest in the ranks of our party. . . .

The opposition in all its shades has revealed a completely un-Bolshevik view on the significance of party discipline. The moves of a whole series of representatives of the opposition represent a crying violation of party discipline, and recall the times when Lenin had to struggle against the "anarchism of the intellectuals" in organizational questions and defend the foundations of proletarian discipline in the party.

The opposition clearly violated the decision of the Tenth Congress of the Russian Congress Party which prohibited the formation of factions within the party. The opposition has replaced the Bolshevik view of the party as a monolithic whole with the view of the party as the sum of all possible tendencies and factions. These tendencies, factions and groupings, according to the "new" view of the opposition, must have equal rights in the party, and the Central Committee of the party must not be so much the leader of the party as a simple registrar and intermediary between the tendencies and groupings. Such a view of the party has nothing in common with Leninism. The factional work of the opposition cannot but become a threat to the unity of the state apparatus. The factional moves of the opposition have enlivened the hopes of all enemies of the party, including the West-European bourgeoisie, for a split in the ranks of the Russian Communist Party. These factional moves again pose before the party in all its sharpness the question whether the Russian Communist Party, since it is in power, can allow the formation of factional groupings within the party.

Adding up the sum of these differences and analyzing the whole character of the moves by the representatives of the opposition, the All-Union Party Conference comes to the conclusion that in the person of the present opposition we have before us not only an attempt at the revision of Bolshevism, not only a direct departure from Leninism, but also a clearly expressed *petty-bourgeois deviation.* There is no doubt that this 'opposition' objectively reflects the pressure of the petty bourgeoisie on the position of the proletarian party and its policy. The principle of intraparty democracy is already beginning to be interpreted broadly beyond the limits of the party, in the sense of weakening the dictatorship of the proletariat and extending political rights to the new bourgeoisie.

In the situation where the Russian Communist Party, embodying the dictatorship of the proletariat, enjoys a monopoly of legality in the country, it is unavoidable that the least stable groups of Communists should sometimes give in to nonproletarian influences. The party as a whole must see these dangers and watchfully guard the proletarian line of the party.

A systematic and energetic struggle of our whole party against this petty-bourgeois deviation is essential. . .

The Formation of the USSR

The Union of Soviet Socialist Republics officially came into being in January, 1924, as a federal union of four states which had been nominally independent though controlled by the single Russian Communist Party: the Russian Republic, the Ukraine, White Russia, and the Transcaucasian Federation. The forms of national autonomy, complete with the right of secession, were carefully observed, but in point of fact language was the only real distinction among the Soviet nationalities, who remain to the present under the strictly centralized control of the Communist Party.

Constitution of the Union of Soviet Socialist Republics

PART I: Declaration

Since the foundation of the Soviet Republics, the States of the world have been divided into two camps; the camp of Capitalism and the camp of Socialism.

There, in the camp of Capitalism: national hate and inequality, colonial slavery and chauvinism, national oppression and massacres, brutalities and imperialistic wars.

Here, in the camp of Socialism: reciprocal confidence and peace, national liberty and equality, the pacific co-existence and fraternal collaboration of peoples.

The attempts made by the capitalistic world during the past ten years to decide the question of nationalities by bringing together the principle of the free development of peoples with a system of exploitation of man by man have been fruitless. In addition, the number of national conflicts becomes more and more confusing, even menacing the capitalistic regime. The bourgeoisie has proven itself incapable of realizing a harmonious collaboration of the peoples.

It is only in the camp of the Soviets; it is only under the conditions of the dictatorship of the proletariat that has grouped around itself the majority of the people, that it has been possible to eliminate the oppression of nationalities, to create an atmosphere of mutual confidence and to establish the basis of a fraternal collaboration of peoples. . . .

. . . National economic reestablishment is impossible as long as the Republics remain separated.

On the other hand, the instability of the international situation and the danger of new attacks make inevitable the creation of a united front of the Soviet Republics in the presence of capitalistic surroundings.

FROM: Constitution of the USSR, Ratified by the Second Congress of Soviets of the USSR, January 13, 1924 (English translation in Milton H. Andrew, *Twelve Leading Constitutions*, Compton, Cal., American University Series, 1931, pp. 327 ff.).

Finally, the very structure of Soviet power, international by nature of class, pushes the masses of workers of the Soviet Republics to unite in one socialist family.

All these considerations insistently demand the union of the Soviet Republics into one federated State capable of guaranteeing security against the exterior, economic prosperity internally, and the free national development of peoples.

The will of the peoples of the Soviet Republics recently assembled in Congress, where they decided unanimously to form the "Union of Socialist Soviet Republics," is a sure guarantee that this Union is a free federation of peoples equal in rights, that the right to freely withdraw from the Union is assured to each Republic, that access to the Union is open to all Republics already existing, as well as those that may be born in the future, that the new federal state will be the worthy crowning of the principles laid down as early as October 1917, of the pacific co-existence and fraternal collaboration of peoples, that it will serve as a bulwark against the capitalistic world and mark a new decisive step towards the union of workers of all countries in one World-Wide Socialist Soviet Republic.

PART II: Treaty

The Russian Socialist Federated Soviet Republic, the Socialist Soviet Republic of the Ukraine, the Socialist Soviet Republic of White Russia, and the Socialist Soviet Republic of Transcaucasia (including the Socialist Soviet Republic of Azerbaijan, the Socialist Soviet Republic of Georgia, and the Socialist Soviet Republic of Armenia) unite themselves in one federal State—"The Union of Soviet Socialist Republics." . . .

Chapter II: Sovereign Rights of the Member Republics

Article 3. The Sovereignty of the member Republics is limited only in the matters indicated in the present Constitution, as coming within the competence of the Union. Outside of those limits, each member Republic exerts its public powers independently; the Union of S.S.R. protects the rights of member Republics.

Article 4. Each one of the member Republics retains the right to freely withdraw from the union. . . .

Stalin on Leninism and the Party

Lenin died on January 21, 1924. He was succeeded as Chairman of the Council of Peoples' Commissars of the USSR by Alexei Rykov, but the real leadership of the Communist Party was temporarily shared by Stalin and Zinoviev. Stalin had the decisive advantage with his control of the party Secretariat, and in the spring of 1924 began to assert himself in the theoretical field with a series of lectures on "Leninism." Stalin proved to be Lenin's most adept pupil in both the theory and practice of the disciplined party organization.

. . . The Party is not only the *vanguard* detachment of the working class. If it desires really to direct the struggle of the class it must at the same time be the *organized* detachment of its class. The Party's tasks under the conditions of capitalism are immense and extremely varied. The Party must direct the struggle of the proletariat under the exceptionally difficult conditions of internal and external development; it must lead the proletariat in the offensive when the situation calls for an offensive; it must lead the proletariat in retreat when the situation calls for retreat in order to ward off the blows of a powerful enemy; it must imbue the millions of unorganized non-Party workers with the spirit of discipline and system in the struggle, with the spirit of organization and endurance. But the Party can fulfil these tasks only if it is itself the embodiment of discipline and organization, if it is itself the *organized* detachment of the proletariat. Without these conditions there can be no talk of the Party really leading the proletarian millions. . . .

. . . The Party is the organized detachment of the working class. But the Party is not the only organization of the working class. The proletariat has also a number of other

FROM: Stalin, "The Foundations of Leninism" (April, 1924; English translation in J. Stalin, *Problems of Leninism,* Moscow, Foreign Languages Publishing House, 1953, pp. 100, 102-12).

organizations, without which it cannot properly wage the struggle against capital: trade unions, cooperative societies, factory organizations, parliamentary groups, non-Party women's associations, the press, cultural and educational organizations, youth leagues, revolutionary fighting organizations (in times of open revolutionary action), Soviets of deputies as the form of state organization (if the proletariat is in power), etc. The overwhelming majority of these organizations are non-Party, and only some of them adhere directly to the Party, or represent its offshoots. All of these organizations, under certain conditions, are absolutely necessary for the working class, for without them it would be impossible to consolidate the class positions of the proletariat in the diverse spheres of struggle; for without them it would be impossible to steel the proletariat as the force whose mission it is to replace the bourgeois order by the socialist order. . . . The question then arises: who is to determine the line, the general direction, along which the work of all these organizations is to be conducted? Where is that central organization which is not only able, because it has the necessary experience, to work out such a general line, but, in addition, is in a position, because it has sufficient prestige, to induce all these organizations to carry out this line, so as to attain unity of leadership and to preclude the possibility of working at cross purposes?

This organization is the Party of the proletariat.

The Party possesses all the necessary qualifications for this because, in the first place, it is the rallying centre of the finest elements in the working class, who have direct connections with the non-Party organizations of the proletariat and very frequently lead them; because, secondly, the Party, as the rallying centre of the finest members of the working class, is the best school for training leaders of the working class, capable of directing every form of organization of their class; because, thirdly, the Party, as the best school for training leaders of the working class, is, by reason of its experience and prestige, the only organization capable of centralizing the leadership of the struggle of the proletariat, thus transforming each and every non-Party organization of the working class into an auxiliary body and transmission belt linking the Party with the class.

The Party is the highest form of class organization of the proletariat. . . .

. . . The Party is the principal guiding force within the class of the proletarians and among the organizations of that class. But it does not by any means follow from this that the Party can be regarded as an end in itself, as a self-sufficient force. The Party is not only the highest form of class association of the proletarians; it is at the same time an *instrument* in the hands of the proletariat *for* achieving the dictatorship when that has not yet been achieved and *for* consolidating and expanding the dictatorship when it has already been achieved. The Party could not have risen so high in importance and could not have overshadowed all other forms of organization of the proletariat, if the latter had not been confronted with the problem of power, if the conditions of imperialism, the inevitability of wars, and the existence of a crisis had not demanded the concentration of all the forces of the proletariat at one point, the gathering of all the threads of the revolutionary movement in one spot in order to overthrow the bourgeoisie and to achieve the dictatorship of the proletariat. The proletariat needs the Party first of all as its General Staff, which it must have for the successful seizure of power. It need hardly be proved that without a Party capable of rallying around itself the mass organizations of the proletariat, and of centralizing the leadership of the entire movement during the progress of the struggle, the proletariat in Russia could never have established its revolutionary dictatorship.

But the proletariat needs the Party not only to achieve the dictatorship; it needs it still more to maintain the dictatorship, to consolidate and expand it in order to achieve the complete victory of socialism.

"Certainly, almost everyone now realizes," says Lenin, "that the Bolsheviks could not have maintained themselves in power for two-and-a-half months, let alone two-and-a-half years, unless the strictest, truly iron discipline had prevailed in our Party, and unless the latter had been rendered the fullest and unreserved support of the whole mass of the working class, that is, of all its thinking, honest, self-sacrificing and influential elements who are capable of leading or of carrying with them the backward strata."

Now, what does to "maintain" and "expand" the dictatorship mean? It means imbuing the millions of proletarians with the spirit of discipline and organization; it means creating among the proletarian masses a cementing force and a bulwark against the corrosive influences of the petty-bourgeois elements and petty-bourgeois habits; it means enhancing the organizing work of the proletarians in re-educating and remoulding the petty-bourgeois strata; it means helping the masses of the proletarians to educate themselves as a force capable of abolishing classes and of preparing the conditions for the organization of socialist production. But it is impossible to accomplish all this without a party which is strong by reason of its solidarity and discipline.

> "The dictatorship of the proletariat," says Lenin, "is a persistent struggle—bloody and bloodless, violent and peaceful, military and economic, educational and administrative—against the forces and traditions of the old society. The force of habit of millions and tens of millions is a most terrible force. Without an iron party tempered in the struggle, without a party enjoying the confidence of all that is honest in the given class, without a party capable of watching and influencing the mood of the masses, it is impossible to conduct such a struggle successfully."

The proletariat needs the Party *for* the purpose of achieving and maintaining the dictatorship. The Party is an instrument of the dictatorship of the proletariat.

But from this it follows that when classes disappear and the dictatorship of the proletariat withers away, the Party will also wither away.

. . . The achievement and maintenance of the dictatorship of the proletariat is impossible without a party which is strong by reason of its solidarity and iron discipline. But iron discipline in the Party is inconceivable without unity of will, without complete and absolute unity of action on the part of all members of the Party. This does not mean, of course, that the possibility of contests of opinion within the Party is thereby precluded. On the contrary, iron discipline does not preclude but presupposes criticism and contest of opinion within the Party. Least of all does it mean that discipline must be "blind." On the contrary, iron discipline does not preclude but presupposes conscious and voluntary submission, for only conscious discipline can be truly iron discipline. But after a contest of opinion has been closed, after criticism has been exhausted and a decision has been arrived at, unity of will and unity of action of all Party members are the necessary conditions without which neither Party unity nor iron discipline in the Party is conceivable. . . .

. . . It follows that the existence of factions is incompatible either with the Party's unity or with its iron discipline. It need hardly be proved that the existence of factions leads to the existence of a number of centres, and the existence of a number of centres connotes the absence of one common centre in the Party, the breaking up of the unity of will, the weakening and disintegration of discipline, the weakening and disintegration of the dictatorship. . . .

. . . The source of factionalism in the Party is its opportunist elements. The proletariat is not an isolated class. It is constantly replenished by the influx of peasants, petty bourgeois and intellectuals proletarianized by the development of capitalism. . . .

In one way or another, all these petty-bourgeois groups penetrate into the Party and introduce into it the spirit of hesitancy and opportunism, the spirit of demoralization and uncertainty. It is they, principally, that constitute the source of factionalism and disintegration, the source of disorganization and disruption of the Party from within. To fight imperialism with such "allies" in one's rear means to expose oneself to the danger of being caught between two fires, from the front and from the rear. Therefore, ruthless struggle against such elements, their expulsion from the Party, is a prerequisite for the successful struggle against imperialism.

The theory of "mastering" opportunist elements by ideological struggle within the Party, the theory of "overcoming" these elements within the confines of a single Party, is a rotten and dangerous theory, which threatens to condemn the Party to paralysis and chronic infirmity, threatens to make the Party a prey to opportunism, threatens to leave the proletariat without a revolutionary party, threatens to deprive the proletariat of its main weapon in the fight against imperialism. . . . Proletarian parties develop and become strong by purging themselves of opportunists and reformists, social-imperialists and social-chauvinists, social-patriots and social-pacifists.

The Party is strengthened by purging itself of opportunist elements. . . .

. . . Leninism is a school of theory and practice which trains a special type of Party and state worker, creates a special Leninist style in work.

What are the characteristic features of this style? What are its peculiarities?

It has two specific features:

a) the Russian revolutionary sweep and

b) American efficiency.

The style of Leninism is a combination of these two specific features in Party and state work.

The Russian revolutionary sweep is an antidote to inertness, routine, conservatism, mental stagnation and slavish submission to ancestral traditions. The Russian revolutionary sweep is the life-giving force which stimulates thought, impels things forward, breaks the past and opens up perspectives. Without it no progress is possible.

But Russian revolutionary sweep has every chance of degenerating in practice into empty "revolutionary" Manilovism if it is not combined with American efficiency in work. . . .

. . . American efficiency is that indomitable force which neither knows nor recognizes obstacles; which with its businesslike perseverance brushes aside all obstacles; which continues at a task once started until it is finished, even if it is a minor task; and without which serious constructive work is inconceivable.

But American efficiency has every chance of degenerating

into narrow and unprincipled commercialism if it is not combined with the Russian revolutionary sweep. . . .

The combination of the Russian revolutionary sweep with American efficiency is the essence of Leninism in Party and state work.

This combination alone produces the finished type of Leninist worker, the style of Leninism in work.

Stalin on Socialism in One Country

In the fall of 1924 some critical publications by Trotsky were taken as the signal for the party leaders to direct a series of scathing denunciations at him for his alleged ideological heresies. The "theory of permanent revolution" figured prominently as the basis for asserting a fundamental opposition between Trotsky and Lenin, although the more immediate reason for scotching the theory was its implication that the Soviet regime, unsupported by international revolution, was in danger of losing its socialist qualities. Stalin's contribution to the defense against Trotsky was the theory of "socialism in one country," which he contrived out of one distorted quotation from Lenin.

. . . According to Lenin, the revolution draws its strength primarily from among the workers and peasants of Russia itself. According to Trotsky, the necessary strength can be found *only* "in the arena of the world proletarian revolution."

But what if the world revolution is fated to arrive with some delay? Is there any ray of hope for our revolution? Trotsky offers no ray of hope, for "the contradictions in the position of a workers' government . . . can be solved *only* . . . in the arena of the world proletarian revolution." According to this plan, there is but one prospect left for our revolution: to vegetate in its own contradictions and rot away while waiting for the world revolution. . . .

FROM: Stalin, "The October Revolution and the Tactics of the Russian Communists" (December, 1924; *Problems of Leninism*, pp. 121-130).

. . . "Permanent revolution" is not a mere underestimation of the revolutionary potentialities of the peasant movement. "Permanent revolution" is an underestimation of the peasant movement which leads to the *repudiation* of Lenin's theory of the dictatorship of the proletariat.

Trotsky's "permanent revolution" is a variety of Menshevism. . . .

The second peculiar feature of the October Revolution lies in the fact that this revolution represents a model of the practical application of Lenin's theory of the proletarian revolution.

He who has not understood this peculiar feature of the October Revolution will never understand either the international nature of this revolution, or its colossal international might, or the specific features of its foreign policy.

> "Uneven economic and political development," says Lenin, "is an absolute law of capitalism. Hence, the victory of socialism is possible first in several or even in one separate capitalist country. The victorious proletariat of that country, having expropriated the capitalists and organized socialist production, would stand up *against* the rest of the world, the capitalist world, attracting to its cause the oppressed classes of other countries, raising revolts in those countries against the capitalists, and in the event of necessity coming out even with armed force against the exploiting classes and their states." For "the free union of nations in socialism is impossible without a more or less prolonged and stubborn struggle of the socialist republics against the backward states."

The opportunists of all countries assert that the proletarian revolution can begin—if it is to begin anywhere at all, according to their theory—only in industrially developed countries, and that the more highly developed these countries are industrially the more chances there are for the victory of socialism. Moreover, according to them, the possibility of the victory of socialism in one country, and in a country little developed in the capitalist sense at that, is excluded as something absolutely improbable. As far back as the period of the war, Lenin, taking as his basis the law of the uneven development of the imperialist states, opposed to the opportunists his theory of the proletarian revolution on the victory of socialism in one country, even if that country is less developed in the capitalist sense.

It is well known that the October Revolution fully confirmed the correctness of Lenin's theory of the proletarian revolution.

How do matters stand with Trotsky's "permanent revolution" in the light of Lenin's theory of the victory of the proletarian revolution in one country?

Let us take Trotsky's pamphlet *Our Revolution* (1906).

Trotsky writes:

> "Without direct state support from the European proletariat, the working class of Russia will not be able to maintain itself in power and to transform its temporary rule into a lasting socialist dictatorship. This we cannot doubt for an instant."

What does this quotation mean? It means that the victory of socialism in one country, in this case Russia, is impossible "*without* direct state support from the European proletariat," i.e., before the European proletariat has conquered power.

What is there in common between this "theory" and Lenin's thesis on the possibility of the victory of socialism "in one separate capitalist country"?

Clearly, there is nothing in common. . . .

It goes without saying that for the *complete* victory of socialism, for *complete* security against the restoration of the old order, the united efforts of the proletarians of several countries are necessary. It goes without saying that, without the support given to our revolution by the proletariat of Europe, the proletariat of Russia could not have held out against the general onslaught, just as without the support the revolution in Russia gave to the revolutionary movement in the West the latter could not have developed at the pace at which it has begun to develop since the establishment of the proletarian dictatorship in Russia. It goes without saying that we need support. But what does support of our revolution by the West-European proletariat imply? Is not the sympathy of European workers for our revolution, their readiness to thwart the imperialists' plans of intervention—

is not all this support? Is this not real assistance? Unquestionably it is. . . .

. . . Let us take, for example, Trotsky's "Postscript," written in 1922, for the new edition of his pamphlet *Peace Program*. Here is what he says in this "Postscript":

> "The assertion reiterated several times in the *Peace Program* that a proletarian revolution cannot culminate victoriously within national bounds may perhaps seem to some readers to have been refuted by the nearly five years' experience of our Soviet republic. But such a conclusion would be unwarranted. The fact that the workers' state has held out against the whole world in one country, and a backward country at that, only testifies to the colossal might of the proletariat, which in other, more advanced, more civilized countries will be truly capable of performing miracles. But while we have held our ground as a state politically and militarily, we have not arrived, or even begun to arrive, at the building of a socialist society. . . . As long as the bourgeoisie remains in power in the other European countries we will be compelled, in our struggle against economic isolation, to strive for agreement with the capitalist world, at the same time it may be said with certainty that these agreements may at best help us to mitigate some of our economic ills, to take one or another step forward, but real progress of a socialist economy in Russia will become possible *only after the victory* of the proletariat in the major European countries." [Stalin's italics.]

Thus speaks Trotsky, plainly sinning against reality and stubbornly trying to save his "permanent revolution" from final shipwreck.

It appears, then, that, twist and turn as you like, we not only have "not arrived," but we have "not even begun to arrive" at the building of a socialist society. It appears that some people have been hoping for "agreements with the capitalist world," but it also appears that nothing will come of these agreements, for, twist and turn as you like, a "real progress of a socialist economy" will not be possible until the proletariat has been victorious in the "major European countries."

Well, then, since there is still no victory in the West, the only "choice" that remains for the revolution in Russia is: either to rot away or to degenerate into a bourgeois state.

It is no accident that Trotsky has been talking for two years now about the "degeneration" of our Party. . . .

. . . Trotsky's "permanent revolution" is the negation of Lenin's theory of the proletarian revolution; and conversely, Lenin's theory of the proletarian revolution is the negation of the theory of "permanent revolution."

Lack of faith in the strength and capabilities of our revolution, lack of faith in the strength and capabilities of the Russian proletariat—that is what lies at the root of the theory of "permanent revolution."

Hitherto only *one* aspect of the theory of "permanent revolution" has usually been noted—lack of faith in the revolutionary potentialities of the peasant movement. Now, in fairness, this must be supplemented by *another* aspect—lack of faith in the strength and capabilities of the proletariat in Russia.

What difference is there between Trotsky's theory and the ordinary Menshevik theory that the victory of socialism in one country, and in a backward country at that, is impossible without the preliminary victory of the proletarian revolution "in the principal countries of Western Europe"?

As a matter of fact, there is no difference.

There can be no doubt at all. Trotsky's theory of "permanent revolution" is a variety of Menshevism. . . .

Bukharin on the Worker-Peasant Alliance

Bukharin's contribution to the anti-Trotsky argument was to stress the support which the "workers' state" in Russia commanded through its "alliance" with the peasantry—a line of reasoning which made him adhere closely to the circumspectful agricultural policies of the NEP. He went so far as to suggest that the worker-peasant alliance must serve as the model for the world revolution as a whole, considering the great peasant majority of the world's population.

For Comrade Trotsky the posing of the question was extremely simple: there can *only* be a proletarian revolution in Russia . . . , but *this proletarian revolution in a petty-bour-*

geois country is condemned to perish unless governmental aid on the part of the victorious proletariat of Western Europe is provided for it. . . .

Comrade Trotsky began by failing to understand the *peculiar* course of our revolution, which consists of the unique binding together of a *peasant war* against the landlord and the *proletarian revolution.* Comrade Trotsky did not understand the *peculiarity of the initial stage of this* revolution, the essence of which consists of liberation from feudal ways and the destruction of landlord property-holding. . . .

Comrade Trotsky furthermore did not see those special *international* conditions which—even without governmental aid from the victorious West-European proletariat—permit our socialist revolution to sit it out, become stronger, *grow,* in order that it may finally be victorious together with the victory of the working class of other countries.

Comrade Trotsky has here reasoned schematically: *either* a bourgeois revolution *or* a proletarian one; *either* the classical proletarian revolution—and a firm victory, *or* a half-breed proletarian revolution—and death. Either there is governmental aid from the Western proletariat—and salvation, *or* there is no such aid—and no such salvation.

But in fact life has completely refuted these schemes and has given altogether different answers. *Both* bourgeois *and* proletarian (one flows into the other); no state aid from the proletariat, but nevertheless aid on the part of the proletariat, and on the part of the colonies (and even aid on the part of the capitalists, who by their internecine fighting assist proletarian states); no classical proletarian revolution, but nevertheless not death but life, etc. Reality has proven to be much more varicolored that the dry schemes of the carefully drawn diagrams of "permanent revolution."

Trotsky's *political impotence* stems from the fact that he did not see reality. . . .

The disputes which we have been having can be reduced to a considerable degree, as we know, to the question of the

FROM: Bukharin, "The Theory of Permanent Revolution" (Speech of December 13, 1924, in the symposium *For Leninism,* Moscow—Leningrad, Party Press, 1925, pp. 347-51, 353, 367; editor's translation.)

worker-peasant bloc, of the alliance between the working class and the peasantry, and of the hegemony of the proletariat in this "alliance" or "bloc." . . . Only now has this question assumed its vast full magnitude. For, in essence, we are speaking here not only about the problem of the worker-peasant *smychka* ["bond"] in our Soviet republics, but also about a vast and in a certain sense decisive problem of the *international revolution.* For such a burning question of the present like the question of the *colonies,* which is a question of life and death for capitalism, is from the point of view of world revolution none other than the question of the *smychka* between the West-European and American industrial proletariat on the one hand and the colonial peasantry on the other. . . .

If we ask the question how things will be in the framework of the world economy when the workers conquer power, then just this question of the relation of the victorious proletariat to the colonial peasantry will come before us. Insofar as we ask why the European Social Democrats have completely failed to understand the significance of the peasant question, have paid it so little attention, and have failed to pose the problems which are so characteristic for us, the matter does not at all reduce to the fact that we have a peasant country and there the countries are industrialized. They also have had their "agrarian complement," but it is situated not in the metropolitan country but in the separate colonial periphery. And the fact that the European Social-Democrats have paid insufficient attention to the peasant question is unconditionally linked to the circumstance that they have a careless attitude toward the revolutionary posing of the question of the colonies. . . . When Comrade Trotsky, carried away by his "Europeanism," repeatedly underscored the Asiatic-peasant character of the ideology of the "immature" proletariat (and just thus did he evaluate the Bolsheviks), in this Europeanism there was something of the contemptuous attitude of the Social Democrats toward the peasant and colonial question, although Comrade Trotsky personally devoted rather much attention to the colonial question.

From this general context regarding classes, from this "European" evaluation of their role, stemmed Comrade Trotsky's quite concrete presentation of the idea that the revolution in Russia will inevitably perish if there is no governmental support on the part of the victorious proletariat. . . .

The classical proletarian revolution is one where the proletariat is the only "popular" class. In other words, only in a society where there is no peasantry could this ideal revolution occur.

However, this "ideal" presentation completely fails to conform to reality. If we take the *world economy,* we see that the proletariat in the real sense of the word constitutes an insignificant minority of the population. . . .

Before the seizure of power the working class must have the support of the peasants in the *struggle against the capitalists and landlords.* . . .

The proletariat after its victory must *get along* with the peasantry *no matter what,* for it is the majority of the population with great economic and social weight. . . . It is necessary, accordingly, to understand that the proletariat has *no* choice here; it is *compelled,* in building socialism, to get the peasantry behind it; it must *learn how* to accomplish this, for without this its regime will not last. . . .

If a conflict between the proletariat and the peasantry were unavoidable, inevitable, then it would be unavoidable and inevitable even with the *world* victory of the proletariat. Peasants are the overwhelming majority on our planet. If the proletariat does not have the means to get this majority *behind it,* then: *either* the international revolution is also doomed to collapse, *or* it must be postponed until the time when the proletariat becomes a majority on the earth. We cannot hope to burst our "terrestrial boundaries" and expect aid from purely proletarian *heavenly* forces, in "governmental form" besides! . . .

Trotsky's mistake is to consider the conflict between the proletariat and the peasantry inevitable, when it is only *possible.* And this is not one and the same thing. It is inevitable only in the event that the proletarian regime proves to be less advantageous for the peasantry than a bourgeois regime, if the peasantry slips out from under the leadership of the proletariat. But this is not at all bound to happen, and will not, if the party of the victorious proletariat makes care for supporting and strengthening the worker-peasant bloc its main policy. . . .

. . . It is perfectly natural that when Comrade Trotsky insists on his errors we must say: if now when the country is again in a state of crisis they raise the question of the peasantry in its full scope, raising the question of the permanent revolution; when they continue to take the point of view of permanent revolution and want to turn the whole party onto this road—we cannot take this path, because we do not want to give up the Leninist position, because without this position we will destroy our cause. Therefore, we must ideologically liquidate Trotskyism and conquer the whole party under the Leninist banner no matter what, for the question of the worker-peasant bloc is the central question, it is the question of all questions.

Preobrazhensky on the Economics of Industrialization

While organizationally defeated, the Trotskyists remained intellectually active. Evgeny Preobrazhensky, the leading Opposition economist, worked out a penetrating analysis of the obstacles standing in the way of the industrial progress on which all the Communists set their hopes. In his view only a systematic exploitation of the peasant majority could support industrialization by the socialist state. Essentially this was the analysis on which Stalin later based the Five-Year Plans and the collectivization of the peasants.

. . . It will be no exaggeration to say that for all our theoreticians, and practitioners as well, the most interesting, vital, exciting question since the October coup of 1917 and the military victory of the revolution is the question of what

FROM: Preobrazhensky, *The New Economics: An Essay in the Theoretical Analysis of the Soviet Economy* (Second edition, Moscow, Communist Academy, 1926, pp. 86, 89-90, 92-94, 99, 136-37; editor's translation).

the Soviet system represents, in what direction it is developing, what the basic laws of this development are, and, finally, what relation this first experience of an economy whose main links go outside the limits of capitalism has to our old and habitual images of socialism. The last question could be correctly phrased thus: How after eight years of the dictatorship of the proletariat in a vast country, should we view our former images of socialism? . . .

. . . The complex of state socialist production can appear only as the result of breaking up the old system on all fronts, only as the result of social revolution. This fact has colossal significance for understanding not only the genesis of socialism but also the socialist construction that follows. On the other hand, insufficient understanding or neglect of the essence of what socialism is has more than once led and is leading a series of comrades to purely Philistine and sometimes outright reformist notions about the Soviet economy and the paths of its development. . . .

Primary socialist accumulation, as the period of creating the material prerequisites for socialist production in the proper sense of the word, can only begin with the seizure of power and nationalization. . . .

. . . On a private or limited scale socialist accumulation is not able to resolve the basic problem of the socialist organization of the economy. In particular, insofar as we are concerned with the economy of the Soviet Union, it is essential to have: 1) accumulation which makes it possible for the state economy to achieve the technical level of contemporary capitalism wherever it is not possible to move gradually on to the base of the new technology; 2) accumulation which makes possible the change in the technological base of the state economy, the scientific organization of labor, the planned direction of the whole complex of the state economy, everything that is not possible without large supplies for insurance and planned reserves; 3) accumulation which guarantees progress for the whole complex, not just its individual parts, since the chain of dependence in the movement of the whole complex makes progress on different levels, in the manner of capitalist "partisan warfare," individual initiative, and competition, completely impossible. . . .

We term *socialist* accumulation the assimilation to the functioning means of production of the surplus product which is created within the amalgamated socialist economy and which is not distributed as a supplement among the agents of socialist production and the socialist state, but contributes to expanded reproduction.* On the other hand, we term *primary socialist* accumulation the accumulation in the hands of the state of most or all of the material resources from sources lying outside the complex of the state economy. In a backward peasant country this accumulation must play a colossally important role, to a vast degree hastening the arrival of the moment when the technological and scientific reconstruction of the state economy can begin and when this economy can finally achieve purely economic predominance over capitalism. . . . The basic law of our Soviet economy, which at the present moment is coursing through this stage, is precisely the law of primary or preliminary socialist accumulation. To this law are subordinated all the basic processes of economic life in the sphere of the state economy. This law, on the other hand, changes and partly liquidates the law of value and all the laws of the commodity and commodity-capitalistic economy insofar as they manifest themselves or can manifest themselves in our system of economy. Consequently, *we can not only speak of primary socialist accumulation, we cannot even understand the essence of the Soviet economy unless we understand the central role which the law of primary socialist accumulation plays in this economy, how it determines, in the struggle with the law of value, the distribution of the means of production in the economy, the distribution of the working force, and the extent of alienation of the country's surplus product for the expansion of socialist reproduction. . . .*

In regard to alienation of part of the surplus product for the benefit of socialism, matters are entirely different from all pre-socialist economic forms. Exactions from the non-socialist forms must not only have a place inevitably in the period of

* I.e., an increased investment in industrial plant—Ed.

primary socialist accumulation—they must inevitably assume a vast, directly decisive role in peasant countries like the Soviet Union. . . .

In the period of primary socialist accumulation the state economy cannot do without alienating part of the surplus product of the village and of craft production, in sum, without deductions from capitalistic accumulation for the benefit of socialist accumulation. We do not know to what extent other countries will emerge devastated from the civil war in which the dictatorship of the proletariat triumphs. But a country like the U.S.S.R., with its devastated and in general rather backward economy, must go through the period of primary accumulation with very broad use of the sources of the presocialist forms of the economy. We should not forget that the period of primary socialist accumulation is the most critical period in the life of the socialist state after the termination of the civil war. In this period the socialist system is not yet in a condition to develop organically all its own advantages, while at the same time it inevitably liquidates a series of economic advantages which are characteristic of the developed capitalist system. To traverse this period rapidly, to reach quickly the moment when the socialist system will have developed all its natural advantages over capitalism—this is a question of life or death for the socialist state. At least this is how the question stands right now for the U.S.S.R., and perhaps it will stand thus for some time in a series of European countries where the proletariat is victorious. Under such conditions to rely only on accumulation within the socialist sphere means to risk the very existence of socialist economics, or to extend indefinitely the period of preliminary accumulation. . . .

. . . At the moment of its victory the working class changes from the object of exploitation into the subject of it. It cannot regard its own working power, health, labor and conditions as the capitalists regard them. This constitutes the definition of the limit to the tempo of socialist accumulation, a limit which capitalistic industry in the first period of its development did not know. . . .

. . . In this period the law of wages is subordinated to

the law of socialist accumulation, which finds its expression in conscious self-restraint by the working class. . . . Socialist accumulation is a necessity for the working class, but now it proceeds as a consciously understood necessity. . . .

Soviet Cultural Policy—the Liberal Period

While the Communists were firmly wedded to the Marxian proposition that all aspects of life are affected by the class struggle and must be considered in waging class war, the party leaders during the first decade after the revolution did not imagine that they had the competence to make commanding decisions in the artistic realm. They dealt severely with overtly anti-Communist political opinions, but otherwise they were content to give encouragement to "proletarian" cultural contributions, and, as the 1925 party statement on literature illustrates, allow a variety of aesthetic currents to exist.

. . . As the class war in general has not ended, neither has it ended on the literary front. In a class society there is not, nor can there be a neutral art, though the class nature of art generally and of literature in particular is expressed in forms which are infinitely more various than, for instance, in politics. . . .

It must be remembered, however, that this problem is infinitely more complicated than other problems being solved by the proletariat. Even within the limitations of a capitalist society the working class could prepare itself for a victorious revolution, build cadres of fighters and leaders and produce a magnificent ideological weapon for the political struggle. But it could work out neither the problems of natural science nor the tasks of technical development; and by the same token the proletariat, the class which was culturally deprived, was unable to develop its own literature, its own

FROM: Resolution of the Central Committee of the Russian Communist Party, "On the Policy of the Party in the Field of Literature," July 1, 1925 (English translation in Edward J. Brown, *The Proletarian Episode in Russian Literature, 1928-1932*, New York, Columbia University Press, 1952, pp. 235-40; reprinted by permission of the publisher).

characteristic artistic forms, its own style. Although the proletariat has ready infallible criteria regarding the socio-political content of any literary work, it does not have such definite answers to all questions of artistic form. . . .

With relation to the "fellow-travelers" we must bear in mind: (1) their differentiation, (2) the importance of many of them as qualified specialists of literary technique; and (3) the presence of vacillation in this group of writers. The general directive should be for tactful and careful relations with them, and for such an approach as will guarantee all the conditions for their earliest possible movement in the direction of Communist ideology. While discouraging anti-proletarian and antirevolutionary elements (now quite insignificant), and while fighting to expose the ideology of the new *bourgeoisie* which is taking form among a part of the fellow-travelers—those of the "change-of-landmarks" stripe—the Party should have a patient attitude toward intermediate ideological formations, patiently aiding those inevitably numerous formations to develop in the process of ever closer comradely coöperation with the cultural forces of communism. . . .

Communist criticism should fight mercilessly against counterrevolutionary phenomena in literature; and yet at the same time show the greatest tact, attention and patience toward all those groups which can and will join the proletariat. Communist criticism must drive out the tone of literary command. Such criticism can have deep educational significance only when it relies on its own ideological superiority. Marxist criticism should once and for all drive out of its midst all pretentious, half-literate, and self-satisfied Communist conceit. Marxist criticism should have as its slogan "to learn," and should resist every appearance of cheap judgment and ignorant arrogance in its own milieu.

While it has infallible criteria of judgment regarding the class content of literary tendencies, the Party as a whole must not bind itself to any one tendency in the field of literary form. Giving general leadership to literature, the Party cannot support any one faction in literature (classifying these factions according to their different views on form and style), just as it cannot by resolutions settle questions of the form of the family, though in general it does and should lead in the development of new ways of life. Everything indicates that a style proper to the epoch will be created, but it will be created by different methods, and the solution of this problem has not yet been begun. In the present phase of cultural development any attempt to bind the Party in this direction must be repulsed.

Therefore the Party should declare itself in favor of the free competition of various groups and tendencies in this province. Any other solution of the problem would be an official, bureaucratic pseudo-solution. In the same way it is inadmissible to legalize by a decree the monopoly of the literary printing business by any one group or literary organization. While morally and materially supporting proletarian and proletarian-peasant literature, and aiding the fellow-travelers, the Party cannot offer a monopoly to any of these groups, even the one most proletarian in its ideology. For this would be to destroy proletarian literature itself. . . .

Soviet Educational Policy—the Revolutionary Period

The early Communist position on social problems held, according to Marxian logic, that individual development or defects were the product of social and economic conditions. The ideal was the spontaneous blossoming of the individual proletarian, freed from legal, family and educational restraints. (Industrial and political discipline would also have been eliminated had the early left-wing opposition groups had their way.) In education the authority of school and teacher was deëmphasized in favor of letting the child develop freely amid the proper conditioning influences. This was closely akin to the "learning by doing" of American progressive education, as A. P. Pinkevich, one of the leading Soviet educational theorists, freely conceded.

FROM: Pinkevich, *Outlines of Pedagogy* (1927; translated as *The New Education in the Soviet Republic* by Mucia Perlmutter and edited by George S. Counts, New York, The John Day Co., 1929, pp. vi, 198-99, 202, 214, 288, 301-2; reprinted by permission of the editor).

. . . The mere enumeration of the names of Hall, Dewey, Russell, Monroe, Judd, Thorndike, Kilpatrick, and many others, known to every educator in our country, is a sufficient reminder of the tremendous influence which American education has exerted upon us. In spite of the undoubted differences in ideology which divide Soviet from western educational leaders, mutual understanding and recognition of scientific attainments are indispensable. . . .

In his volume entitled *Fundamental Questions of Social Education* Shulgin* has given an excellent exposition of the demands of the party. He presents the Communist conception of the role of labor in education and the role of the labor school in society as follows:

"To our mind labor is the best method of so introducing young children to the laboring class and of so merging them with the class-builder that they may not only understand the proletarian ideology, but may actually begin to live, to strive, and to build according to that ideology. But this is not all. Labor to us is a means of inducting children into the working world family in order that they may participate in and understand the struggle of the masses, follow the history of human society, acquire working, organizing, and collective habits, and come into possession of the discipline of work. To us labor, because of its superior integrating power, is the best method of teaching children how to live the contemporary life. The factory is the first and most sensitive place of modern society. Since labor, self-government, and contemporary life merge into an inseparable union, the march of economic events calls for schools which will train the warrior and builder of life. . . ."

In every school a distinction may be drawn between the teaching of the materials of instruction and the teaching of behavior. In our schools the latter could more properly be called the organization of the children's collective or the organization of behavior. The term behavior is used here in the sense in which it is employed by the psychologist.

At the beginning of our discussion of the question of the organization of conduct we wish to emphasize one guiding principle of Soviet pedagogy. We assign to the teacher the

* Shulgin: an early Soviet educational theorist—Ed.

role of organizer, assistant, instructor, and older comrade, but not the role of superior officer. In the old school the teacher was a dictator. In the liberal bourgeois school he is at best a leader. With us he is primarily an organizer. . . .

In our opinion the children should organize their own social life in school in order to develop those collectivistic traits which are indispensable for the creation of new forms of social life. Naturally they should not be left entirely to themselves. In order to make full pedagogical use of the efforts of children at self-organization the teacher should place certain limitations on their social activity. . . .

The most fundamental characteristic, however, which distinguishes our theory of self-government from that obtained in other countries is its communistic coloring, or at least its communistic foundation. We need organizers and builders of a new society, we need warriors for a new way of life. Self-government is our most effective educational instrument for producing such organizers, builders, and warriors. . . .

Our aim is to take the project method and put our own content into it. All forms of our community purposeful undertakings are as a matter of fact "projects." . . . The bourgeois American school fails to give to the method that community quality which is characteristic of our socialistic school. There is no doubt, however, that of all the contemporary attempts to reform the school, the project system with appropriate changes is best adapted to the nature and purposes of the Soviet school. It affords the children greater freedom of activity, encourages them to engage in practical work, demands of them independent planning, and trains them in the methods of investigation. . . .

The center of all the work of the school should be human labor. Every school activity is consequently closely related to this central aim. But an understanding of labor requires a penetrating study of the productive forces which man utilizes as well as those social relations which grow out of the particular organization of labor in a given society. These considerations have led us to adopt as a fundamental scheme for organizing the curriculum of the labor school the three-fold concept of nature, labor, and society, or, to put it another way, productive energies, productive relations, and superstructure. And all teaching is unified through one central synthetic theme of colossal importance—*human labor*. Obviously this scheme is distinctly Marxian. Moreover, it is the first truly Marxian educational plan; and, regardless of the extent to which the program itself may change, we are confident that the basic scheme of the Soviet school will remain unshaken.

In complete harmony with the content of the new program are the methods of instruction which it suggests. First of all, it calls for a completely objective method of teaching, understanding the term in the light of our discussion above. This means that children are not to study verbal descriptions of phenomena and things but rather the phenomena and things themselves. In other words the program of the [State Scientific] Council calls for direct contact with the surrounding nature, labor, and society in which the child lives. This environment is the starting point of all the work of the school. . . .

The Zinoviev-Kamenev Opposition

In 1925 the party leadership split. Zinoviev and Kamenev, with the Leningrad party organization which Zinoviev controlled, went into opposition against the party majority led by Stalin, Bukharin and Rykov. At the Fourteenth Party Congress in December, 1925, the new opposition vainly attacked the leadership. Zinoviev raised again the theoretical problem of "state capitalism" and progress toward socialism, while Kamenev bluntly warned of the danger of Stalin's becoming a personal dictator. Stalin's dominance in the party organization decided the issue, and Zinoviev and Kamenev were overwhelmingly defeated.

a) Zinoviev on State Capitalism

What are the chief difficulties in our work? In my opinion there are three. They form, as it were, the background of the whole picture of our construction. *The first difficulty* is the delay of the world revolution. At the beginning of the October Revolution we were convinced that the workers of other countries would provide us with direct support in a matter of months, or in any case within a few years. Now, unfortunately, it has been demonstrated that the delay of the world revolution is a fact, that the partial stabilization of capitalism characterizes a whole period, and that a new, more complicated set of difficulties is connected with this stabilization.

The second difficulty is well known—this is the building of socialism in a backward country with such an enormous predominance of the peasantry. This is a difficulty for which we gave ourselves the answer in the first days of the revolution and which we have been successfully overcoming.

The third difficulty is the creation of a collective leadership for our party after the death of Vladimir Ilich. Only now, it seems to me, is this being drawn in full clarity. This difficulty is not unimportant, because leading the party means at the same time directing the state. This is not only an organizational question—this is a political problem of the most profound importance. . . .

Recently a dispute about the question of *state capitalism* descended upon us quite unexpectedly, out of a clear blue . . . To take the bull by the horns, Comrades, I think it is first of all necessary to answer those who are now trying to represent the matter as though we have no state capitalism and practically nothing of capitalism in general. I feel that the thing here is really the attempt of certain comrades to declare that the NEP is socialism. (*Laughter, noise*) Such a point of view, such a position represents the idealization of the NEP, the idealization of capitalism. (*Voice: "Who thinks so?"*) It is indisputable that the NEP is the *road* to socialism, but the assertion that the NEP is not socialism also seems to me indisputable. (*Voice: "These are questions from political grammar school."*) So, Comrades, it appears to me that this is just what the dispute is about. Of course, he

FROM: Zinoviev, Minority Report to the Fourteenth Party Congress, December, 1925 (*Fourteenth Congress of the All-Union Communist Party [of Bolsheviks]: Stenographic Report,* Moscow, Party Press, 1926, pp. 98, 101, 108-9; editor's translation).

who idealizes the NEP cannot but dispute Lenin's formulation on the question of state capitalism. . . .

Comrade Bukharin has said . . . that if we allow the idea that nationalized enterprises are state-capitalist enterprises, if we say this directly, then how can we conduct a campaign to raise the productivity of labor? The workers will not begin to raise the productivity in factories which are not purely socialist. This is actually real pessimism. . . .

The workers are not children, we don't need to offer the workers anything tinseled or gilded or lull them to sleep—they know perfectly well the strong and weak sides of our economy and in particular of our state industry. They know perfectly well that our Soviet factories and mills are basically enterprises of a type consistent with socialism. We are not arguing about this. They give themselves the answer that we have conquered these enterprises, that we have driven the exploiters out of them, that our factories and mills are working for the working class, that we have there the basic prerequisites for building socialism and completing it. But together with this they know perfectly well that their factories are connected with the market. They know all the shady sides, all the backwardness of our technology; they know the backwardness of our forms of wages, their relatively low level, and they take things as they are. They know well enough what circumstances surround us, so that we do not need to sweeten or sugar-coat the real state of affairs. Look the truth boldly in the face. And rest assured that the worker will understand that all our industry belongs to the working class, that in his own factory he ought to work as one needs to work for one's own class, as genuine builders of socialism need to work.

So, Comrades, I think it is indisputable . . . that our state industry consists of enterprises which are of a type consistent with socialism but are not yet fully socialist, as Bukharin admitted in the spring of 1922. Finally, it is indisputable that the simplest and clearest example of state capitalism in a country like ours is concessions and leases. But it must be just as indisputable for us that this does not exhaust state capitalism, that we cannot forget about free trade and its forms, about planning and distribution, about the revival of capitalism in individual farms. We cannot forget that all this, insofar as it is subordinated to the control of the state—all this Vladimir Ilich called state capitalism, adding the qualification that this is a *unique* state capitalism, radically distinguished from the state capitalism of the bourgeois countries in that it is subordinated and limited by the working class, by the proletarian state. But at the same time Vladimir Ilich said that in order for the workers to see that we do have capitalism we must not idealize or gloss over reality.

b) Kamenev on Stalin

I turn to intraparty questions. To these questions I give three answers.

The first concerns the organizational forms of our intraparty life. Comrade Bukharin has said that we bought the controversy with Comrade Trotsky at the price, as he expressed it, of a convulsion in intraparty life. You must resolve this question in the sense that in the background of a general enlivening and heightening of the activity of all strata of the population, intraparty democracy is essential, its further development is essential. According to the testament of Lenin this has now become possible precisely because the de-classing of the proletariat has ceased.

In the contrary case with this background you will inevitably have a new convulsion in intraparty life. This will be a phenomenon on a catastrophic order. I appeal to you not to choose this path, but the other path.

The things you hear about that path at the congress—about defeatists, liquidators, Axelrodists, etc.—cannot be true; such things had not entered the party's head even after it assembled at the congress. *This must be avoided. This can be avoided only if the minority, which is not made up of newcomers, which you know about fully—if this minority*

FROM: Kamenev, Speech to the Fourteenth Party Congress, December, 1925 (Stenographic Report, pp. 273-75; editor's translation).

is given an opportunity to defend its views in the party, of course with the full responsibility which the party and the dictatorship impose upon us.

Second: Besides the invigoration of party discussion, besides granting the minority an opportunity to express its views to the whole party, as becomes Bolsheviks, within those limits which are set by the party statutes and the dictatorship of the party and the proletariat—it seems to me that you must *resist this new tendency in the party which I have tried to sketch out to you.* I am sure that if you find it impossible to do this now because of some organizational consideration or another—the facts of life, the course of the class struggle in our country, the growth of differentiation in the village will compel you to do this, and to say that the school which Bukharin has established is based on a departure from Lenin. What we need right now is in the slogan, back to Lenin! (Voice from a seat: "Why back?") Because this is going forward. Comrades, I know that in the first part of my speech you tried to attribute the matter to malice. We see that the matter is not one of malice, and I hope you will say this after a few months.

And finally, the third point: *We are against creating a theory of the "Duce,"* * *we are against establishing a "Duce."* We are against the Secretariat, which has in practice combined both policy and organization, standing over the political organ. *We are for our upper level being organized in such a fashion that there would be a really all-powerful Politbureau, bringing together all our party's policies, and at the same time the Secretariat would be subordinate to it and execute the technical aspects of its decisions.* (Noise) We cannot consider it normal but think it harmful to the party, if such a situation is continued where the Secretariat combines both policy and organization, and in fact predecides policy. (Noise) Here, Comrades, is what we need to do. Everyone who does not agree with me will draw his own conclusions. (Voice from a seat: "You should have begun with this.") The speaker has the right to begin with what he wants. You

* Russian *vozhd*—"leader," in a then derogatory sense—Ed.

think I ought to have begun with what I have said, that personally I assert that our General Secretary is not the kind of figure that can unite the old Bolshevik staff around himself. I don't consider this a basic political question. I don't consider this question more important than the question of the theoretical line. I feel that if the party adopted (Noise) a definite political line which was clearly marked off from those deviations which part of the Central Committee is now supporting, this question would not now be on the agenda. But I must say this out to the end. Precisely because I more than once told Comrade Stalin this, precisely because I more than once told a group of Leninist comrades, I repeat it here at the congress: *I have arrived at the conviction that Comrade Stalin cannot fulfill the role of unifier of the Bolshevik staff*. (Voices from the audience: "Untrue!" "Nonsense!" "So that's what it is!" "He's shown his cards!" Noise. Applause by the Leningrad delegation. Shouts: "We won't surrender the commanding heights to you." "Stalin! Stalin!" The delegates stand and cheer Comrade Stalin. Stormy applause. Shouts: "Here's where the party has become united. Now the Bolshevik staff must be united.")

(Yevdokimov, from his seat) "Long live the Russian Communist Party! Hurrah! Hurrah!" (The delegates stand and shout "Hurrah!" Noise. Stormy, long-sustained applause)

(Yevdokimov, from his seat) "Long live the Central Committee of our party! Hurrah!" (The delegates shout "Hurrah!") "The party above all! Right!" (Applause and shouts, "Hurrah!")

(Voice from a seat) "Long live Comrade Stalin!" (Stormy, continued applause, shouts) "Hurrah!" (Noise)

(Chairman) "Comrades, I beg you to quiet down. Comrade Kamenev will now finish his speech."

I began this part of my speech with the words, "We are against the theory of individual preëminence, we are against creating a Duce!" With these same words I end my speech. (Applause by the Leningrad delegation)

(Voice from a seat) "And who do you propose?"

(Chairman) "I declare a ten minute recess." . . .

The United Opposition

In 1926, the two defeated opposition groups, Trotskyist and Zinovievist, merged and undertook a major appeal to the party rank-and-file against the leadership. They had to resort to conspiratorial organization, and when this activity was detected (the "Lashevich affair"), the leadership prepared a new condemnation of the Opposition's factionalism. In reply, the leaders of the Opposition drew up a detailed statement of their case which they vainly tried to present to the party membership.

. . . 1. Bureaucratism as the Source of Factionalism

The immediate cause of all of the sharpening crises in the party is in bureaucratism, which has grown amazingly in the period following the death of Lenin, and continues to grow.

The Central Committee of the ruling party has at its disposal for action upon the party not only ideological and organizational, i.e., not only party means, but also governmental and economic means. Lenin always took into account the danger that the concentration of administrative power in the hands of the party would lead to bureaucratic pressure on the Party. Precisely from this arose Vladimir Ilich's idea about organizing the Control Commission, which, while it had no administrative power in its hands, would have all the power essential for the struggle with bureaucratism, for the defense of the right of a party member to express his convictions freely and to vote according to his conscience without fearing any punitive consequences. . . .

Meanwhile, in fact—and this must be said here before anything else—the Central Control Commission itself has become a purely administrative organ, which assists the repression conducted by other bureaucratic organs, executing for them the punitive part of the work, prosecuting any independent thought in the party, any voice of criticism, any concern expressed aloud about the fate of the party, any critical remarks about certain leaders of the party. . . .

FROM: The Declaration of the Thirteen, July, 1926 (editor's translation from copy in the Trotsky Archive).

The resolution of December 5, 1923, adopted unanimously at that time, refers to the fact that bureaucratism, suppressing free discussion, striking down criticism, unavoidably pushes conscientious party members onto the road of reticence and factionalism. The correctness of this point has been fully and completely confirmed by the events of the recent period, especially by the affair of Comrades Lashevich, Belenki, Chernishov, et al. It would be criminal blindness to represent this affair as the result of the evil party will of an individual person or an individual group. Indeed, before us here is the obvious and indubitable consequence of the prevailing course, under which people talk only on top, while below they think and think to themselves under cover. (And what they think they keep to themselves.) Those who are dissatisfied, disagree, or doubt, are afraid to raise their voices in party meetings. The party mass always hears only the speech of the party command on the one and only "crib." The mutual tie and trust for the leadership are weakening.

An official show prevails in the meetings, together with the apathy which is unavoidably connected with it. Frequently only an insignificant minority remains at the time of voting; the participants in the meeting hasten to leave so that they will not be compelled to vote for decisions dictated earlier. No resolutions anywhere are ever adopted otherwise than "unanimously." All this is gravely reflected in the internal life of the Party organizations. Members of the Party are afraid openly to express aloud their most cherished thoughts, wishes and demands. This is what constitutes the cause of the "affair" of Comrade Lashevich et al.

2. The Cause of the Growth of Bureaucratism

It is completely obvious that the more difficult it is for the ruling centers to carry through their decisions by the methods of party democracy, the less the vanguard of the working class sees their policy as its own.

The divergence between the direction of economic policy and the direction of the feelings and thoughts of the proletarian vanguard inevitably strengthens the need for repression and gives all policy an administrative-bureaucratic character.

Any other explanation of the growth of bureaucratism is secondary and does not encompass the essence of the question.

The lag of industry behind the economic development of the country as a whole signifies, in spite of the growth in the number of workers, a lowering of the specific gravity of the proletariat in the society. The lag in the influence of industry on agriculture and the rapid growth of the *kulaks** lowers in the village the specific gravity of the hired workers and poor peasants and their trust in the state and in themselves. The lag of wage raises behind the rising living standard of the nonproletarian elements of the city and the upper groups of the village inevitably signifies the lowering of the political and cultural self-esteem of the proletariat as the ruling class. From this, in particular, comes the clear decrease in the activity of the workers and poor peasants in the elections to the soviets, which is a most serious warning for our Party. . . .

4. The Question of Industrialization

The present year again reveals with all clarity that state industry is lagging behind the development of the economy as a whole. The new harvest again catches us without supplies of goods. But movement toward socialism is assured only when the tempo of development of industry does not lag behind the general development of the economy, but leads it, systematically bringing the country closer to the technical level of the advanced capitalist countries. Everything must be subordinated to this task, equally vital both for the proletariat and for the peasantry. . . .

The question of the *smychka* is under present conditions above all a question of industrialization.

Meanwhile the party sees with alarm that the resolution of the Fourteenth Congress on industrialization in reality draws back more and more, following the example of what was not carried out in the party's resolution on democracy. In this fundamental question, on which the life and death of the

* *Kulak:* Russian "fist," colloquial expression for a prosperous peasant—Ed.

October Revolution depend, the party cannot and does not want to live with official "cribs," which are dictated, frequently, not by the interests of the matter but by the interests of factional struggle. The party wants to know, to think, to check, to decide. The present regime prevents this, and precisely from this stems the secret distribution of party documents on the "affair" of Lashevich, etc.

5. Policy in the Village

In questions of agricultural policy in the village the danger of shifts to the side of the upper groups in the village is all the more clearly defined. . . .

The fact is that under the guise of a union of the poor peasantry with the middle peasant, we observe steadily and regularly the political subordination of the poor peasantry to the middle peasants, and through them to the *kulaks*.

6. The Bureaucratic Perversion of the Workers' State

The number of workers in our state industry does not now reach two million; together with transport, it is less than three million. The soviet, trade-union, coöperative and all other employees certainly do not number less than that figure, and this comparison alone testifies to the colossal political and economic role of the bureaucracy; it is entirely obvious that the state apparatus, in its composition and level of life, is to an overwhelming degree bourgeois and petty-bourgeois, and inclines away from the proletariat and the village poor, on the one hand, toward the displaced intelligentsia, and on the other toward the land-leaser, the merchant, the *kulak*, the new bourgeois. How many times did Lenin remind us of the bureaucratic perversion of the state apparatus and about the frequent necessity for the trade unions to defend the workers from the state, while the party bureaucrat in just this region is infected with the most dangerous self-deception. . . .

7. The Bureaucratic Perversion of the Party Apparatus

In 1920 a party conference under Lenin's direction considered it essential to point out the impermissibility of the fact that in the mobilization of the comrades, party organs and individual comrades were guided by some considerations other than business ones. Any repression whatever against comrades because they think differently about one or another question or party decision is impermissible. The whole present practice contradicts this decision at every step. Genuine discipline is shaken apart and replaced by subordination to the influential figures in the apparatus. The comrades on whom the party can rely in the most difficult days are pushed out of the staff in ever greater numbers, they are thrown around, exiled, persecuted, and replaced steadily and regularly by casual people, untested, but who are distinguished by silent obedience. Now these bureaucratic sins of the party regime are transferred to the accused comrades Lashevich and Belenki, whom the party has known in the course of more than two decades as devoted and disciplined members. The act of accusing them is therefore an act of accusing the bureaucratic perversion of the party apparatus.

The significance of a firmly welded, centralized apparatus in the Bolshevik Party needs no explanation. Without this skeleton the proletarian revolution would be impossible. The party apparatus in its majority is composed of devoted and irreproachable party members who have no stimulus other than the struggle of the working class. Under the correct regime and the proper distribution of forces the very same party workers could successfully help realize party democracy.

8. Bureaucratism and the Everyday Life of the Working Masses

. . . The bureaucratic regime has spread like rust into the life of every plant and workshop. If the members of the party are in fact deprived of the right to criticize by the district committee, the provincial committee, or the Central Committee, in the plant, they are deprived of the right to subject the immediate authorities to criticism. Party members are scared. The administrator who is able as a loyal person to guarantee himself the support of the secretary of the next higher organization thus insures himself against criticism from below and not infrequently also from responsibility for mismanagement or actual stupidity.

In a socialist economy which is under construction, the fundamental condition for economic expenditure of the nation's resources is vigilant control by the masses, above all by the workers in the factories and plants. As long as they cannot move openly against disorders and abuses and expose their perpetrators by name, without the danger of being counted in the Opposition, among the "dissidents," among the troublemakers, or of being driven out of the cell and even from the plant, the struggle for a regime of economy as well as for the productivity of labor will inevitably be viewed on bureaucratic lines, i.e., they will most often strike at the vital interests of the workers. Precisely this is observed right now.

Clumsy or slovenly rate-setting work, harshly striking the workers, is in nine cases out of ten the direct result of bureaucratic inattention to the most elementary interests of the workers and even of production itself. It is to this that we must account the delayed payment of wages, i.e., relegating to the last consideration that which ought to constitute the prime concern.

The question of the so-called excesses at the top is fully linked to the repression of criticism. Many circulars are written against the excesses. Not a few cases against them are conducted in the Control Commissions. But the masses are suspicious of this kind of office-routine struggle with the excesses. There is one serious solution here—the masses must not be afraid to say what they think.

Where are these burning questions being discussed? Not in official party meetings but in corners and alleys, under cover, always in danger. From these intolerable conditions has stemmed the affair of Comrades Lashevich et al. The basic conclusion from this affair is: it is necessary to change conditions. . . .

10. The Comintern

Straightening out the class line of the Party means straightening out its international line. We must cast aside all doubting survivals of the innovation which represents the matter as though the victory of socialist construction in our country is not linked indissolubly with the course and outcome of the struggle of the European and world proletariat for power. We are building socialism and will go on building it. The European proletariat will struggle for power. The colonial peoples are struggling for independence. This is the common front. Each unit in each sector must give the maximum that it can give without waiting for the initiative of the others. Socialism will be victorious in our country in direct connection with the revolution of the European and world proletariat and with the struggle of the East against the imperialist yoke. . . .

11. On Factionalism

. . . The idea that by mechanically settling with the so-called opposition, it is possible to broaden the frame of party democracy is a crude self-deception; on the basis of all its experience the party cannot believe these lullabies any more. The methods of mechanical adjudication are preparing new splits and cleavages, new removals, new expulsions, new pressure with respect to the party as a whole. This system inevitably constricts the leading summit, reduces its authority and compels it to replace its ideological authority with doubled and tripled pressure. Whatever it does, the party must put a stop to this pernicious process. Lenin showed that firm leadership of the party does not mean strangling it.

12. For Unity

There cannot be the slightest doubt that the Party is able to straighten out its difficulties. The idea that there is no way out for the Party on the path of unity would be the supreme nonsense. There is a way out—moreover, only on the path of unity. . . .

Only on the foundation of party democracy is healthy, collective leadership possible. There is no other path. In struggle and in work on this, the only correct path, our unrecriminating support is guaranteed to the Central Committee wholly and in full.

Bukharin on the Opposition

Bukharin was the main spokesman of the party leadership on matters of theory during the controversy of 1926-27. In the summer of 1926 he replied to the Opposition with a defense of the cautious economics of the NEP and a warning that Opposition challenges to the unity of the party endangered the Soviet regime as a whole. The latter argument prepared the ground for the expulsion of the Opposition in 1927.

. . . The first thesis advanced by the opposition is the assertion that our industry is retrogressing, and that the disproportion between agriculture and city industry is increasing, to the detriment of city industry. . . . The total balance is undoubtedly in favor of the growth of industry as compared with agriculture.

The second thesis advanced by the opposition in the sphere of economic policy in its relation to the industrialization of the country is the thesis that we must now carry on a greatly intensified industrial policy, this to be accomplished in the first place by increasing the prices of our industrial products. . . .

We believe this policy to be entirely *wrong*, and we cannot agree to its pursuance. . . .

Every *monopoly* runs a *certain danger of rusting*, of resting on its laurels. The private capitalist and private owner is constantly being spurred onward by competition. . . . But if we, who have practically all big industry in our hands, who have a state super-monopoly and own all essentials, do not stimulate the leading staff of our industry to cheapen production, and to produce on more rational lines, then indeed we have arrived at the prerequisite stage for the rusting of our industry on the basis of its monopoly. That which is accomplished by competition . . . in a capitalist state, we

FROM: Bukharin, "The Party and the Opposition Bloc" (Report to the Leningrad Party Organization, July 28, 1926; slightly adapted from English translation in *International Press Correspondence*, no. 58, August 26, 1926, pp. 978-81, 983-84, 986-87)

must attain by conscious pressure under the impetus of the needs of the masses: *produce better and cheaper, supply better goods, supply cheap goods!* . . .

It would be entirely wrong to say industry should develop solely upon what is produced within this industry itself. On the contrary, the whole question is; *How much* can we take away from the peasantry, *to what extent* and *by what methods* can we accomplish the pumping-over process, what are the limits of the pumping-over, and how shall we calculate in order to arrive at favorable results? This is the question. Here lies the difference between us and the opposition, a difference which may be defined by saying that the comrades of the opposition are in favor of an immoderate amount of pumping-over, and are desirous of putting so severe a pressure upon the peasantry that in our opinion the result would be economically irrational and politically unallowable. . . .

Now the character, the class character of our soviet power in our country is being questioned. This is another step in the development of the oppositional idea, another step away from the true Leninist standpoint.

Comrade Trotsky, in one of his speeches at the Plenum of the Central Committee, advanced the thesis of the "extremely non-proletarian character" of the soviet power existing in our country. When the peasant question came under discussion, in connection with the results of the elections, the opposition stated that we are threatened by a deviation in the direction of the rich peasantry, and demanded decisive intervention on the part of the party, in order to prevent any further shifting in a state already far from being proletarian. . . .

Our proletarian dictatorship, our workers' state, has the peculiarities of working in an agricultural country and of having its state apparatus burdened with various bureaucratic aberrations.

This is perfectly true. But what is the *class character* of the state? It is a *workers' state*. To state that our state is not a workers' state, that it is already semi-bourgeois, is to assert that our state is already in a condition of degeneration, and to throw doubts upon the existence of the proletarian dictatorship in our country. . . . If this were really the case, it would be a very serious matter indeed. If we really had no proletarian dictatorship, then we should have to pursue a very different line, and our party, in so far as it is a proletarian party, would obviously place questions on the agenda aiming at a radical purging of the present Soviet power. . . .

This brings us to the thesis of the degeneration of our whole state apparatus, and of the deviation of our policy, and of the policy of the present Soviet state, from the interests of the broad proletarian masses. . . . The opposition has pointed out that the numerous bureaucratic groups in our state apparatus are complemented by the equally numerous bureaucratic groups in the economic organs, the cooperatives, the trade unions, etc. It would thus seem that the whole of the groups composing our apparatus have practically nothing in common with the interests of the broad masses.

We have been believing in our simplicity that our party is the vanguard of the proletariat; but now it turns out that it is a bureaucratic clique entirely detached from the masses. We believe the soviet power to represent a form of the dictatorship of the proletariat, but it appears that all we have is an extremely non-proletarian state, headed by a completely declassed caste. The logical continuance of this train of thought is bound to lead sooner or later to the idea of the overthrow of the soviet power—it can lead nowhere else. . . .

You are aware that up to now we Leninists have regarded the unity and coherence of our party as the first prerequisite for the maintenance and firmer establishment of the proletarian dictatorship. We Leninists have always imagined that the proletarian dictatorship can only be secure in our country if our party plays its role properly and when this party is in the first place the *sole* party in our country, that is, when the legal existence of other parties is made impossible, and in the second place the party is *unitary* in its structure, that is, represents a structure excluding any independent and autonomous groups, factions, organized currents, etc. . . . Now this has all changed at one blow. Now the whole opposition, the whole oppositional bloc—Trotsky, Kamenev, Zinoviev, Krupskaia,* etc.—demands freedom for factions within the party. . . .

It is to be observed that oppositional circles seem to like to dally with the idea of *two parties.* Ossovsky** prophesies that we shall have two parties in the immediate future, both of which will call themselves Communist at first: one party which will be in favor of withdrawal from the Anglo-Russian Committee and will stand for a very "international standpoint," and another party which imagines that socialism can be built up in our country alone, a sort of "national-communist" party. This entertaining of the idea of two parties has already become extremely popular in oppositional circles. The standpoint taken by the opposition on the freedom to form groups and factions is one step on the road to this idea, which in its actual essence is the idea of the justification of a split in the Party. . . .

. . . The Central Committee and the Central Control Commission have been faced by the fact that a number of comrades, including some holding extremely responsible positions, had actually taken such steps as the convocation of an illegal meeting against the party and its leaders. *Were we to tolerate such actions, our party would cease to exist tomorrow as a Leninist party.* We cannot tolerate this. We say to these comrades: Defend your principles, declare your standpoint, *speak in the party meetings;* but if you take to the forest, if you will not reply to our questions, if you refuse to make statements before the Control Commission, if you choose the method of organizing a new party within our party, the method of illegal organization, then we shall fight you relentlessly. . . .

We must increase our activity in the work of strengthening the ideology of all party members, of closing the ranks of

* Nadezhda Krupskaia: Lenin's widow, who sided with the opposition in 1925 and 1926—Ed.

** Ossovsky: one of Zinoviev's supporters, who argued that factions were natural—Ed.

the party on the basis of a definite political standpoint. May every member of the party know and realize that the majority of the Central Committee has a clearly defined standpoint, one for which it stands, which it continues, and which serves as a rule for its guidance of the party. . . . We have our line of policy, and we follow it *consistently*. We shall continue to stand for this line, to fight for it, to lead the party unwaveringly by it, and we are firmly convinced that the whole party . . . will pursue this line in every respect. The most important point is: the struggle for the right political line; everything else depends upon this, everything else is determined by the struggle for the right political line. Our line is actually a *Leninist* political line, from which we never deviate, for which we fight without ceasing, and which will be the means of leading us to victory.

The Theoretical Debate on Socialism in One Country

At the Fifteenth Party Conference in November, 1926, the opposition leaders tried to expose the forced nature of Stalin's theoretical innovations. A battle of quotations and hair-splitting distinctions ensued, indicative of the new Communist scholasticism. Stalin had the last word, thanks to his control of the party organization, and the manipulation of scripture to fit the political needs of the moment became a permanent feature of communism.

a) Kamenev's Criticism of Stalin

. . . Our whole Party holds the standpoint that our revolution is a socialist revolution, that it represents the basis for the further development of international revolution, and that it forms the transitional period from capitalism to socialism. . . .

Why is it then necessary, comrades, to invent differences of opinion on the character of our revolution and its future, since we are able to agree wholly and entirely with everything expressed in this resolution as the point of departure of the

FROM: Kamenev, Speech at the Fifteenth Party Conference (English translation in *International Press Correspondence*, no. 79, November 25, 1926, pp. 1365-67).

Party in the question of the nature of our revolution? (A voice: "Can socialism be established?") Wait, comrades. I cannot say everything at once. Wait till I come to that. . . .

Yes, in the course of the transition period between capitalism and Communism the proletariat will be able to establish the completely socialist state of society, provided it pursues a correct policy in its relations with the peasantry. . . .

. . . But why did Comrade Rykov write, and why did you unanimously decide—we are in perfect agreement with this standpoint—that we must catch up to and pass the level of development in the advanced capitalist countries within a historically comparative minimum of time? . . .

The point is, comrades, that this speed is necessary, and we must ask why it is considered necessary. It is necessary because the Soviet Union, as the first country of Socialism, must prove to the millions of the working people, the workers and peasants, the real superiority of socialist economy. This means that this country must and can provide for the needs of the population much more completely and cheaply than capitalist economics are capable of doing. (Comrade: "Thank God for that!" Laughter.)

. . . It is not only military intervention which may prove an obstacle in the path of the realisation of the completely socialist state of society, but the failure to carry out the above instructions. For this reason we raise the question of the rate of development of our economics, and not only the question of military intervention. The rate of our economic development, as compared with the rate of capitalist development, the necessity of rapidly attaining and passing the level of capitalism, is as important a prerequisite for the final victory of Socialism in our country as the necessity of safeguarding against military intervention. . . .

Comrade Stalin has here given us a detailed analysis of Lenin's views on the possibility of the realisation of Socialism in one country. In this he referred to an article of Lenin published in 1915. He proved that the theory and practice of the establishment of Socialism in the Soviet Union arise, so to speak, from his quotations, and from this law of the inequality of capitalist development. I cannot deal with this in detail, as the time is too short, and I must still speak of a number of other questions. But I cannot but observe that one must not refer to this quotation as indicating how Lenin conceived the tasks of the revolution in Russia at that time.

The simple duty of being perfectly accurate with respect to quotations from Lenin forces me to this explanation. This quotation, adduced correctly and completely by Comrade Stalin, was published in the "Social Democrat," the then central organ of our Party, on 25 August 1915. The article from which it is taken contains a general criticism of the standpoint of those social traitors who had said: We cannot begin the social revolution in Germany or in England or in Italy, we must begin everywhere at once. Lenin replied to them: You are traitors, for under the cloak of this theory, which compels one country to wait for another, you wish to avoid fulfilling your duty of kindling the proletarian revolution in every country. This was during the epoch of the imperialist war, in 1915. A month and a half later, in number 47 of the "Social Democrat," published on 13 October, exactly six weeks afterwards, Lenin wrote an article dealing specially with the tasks then confronting the Bolsheviki in Russia. Since Lenin stated in September that the victory of Socialism is possible in one country, even a backward country, and since he stated that it was the duty of every proletarian revolutionist to maintain this standpoint, we should naturally expect that he would apply the standpoint first of all to Russia.

But, comrades, this is not the case. We must not carelessly represent the true history of Lenin's views in order to score points in debate. Six weeks after the publication of the passage quoted by comrade Stalin, Lenin wrote in his famous article "Some Theses":

"While paying due regard to the demands made by our comrades from Russia, we formulate some theses on the actual questions of our present work."

A number of these are then enumerated, of which the fifth runs as follows:

"The social import of the next revolution in Russia can only be the revolutionary democratic dictatorship of the proletariat and the peasantry."

The sixth thesis reads:

"It is the task of the proletariat of Russia to carry through the bourgeois democratic revolution to its end, in order to arouse socialist revolution in Europe. This second task is now following very closely upon the first, but it still continues to remain a special and second task."

(Voices: "What of it?" "We have read that for ourselves." "That will not do. Nothing can be made of that!") Comrades, I cannot help it if it is disagreeable for you to hear these sentences. (Voices: "We not only hear them, but we understand them as well!")

If you will accord a straightforward consideration to the declaration of Lenin, made six weeks after the appearance of the article correctly quoted by Comrade Stalin, you will be bound to admit that Lenin's words in 1915 on the establishment of Socialism in one country referred clearly to the West European States . . . (A voice: "Nothing of the sort!") and that at the same time he pointed out another urgent task for Russia. That which I have read to you is his definition of the social import of the impending revolution. . . .

We regard our State as a proletarian State, not only because it is a State ruled by the dictatorship of the proletariat, but because the proletariat is utilising state power and state organisation as an instrument for raising up to Socialism the whole of the non-proletarian strata of the workers.

But, comrades, we must add—and it is our duty to do this—all that Lenin said on this question. Were we to state that we have a proletarian State and nothing more, then we should not be stating the truth, nor what Lenin said. For Lenin told us that we have a proletarian State in a double sense: the dictatorship of the proletariat, and the raising of the whole stratum of the workers to an ever higher level; but we have a proletarian State in a country with a preponderant peasant population and with bureaucratic deformations. . . .

But when a proletarian dictatorship is realised in a country with a preponderantly peasant population, the inevitable practical result is that in ordinary daily work the lowest stories of the building of state power will not be found to be in the hands of the purely industrial proletariat, but in the hands of the peasantry. (Disturbance. Voices: "Where then is the proletariat?" "Should we send the proletariat into the village Soviets, instead of to work in the factories?") Permit me to ask, comrades, is this a fact or is it not? . . . If we have 100 million peasants, and if we pursue the correct line of Soviet democracy, the certain result is the fact which I have just stated. It is to redouble our efforts towards adapting the proletarian methods of leadership to those subordinate organs of the Soviet apparatus and the Soviet power which are unavoidably in the hands of the peasantry. (Voices: "What object do these facts serve?") As soon as we touch upon this necessary task, then you begin to say: You are exaggerating, that is not a fact at all. In this way we can come to no understanding, comrades.

And precisely as this fact is the inevitable consequence of the realisation of the dictatorship of the proletariat and of the proletarian State in an agrarian country, in the same manner the bureaucratic deformations of the state apparatus are an expression of class.

What does this mean? In my opinion it means that the state apparatus, viewed from the class standpoint, is endeavouring to oust the workers from immediate participation in the administration of the State. . .

b) Stalin's Reply to Kamenev

. . . Engels said that the proletarian revolution . . . could not succeed in one single country alone. The facts, however, show that under the new conditions of imperialism, such a revolution in its most essential parts has already been carried through in one single country alone, for we have carried out nine tenths of this programme in our country.

Comrade Zinoviev may say that we have committed a

FROM: Stalin, Concluding Remarks at the Fifteenth Party Conference (English translation in *International Press Correspondence,* no. 78, November 25, 1926, pp. 1350, 1353-54).

mistake by carrying out the points of this programme (laughter). It is very easily possible that in carrying out these points we have shown a certain "national limitedness" (laughter). That is very easily possible. One thing is nevertheless true; that which Engels wrote in the forties of the last century under the conditions of pre-monopolistic capitalism and which was impossible for one country alone has become possible under the conditions of imperialism in our own country.

Naturally, if Engels were alive today, he would not cling to the old formula. On the contrary, he would welcome our revolution and say: To hell with all old formulas! Long live the victorious revolution in the Soviet Union! The gentlemen in the ranks of the Social Democracy, however, do not think like that. They cling to the old formulation of Engels in order to facilitate their struggle against the revolution, against the Bolsheviks. That is naturally their affair. It is only serious when Comrade Zinoviev attempts to imitate these gentlemen and in this matter to go the way of the Social Democracy. . . .

One must recognise, comrades, that it was Lenin and no other who first of all established the proof of the possibility of the victory of socialism in one country alone. One may not deny Lenin that which is due to him. One must not be afraid of the truth, one must have the courage to speak the truth, one must have the courage to declare that Lenin was the first Marxist who formulated the question of the victory of socialism in one country alone in a new form and answered it in the affirmative.

I do not wish with this to say that Lenin as a thinker stood higher than Marx or Engels. I only wish to say two things: First of all, one must not demand of Marx and Engels, although they were tremendous thinkers and geniuses, that in the period of pre-monopolistic capital they could foresee all the possibilities of the proletarian class struggle and the proletarian revolution which developed half a century later in the period of developed monopolistic capitalism. Secondly, there is nothing particularly wonderful in the fact that Lenin, himself a genius and a follower of Engels and Marx, should have understood the new possibilities of the proletarian revolution under the new conditions of capitalist development and thus establish the truth that the victory of socialism in one country alone is possible. . . .

. . . Comrade Kamenev took the "trouble" to prove that the basic article of Comrade Lenin (1915) which deals with the possibility of socialism in one country alone, allegedly did not refer to Russia, but that when Lenin spoke of such a possibility he was thinking not of Russia but of other capitalist countries. Comrade Kamenev took this doubtful "trouble" in order to clear the way for Comrade Trotsky whose "scheme" was refuted by the article of Lenin written in 1915.

To put it vulgarly, Comrade Kamenev has played the role of housemaid to Comrade Trotsky by cleaning the way for him (laughter). It is naturally a sad sight to observe the director of the Lenin Institute in the role of Housemaid to Comrade Trotsky. Not that there is anything undignified in the work of a housemaid, but because comrade Kamenev is without doubt a capable person who might very well concern himself with more qualified work. He adopted this role, however, perfectly voluntarily, as of course he was fully entitled to do, so that nothing is to be done in the matter. How has Comrade Kamenev carried out this peculiar role? Comrade Kamenev declared in his speech that the chief theses of Lenin in his article written in 1915, the theses which have determined the whole policy of our revolution and its work of reconstruction, the theses which speak of the possibility of the victory of socialism in one country alone, do not refer to Russia and could not refer to Russia and that when Lenin spoke of the victory of socialism in one country alone, he was not thinking of Russia but of other capitalist countries. That is unbelievable and unheard of, that sounds like a direct slander against Comrade Lenin. But Comrade Kamenev evidently does not care what the party thinks about such a falsification of Lenin. He is only concerned to clear the way for Comrade Trotsky at any price.

How has he attempted to justify this peculiar contention? He said that two weeks after the publication of the article mentioned, Comrade Lenin published his well-known theses concerning the character of the coming revolution in which he said that the task of Marxists would be exhausted with the efforts to achieve the victory of the bourgeois democratic revolution in Russia and that Lenin, when he said this, spoke on the assumption that the Revolution in Russia would retain its bourgeois stage and not develop into a socialist revolution. As, however, the article of Lenin upon the possibility of the victory of socialism in one country alone deals not with the bourgeois revolution but with the socialist revolution, it is clear that Lenin in his article could not have been thinking of Russia.

According to Kamenev it turns out that Lenin interpreted the extent of the Russian revolution just as a left bourgeois revolutionary or a reformist of the social democratic type would have done, according to whose opinions a bourgeois revolution would not develop into a socialist revolution and that between a bourgeois and a socialist revolution a long historical interval, a long pause of at least several decades must intervene whilst capitalism develops and the proletariat vegetates.

According to Kamenev it turns out that in 1915 when he wrote his article, Lenin did not think and did not conceive of directly going on to the socialist revolution after the victory of the bourgeois revolution. You will say, this is unbelievable and unheard of. Yes, this contention of Comrade Kamenev is really unbelievable and unheard of. But Kamenev does not mind about that in the least.

Permit me to mention a few documents which prove that Comrade Kamenev has vulgarly falsified the opinions of Comrade Lenin in this question. . . .

. . . Where are we to fit in the theses of Lenin from 1915 to which Comrade Kamenev appealed in his speech and which deal with the tasks of the bourgeois democratic revolution in Russia? Do not these theses contradict the idea of the development of the bourgeois revolution into a socialist revolution? No, they do not, on the contrary. The basis of these theses is just the idea of the development of the bourgeois revolution into the socialist revolution, the idea of the development of the first stage of the Russian revolution into its second stage.

First of all Lenin by no means says in these theses that the extent of the Russian revolution and the tasks of the Marxists in Russia are exhausted with the fall of the Czar and the landowners, by the fulfilment of the tasks set by the bourgeois democratic revolution. Secondly, Lenin in these theses limited himself to characterising the tasks of the bourgeois democratic revolution because he regarded this revolution as the first stage and as the immediate task of the Russian Marxists. Thirdly, Lenin proceeds from the assumption that the Russian Marxists must not commence their task with the second stage (as comrade Trotsky proposed with his slogan "down with the Czar, form a workers government") but with the first stage, with the stage of the bourgeois democratic revolution.

Is there any contradiction here? Is even the shadow of a contradiction with the idea of the development of the bourgeois revolution into the socialist revolution here? The opposite is the case.

We see that Comrade Kamenev has definitely falsified the standpoint of Lenin. . . .

Stalin on the Expulsion of the Left Opposition

Bitter controversy between the Opposition and the party leadership raged from the summer of 1926 to the fall of 1927, though Stalin's control of the party organization left no doubt as to the outcome of the contest. The Opposition leaders were removed from one post after another, and at the Fifteenth Party Congress in December, 1927, the active oppositionists were expelled from the party. Stalin justified this as the elimination of deviant individualists who refused to respect the principle of party discipline. Zinoviev and Kamenev with their followers thereupon recanted, and were temporarily reinstated in the party. The Trotskyists were exiled to remote points in Siberia and elsewhere. A year later, in February, 1929, Trotsky was ousted from the country altogether.

How could it happen that the entire Party, as a whole, and following it the working class too, so thoroughly isolated the opposition? After all, the opposition are headed by well-known people with well-known names, people who know how to advertise themselves (*voices:* "Quite right!"), people who are not afflicted with modesty (*applause*) and are able to blow their own trumpets.

It happened because the leading groups of the opposition proved to be a group of petty-bourgeois intellectuals divorced from life, divorced from the revolution, divorced from the Party, from the working class. (*Voices:* "Quite right!" *Applause*). . . .

Have we the dictatorship of the proletariat or not? Rather a strange question. (*Laughter*) Nevertheless, the opposition raise it in every one of their statements. The opposition say that we are in a state of Thermidor degeneration. What does that mean? It means that we have not the dictatorship of the proletariat, that our economics and our politics are a failure, are going backwards, that we are not going towards Socialism, but towards capitalism. This, of course, is strange and foolish. But the opposition insist on it. . . .

. . . The opposition utterly break away from the Leninist principle of organization and take the path of organizing a second party, the path of organizing a new International. . . . On all these questions the opposition have slipped into Menshevism. Can these Menshevik views of the opposition be regarded as compatible with the Party's ideology, with our Party's program, with its tactics, with the tactics of the Comintern, with the organizational principles of Leninism?

Under no circumstances; not for a single moment!

You will ask: how could such an opposition come into being among us; where are their social roots? I think that the social roots of the opposition lie in the fact that the urban petty-bourgeois strata are being ruined under the conditions of our development, in the fact that these strata are discontented with the regime of the dictatorship of the proletariat, in the striving of these strata to change this regime, to "improve" it in the spirit of establishing bourgeois democracy.

I have already said that as a result of our progress, as a

FROM: Stalin, *Political Report of the Central Committee to the Fifteenth Congress of the C.P.S.U.(B.)* (December 3, 1927; English translation, Moscow Foreign Languages Publishing House, 1950, pp. 92, 99, 105-6, 110-11).

result of the growth of the relative weight of the socialist forms of economy, a section of the petty-bourgeoisie, particularly the urban bourgeoisie, is being ruined and is going under. The opposition reflect the grumbling and discontent of these strata with the regime of the proletarian revolution.

Such are the social roots of the opposition. . . .

Why did the Party expel Trotsky and Zinoviev? Because they are the *organizers* of the entire anti-Party opposition (*voices:* "Quite right!"), because they set themselves the aim of breaking the laws of the Party, because they thought that nobody would dare to touch them, because they wanted to create for themselves the privileged position of nobles in the Party. . . .

If the opposition want to be in the Party let them submit to the will of the Party, to its laws, to its instructions, without reservations, without equivocation. If they refuse to do that, let them go wherever they please. (*Voices:* "Quite right!" *Applause*). We do not want new laws providing privileges for the opposition, and we will not create them. (*Applause*).

The question is raised about terms. We have only one set of terms: the opposition must disarm wholly and entirely, in ideological and organizational respects. (*Voices:* "Quite right!" *Prolonged applause*).

They must renounce their anti-Bolshevik views openly and honestly, before the whole world. (*Voices:* "Quite right!" *Prolonged applause*). . . .

Stalin on the Grain Crisis

In 1928, after disposing of the Trotsky-Zinoviev opposition, Stalin began to turn to a more vigorous policy of industrial development and exploitation of the peasants. While there is evidence that he was at least partly motivated in this by the desire to embarrass Bukharin and Rykov, Stalin nonetheless put his case effectively.

. . . The underlying cause of our grain difficulties is that the increase in the production of grain for the market is not keeping pace with the increase in the demand for grain.

Industry is growing. The number of workers is growing. Towns are growing. And, lastly, the regions producing industrial crops (cotton, flax, sugar beet, etc.) are growing, creating a demand for grain. All this leads to a rapid increase in our requirements as regards grain—grain available for the market. But the production of grain for the market is increasing at a disastrously slow rate. . . .

. . . Is it not a fact that the grain crop area has already reached the prewar mark? Yes, it is a fact. Is it not a fact that already last year the gross production of grain was equal to the prewar output, i.e., 5,000,000,000 *puds*?* Yes, it is a fact. How, then, is it to be explained that, in spite of these facts, the amount of grain we are producing for the market is only one-half, and the amount we are exporting is only about one-twentieth of what it was in prewar times?

The reason is primarily and chiefly the change in the structure of our agriculture brought about by the October Revolution, the change from large-scale landlord and large-scale kulak farming, which provided the largest proportion of marketed grain, to small- and middle-peasant farming, which provides the smallest proportion of marketed grain. The mere fact that before the war there were fifteen to sixteen million individual peasant farms, whereas at present there are 24,000,000 to 25,000,000 peasant farms, shows that now the basis of our agriculture is essentially small-peasant farming, which provides a minimum amount of grain for the market. . . .

. . . The abolition of landlord (large-scale) farming, the reduction of the kulak (large-scale) farming to less than one-third, and the change to small-peasant farming with only 11 per cent of its output available for the market, in the absence, in the sphere of grain growing, of any more or less developed large-scale socialized farming (collective farms and state farms), was bound to lead, and in fact has led, to a sharp reduction in the output of grain for the market as

FROM: Stalin, "On the Grain Front" (*Talk to Students of the Institute of Red Professors, the Communist Academy and the Sverdlov University, May 28, 1928; Problems of Leninism,* pp. 248-249, 251-59).

* One *pud* = approximately 36 lbs.—Ed.

compared with prewar times. It is a fact that the amount of marketed grain in our country is now half of what it was before the war, although the gross output of grain has reached the prewar level. . . .

What is the way out of this situation?

Some people see the way out of this situation in a return to kulak farming, in the development and extension of kulak farming. These people dare not advocate a return to landlord farming, for they realize, evidently, that such talk is dangerous in our times. All the more eagerly, therefore, do they urge the necessity of the utmost development of kulak farming in the interest of—the Soviet power. These people think that the Soviet power can simultaneously rely on two opposite classes—the class of the kulaks, whose economic principle is the exploitation of the working class, and the class of the workers, whose economic principle is the abolition of all exploitation. A trick worthy of reactionaries.

There is no need to prove that these reactionary "plans" have nothing in common with the interests of the working class, with the principles of Marxism, with the tasks of Leninism. . . .

What, then, is the way out of the situation?

1. The way out lies, firstly, in the transition from the small, backward and scattered peasant farms to amalgamated, large-scale socialized farms, equipped with machinery, armed with scientific knowledge and capable of producing a maximum of grain for the market. The solution lies in the transition from individual peasant farming to collective, socialized farming. . . .

2. The way out lies, secondly, in expanding and strengthening the old state farms, and in organizing and developing new, large state farms. . . .

3. Finally, the way out lies in systematically increasing the yield of the small and middle individual peasant farms. We cannot and should not lend any support to the individual large kulak farms. But we can and should assist the individual small- and middle-peasant farms, helping them to increase their crop yields and drawing them into the channel of cooperative organizations. . . .

Thus, if all these tasks are fulfilled, the state can in three or four years' time have at its disposal 250,000,000 to 300,-000,000 additional *puds* of marketable grain—a supply more or less sufficient to enable us to manoeuvre within the country as well as abroad. . . .

Should not, in addition to these measures, a number of other measures be adopted—measures, say, to reduce the rate of development of our industry, the growth of which is causing a considerable increase in the demand for grain which at present is outstripping the increase in the production of grain for the market? No, not under any circumstances! To reduce the rate of development of industry would mean to weaken the working class; for every step forward in the development of industry, every new factory, every new works, is, as Lenin expressed it, "a new stronghold" of the working class, which strengthens its position in the fight against the petty-bourgeois element, in the fight against the capitalist elements in our economy. On the contrary, we must maintain the present rate of development of industry; we must at the first opportunity speed it up in order to pour goods into the rural districts and obtain from them more grain, in order to supply agriculture, primarily the collective farms and state farms, with machines, in order to industrialize agriculture and to increase the proportion of its output for the market.

Should we, perhaps, for the sake of greater "caution," retard the development of heavy industry and make light industry, which produces chiefly for the peasant market, the basis of our industry as a whole? Not under any circumstances! That would be suicidal; it would undermine our whole industry, including light industry. It would mean abandoning the slogan of industrializing our country, it would transform our country into an appendage of the world capitalist system of economy. . . .

How will the measures proposed affect the alliance between the workers and the peasants? I think that these measures can only help to strengthen the alliance between the workers and the peasants.

Indeed, if the collective farms and the state farms develop

at increased speed; if, as a result of direct assistance given to the small and middle peasants, the yield of their farms increases and the cooperative societies embrace wider and wider masses of the peasantry; if the state obtains the hundreds of millions of *puds* of additional marketable grain required for the purposes of manoeuvering; if, as a result of these and similar measures, the kulaks are curbed and gradually overcome—is it not clear that the contradictions between the working class and the peasantry within the alliance of workers and peasants will thereby be smoothed out more and more; that the need for emergency measures in the purchase of grain will disappear; that the large masses of peasantry will turn more and more to collective forms of farming and that the fight to overcome the capitalist elements in the rural districts will assume an increasingly mass and organized character?

Is it not clear that the cause of the alliance between the workers and the peasants can only benefit by these measures? . . .

. . . The alliance of the proletariat with the peasantry under the conditions of the dictatorship of the proletariat should not be regarded as an alliance with the whole of the peasantry. The alliance of the proletariat with the peasantry is an alliance of the working class with the labouring masses of the peasantry. Such an alliance cannot be effected without a struggle against the capitalist elements of the peasantry, against the kulaks. . . .

The Right Opposition

Stalin's political tactics and his desire for stepped-up industrialization and increased pressure on the peasants produced acute anxiety among many of his colleagues. Bukharin, together with Rykov and the trade-union chief Tomsky, formed a "Right Opposition" which endeavored to check Stalin in behind-the-scenes maneuvers. In July, 1928, Bukharin addressed the Central Committee with a vain plea for caution, and then turned to the broken Left Opposition to reveal his fears and seek help.

a) Bukharin on Peasant Policy

. . . If we want to catch up with Western Europe—and we want to do this—if we want to increase the tempo of accumulation for socialist industry—and we want to do this —if we take into account our general economic backwardness, our poverty, then it is perfectly clear that great difficulties for our building stem from all this. We want to solve a series of great tasks at once: the maximum accumulation in socialist industry, the maximum increase in agriculture, the maximum consumption for the working class and the toiling masses in general, their maximum uplift, etc. These tasks cannot be solved simultaneously. We solve them as we come to them, heeling over now to one side, now to the other, contradicting ourselves. We are moving all the time in contradictions. It stands to reason that difficulties of such a kind really lie in the nature of our reconstruction period. I call your attention, for example, to the curious fact that we complain of economic disproportions now from one end and now from the other.

Voroshilov: Give us your panacea.

Bukharin: I don't want to give a panacea, and you, please, don't make fun of me. I want to say that the reconstruction period quite naturally evokes a series of complications and difficulties, but at the same time there is no doubt in my mind that there are different kinds of difficulties. . . . When, taking Comrade Stalin's formulation, we say now, "We have a threat to the *smychka,*" does this fit into the category of circumstances from which a split could issue? Of course it does. A threat to the *smychka* is a circumstance from which a split could issue. But Lenin wrote that the main task of our Central Committee and Central Control Commission, as of our party as a whole, consists of not allowing these disagreements to grow to the level of serious class disagreements. . . . To undertake the slightest campaign in the country reversing our election instruction means to mobilize

FROM: Bukharin, Speech to the Central Committee, July 10, 1928 (editor's translation from partial copy of the minutes of the meeting in the Trotsky Archive).

against us to an ever greater degree the *kulak* element, the petty bourgeoisie of a whole series of cities, the middle bourgeoisie, petty-bourgeois strata, etc. The reserves of these forces remain very great, and the slightest vacillation on this question in the ranks of our party will have a disproportionately great political significance. . . . Should we correct the situation we now have as a result of the grain collections by making concessions in the direction of the *kulak*, by dropping the slogan of an intensified offensive against the *kulaks?* Absolutely not. The problem at the present time is to remove the threat to the alliance with the middle peasant which we now find. We are dropping the extraordinary measures,* and in no case do we identify the extraordinary measures with the decisions of the Fifteenth Congress. . . . Can we have such difficulties this year as we had last year? We can. How will we react to this? We will turn to the application of extraordinary measures if such difficulties are met within the coming year, but if we apply them, will we do so to the same extent or not? It seems to me that this is the most agonizing and important question that faces us. As a preliminary I would like to suggest a consideration or analogy which at first glance will appear wild or joking.

Imagine that you are the proletarian power in a petty-bourgeois country, but that you are forcibly driving the *muzhik* [peasant] into communes.

Voroshilov: As in 1918 and 1919, let's say.

Bukharin: Then you will get an uprising of the *muzhik*, of which the *kulak* is the driver; the *kulak* organizes and leads it.

The petty-bourgeois element rises against the proletariat, beats it on the head, and as the result of a cruel class war the proletarian dictatorship disappears. What do you get here?

Stalin: The Son is terrifying but God is gracious. (Laughter). . . .

Bukharin: We must in no case turn toward allowing the expanded reproduction of extraordinary measures.

Kossior: This is true.

Lozovsky: Right now this doesn't depend on us.

* I.e., the pressure applied to the peasants to get grain during the winter of 1928-29—Ed.

Bukharin: Right now a great deal still depends on us. Therefore, the center of our policy is the following: We must in no case allow a threat to the *smychka*. Otherwise we will not fulfill the basic testament of Lenin. . . .

b) *Bukharin on the Menace of Stalin*

Kamenev: Is the struggle really serious?

Bukharin: That's just what I wanted to talk about. We feel that Stalin's line is ruinous for the whole revolution. We could be overthrown on account of it. The disagreements between us and Stalin are many times more serious than the disagreements which we used to have with you. Rykov, Tomsky and I agree on formulating the situation thus: "It would be much better if Zinoviev and Kamenev were in the Politbureau instead of Stalin." I have spoken with Rykov and Tomsky about this quite frankly. I have not spoken with Stalin for several weeks. He is an unprincipled intriguer, who subordinates everything to the preservation of his own power. He changes his theory according to whom he needs to get rid of. In the "seven" * our arguing with him reached the point of saying, "false," "you lie," etc. Now he has made concessions, so that he can cut our throats. We understand this, but he maneuvers so as to make us appear to be the schismatics. . . . This is the line which he pronounced at the plenum: 1) Capitalism grew either on account of colonies, or loans, or the exploitation of the workers. We have no colonies, we can get no loans, therefore our basis is tribute from the peasantry. You understand that this is just what Preobrazhensky's theory is. 2) The more socialism grows, the greater will be the resistance [to it]. . . . This is idiotic illiteracy. 3) Since tribute is necessary and resistance will grow, we need firm leadership. Self-criticism must not apply to the leadership, but only to those who carry out orders. Self-criticism is in fact aimed at Tomsky and Uglanov.** As

FROM: Bukharin-Kamenev Talk, July 11, 1928 (Notes by Kamenev; editor's translation from copy in the Trotsky Archive).

* The informal leadership group, including most of the Politbureau—Ed.

** Uglanov: pro-Bukharin secretary of the Moscow party organization, removed in the fall of 1928—Ed.

a result we are getting a police regime. This is not a "cuckoo" matter, but will really decide the fate of the revolution. With this theory everything can perish. . . .

The Petersburg [Leningrad] people are in general with us, but they got scared when the talk got to the possibility of removing Stalin. . . . Our potential forces are vast, but 1) the middle-ranking Central Committee member still does not understand the depth of the disagreements, 2) there is a terrible fear of a split. Therefore, when Stalin conceded on the extraordinary measures, he made it difficult for us to attack him. We don't want to come forth as schismatics, for then they would slaughter us. But Tomsky in his latest speech showed clearly that Stalin is the schismatic. . . .

Kuibyshev on Industrialization

Stalin's chief spokesman on industrial development was Valerian V. Kuibyshev, head of the Supreme Economic Council. In September, 1928, Kuibyshev set forth the basic intention of developing heavy industry at the maximum possible rate, and dismissed all criticism of this course as a "petty-bourgeois" deviation.

The occurrence of a deficit in the coming year too forces us once more to return to the question of the rate of development of our industry. At any price we must absolutely accelerate the growth of our industry as far as possible. What are we likely to attain in the coming twelvemonth? We reckon with an increase of 20 per cent, i.e., 22 per cent in the case of the industry producing means of production, and 18 per cent in the case of the industry catering for direct consumption. The heavy industries manufacturing articles of production will be the object of particular attention in this connection.

FROM: Kuibyshev, "The Economic Situation of the Soviet Union" (Report to the Leningrad Party Organization, September 19, 1928; English translation in *International Press Correspondence*, no. 73, October 19, 1928, pp. 1337-38, and no. 75, October 26, 1928, p. 1383).

The question arises whether we are right in our programme. Is it right that we should particularly accelerate the rate of development of industry producing the means of production in regard both to the investment of funds and to an augmentation of the quantities produced, while the peasant question becomes more and more acute and there is an ever-increasing demand for mass-articles on the rural markets? I believe such a line of procedure to be absolutely correct. . . .

. . . Those assertions cannot be too energetically repudiated which speak of an "over-industrialisation" and accuse us of employing unduly great funds for the manufacture of means of production, i.e., for the metal industry, engineering, for hard coal, petroleum, and the like, also maintaining that the rate of development of our industry is exceeding our strength and must therefore be reduced. Such talk, which arises out of a feeling of panic in view of the difficulties with which we are faced and which can only be overcome by as great as possible an increase in the output capacity of our industry, is in direct opposition to the interests and requirements of our country. We are confronted with the immediate danger of a deficit in regard to metals. The Presidium of the Supreme Economic Council recently treated the question of an importation of cast iron. That suffices to show how disagreeable and anomalous is the position in which we are at present. It is altogether absurd to assert that part of the money we spend on great industrial constructions ought to be employed for the lighter industries. . . .

Our economic development cannot be expected to proceed quite without failure, disproportions, or anomalies. We shall constantly be involved in anomalies, seeing that we had not the possibility during the first years of the existence of the Soviet Union to live in peace and to proceed smoothly and uninterruptedly with all branches of our development. We were deprived of this possibility because a great number of contradictions existed even in former times in our industry and in all other branches of our economy, in which connection it must be borne in mind that the more successfully we progress in our socialist development, the greater will be the difficulties that will be laid in our path by our opponents at home and abroad. The elimination of class differences, which is the final aim of our entire development, will and must be effected in the form of ever greater class struggle. Naturally we shall need more than a decade to eradicate these differences and to ensure a smooth and harmonious development of our economic organism without disproportions and anomalies. These differences and anomalies are inevitable and we shall be occupied with them for a long time to come. They will lead to new difficulties and complications in our economic life. But they will not hinder us, they must not be allowed to diminish the energy with which we carry on development along the lines laid down by our Party. The industrialisation of the country and the enhancement of the rate of industrialisation are both tasks continually confronting us. . . .

. . . We must be prepared to meet with discontent and active resistance in certain sections of the population, which will increase the difficulties with which we are faced in an economic respect. On the other hand, this same discontent penetrates through all sorts of channels even as far as certain parts of our Soviet apparatus, the result being doubts as to the possibility of executing such great tasks and as to the wisdom of aspiring to such difficult objectives as are involved in the industrialisation of agriculture and the industrialisation of our entire economy. By penetrating into our Soviet apparatus, such sentiments also find ingress in a small measure into our Party. The Party will have recourse to all available measures for the purpose of nipping in the bud such sentiments as pessimism or lack of confidence. The July plenum of the C[entral] C[ommittee] openly stated that, apart from its energetic struggle against pseudo-radical tendencies of the nature of Trotskyism, "left" tendencies which in reality hide a Social Democratic core, the Party must also combat such pessimistic currents as are occasioned by the existing difficulties and tend to diminish the energy and activity essential for the solution of the tremendous tasks with which we are faced. Seeing that the difficulties before us are very great and that the unity, discipline, and solidarity of our Party are our only guarantee of success, we must seek not only to combat the pessimistic tendencies, which are to a great part no more than the reflection of the discontent of the petty-bourgeois chaos at our policy of industrialisation, but also to combat the attitude of tolerance observed with regard to these tendencies. . . .

. . . We are told we are "over-industrialising" and "biting off more than we can chew." History, however, will not permit us to proceed more slowly, otherwise the very next year may lead to a series of even more serious anomalies than are apparent to-day. Any careful student of our economy will, I am sure, agree with me that the most serious misproportion, which is most disadvantageous in its effect on our economy, is that between the output of the means of production and the requirements of the country. . . .

The difficulty of the economic tasks before us upon the one hand and the growth of the hostile forces arrayed against us (both by international capitalism and by the capitalistic elements within our country) upon the other, are naturally reflected in the attitude of the engineers and other technical staffs.

The process of differentiation among the technical staffs has greatly increased, dividing them into a very small group of outright enemies of the Soviet authority and underminers of our economy on the one side, and upon the other such of the engineers and technical operatives as are wholly devoted to the object of socialist development and inspired with the [sense] of the grand task before us. This process of differentiation not only deserves our closest attention, but must also furnish us with various valuable conclusions. While most energetically opposing the enemies of our economy, who are direct agents of the bourgeoisie, we must give all possible aid and encouragement to the honest and devoted technical operatives and see to it that the conditions of their activity are such as will facilitate the execution of the tasks with which they are charged. . . .

All organisations that are in touch with the technical staffs are beginning to understand that without a healthy relationship and without the honest co-operation of the technical staffs with the Soviet authorities, we shall not be able to realise the gigantic plan of the reconstruction of our industry, which is not only completely indispensable to us but which is also the very best guarantee for our economy and for the development of socialism. Without technical staffs, the technical equipment of our industry is an impossibility. At the same time, however, all the necessary steps must naturally be taken to train new cadres of Red engineers. This side of the question deserves more attention than has ever been paid to it before. . . .

Bukharin on Equilibrium

In reply to the Stalinists' new industrialization emphasis, Bukharin published a plea for caution and balance in which he opposed sacrificing the standard of living of the population. This "consumptionist" attitude has recurred from time to time in the Communist movement, particularly in the Communist regimes of Eastern Europe.

. . . The relative *planlessness*—or *relative planfulness*—of the economy of the transition period has its basis in the existence of small enterprises, of market connections, i.e., significant elements of . . . spontaneity. . . . Hence the very plan has a special nature: it is by no means the more or less 'finished' plan of a developed socialist society. In this plan there are many elements of the forecasting of the spontaneous or incalculable (for example, estimate of the crop, the amount of grain coming to market, the amount of products of peasant production as a whole that will be offered on the market, and, consequently, also the estimate of prices, etc. etc.), and these forecasts become the starting point of one or another directive. It is just for this reason that with us there is no possibility of an "ideal" plan. And just for this reason there is room up to a *certain* point for errors. But the fact that an error can be explained and may even be *unavoidable* does not prevent it from being an *error*. This

FROM: Bukharin, "Notes of an Economist" (September 30, 1928; English translation by Bertram D. Wolfe in *Khrushchev and Stalin's Ghost*, New York, Praeger, 1957, pp. 299-302, 304-6, 309-11, 314-15; reprinted by permission of the publisher).

is the first point. Secondly, the gravest violations of fundamental proportions (as was the case with us in the grain economy, of which more below), and the resultant miscalculations are *by no means unavoidable* errors. Thirdly, even if a good plan is not omnipotent, then a bad "plan" and bad economic maneuvering in general can ruin even a good cause. . . .

. . . For this reason, despite the relativism of our planning, its role is really *enormous.* Major errors in the directing of the economy which result in a violation of the basic economic proportions in the country, therefore, of themselves may engender a highly unfavorable change in the relations of the classes. The reverse side of such a violation of the necessary *economic* proportions would be a resultant upsetting of the *political* equilibrium in the country.

To avoid a "goods famine" and a "crisislike" violation of the basic economic proportions, which are by no means inevitable or absolute laws, it follows that:

In order to attain the most favorable possible march of social reproduction (the most crisis-free), and to attain the systematic growth of socialism, and, in consequence, to attain the most favorable possible situation for the proletariat in the relations of class forces in the country—it is necessary to achieve a coordination of the basic elements of the national economy, to 'balance' them, arrange them, arrange them in such fashion that they best fulfill their respective functions, and actively influence the course of economic life and the class struggle so as to attain the best possible balance or equilibrium. . . .

In their simplicity, the ideologists of Trotskyism assume that the maximum annual pumping out of resources from the peasant economy into industry will assure the maximum tempo of the development of industry. But that is clearly not so. The greatest *not temporary but continuous* tempo can be attained by such a coordination in which industry develops on the foundation of a *rapidly growing* agricultural economy. It is then that industry attains its own record-breaking figures in its development. . . .

. . . What the Trotskyites fail to comprehend is that the

development of industry is dependent on the development of agriculture. . . .

. . . *Along with a stormy growth of industry, along with a significant growth in the population and a rise in the needs of the population, the quantity of grain has not grown in the country.* Isn't it clear that a contemptuous attitude to the grain problem under such conditions would be a real crime? And is it not clear . . . that a Trotskyist "solution" would lead straight to a real, and not an imaginary collapse? . . .

. . . One thing is clear: if any branch of production systematically fails to receive in return for its products the costs of production, plus a certain addition corresponding to a *part* of the surplus labor which can serve as a source of expanding reproduction, then that branch of industry either stagnates or *retrogresses.* This law "applies" to grain growing as it does to any other branch of the economy. . . .

Those who believe that the growth of the planned economy brings with it the possibility—as a result of the dying out of the law of value—of doing whatever one pleases, simply do not understand the ABC of economics. These considerations are sufficient to define the limit of the process of "pumping over" resources from agriculture to *industry. The opponents of industrialization* come out against any alienation even of a part of the surplus product, i.e. against all "pumping over" whatsoever. But in that case the tempo of industrialization will be slowed up. The Trotskyists define the magnitude of the pumping over by the limits of the "technically achievable," i.e., they go even beyond the limits of the entire surplus product. It is clear that in that case there can be no thought of the *development* of agriculture or its grain section, which in turn is required for the development of industry itself. Here the truth lies somewhere in between. . . .

The center of all our plan calculations, of all our economic policy, must be concern for the steadily developing *industrialization of our country.* . . . From every point of view—development of the productive forces, development of agriculture, growth of the specific gravity of socialism in the total economy, strengthening of the class alliances within the country, strengthening of our powers of self-defense, growth of mass consumption, etc. etc.—the industrialization of the country is for us a *law*.

But in carrying this out we must always remember that our socialist industrialization must differ from capitalist industrialization in that it is carried out *by the proletariat*, for the purposes of *socialism*, that its effect upon the peasant economy must be quite different and distinct in character, that its whole attitude towards the village economy must be different and distinct. Capitalism effected the *debasement* of agriculture. Socialist industrialization, however, is not a parasitic process in its relations with the village (under capitalism, despite the development of agriculture under the influence of industry, the elements of such a parasitism are present), but a means of its great *transformation and upswing*. The industrialization of the country therefore signifies also the industrialization of agriculture and thereby it prepares the abolition of the antagonism between city and village. . . .

We should strive for the fastest possible tempo of industrialization. Does that mean that we ought to put everything into capital construction? The question is quite a meaningless one. But behind this meaningless question there is hidden another that is quite meaningful: namely, the question of the limits of accumulation, of the upper limit for the sum of capital investment.

Above all, when we are drawing up our program of capital construction we must keep in mind the directive of the party on reserves (of valuta, gold, grain, goods). Of late it has become the fashion to keep quiet about the question of reserves. . . . Though silence may be golden and we short of gold, still we cannot afford to play at silence in this. We not only have no reserves; but in meeting the current supply problem itself "waiting one's turn" and "queuing up" have become our "way of life," which to a significant degree also disorganizes our *productive* life. . . .

. . . I have the impression that the People's Supreme Economic Council in drawing up its Five-Year Plan has forgotten the policy of reserves altogether . . . and that the excessive demands put upon the budget make it 'unrealistic.' But 'lack of realism' is 'quite' an essential deficiency in a plan.

It's clear that the question of reserves is tied up with the question of consumption, both productive consumption (including capital construction) and personal consumption (the personal consumption of the masses). And we all know that in this the bow is already drawn at high tension. *To increase this tension still further, and increase still more the goods famine, is impossible. . . .*

We must mobilize and put in motion the maximum number and kind of economic factors which work in favor of socialism. This requires a most complicated combination of personal, group, mass, social and state initiative. We have *too much* overcentralized everything. We must ask ourselves: ought we not now to take some steps in the direction of the Leninist commune-state? This does not by any means signify "letting go of the reins." Quite the contrary. The fundamental leadership, the solving of the more important problems, are matters which must be dealt with more firmly, more severely—*but for that reason more carefully thought out* "at the center." But within the strict framework of these decisions the lower organs must act on their own initiative and be responsible for *their own* range of problems, etc. Supercentralization in a number of fields had led to our depriving ourselves of *additional forces, means, resources and possibilities.* And we are in no position to utilize the entire mass of these possibilities, thanks to a number of bureaucratic barriers. We could act with more elasticity, more maneuverability, more successfully, if, beginning with the individual state enterprises, we were in a position to adapt ourselves to the real, concrete conditions, and thereby avoid the thousand small and large stupidities we are committing. . . .

The Condemnation of the Right Opposition

The first overt move against Bukharin, Rykov and Tomsky was made by the Politbureau in February, 1929, after a series of unpublicized maneuvers and conflicts in the party organization. Disclosure of the Bukharin-Kamenev negotiations prompted a broadening series of attacks on the "Right deviation," which finally culminated in the public denunciation of the Right Opposition leaders in the summer of 1929. The latter were removed from their most important posts, though their abject recantation in the fall of 1929 saved them for the time being from being expelled from the party. Stalin's political victory was now complete; he was absolute master of the party and began to cultivate the personal adulation which characterized his rule.

. . . The joint session of the Politbureau of the CC and the Presidium of the CCC determines that the factional activity of Bukharin . . . unfortunately has still continued in one form or another up to the present time. Such facts as Bukharin's refusal to work in the Comintern; his refusal to work as editor of Pravda; the appearance in the press without the knowledge of the CC of Bukharin's "Notes of an Economist," which represents eclectic nonsense that is not permissible for a Marxist and creates the danger of controversy in the party; the submission of their resignations by Bukharin, Rykov and Tomsky to the November Plenum of the CC; Bukharin's declaration of January 30, 1929, confirming in basic content his conversations with Kamenev in July, 1928; Tomsky's submission of his resignation [as trade union chief] in December, 1928; Bukharin's and Tomsky's unwillingness to submit to the decision made by the Politbureau more than once that they withdrew their resignations —all this and similar facts show that Bukharin continues to nurse his grudge and to struggle against the CC.

To justify his factional activity Bukharin has resorted to a series of impermissible slanders of the CC, of its domestic and foreign policies, of its organizational leadership, with the aim of defaming the party and its CC. By thus defaming the party's policy Bukharin has slipped into the position of a

FROM: Resolution of the Joint Session of the Politbureau of the Central Committee and the Presidium of the Central Control Commission, *On Intra-Party Affairs*, February 9, 1929 (CPSU in Resolutions, II, 558-562; editor's translation).

diplomatic defense of the right elements in the CPSU (Frumkin* & Co.) which demand the unfettering of the capitalist elements in town and country, and of the conciliationist elements in the Comintern (Humbert-Droz** & Co.) who deny the precariousness of the stabilization of capitalism and revise the decisions of the Presidium of the Executive Committee of the Communist International on the expulsion of the rightists from the German Communist Party.

In connection with these points the joint session of the Politbureau of the CC and the Presidium of the CCC determines the following facts:

1) Bukharin's declaration that the policy of the party after the July Plenum was determined by "the slogan of tribute, i.e., military-feudal exploitation of the peasantry," supposedly proclaimed by Comrade Stalin in his speech at the Plenum, is inherently deceitful and false through and through. The party as a whole, like Comrade Stalin, has always struggled and will continue to struggle against the Trotskyist theory of "military feudal exploitation of the peasantry." Bukharin knows this just as well as the whole party does. The party as a whole, like Comrade Stalin, proceeds from the fact that the peasantry is still paying excessively high prices for industrial products and receives excessively low prices for agricultural products, that this surtax ("tribute") cannot be eliminated now unless we want to abandon industrialization, that it has to be curtailed step by step in order to eliminate it altogether after a period of several years. . . .

. . . This is not the first time that Bukharin has resorted to slander against the party. The history of our party contains facts from the period of the Treaty of Brest-Litovsk, when Bukharin, himself sitting in the petty-bourgeois opportunist swamp, accused Lenin and his party of opportunism and petty-bourgeois tendencies, when in the theses of the "left" Communists submitted to the Seventh Congress of

* Frumkin: Commissar of Finance, 1926-28, and a strong advocate of concessions to the peasantry—Ed.

** J. Humbert-Droz: a Swiss Communist leader, advocate of cooperation with democratic socialists—Ed.

the party he wrote that "the policy of the leading institutions of the party has been a policy of vacillation and compromises," that "the social basis of such a policy is the process of the degeneration of our party from a purely proletarian one to a nation-wide one," that "the party, instead of lifting up the peasant masses, has itself slipped down to their level; from the vanguard of revolution it has turned into a middle peasant."

2) Bukharin's declaration that a "super-tax" imposition on the peasantry is a constituent part of the party's policy, that the party and the CC are not carrying out the decisions of the plenums of the CC on the stimulation of individual peasant farming and increasing its output, is incorrect and false. . . .

In the party there cannot be two lines. Either the party line is incorrect—and then Bukharin is right, marking himself off from the CC. Or the party line is correct—and then Bukharin's "new" line on the peasant question cannot be anything but an approach to Frumkin's line, which is calculated on the unfettering of the capitalist elements. It is impossible to dangle endlessly between the slogan "get rich" and the slogan "attack the *kulak*." In essence Bukharin is slipping into Frumkin's position.

3) Bukharin's declaration about the hopelessness of our foreign-exchange position, about his having "predicted" all this, and no one listening to him, etc., is entirely incorrect. This declaration of Bukharin's represents nothing but bragging. . . .

4) Bukharin's declaration that we have no intraparty democracy, that the party is becoming "bureaucratized," that "we are cultivating bureaucracy," that there are no elected secretaries in the party, that we have established as it were a system of political commissars at *Pravda,* in the Comintern, in the Central Trade Union Council, that the present regime in the party has become unbearable, etc., is entirely incorrect and false through and through. We cannot help noting that Bukharin has here slid into the position of Trotsky in his notorious letter of October 8, 1923. It is only necessary to compare Trotsky's words in this letter about the "intraparty

regime," about "secretarial bureaucratism," or to the effect that "the bureaucratization of the party apparatus has reached unheard of proportions by applying the methods of secretarial selection"—it is only necessary to compare these words of Trotsky's with Bukharin's declaration, to understand to what depths Bukharin has fallen. Only people who are dissatisfied with the presence of iron intraparty discipline, only people who are dissatisfied with the fact that the party's majority does not agree with their panicky "platforms" and "theses," only people who are dissatisfied with the present composition of the leading organs of our party—only such people are capable of accusing our party, with its methods of self-criticism, of bureaucratism and bureaucratization. Lenin was right when he called such comrades people who are overcome by "lordly anarchism." Lenin was right when he said in regard to such people, "It clearly appears that cries about notorious bureaucratism are simply to conceal dissatisfaction with the personal composition of the center—it is a fig leaf" ("One Step Forward"). . . .

In essence in his attacks on the "intraparty regime" Bukharin is slipping into the same position on the "freedom of ideological groupings" which the Trotskyist opposition held in the initial stage of its development. . . .

Bukharin's and Tomsky's declaration is completely without substance in saying that they are being "worked over" in the party, that an "organizational encirclement" has been created, in view of which they are compelled to insist on resigning. . . . Of what does intraparty democracy consist? No one can compel a party of a million and a half to hold their spit in their mouths and not ask questions about intraparty affairs for the sake of Bukharin's and Tomsky's tranquility. If the activity of the party masses and their wish to know the truth about Bukharin and Tomsky lead to justified criticism of these comrades' form of action, Bukharin and Tomsky are themselves guilty for committing incorrect actions which have made the party anxious and agitated. . . .

Volume II

Chapter Four: Soviet Communism: The Transformation under Stalin, 1929-1941

The Communist movement, despite the impersonal sociology contained in its doctrine, bears to an almost unique degree the impress of dominant individual personalities—specifically, Lenin and Stalin. Lenin launched the movement and gave it the qualities necessary for seizing and holding power; Stalin accomplished the permanent adaptation of the movement to the circumstances of its time and setting. The insane purging and self-glorification in which Stalin indulged were perhaps transitory, but the other changes for which he was responsible have been permanently assimilated into the Communist movement the world over—the priority of the industrialization effort and national power, the shift to conservative social and intellectual norms, and the monolithic control of all communication to enforce the pseudo-Marxist rationalization of the system.

Stalin's Revolution

Wielding the unchallenged personal control over the Communist Party and the Soviet state which he had attained with the defeat of the Right Opposition, Stalin commenced a drastic program of reconstructing the economic foundations of Soviet society. The two cardinal lines of effort, as he set them forth in his final attack on the Bukharin group in April, 1929, were the collectivization of the peasantry and the intensive development of heavy industry. Shortly afterward the First Five-Year Plan was formally approved by the Sixteenth Party Conference, with its commencement set retroactively back to October, 1928.

. . . What is the theoretical basis for the blindness and bewilderment of Bukharin's group?

I think that the theoretical basis for this blindness and bewilderment is Bukharin's incorrect, non-Marxian approach to the question of the class struggle in our country. I have in mind Bukharin's non-Marxian theory that the kulaks will grow into socialism, his failure to understand the mechanism of the class struggle under the dictatorship of the proletariat. . . .

Hitherto, we Marxist-Leninists thought that between the capitalists of town and country, on the one hand, and the working class, on the other, there is an *irreconcilable* antagonism of interest. This is exactly what the Marxian theory of the class struggle rests on. But now, according to Bukharin's theory that the capitalists will *peacefully grow* into socialism, all this is turned topsy-turvy; the irreconcilable antagonism of class interests between the exploiters and the exploited disappears, the exploiters grow into socialism. . . .

Either one thing or the other: either there is an irreconcilable antagonism of interests between the capitalist class and the class of the workers who have assumed power and have organized their dictatorship, or there is no such antagonism of interests, in which case only one thing remains: to proclaim the harmony of class interests. . . .

What can there be in common between Bukharin's theory that the kulaks will grow into socialism and Lenin's theory of the dictatorship as a fierce class struggle? Obviously, there is not, nor can there be, anything in common between them.

Bukharin thinks that under the dictatorship of the proletariat the class struggle must *subside* and *pass away* so that the abolition of classes may be brought about. Lenin, on the contrary, teaches us that classes can be abolished only by means of a stubborn class struggle, which under the dictatorship of the proletariat becomes *ever fiercer* than it was before the dictatorship of the proletariat. . . .

. . . In addition to the ordinary taxes, direct and indirect, which the peasantry is paying to the state, it also pays a certain supertax in the form of an overcharge on consumer goods, and in the form of low prices received for agricultural produce. . . .

FROM: Stalin, "The Right Deviation in the CPSU(B)" (Speech to the Central Committee, April, 1929; *Problems of Leninism*, pp. 309-13, 326-27, 331, 336-37, 371-72).

. . . We also call it "the scissors," "drainage" of resources from agriculture into industry for the purpose of speeding up industrial development.

Is this "drainage" really necessary? Everybody agrees that it is, as a temporary measure, if we really wish to maintain a speedy rate of industrial development. Indeed, we must at all cost maintain a rapid growth of our industry, for this growth is necessary not solely for our industrial production, but primarily for our agriculture, for our peasantry, which at the present time needs most of all tractors, agricultural machinery and fertilizers.

Can we abolish this supertax at the present time? Unfortunately, we cannot. We must abolish it at the first opportune moment, in the coming years. But we cannot abolish it right now.

Now, as you see, this supertax obtained by means of "the scissors" is in fact "something like a tribute." Not a tribute, but "something like a tribute." It is "something like a tribute" which we are paying for our backwardness. We need this supertax to stimulate the development of our industry and to do away with our backwardness. . . .

. . . It was no accident that Bukharin and his friends took exception to the word "tribute" and began to speak of military-feudal exploitation of the peasants. Their outcry about military-feudal exploitation was undoubtedly an expression of their extreme discontent with the Party policy toward the kulaks, which is being applied by our organizations. Discontent with the Leninist policy of the Party in its leadership of the peasantry, discontent with our grain-purchasing policy, with our policy of developing collective and state farms to the utmost, and lastly, the desire to "unfetter" the market and to establish complete freedom of private trade—there you have the underlying reason for Bukharin's screams about military-feudal exploitation of the peasantry.

In the whole history of our Party I cannot recall another single instance of the Party being accused of carrying on a policy of military-feudal exploitation. This anti-Party weapon was not borrowed from a Marxian arsenal. From where, then, was it borrowed? From the arsenal of Milyukov, the leader of the Constitutional-Democrats. . . .

. . . We have two different plans of economic policy.

The Party's Plan:

1. We are re-equipping industry (reconstruction).

2. We are beginning seriously to re-equip agriculture (reconstruction).

3. For this we must expand the development of collective farms and state farms, employ on a mass scale the contract system and machine and tractor stations as means of establishing a *bond* between industry and agriculture in the sphere of *production*.

4. As for the present grain-purchasing difficulties, we must admit the necessity for temporary emergency measures that are bolstered up by the popular support of the middle- and poor-peasant masses, as one of the means of breaking the resistance of the kulaks and of obtaining from them the maximum grain surplus necessary to be able to dispense with imported grain and to save foreign currency for the development of industry.

5. Individual poor- and middle-peasant farming plays, and will continue to play, a predominant part in supplying the country with food and raw materials; but alone it is no longer adequate—the development of individual poor- and middle-peasant farming must therefore be *supplemented* by the development of collective farms and state farms, by the contract system applied on a mass scale, by accelerating the development of machine-and-tractor stations, in order to facilitate the squeezing out of the capitalist elements from agriculture and the gradual transfer of the individual peasant farms to large-scale collective farming, to collective labour.

6. But in order to achieve all this, it is necessary first of all to accelerate the development of industry, of metallurgy, chemicals, machine building, of tractor works, agricultural-machinery works, etc. Failing this it will be impossible to solve the grain problem just as it will be impossible to reconstruct agriculture.

Conclusion: *The key to the reconstruction of agriculture is the speedy rate of development of our industry.*

Bukharin's Plan:

1. "Normalize" the market; permit the free play of prices on the market and a rise in the price of grain, undeterred by the fact that this may lead to a rise in the price of manufactured goods, raw materials and bread.

2. The utmost development of individual peasant farming accompanied by a certain reduction of the rate of development of collective farms and state farms (Bukharin's theses of July and his speech at the July Plenum).

3. Grain purchasing on the spontaneity principle, precluding under all circumstances even the partial application of emergency measures against the kulaks, even though such measures are supported by the middle- and poor-peasant masses.

4. In the event of shortage of grain, to import about 100,000,000 rubles worth of grain.

5. And if there is not enough foreign currency to pay for imports of grain and equipment for industry, to reduce imports of equipment and, consequently, the rate of development of our industry—otherwise our agriculture will simply "mark time," or will even "directly decline."

Conclusion: *The key to the reconstruction of agriculture is the development of individual peasant farming.*

This is how it works out, comrades.

Bukharin's plan is a plan to *reduce* the rate of development of industry and to *undermine* the new forms of the [worker-peasant] bond.

Such are our divergencies. . . .

. . . The fight against the Right deviation is one of the most decisive duties of our Party. If we, in our own ranks, in our own Party, in the political General Staff of the proletariat, which is directing the movement and is leading the proletariat forward—if we in this General Staff should tolerate the free existence and the free functioning of the Right deviationists, who are trying to demobilize the Party, to demoralize the working class, to adapt our policy to the tastes of the "Soviet" bourgeoisie, and thus yield to the difficulties of our socialist construction—if we should tolerate all this, what would it mean? Would it not mean that we want to send the revolution downhill, demoralize our socialist construction, flee from difficulties, surrender our positions to the capitalist elements?

Does Bukharin's group understand that to refuse to fight the Right deviation is to betray the working class, to betray the revolution?

Does Bukharin's group understand that unless we overcome the Right deviation and the conciliationist tendency, it will be impossible to overcome the difficulties facing us, and that unless we overcome these difficulties it will be impossible to achieve decisive successes in socialist construction?

Compared with this, what is the value of this pitiful talk about the "civil execution" of three members of the Political Bureau?

No, comrades, the Bukharinites will not frighten the Party with liberal chatter about "civil execution." The Party demands that they should wage a determined struggle against the Right deviation and the conciliationist tendency side by side with all the members of the Central Committee of our Party. It demands this of the Bukharin group in order to help to mobilize the working class, to break down the resistance of the class enemies and to make sure that the difficulties of our socialist construction will be overcome.

Either the Bukharinites will fulfill this demand of the Party, in which case the Party will welcome them, or they will not, in which case they will have only themselves to blame. . . .

Disciplining the Intellectuals

Simultaneously with his forceful new economic policies Stalin imposed stringent party controls over most fields of intellectual life. The toleration of variety came to an end with the silencing or imprisonment of large numbers of nonconforming thinkers, Communist and non-Communist alike. A spirit of class war, devotion to the interests of the party, and unqualified acceptance of the official version of Marxist orthodoxy became the guide lines for Soviet intellectual life, as was made clear in the 1929 purge of philosophers.

. . . 1. The Marxist-Leninist philosophy—dialectical materialism—is the only scientific theory which gives the proletariat a complete world view and weapon in the struggle for the proletarian dictatorship and the socialist reconstruction of society. It is the outcome of the whole accumulation of knowledge which mankind has achieved, and is confirmed by the everyday experience of the class struggle and every forward step of scientific research.

The significance of the materialistic dialectic in particular grows under the conditions of the present epoch—the epoch of dying capitalism, of proletarian revolution, and of socialism under construction. The deep contradictions of contemporary bourgeois society, the unusual complexity of all social phenomena, the rapid flux of events, the struggle of nascent social forms with dying ones, can be comprehended only from the point of view of dialectical materialism.

2. The condition of contemporary bourgeois philosophy reflects the disruption of capitalist society. Contemporary bourgeois philosophy not only does not fructify positive knowledge, but in every way retards its development. Sad epigonism, creeping empiricism, formalism, open acceptance of priests and mysticism—such is the philosophical countenance of the contemporary bourgeoisie. . . .

3. At the same time, in the USSR, dialectical materialism is steadily broadening its influence on the broadest masses and more and more is penetrating into all areas of scientific knowledge. . . . The solution of the problems of contemporary natural science from the point of view of dialectical materialism has begun. A cadre of Communist workers in the area of philosophy and natural science has been established and has grown.

4. Meanwhile, however, it is necessary to note that the successes which have been achieved are far from sufficient in comparison to the needs and great tasks facing Marxism-Leninism at the present time. In particular, in the area of

FROM: Resolution of the Second All-Union Conference of Marxist-Leninist Scientific Research Institutions, April, 1929, "On Contemporary Problems of the Philosophy of Marxism-Leninism" (*Under the Banner of Marxism*, No. 5, 1929, pp. 6-8; editor's translation).

natural science only the first steps have been taken to apply the Marxist method. It is essential to strengthen and deepen the connection of work in the field of philosophy with a series of actual problems in the field of social science; it is essential to develop to a significantly broader degree work in instilling the methodology of Marx, Engels and Lenin in the various fields of specialized knowledge. Finally, it is essential to adopt all measures to broaden the cadres of trained workers in the field of Marxist philosophy.

5. The class struggle which is going on under the conditions of developing socialist construction leads to the familiar invigoration of ideological tendencies openly inimical to Marxism-Leninism, as well as various revisionist deviations from it. The purest idealism and revisionism, adapting themselves to the conditions of the dictatorship of the proletariat, sometimes array themselves in Marxist dress and come forth under the flag of specialized knowledge, or else they distort Marx, Engels and Lenin, and conceal themselves with incorrectly explained citations from their works.

On the other hand, the failure to understand all the complexity of the transitional period and the contradictory character of our development, and the consequences of this—narrow practicality, oversimplification, and failure to understand the vast theoretical tasks posed by our epoch—and on the other hand, the resistance to the penetration of Marxist-Leninism into new fields of knowledge, all feed the various anti- and pseudo-Marxist deviations in philosophy: positivism, the denial of the significance of the materialist dialectic or the distortion of it, deviations from the Marxist and Leninist understanding of the problems of historical materialism, etc. . . .

7. . . . The crisis which contemporary theoretical natural science is undergoing is a continuation of that crisis the analysis of which was made by Lenin. The latest successes of natural science cannot be fitted into the framework of the old, mechanistic and formally logical theories. Bourgeois philosophy lives on the crisis like a parasite, trying to utilize the crisis in natural science for its own ends. However, a real solution of the basic methodological difficulties in scientific

research can be achieved only by applying the method of the materialist dialectic. Contemporary natural science "lies in child-birth. It is giving birth to dialectical materialism" (Lenin).

The conference observes that the solution of the tasks of working out the theory of the materialist dialectic and the methodology of contemporary natural science is possible only on the basis of the closest link of the work of Marxists in the field of philosophy and natural science.

8. The proletarian revolution, after shaking up old notions and prejudices among the broad masses, puts forth the task of working out a new world view among the broadest strata of the working class.

A decisive blow to religious ideology can be dealt only by disseminating the dialectical-materialist world view among the masses. Antireligious propaganda can be given positive content only by building it on the foundation of dialectical materialism.

Therefore the conference considers it essential to expand the publishing of atheistic literature, in order to satisfy the new stage of antireligious propaganda. . . .

Rakovsky on Bureaucracy

Christian Rakovsky, a Rumanian-born Bulgarian who had served as prime minister of the Ukraine and Soviet ambassador to Great Britain, was one of the most articulate and determined critics of Stalin among the exiled Trotskyists. He began to analyze Soviet social trends in terms that recalled the warnings of the early left-wing Communist deviations: the "workers' state" had come under the domination of a bureaucratic social group which was well on the way to becoming a ruling class in its own right. This view was elaborated by Trotsky in his book *The Revolution Betrayed,* and paralleled later on in *The New Class* by Milovan Djilas.

a) Letter on the Causes of the Degeneration of the Party and Governmental Apparatus

. . . When a class seizes power, a certain part of this class is transformed into agents of the power itself. In this way the bureaucracy arises. In the proletarian state, where capitalistic accumulation is not permitted for members of the ruling party, this differentiation is at first functional, but then it becomes social. I do not say class, but social. I mean that the social position of the Communist who has an automobile at his disposal, a good apartment, regular leaves, and earns the party maximum, is distinct from the position of that same Communist if he works in the coal mines where he gets fifty to sixty rubles a month. (While we are speaking of workers and employees, you know that they are classified among eighteen different grades.)

The second consequence is that part of those functions which formerly the whole party or the whole class itself carried out has now shifted to the power, i.e., to a certain number of people from this party, from this class.

The unity and solidarity which formerly were a natural consequence of the revolutionary class struggle can now be preserved only through a whole system of actions which have as their aim the preservation of the equilibrium between the different groups of that class and that party and their subordination to the common goal.

But this is a long, difficult process, comprising the political education of the ruling class and the knowledge which it must acquire to keep its hands on the governmental, party and union apparatuses, to control them and direct them.

I repeat, this is a matter of education. No one class has been born with the skill to rule—this is acquired only through experience, by making mistakes and learning from one's mistakes. The most ideal Soviet constitution is not in a position to guarantee to the working class the unimpeded application of its dictatorship and its class control, if it does not know how to make use of the constitutional rights granted to it. . . .

I feel that we should note above all that when we manipulate the concepts "party" and "masses" we should not over-

FROM: Rakovsky, Letter on the Causes of the Degeneration of the Party and Governmental Apparatus, August 2, 1928 (*Bulletin of the Opposition,* No. 6, October, 1929, editor's translation, pp. 15, 17).

look the content with which a decade of history has invested them.

Neither the working class nor the party is *physically or morally* what it was ten years ago. I think I do not exaggerate when I say that the party member of 1917 would hardly recognize himself in the person of the party member of 1928. . . .

b) Evaluation of the Situation

. . . The causes of this deep crisis which has appeared with unusual suddenness between the Fifteenth Congress and the present conference are rooted in the direction of the line which the party leadership has now been following for many years. To seek these causes only in objective conditions, in the growth of internal contradictions arising from the presence of the internal petty-bourgeois and external capitalist encirclements, is a cowardly attempt by the party leadership to escape responsibility for the unforgivable mistakes which they have committed. The proletarian dictatorship has known incomparably more difficult international and internal situations, but this is the first time it has faced such a sharp crisis in the party and such burning awareness that it has gotten into a blind alley. . . .

The Politbureau, concealing from the party and from the working class its crude and systematic errors on the questions of the village, of industry, on the labor question, complications in the guiding policy of the Comintern and the party, has concealed from the latter and from the working masses the platform of the opposition. Clinging to its unlimited apparatus absolutism, afraid of losing power, the party leadership has sacrificed the interests of the dictatorship of the proletariat, of the Soviet state, and of the world revolution, for the sake of preserving itself. The efforts of the opposition to make its point of view known to the party before the convocation of the congress ran into furious resistance by the apparatus. The opposition was organizationally de-

FROM: Rakovsky, "Evaluation of the Situation: On the Eve of the Sixteenth Party Conference, April, 1929" (*Bulletin of the Opposition,* No. 3-4, September, 1929, p. 12).

stroyed and placed outside the party, except for those who agreed to disavow their own correct views and subscribe to the pretended correctness of the policy of the leadership which is actually leading to the ruin of the proletarian dictatorship and the proletarian state. . . .

c) *Declaration to the Central Committee*

. . . The danger of disproportionately swollen bureaucracy is that it gradually pushes the toiling masses out of the real leadership of the state, the trade unions and the party.

Even Lenin indicated that there is no real control by the masses over the apparatus without their real and direct participation in the administration of the country.

Therefore we feel that only an apparatus based on the confidence of the masses, an apparatus whose basis is election and replacement and the observance of revolutionary legality—corresponds to the interests of the toiling masses and the demands of the proletarian dictatorship.

Under the conditions of the capitalist encirclement the proletarian dictatorship is realized through the Communist Party with the co-operation of the trade unions. Of necessity a significant share of the power will long remain concentrated in the hands of the party and its leadership, and as *elective power and replaceable power* it must be under the *vigilant control and free criticism of the whole party. Party democracy,* which was foreseen in the program and statutes and confirmed by the decisions of the congresses and plenums and in particular by the resolution of December, 1923—party democracy, based on the initiative of the party and the working class, must be realized in full. . . .

d) *Theses of August*

. . . In its attitude toward the poor peasants as in its attitude toward the working class centrism [i.e., Stalinism] continues its previous policy of fear and distrust, of this

FROM: Rakovsky, Kossior and Okudzhava, Declaration to the Central Committee and the Central Control Commission, August 22, 1929 (*Bulletin of the Opposition,* No. 6, October, 1929, p. 6).

quality of bureaucracy in general. Centrism fears the real participation of the toiling masses in Socialist construction. Of course, it would like to rely on them, but only on condition that the masses not involve themselves in "politics," i.e., not even discuss, much less criticize, the "general line." Centrism kills all real initiative of the masses. . . . Bureaucratism has castrated the class and revolutionary content of the trade unions. If industrialization and the struggle with agrarian capitalism rest on an apparatus which is partly worn out, has partly lost its revolutionary enthusiasm and has broken down in many of its links, they will find themselves under the constant threat of disruption.

The opposition of 1923-1924 foresaw the vast harm to the proletarian dictatorship which stems from the perversion of the party regime. Events have fully justified its prognosis: the enemy crept in through the bureaucratic window.

At the present moment, more than ever, it is necessary to say loudly, the correct democratic party regime *is the touchstone of a real left course. . . .*

e) Circular of the Bolshevik-Leninist Opposition

In our declaration to the Central Committee and the Central Control Commission of October 4 of last year the Bolshevik-Leninist opposition warned against extraordinary administrative measures in the villages because they are followed by negative political consequences.

We also warned against the harmful theory of the possibility of building a socialist society in one country, a theory which could arise only in the imagination of a bureaucracy believing in the omnipotence of the apparatus, the theory advanced by Stalin-Bukharin after Lenin's death. We wrote

FROM: Rakovsky, Kossior and Okudzhava, Theses of August, 1929 (*Bulletin of the Opposition,* No. 7, November-December, 1929, p. 9).

FROM: Rakovsky, Kossior, Muralov and Kasparova, "Circular of the Bolshevik-Leninist Opposition to the Central Committee, the Central Control Commission, and All Members of the CPSU," April, 1930 (*Bulletin of the Opposition,* No. 17-18, November-December, 1930, pp. 11-12, 16).

that this theory creates harmful illusions, that it leads to underestimation of the very great difficulties which stand in the path of socialist construction and thus leaves the party and the proletariat unprepared to overcome them. In our declaration we also pointed out that the correct assumptions of principle which were embodied in the decisions of the Sixteenth Party Conference on industrialization and collectivization lead, under conditions of bureaucratic administration, when the class has been replaced by officials who have been transformed into a specialized ruling stratum, not to the development but to the disruption of socialist construction.

We pointed out that the restoration and strengthening of party and workers' democracy is the primary condition for eliminating the avarice, irresponsibility, stubbornness and arbitrariness of the apparatus, the reverse side of which is the oppression, humiliation and lack of rights of the toiling masses. . . .

The Central Committee has issued a directive which is *per se the crudest deviation from socialism.* The slogan of *intensive* collectivization—no matter whether a term of fifteen years is assigned for this, as it was at first, or one year, as they have made it since—is *per se* the greatest economic absurdity. We are Marxists, and we know that new forms of ownership can be created on the basis of new productive relations. But these productive relations still do not exist. . . .

Secretaries, chairmen of executive committees, procurement officials, heads of co-operatives, heads of state farms, party and nonparty directors of enterprises, specialists, foremen, who, following the line of least resistance, install in our industry the sweat-shop system and factory despotism—here is the real power in the period of the proletarian dictatorship which we are now experiencing. This stage can be characterized as domination by the corporative interests of the various categories of the bureaucracy, and internecine struggle between them.

From the workers' state with bureaucratic perversions—as Lenin defined our form of government—we have developed into *a bureaucratic state with proletarian-Communist survivals.*

Before our eyes a great *class of rulers* has been *taking shape* and is continuing to develop. It has its own internal subdivisions, and grows by way of calculated co-optation, through the direct or indirect appointment system (by way of bureaucratic promotion or the system of fictitious elections). The unifying factor of this unique class is that unique form of private property, governmental power. "The bureaucracy has the state in its possession," wrote Marx, "as rights of private property."

Stalin on the Liquidation of the Kulaks

Late in 1929 the collectivization of the peasants was shifted from a relatively gradual and nonviolent basis to one of urgency and violence. There was much uneasiness in the party about this, but Stalin identified such qualms with the Right Opposition and denounced them as evidence of pro-capitalist sentiment. In the winter of 1929-1930 over half of the Soviet peasantry was collectivized, but at the cost of such a growth in mass hostility to the regime that Stalin himself had to call a temporary retreat. Collectivization was then resumed at a more gradual pace and on the basis of a compromise that allowed small private plots to each peasant family, but the damage to agriculture which the program caused undoubtedly contributed to the grave famine of 1932-33. By the mid-1930's collectivization was virtually complete.

. . . The so-called theory of the "equilibrium" between the sectors of our national economy is still current among Communists. This theory has, of course, nothing in common with Marxism. Nevertheless, this theory is advocated by a number of people in the camp of the Right deviators.

This theory is based on the assumption that to begin with we have a socialist sector—which is one compartment, as it were—and that in addition we also have a nonsocialist or, if you like, capitalist sector—which is another compartment.

FROM: Stalin, "Problems of Agrarian Policy in the USSR" (Speech at a conference of Marxist students of the agrarian question, December 27, 1929; *Problems of Leninism,* pp. 391-93, 408-9, 411-12).

These two "compartments" move on different rails and glide peacefully forward, without touching each other. Geometry teaches that parallel lines do not meet. But the authors of this remarkable theory believe that these parallel lines will meet eventually, and that when they do, we will have socialism. This theory overlooks the fact that behind these so-called "compartments" there are classes, and that these compartments move as a result of a fierce class struggle, a life-and-death struggle, a struggle on the principle of "who will win?"

It is not difficult to see that this theory has nothing in common with Leninism. It is not difficult to see that, objectively, the purpose of this theory is to defend the position of individual peasant farming, to arm the kulak elements with a "new" theoretical weapon in their struggle against the collective farms, and to destroy confidence in the collective farms. . . .

. . . Can we advance our socialized industry at an accelerated rate as long as we have an agricultural base, such as is provided by small-peasant farming, which is incapable of expanded reproduction, and which, in addition, is the predominant force in our national economy? No, we cannot. Can Soviet power and the work of socialist construction rest for any length of time on two *different* foundations: on the most large-scale and concentrated socialist industry, and the most scattered and backward, small-commodity peasant farming? No, they cannot. Sooner or later this would be bound to end in the complete collapse of the whole national economy.

What, then, is the solution? The solution lies in enlarging the agricultural units, in making agriculture capable of accumulation, of expanded reproduction, and in thus transforming the agricultural bases of our national economy.

But how are the agricultural units to be enlarged?

There are two ways of doing this. There is the *capitalist* way, which is to enlarge the agricultural units by introducing capitalism in agriculture—a way which leads to the impoverishment of the peasantry and to the development of capitalist enterprises in agriculture. We reject this way as incompatible with the Soviet economic system.

There is a second way: the *socialist* way, which is to introduce collective farms and state farms in agriculture, the way which leads to the amalgamation of the small-peasant farms into large collective farms, employing machinery and scientific methods of farming, and capable of developing further, for such agricultural enterprises can achieve expanded reproduction.

And so, the question stands as follows: either one way or the other, either *back*—to capitalism, or *forward*—to socialism. There is no third way, nor can there be.

The "equilibrium" theory is an attempt to indicate a third way. And precisely because it is based on a third (non-existent) way, it is utopian and anti-Marxian. . . .

The characteristic feature in the work of our Party during the past year is that we, as a Party, as the Soviet power,

a) have developed an offensive along the whole front against the capitalist elements in the countryside;

b) that this offensive, as you know, has brought about and is bringing about very palpable, *positive* results.

What does this mean? It means that we have passed from the policy of *restricting* the exploiting proclivities of the kulaks to the policy of *eliminating* the kulaks as a class. This means that we have made, and are still making, one of the decisive turns in our whole policy.

Until recently the Party adhered to the policy of *restricting* the exploiting proclivities of the kulaks. . . .

. . . Could we have undertaken such an offensive against the kulaks five years or three years ago? Could we then have counted on success in such an offensive? No, we could not. That would have been the most dangerous adventurism. It would have been playing a very dangerous game at offensive. We would certainly have failed, and our failure would have strengthened the position of the kulaks. Why? Because we still lacked a wide network of state and collective farms in the rural districts which could be used as strongholds in a determined offensive against the kulaks. Because at that time we were not yet able to *substitute* for the capitalist production of the kulaks the socialist production of the collective farms and state farms. . . .

. . . Now we are able to carry on a determined offensive

against the kulaks, to break their resistance, to eliminate them as a class and substitute for their output the output of the collective farms and state farms. Now, the kulaks are being expropriated by the masses of poor and middle peasants themselves, by the masses who are putting solid collectivization into practice. Now, the expropriation of the kulaks in the regions of solid collectivization is no longer just an administrative measure. Now, the expropriation of the kulaks is an integral part of the formation and development of the collective farms. Consequently it is now ridiculous and foolish to discourse on the expropriation of the kulaks. You do not lament the loss of the hair of one who has been beheaded.

There is another question which seems no less ridiculous: whether the kulaks should be permitted to join the collective farms. Of course not, for they are sworn enemies of the collective-farm movement. . . .

The Socialized Economy and Revolutionary Law

For the first two decades after the revolution the Communists took the Marxian view that law was a manifestation of the class struggle, and hence anticipated the eventual "withering away" of law. Meanwhile, jurists like Pashukanis argued, law was to be employed by the Soviet state not as a set of absolute norms but as a flexible instrument of policy in the transition from economic individualism to socialism.

. . . Our transition period cannot be regarded as a final social-economic conception but must be regarded as a movement—an ever accelerating movement—to socialism. The social-economic conception for whose sake the proletarian dictatorship exists and actively manifests itself is socialism and communism. Behind us lies capitalism. Now we are achieving the revolutionary transition from capitalism to socialism. The production of petty goods is being socialized

FROM: Pashukanis, "The Soviet State and the Revolution in Law" (1930; English translation in Hugh W. Babb and John Newbold Hazard, *Soviet Legal Philosophy*, Cambridge, Mass., Harvard University Press, 1951, pp. 278-79; reprinted by permission of the publisher).

and becoming socialist production. But we shall be told there is, of course, a "dominant leading sector." That is true. But, of course, when this dominant sector shall have absorbed everything, the disappearance of law will begin thereupon. How do you wish to build a final legal system when you start from social relationships which already comprise the necessity that law of every sort wither away? This is a task completely unthinkable. But if you reduce everything merely to the subjective will element—"to constraint"—then it is inconceivable why Marx and Engels spoke of the "bourgeois" form of law. It is specifically because we are starting from the objective relationships which the proletarian dictatorship is remaking every hour—it is specifically for this reason that we cannot be occupied with the creation of a system of proletarian law. What is it that you are pleased to consider the basic part of this system? The Land Code of 1922? Or the Code now being worked out? Or the relationships that will be formed among us when 100 per cent collectivization shall have been realized? Or the relationships which will be formed among us when the contradictions between city and hamlet shall have disappeared?

I think that this aspiration—at whatever cost—to palm off a special and final system of law upon us is an attempt to deprive us in our practical work of that which is more necessary to us than anything else—political elasticity—to the end that we follow policy for the reason that policy is sufficient, for the reason that the relationships between policy and the juridic superstructure (the legal superstructure in the transition period) are completely different from those to be found in a bourgeois state. Accordingly to offer ideas borrowed from the domain of bourgeois-capitalist relationships is completely unsuited to the transition epoch. This pseudo-revolutionary challenge exalts the class essence of our law, as it were, in that it terms our law proletarian law and liquidates the bourgeois form. In reality there is latent here a desire to hold development back at a given stage: to elevate this stage into a final system. This is the misfortune of those who have chosen for themselves the profession of Soviet jurists.

The relationship of law to policy and to economics is utterly different among us from what it is in bourgeois society. In bourgeois-capitalist society, the legal superstructure should have maximum immobility—maximum stability—because it represents a firm framework for the movement of the economic forces whose bearers are capitalist entrepreneurs. Accordingly, the aspiration to create final and integrated systems of law, free from inner contradictions, is characteristic of bourgeois jurists. Among us it is different. We require that our legislation possess maximum elasticity. We cannot fetter ourselves by any sort of system, because every day we are demolishing the structure of production relationships and replacing them by new production relationships: we are doing this consciously and through the medium of the state—which the bourgeois state does not do. The bourgeois state is oriented in form. All the activity of the proletarian state is oriented in the attainment of results according to the essence of the matter. Accordingly, at a time when bourgeois political scientists are striving to depict policy itself as law—to dissolve policy in law—law occupies among us, on the contrary, a subordinate position with reference to policy. We have a system of proletarian policy, but we have no need for any sort of juridic system of proletarian law. The system of proletarian policy consists in this, that—resting upon our attainments in the economic and cultural fields—we transfer production relationships (utilizing the lever of state constraint) into another phase: we make them different. It is sufficient to enumerate such things as industrialization, grain collections under contract with the state, collectivization, the liquidation of the kulaks as a class, the struggle for an industrial and financial plan—all these are examples of how we are achieving a change of arrangements, drawing nearer to socialism and actively changing production relationships and replacing them by others. . . .

Stalin on the Ends and Means of Industrialization

In two speeches in 1931 Stalin spelled out some of the political and social implications of a socialist state dedicated to industrial development. He discarded the last pretenses of collectivistic equality in favor of a system of strict individual responsibility and incentives, with rewards in proportion to effort and skill. He recognized that the technical officialdom, properly trained, paid, and respected, is the backbone of a modern industrial system. At the same time he lent urgency to the industrialization effort by pointing to considerations of national power and defense.

a) The Tasks of Business Executives

. . . The underlying cause of wrecking activities is the class struggle. Of course, the class enemy is furiously resisting the socialist offensive. This alone, however, is not an adequate explanation for the luxuriant growth of wrecking activities.

How is it that sabotage has assumed such wide dimensions? Who is to blame for this? We are to blame. Had we handled the business of industrial management differently, had we started much earlier to learn the technique of the business, to master technique, had we more frequently and efficiently intervened in the management of production, the wreckers could not have done so much damage.

We must ourselves become experts, masters of the business; we must turn to technical science—such was the lesson life itself was teaching us. But neither the first warning nor even the second brought about the necessary change. It is time, it is high time that we turned towards technique. It is time we cast aside the old slogan, the obsolete slogan of noninterference in technique, and ourselves become specialists, experts, complete masters of our economy.

It is frequently asked: Why have we not one-man management? We do not have it and will not have it until we have mastered technique. Until there are among us Bolsheviks a sufficient number of people thoroughly familiar with technique, economics and finance, we will not have real one-man management. You can write as many resolutions as you please, take as many vows as you please, but, unless you master the technique, economics and finance of the mill,

FROM: Stalin, "The Tasks of Business Executives" (Speech at the First All-Union Conference of Managers of Socialist Industry, February, 1931; *Problems of Leninism*, pp. 454-58).

factory or mine, nothing will come of it, there will be no one-man management.

Hence, the task is for us to master technique ourselves, to become the masters of the business ourselves. This is the sole guarantee that our plans will be carried out in full, and that one-man management will be established.

This, of course, is no easy matter; but it can certainly be accomplished. Science, technical experience, knowledge, are all things that can be acquired. We may not have them today, but tomorrow we will. The main thing is to have the passionate Bolshevik desire to master technique, to master the science of production. Everything can be achieved, everything can be overcome, if there is a passionate desire to do so.

It is sometimes asked whether it is not possible to slow down the tempo somewhat, to put a check on the movement. No, comrades, it is not possible! The tempo must not be reduced! On the contrary, we must increase it as much as is within our powers and possibilities. This is dictated to us by our obligations to the workers and peasants of the U.S.S.R. This is dictated to us by our obligations to the working class of the whole world.

To slacken the tempo would mean falling behind. And those who fall behind get beaten. But we do not want to be beaten. No, we refuse to be beaten! One feature of the history of old Russia was the continual beatings she suffered because of her backwardness. She was beaten by the Mongol khans. She was beaten by the Turkish beys. She was beaten by the Swedish feudal lords. She was beaten by the Polish and Lithuanian gentry. She was beaten by the British and French capitalists. She was beaten by the Japanese barons. All beat her—because of her backwardness, military backwardness, cultural backwardness, political backwardness, industrial backwardness, agricultural backwardness. They beat her because to do so was profitable and could be done with impunity. Do you remember the words of the prerevolutionary poet: "You are poor and abundant, mighty and impotent, Mother Russia." * Those gentlemen were quite familiar with

* *From* Nekrasov's "Who Is Happy in Russia?" (1876)—Ed.

the verses of the old poet. They beat her, saying: "You are abundant," so one can enrich oneself at your expense. They beat her, saying: "You are poor and impotent," so you can be beaten and plundered with impunity. Such is the law of the exploiters—to beat the backward and the weak. It is the jungle law of capitalism. You are backward, you are weak—therefore you are wrong; hence, you can be beaten and enslaved. You are mighty—therefore you are right; hence, we must be wary of you.

That is why we must no longer lag behind.

In the past we had no fatherland, nor could we have one. But now that we have overthrown capitalism and power is in our hands, in the hands of the people, we have a fatherland, and we will defend its independence. Do you want our socialist fatherland to be beaten and to lose its independence? If you do not want this you must put an end to its backwardness in the shortest possible time and develop genuine Bolshevik tempo in building up its socialist system of economy. There is no other way. That is why Lenin said on the eve of the October Revolution: "Either perish, or overtake and outstrip the advanced capitalist countries."

We are fifty or a hundred years behind the advanced countries. We must make good this distance in ten years. Either we do it, or we shall be crushed.

This is what our obligations to the workers and peasants of the U.S.S.R. dictate to us.

But we have other, still more serious and more important obligations. They are our obligations to the world proletariat. They coincide with our obligations to the workers and peasants of the U.S.S.R. But we place them higher. The working class of the U.S.S.R. is part of the world working class. We achieved victory not solely through the efforts of the working class of the U.S.S.R., but also thanks to the support of the working class of the world. Without this support we would have been torn to pieces long ago. It is said that our country is the shock brigade of the proletariat of all countries. This is a fitting definition. But this imposes very serious obligations upon us. Why does the international proletariat support us? How did we merit this support? By the fact that we were the first to hurl ourselves into the battle against capitalism, we were the first to establish a working-class state, we were the first to start building socialism. By the fact that we are doing work which, if successful, will change the whole world and free the entire working class. But what is needed for success? The elimination of our backwardness, the development of a high Bolshevik tempo of construction. We must march forward in such a way that the working class of the whole world, looking at us, may say: This is my vanguard, this is my shock brigade, this is my working-class state, this is my fatherland; they are promoting their cause, which is *our* cause, and they are doing this well; let us support them against the capitalists and promote the cause of the world revolution. Must we not live up to the hopes of the world's working class, must we not fulfill our obligations to them? Yes, we must if we do not want utterly to disgrace ourselves.

Such are our obligations, internal and international.

As you see, they dictate to us a Bolshevik tempo of development.

I will not say that we have accomplished nothing in regard to economic management during these years. In fact, we have accomplished a good deal. We have doubled our industrial output as compared with the prewar level. We have created the largest-scale agricultural production in the world. But we could have accomplished more had we tried hard during this period really to master production, the technique of production, the financial and economic side of it.

In ten years at most we must make good the distance which separates us from the advanced capitalist countries. We have all the "objective" possibilities for this. The only thing lacking is the ability to take proper advantage of these possibilities. And that depends on us. *Only* on us! It is time we learned to take advantage of these possibilities. It is time to put an end to the rotten policy of noninterference in production. It is time to adopt a new policy, a policy adapted to the present times—the policy of *interfering in everything*. If you are a factory manager, then interfere in all the affairs of the factory, look into everything, let nothing escape you, learn and learn again. Bolsheviks must master technique.

It is time Bolsheviks themselves became experts. In the period of reconstruction technique decides everything. And a business executive who does not want to study technique, who does not want to master technique, is a joke and not an executive.

It is said that it is hard to master technique. That is not true! There are no fortresses which Bolsheviks cannot capture. We have solved a number of most difficult problems. We have overthrown capitalism. We have assumed power. We have built up a huge socialist industry. We have swung the middle peasants to the path of socialism. We have already accomplished what is most important from the point of view of construction. What remains to be done is not so much: to study technique, to master science. And when we have done that we will develop a tempo of which we dare not even dream at present.

And we will do that if we really want to.

b) New Conditions—New Tasks in Economic Construction

. . . What is the cause of the heavy turnover of labour power?

The cause is the wrong structure of wages, the wrong wage scales, the "Leftist" practice of wage equalization. In a number of our factories wage scales are drawn up in such a way as to practically wipe out the difference between skilled and unskilled labour, between heavy and light work. The consequence of wage equalization is that the unskilled worker lacks the incentive to become a skilled worker and is thus deprived of the prospect of advancement; as a result he feels himself a "visitor" in the factory, working only temporarily so as to "earn a little" and then go off to "seek his fortune" elsewhere. The consequence of wage equalization is that the skilled worker is obliged to wander from factory to factory until he finds one where his skill is properly appreciated.

FROM: Stalin, "New Conditions—New Tasks in Economic Construction" (Speech at a conference of business executives, June, 1931; *Problems of Leninism*, pp. 463-64, 466-67, 471-73).

Hence, the "general" drift from factory to factory; hence, the heavy turnover of labour power.

In order to put an end to this evil we must abolish wage equalization and discard the old wage scales. In order to put an end to this evil we must draw up wage scales that will take into account the difference between skilled and unskilled labour, between heavy and light work. We cannot tolerate a situation where a rolling-mill hand in a steel mill earns no more than a sweeper. We cannot tolerate a situation where a locomotive driver earns only as much as a copying clerk. Marx and Lenin said that the difference between skilled and unskilled labour would exist even under socialism, even after classes had been abolished; that only under communism would this difference disappear and that, consequently, even under socialism "wages" must be paid according to work performed and not according to needs. But the equalitarians among our business executives and trade union officials do not agree with this and believe that under our Soviet system this difference has already disappeared. Who is right, Marx and Lenin, or the equalitarians? We must take it that it is Marx and Lenin who are right. But if that is so, it follows that whoever draws up wage scales on the "principle" of wage equalization, without taking into account the difference between skilled and unskilled labour, breaks with Marxism, breaks with Leninism. . . .

. . . Can it be said that the present organization of labour in our factories meets the modern requirements of production? Unfortunately, this cannot be said. At all events, there are still a number of factories where work is organized abominably, where instead of order and coordination of work there is disorder and confusion, where instead of responsibility for the work there is absolute irresponsibility, absolute *lack of personal responsibility.*

What does lack of personal responsibility mean? It means complete lack of responsibility for work that is entrusted to anyone, lack of responsibility for machinery and tools. Naturally, when there is no personal responsibility we cannot expect a tangible increase in productivity of labour, an improvement in the quality of the goods, the exercise of care in handling machinery and tools. You know what lack of personal responsibility led to on the railways. It is leading to the same result in industry. We have abolished the system under which there was lack of personal responsibility on the railways and have thus improved their work. We must do the same in industry in order to raise its work to a higher level.

Formerly, we could "manage" somehow or other with bad organization of labour, which gets on quite nicely without personal responsibility, without every man being responsible for the job entrusted to him. Now it is a different matter. Conditions have entirely changed. With the present vast scale of production and the existence of giant enterprises, lack of personal responsibility has become the plague of industry which is jeopardizing all our achievements in our factories in the sphere of production and organization. . . .

. . . We can no longer manage our industry with the very small engineering, technical and administrative staffs with which we managed it formerly. It follows that the old centres for training engineering and technical forces are no longer adequate, that we must create a network of new centres—in the Urals, in Siberia and in Central Asia. We must now ensure the supply of three times, five times the number of engineering, technical and administrative staffs for industry if we really intend to carry out the program of the socialist industrialization of the U.S.S.R.

But we do not need just *any kind* of administrative, engineering and technical forces. We need *such* administrative, engineering and technical forces as are capable of understanding the policy of the working class of our country, are capable of assimilating that policy and are ready to carry it out conscientiously. And what does this mean? This means that our country has entered a phase of development in which the *working class must create its own industrial and technical intelligentsia,* one that is capable of upholding the interests of the working class in production as the interests of the ruling class.

No ruling class has managed without its own intelligentsia.

There are no grounds for believing that the working class of the U.S.S.R. can manage without its own industrial and technical intelligentsia.

The Soviet government has taken this fact into account and has opened wide the doors of all the higher educational institutions in every branch of national economy to members of the working class and labouring peasantry. You know that tens of thousands of working class and peasant youths are now attending higher educational institutions. Formerly, under capitalism, the higher educational institutions were the monopoly of the scions of the rich—today, under the Soviet system, the working class and peasant youth predominate in these institutions. There is no doubt that our educational institutions will soon be turning out thousands of new technicians and engineers, new leaders for our industries.

But that is only one side of the matter. The other side is that the industrial and technical intelligentsia of the working class will be recruited not only from among those who have passed through the institutions of higher learning, but also from among practical workers in our factories, from the skilled workers, from among the working-class cultural forces in the mills, factories and mines. The initiators of socialist emulation, the leaders of shock brigades, those who inspire in practice labour enthusiasm, the organizers of work in the various sections of our construction—such is the new stratum of the working class that, together with the comrades who have passed through the institutions of higher learning, must form the core of the intelligentsia of the working class, the core of the administrative staffs of our industry. It is our duty not to discourage these "rank-and-file" comrades who show initiative, but boldly to promote them to responsible positions; to give them the opportunity to display their organizing abilities and the opportunity to supplement their knowledge; to create suitable conditions for their work, not stinting money for this purpose.

Among these comrades not a few are non-Party people. But that should not prevent us from boldly promoting them to responsible positions. On the contrary, it is particularly these non-Party comrades who must receive our special attention, who must be promoted to responsible positions so that they may see for themselves that the Party appreciates capable and gifted workers.

Some comrades think that only Party members may be placed in leading positions in the mills and factories. This is the reason why they not infrequently shove aside non-Party comrades who possess ability and initiative and promote Party members instead, although they may be less capable and show no initiative. Needless to say, there is nothing more stupid and reactionary than such a "policy," so-called. It need hardly be proved that such a "policy" can only discredit the Party and repel the non-Party workers from it. Our policy is by no means to transform the Party into an exclusive caste. Our policy is to create an atmosphere of mutual confidence," of "mutual control" (*Lenin*) between Party and non-Party workers. One of the reasons why our Party is strong among the working class is that it pursues such a policy.

Hence, the task is *to see to it that the working class of the U.S.S.R. has its own industrial and technical intelligentsia. . . .*

Stalin on the Sanctity of Leninism

In 1931, reacting to an article which cast doubt on Lenin's infallibility, Stalin made it clear that the pursuit of truth—"rotten liberalism"—would henceforth be subordinated to considerations of the glory and discipline of the party.

Dear Comrades!

I emphatically protest against the publication in *Proletarskaya Revolyutsia* (No. 6, 1930) of Slutsky's anti-Party and semi-Trotskyite article, "The Bolsheviks on German Social-Democracy in the Period of its Prewar Crisis," as a discussion article.

Slutsky asserts that Lenin (the Bolsheviks) underestimated the danger of *centrism* in German Social-Democracy and in

FROM: Stalin, "Some Questions Concerning the History of Bolshevism" (Letter to the Editorial Board of *Proletarian Revolution,* 1931; *Problems of Leninism,* pp. 483-84, 493-94).

pre-war Social-Democracy in general; that is, he underestimated the danger of camouflaged opportunism, the danger of conciliation with opportunism. In other words, according to Slutsky, Lenin (the Bolsheviks) did not wage a relentless struggle against opportunism, for, in essence, underestimation of centrism is tantamount to the renunciation of a forceful struggle against opportunism. Thus, it is suggested that in the period before the war Lenin was not yet a real Bolshevik; that it was only in the period of the imperialist war, or even at the close of that war, that Lenin became a real Bolshevik.

This is the tale Slutsky tells in his article. And you, instead of branding this new-found "historian" as a slanderer and falsifier, enter into discussion with him, provide him with a forum. I cannot refrain from protesting against the publication of Slutsky's article in your journal as a discussion article, for the question of Lenin's *Bolshevism,* the question as to whether Lenin *did* or *did not* wage a relentless principled struggle against centrism as a certain form of opportunism, the question as to whether Lenin *was* or *was not* a real Bolshevik, cannot be made the subject of discussion. . . .

Everyone knows that Leninism was born, grew up and became strong in its ruthless struggle against opportunism of every brand, including centrism in the West (Kautsky) and centrism in our country (Trotsky, etc.). This cannot be denied even by the outspoken enemies of Bolshevism. It is an axiom. But you are trying to drag us back by turning an axiom into a problem requiring "further analysis." Why? On what grounds? Perhaps through ignorance of the history of Bolshevism? Perhaps for the sake of a rotten liberalism, so that the Slutskys and other disciples of Trotsky may not be able to say that they are being gagged? A rather strange sort of liberalism, this, exercised at the expense of the vital interests of Bolshevism. . . .

. . . The more reliable method of testing the Bolsheviks by their deeds would have upset Slutsky's whole position in a flash.

Because a test of the Bolsheviks by their deeds would have shown that the Bolsheviks are the *only* revolutionary organization in the world which has completely smashed the opportunists and centrists and driven them out of the Party.

Because the real deeds and the real history of the Bolsheviks would have shown that Slutsky's teachers, the Trotskyites, were the *principal* and *basic* group which fostered centrism in Russia, and for this purpose created a special organization —the August Bloc,* which was a hotbed of centrism.

Because a test of the Bolsheviks by their deeds would have exposed Slutsky once and for all as a falsifier of the history of our Party, who is trying to cover up the centrism of prewar Trotskyism by slanderously accusing Lenin and the Bolsheviks of underestimating the danger of centrism.

That, comrade editors, is how matters stand with Slutsky and his article.

As you see, the editorial board made a mistake in permitting a discussion with a falsifier of the history of our Party.

What induced the editorial board to take this wrong road?

I think that they were induced to take that road by the rotten liberalism which has spread to some extent among a section of the Bolsheviks. Some Bolsheviks think that Trotskyism is a faction of communism—one which makes mistakes, it is true, which does many foolish things, is sometimes even anti-Soviet, but which, nevertheless, is a faction of communism. Hence, there is a somewhat liberal attitude towards the Trotskyites and Trotskyite-minded people. It need hardly be proved that such a view of Trotskyism is profoundly wrong and pernicious. As a matter of fact, Trotskyism has long since ceased to be a faction of communism. As a matter of fact, Trotskyism is the vanguard of the counterrevolutionary bourgeoisie which is fighting communism, fighting the Soviet regime, fighting the building of socialism in the U.S.S.R. . . .

The New Educational Policy

The impact of the industrialization drive was quickly felt in various areas of social policy, where revolutionary notions

* "August Bloc": the largely Menshevik group which met in Vienna in August, 1912—Ed.

about conditioning the ideal man gave way to the practical necessity for imparting knowledge and evoking effort. In a series of decrees beginning in 1931, the experiment in progressive education was repudiated in favor of academic education of the traditional disciplinarian type.

The "polytechnical" approach stressed at this time (to combine regular instruction with practical labor training) was abandoned between the late thirties and Stalin's death, but has been heavily reëmphasized since then.

. . . The Soviet school, taking as its task "the preparation of the all-around developed member of communist society," gives the children an incomparably broader social-political outlook and more general development than the pre-revolutionary and bourgeois school. In the last few years the level of general education of the children in the Soviet school has risen.

Especially significant successes have been achieved by the school since the historic decision of the Sixteenth Party Congress [July, 1930] on the introduction of universal primary education. Just in the last year the number of students in the primary and secondary school has risen from 13.5 million to 20 million. In addition to this the factory-plant schools and technicums have 1,400,000 students.

Together with decisive steps toward the realization of compulsory instruction for children of school age the school has moved significantly forward on the path of combining school instruction with productive labor and social work, thanks to which the fundamental reconstruction of the school on the basis of polytechnicism has been started. . . .

However, in spite of all these achievements, the Central Committee states that the Soviet school is still far from meeting the tremendous demands which are placed upon it in the present stage of socialist construction. The Central Committee considers that a radical inadequacy of the school at the present moment lies in the fact that instruction in the school does not give sufficient breadth of general educational

FROM: Decision of the Central Committee of the All-Union Communist Party on the Primary and Secondary School, September 5, 1931 (*On the Path to the New School,* October, 1931, pp. 3-4, 8; editor's translation).

knowledge, and does not satisfactorily meet the task of preparing literate people who have mastered the basic sciences (physics, chemistry, mathematics, the native language, geography, etc.), for the technicums and higher schools. As a result of this, the polytechnicization of the school in many cases acquires a formal character and does not prepare children as all-around developed builders of socialism who have tied theory and practice together and have mastered technique. . . .

While applying in the Soviet school various new methods of instruction which can facilitate the education of energetic and initiative-possessing participants in the building of socialism, it is essential to unleash a decisive struggle against light-minded methodological projectism, the dissemination on a mass scale of methods not verified in preliminary practice, which has recently been revealed with special clarity in the application of the so-called "project method." Attempts, stemming from the anti-Leninist theory of the "withering-away of the school," to put all school work on the basis of the so-called "project method" have actually led to the ruin of the school. . . .

In the period of socialism, when the proletariat is accomplishing the final destruction of classes under conditions of sharpened class struggle, sustained communist education in the Soviet school and intensification of the struggle against all attempts to inoculate children in the Soviet school with elements of anti-proletarian ideology assume exceptionally weighty significance.

In connection with this the Central Committee proposes that the party organizations strengthen their guidance of the school and take under their immediate supervision the setting up of the teaching of social-political discipline in the seven-year schools, pedagogical technicums and higher pedagogical institutes.

Confirming the necessity of the timely fulfillment of the decision of the Central Committee of July 25, 1930, on universal compulsory primary instruction, the Central Committee proposes, toward the end of the quickest realization of the demands of the party program on general and polytechnical education for all children and youth up to 17 years of age, that the Council of People's Commissars of the USSR work out a plan of *universal compulsory seven-year instruction*. . . .

The Central Committee underscores the growing significance and role of the school in the building of socialism. The Central Committee proposes that all organizations systematically and undeviatingly conduct a struggle against opportunist anti-Leninist perversions of the policy of the party in the region of school work. The success of the struggle with the chief danger on the path of setting up the polytechnical school—the right-opportunist claimants of party policy, who would lead it to reject the polytechnicization of the school, to attempt to preserve the old, verbalistic school, to divorce theoretical instruction and practice—requires the intensification of the struggle against left-opportunist perversions, against theories of the "withering-away of the school" and reduction of the role of the teacher.

The Central Committee directs the attention of all party organizations to the necessity of decisively heightening attention on the mass school, the work of the teacher, and the strengthening of day-to-day concrete guidance of the school.

Stalin's Social Ideal

At the Seventeenth Party Congress in 1934, Stalin set forth his revised conception of the positive virtues of socialism—class struggle instead of the withering away of the state, inequality instead of equality, and the decisiveness of individual effort instead of the sway of economic circumstances. By this time Stalin's reinterpretation of doctrine under cover of a pretended orthodoxy had cut the Communist movement entirely off from any guiding influence of Marxist principle.

. . . It goes without saying that a classless society cannot come of itself, spontaneously, as it were. It has to be achieved

FROM: Stalin, Report on the Work of the Central Committee, to the Seventeenth Congress of the CPSU(B) (January, 1934; *Problems of Leninism*, pp. 631-32, 634-35, 643-45).

and built by the efforts of all the working people, by strengthening the organs of the dictatorship of the proletariat, by intensifying the class struggle, by abolishing classes, by eliminating the remnants of the capitalist classes, and in battles with enemies both internal and external.

The point is clear, one would think.

And yet, who does not know that the promulgation of this clear and elementary thesis of Leninism has given rise to not a little confusion and to unhealthy sentiments among a section of Party members? The thesis that we are advancing towards a classless society—which was put forward as a slogan—was interpreted by them to mean a spontaneous process. And they began to reason in this way: If it is a classless society, then we can relax the class struggle, we can relax the dictatorship of the proletariat, and get rid of the state altogether, since it is fated to wither away soon in any case. They dropped into a state of moon-calf ecstasy, in the expectation that soon there will be no classes, and therefore no class struggle, and therefore no cares and worries, and therefore we can lay down our arms and retire—to sleep and to wait for the advent of a classless society. (*General laughter*). . . .

It goes without saying that if this confusion of mind and these non-Bolshevik sentiments obtained a hold over the majority of our Party, the Party would find itself demobilized and disarmed.

Now take the question of the agricultural *artel* and the agricultural *commune*. Everybody admits now that under present conditions the artel is the only proper form of the collective-farm movement. . . .

Unlike the artel, where only the means of production are socialized, the communes, until recently, socialized not only the means of production, but also the appurtenances of life of every member of the commune; that is to say, the members of a commune, unlike the members of an artel, did not individually own poultry, small livestock, a cow, grain, or household land. This means that in the commune the individual, everyday interests of the members have not so much been taken into account and combined with the public interests as they have been eclipsed by the latter in the pursuit of petty-bourgeois equalization. . . .

. . . There are those who think that in declaring the artel to be the fundamental form of the collective-farm movement the Party has drifted away from socialism, has retreated from the commune, from the higher form of the collective-farm movement, to a lower form. The question arises—why? Because, it is suggested, there is no equality in the artel, since differences in the requirements and in the individual lives of the members of the artel are preserved; whereas in the commune there is equality, because the requirements and the individual life of all its members have been made equal. But in the first place, there are no longer any communes which practise levelling, equalization in requirements and in individual life. Practice has shown that the communes would certainly have been doomed had they not abandoned equalization and had they not actually assumed the status of artels. Hence, it is useless talking about what no longer exists. Secondly, every Leninist knows (that is, if he is a real Leninist) that equalization in the sphere of requirements and individual life is a piece of reactionary petty-bourgeois absurdity worthy of a primitive sect of ascetics, but not of a socialist society organized on Marxian lines; for we cannot expect all people to have the same requirements and tastes, and all people to live their individual lives on the same model. And, finally, are not differences in requirements and in individual life still preserved among the workers? Does that mean that the workers are more remote from socialism than the members of the agricultural communes?

These people evidently think that socialism calls for equalization, for levelling the requirements and the individual lives of the members of society. Needless to say, such an assumption has nothing in common with Marxism, with Leninism. By equality Marxism means, not equalization of individual requirements and individual life, but the abolition of classes, i.e., a) the equal emancipation of all working people from exploitation after the capitalists have been overthrown and expropriated; b) the equal abolition for all of private property in the means of production after they have been converted into the property of the whole of society; c) the equal duty of all to work according to their ability, and the equal right of all working people to receive remuneration according to the amount of work performed (*socialist* society); d) the equal duty of all to work according to their ability, and the equal right of all working people to receive remuneration according to their needs (*communist* society). Furthermore, Marxism proceeds from the assumption that people's tastes and requirements are not, and cannot be, identical, equal, in regard to quality or quantity, either in the period of socialism or in the period of communism.

That is the Marxian conception of equality. . . .

. . . Victory never comes of itself—it usually has to be attained. Good resolutions and declarations in favour of the general line of the Party are only a beginning; they merely express the desire for victory, but not the victory itself. After the correct line has been laid down, after a correct solution of the problem has been found, success depends on how the work is organized; on the organization of the struggle for the application of the Party line; on the proper selection of personnel; on the way a check is kept on the fulfilment of the decisions of the leading bodies. Otherwise the correct line of the Party and the correct solutions are in danger of being seriously prejudiced. Furthermore, after the correct political line has been laid down, organizational work decides everything, including the fate of the political line itself, its success or failure.

As a matter of fact, victory was achieved and won by a stern and systematic struggle against all sorts of difficulties that stood in the way of carrying out the Party line; by overcoming the difficulties; by mobilizing the Party and the working class for the purpose of overcoming the difficulties; by organizing the struggle to overcome the difficulties; by removing inefficient executives and choosing better ones, capable of waging the struggle against difficulties.

What are these difficulties; and wherein are they lodged?

They are difficulties attending our organizational work, difficulties attending our organizational leadership. They are lodged in ourselves, in our leading people, in our organizations, in the apparatus of our Party, state, economic, trade union, Young Communist League, and all other organizations.

We must realize that the strength and prestige of our Party, state, economic, and all other organizations, and of their leaders, have grown to an unprecedented degree. And precisely because their strength and prestige have grown to an unprecedented degree, it is their work that now determines everything, or nearly everything. There can be no justification for references to so-called objective conditions. Now that the correctness of the Party's political line has been confirmed by the experience of a number of years, and that there is no longer any doubt as to the readiness of the workers and peasants to support this line, the part played by so-called objective conditions has been reduced to a minimum; whereas the part played by our organizations and their leaders has become decisive, exceptional. What does this mean? It means that from now on nine tenths of the responsibility for the failures and defects in our work rest, not on "objective" conditions, but on ourselves, and on ourselves alone. . . .

Bureaucracy and red tape in the administrative apparatus; idle chatter about "leadership in general" instead of real and concrete leadership; the functional structure of our organizations and lack of individual responsibility; lack of personal responsibility in work, and wage equalization; the absence of a systematic check upon the fulfilment of decisions; fear of self-criticism—these are the sources of our difficulties; this is where our difficulties are now lodged. . . .

The New History

In keeping with Stalin's stress on individual responsibility, the old ultra-Marxist line of economic determinism in history and social science was sharply criticized in 1934. A much more conventional presentation of history, with emphasis on individuals and nations, was enjoined upon Soviet schools and historians. This was followed by the repudiation of anti-nationalist attacks on the past of Czarist Russia.

The Council of People's Commissars of the USSR and the Central Committee of the All-Union Communist Party (Bolsheviki) state that the teaching of history in schools of the USSR is unsatisfactory. The textbooks and oral instruction are of an abstract schematic character. Instead of the teaching of civic history in an animated and entertaining form with an exposition of the most important events and facts in their chronological sequence and with sketches of historical personages, the pupils are given abstract definitions of social and economic formations, which thus replace the consecutive exposition of civic history by abstract sociological schemes.

The decisive condition of a permanent mastery of history is the observance of historical and chronological sequence in the exposition of historical events, with a due emphasis in the memory of the pupils of important historical facts, the names of historical persons and chronological dates. Only such a course of historical teaching can ensure the necessary understanding, fidelity of presentation and a real use of historical material; correct analysis and correct explanation of historical events, leading pupils to the Marxist conception of history, are possible only on this basis. . . .

The New Nationalism

After an accumulation of hints about the paramountcy of national interest, the Soviet government proclaimed the supreme virtue of national tradition and patriotism—which, incidentally, served as the justification for intensifying the penalties for treason.

FROM: Decree of the Council of People's Commissars of the USSR and of the Central Committee of the All-Union Communist Party (Bolsheviks), "On the Teaching of Civic History in Schools of the USSR," May 16, 1934 (English translation in *The Slavonic Review,* July, 1934, p. 204, reprinted by permission of the Editorial Board).

FROM: "For the Fatherland!" *Pravda,* June 9, 1934 (English translation in *The Communist Conspiracy, Part I: Communism outside the U. S., Section B: the USSR;* U. S. House of Representatives Report No. 2241, 84th Congress, 2nd Session, Washington, Government Printing Office, 1956, pp. 287-88).

. . . The country of the October Revolution is endlessly dear to the workers, the kolkhozniks [collective farmers] and the Soviet intelligentsia. The working people are bound to their factories, sovkhozes [state farms] and kolkhozes [collective farms], to their soil and to their culture by the indissoluble links of blood, heroism and love. For proletarians and kolkhozniks, for honest Soviet specialists, there is nothing more beautiful and more clear than their own country liberated from the yoke of landowners and capitalists.

The best traditions of the Civil War and of the struggle with the interventionists, when the workers and peasants were armed to defend their right to a new life, are now being multiplied in the progress of techniques and Socialistic culture. That is why the Soviet Union has become an impregnable fortress and is capable of crushing all those who would dare to attempt to violate the sanctity of its boundaries.

For our fatherland! This call fans the flame of heroism, the flame of creative initiative in pursuits and all fields of our rich life. For our fatherland! This call arouses millions of workers and alerts them in the defence of their great country.

The defence of the fatherland is the supreme law of life. And he who raises his hand against his country, he who betrays his country should be destroyed.

Today we publish the decree of the Central Executive Committee of the U.S.S.R. regarding the supplementing of the statutes of the state criminal code with articles on treason. The Soviet country is very dear to the workers and kolkhozniks. They have paid for it dearly in blood and suffering in their struggle with exploiters and interventionists and they will not allow anyone to betray their country and will not allow anyone to bargain with her interests.

For high treason, for acts detrimental to the country's military might, or state independence, or inviolability of her territories, for espionage, for divulging military or state secrets, for deserting to the enemy, or escaping across the border, the Soviet court will punish the guilty by shooting or by confiscating all his property. In the case of a civilian, some leniency will be shown according to circumstances, and for the death penalty will be substituted the confiscation of his property or imprisonment for ten years. For a person in military service, however, for treason there will be only one measure of punishment—execution by shooting with confiscation of all his property. Individual members of his family are also responsible for the acts of traitors. In the case of the escape or flight across the border of a person in military service, all mature members of his family, if they are implicated in aiding the criminal, or knew of his intentions and did not report them to the authorities, the punishment is imprisonment from five to ten years with confiscation of all their property.

The other members of the family of the traitor and all his dependents at the time he committed treason are subject to disfranchisement and exile to some remote region in Siberia for five years.

Traitors should be punished unmercifully. On the other hand, if a person in military service was aware of a plot to betray the government or of an act of betrayal and did not report this to the authorities, he is subject to imprisonment for ten years. One cannot be a neutral observer where the interests of the country or the workers and peasants are concerned. This is a terrible crime; this is complicity in the crime.

This decree of the Central Executive Committee gives the workers of the great Soviet Union a new weapon in their hands in the struggle against the enemies of the proletariat dictatorship. The one hundred and seventy million working people who regard the Soviet land as their own mother who has nursed them to a happy and joyous life will deal with the traitors of their fatherland with all their force.

For the fatherland, for its honor and glory, might and well-being!

Socialist Realism

Artistic activity, like other fields of intellectual endeavor in the USSR, was subjected to stringent party control from 1929 on. After a dismal experiment in "proletarian" art the party line shifted to conservative nineteenth-century fashions which were applied to the task of propagandizing an official optimism. The famous revolutionary writer Maxim Gorky was restored to favor as the leading exponent of the "new" literature, which he extolled at a writer's congress in 1935 as "socialist realism." With some variation in the rigor of its enforcement, this has been the Communist line in the arts ever since, while modernistic experiments have been systematically condemned as "bourgeois formalism."

The Communist-Leninist Party, the workers' and peasants' government of the Union of Socialist Soviets, which have destroyed capitalism throughout the length and breadth of tsarist Russia, which have handed over political power to the workers and the peasants, and which are organizing a free classless society, have made it the object of their daring, sage and indefatigable activity to free the working masses from the age-old yoke of an old and outworn history, of the capitalist development of culture, which today has glaringly exposed all its vices and its creative decrepitude. And it is from the height of this great aim that we honest writers of the Union of Soviets must examine, appraise and organize our work. . . .

. . . We must grasp and fully realize the fact that in our country the socially organized labour of semi-literate workers and a primitive peasantry has in the short space of ten years created stupendous values and armed itself superbly for defence against an enemy's attack. Proper appreciation of this fact will reveal to us the cultural and revolutionary power of a doctrine which unites the whole proletariat of the world.

All of us—writers, factory workers, collective farmers—still work badly and cannot even fully master everything that has been made by us and for us. Our working masses do not yet quite grasp the fact that they are working only for themselves. This feeling is smouldering everywhere, but it has

FROM: Gorky, "Soviet Literature" (Speech at The First All-Union Congress of Soviet Writers, August, 1934; English translation in H. G. Scott, ed., *Problems of Soviet Literature,* Moscow, Cooperative Publishing Society of Foreign Workers in The U.S.S.R., 1935, pp. 53-54, 64-67).

not yet blazed up into a mighty and joyous flame. But nothing can kindle until it has reached a certain temperature, and nobody ever was so splendidly capable of raising the temperature of labour energy as is the party organized by the genius of Vladimir Lenin, and the present-day leader of this party.

As the principal hero of our books we should choose labour, *i.e.*, a person, organized by the processes of labour, who in our country is armed with the full might of modern technique, a person who, in his turn, so organizes labour that it becomes easier and more productive, raising it to the level of an art. . . .

The party leadership of literature must be thoroughly purged of all philistine influences. Party members active in literature must not only be the teachers of ideas which will muster the energy of the proletariat in all countries for the last battle for its freedom; the party leadership must, in all its conduct, show a morally authoritative force. This force must imbue literary workers first and foremost with a consciousness of their collective responsibility for all that happens in their midst. Soviet literature, with all its diversity of talents, and the steadily growing number of new and gifted writers, should be organized as an integral collective body, as a potent instrument of socialist culture.

The Writers' Union is not being created merely for the purpose of bodily uniting all artists of the pen, but so that professional unification may enable them to comprehend their corporate strength, to define with all possible clarity their varied tendencies, creative activity, guiding principles, and harmoniously to merge all aims in that unity which is guiding all the creative working energies of the country.

The idea, of course, is not to restrict individual creation, but to furnish it with the widest means of continued powerful development.

It should be realized that critical realism originated as the individual creation of "superfluous people," who, being incapable of the struggle for existence, not finding a place in life, and more or less clearly realizing the aimlessness of personal being, understood this aimlessness merely as the senselessness of all phenomena in social life and in the whole historical process.

Without in any way denying the broad, immense work of critical realism, and while highly appreciating its formal achievements in the art of word painting, we should understand that this realism is necessary to us only for throwing light on the survivals of the past, for fighting them, and extirpating them.

But this form of realism did not and cannot serve to educate socialist individuality, for in criticizing everything, it asserted nothing, or else, at the worst, reverted to an assertion of what it had itself repudiated.

Socialist individuality, as exemplified by our heroes of labour, who represent the flower of the working class, can develop only under conditions of collective labour, which has set itself the supreme and wise aim of liberating the workers of the whole world from the man-deforming power of capitalism.

Life, as asserted by socialist realism, is deeds, creativeness, the aim of which is the uninterrupted development of the priceless individual faculties of man, with a view to his victory over the forces of nature, for the sake of his health and longevity, for the supreme joy of living on an earth which, in conformity with the steady growth of his requirements, he wishes to mould throughout into a beautiful dwelling place for mankind, united into a single family. . . .

The high standard demanded of literature, which is being rapidly remoulded by life itself and by the cultural revolutionary work of Lenin's party, is due to the high estimation in which the party holds the importance of the literary art. There has never been a state in the world where science and literature enjoyed such comradely help, such care for the raising of professional proficiency among the workers of art and science.

The proletarian state must educate thousands of first-class "craftsmen of culture," "engineers of the soul." This is necessary in order to restore to the whole mass of the working people the right to develop their intelligence, talents and faculties—a right of which they have been deprived everywhere else in the world. This aim, which is a fully practicable one, imposes on us writers the need of strict responsibility for our work and our social behaviour. This places us not only in the position, traditional to realist literature, of "judges of the world and men," "critics of life," but gives us the right to participate directly in the construction of a new life, in the process of "changing the world." The possession of this right should impress every writer with a sense of his duty and responsibility for all literature, for all the aspects in it which should not be there. . . .

The New Family Ideal

Together with the rejection of most other early revolutionary social norms in the mid-1930's, the Soviet government discarded the ideal of sexual freedom in favor of the stable family and parental responsibility.

The published draft of the law prohibiting abortion and providing material assistance to mothers has provoked a lively reaction throughout the country. It is being heatedly discussed by tens of millions of people and there is no doubt that it will serve as a further strengthening of the Soviet family. Parents' responsibility for the education of their children will be increased and a blow will be dealt at the lighthearted, negligent attitude towards marriage.

When we speak of strengthening the Soviet family, we are speaking precisely of the struggle against the survivals of a bourgeois attitude towards marriage, women and children. So-called "free love" and all disorderly sex life are bourgeois through and through, and have nothing to do with either socialist principles or the ethics and standards of conduct of the Soviet citizen. Socialist doctrine shows this, and it is proved by life itself.

FROM: Discussion of the Law on Abolition of Legal Abortion, *Pravda,* Editorials of May 28 and June 9, 1936 (English translation in Rudolf Schlesinger, ed., *Changing Attitudes in Soviet Russia: The Family in the USSR,* London, Routledge & Kegan Paul, 1949, pp. 251-54, 268-69; reprinted by permission of the publisher).

The *elite* of our country, the best of the Soviet youth, are as a rule also excellent family men who dearly love their children. And *vice versa:* the man who does not take marriage seriously, and abandons his children to the whims of fate, is usually also a bad worker and a poor member of society.

Fatherhood and motherhood have long been virtues in this country. This can be seen at the first glance, without searching enquiry. Go through the parks and streets of Moscow or of any other town in the Soviet Union on a holiday, and you will see not a few young men walking with pink-cheeked, well-fed babies in their arms.

The rise in the standard of living has brought the joy of parenthood within the reach of all adults. The Soviet land cannot complain of too low a birth-rate. The birth-rate is rising steadily, and the mortality rate is as steadily going down. . . .

More than once the enemies of the people suggested to us the foul and poisonous ideal of liquidating the family and disrupting marriage. The bourgeoisie has tried to use it as a weapon in the struggle against socialist progress. It is enough to recall with what persistence they spread the slander about the "nationalization of women." And during the great move to collectivize the villages, the *kulaks* again broadcast this favourite bourgeois allegation. The *kulaks* used it to scare the peasants: "In the collective farms you will all sleep under the same 30-yard-wide blanket."

The bourgeois who establishes his family order with the aid of a knout, the bourgeois for whom his own family is but a thin veneer covering prostitution and sexual debauchery, naturally thought that everyone would fall for his lie about "free love" in the country where the exploitation of man by man has been abolished and women have been liberated. But he failed. This weapon, too, was shattered by the stubborn facts of Soviet reality. . . .

There is no point in denying that in towns and villages there are still men and women whose attitude towards family and children is superficial and devil-may-care. Marriage and divorce are, of course, private affairs—but the State cannot allow anyone to mock at women or to abandon his children to the mercy of fate. The irresponsible profligate who gets married five times a year cannot enjoy the respect of Soviet youth. Nor can a girl who flutters from one marriage into the next with the swiftness of a butterfly enjoy respect. Men and women of this sort merely deserve social contempt. Marriage is a serious, responsible business and one that must not be approached lightheartedly. . . .

Social education is being widely developed in this country. The State is coming to the aid of the family. But the State in no wise relieves the mother or the father of their care of the children. Under Soviet conditions the father is the social educator. He has to prepare good Soviet citizens: that is his duty, that is also his pride—and the Soviet land has heard many proud declarations by fathers and mothers about the sons and daughters they gave to the Soviet fatherland, about gallant pilots and parachutists, engineers, doctors, teachers. . . .

A man who cowardly and basely abandons his children, shuns his responsibility, hides in corners and puts all the paternal duties on the mother's shoulders, shames the name of a Soviet citizen. Evading the payment of alimony is not a weakness, though it is treated with such leniency by some of our institutions. It is a crime, and not only the man who befouls the name of Soviet citizen, but all those who protect him are guilty of this crime. . . .

A Soviet child has a right to a real father, an educator and friend. A father who abandons his children is guilty both before them and before the socialist State which has entrusted the children to his care. An irresponsible attitude towards marriage and family is a bad recommendation as a citizen.

Socialism provides every toiler with a happy, beautiful life. For the first time in history it creates for the workers a possibility of fatherhood and motherhood in the fullest sense of the word. It therefore makes serious demands on mother and father. A bourgeois attitude towards the family cannot be tolerated.

The published law-project and its widespread discussion are signs of a new socialist morality, imbued with force, confidence and vitality. It lies in the flowering and enrichment of human personality, in love for Man. In the light of this morality, the mother wears a new face, and so does the father. "Paternal pride"—these words sound real only in the Soviet land, because a father who has raised new builders of socialism can feel a worthy citizen of his country. . . .

Trotsky on the New Soviet Society

In 1937 Trotsky published a general critique of Stalin's regime, "The Revolution Betrayed." He elaborated Rakovsky's argument, with the thesis that the bureaucracy dominated the Soviet state and had raised Stalin to power as a "Bonaparte" to protect its group interests. While Trotsky explained this phenomenon as the inevitable result of Russian backwardness, he nonetheless defended the "socialist" character of the Soviet economy and expressed hope that a new proletarian movement would restore the ideals of the revolution.

. . . Marx expected that the Frenchman would begin the social revolution, the German continue it, the Englishman finish it; and as to the Russian, Marx left him far in the rear. But this conceptual order was upset by the facts. Whoever tries now mechanically to apply the universal historic conception of Marx to the particular case of the Soviet Union at the given stage of its development, will be entangled at once in hopeless contradictions.

Russia was not the strongest, but the weakest link in the chain of capitalism. The present Soviet Union does not stand above the world level of economy, but is only trying to catch up to the capitalist countries. If Marx called that society which was to be formed upon the basis of a socialization of the productive forces of the most advanced capitalism of its epoch, the lowest stage of communism, then this designation obviously does not apply to the Soviet Union, which is still today considerably poorer in technique, culture and the

FROM: Trotsky, *The Revolution Betrayed: What Is the Soviet Union and Where Is It Going?* (English translation by Max Eastman, Garden City, N. Y., Doubleday, Doran & Co., 1937, pp. 47, 51-52, 89, 93, 111-13, 255, 277-78, 288-90; reprinted by permission of the copyright holder, Pioneer Publishers).

good things of life than the capitalist countries. It would be truer, therefore, to name the present Soviet regime in all its contradictoriness, not a socialist regime, but a *preparatory* regime *transitional* from capitalism to socialism. . . .

However you may interpret the nature of the present Soviet state, one thing is indubitable: at the end of its second decade of existence, it has not only not died away, but not begun to "die away." Worse than that, it has grown into a hitherto unheard of apparatus of compulsion. The bureaucracy not only has not disappeared, yielding its place to the masses, but has turned into an uncontrolled force dominating the masses. The army not only has not been replaced by an armed people, but has given birth to a privileged officers' caste, crowned with marshals, while the people, "the armed bearers of the dictatorship," are now forbidden in the Soviet Union to carry even nonexplosive weapons. With the utmost stretch of fancy it would be difficult to imagine a contrast more striking than that which exists between the schema of the workers' state according to Marx, Engels and Lenin, and the actual state now headed by Stalin. While continuing to publish the works of Lenin (to be sure, with excerpts and distortions by the censor), the present leaders of the Soviet Union and their ideological representatives do not even raise the question of the causes of such a crying divergence between program and reality. We will try to do this for them. . . .

The proletarian character of the October revolution was determined by the world situation and by a special correlation of internal forces. But the classes themselves were formed in the barbarous circumstances of tsarism and backward capitalism, and were anything but made to order for the demands of a socialist revolution. The exact opposite is true. It is for the very reason that a proletariat still backward in many respects achieved in the space of a few months the unprecedented leap from a semifeudal monarchy to a socialist dictatorship, that the reaction in its ranks was inevitable. . . .

Before he felt out his own course, the bureaucracy felt out Stalin himself. He brought it all the necessary guarantees:

the prestige of an old Bolshevik, a strong character, narrow vision, and close bonds with the political machine as the sole source of his influence. The success which fell upon him was a surprise at first to Stalin himself. It was the friendly welcome of the new ruling group, trying to free itself from the old principles and from the control of the masses, and having need of a reliable arbiter in its inner affairs. A secondary figure before the masses and in the events of the revolution, Stalin revealed himself as the indubitable leader of the Thermidorian bureaucracy, as first in its midst. . . .

The present Soviet society cannot get along without a state, nor even—within limits—without a bureaucracy. But the cause of this is by no means the pitiful remnants of the past, but the mighty forces and tendencies of the present. The justification for the existence of a Soviet state as an apparatus of compulsion lies in the fact that the present transitional structure is still full of social contradictions, which in the sphere of consumption—most close and sensitively felt by all—are extremely tense, and forever threaten to break over into the sphere of production. The triumph of socialism cannot be called either final or irrevocable.

The basis of bureaucratic rule is the poverty of society in objects of consumption, with the resulting struggle of each against all. When there is enough goods in a store, the purchasers can come whenever they want to. When there is little goods, the purchasers are compelled to stand in line. When the lines are very long, it is necessary to appoint a policeman to keep order. Such is the starting point of the power of the Soviet bureaucracy. It "knows" who is to get something and who has to wait.

A raising of the material and cultural level ought, at first glance, to lessen the necessity of privileges, narrow the sphere of application of "bourgeois law," and thereby undermine the standing ground of its defenders, the bureaucracy. In reality the opposite thing has happened: the growth of the productive forces has been so far accompanied by an extreme development of all forms of inequality, privilege and advantage, and therewith of bureaucratism. That too is not accidental.

In its first period, the Soviet regime was undoubtedly far more equalitarian and less bureaucratic than now. But that was an equality of general poverty. The resources of the country were so scant that there was no opportunity to separate out from the masses of the population any broad privileged strata. At the same time the "equalizing" character of wages, destroying personal interestedness, became a brake upon the development of the productive forces. Soviet economy had to lift itself from its poverty to a somewhat higher level before fat deposits of privilege became possible. The present state of production is still far from guaranteeing all necessities to everybody. But it is already adequate to give significant privileges to a minority, and convert inequality into a whip for the spurring on of the majority. That is the first reason why the growth of production has so far strengthened not the socialist, but the bourgeois features of the state.

But that is not the sole reason. Alongside the economic factor dictating capitalistic methods of payment at the present stage, there operates a parallel political factor in the person of the bureaucracy itself. In its very essence it is the planter and protector of inequality. It arose in the beginning as the bourgeois organ of a workers' state. In establishing and defending the advantages of a minority, it of course draws off the cream for its own use. Nobody who has wealth to distribute ever omits himself. Thus out of a social necessity there has developed an organ which has far outgrown its socially necessary function, and become an independent factor and therewith the source of great danger for the whole social organism.

The social meaning of the Soviet Thermidor now begins to take form before us. The poverty and cultural backwardness of the masses has again become incarnate in the malignant figure of the ruler with a great club in his hand. The deposed and abused bureaucracy, from being a servant of society, has again become its lord. On this road it has attained such a degree of social and moral alienation from the popular masses, that it cannot now permit any control over either its activities or its income. . . .

The Soviet Union is a contradictory society halfway between capitalism and socialism, in which: (a) the productive forces are still far from adequate to give the state property a socialist character; (b) the tendency toward primitive accumulation created by want breaks out through innumerable pores of the planned economy; (c) norms of distribution preserving a bourgeois character lie at the basis of a new differentiation of society; (d) the economic growth, while slowly bettering the situation of the toilers, promotes a swift formation of privileged strata; (e) exploiting the social antagonisms, a bureaucracy has converted itself into an uncontrolled caste alien to socialism; (f) the social revolution, betrayed by the ruling party, still exists in property relations and in the consciousness of the toiling masses; (g) a further development of the accumulating contradictions can as well lead to socialism as back to capitalism; (h) on the road to capitalism the counterrevolution would have to break the resistance of the workers; (i) on the road to socialism the workers would have to overthrow the bureaucracy. In the last analysis, the question will be decided by a struggle of living social forces, both on the national and the world arena. . . .

The increasingly insistent deification of Stalin is, with all its elements of caricature, a necessary element of the regime. The bureaucracy has need of an inviolable superarbiter, a first consul if not an emperor, and it raises upon its shoulders him who best responds to its claim for lordship. That "strength of character" of the leader which so enraptures the literary dilettantes of the West, is in reality the sum total of the collective pressure of a caste which will stop at nothing in defense of its position. Each one of them at his post is thinking: *l'état—c'est moi.* In Stalin each one easily finds himself. But Stalin also finds in each one a small part of his own spirit. Stalin is the personification of the bureaucracy. That is the substance of his political personality.

Caesarism, or its bourgeois form, Bonapartism, enters the scene in those moments of history when the sharp struggle of two camps raises the state power, so to speak, above the nation, and guarantees it, in appearance, a complete independence of classes—in reality, only the freedom necessary for a defense of the privileged. The Stalin regime, rising above a politically atomized society, resting upon a police and officers' corps, and allowing of no control whatever, is obviously a variation of Bonapartism—a Bonapartism of a new type not before seen in history.

Caesarism arose upon the basis of a slave society shaken by inward strife. Bonapartism is one of the political weapons of the capitalist regime in its critical period. Stalinism is a variety of the same system, but upon the basis of a workers' state torn by the antagonism between an organized and armed Soviet aristocracy and the unarmed toiling masses.

As history testifies, Bonapartism gets along admirably with a universal, and even a secret, ballot. The democratic ritual of Bonapartism is the *plebiscite.* From time to time, the question is presented to the citizens: *for* or *against* the leader? And the voter feels the barrel of a revolver between his shoulders. Since the time of Napoleon III, who now seems a provincial dilettante, this technique has received an extraordinary development. The new Soviet constitution which establishes *Bonapartism on a plebiscite basis* is the veritable crown of the system.

In the last analysis, Soviet Bonapartism owes its birth to the belatedness of the world revolution. But in the capitalist countries the same cause gave rise to fascism. We thus arrive at the conclusion, unexpected at first glance, but in reality inevitable, that the crushing of Soviet democracy by an all-powerful bureaucracy and the extermination of bourgeois democracy by fascism were produced by one and the same cause: the dilatoriness of the world proletariat in solving the problems set for it by history. . . .

This is the first time in history that a state resulting from a workers' revolution has existed. The stages through which it must go are nowhere written down. It is true that the theoreticians and creators of the Soviet Union hoped that the completely transparent and flexible Soviet system would permit the state peacefully to transform itself, dissolve, and die away, in correspondence with the stages of the economic and cultural evolution of society. Here again, however, life proved more complicated than theory anticipated. The proletariat of a backward country was fated to accomplish the first socialist revolution. For this historic privilege, it must, according to all evidences, pay with a second supplementary revolution—against bureaucratic absolutism. . . .

It is not a question of substituting one ruling clique for another, but of changing the very methods of administering the economy and guiding the culture of the country. Bureaucratic autocracy must give place to Soviet democracy. A restoration of the right of criticism, and a genuine freedom of elections, are necessary conditions for the further development of the country. This assumes a revival of freedom of Soviet parties, beginning with the party of Bolsheviks, and a resurrection of the trade unions. The bringing of democracy into industry means a radical revision of plans in the interests of the toilers. Free discussion of economic problems will decrease the overhead expense of bureaucratic mistakes and zigzags. Expensive playthings—palaces of the Soviets, new theaters, show-off subways—will be crowded out in favor of workers' dwellings. "Bourgeois norms of distribution" will be confined within the limits of strict necessity, and, in step with the growth of social wealth, will give way to socialist equality. Ranks will be immediately abolished. The tinsel of decorations will go into the melting pot. The youth will receive the opportunity to breathe freely, criticize, make mistakes, and grow up. Science and art will be freed of their chains. And, finally, foreign policy will return to the traditions of revolutionary internationalism. . . .

The Great Purge

The era of the purges commenced late in 1934 with the assassination of Stalin's heir-apparent, Sergei Kirov. This was the pretext for the elaborately staged "Moscow Trials" of 1936, 1937 and 1938, in which most of the old opposition

FROM: Stalin, "On Inadequacies of Party Work and Measures for Liquidating Trotskyist and Other Double-Dealers" (Speech to the Plenum of the Central Committee of the CPSU, March 3, 1937; *Pravda*. March 29, 1937; editor's translation).

leaders were sentenced to death after confessing to a fantastic series of imaginary crimes. By 1937 the purge began to spread from the ranks of old opposition sympathizers to the government, the army, and the party itself, as more and more people were implicated in the false confessions of "plots" which the NKVD extracted from its victims. Stalin apparently convinced himself that the menace of "Trotskyist wreckers" employed by "intelligence services of foreign states" was real, and warned the party to prepare for ever sharper struggle with the hidden enemies of socialism.

Comrades!

From the reports and the discussions of them heard at this Plenum it is obvious that we have to deal here with the following three basic facts.

In the first place, the wrecking and diversionary-spying work of agents of foreign states, among whom a rather active role has been played by the Trotskyists, has touched to one degree or another all or almost all of our organizations, administrative and party as well as economic.

In the second place, agents of foreign states, including Trotskyists, have penetrated not only into the lower organizations, but even into certain responsible posts.

In the third place, certain of our leading comrades, at the center as well as in the provinces, have not only been unable to see the real face of these wreckers, diversionists, spies and murderers, but have proved to be careless, indifferent and naïve about it, and not uncommonly have coöperated in promoting agents of foreign states to some responsible post or other. . . .

. . . Our party comrades . . . have forgotten that the Soviet power has won only in one-sixth of the earth, that five-sixths of the earth constitute the realm of the capitalist states. They forget that the Soviet Union finds itself in the circumstances of a capitalistic encirclement. . . .

Capitalistic encirclement means that there is one country, the Soviet Union, which has established the socialist order, and that apart from this there are many countries—bourgeois countries—which continue to lead the capitalistic way of life and which surround the Soviet Union, awaiting the chance to attack it and destroy it, or in any case to undermine its might and weaken it. . . .

Is it not clear that as long as the capitalist encirclement exists we will have wreckers, spies, diversionists and murderers sent into our interior by agents of foreign states?

Our party comrades have forgotten about all this, and having forgotten this, have been caught completely off guard.

This is why the spying and diversionary work of the Trotskyist agents of the Japanese-German police force has proved to be a complete surprise for some of our comrades.

Further: While struggling with Trotskyist agents our party comrades did not notice—they overlooked the fact—that present-day Trotskyism is no longer what it was, say, seven or eight years ago; that during this time Trotskyism and the Trotskyists have undergone an important evolution which has radically changed the face of Trotskyism; that in view of this the struggle with Trotskyism and the methods of struggle with it must be radically changed. Our party comrades have not noticed that Trotskyism has ceased to be a political tendency in the working class . . . and has turned into a frantic and unprincipled band of wreckers, diversionists, spies and murderers working under the orders of the intelligence organs of foreign states. . . .

At the 1937 trial Piatakov, Radek and Sokolnikov* . . . admitted that they had a definite political platform . . . , an antipopular and antiproletarian platform. The restoration of capitalism, the liquidation of the collective farms and state farms, the restoration of the system of exploitation, alliance with the fascist forces of Germany and Japan to bring war to the Soviet Union, the struggle for war and against the policy of peace, the territorial dismemberment of the Soviet Union with the cession of the Ukraine to the Germans and of the Maritime Province to Japan, preparations for the military defeat of the Soviet Union in the event of an attack on it by hostile powers, and—as the means of fulfilling these tasks—wrecking, diversion, individual terror against

* Sokolnikov: Commissar of Finance, 1922-26, and a follower of Zinoviev—Ed.

the leaders of the Soviet government, espionage in the service of the Japanese-German fascist forces—such is the political platform of present-day Trotskyism set forth by Piatakov, Radek and Sokolnikov. . . .

. . . Now that we have technically well-trained Bolshevik cadres, the role of wrecker is played not by openly alien people . . . but by people who possess party cards and enjoy all the rights of party members. Now the weakness of our people consists not in technical backwardness but in political carelessness, in blind trust of people who have accidently acquired party cards, in the absence of checkups on people not just on the basis of their political declarations but according to the results of their work. Now the key question for us is not the liquidation of the technical backwardness of our cadres, for this has basically already been liquidated, but the liquidation of political carelessness and political trustingness toward wreckers who have accidentally acquired party cards. . . .

We must smash and throw out the rotten theory that with each forward movement we make the class struggle will die down more and more, that in proportion to our successes the class enemy will become more and more domesticated.

This is not only a rotten theory but a dangerous theory, for it lulls our people to sleep, leads them into a trap, and makes it possible for the class enemy to rally for the struggle against the Soviet power.

On the contrary, the more we move forward, the more success we have, then the more wrathful become the remnants of the beaten exploiter classes, the more quickly they turn to sharper forms of struggle, the more mischief they do the Soviet state, the more they grasp at the most desperate means of struggle, as the last resort of the doomed. . . .

We must smash and throw out a second rotten theory which says that he who does not always wreck things and sometimes may be successful in his work cannot be a wrecker.

This strange theory reveals the naïveté of its authors. No wrecker wrecks things all the time if he doesn't want to be exposed very quickly. On the contrary, the real wrecker must from time to time be successful in his work, for this is the only way for the wrecker to get people's confidence and continue his wrecking work. . . .

We must smash and throw out a third rotten theory which says that the systematic fulfillment of the economic plans reduces wrecking and the results of wrecking to nothing.

Such a theory can serve only one end—to tickle the bureaucratic conceit of our functionaries, soothe them and weaken their struggle against wrecking. . . .

We must smash and throw out [another] rotten theory which says that the Trotskyist wreckers do not have large reserves, that they are assembling their last cadres, as it were.

This is untrue, comrades. Only naïve people could think up such a theory. The Trotskyist wreckers have their reserves. They consist above all of the remnants of the beaten exploiter classes in the USSR. They consist of a whole series of groups and organizations outside the borders of the USSR which are hostile to the Soviet Union.

Take, for example, the Trotskyist counterrevolutionary Fourth International, which is two-thirds made up of spies and diversionists. Isn't this a reserve? Is it not clear that this International of spies will spawn cadres for the spying and wrecking work of the Trotskyists? . . .

The Moscow Trials

Bukharin and Rykov were brought to trial in 1938 together with the Trotskyists Rakovsky and Krestinsky and the former secret police chief Yagoda. Andrei Vyshinsky was prosecutor in this as in the earlier trials; new heights of fantasy were reached in the charges which he pressed, ranging from a conspiracy to kill Lenin in 1918 to a recent plot with Germany and Japan to partition the USSR and restore capitalism. All the defendants except Krestinsky confessed readily, probably as the result of promises, threats, torture, and ideological arguments in combination. Bukharin's last plea is interesting evidence of the latter factor. As in the previous

FROM: *Report of Court Proceedings: The Case of the Anti-Soviet Bloc of Rights and Trotskyites* (Moscow, People's Commissariat of Justice of the USSR, 1938, English edition, pp. 5-6, 36, 626, 648, 696-97, 767, 778-79).

trials most of the defendants were shot, and those who received prison terms were never heard of again.

a) The Indictment

. . . The investigation instituted by the organs of the People's Commissariat of Internal Affairs has established that on the instructions of the intelligence services of foreign states hostile to the U.S.S.R. the accused in the present case organized a conspiratorial group named the "bloc of Rights and Trotskyites," the object of which was to overthrow the Socialist social and state system existing in the U.S.S.R., to restore capitalism and the power of the bourgeoisie in the U.S.S.R., to dismember the U.S.S.R. and to sever from it for the benefit of the aforementioned states the Ukraine, Byelorussia, the Central Asiatic Republics, Georgia, Armenia, Azerbaijan and the Maritime Region. . . .

Lacking all support within the U.S.S.R., the members of the "bloc of Rights and Trotskyites" in their struggle against the Socialist social and state system existing in the U.S.S.R. and for seizing power placed all their hopes exclusively upon the armed assistance of foreign aggressors, who promised the conspirators this assistance on the condition that the U.S.S.R. was to be dismembered and that the Ukraine, the Maritime region, Byelorussia, the Central Asiatic Republics, Georgia, Armenia and Azerbaijan were to be severed from the U.S.S.R.

This agreement between the "bloc of Rights and Trotskyites" and the representatives of the aforementioned foreign states was facilitated by the fact that many of the leading participants of this conspiracy had long been agents of foreign intelligence services and had for many years carried on espionage activities on behalf of these intelligence services.

This applies first of all to one of the inspirers of the conspiracy, enemy of the people TROTSKY. His connection with the Gestapo was exhaustively proved at the trials of the Trotskyite-Zinovievite Terrorist Centre in August 1936, and of the Anti-Soviet Trotskyite Centre in January 1937.

However, the materials in the possession of the investigating authorities in the present case establish that the connections between enemy of the people TROTSKY and the German political police and the intelligence services of other countries were established at a much earlier date. The investigation has definitely established that TROTSKY has been connected with the German intelligence service since 1921, and with the British Intelligence Service since 1926. . . .

b) The Pleas

THE PRESIDENT: Accused Bukharin, do you plead guilty to the charges brought against you?

BUKHARIN: Yes, I plead guilty to the charges brought against me.

THE PRESIDENT: Accused Rykov, do you plead guilty to the charges brought against you?

RYKOV: Yes, I do.

THE PRESIDENT: Accused Yagoda, do you plead guilty to the charges brought against you?

YAGODA: Yes, I do.

THE PRESIDENT: Accused Krestinsky, do you plead guilty to the charges brought against you?

KRESTINSKY: I plead not guilty. I am not a Trotskyite. I was never a member of the bloc of Rights and Trotskyites, of whose existence I was not aware. Nor have I committed any of the crimes with which I personally am charged, in particular I plead not guilty to the charge of having had connections with the German intelligence service.

THE PRESIDENT: Do you corroborate the confession you made at the preliminary investigation?

KRESTINSKY: Yes, at the preliminary investigation I confessed, but I have never been a Trotskyite.

THE PRESIDENT: I repeat the question, do you plead guilty?

KRESTINSKY: Before my arrest I was a member of the Communist Party of the Soviet Union (Bolsheviks) and I remain one now.

THE PRESIDENT: Do you plead guilty to the charge of participating in espionage activities and of participating in terrorist activities?

KRESTINSKY: I have never been a Trotskyite, I have never

belonged to the bloc of Rights and Trotskyites and have not committed a single crime.

THE PRESIDENT: Accused Rakovsky, do you plead guilty to the charges brought against you?

RAKOVSKY: Yes, I do. . . .

c) Vyshinsky's Summation

. . . The Trotskyites and Bukharinites, that is to say, the "bloc of Rights and Trotskyites," the leading lights of which are now in the prisoners' dock, is not a political party, a political tendency, but a band of felonious criminals, and not simply felonious criminals, but of criminals who have sold themselves to enemy intelligence services, criminals whom even ordinary felons treat as the basest, the lowest, the most contemptible, the most depraved of the depraved. . . .

The investigation established, and I deem it necessary to remind you of this here in its full scope, Comrades Judges, that in 1918, immediately following the October Revolution, in the period of the conclusion of the Brest-Litovsk Peace, Bukharin and his group of so-called "Left Communists," and Trotsky with his group, together with the "Left" Socialist-Revolutionaries, organized a conspiracy against Lenin as the head of the Soviet government.

Bukharin and the other conspirators, as can be seen from the materials of the investigation, aimed at frustrating the Brest-Litovsk Peace, overthrowing the Soviet government, arresting and killing Lenin, Stalin and Sverdlov,* and forming a new government made up of Bukharinites, who then for purposes of camouflage called themselves "Left Communists," and of Trotskyites and "Left" Socialist-Revolutionaries. . . .

All the accused stand convicted of having, according to the indictment, in 1932-33 organized, on the instructions of intelligence services of foreign states, a conspiratorial group called the "bloc of Rights and Trotskyites," which set itself the aim of committing the crimes which have been fully proved here.

* Sverdlov: Secretary of the party from 1917 until his death in 1919—Ed.

It has been proved that this bloc consisted of agents of the intelligence services of several foreign states, it has been proved that the "bloc of Rights and Trotskyites" maintained regular illegitimate relations with certain foreign states with the object of obtaining their help for putting into effect its criminal designs, for the overthrow of the Soviet government and for establishing the power of the landlords and capitalists in the U.S.S.R.

It has been proved that the "bloc of Rights and Trotskyites" regularly engaged in espionage on behalf of these states and supplied their intelligence services with most important state secret material.

It has been proved that in pursuance of the same aims the "bloc of Rights and Trotskyites" systematically perpetrated wrecking and diversionist acts in various branches of our national economy—in the sphere of industry, agriculture, finance, municipal economy, railways, etc.

It has been proved that the "bloc of Rights and Trotskyites" organized a number of terrorist acts against leaders of the Communist Party of the Soviet Union (Bolsheviks) and of the Soviet government, that this "bloc of Rights and Trotskyites" perpetrated terrorist acts against S. M. Kirov, V. R. Menzhinsky,* V. V. Kuibyshev, A. M. Gorky, and also brought about the death of M. A. Peshkov.**

It has been proved that the bloc had organized, but fortunately for us had not succeeded in effecting, a number of terrorist acts against the leaders of our Party and government.

Such are the circumstances of the present case. Such is the part taken in this case by each of the accused who are now awaiting your verdict, Comrades Judges.

There exist no words with which one could depict the monstrousness of the crimes committed by the accused. But, I ask, do we need any more words for that? No, Comrades Judges, these words are not needed. All the words have al-

* Menzhinsky: Head of the GPU, 1922-34. He and the following men had apparently died natural deaths, but were now alleged to be the victims of medical murders.—Ed.

** Peshkov: Gorky's son—Ed.

ready been spoken. Everything has been analysed to the minutest details. The entire people now sees what these monsters are.

Our people and all honest people throughout the world are waiting for your just verdict. May this verdict of yours resound through the whole of our great country like a bell calling to new feats of heroism and to new victories! May your verdict resound as the refreshing and purifying thunderstorm of just Soviet punishment!

Our whole country, from young to old, is awaiting and demanding one thing: the traitors and spies who were selling our country to the enemy must be shot like dirty dogs!

Our people are demanding one thing: crush the accursed reptile!

Time will pass. The graves of the hateful traitors will grow over with weeds and thistle, they will be covered with eternal contempt of honest Soviet citizens, of the entire Soviet people. But over us, over our happy country, our sun will shine with its luminous rays as bright and as joyous as before. Over the road cleared of the last scum and filth of the past, we, our people, with our beloved leader and teacher, the great Stalin, at our head, will march as before onwards and onwards, towards communism!

d) Bukharin's Last Plea

Citizen President and Citizens Judges, I fully agree with Citizen the Procurator regarding the significance of the trial, at which were exposed our dastardly crimes, the crimes committed by the "bloc of Rights and Trotskyites," one of whose leaders I was, and for all the activities of which I bear responsibility.

This trial, which is the concluding one of a series of trials, has exposed all the crimes and the treasonable activities, it has exposed the historical significance and the roots of our struggle against the Party and the Soviet government.

I have been in prison for over a year, and I therefore do not know what is going on in the world. But, judging from those fragments of real life that sometimes reached me by chance, I see, feel and understand that the interests which we so criminally betrayed are entering a new phase of gigantic development, are now appearing in the international arena as a great and mighty factor of the international proletarian phase.

We, the accused, are sitting on the other side of the barrier, and this barrier separates us from you, Citizens Judges. We found ourselves in the accursed ranks of the counter-revolution, became traitors to the Socialist fatherland. . . .

. . . At such moments, Citizens Judges, everything personal, all the personal incrustation, all the rancour, pride, and a number of other things, fall away, disappear. And, in addition, when the reverberations of the broad international struggle reach your ear, all this in its entirety does its work, and the result is the complete internal moral victory of the U.S.S.R. over its kneeling opponents. I happened by chance to get Feuchtwanger's book* from the prison library. There he refers to the trials of the Trotskyites. It produced a profound impression on me; but I must say that Feuchtwanger did not get at the core of the matter. He stopped half way, not everything was clear to him; when, as a matter of fact, everything is clear. World history is a world court of judgment: A number of groups of Trotskyite leaders went bankrupt and have been cast into the pit. That is true. But you cannot do what Feuchtwanger does in relation to Trotsky in particular, when he places him on the same plane as Stalin. Here his arguments are absolutely false. For in reality the whole country stands behind Stalin; he is the hope of the world; he is a creator. Napoleon once said that fate is politics. The fate of Trotsky is counter-revolutionary politics.

I am about to finish. I am perhaps speaking for the last time in my life.

I am explaining how I came to realize the necessity of capitulating to the investigating authorities and to you, Citizens Judges. We came out against the joy of the new life with the most criminal methods of struggle. I refute

* Evidently Lion Feuchtwanger, *Moscow, 1937: A Travel Report for My Friends* (original German edition, Amsterdam, 1937) —Ed.

the accusation of having plotted against the life of Vladimir Ilyich, but my counter-revolutionary confederates, and I at their head, endeavoured to murder Lenin's cause, which is being carried on with such tremendous success by Stalin. The logic of this struggle led us step by step into the blackest quagmire. And it has once more been proved that departure from the position of Bolshevism means siding with political counter-revolutionary banditry. Counter-revolutionary banditry has now been smashed, we have been smashed, and we repent our frightful crimes. . . .

. . . I am kneeling before the country, before the Party, before the whole people. The monstrousness of my crimes is immeasurable especially in the new stage of the struggle of the U.S.S.R. May this trial be the last severe lesson, and may the great might of the U.S.S.R. become clear to all. Let it be clear to all that the counter-revolutionary thesis of the national limitedness of the U.S.S.R. has remained suspended in the air like a wretched rag. Everybody perceives the wise leadership of the country that is ensured by Stalin.

It is in the consciousness of this that I await the verdict. What matters is not the personal feelings of a repentant enemy, but the flourishing progress of the U.S.S.R. and its international importance. . . .

The Purges and Torture

In 1939 Stalin issued in the name of the Central Committee his retroactive approval of the methods of torture which the NKVD used to obtain confessions.

The Central Committee of the All-Union Communist Party (Bolsheviks) explains that the application of methods of physical pressure in NKVD practice is permissible from

FROM: Stalin, Telegram to regional and republic secretaries of Communist Party committees, to the People's Commissars of Internal Affairs, and to the heads of NKVD organizations, January 20, 1939 (quoted by Khrushchev in his secret speech of February 25, 1956; English translation by the United States Department of State, in *The Anti-Stalin Campaign,* New York, Columbia University Press, 1956, p. 41).

1937 on in accordance with permission of the Central Committee of the All-Union Communist Party (Bolsheviks). . . . It is known that all bourgeois intelligence services use methods of physical influence against the representatives of the socialist proletariat and that they use them in their most scandalous form. The question arises as to why the socialist intelligence service should be more humanitarian against the mad agents of the bourgeoisie, against the deadly enemies of the working class and the kolkhoz workers. The Central Committee of the All-Union Communist Party (Bolsheviks) considers that physical pressure should still be used obligatorily, as an exception applicable to known and obstinate enemies of the people, as a method both justifiable and appropriate.

The Plea of a Purge Victim

The secret purges of 1937-38 struck the party hierarchy severely. A large majority of the Central Committee, all but one of the six candidate members of the Politbureau, and two members of the Politbureau itself—all tested Stalinists—were secretly arrested, tortured and shot. The statement by one of the candidate members of the Politbureau, Robert Eikhe, repudiating the confession extorted from him, was revealed by Khrushchev in 1956.

I have not been guilty of even one of the things with which I am charged and my heart is clean of even the shadow of baseness. I have never in my life told you a word of falsehood and now, finding my two feet in the grave, I am also not lying. My whole case is a typical example of provocation, slander and violation of the elementary basis of revolutionary legality. . . .

. . . The confessions which were made part of my file are not only absurd but contain some slander toward the Central Committee of the All-Union Communist Party (Bolsheviks) and toward the Council of People's Commissars because cor-

FROM: Eikhe, Declaration to Stalin, October 27, 1939 (quoted by Khrushchev in his secret speech of February 25, 1956; in *The Anti-Stalin Campaign*, pp. 32-33).

rect resolutions of the Central Committee of the All-Union Communist Party (Bolsheviks) and of the Council of People's Commissars, which were not made on my initiative and without my participation, are presented as hostile acts of counter-revolutionary organizations made at my suggestion. . . .

I am now alluding to the most disgraceful part of my life and to my really grave guilt against the Party and against you. This is my confession of counter-revolutionary activity. . . . The case is as follows: not being able to suffer the tortures to which I was submitted by Ushakov and Nikolayev —and especially by the first one—who utilized the knowledge that my broken ribs have not properly mended and have caused me great pain—I have been forced to accuse myself and others.

The majority of my confession has been suggested or dictated by Ushakov, and the remainder is my reconstruction of NKVD materials from western Siberia for which I assumed all responsibility. If some part of the story which Ushakov fabricated and which I signed did not properly hang together, I was forced to sign another variation. The same thing was done to Rukhimovich,* who was at first designated as a member of the reserve net and whose name later was removed without telling me anything about it; the same was also done with the leader of the reserve net, supposedly created by Bukharin in 1935. At first I wrote my name in, and then I was instructed to insert Mezhlauk.** There were other similar incidents.

. . . I am asking and begging you that you again examine my case and this not for the purpose of sparing me but in order to unmask the vile provocation which like a snake wound itself around many persons in a great degree due to my meanness and criminal slander. I have never betrayed you or the Party. I know that I perish because of vile and mean work of the enemies of the Party and of the people, who fabricated the provocation against me.

* Rukhimovich: a member of the Central Committee who fell in the purge—Ed.

** Mezhlauk: a vice-premier and purge victim—Ed.

Stalin as a Philosopher

A new history of the Communist Party of the Soviet Union, written under Stalin's direction, was published in 1938 to bring the past into line with the purge charges. Stalin personally contributed a chapter on the philosophy of Marxism, in which he put special stress on the historical role of the proper ideas and theories.

. . . The strength and vitality of Marxism-Leninism lies in the fact that it does base its practical activity on the needs of the development of the material life of society and never divorces itself from the real life of society.

It does not follow from Marx's words, however, that social ideas, theories, political views and political institutions are of no significance in the life of society, that they do not reciprocally affect social being, the development of the material conditions of the life of society. We have been speaking so far of the *origin* of social ideas, theories, views and political institutions, of *the way they arise*, of the fact that the spiritual life of society is a reflection of the conditions of its material life. As regards the *significance* of social ideas, theories, views and political institutions, as regards their *role* in history, historical materialism, far from denying them, stresses the important role and significance of these factors in the life of society, in its history.

There are different kinds of social ideas and theories. There are old ideas and theories which have outlived their day and which serve the interests of the moribund forces of society. Their significance lies in the fact that they hamper the development, the progress of society. Then there are new and advanced ideas and theories which serve the interests of the advanced forces of society. Their significance lies in the fact that they facilitate the development, the progress of society; and their significance is the greater the more accurately they reflect the needs of development of the material life of society.

FROM: Stalin, "Dialectical and Historical Materialism" (from the *History of the CPSU(B): Short Course,* 1938; in *Problems of Leninism,* pp. 726-28).

New social ideas and theories arise only after the development of the material life of society has set new tasks before society. But once they have arisen they become a most potent force which facilitates the carrying out of the new tasks set by the development of the material life of society, a force which facilitates the progress of society. It is precisely here that the tremendous organizing, mobilizing and transforming value of new ideas, new theories, new political views and new political institutions manifests itself. New social ideas and theories arise precisely because they are necessary to society, because it is *impossible* to carry out the urgent tasks of development of the material life of society without their organizing, mobilizing and transforming action. Arising out of the new tasks set by the development of the material life of society, the new social ideas and theories force their way through, become the possession of the masses, mobilize and organize them against the moribund forces of society, and thus facilitate the overthrow of these forces, which hamper the development of the material life of society.

Thus social ideas, theories and political institutions, having arisen on the basis of the urgent tasks of the development of the material life of society, the development of social being, themselves then react upon social being, upon the material life of society, creating the conditions necessary for completely carrying out the urgent tasks of the material life of society, and for rendering its further development possible.

In this connection, Marx says: "Theory becomes a material force as soon as it has gripped the masses."

Hence, in order to be able to influence the conditions of material life of society and to accelerate their development and their improvement, the party of the proletariat must rely upon such a social theory, such a social idea as correctly reflects the needs of development of the material life of society, and which is therefore capable of setting into motion broad masses of the people and of mobilizing them and organizing them into a great army of the proletarian party, prepared to smash the reactionary forces and to clear the way for the advanced forces of society.

The fall of the "Economists" and Mensheviks was due,

among other things, to the fact that they did not recognize the mobilizing, organizing and transforming role of advanced theory, of advanced ideas and, sinking to vulgar materialism, reduced the role of these factors almost to nothing, thus condemning the Party to passivity and inanition.

The strength and vitality of Marxism-Leninism is derived from the fact that it relies upon an advanced theory which correctly reflects the needs of development of the material life of society, that it elevates theory to a proper level, and that it deems it its duty to utilize every ounce of the mobilizing, organizing and transforming power of this theory.

That is the answer historical materialism gives to the question of the relation between social being and social consciousness, between the conditions of development of material life and the development of the spiritual life of society. . . .

Vyshinsky on the New Law

> The final step in the enunciation of the new Soviet set of social ideals was the purge of Pashukanis and his theory of the diminishing role of law. In place of this Vyshinsky proclaimed that law of the socialist type would remain firmly in effect until that distant date when the state withered away.

The proletariat requires the state, state apparatus, a definite state order—the socialist legal order, which signifies the stability of socialist social relationships and of socialist discipline, respect for the rules of socialist life in common, respect and preservation inviolate of social, socialist property—the bases of the entire Soviet order, the observance of all Soviet laws. Special forms of the class struggle correspond to the epoch of the proletarian dictatorship, and the state during this period is confronted with special problems related

FROM: Vyshinsky, ed., *The Law of the Soviet State* (1938; English translation by Hugh W. Babb, New York, The Macmillan Co., 1948, pp. 47-48, 52, 54-57; reprinted by permission of the publisher).

to those forms and responsive to the demands of this period. . . .

The dictatorship of the proletariat solves the problems of the proletarian revolution both with the aid of law and with the assistance of measures strictly defined by statute, through administrative and judicial organs. The dictatorship of the proletariat is authority unlimited by any statutes whatever. But the dictatorship of the proletariat, creating its own laws, makes use of them, demands that they be observed, and punishes breach of them. Dictatorship of the proletariat does not signify anarchy and disorder but, on the contrary, strict order and firm authority which operates upon strict principles, set out in the fundamental law of the proletarian state—the Soviet Constitution. . . .

The greatest expression of the development of proletarian democracy—and at the same time of the organic synthesis of the principles thereof and of the proletarian dictatorship—is the Stalin Constitution, which records in the form of law the brilliant and epoch-making triumphs of socialism. It is at the same time the greatest monument of Soviet socialist law, the greatest historical act, in which is expressed the will of the Soviet people, the will of the working classes. The Stalin Constitution signifies the ultimate strengthening of the Soviet order, of the proletarian dictatorship, which rests on a still more mighty socialist basis than had ever existed in the previous twenty years of the history of our socialist revolution. It reveals the ultimate essence of socialist democracy, which is the direct consequence of the triumph of the proletarian dictatorship and the integration of the development of the Soviet socialist state order. . . .

As a means of control on the part of society, a means of regulating social relationships, a method and means of preserving the interests of socialist society and the rights and interests of citizens, Soviet law carries out a social function of gigantic importance—without which the socialist state could not get along until that time when it completely withers away.

Law—like the state—will wither away only in the highest

phase of communism, with the annihilation of the capitalist encirclement; when all will learn to get along without special rules defining the conduct of people under the threat of punishment and with the aid of constraint; when people are so accustomed to observe the fundamental rules of community life that they will fulfill them without constraint of any sort. Until then, however, there is necessity for general control, firm discipline in labor and in community life, and complete subordination of all the new society's work to a truly democratic state. . . .

Stuchka* characterized Soviet civil law and the Soviet Civil Code as basically bourgeois phenomena. He flatly declared all the law of the period of the New Economic Policy to be bourgeois, asserting that we have simply "imported, borrowed, bourgeois law."

Our new (and we may say here our first) codes were to him the result of "concessions to bourgeois law," as "landmarks of retreat"—thus repeating the anti-Leninist fabrications of Zinoviev and Bukharin and transferring Trotskyist-Zinovievist principles into the field of legal theory. In *The Revolutionary Role of Soviet Law*, Stuchka wrote that he had succeeded "with the help of his comrades" in formulating a new revolutionary dialectic conception of civil law in general and of our Soviet civil law in particular. This new conception, for whose invention Stuchka takes special credit, was the notorious theory of so-called "economic" law whereby, as everyone knows, Stuchka and some of his pupils understood a part of the civil law embracing questions of an administrative-economic character. . . .

The "new, revolutionary-dialectic conception," proudly proclaimed by Stuchka, dwindled to the right-opportunist "theory" of "two-section law," merely contrasting the interests of socialist economy with those of the socialist man, and underestimating the civil law as law which regulates, affirms, and preserves the individual and property interests of the toiling citizens of the USSR, the builders of socialism.

This is a coarse perversion of the Marx-Engels-Lenin-Stalin

* Stuchka: a leading Soviet jurist of the nineteen-twenties—Ed.

theory of socialism—as to the place and part of individuality in socialist society.

"Socialism does not deny individual interests—it amalgamates them with those of the group. Socialism cannot be isolated from individual interests—only socialist society can most completely satisfy them. Moreover, socialist society represents the only firm guarantee that individual interests will be preserved" (Stalin).

These teachings of Stalin define also the path of development of Soviet civil law and the problems before us in this field—problems of developing and reinforcing Soviet civil law.

The extent of the perversions in the field of the Marxist-Leninist theory of law is particularly apparent in the liquidation of the discipline of Soviet civil law by Stuchka and his followers, who have now come actually to be wreckers and traitors. The whole depth of these perversions is particularly conspicuous in our time, when the greatest of human constitutions, the Stalin Constitution, allots a particularly honored place to the civil rights of Soviet people, when civil legal relationships are raised, in conditions of socialist society, to the highest degree of their development. Unfortunately the perversions of the Marxist theory of law went far deeper than would be inferred from the foregoing. A group of traitors, headed by Pashukanis and others, sat for a number of years in the former Institute of Soviet Construction and Law, and systematically practiced the distortion of the fundamental and most important principles of Marxist-Leninist methodology in the field of law. . . .

. . . Each in his field wrought not a little to pervert the great doctrine of Marx-Engels-Lenin-Stalin, so as to disarm Soviet jurists and expose them to the putrid vapor of all kinds of anti-Marxist, anti-Leninist "theories" whereby our enemies sought to sully the pure source of great and truly scientific thought. Because of the work of these wreckers over a period of years, the extremely rich scientific inheritance of Marx-Engels-Lenin, and the equally rich works of Stalin, which guarantee the further development of Soviet legal science, remained unutilized and insufficiently elaborated. . . .

They denied the very possibility of the development of Soviet law as socialist law. They tried mechanically to transfer the legal institutions of one epoch (that of imperialistic capitalism) into another (that of socialism), perverting the basic methodological settings of Marxism-Leninism, which teaches that law, or the legal superstructure, can and must be explained in the last analysis out of the economic structure of society, out of its relationships of production. . . .

Labor Discipline

Following the enunciation of the principles of industrial discipline and individual responsibility during the period of the First Five-Year Plan, the Soviet government found intensive efforts necessary to instill these qualities into the industrial labor force. The urban labor shortage occasioned by the rapid expansion of industry made the traditional threat of discharge ineffective, and in 1938 habitual infraction of industrial discipline was made a criminal offense.

The U.S.S.R. Council of People's Commissars, the Central Committee of the All-Union Communist Party (Bolshevik) and the All-Union Central Council of Trade Unions resolve:

1. To oblige the managements of enterprises and establishments (offices) along with trade union organs to lead a determined struggle against all violators of labor discipline and internal labor regulations, against shirkers, idlers, and self-seekers—against all who have a dishonest concern toward their labor obligations, be it a worker (wage-earner) or employee (salaried worker).

The law requires the dismissal of a worker or employee for absence without sufficient reason. This measure is directed against parasites who do not want to work but try to live

FROM: Resolution Concerning Consolidation of Labor Discipline, Improvement of the Practice of Social Security, and Suppression of Abuses in This Field, December 28, 1938 (English translation by Edward S. Kozera in Meisel and Kozera, *Materials for the Study of the Soviet System*, pp. 303-4; reprinted by permission of the publisher).

at the expense of the state, at the expense of the people. The requirements of the law regarding the dismissal of slackers should be carried out without fail.

The eight-, seven-, and six-hour day, depending on the conditions of the job, is established by law and accepted by the working class. In addition, the overwhelming majority of workers have a seven-hour working day. The state demands, and the working class supports this requirement, that the duration of the working day, established by law, be observed precisely and without any violations; that where the six-, seven-, and eight-hour day is prescribed, work should be carried out in full conformity with the law, namely, a full six-, seven-, or eight-hour day. Tardiness, early departure for and late return from lunch, leaving work before the scheduled time, and also loafing on the job—all these constitute a rude violation of labor discipline, a violation of the law, involving an undermining of the economic and defensive strength of country, and the well-being of the people.

A worker or employee coming late to work without sufficient reason, or leaving early for lunch or returning too late, or leaving the enterprise or establishment before the scheduled time, or loafing during working hours is subject to administrative penalties: reproof or reprimand, reprimand with a warning of dismissal, transfer to another, lower-paying job for a period up to three months, or demotion to a lower-grade job.

A worker or employee committing three such infractions in one month or four infractions in two consecutive months is subject to dismissal as a shirker and violator of labor law and labor discipline.

2. To establish that managers of enterprises, establishments, sections, and shops are subject to dismissal and penal prosecution for deviation from execution of measures for strengthening labor discipline and rejection of measures against shirkers, idlers, and self-seekers. . . .

Stalin on the State and the Intelligentsia

At the Eighteenth Party Congress in March, 1939, Stalin undertook to explain theoretically the role of the Soviet state (to all intents and purposes permanent), both in developing the country and in protecting it against the "capitalist encirclement." He added a defense of the "Soviet intelligentsia" —meaning all the middle and upper strata of white-collar, technical, and managerial employees of the government— which confirmed that political preference for "proletarians" had come to an end.

. . . The state arose because society split up into antagonistic classes; it arose in order to keep in check the exploited majority in the interests of the exploiting minority. The instruments of state power became concentrated mainly in the army, the penal organs, the intelligence service, the prisons. Two basic functions characterize the activity of the state: at home (the main function), to keep in check the exploited majority; abroad (not the main function), to extend the territory of its class, the ruling class, at the expense of the territory of other states, or to defend the territory of its own state from attack by other states. Such was the case in slave society and under feudalism. Such is the case under capitalism.

In order to overthrow capitalism it was necessary not only to remove the bourgeoisie from power, not only to expropriate the capitalists, but also to smash entirely the bourgeois state machine, its old army, its bureaucratic officialdom and its police force, and to substitute for it a new, proletarian form of state, a new, socialist state. And that, as we know, is exactly what the Bolsheviks did. But it does not at all follow that the new, proletarian state may not retain certain functions of the old state, modified to suit the requirements of the proletarian state. Still less does it follow that the forms of our socialist state must remain unchanged, that all the original functions of our state must be fully retained in the future. As a matter of fact, the forms of our state are changing and will continue to change in line with the development of our country and with the changes in the international situation.

Lenin was absolutely right when he said:

FROM: Stalin, Report on the Work of the Central Committee, to the Eighteenth Congress of the CPSU(B) (March, 1939; *Problems of Leninism*, pp. 795-800).

"The forms of bourgeois states are extremely varied, but their essence is the same: all these states, whatever their form, in the final analysis are inevitably the *dictatorship of the bourgeoisie.* The transition from capitalism to communism certainly cannot but yield a great abundance and variety of political forms, but the essence will inevitably be the same: *the dictatorship of the proletariat.*"

Since the October Revolution, our socialist state has in its development passed through two main phases.

The first phase was the period from the October Revolution to the elimination of the exploiting classes. The principal task in that period was to suppress the resistance of the overthrown classes, to organize the defence of the country against the attack of the interventionists, to restore industry and agriculture, and to prepare the conditions for the elimination of the capitalist elements. Accordingly, in this period our state performed two main functions. The first function was to suppress the overthrown classes within the country. In this respect our state bore a superficial resemblance to previous states, whose functions had also been to suppress recalcitrants, with the fundamental difference, however, that our state suppressed the exploiting minority in the interests of the labouring majority, while previous states had suppressed the exploited majority in the interests of the exploiting minority. The second function was to defend the country from foreign attack. In this respect it likewise bore a superficial resemblance to previous states, which also undertook the armed defence of their countries, with the fundamental difference, however, that our state defended from foreign attack the gains of the labouring majority, while previous states in such cases defended the wealth and privileges of the exploiting minority. Our state had yet a third function: this was economic and organizational work and cultural and educational work performed by our state bodies with the purpose of developing the young shoots of the new, socialist economic system and re-educating the people in the spirit of socialism. But this new function did not attain any considerable development in that period.

The second phase was the period from the elimination of

the capitalist elements in town and country to the complete victory of the socialist economic system and the adoption of the new Constitution. The principal task in this period was to organize socialist economy throughout the country and to eliminate the last remnants of the capitalist elements, to organize a cultural revolution, and to organize a thoroughly modern army for the defence of the country. And the functions of our socialist state changed accordingly. The function of military suppression inside the country ceased, died away; for exploitation had been abolished, there were no more exploiters left, and so there was no one to suppress. In place of this function of suppression the state acquired the function of protecting socialist property from thieves and pilferers of the property of the people. The function of armed defence of the country from foreign attack fully remained; consequently, the Red Army and the Navy also fully remained, as did the penal organs and the intelligence service, which are indispensable for the detection and punishment of the spies, assassins and wreckers sent into our country by foreign intelligence services. The function of the state organs as regards economic and organizational work, and cultural and educational work, remained and was developed to the full. Now the main task of our state inside the country lies in peaceful economic and organizational work, and cultural and educational work. As for our army, penal organs, and intelligence service, their edge is no longer turned to the inside of the country but to the outside, against external enemies.

As you see, we now have an entirely new, socialist state, one without precedent in history and differing considerably in form and functions from the socialist state of the first phase.

But development cannot stop there. We are moving ahead, towards communism. Will our state remain in the period of communism also?

Yes, it will, if the capitalist encirclement is not liquidated, and if the danger of foreign military attack is not eliminated, although naturally, the forms of our state will again change in conformity with the change in the situation at home and abroad.

No, it will not remain and will wither away if the capitalist encirclement is liquidated and is replaced by a socialist encirclement.

That is how the question stands with regard to the socialist state. . . .

In spite of the fact that the position of the Party on the question of the Soviet intelligentsia is perfectly clear, there are still current in our Party views hostile to the Soviet intelligentsia and incompatible with the Party position. As you know, those who hold these false views practise a disdainful and contemptuous attitude towards the Soviet intelligentsia and regard it as a force alien and even hostile to the working class and the peasantry. True, during the period of Soviet development the intelligentsia has undergone a radical change both in composition and status. It has become closer to the people and is honestly collaborating with it, in which respect it differs fundamentally from the old, bourgeois intelligentsia. But this apparently means nothing to these comrades. They go on harping on the old tune and wrongly apply to the Soviet intelligentsia views and attitudes which were justified in the old days when the intelligentsia was in the service of the landlords and capitalists. . . .

But the position with regard to the intelligentsia has radically changed since the October Revolution, since the defeat of the foreign armed intervention, and especially since the victory of industrialization and collectivization, when the abolition of exploitation and the firm establishment of the socialist economic system made it effectively possible to give the country a new Constitution and to put it into effect. . . . Parallel with this painful process of differentiation and break-up of the old intelligentsia there was going on a rapid process of formation, mobilization and mustering of forces of a new intelligentsia. Hundreds of thousands of young people from the ranks of the working class, the peasantry and the working intelligentsia entered the universities and technical colleges, from which they emerged to reinforce the attenuated ranks of the intelligentsia. They infused fresh blood into it and animated it with a new, Soviet spirit. They radically changed the whole aspect of the intelligentsia, moulding it in their own form and image. The remnants of the old intelligentsia were dissolved in the new, Soviet intelligentsia, the intelligentsia of the people. There thus arose a new, Soviet intelligentsia, intimately bound up with the people and, for the most part, ready to serve them faithfully and loyally.

As a result, we now have a numerous, new, popular, socialist intelligentsia, fundamentally different from the old, bourgeois intelligentsia both in composition and in social and political character.

The old theory about the intelligentsia, which taught that it should be distrusted and combated, fully applied to the old prerevolutionary intelligentsia, which served the landlords and capitalists. That theory is now out-of-date and does not fit our new, Soviet intelligentsia. A new theory is needed for our new intelligentsia, one teaching the necessity for a cordial attitude towards it, solicitude and respect for it, and cooperation with it in the interests of the working class and the peasantry. . . .

Malenkov on Bureaucratic Efficiency

Georgi Malenkov, a member of the party Secretariat, first achieved note at the Eighteenth Party Conference in February, 1941, with a blistering attack on the weaknesses of party control over the economy and on the intrusion of ideological considerations into the realm of personnel selection and incentives. Henceforth proletarian background counted for nothing; industrialist expediency had eliminated the last vestiges of real revolutionary sentiment in the USSR.

. . . The causes of unsatisfactory work in industry and transportation are comprised in the inadequacies of direction on the part of the commissariats and in the fact that the regional committees and the city committees of the party

FROM: Malenkov, Report to the Eighteenth Party Conference, February 15, 1941, "On the Tasks of Party Organizations in the Field of Industry and Transportation" (*Pravda*, February 16, 1941; editor's translation).

have weakened their work in the field of industry and transportation.

As to the commissariats it must be said first of all that in many cases they conduct their work bureaucratically; they still do not reach each individual enterprise; they "direct" their enterprises not in substance but only in form, by way of correspondence. . . .

The inadequacies of the work of the party organizations in the field of industry and transportation are mainly comprised in the fact that the party organizations do not assist the commissariats or enterprises of their region, city or district.

The party organizations have weakened their work both in industry and in transportation, incorrectly assuming that they do not bear responsibility for the work of industry and transportation.

The local party organizations, like the economic organizations, do not understand the meaning and significance of checking upon execution, and because of this, do not aid the commissariats and head offices to arrange everyday checking up on the execution of the decisions of the commissariats by the directors of the enterprises subordinated to them. . . .

The correct organization of wages is the chief condition for the growth of production. The guiding principle of our whole policy in the field of wages is the principle of getting the toilers materially interested in the results of their labor. We realize this principle through the piecework system of payment for workers, the bonus system for directing functionaries, and through encouraging skilled labor in comparison with unskilled labor. . . .

The task consists of encouraging those who work well and completely liquidating the rotten practice of leveling in the field of wages. The directors of enterprises, the heads of divisions and workshops are obliged to carry out the raising of norms for earnings in connection with the introduction of progressive technology and measures of business organization. . . .

. . . A very important organizational task is the significant heightening of the attention of party organizations in the matter of the selection of cadres working in industry and transportation.

First of all, it is essential *to study, to know well the administrative and technical-engineering functionaries of the industrial enterprises and the railroads.* Without such knowledge and without knowing the people it is impossible to decide correctly and promptly the question of replacing worthless functionaries and of promoting people who have ability and initiative.

It is essential, comrades, to stop studying functionaries only on paper, in the office-routine way.

It is necessary to put an end to the biological approach* to the selection of cadres, and actually to check up on the functionaries, to evaluate them by their work, and not to be guided by questionnaire data.

Up to now, in spite of the party's directives, the appointment of a functionary in many party and economic organs is based more on the evidence of his genealogy, on the evidence of who his grandfather and grandmother were,** and not on the study of his personal, business, and political qualities, his abilities.

The basic question in the matter of the selection of cadres is the question of the correct promotion of new workers. We must more boldly promote the good workers who have ability and initiative, who know how to organize real-life business.

In this connection it is necessary to understand that *I speak of promoting not only party members but also nonparty Bolsheviks.*

Among the nonparty members are many honorable and able functionaries who, although they are not in the party and do not have Communist status, nevertheless often work better

* "Biological approach": evidently an analogy with the practice of computing theoretical agricultural yields rather than the actual crop harvested—Ed.

** I.e., a proletarian family background—Ed.

and more conscientiously than certain Communists with status. . . .

While promoting functionaries with ability and initiative, it is necessary *simultaneously to pose the question of replacing worthless, weak, indecisive functionaries, to replace the windbags who are not capable of organizing real-life business. . . .*

Chapter Five: International Communism, 1919-1941

The international Communist movement had its origins in the splits brought about in the socialist parties almost everywhere by the First World War and the Russian Revolution. Left-wing elements were gathered together under Russian leadership and recast into a distinctively Russian-type revolutionary organization. Country by country the history of the Communist International was exceedingly complex, but the system of organization and the major developments in the movement were determined in Russia. Over the years the expedient interests of the Russian state figured ever more prominently in guiding the movement, at the expense of the fortunes of communism in any other particular country.

•

The Prospect of International Revolution—Germany

The world revolution expected and relied on by the Bolsheviks seemed to be imminent in the months immediately after the end of World War I. Left-wing socialists in sympathy with Soviet Russia prepared for revolutionary struggle. In Germany Karl Liebknecht and Rosa Luxemburg organized the Spartacus League—the nucleus of the future German Communist Party—and in January, 1919, attempted to seize power. The revolt was put down by the moderate socialist government of the new German republic, and both Spartacus leaders were killed.

Proletarians! Men and Women of Labor! Comrades!

The revolution has made its entry into Germany. The

FROM: "Manifesto of the Spartacus Group," December, 1918 (English translation in *The New York Times,* January 24, 1919).

masses of the soldiers, who for four years were driven to the slaughterhouse for the sake of capitalistic profits, the masses of workers, who for four years were exploited, crushed, and starved, have revolted. That fearful tool of oppression—Prussian militarism, that scourge of humanity—lies broken on the ground. Its most noticeable representatives, and therewith the most noticeable of those guilty of this war, the Kaiser and the Crown Prince, have fled from the country. Workers' and Soldiers' Councils have been formed everywhere.

Proletarians of all countries, we do not say that in Germany all the power has really been lodged in the hands of the working people, that the complete triumph of the proletarian revolution has already been attained. There still sit in the government all those Socialists who in August, 1914, abandoned our most precious possession, the International, who for four years betrayed the German working class and at the same time the International.

But, proletarians of all countries, now the German proletarian himself is speaking to you. We believe we have the right to appear before your forum in his name. From the first day of this war we endeavored to do our international duty by fighting that criminal government with all our power and branding it as the one really guilty of the war. . . .

We know that also in your countries the proletariat made the most fearful sacrifices of flesh and blood, that it is weary of the dreadful butchery, that the proletarian is now returning to his home, and is finding want and misery there, while fortunes amounting to billions are heaped up in the hands of a few capitalists. He has recognized, and will continue to recognize, that your governments, too, have carried on the war for the sake of the big money bags. And he will further perceive that your governments, when they spoke of "justice and civilization" and of the "protection of small nations," meant the profits of capital just as did ours when it talked about the "defense of the home"; and that the peace of "justice" and of the "League of Nations" amounts to the same base brigandage as the peace of Brest-Litovsk. Here, as well as there, the same shameless lust for booty, the same desire for oppression, the same determination to exploit to the limit the brutal preponderance of murderous steel.

The imperialism of all countries knows no "understanding," it knows only one right—capital's profits; it knows only one language—the sword; it knows only one method—violence. And if it is now talking in all countries, in yours as well as ours, about the "League of Nations," "disarmament," "rights of small nations," "self-determination of the peoples," it is merely using the customary lying phrases of the rulers for the purpose of lulling to sleep the watchfulness of the proletariat.

Proletarians of all countries! This must be the last war! We owe that to the 12,000,000 murdered victims, we owe that to our children, we owe that to humanity. . . .

Socialism alone is in a position to complete the great work of permanent peace, to heal the thousand wounds from which humanity is bleeding, to transform the plains of Europe, trampled down by the passage of the apocryphal horseman of war, into blooming gardens, to conjure up ten productive forces for every one destroyed, to awaken all the physical and moral energies of humanity, and to replace hatred and dissension with fraternal solidarity, harmony, and respect for every human being.

If representatives of the proletarians of all countries stretch out their hands to each other under the banner of socialism for the purpose of making peace, then peace will be concluded in a few hours. . . .

. . . The proletariat of Germany is looking toward you in this hour. Germany is pregnant with the social revolution, but socialism can only be realized by the proletariat of the world.

And therefore we call to you: "Arise for the struggle! Arise for action! The time for empty manifestos, platonic resolutions, and high-sounding words has gone by! The hour of action has struck for the International!" We ask you to elect Workers' and Soldiers' Councils everywhere that will seize political power and, together with us, will restore peace.

Not Lloyd George and Poincaré, not Sonnino, Wilson, and

Erzberger or Scheidemann,* must be allowed to make peace. Peace is to be concluded under the waving banner of the socialist world revolution.

Proletarians of all countries! We call upon you to complete the work of socialist liberation, to give a human aspect to the disfigured world, and to make true those words with which we often greeted each other in the old days and which we sang as we parted: "And the International shall be the human race."

Klara Zetkin
Rosa Luxemburg
Karl Liebknecht
Franz Mehring

The Founding of the Communist International

In March, 1919, the Soviet Communist leaders assembled a casual group of foreign sympathizers in Moscow and proclaimed this to be the founding congress of the Third or Communist International (the "Comintern," following Marx's "International Workingmen's Association" and the Social-Democratic Second International). Designed as a sort of general staff of world revolution, the Comintern remained under firm Russian control (Zinoviev was its chairman from 1919 to 1926), though it attracted widespread foreign support in the years immediately after its establishment. The initial manifesto, written by Trotsky, summoned all the victims of "imperialism," proletarians and colonials, to rally to the Communist cause.

FROM: "Manifesto of the Communist International to the Proletariat of the Entire World," March, 1919 (written by Trotsky; English translation in Jane Degras, ed., *The Communist International, 1919-1943: Documents,* London, Oxford University Press, 1956, Vol. I, pp. 38, 41-45, 47).

* David Lloyd George, Prime Minister of Great Britain; Raymond Poincaré, President of the French Republic; Baron Sidney Sonnino, Italian Foreign Minister; Woodrow Wilson, President of the United States; Matthias Erzberger, leader of the German Catholic Center Party and signer of the 1918 armistice; Philip Scheidemann, Social-Democratic head of the provisional government in Germany—Ed.

. . . The epoch of final, decisive struggle came later than the apostles of the social revolution had expected and hoped. But it has come. We Communists, the representatives of the revolutionary proletariat of various countries of Europe, America, and Asia, who have gathered in Soviet Moscow, feel and consider ourselves to be the heirs and executors of the cause whose programme was announced 72 years ago. Our task is to generalize the revolutionary experience of the working class, to cleanse the movement of the disintegrating admixtures of opportunism and social-patriotism, to mobilize the forces of all genuinely revolutionary parties of the world proletariat and thereby facilitate and hasten the victory of the Communist revolution throughout the world. . . .

State control of economic life, which capitalist liberalism resisted so strongly, has become a fact. There is no return to free competition, nor even to the domination of trusts, syndicates, and other economic monsters. There is only one question: Who shall henceforth take charge of nationalized production—the imperialist State or the State of the victorious proletariat?

In other words: Shall all toiling mankind become the bond slaves of a victorious world clique who, under the name of the League of Nations and aided by an "international" army and "international" navy, will plunder and strangle in one place and cast crumbs elsewhere, while everywhere shackling the proletariat, with the sole object of maintaining their own rule; or shall the working class of Europe and of the advanced countries in other parts of the world themselves take in hand the disrupted and ruined economy in order to assure its reconstruction on socialist foundations?

It is possible to shorten the present epoch of crisis only by means of the proletarian dictatorship which does not look back to the past, which respects neither hereditary privileges nor property rights, but takes as its starting-point the need of saving the starving masses and to this end mobilizes all forces and resources, introduces universal labour conscription, establishes the regime of labour discipline, in order in the course of a few years not only to heal the gaping wounds inflicted by war but also to raise mankind to new and unimagined heights. . . .

While oppressing and coercing the small and weak peoples, condemning them to hunger and degradation, the Allied imperialists, like the imperialists of the Central Powers a short while ago, do not stop talking about the right of national self-determination, which is today trampled underfoot in Europe as in all other parts of the world.

The small peoples can be assured the opportunity of a free existence only by the proletarian revolution, which will liberate the productive forces of all countries from the constraint of the national State, unite the peoples in closest economic collaboration on the basis of a common economic plan, and afford even the smallest and weakest people the opportunity of conducting their national cultural affairs freely and independently, without detriment to the unified and centralized European and world economy. . . .

The emancipation of the colonies is possible only in conjunction with the emancipation of the metropolitan working class. The workers and peasants not only of Annam, Algiers, and Bengal, but also of Persia and Armenia, will gain their opportunity of independent existence only when the workers of England and France have overthrown Lloyd George and Clemenceau and taken State power into their own hands. Even now the struggle in the more developed colonies is more than the struggle for national liberation; it is assuming an explicitly social character. If capitalist Europe forcibly dragged the backward sections of the world into the capitalist whirlpool, then socialist Europe will come to the aid of liberated colonies with its technology, its organization, its spiritual forces, in order to facilitate their transition to a planned and organized socialist economy.

Colonial slaves of Africa and Asia! The hour of proletarian dictatorship in Europe will also be the hour of your own liberation!

The entire bourgeois world accuses the communists of abolishing freedom and political democracy. That is not true. Having taken power, the proletariat merely asserts the utter impossibility of employing the methods of bourgeois democracy, and creates the conditions and forms of a new and higher workers' democracy. The whole course of capitalist development, especially during its final imperialist epoch, has undermined political democracy not only by condemning the numerous petty-bourgeois and semi-proletarian strata, as well as the lowest strata of the proletariat, to permanent economic deprivation and political impotence. . . .

In this realm of destruction, where not only the means of production and exchange but also the institutions of political democracy lie in bloody ruins, the proletariat must create its own apparatus, designed first and foremost to bind together the working class and to ensure the possibility of its revolutionary intervention in the further development of mankind. This apparatus is the workers' Soviets. The old parties, the old trade unions, have in the persons of their leaders proved incapable of carrying out, even of understanding, the tasks presented by the new epoch. The proletariat has created a new kind of apparatus, which embraces the entire working class regardless of occupation or political maturity; a flexible apparatus capable of continual renewal and extension, of drawing broader and broader strata into its orbit, opening its doors to the working people in town and country who stand close to the proletariat. This irreplaceable organization of working-class self-government, of its struggle, and later of its conquest of State power, has been tested in the experience of various countries and represents the greatest achievement and mightiest weapon of the proletariat of our time. . . .

Civil war is forced on the working class by its arch-enemies. Unless it renounces itself and its own future, which is also the future of all mankind, the working class must give blow for blow. The Communist parties, which never conjure up civil war artificially, try to shorten it as much as possible whenever with iron necessity it does break out, to reduce to a minimum the number of victims and, above all, to assure victory to the proletariat. Hence arises the necessity of disarming the bourgeoisie in time, of arming the workers, of creating a communist army to defend the proletarian power and the inviolability of its socialist construction. Such is the Red Army of Soviet Russia which arose to defend the conquests of the working class against all attacks from within and without. The Soviet Army is inseparable from the Soviet State. . . .

The bourgeois world order has been sufficiently lashed by socialist criticism. The task of the international communist party consists in overthrowing that order and erecting in its place the edifice of the socialist order.

We summon the working men and women of all countries to unite under the communist banner under which the first great victories have already been won.

Proletarians of all countries! In the struggle against imperialist savagery, against monarchy, against the privileged estates, against the bourgeois State and bourgeois property, against all kinds and forms of social and national oppression—*Unite!*

Under the banner of workers' Soviets, under the banner of revolutionary struggle for power and the dictatorship of the proletariat, under the banner of the Third International—proletarians of all countries, unite! . . .

The Hungarian Soviet Republic

Aside from Russia, the only country in which Communists came to power during the era of the Comintern was Hungary, where the leftists under Bela Kun, in default of effective opposition, seized the opportunity in March, 1919, to establish a dictatorship on the Soviet model. The regime lasted only until August, 1919, when it was overthrown by Rumanian intervention with Anglo-French backing.

To All!

Today the proletariat of Hungary takes all authority into its hands. The collapse of the bourgeois world and the bankruptcy of the coalition compel the workers and peasants to take this step. Capitalistic production has collapsed. Communism alone can preserve the country from anarchy.

FROM: Proclamation of the Revolutionary Governing Council of Hungary, March 22, 1919 (English translation in Enemy Press Supplement, London, April 10, 1919).

In foreign politics we are also faced by a complete catastrophe. The Paris Conference has decided to occupy nearly the whole of Hungary by arms, and regards the line of occupation as a definitive political frontier, thus making the supply of food and coal impossible. In the dictatorship of the proletariat lies our salvation. For this purpose the perfect unity of the proletariat is necessary. The Social Democratic Party and the Communist Party have therefore joined. The Hungarian Socialistic Party henceforth receives as members all the working men and women of the country.

This party empowers the Revolutionary Governing Council to assume the Government. It will develop the Workers', Peasants' and Soldiers' Councils throughout the country, which will exercise legislative, executive, and judicial powers. Hungary becomes a Soviet Republic, which will immediately proceed to carry into effect the principles of Socialism and Communism. The large estates, mines, large industrial concerns, banks and means of traffic will be socialized. Agrarian reform will be effected not by division into small lots, but by cooperative societies. Profiteers, and those who speculate on hunger and want, will be pitilessly dealt with.

The Governing Council demands iron discipline. The bandits of counter-revolution and the brigands of plunder will be punished with death. The Council organizes a powerful proletarian army to assert the dictatorship of workers and peasants against Hungarian capitalists and landlords as well as against Rumanian boiars [noblemen] and Czech bourgeois.

It declares its entire ideal and spiritual community with the Russian Soviet Government, to which it offers an armed alliance. It sends its fraternal greetings to the workers of England, France, Italy, and America, and calls upon them not to tolerate for one moment the wicked predatory campaign of their capitalistic governments against the Hungarian Soviet Republic. It invites to an armed alliance the workers of Czechoslovakia, Rumania, Serbia and Croatia against bourgeois, boiars, landlords, and dynasties. It calls on the workers of German-Austria and Germany to break with Paris and ally themselves with Moscow, to set up the Soviet Republic, and to face the conquering imperialists with arms in their hands.

We are conscious of the hardships and sacrifices before us. We must fight to free our food supplies and our mines, for the liberty of our brothers and our own existence. We trust in the heroism of the proletariat. We choose a course that will bring us hardships, misery and suffering, because only thus can we help to victory the cause of Socialism which will redeem the world. We call on all to work or to enter the proletarian army.

Lukacs on Force and Consciousness

The outstanding non-Soviet Communist theoretician in the early period of the International was the Hungarian literary critic Georg Lukacs. While serving as Commissar of Education in the Bela Kun government Lukacs announced a frankly revised conception of Marxism which put heavy stress on the factors of thought and power, in opposition to the strict economic determinism of the "vulgar Marxists." Theoretically speaking Lukacs was a Stalinist before Stalin, though the straightforwardness of his innovations brought him Moscow's disfavor. Also distinguished by a humanitarian bent, Lukacs once again gained note by participating in the short-lived Hungarian national Communist movement of 1956.

. . . *Paralleling the economic struggle a struggle is waged for society's consciousness. However, society's development of consciousness is synonymous with the possibility of leading society.* The proletariat achieves victory in its class struggle not only in the sphere of force, but equally in this struggle for the social consciousness, as during the last fifty or sixty years it has in an ascending line broken up bourgeois ideology and developed its own consciousness as henceforth the only standard social consciousness.

The most important weapon in this contest over conscious-

FROM: Lukacs, "The Change in the Function of Historical Materialism" (1919; in *History and Class Consciousness*, Berlin, Malik Verlag, 1923, pp. 234, 244-47, 251-52; editor's translation).

ness, over social leadership, is historical materialism. Therefore historical materialism is just as much a function of the development and break-up of capitalist society as all other ideologies. . . .

. . . Historical materialism cannot at all be applied to the pre-capitalist social structure in the same way as to that of capitalistic development. Here we need much more developed, much more refined analyses, to indicate on the one hand what role among the forces which move society has been played by purely economic forces—insofar as such have ever existed in the strict sense of "purity"—and on the other hand to point out how these economic forces have influenced the rest of the structure of society. . . . Historical materialism has attained its greatest success in the analysis of the structure of society, of law, and of other structures on the same plane. . . . It becomes far less conclusive and creative when it is applied to literary, scientific, and religious creations.

Vulgar Marxism has completely neglected this distinction. . . .

This historical attitude of vulgar Marxism has by itself decisively influenced the conduct of the labor parties, their political theory and tactics. The question in which this divorce from vulgar Marxism is most clearly expressed is that of *force:* the role of force in the struggle to achieve and preserve victory in the proletarian revolution. . . .

Vulgar Marxist economism specifically disputes the significance of force in the transition from one economic system of production to another. It appeals to the "natural lawfulness" of economic development, which accomplishes this transition by its own supreme authority, without the assistance of crude, "non-economic" force. . . .

. . . For Marx the "ripeness" of the production relations for the transition from one form of production to another meant something entirely different from what it means for vulgar Marxism. The organization of the revolutionary elements as a class—not just "against capital," but "for itself," to change the simple forces of production into a lever for social transformation—is not only a problem of class consciousness, of the practical effectiveness of conscious action, but also the beginning of the suspension of the pure "natural lawfulness" of economism. It means that the "greatest productive force" [the workers] finds itself in rebellion against the system of production of which it is a part. A situation has arisen which can be resolved only by force. . . .

The qualitative distinction between the decisive, "last" crisis of capitalism . . . and the earlier ones is not just a simple change of its duration and depth, of quantity into quality. . . . This change is expressed in the fact that the proletariat ceases to be a simple object of the crisis; that the internal antagonism in capitalistic production . . . comes out into the open. The organization of the proletariat, whose aim has always been "to halt the ruinous consequences for its class of that natural law of capitalistic production" (Marx), moves from the stage of negativity . . . to activity. With this the structure of the crisis has decisively, qualitatively changed. . . . Force becomes the decisive economic factor in this situation.

This shows again that these "eternal natural laws" are valid only for a certain period of development. . . .

Vulgar Marxism . . . denies the significance of force "as an economic factor." For vulgar Marxism the theoretical underestimation of the significance of force in history and the denial of its role in the history of the past is a theoretical preparation for opportunistic tactics. This elevation of the specific developmental laws of capitalist society to general laws is the theoretical foundation for the effort to make the existence of capitalist society practically eternal.

. . . The demand that socialism be realized without "noneconomic" force, through the immanent laws of economic development, is actually synonymous with the eternal survival of capitalist society. . . .

Leninist Discipline in the Comintern

The early years of the Communist International were a period of turmoil from the organizational point of view, as the Russian Communists strove to split the European socialist parties and bring their left-wing elements under firm international discipline. The Second Comintern Congress, in August, 1920, laid down "twenty-one conditions"—largely drafted by Lenin—to which member Communist parties would have to subscribe. They were required to commit themselves to the political pattern which had emerged in Russia—violent revolution under the exclusive leadership of a strictly disciplined Communist party—as well as to unquestioning acceptance of the decisions of the International and the interests of the Soviet Republic.

. . . The second congress of the Communist International puts forward the following conditions of adherence to the Communist International:

1. *All propaganda and agitation* must be of a genuinely communist character and in conformity with the programme and decisions of the Communist international. The entire party press must be run by reliable communists who have proved their devotion to the cause of the proletariat. The dictatorship of the proletariat is to be treated not simply as a current formula learnt by rote; it must be advocated in a way which makes its necessity comprehensible to every ordinary working man and woman, every soldier and peasant, from the facts of their daily life, which must be systematically noted in our press and made use of every day. . . .

2. Every organization which wishes to join the Communist International must, in an orderly and planned fashion, remove reformists and centrists from all responsible positions in the workers' movement (party organizations, editorial boards, trade unions, parliamentary fractions, co-operatives, local government bodies) and replace them by tried communists, even if, particularly at the beginning, "experienced" opportunists have to be replaced by ordinary rank and file workers.

3. In practically every country of Europe and America the class struggle is entering the phase of civil war. In these cir-

FROM: Conditions of Admission to the Communist International, Approved by the Second Comintern Congress, August, 1920 (in *The Communist International: Documents*, Vol. I, pp. 168-72).

cumstances communists can have no confidence in bourgeois legality. They are obliged everywhere to create a parallel illegal organization which at the decisive moment will help the party to do its duty to the revolution. In all those countries where, because of a state of siege or of emergency laws, communists are unable to do all their work legally, it is absolutely essential to combine legal and illegal work.

4. The obigation to spread communist ideas includes the special obligation to carry on systematic and energetic propaganda in the army. Where such agitation is prevented by emergency laws, it must be carried on illegally. Refusal to undertake such work would be tantamount to a dereliction of revolutionary duty and is incompatible with membership of the Communist International.

5. Systematic and well-planned agitation must be carried on in the countryside. The working class cannot consolidate its victory if it has not by its policy assured itself of the support of at least part of the rural proletariat and the poorest peasants, and of the neutrality of part of the rest of the rural population. . . .

6. Every party which wishes to join the Communist International is obliged to expose not only avowed social-patriotism, but also the insincerity and hypocrisy of social-pacifism; to bring home to the workers systematically that without the revolutionary overthrow of capitalism no international court of arbitration, no agreement to limit armaments, no "democratic" reorganization of the League of Nations, will be able to prevent new imperialist wars.

7. Parties which wish to join the Communist International are obliged to recognize the necessity for a complete and absolute break with reformism and with the policy of the "centre," and to advocate this break as widely as possible among their members. Without that no consistent communist policy is possible. . . .

8. A particularly explicit and clear attitude on the question of the colonies and the oppressed peoples is necessary for the parties in those countries where the bourgeoisie possess colonies and oppress other nations. Every party which wishes to join the Communist International is obliged to expose the

tricks and dodges of "its" imperialists in the colonies, to support every colonial liberation movements not merely in words but in deeds, to demand the expulsion of their own imperialists from these colonies, to inculcate among the workers of their country a genuinely fraternal attitude to the working people of the colonies and the oppressed nations, and to carry on systematic agitation among the troops of their country against any oppression of the colonial peoples.

9. Every party which wishes to join the Communist International must carry on systematic and persistent communistic activity inside the trade unions, the workers' councils and factory committees, the co-operatives, and other mass workers' organizations. Within these organizations communist cells must be organized which shall by persistent and unflagging work win the trade unions, etc., for the communist cause. In their daily work the cells must everywhere expose the treachery of the social-patriots and the instability of the "centre." The communist cells must be completely subordinate to the party as a whole.

10. Every party belonging to the Communist International is obliged to wage an unyielding struggle against the Amsterdam "International" of the yellow trade unions.*. . .

11. Parties which wish to join the Communist International are obliged to review the personnel of their parliamentary fractions and remove all unreliable elements, to make these fractions not only verbally but in fact subordinate to the party presidium, requiring of each individual communist member of parliament that he subordinate his entire activity to the interests of genuinely revolutionary propaganda and agitation.

12. Parties belonging to the Communist International must be based on the principle of *democratic centralism*. In the present epoch of acute civil war the communist party will be able to fulfil its duty only if its organization is as centralized as possible, if iron discipline prevails, and if the party centre, upheld by the confidence of the party membership,

* I.e., the socialist International Federation of Trade Unions, with headquarters in Amsterdam—Ed.

has strength and authority and is equipped with the most comprehensive powers.

13. Communist parties in those countries where communists carry on their work legally must from time to time undertake cleansing (re-registration) of the membership of the party in order to get rid of any petty-bourgeois elements which have crept in.

14. Every party which wishes to join the Communist International is obliged to give unconditional support to any Soviet republic in its struggle against counter-revolutionary forces. Communist parties must carry on unambiguous propaganda to prevent the dispatch of munitions transports to the enemies of the Soviet republics; they must also carry on propaganda by every means, legal or illegal, among the troops sent to strangle workers' republics.

15. Parties which still retain their old social-democratic programmes are obliged to revise them as quickly as possible, and to draw up, in accordance with the special conditions of their country, a new communist programme in conformity with the decisions of the Communist International. . . .

16. All the decisions of the Congresses of the Communist International, as well as the decisions of its Executive Committee, are binding on all parties belonging to the Communist International. . . .

17. . . . All parties which wish to join the Communist International must change their names. Every party which wishes to join the Communist International must be called: *Communist* party of such and such a country (section of the Communist International). This question of name is not merely a formal matter, but essentially a political question of great importance. The Communist International has declared war on the entire bourgeous world and on all yellow social-democratic parties. The difference between the communist parties and the old official "social-democratic" or "socialist" parties, which have betrayed the banner of the working class, must be brought home to every ordinary worker. . . .

21. Those members of the party who reject in principle the conditions and theses put forward by the Communist International are to be expelled from the party. . . .

Zinoviev on the German Revolution

Early Communist hopes for international revolution rested on Germany, which they regarded as the country with the most powerful working class. The German Communists attempted a series of uprisings, and in 1923, at the time of the inflation, it appeared to the Russians that the proletariat was about to take power in Germany. As it happened, the main attempt was called off, isolated Communist risings were put down, and the German Communist Party remained more or less on the defensive until it was broken up by Hitler.

The 1923 setback to their revolutionary hopes induced the Soviet leaders to adopt the "united front" policy of alliance with whatever reformist or nationalist groups would agree to cooperate with the USSR. Meanwhile conventional diplomatic relations were established between the USSR and most other countries.

. . . German events are developing with the certainty of fate. . . .

. . . Soon everyone will see that the autumn months of 1923 mark a turning point not only for Germany, but also for the world in general. . . .

The social basis of the coming revolution is absolutely clear. In the cities the workers are definitely numerically superior (to the rest of the population). These workers have followed the counterrevolutionary German Social Democratic Party in one way or another . . . (but) this worker-giant is now convinced that the country and the working class can be saved only by revolution.

From the moment the German working class turns its back upon the German Social Democrats and follows the Communist Party, the fate of Germany is sealed. . . .

The forthcoming German revolution will be a proletarian class revolution. The twenty-two million German workers who make up its army represent the cornerstone of the

FROM: Zinoviev, *Problems of the German Revolution* (1923; excerpts translated in Xenia J. Eudin and Harold H. Fisher, *Soviet Russia and the West,* pp. 214-15; reprinted by permission of the publisher, Stanford University Press. Copyright, 1957, by the Board of Trustees of Leland Stanford Junior University).

international proletariat. They will meet the capitalists with an international revolution. According to the highest estimates, in 1917 Russia had eight to ten million workers among a population of 160 million. Germany, with a population of sixty million, has more than twenty million workers. With us, the working class was only a small minority; in Germany it is the principal element, the majority of the population.

Most important of all, the German revolution will operate from a powerful industrial base. It is true that German industries are in a very difficult position. . . . But even so, German industries represent a formidable power. In that sense, Lenin was correct when he said: "In Western Europe, and especially in a country such as Germany, it will be much more difficult to start a proletarian revolution than in Russia. But it will be much easier to continue and to finish it." The German proletariat has preponderance both in industry and in agriculture. . . .

. . . One can say that the role of the peasants in Russia, war-weary, exhausted by continued ravages and devastation, and pushed to the abyss by the actions of capitalists, will be played in Germany by the middle class in the towns. The middle class will naturally vacillate between the proletariat and the bourgeoisie. It may even support the enemies of the revolution more often than not. But in the end it will provide (us with) auxiliary forces. The urban and rural proletariat will under no circumstances abandon revolutionary ideas. Today it has succeeded, and in a truly short time, in neutralizing the petty bourgeois elements and in gaining the sympathy of some of them. . . .

The attitude of the German petty bourgeoisie in the cities is due partly to the brutal policies of the Entente . . . and partly to the egotism of the German capitalist bourgeoisie, which has been ruinous to the middle classes. We, the Marxists, know that industrial capital destroys the petty bourgeoisie, and consequently proletarianizes most of them. But it is in Germany that we see for the first time that process being accomplished on a considerable scale. . . .

All the difficulties (of the German proletarian revolution)

in achieving a domestic correlation of forces are secondary to the difficulties from the outside that will come into being the day after victory is won. The threat of an immediate war on the part of the French, Czech, and Polish bourgeoisie, the possibility of an English blockade—these are the main international political difficulties that will confront the German revolution. . . .

Imperialism will undoubtedly attempt to organize an international front against the German proletarian revolution. But its success is doubtful. Six years of struggle against the Russian revolution have shown that to erect a united front is no easy matter. There is bound to be a struggle in the camp of the imperialist bourgeoisie between two types of policy: an imperialist policy of conquest, and a social-class policy in the broad sense. . . .

It goes without saying that the German proletariat must prepare for the worst, that is, it must expect international imperialism to interpret its revolution not as an isolated episode but as affecting the face of all European bourgeoisie. It must make its plans accordingly. . . .

The Trotskyists on the Comintern

At the time of their last stand in 1927 the Trotsky Opposition made a burning issue out of the mistakes which they alleged the Soviet leadership to have committed in pursuance of the "united front" policy. The purge of the Chinese Communists by Chiang Kai-shek was the occasion for a bitter Trotskyist attack on the "petty-bourgeois" compromises made by the leadership and on the effort to cover up failure by muzzling the Opposition. The international issue contributed to Stalin's determination to destroy the Opposition. Trotsky's expulsion evoked serious disagreements in the foreign Communist parties, which gave Stalin the opportunity to tighten Russian control over the Comintern in the course of disciplining the Trotskyist dissidents.

Comrades,

The serious mistakes which have been permitted in the

work of leading the Chinese revolution have contributed to a severe defeat, from which it is possible to escape only by returning to Lenin's path. The extremely abnormal circumstances under which the discussion of questions connected with the Chinese revolution is going on create an extraordinarily tense situation in the party. The one-sided "discussion" being conducted in the pages of *Pravda* and *Bolshevik*, and the intentional distortion of the views of the opposition (for example, attributing to it the demand to quit the Kuomintang), testify to the desire of the leading group in the Central Committee to cover its mistakes by hunting down the opposition. All this directs the party's attention on a false path. . . .

All the prerequisites were present for arming the Chinese workers (primarily in Shanghai and Hankow). And nevertheless the heroic proletariat of Shanghai was revealed to be unarmed, and the mass of the Hankow workers are not armed even now, in spite of the fact that the "Left" Kuomintang men are ruling in Hankow.

The "leadership" in China *in fact* concluded that it could not arm the workers, could not organize revolutionary strikes, could not finally support the peasants against the landlords, could not issue a daily Communist newspaper, could not criticize the domination of the bourgeois of the Right Kuomintang and the petty-bourgeois of the "Left" Kuomintang, could not organize Communist cells in Chiang Kai-shek's army, could not proclaim the slogan of soviets—in order "not to drive away" the bourgeoisie, in order "not to frighten" the petty-bourgeoisie, in order not to shake the government of the "bloc of four classes." In answer to this, thanks to this, one ought to expect, the Chinese "national" bourgeoisie, after waiting for a convenient moment, mercilessly shoots down the Chinese workers, and appeals for the help of the imperialists, today the Japanese, tomorrow the Americans, and the day after tomorrow the English. . . .

The Chinese defeat can be reflected in the most direct

FROM: The Declaration of the Eighty-Four, May, 1927 (editor's translation from copy in the Trotsky Archive).

manner in the fate of the USSR in the immediate future. If the imperialists succeed for an extended period in pacifying China, they will then move against us, against the USSR. The defeat of the Chinese revolution can bring war against the USSR vastly nearer. Meanwhile, the party is deprived of the opportunity of judging the Chinese question, which is now for it, the first party of the Comintern, the most important question. Principled consideration of the questions of the Chinese revolution is suppressed. And at this very time in fact only a furious one-sided discussion is being conducted, i.e., in the sense of hunting down the opposition, with the objective of concealing the incorrect line of the leading core of the Central Committee. . . .

Between the incorrect line in the Chinese question and the incorrect line in the question of the Anglo-Russian Committee* there is a close internal connection. That same line is proceeding now in the whole policy of the Comintern. In Germany hundreds of skilled Left proletarians are being expelled from the party merely because they have shown solidarity with the Russian Opposition. The Right elements in all the parties are getting more and more preponderance. The crudest Right mistakes (in Germany, Poland, France, etc.) go unpunished. The slightest voice of criticism on the Left leads to lopping off. The authority of the All-Union Communist Party and the October Revolution are thus utilized for the turn of the Communist parties to the right, away from the Leninist line. All this taken together deprives the Comintern of the possibility of preparing and conducting the struggle against war in a Leninist manner.

For any Marxist it is indisputable that the incorrect line in China and in the question of the Anglo-Russian Committee is not accidental. It continues and completes the incorrect line in internal policy.

The economy of the Soviet Union has completed, in general and as a whole, its restoration period. In the course of this

* The Anglo-Russian Committee of Trade-Union Unity, an organ of tenuous cooperation which the Russian oppositionists wanted to abandon after the failure of the British general strike in 1926—Ed.

period substantial success was achieved in economic construction. In industry, agriculture, and the other branches of the economy of the Union of Soviet Socialist Republics we are either approaching or have overtaken the pre-war level. . . .

But . . . instead of a Marxist analysis of the real situation of the proletarian dictatorship in the USSR, the party offers up the false, petty-bourgeois "theory of socialism in one country," which has nothing in common with Marxism, with Leninism. This crude retreat from Marxism makes it more difficult for the party to see the *class content* of the economic processes which are going on. Meanwhile it is precisely in the turns unfavorable for the workers and in the burdensome position of the broad popular masses that the *negative manifestations* of the period of the revolution through which we are living are comprised. . . .

The basic condition for the solution of the questions which at the present time stand before the party in the region of economic construction, in a most complicated class context internally and with the build-up of a hostile attack on the USSR from without, under the circumstance of the delay of the international proletarian revolution, *is the question of reviving intraparty democracy and strengthening the living, active connection of the party with the working class.*

Iron party discipline is essential for us—as under Lenin. But intraparty democracy is also essential for us—as under Lenin.

The whole party from top to bottom must be, in a Bolshevik manner, ideologically and organizationally, a firmly welded collective, increasing among all the masses their real and not just official-formal participation in deciding all of the questions which stand before the party, the working class, and the whole country.

The intraparty regime which has been established in the recent period leads to a vast reduction in the activity of the party, this leading force of the proletarian revolution. The possibility for conscious participation in deciding the most important questions of the proletarian revolution by the broad, lower party masses, has been diminished and constricted to an extreme degree. . . .

The *international situation* is becoming more and more tense. The danger of war is increasing. The central task of the All-Union Communist Party and of the whole vanguard of the international proletariat now consists of *preventing war (or perhaps just postponing it for as long a time as possible), in order to support and defend in whatever way the policy of peace, which only our party and soviet rule are able to carry out in the end.*

The cause of the USSR is the cause of the international proletariat. The most important task of the international proletariat is to avert the danger of a new war which hangs over the head of the USSR. But this cannot be done through the path of a bloc with the traitors of the General Council [of the British Trades Union Congress]. Any serious struggle for the prevention of war is impossible in alliance with Purcell and Citrine. It is possible to get closer to the Social-Democratic and nonparty *workers,* to draw them into the struggle against war, only by going *over the heads* of these treacherous leaders, and in struggle with them. . . .

Our party's whole policy suffers from the course to the right. If the new blow now being prepared against the Left, the Opposition, is launched, this will finally free the hands of the Right, nonproletarian, and antiproletarian elements, in part within our party and especially outside its ranks. A blow against the Left will have as its inevitable consequence the triumph of the Ustrialov movement. Ustrialov* has long demanded such a blow against the Opposition in the name of the neo-NEP. Ustrialov is the most consistent, most principled and irreconcilable foe of Bolshevism. Self-satisfied administrators, rivaling the old bureaucrats in authority, the petty-bourgeois who has risen to a post of command and looks down haughtily on the masses, all these feel the ground firm under their feet and all are raising their heads more. These are all elements of the neo-NEP. Behind them stands the Ustrialovist-specialist and in the next rank the Nepman and

* Ustrialov: a Russian émigré economist who expounded the view that under the NEP Russia was inevitably returning to capitalism—Ed.

the kulak, labeled strong muzhik. Here is where the real danger comes from.

In internal questions the turns are not so obviously discovered as in external questions because the internal processes develop much more slowly than the general strike in England or the revolution in China. But the basic tendency of the policy is present here, and the more slowly it grows internally, the more serious it can become.

Lenin defined the Soviet state as a workers' state in a country whose population has a peasant majority, and with a bureaucratic perversion. This was said at the beginning of 1921. Lenin's definition is now more vital than ever. During the years of the NEP the new bourgeoisie of town and village has grown into a serious force. Under such circumstances striking a blow at the Opposition signifies nothing else but an attempt, behind hypocritical cries of defending unity ("the initiators of any split cry most of all about unification," said Engels), to discredit and destroy the *left proletarian, Leninist wing of our party*. Such a destruction would mean the inevitable and rapid strengthening of the right wing of the AUCP and just as inevitably the prospect of the subordination of the interests of the proletariat to the interests of other classes.

We always need unity of the party, especially under the present conditions. We all learned in Lenin's school that a Bolshevik must obtain unity *on the basis of a revolutionary-proletarian political line*. In the most difficult historical conditions—in the years of the underground, then in 1917 when in the midst of war we struggled for power; in 1918, when the question of the Brest-Litovsk peace was decided under unprecedentedly hard conditions, and in the following years under Lenin, the party openly considered disputed questions and found the correct path to real, not show-window, unity. We were able to do this under conditions incomparably more difficult than the present. . . .

The "Third Period"

In 1928, simultaneously with his attack on the Bukharin group in Russia, Stalin initiated a new ultra-left line for the

Comintern and proceeded to weed Bukharin's right-wing sympathizers out of the leadership of the foreign Communist parties, just as he had with the Trotskyists. As a result of these expulsions, most of the original founders of the Communist parties were eliminated from the movement, which from this time on was completely subservient to Moscow. The line enjoined on the foreign Communists until 1934 was one of uncompromising hostility to democratic and reformist movements. Hitler's seizure of power in Germany was thereby facilitated, while Earl Browder of the Communist Party of the USA denounced Roosevelt's New Deal as fascist.

The situation of the United States confirms most strikingly the correctness of the draft thesis before us, when it speaks of "the tremendous strain of the internal antagonism . . . as well as of the international antagonisms." The policies of the Roosevelt administration, known as the "New Deal," called into being by the crisis and by these "tremendous strains," have by no means softened these strains and antagonisms, but on the contrary have intensified them. Precisely the period of the Roosevelt regime has marked not alone the sharpening of the international relations of the U.S., but also the internal class relations.

Roosevelt's policy called for "national concentration" and "class peace." But in spite of the apparent surface successes of his regime, even the "honeymoon period" of the New Deal has been marked by rising mass struggles, by great class battles, by a radicalization of large sections of all the toiling masses of the population. . . . Never before in modern times has the "strain of internal class antagonisms" in the U.S. been so sharp and so general.

Characteristic for the whole system of policies known as the New Deal is their nature as preparations for war. The economic contents of these measures are those of war economy. . . . Simultaneously, U. S. oppression of the colonies and semi-colonies takes on sharper forms, as the resistance of the colonial masses grows. . . .

FROM: Earl Browder, Speech at the Thirteenth Plenum of the Executive Committee of the Communist International, January 1934 (in *The Communist International*, January 15, 1934, pp. 75-77).

If we witness all these developments during what may be called the "honeymoon" period of the Roosevelt regime, when the illusions created by an unprecedented demagogy were bolstered up for a time by a rapid rise in production stimulated by an enormous speculative market (the flight from the dollar)—then we have every reason to expect the growth and intensification of class conflicts, and of all the contradictions of capitalism, now when the Roosevelt program has already exposed its inability to improve the condition of the masses, when production again declines precipitately, when rising prices and inflation cut further sharply into the living standards of the masses, and when demagogy is rapidly being reinforced with a sharp development of fascist ideology and terror directed against the struggling masses.

International social-fascism* has hailed the Roosevelt policies as "steps in the direction of socialism." The British Labor Party and Trade Union Congress have adopted the Roosevelt program as their own, demanding that it can be imitated in Britain. In this way they are but continuing, in the period of crisis, that complete ideological subordination to the bourgeoisie which, during the period of American prosperity, created out of the figure of Henry Ford the reformist "saviour." The American Socialist Party has not lagged behind in this respect; Norman Thomas and Morris Hillquit hastened to pay a public visit to Roosevelt, upon his assumption of office, to congratulate him upon his policies, which they hailed as nothing less than a "revolution" in the interests of the masses.

But the fascist direction in which the Roosevelt policies are carrying the U.S. is becoming clear to the whole world. Nowhere is this more manifest than in the efforts to merge the reformist American Federation of Labor into the machinery of government, under the avowed banner of the fascist conception of the "corporate state," prohibition of strikes, compulsory arbitration, governmental fixing of wages, and even control of the inner life of the trade unions. For the

* I.e., democratic Socialists—Ed.

edification of the masses this was spoken of as a "partnership of capital and labor, together with the government." Under this program the A.F. of L. is given governmental support and even financial assistance, and a determined effort is made to control and eventually choke off the strike movement, by driving the workers into the A.F. of L. where it is hoped the official leadership will be able to bring the masses under control. . . .

The Fourth International

Trotsky's sympathizers in the Communist parties outside Russia, after vainly trying to hold on as left opposition groups within their respective organizations, began to build an independent movement. In 1934 they proclaimed the establishment of a "Fourth International" to challenge the Third, which, they contended, had betrayed the world revolution because of its identification with Stalin's bureaucratic nationalism. Apart from a considerable response in South-East Asia the Fourth International never advanced beyond the status of a splinter group; it ceased to be a significant force after Trotsky's assassination in 1940.

. . . The two parties of the proletariat, into whose hands history successively gave the imposing task of overthrowing the bourgeoisie and opening the road to socialism, have failed abysmally. Social democracy and Stalinism both collapsed at the first blow, like eggshells sucked dry, in Germany, then in Austria, then in Latvia, then in Bulgaria. (The social democracy, be it noted, died politically twenty years ago; it proved no less despicable in its second incarnation.)

The whole history of the modern proletarian movement has only served to underscore the all-importance and indispensability of that most highly perfected of all its instruments: the political party. Especially in our time has it become the master key to all problems. The class war is fought by class armies. The working class as a whole—to say nothing of its necessary allies in other sections of the

FROM: "For the Fourth International!," lead article in *The New International,* Vol. I, No. 1, July, 1934 (pp. 1-3).

population—is not characterized by firm homogeneity. It is stratified at different levels of consciousness, it is divided by conflicting ideologies, by separatist interests of caste, religion, nationality, sex, age. Emerging from its ranks—but transcending these differences and consequently able to overcome them—is its vanguard, the revolutionary political party. The party embodies the accumulated experiences of the proletariat distilled into its revolutionary theory. It is the repository of the consciousness of the class. It embraces the most advanced, the most militant, the most devoted, unites them firmly on the basis of tested principles and welds them together in rigorous discipline.

The proletariat as a class, as a whole, cannot directly plan and guide its battles, any more than each platoon in an army can elaborate the strategy and tactics of war. For that a staff, a vanguard is imperative—not imposed from above as in a capitalist army, without the possibility of control and verification from the ranks, but rising from the ranks by tested ability and common approval. It is all the more imperative in this epoch because of the extreme concentration of power in the enemy camp, its increased mobility, and because of the abruptness with which changes take place in the objective situation. These necessitate a trained, vigilant vanguard equipped with foresight and consequently capable of pre-arrangement. Foresight is made possible by the searchlight of Marxism, whose powerful batteries are merely the condensed experiences of history, illuminating the path ahead.

For lack of just such a party, the working class has suffered one defeat after another, until the dreadful climax in 1933-1934 fully disclosed the bankruptcy of the existing organizations.

Neither of the two parties came to their miserable end because of some aberration, springing out of conditions peculiar to Germany, or Austria. Their demolition is rather to be traced to the fundamental theories and practices common to their respective Internationals. The generic name of these theories is nationalistic opportunism.

The modern social democratic parties were nurtured on the skimmed milk of the imperialist expansion of their respective national fatherlands. Grown mighty and fabulously wealthy on the vast profits of colonial exploitation, the imperialist powers found it necessary and possible to corrupt and thus enlist the support of a whole section of its own working class. The social democracy based itself upon the aristocracy of labor, upon the reforms which an indulgent imperialism vouchsafed it, and upon sections of the middle class. It was gradually absorbed into the machinery of the capitalist state and interlaced its destiny with the fate of the bourgeois nation. Thence the unforgettable treason of the social democracy during the war, each party digging bloodsoaked fingers into the throat of the other for the greater glory of its own fatherland. Thence the rabid loyalty to the capitalist state when the spontaneous post-war revolutionary wave threatened to inundate the bourgeoisie. Thence the theory of gradually converting capitalism into socialism just as smoothly and miraculously as the transubstantiation of the wafer and the wine into the body and blood of Christ. Thence the repudiation of the dictatorship of the proletariat and its replacement by the theory and practise of coalitions with the democratic bourgeoisie for the preservation of capitalism, as a necessary transition to socialism. Thence the theory of the lesser evil—capitalism is preferable to Bolshevism—the theory which facilitated the victory of Fascism.

What distinguishes the Stalinist parties from the social democratic is not so much the outcome of their policy—the effects have been equally calamitous in both cases—as it is the different origin of their nationalism. The Stalinist parties were not poisoned at the well of imperialist nationalism, but at the well once fed exclusively by the springs of a proletarian revolution. The theory of "socialism in one country" is an expression of the nationalist degeneration of the Soviet Union. There is not, nor can there be, an inherent conflict between the interests of the Soviet Union and the interests of the world revolution. The interests of a parasitic Soviet bureaucracy, however, can and do conflict with the interests of the world revolution. The generalized formulation of this conflict is implicit in the theory of "socialism in one country."

The Soviet bureaucracy, myopically attributing longevity to

phenomena of a temporary character, does not believe in the possibilities of a world revolution for several decades to come. With this conviction pervading all their thoughts, the bureaucrats want above all else the safeguarding of Russia's territorial integrity in order to construct a nationally walled-off utopia. This course has led inexorably to the transformation of the Third International from the general staff of the world revolution into a Soviet border patrol. Internationalism requires the subordination of each country to the interests of the world revolution. Nationalism means the subordination of the world movement to the interests of the Stalinist bureaucracy in the Soviet Union. . . .

The revolutionary vanguard needs a new Communist International. The masses are confused, it is true. They are being confused by the social democrats of all shades and disguises, who tell them that the Second International is good enough, that it can be reformed, if not today then tomorrow, if not tomorrow then . . . after Fascism triumphs in a few more countries. They are being confused by the Stalinists who tell them that the Third International was right yesterday, today, tomorrow and forever. They are being confused by the vacillators and opportunists who deceive them with stories about uniting the Second and the Third, or about forming some other International—not a "sectarian" one, God forbid! but one in which all "good revolutionary parties outside the Second and the Third" will find shelter for the night. The Fourth International will not bring confusion into the ranks of the working class. It will bring a flaming sword whose edge cuts through the web of lies and deceit and hypocrisy, and whose light brings clarity. . . .

The Fourth International? This is no meaningless phrase. *It is a fighting program!* It means a fight to the death against Fascism, imperialism, war. It means an intransigent struggle against treacherous social reformism, bureaucratic Stalinism, cowardly compromising centrism of all species. It means the unconditional struggle to defend the Soviet Union which social democrats and Stalinists left in the lurch in Germany when they permitted the arch-anti-Sovietist Hitler to come to power without a battle. It means the militant struggle for revolutionary Marxism, for the final victory of the working class. . . .

. . . As yesterday, so today, we shall continue to work with all our strength for all the fundamental theories of Marx, Engels, Lenin and Trotsky, which have been tested through and through and confirmed a thousand times over and from every angle. With its modest resources, *The New International* will defend the revolutionary teachings of Marxism in every domain, taking up every challenge and refuting all over again those "new" anti-Marxists who have merely refurbished the well-riddled views of old revisionists. Our banner is hoisted and unfurled. The class-conscious militants will rally to it and plant it on the citadels of capitalism.

For the Fourth International! For revolutionary Marxism!

The Popular Front

In 1934 the Soviet government revised its foreign policy abruptly, to press for "collective security" against the threat of Germany and Japan. The USSR joined the League of Nations, and in 1935 concluded a military alliance with France. In conformity with this shift, the Communist International received instructions at its Seventh (and last) Congress in August, 1935, to promote cooperation with liberal and socialist groups wherever such "Popular Front" alliances could be arranged. By thus playing revolution down, the Communists experienced a considerable heightening of their appeal, and Popular Front governments came to power temporarily in France and Spain.

In face of the towering menace of fascism to the working class and all the gains it has made, to all toilers and their elementary rights, to the peace and liberty of the peoples, the Seventh Congress of the Communist International declares that *at the present historical stage it is the main and*

FROM: Resolution of the Seventh World Congress of the Communist International, August, 1935, "The Offensive of Fascism and the Tasks of the Communist International in the Fight for the Unity of the Working Class against Fascism" (English translation in *Seventh World Congress of the Communist International,* New York, Workers' Library Publishers, 1935).

immediate task of the international labor movement to establish the united fighting front of the working class. For a successful struggle against the offensive of capital, against the reactionary measures of the bourgeoisie, against fascism, the bitterest enemy of all the toilers, who, without distinction of political views, have been deprived of all rights and liberties, it is imperative that unity of action be established between all sections of the working class, irrespective of what organization they belong to, even before the majority of the working class unites on a common fighting platform for the overthrow of capitalism and the victory of the proletarian revolution. But it is precisely for this very reason that this task makes it the duty of the Communist Parties to take into consideration the changed circumstances and to apply the united fronts tactics *in a new manner,* by seeking to reach agreements with the organizations of the toilers of various political trends for joint action on a factory, local, district, national and international scale.

With this as its point of departure, the Seventh Congress of the Communist International enjoins the Communist Parties to be guided by the following instructions when carrying out the united front tactics:

1. *The defense of the immediate economic and political interests of the working class, the defense of the latter against fascism,* must be the starting point and form the main content of the worker's united front in all capitalist countries. In order to set the broad masses in motion, such slogans and forms of struggle must be put forward as arise from the vital needs of the masses and from the level of their fighting capacity at the given stage of development. Communists must not limit themselves to merely issuing appeals to struggle for proletarian dictatorship, but must show the masses *what they are to do today* to defend themselves against capitalist plunder and fascist barbarity. They must strive, through the joint action of the labor organizations, to mobilize the masses around *a program of demands that are calculated to really shift the burden of the consequences of the crisis on to the shoulders of the ruling classes; demands,*

the fight to realize which, disorganizes fascism, hampers the preparations for imperialist war, weakens the bourgeoisie and strengthens the positions of the proletariat. . . .

2. Without for a moment giving up their independent work in the sphere of Communist education, organization and mobilization of masses, the Communists, in order to render the road to unity of action easier for the workers, *must strive to secure joint action with the Social-Democratic Parties, reformist trade unions and other organizations of the toilers against the class enemies of the proletariat, on the basis of short or long-term agreements. . . .*

5. Joint action with the Social-Democratic Parties and organizations not only does not preclude, but on the contrary, *renders still more necessary the serious and well-founded criticism of* reformism, of Social-Democracy as the ideology and practice of class collaboration with the bourgeoisie, and the patient exposition of the principles and program of Communists to the Social-Democratic workers. . . .

6. *Election campaigns* must be utilized for the further development and strengthening of the united fighting front of the proletariat. While coming forward independently in the elections and unfolding the program of the Communist Party before the masses, the Communists must seek to establish a united front with the Social-Democratic Parties and the trade unions (also with the organizations of the toiling peasants, handicraftsmen, etc.), and exert every effort to prevent the election of reactionary and fascist candidates. In face of fascist danger, the Communists may, *while reserving for themselves freedom of political agitation and criticism,* participate in election campaigns on *a common platform and with a common ticket of the anti-fascist front,* depending on the growth and success of the united front movement, also depending on the electoral system in operation. . . .

Emphasizing the special importance of forming a united front in the sphere of the economic struggle of the workers and the establishment of the unity of the trade union movement as a most important step in consolidating the united front of the proletariat, the Congress makes it a duty of the Communists to adopt all practical measures for the realization of the unity of the trade unions by industries and on a national scale. . . .

The Spanish Civil War

In accordance with the Popular Front policy, the Spanish Communists gave their full support to the republican government of Spain during the civil war which followed General Franco's rebellion of July, 1936. Thanks to this line and the importance of Soviet aid, the Communists exercised strong (but neither exclusive nor revolutionary) influence in the government of the republic until it was overwhelmed by Franco in March, 1939.

José Diaz, General Secretary of the Communist Party of Spain, made it clear in a speech to the Central Committee in March, 1937, that revolutionary policies would be postponed until after the defeat of the fascists. The Communists denounced the revolutionary extremism of the Trotskyist POUM ("Workers' Party of Marxist Unity"), and supported the government's suppression of the Anarchist uprising in Barcelona in May, 1937.

The Communist position in Spain is significant as a link between their old avowedly revolutionary line and their post-World-War-II appeal on an ostensibly reformist or nationalist basis—*vide* Diaz's stress on the role of the "new" type of "democratic" republic.

. . . Realizing the new character which our struggle acquired when the war began, our party announced the slogan of broadening the Popular Front, of turning toward the union of all Spaniards. For this it took account of the fact that the civil war was now transformed into a war of independence, a war of national liberation. . . .

Our struggle, which in its basic content is a national one, also has a marked international character. This international character of our struggle has been defined, in a few words but in the manner of a genius, by our great comrade Stalin. . . . Stalin, in his historic telegram to the Central Committee of our party says the following:

FROM: Diaz, "For Unity, until Victory" (Report to the Central Committee of the Communist Party of Spain, March 5, 1937, pp. 10, 12-14, 17-18, 38, 46-48; editor's translation).

"In helping the revolutionary masses of Spain as much as possible, the workers of the Soviet Union are only doing their duty. They realize that to liberate Spain from the oppression of the fascist reactionaries is not the private affair of the Spaniards, but the common cause of all advanced and progressive humanity." . . .

We are fighting for the Democratic Republic, for a Democratic and Parliamentary Republic of a new type, with deep social content. The struggle which is going on in Spain does not have as its object the establishment of a democratic republic such as can be seen in France or in any other capitalist country. No; the Democratic Republic for which we are fighting is different. We are fighting to destroy the material bases on which reaction and fascism rest, for without the destruction of these bases a true political democracy cannot exist.

In our struggle we are pursuing *the annihilation of the material bases of semifeudal Spain,* tearing out the roots of fascism. . . .

We must annihilate the big landholders. . . .

We must also *destroy the economic and political power of the Church,* which was a center of conspiracy against the popular masses and one of the firmest supports of semifeudal Spain, and for this we must proceed with the confiscation and nationalization of its property. Let it be well understood that *fighting the Church* in its semifeudal economic and political structure is not the same thing as *fighting religion,* but the contrary, for only a republican and democratic Spain, liberal and progressive, will be able to guarantee freedom of religion in our country.

We must also proceed with the *liquidation of militarism*. . . .

We must likewise *break up the great financial oligarchies*. . . .

In addition to these fundamental points, whose solution will mean the disappearance of the semifeudal castes which have been dominant in Spain, and the transformation of the material and social base of our new Democratic and Parliamentary Republic, it is necessary to proceed, as the complement of what this should be, to the establishment of *true* universal suffrage, to the direct participation of all the people in elections and in the posts of political and economic leadership of the country. Thus we will move directly to the inauguration of a true democracy, which will permit wide channels to be opened for the economic, political, and cultural progress of our people. . . .

. . . The fact of not having clearly understood the character of our struggle leads organizations and parties associated with ours to adopt extremist attitudes which in no way benefit the cause of the people, but far from carrying us rapidly to victory, seriously obstruct the attainment of it. To these equivocal positions correspond those premature attempts at "socialization" and "collectivization." . . . Today, when there is a Popular Front government in which all the forces who are fighting against fascism are represented, this is not advisable, but is self-defeating. Now it is necessary to move rapidly to coordinate production and intensify it under a single administration to provide everything necessary for the front and the rear. To persist now in these attempts is to go against the interests which are supposedly being defended. To announce those premature attempts at "socialization" and "collectivization" while the war has still not been decided, at moments when the enemy within, aided by fascism without, is violently attacking our positions and endangering the fate of our country, is absurd and equivalent to becoming accomplices of the enemy. Such attempts reveal the failure to understand the character of our struggle, which is the struggle for the defense of the Democratic Republic, in which all the popular forces needed to win the war can and must combine.

It is said that the Communists have renounced their revolutionary program. No; what has happened is that we conform to the realities of the struggle and the necessities of the war. . . .

We have not abandoned our revolutionary program just because we did not carry forward these unfortunate attempts. What is happening is that today it is impossible to have a more revolutionary program than the one which the Communist Party has placed before the people. We plan our tactics and our strategy in accordance with the given situation. That is, we Marxist-Leninists apply to each concrete situation the tactics and strategy which correspond to that situation; and he who pretends to jump stages, with resounding names, wishing to do the impossible, will smash against the difficulties of the situation. But the harm is not that they smash themselves; the harm is that with their lack of understanding they compromise everyone's cause and endanger the freedom of Spain. . . .

In spite of everything, at all cost, we must maintain the Popular Front. Whatever the difficulties which are found in our path, the Communist Party will continue to be the most vigorous defender of the Popular Front and of its expression in power: the legitimate government. Our party will permit no one to attack the union of the anti-fascist forces with impunity. Our slogan is, "United now to win the war, and united afterward to reap the fruits of victory"; he who tries to break the union of the Popular Front, he who tries to break the union of the Spanish people struggling for the independence of Spain and staking everything on this struggle, is working consciously or unconsciously in favor of our enemies. . . .

Who are the enemies of the people? The enemies of the people are the fascists, the Trotskyists, and the "uncontrollables." . . . Our principal enemy is fascism. Against it we are concentrating all of the people's vigor and hatred. Against it we are setting all the forces ready to annihilate it; but our hatred is also directed, with the same concentrated force, against the agents of fascism who hide themselves behind pretended revolutionary slogans as POUM'ists, disguised Trotskyists, the better to accomplish their mission as agents of our enemies waiting in ambush in our own territory. We cannot annihilate the Fifth Column without also annihilating those who also defend politically the enemy's slogans directed at disrupting and disuniting the anti-fascist forces. The slogans of the enemy are: Against the Democratic Republic, against the anti-Fascist Popular Front, against the Popular Front government, against the regular army, etc., and above all against the Soviet Union on account of its magnificent solidarity with the Spanish people in this struggle. Although the Trotskyists try to conceal themselves with other apparently more revolutionary slogans, such as the social republic, workers' government, red militia, they cannot avoid revealing their fascist ears. . . .

It is a serious error to consider the Trotskyists as a fraction of the workers' movement. This is an unprincipled group of counterrevolutionaries classified as agents of international fascism. The recent Moscow trial has shown in the light of day that the chief of the band, Trotsky, is a direct agent of the Gestapo. In his hatred of the Soviet Union, of the great Bolshevik Party and of the Communist International, he joined hands with the fascists. . . .

The Nazi-Soviet Pact

In 1939, after mutual suspicion wore Russia's ties with Britain and France thin, the Soviet government commenced negotiations with Germany and threw the world (and especially the international Communist movement) into consternation by concluding the nonaggression treaty of August, 1939. Molotov, at the time both premier (1930-1941) and foreign commissar (1939-1949 and 1953-1956), defended the deal strictly in terms of power politics and national interest. The loyalties of many foreign Communists were rudely shaken by the maneuver, which registered the clear ascendancy of Soviet national security over the fortunes of the international revolutionary movement.

. . . The conclusion of a pact of non-aggression between the U.S.S.R. and Germany is of tremendous positive value, eliminating the danger of war between Germany and the Soviet Union. . . .

The decision to conclude a non-aggression pact between the U.S.S.R. and Germany was adopted after military negotiations with France and Great Britain had reached an impasse

FROM: Molotov, "The Meaning of the Soviet-German Non-Aggression Pact" (Speech to the Supreme Soviet, August 31, 1939; English translation in *The Strategy and Tactics of World Communism: Supplement I,* "One Hundred Years of Communism, 1848-1948" (U. S. House of Representatives Document No. 619, 80th Congress, 2nd Session), Washington, Government Printing Office, 1948, pp. 158, 160-63).

owing to the insuperable differences I have mentioned. As the negotiations had shown that the conclusion of a pact of mutual assistance could not be expected, we could not but explore other possibilities of ensuring peace and eliminating the danger of war between Germany and the U.S.S.R. If the British and French governments refused to reckon with this, that is their affair. It is our duty to think of the interests of the Soviet people, the interests of the Union of Soviet Socialist Republics. (*Prolonged applause*) All the more since we are firmly convinced that the interests of the U.S.S.R. coincide with the fundamental interests of the peoples of other countries. (*Applause*) But that is only one side of the matter.

Another circumstance was required before the Soviet-German Non-Aggression Pact could come into existence. It was necessary that in her foreign policy Germany should make a turn towards good-neighborly relations with the Soviet Union.

Only when this second condition was fulfilled, only when it became clear to us that the German Government desired to change its foreign policy so as to secure an improvement of relations with the U.S.S.R., was the basis found for the conclusion of a Soviet-German Non-Aggression Pact. Everybody knows that during the last six years, ever since the National-Socialists (Nazis) came into power, political relations between Germany and the U.S.S.R. have been strained. Everybody also knows that despite the differences of outlook and political systems, the Soviet Government endeavored to maintain normal business and political relations with Germany. . . .

. . . Stalin declared . . . that the Soviet Union stands for strengthening business relations with all countries. But at the same time Stalin warned us against warmongers who are anxious in their own interests to involve our country in conflicts with other countries.

Exposing the hullabaloo raised in the British, French, and American press about Germany's "plans" for the seizure of the Soviet Ukraine, Stalin said:

"It looks as if the object of this suspicious hullabaloo was to incense the Soviet Union against Germany, to poison the atmosphere and to provoke a conflict with Germany without any visible grounds."

As you see, Stalin hit the nail on the head when he exposed the machinations of the Western European politicians who were trying to set Germany and the Soviet Union at loggerheads.

It must be confessed that there were some short-sighted people even in our own country who, carried away by oversimplified anti-fascist propaganda, forgot about this provocative work of our enemies. Mindful of this, Stalin even then suggested the possibility of other, unhostile, good-neighborly relations between Germany and the U.S.S.R. It can now be seen that on the whole Germany correctly understood these statements of Stalin and drew practical conclusions from them. . . . The conclusion of the Soviet-German Non-Aggression Pact shows that Stalin's historic pre-vision has been brilliantly confirmed. (*Loud applause*).

Voices are now being heard testifying to the lack of understanding of the most simple reasons for the improvement of political relations between the Soviet Union and Germany which has begun. For example, people ask with an air of innocence how the Soviet Union could consent to improve political relations with a state of a fascist type. "Is that possible?" they ask. But they forget that this is not a question of our attitude towards the internal regime of another country but of the foreign relations between the two states. They forget that we hold the position of not interfering in the internal affairs of other countries and, correspondingly, of not tolerating interference in our own internal affairs. . . .

. . . In our foreign policy towards non-Soviet countries, we have always been guided by Lenin's well-known principle of the peaceful coexistence of the Soviet state and of capitalist countries. . . .

August 23, 1939, the day the Soviet-German Non-Aggression Pact was signed, is to be regarded as a date of great historical importance. The Non-Aggression Pact between the U.S.S.R. and Germany marks a turning point in the history of Europe, and not only of Europe. Only yesterday the

German fascists were pursuing a foreign policy hostile to us. Yes, only yesterday we were enemies in the sphere of foreign relations. Today, however, the situation has changed and we are enemies no longer.

The art of politics in the sphere of foreign relations does not consist in increasing the number of enemies for one's country. On the contrary, the art of politics in this sphere is to reduce the number of such enemies and to make the enemies of yesterday good neighbors, maintaining peaceable relations with one another. . . .

Chapter Six: The Expansion of Communism, 1941-1953

In the critical years of World War II and its aftermath, Communist power moved beyond the boundaries of the USSR and became really international. In most instances, the essential characteristics of the movement remained as they had been fixed during the first decade of Stalinism in Russia, with unrelenting emphasis on industrialization and totalitarian controls. Soviet Russia went through this period with no structural change apart from further tightening of the control system, and Soviet norms were imposed on or accepted by foreign Communists as they came to power in Eastern Europe or the Far East.

In the expansion of Communism after World War II the nature of its appeal and the methods of acquiring power had become quite different from what the movement originally envisaged. Instead of leading a mass revolutionary upsurge the Communists won their new footholds either through wartime national resistance movements or in consequence of Soviet occupation and secret intrigue. Communists have come to power nowhere except in countries where the authority of the old government was actually dissolved in the course of the war. It was no longer the "proletarian revolution" but a military and police usurpation.

Russia in the Second World War

After the German invasion of the USSR in June, 1941, the Communist view of the world was once again revised. Stalin

FROM: Stalin, Speech on the Twenty-Fourth Anniversary of the October Revolution, to the Moscow Soviet and Representatives of Moscow Party and Public Organizations, November 6, 1941 (English translation in Stalin, *On the Great Patriotic War of the Soviet Union*, Moscow, Foreign Languages Publishing House, 1954, pp. 35-37, 44-45).

stressed that Russia was fighting a "patriotic war" to defend the sovereign rights of nations, and hailed the positive aspects of his American and British allies. Revolution was to all intents and purposes ignored.

a) Stalin on the Patriotic War

. . . In our country the German invaders, i.e., the Hitlerites, are usually called fascists. The Hitlerites, it appears, consider this wrong and obstinately persist in calling themselves "National-Socialists." Hence, the Germans are trying to assure us that the Hitler party, the party of German invaders, which is plundering Europe and has engineered this dastardly attack on our socialist country, is a socialist party. Is this possible? What can there be in common between socialism and the bestial Hitler invaders who are plundering and oppressing the peoples of Europe?

Can the Hitlerites be regarded as *nationalists*? No, they cannot. Actually, the Hitlerites are now not nationalists but *imperialists*. As long as the Hitlerites were engaged in assembling the German lands and reuniting the Rhine district, Austria, etc., there might have been some ground for calling them nationalists. But after they seized foreign territories and enslaved European nations—the Czechs, Slovaks, Poles, Norwegians, Danes, Netherlanders, Belgians, the French, Serbs, Greeks, Ukrainians, Byelorussians, the inhabitants of the Baltic countries, etc.—and began to reach out for world domination, the Hitler party ceased to be a nationalist party, for from that moment it became an imperialist, predatory, oppressor party.

The Hitler party is a party of imperialists, and of the most rapacious and predatory imperialists in the world at that.

Can the Hitlerites be regarded as *socialists*? No, they cannot. Actually, the Hitlerites are the sworn enemies of socialism, arrant reactionaries and Black-Hundreds, who have robbed the working class and the peoples of Europe of the most elementary democratic liberties. In order to cover up their reactionary, Black-Hundred nature, the Hitlerites denounce the internal regime of Britain and America as a plutocratic regime. But in Britain and the United States there are elementary democratic liberties, there are trade unions of workers and other employees, there are workers' parties, there are parliaments; whereas in Germany, under the Hitler regime, all these institutions have been destroyed. One need but compare these two sets of facts to perceive the reactionary nature of the Hitler regime and the utter hypocrisy of the German fascist buncombe about a plutocratic regime in Britain and in America. In point of fact the Hitler regime is a copy of the reactionary regime which existed in Russia under tsarism. As we know, the Hitlerites suppress the rights of the workers, the rights of the intellectuals and the rights of nations as readily as the tsarist regime suppressed them; they organize medieval pogroms against the Jews as readily as the tsarist regime did.

The Hitler party is a party of enemies of democratic liberties, a party of medieval reaction and Black-Hundred pogroms. . . .

Lenin distinguished between two kinds of war—predatory, and therefore unjust wars, and wars of liberation, just wars.

The Germans are now waging a predatory war, an unjust war, aimed at seizing foreign territory and subjugating foreign peoples. That is why all honest people must rise against the German invaders, as against an enemy.

Unlike Hitler Germany, the Soviet Union and its Allies are waging a war of liberation, a just war, aimed at liberating the enslaved peoples of Europe and the U.S.S.R. from Hitler's tyranny. That is why all honest people must support the armies of the U.S.S.R., Great Britain, and the other Allies, as armies of liberation.

We have not, and cannot have, any such war aims as the seizure of foreign territories and the subjugation of foreign peoples—whether it be the peoples and territories of Europe or the peoples and territories of Asia, including Iran. Our first aim is to liberate our territories and our peoples from the German fascist yoke.

We have not, and cannot have, any such war aims as that of imposing our will and our regime upon the Slavonic or other enslaved nations of Europe, who are expecting our help. Our aim is to help these nations in the struggle for liberation they are waging against Hitler's tyranny and then to leave it to them quite freely to arrange their lives on their lands as they think fit. There must be no interference whatever in the internal affairs of other nations! . . .

b) *Stalin on the Two Camps*

. . . It may now be regarded as beyond dispute that in the course of the war imposed upon the nations by Hitlerite Germany, a radical demarcation of forces and the formation of two opposite camps have taken place: the camp of the Italo-German coalition, and the camp of the Anglo-Soviet-American coalition.

It is equally beyond dispute that these two opposite coalitions are guided by two different and opposite programmes of action.

The programme of action of the Italo-German coalition may be characterized by the following points: race hatred; domination of the "chosen" nations; subjugation of other nations and seizure of their territories; economic enslavement of the subjugated nations and spoliation of their national wealth; destruction of democratic liberties; universal institution of the Hitler regime.

The programme of action of the Anglo-Soviet-American coalition is: abolition of racial exclusiveness; equality of nations and inviolability of their territories; liberation of the enslaved nations and restoration of their sovereign rights; the right of every nation to manage its affairs in its own way; economic aid to war-ravaged nations and assistance in establishing their material welfare; restoration of democratic liberties; destruction of the Hitler regime. . . .

It is said that the Anglo-Soviet-American coalition has every chance of winning, and would certainly win if it did not

FROM: Stalin, Speech on the Twenty-Fifth Anniversary of the October Revolution, to the Moscow Soviet and Representatives of Moscow Party and Public Organizations, November 6, 1942 (*On the Great Patriotic War of the Soviet Union*, pp. 87-88, 90-91).

suffer from an organic defect which might weaken and disintegrate it. This defect, in the opinion of these people, is that this coalition consists of heterogeneous elements having different ideologies, and that this circumstance will prevent them from organizing joint action against the common enemy.

I think that this assertion is wrong.

It would be ridiculous to deny the difference in the ideologies and social systems of the countries that constitute the Anglo-Soviet-American coalition. But does this preclude the possibility, and the expediency, of joint action on the part of the members of this coalition against the common enemy who threatens to enslave them? Certainly not. Moreover, the very existence of this threat imperatively dictates the necessity of joint action among the members of the coalition in order to save mankind from reversion to savagery and medieval brutality. Is not the programme of action of the Anglo-Soviet-American coalition a sufficient basis upon which to organize a joint struggle against Hitler tyranny and to vanquish it? I think it is quite sufficient. . . .

Dissolution of the Comintern

A specifically antirevolutionary gesture was the dissolution of the Communist International in May, 1943, ostensibly on the grounds that it no longer served the interests of the working-class movement in different countries. Victory over Germany was made the supreme goal of the Communist movement. Nevertheless, postwar events were to show that Soviet authority over the Communist movement continued unabated, and that this authority could again turn the movement in the aggressive direction.

The historic rule of the Communist International, which was founded in 1919 as a result of a political union of the great majority of the old pre-war working-class parties, consisted in upholding the principles of the working-class movement, in helping to promote consolidation in a number of

FROM: Resolution of the Presidium of the Executive Committee of the Communist International, May 22, 1943, proposing the dissolution of the International (English translation in *The Strategy and Tactics of World Communism,* pp. 165-68).

countries of the vanguard of the foremost workers in the real working-class parties, and in helping them mobilize workers for the defense of their economic and political interests, and for the struggle against Fascism and the war which the latter was preparing and for the support of the Soviet Union as the chief bulwark against Fascism.

The Communist International from the first exposed the real meaning of the Anti-Comintern Pact* as a weapon for the preparation of war by the Hitlerites. Long before the war it ceaselessly and tirelessly exposed the vicious, subversive work of the Hitlerites, who masked it by their screams about so-called interference of the Communist International in the internal affairs of these states.

But long before the war it became more and more clear that, with increasing complications in internal and international relations of various countries, any sort of international center would encounter insuperable obstacles in solving the problems facing the movement in each separate country.

Deep differences of the historic paths of development of various countries, differences in their character and even contradictions in their social orders, differences in the level and the tempo of their economic and political development, differences finally in the degree of consciousness and organization of workers, conditioned different problems affecting the working class of the various countries.

The whole development of events in the last quarter of a century and the experience accumulated by the Communist International convincingly showed that the organizational form of uniting workers chosen by the First Congress of the Communist International, answered conditions of the first stages of the working-class movement, but it has been outgrown by the growth of this movement and by the complications of its problems in separate countries and has even become a drag on the further strengthening of the national working class parties.

* Anti-Comintern Pact: treaty of alliance between Germany and Japan, 1936, later extended to include Italy and Germany's lesser allies; ostensibly directed against communism—Ed.

The World War that the Hitlerites have let loose has still further sharpened the differences in the situation of the separate countries and has placed a deep dividing line between those countries that fell under the Hitlerite tyranny and those freedom-loving peoples who have united in a powerful anti-Hitlerite coalition.

In countries of the Hitlerite bloc the fundamental task of the working class, toilers and all honest people consists in giving all help for the defeat of this bloc by sabotage of the Hitlerite military machine from within and by helping to overthrow the governments guilty of war.

In countries of the anti-Hitlerite coalition the sacred duty of the widest masses of the people, and in the first place of foremost workers, consists in aiding by every means the military efforts of the governments of these countries aimed at the speediest defeat of [the] Hitlerite bloc and the assurance of the friendship of nations based on their equality. . . .

. . . Taking into account the growth and the political maturity of Communist parties and their leading cadres in separate countries and also having in view the fact that during the present war some sections have raised the question of the dissolution of the Communist International as the directing center of the international working-class movement, the Presidium of the Executive Committee of the Communist International, in the circumstances of the World War, not being able to convene a Congress of the Communist International, puts forth the following proposal for ratification by the sections of the Communist International:

The Communist International, as the directing center of the international working-class movement, is to be dissolved, thus freeing the sections of the Communist International from their obligations arising from the statutes and resolutions of the Congresses of the Communist International.

The Presidium of the Executive Committee of the Communist International calls on all supporters of the Communist International to concentrate their energies on the whole-hearted support of and active participation in the war of liberation of the peoples and the states of the anti-Hitlerite coalition for the speediest defeat of the deadly enemy of the working class and toilers—German Fascism and its associates and vassals.

Guerrilla Revolution—the Yugoslav Partisans

In German-occupied Yugoslavia the Communist Party under Josip Broz Tito won a dominant place in the guerrilla resistance movement. These "Partisans" denounced the monarchy and fought its supporters, though for the time being they denied plans of Communist revolution. When Germany collapsed Yugoslavia was effectively under one-party Communist control, and the reorganization of the country's political and economic life rapidly followed.

a) Statement of the Second Assembly of the Anti-Fascist Council of National Liberation

(a) The so-called Yugoslav Government abroad is deprived of all the rights of a legal Government, as also of the rights of representing the peoples of Yugoslavia in foreign countries.

(b) King Peter II Karadjordjević is forbidden to return to the country until after the liberation of the entire country, when the problem of the king as well as the question of monarchy can be decided.

(c) It is recommended that the Anti-Fascist National Council should re-examine all international treaties or obligations undertaken by the so-called Yugoslav Government abroad.

(d) International treaties or obligations which may in future be contracted by the fugitive Yugoslav Government in the name of Yugoslavia and of her peoples will not be recognized.

FROM: Statement issued by the Second Assembly of the Anti-Fascist Council of National Liberation, Jajce (Bosnia), November 29, 1943 (English translation in *Free Europe*, December 31, 1943, p. 222; reprinted in *Documents on International Affairs, 1939-1946* (London, Royal Institute of International Affairs and Oxford University Press), Vol. II: "Hitler's Europe," p. 334).

b) *Declaration by the National Liberation Committee of Yugoslavia*

The National Liberation Movement, since the very beginning of our struggle against the occupier, endeavoured to unite all the national forces. The leaders of this movement always placed the cause of the liberation of the country from the barbarous Fascist invaders above all other interests of particular political and social groups and classes. For this reason, while the most sanguinary battles with the occupiers and their henchmen were raging, all efforts were made to enable those who love their people and freedom to assemble in one united front of national liberation. These efforts were crowned with success. A United Front of National Liberation, embracing a great majority of the population of Yugoslavia, became the basis of the armed resistance of the entire nation against the occupier, the basis on which the partisan detachments developed and the regular units of the Army of National Liberation of Yugoslavia were formed.

For over two and a half years the true forces of resistance in Yugoslavia witnessed with great bitterness how all the emigrant governments, one after the other, instead of helping the superhuman struggle of the peoples of Yugoslavia for the freedom of their country, stubbornly continued in their hostile attitude towards the National Liberation Movement, and through their Minister Draža Mihajlović waged an armed struggle against their own people at the side of the occupier. The peoples' representatives at the second session of the Anti-Fascist Council of November 29, 1943, in their resolutions condemned the treacherous work of the émigré governments and, expressing the strivings of all the peoples of Yugoslavia, issued historical resolutions on the creation of a federative democratic Yugoslavia.

The National Liberation Movement of Yugoslavia is in its

FROM: Declaration by the National Liberation Committee of Yugoslavia, August, 1944 (English translation in *Free Europe*, September 8, 1944, p. 75; reprinted in *Documents on International Affairs, 1939-1946*, Vol. II: "Hitler's Europe," pp. 337-38).

essence a movement which has been endorsed by the entire people, and is both national and democratic. Therefore, we must emphasise once more that the leaders of the Movement of National Liberation of Yugoslavia have before them one single important aim: to fight against the occupiers and their lackeys and build up a federative democratic Yugoslavia, and not—as our enemies accuse us—the aim of introducing Communism.

Stalin's War Aims

Until the end of World War II Stalin expressed hope for permanent postwar coöperation with the United States and Britain. The menace of Germany still loomed far greater in his thinking than the prospects of Communist expansion.

. . . The past year has witnessed the triumph of the common cause of the anti-German coalition, for the sake of which the peoples of the Soviet Union, Great Britain, and the United States of America have united in a fighting alliance. . . .

. . . There is talk of disagreements among the three powers on certain questions concerning security. Of course there are disagreements, and there will be on a number of other questions too. Disagreements even exist among people who belong to the same party. How much more so must this be the case among representatives of different countries and different parties. The surprising thing is not that differences exist, but that there are so few, and that these are, as a rule, settled almost every time in a spirit of unity and coordination of action of the three Great Powers. It is not the disagreements that count, but the fact that they do not go beyond the limits dictated by the interests of unity among the three Great Powers, and that, in the final analysis, they are settled in conformity with the interests of this unity. It is common

FROM: Stalin, Speech on the Twenty-Seventh Anniversary of the October Revolution, to the Moscow Soviet and Representatives of Moscow Party and Public Organizations, November 6, 1944 (*On the Great Patriotic War of the Soviet Union*, pp. 200-205, 207-8).

knowledge that more serious disagreements existed among us on the question of opening the second front. It is known, however, that, in the final analysis, these disagreements were settled in the spirit of complete harmony. . . .

Since the fighting alliance of the democratic countries has stood the test of over three years of war, and since this alliance is sealed with the blood of the peoples who have risen to defend their freedom and honour, there can be no doubt that it will stand the test of the concluding stage of the war. (Prolonged applause) . . .

To win the war against Germany means consummating a great historical cause. But winning the war does not yet mean ensuring the peoples a durable peace and reliable security in the future. The task is not only to win the war, but also to prevent the outbreak of fresh aggression and another war, if not for ever, then at least for a long time to come.

After her defeat Germany will, of course, be disarmed economically, as well as militarily and politically. It would be naive to think, however, that she will make no attempt to recuperate her strength and embark on new aggression. It is common knowledge that the German rulers are already making preparations for another war. History shows that quite a short period, a matter of twenty or thirty years, is sufficient to enable Germany to recover from defeat and recuperate her strength. What means are available to prevent fresh aggression on Germany's part and, if war breaks out nevertheless, to strangle it at the very outset and prevent it from developing into a big war? . . .

Apart from the complete disarming of aggressor nations there is only one means of achieving this: to set up a special organization consisting of representatives of the peaceful nations, for the protection of peace and for ensuring security; to place at the disposal of the leading body of this organization the minimum of armed forces necessary to prevent aggression; and to make it the duty of this organization to utilize these armed forces without delay, in the event of necessity, to prevent or liquidate aggression and punish those responsible for it.

This must not be a replica of the League of Nations of sad

memory, which possessed neither the powers nor the means with which to prevent aggression. It will be a new, special, fully-empowered international organization, which will have at its disposal all that is necessary for protecting peace and preventing fresh aggression.

Can we count on the activities of this international organization being sufficiently effective? They will be effective if the Great Powers who have borne the brunt of the burden of the war against Hitler Germany continue to act in a spirit of unanimity and harmony. They will not be effective if this essential condition is violated. . . .

Stalin on Poland

When Soviet troops moved into the countries of Eastern Europe in 1944, the Soviet government began to maneuver local Communists into positions of power, ostensibly in the name of creating "friendly" and "democratic" regimes. With respect to Poland, Stalin made it clear to his allies at the time of the Yalta Conference that he intended to back the Communist-dominated "Committee of National Liberation" in opposition to the authority of the London government-in-exile, though he did promise free elections in the future.

The Polish National Committee has made serious achievements in the strengthening of the Polish state and the apparatus of governmental power in the territory of Poland, in the expansion and strengthening of the Polish army, in carrying into practice of a number of important governmental measures and, in the first place, of the agrarian reform in favor of the peasants. All this has lead to consolidation of democratic powers of Poland and to powerful strengthening of authority of the National Committee among the wide masses in Poland and among wide social Polish circles abroad.

It seems to me that now we should be interested in the support of the Polish National Committee and all those who

FROM: Stalin to President Roosevelt, December 27, 1944 (in *Foreign Relations of the United States: The Conferences at Malta and Yalta, 1945* (U. S. House of Representatives Document No. 154, 84th Congress, 1st Session), Washington, Government Printing Office, 1955, pp. 221-22).

want and are capable to work together with it and that is especially important for the Allies and for the solution of our common task—the speeding of the defeat of Hitlerite Germany. For the Soviet Union, which is bearing the whole burden for the liberation of Poland from German occupationists, the question of relations with Poland under present conditions is the task of daily close and friendly relations with a power which has been established by the Polish people on its own soil and which has already grown strong and has its own army which together with the Red Army is fighting against the Germans.

I have to say frankly that if the Polish Committee of National Liberation will transform itself into a Provisional Polish Government then, in view of the above-said, the Soviet Government will not have any serious ground for postponement of the question of its recognition. It is necessary to bear in mind that in the strengthening of a pro-Allied and democratic Poland the Soviet Union is interested more than any other power not only because the Soviet Union is bearing the main brunt of the battle for liberation of Poland but also because Poland is a border state with the Soviet Union and the problem of Poland is inseparable from the problem of security of the Soviet Union. To this we have to add that the successes of the Red Army in Poland in the fight against the Germans are to a great degree dependent on the presence of a peaceful and trustworthy rear in Poland, and the Polish National Committee fully takes into account this circumstance while the *émigré* government and its underground agents by their terroristic actions are creating a threat of civil war in the rear of the Red Army and counteract the success of the latter. . . .

Stalin on the Great-Russians

One aspect of Stalin's later conservatism was his acknowledgment of the national pride of the "Great-Russian" (i.e., Russian-speaking) majority of the Soviet population, together with considerable Russification of the cultures of the minorities. At the close of World War II Stalin singled out the Great-Russians to credit them with the victory.

Comrades, permit me to propose another toast, the last one.

I would like to propose that we drink to the health of the Soviet people, and primarily of the Russian people. (Loud and prolonged applause and cheers)

I drink primarily to the health of the Russian people because it is the most outstanding of all the nations that constitute the Soviet Union.

I drink to the health of the Russian people, because, during this war, it has earned universal recognition as the guiding force of the Soviet Union among all the peoples of our country.

I drink to the health of the Russian people, not only because it is the leading people, but also because it is gifted with a clear mind, a staunch character, and patience.

Our Government committed no few mistakes; at times our position was desperate, as in 1941-42, when our army was retreating, abandoning our native villages and towns in the Ukraine, Byelorussia, Moldavia, the Leningrad Region, the Baltic Region, and the Karelo-Finnish Republic, abandoning them because there was no other alternative. Another people might have said to the government: You have not come up to our expectations. Get out. We shall appoint another government, which will conclude peace with Germany and ensure tranquillity for us. But the Russian people did not do that, for they were confident that the policy their Government was pursuing was correct; and they made sacrifices in order to ensure the defeat of Germany. And this confidence which the Russian people displayed in the Soviet Government proved to be the decisive factor which ensured our historic victory over the enemy of mankind, over fascism.

I thank the Russian people for this confidence!

To the health of the Russian people! (Loud and prolonged applause)

FROM: Stalin, Speech at the Reception in the Kremlin in Honour of the Commanders of the Red Army Troops, May 24, 1945 (*On the Great Patriotic War of the Soviet Union*, pp. 241-42).

The Revival of International Communism

The Communist Party of the United States provided an extreme example of the subordination of revolution to considerations of winning the war and assuring the peace. In May, 1945, Jacques Duclos, second-in-command of the French Communist Party, published an attack on Earl Browder's reformist perspective which led to Browder's replacement by William Z. Foster as the American Communist leader, and signaled the revival of militance throughout the international Communist movement.

The Teheran Conference [of Roosevelt, Churchill, and Stalin, December, 1943] served as Browder's point of departure from which to develop his conceptions favorable to a change of course in the American Communist Party. However, while justly stressing the importance of the Teheran Conference for victory in the war against fascist Germany, Earl Browder drew from the Conference decisions erroneous conclusions in no wise flowing from a Marxist analysis of the situation. Earl Browder made himself the protagonist of a false concept of the ways of social evolution in general, and in the first place, the social evolution of the U.S.

Earl Browder declared, in effect, that at Teheran capitalism and socialism had begun to find the means of peaceful co-existence and collaboration in the framework of one and the same world; he added that the Teheran accords regarding common policy similarly pre-supposed common efforts with a view of reducing to a minimum or completely suppressing methods of struggle and opposition of force to force in the solution of internal problems of each country. . . .

The Teheran agreements mean to Earl Browder that the greatest part of Europe, west of the Soviet Union, will probably be reconstituted on a bourgeois democratic basis and not on a fascist-capitalist or Soviet basis.

"But it will be a capitalist basis which is conditioned by the principle of complete democratic self-determination for

FROM: Duclos, "On the Dissolution of the Communist Party of the United States" (*Daily Worker*, May 24, 1945).

each nation, allowing full expression within each nation of all progressive and constructive forces and setting up no obstacles to the development of democracy and social progress in accordance with the varying desires of the peoples. It means a perspective for Europe minimizing, and to a great extent eliminating altogether, the threat of civil war after the international war.". . .

And Earl Browder adds: "Whatever may be the situation in other lands, in the United States this means a perspective in the immediate postwar period of expanded production and employment and the strengthening of democracy within the framework of the present system—and not a perspective of the transition to socialism.

"We can set our goal as the realization of the Teheran policy, or we can set ourselves the task of pushing the United States immediately into socialism. Clearly, however, we cannot choose both.

"The first policy, with all its difficulties, is definitely within the realm of possible achievement. The second would be dubious, indeed, especially when we remember that even the most progressive section of the labor movement is committed to capitalism, is not even as vaguely socialistic as the British Labor Party.

"Therefore, the policy for Marxists in the United States is to face with all its consequences the perspective of a capitalist postwar reconstruction in the United States, to evaluate all plans on that basis, and to collaborate actively with the most democratic and progressive majority in the country, in a national unity sufficiently broad and effective to realize the policies of Teheran." . . .

1. The course applied under Browder's leadership ended in practice in liquidation of the independent political party of the working class in the U.S.

2. Despite declarations regarding recognition of the principles of Marxism, one is witnessing a notorious revision of Marxism on the part of Browder and his supporters, a revision which is expressed in the concept of a long-term class peace in the United States, of the possibility of the suppres-

sion of the class struggle in the postwar period and of establishment of harmony between labor and capital. . . .

Nationalization of monopolies actually in no sense constitutes a socialist achievement, contrary to what certain people would be inclined to believe. No, in nationalization it is simply a matter of reforms of a democratic character, achievement of socialism being impossible to imagine without preliminary conquest of power.

Everyone understands that the Communists of the United States want to work to achieve unity in their country. But it is less understandable that they envisage the solution of the problems of national unity with the good will of the men of the trusts, and under quasi-idyllic conditions as if the capitalist regime had been able to change its nature by some unknown miracle.

In truth, nothing justifies the dissolution of the American Communist Party, in our opinion. Browder's analysis of capitalism in the United States is not distinguished by a judicious application of Marxism-Leninism. The predictions regarding a sort of disappearance of class contradictions in the United States correspond in no wise to a Marxist-Leninist understanding of the situation. . . .

It is scarcely necessary to recall that the material bases for fascism reside in the trusts, and the great objective of this war, the annihilation of fascism, can only be obtained to the extent in which the forces of democracy and progress do not shut their eyes to the economic and political circumstances which engendered fascism.

The American Communists have an especially important role to play in the struggle taking place between the progressive forces of the earth and the fascist barbarism.

Without any doubt they would have been in a better position to play this role in the interests of their country and human progress if, instead of proceeding to dissolve their Party, they had done everything to strengthen it and make of it one of the elements of the assembling of the broad democratic masses of the United States for the final crushing of fascism, that shame of the 20th Century. It would be useless to hide the fact that fascism has more or less concealed sympathizers in the United States, as it has in France and other countries. . . .

Stalin's Analysis of Victory

In February, 1946, Stalin took the occasion of a "campaign" meeting preceding the usual single-slate election to suggest a Marxist explanation of the war and to claim vindication of his policies of intensive industrialization, collectivization, and purging.

. . . It would be wrong to think that the Second World War was a casual occurrence or the result of mistakes of any particular statesmen, though mistakes undoubtedly were made. Actually, the war was the inevitable result of the development of world economic and political forces on the basis of modern monopoly capitalism. Marxists have declared more than once that the capitalist system of world economy harbors elements of general crises and armed conflicts and that, hence, the development of world capitalism in our time proceeds not in the form of smooth and even progress but through crises and military catastrophes. . . .

. . . Unlike the First World War, the Second World War against the Axis states from the very outset assumed the character of an anti-fascist war, a war of liberation, one the aim of which was also the restoration of democratic liberties. The entry of the Soviet Union into the war against the Axis states could only enhance, and indeed did enhance, the anti-fascist and liberation character of the Second World War.

It was on this basis that the anti-fascist coalition of the Soviet Union, the United States of America, Great Britain and other freedom-loving states came into being—a coalition which subsequently played a decisive part in defeating the armed forces of the Axis states. . . .

Our victory means, first of all, that our Soviet social order

FROM: Stalin, Pre-Election Speech of February 9, 1946 (English translation in *The Strategy and Tactics of World Communism*, pp. 168-78).

has triumphed, that the Soviet social order has successfully passed the ordeal in the fire of war and has proved its unquestionable vitality. . . .

. . . The point now is that the Soviet social order has shown itself more stable and capable of enduring than a non-Soviet social order, that the Soviet social order is a form of organization, a society superior to any non-Soviet social order. . . .

Of course, victory cannot be achieved without gallantry. But gallantry alone is not enough to vanquish an enemy who has a large army, first-class armaments, well-trained officer cadres, and a fairly good organization of supplies. To meet the blow of such an enemy, to repulse him and then to inflict utter defeat upon him required, in addition to the matchless gallantry of our troops, fully up-to-date armaments and adequate quantities of them as well as well-organized supplies in sufficient quantities.

But that, in turn, necessitated having—and in adequate amounts—such elementary things as metal for the manufacture of armaments, equipment and machinery for factories, fuel to keep the factories and transport going, cotton for the manufacture of uniforms, and grain for supplying the Army.

Can it be claimed that before entering the Second World War our country already commanded the necessary minimum material potentialities for satisfying all these requirements in the main? I think it can. In order to prepare for this tremendous job we had to carry out three Five-Year Plans of national economic development. It was precisely these three Five-Year Plans that helped us to create these material potentialities. At any rate, our country's position in this respect before the Second World War, in 1940, was several times better than it was before the First World War, in 1913. . . .

Such an unprecedented increase in production cannot be regarded as the simple and usual development of a country from backwardness to progress. It was a leap by which our Motherland was transformed from a backward into an advanced country, from an agrarian into an industrial country. . . .

By what policy did the Communist Party succeed in providing these material potentialities in the country in such a short time?

First of all, by the Soviet policy of industrializing the country.

The Soviet method of industrializing the country differs radically from the capitalist method of industrialization. In capitalist countries industrialization usually begins with light industry. . . .

. . . Naturally, the Communist Party could not take this course. The Party knew that a war was looming, that the country could not be defended without heavy industry, that the development of heavy industry must be undertaken as soon as possible, that to be behind with this would mean to lose out. The Party remembered Lenin's words to the effect that without heavy industry it would be impossible to uphold the country's independence, that without it the Soviet order might perish.

Accordingly the Communist Party of our country rejected the "usual" course of industrialization and began the work of industrializing the country by developing heavy industry. It was very difficult, but not impossible. A valuable aid in this work was the nationalization of industry and banking, which made possible the rapid accumulation and transfer of funds to heavy industry.

There can be no doubt that without this it would have been impossible to secure our country's transformation into an industrial country in such a short time.

Second, by a policy of collectivization of agriculture.

In order to do away with our backwardness in agriculture and to provide the country with greater quantities of marketable grain, cotton, and so forth, it was essential to pass from small-scale peasant farming to large-scale farming, for only large-scale farming can make use of new machinery, apply all the achievements of agronomical science and yield greater quantities of marketable produce.

There are, however, two kinds of large farms—capitalist and collective. The Communist Party could not adopt the capitalist path of development of agriculture, and not as a matter of principle alone but also because it implies too prolonged a development and involves preliminary ruination of the peasants and their transformation into farm hands. Therefore, the Communist Party took the path of the collectivization of agriculture, the path of creating large-scale farming by uniting peasant farms into collective farms.

The method of collectivization proved a highly progressive method not only because it did not involve the ruination of the peasants but especially because it permitted, within a few years, the covering of the entire country with large collective farms which are able to use new machinery, take advantage of all the achievements of agronomic science and give the country greater quantities of marketable produce.

There is no doubt that without a collectivization policy we could not in such a short time have done away with the age-old backwardness of our agriculture.

It cannot be said that the Party's policy encountered no resistance. Not only backward people, such as always decry everything new, but many prominent members of the Party as well, systematically dragged the Party backward and tried by hook or by crook to divert it to the "usual" capitalist path of development. All the anti-Party machinations of the Trotskyites and the Rightists, all their "activities" in sabotaging the measures of our Government, pursued the single aim of frustrating the Party's policy and obstructing the work of industrialization and collectivization. But the Party did not yield either to the threats from one side or the wails from the other and advanced confidently regardless of everything. . . .

The Communist Party's plans of work for the immediate future . . . are set forth in the new Five-Year Plan which is shortly to be endorsed. The principal aims of the new Five-Year Plan are to rehabilitate the ravaged areas of the country, to restore the prewar level in industry and agriculture, and then to surpass this level in more or less substantial measure. To say nothing of the fact that the rationing system will shortly be abolished (*stormy, prolonged applause*), special attention will be devoted to extending the production of consumer goods, to raising the living standard of the working people by steadily lowering the prices of all goods (*stormy, prolonged applause*), and to the widespread construction of all manner of scientific research institutions (*applause*) that can give science the opportunity to develop its potentialities. (*Stormy applause*)

I have no doubt that if we give our scientists proper assistance they will be able in the near future not only to overtake but to surpass the achievements of science beyond the boundaries of our country. (*Prolonged applause*)

As regards the plans for a longer period ahead, the Party means to organize a new mighty upsurge in the national economy, which would allow us to increase our industrial production, for example, three times over as compared with the prewar period. We must achieve a situation where our industry can produce annually up to 50 million tons of pig iron (*prolonged applause*), up to 60 million tons of steel (*prolonged applause*), up to 500 million tons of coal (*prolonged applause*) and up to 60 million tons of oil. (*Prolonged applause*) Only under such conditions can we consider that our homeland will be guaranteed against all possible accidents. (*Stormy applause*) That will take three more Five-Year Plans, I should think, if not more. But it can be done and we must do it. (*Stormy applause*)

Such is my brief report on the Communist Party's work in the recent past and its plans of work for the future.

It is for you to judge how correctly the Party has been working and whether it could not have worked better. . . .

. . . The Communist Party is prepared to accept the electors' verdict. (*Stormy applause*)

In the election struggle the Communist Party is not alone. It goes to the polls in a bloc with non-Party people. In bygone days the Communists treated non-Party people and non-Party status with some mistrust. This was due to the fact that the non-Party flag was not infrequently used as a camouflage by various bourgeois groups for whom it was not advantageous to face the electorate without a mask.

That was the case in the past. But now we have different times. Our non-Party people are now divided from the bourgeoisie by a barrier known as the Soviet social order. This same barrier unites non-Party people with the Communists in a single community of Soviet men and women. Living in this single community they struggled together to build up the might of our country, fought and shed their blood together on the battle fronts for the sake of our country, and in greatness worked together to forge a victory over the enemies of our country and did forge that victory. The only difference between them is that some belong to the Party, others do not. But that is a formal difference. The important thing is that both are furthering the same common cause. Therefore the bloc of Communists and non-Party people is a natural and vital thing. (*Stormy, prolonged applause*)

In conclusion, allow me to thank you for the confidence you have shown me (*prolonged, unabating applause; shout from the audience: "Hurrah for the great captain of all victories, Comrade Stalin!"*) in nominating me to the Supreme Soviet. You need not doubt that I shall do my best to justify your trust.

(*All rise. Prolonged, unabating applause turning into an ovation. From all parts of the hall come cheers: "Long live our great Stalin! Hurrah!" "Hurrah for the great leader of the peoples!" "Glory to the great Stalin!" "Long live Comrade Stalin, the candidate of the entire nation!" "Glory to Comrade Stalin, the creator of all our victories!"*)

The Zhdanov Movement

Stalin's heir apparent from the end of the war until his death in 1948 was Andrei Zhdanov, who figured particularly in the ideological sphere. In August, 1946, Zhdanov launched an intensive campaign of ideological retightening, in a savage attack on certain writers and literary journals for allowing themselves to fall under "bourgeois" influences. Such criticism was then extended to virtually every other field of culture and learning, and from this time until Stalin's death Soviet intellectual life experienced its most regimented and barren period.

. . . We demand that our comrades, both as leaders in literary affairs and as writers, be guided by the vital force of the Soviet order—its politics. Only thus can our youth be reared, not in a devil-may-care attitude and a spirit of ideological indifference, but in a strong and vigorous revolutionary spirit.

It is known that Leninism incarnated all the best traditions of the Russian revolutionary democrats of the nineteenth century and that our Soviet culture has risen, developed, and flowered on the basis of a critical working over of the cultural heritage of the past. In the sphere of literature our Party, through the words of Lenin and Stalin, has recognized more than once the tremendous significance of the great Russian revolutionary-democratic writers and critics—Belinsky, Dobroliubov, Chernyshevsky, Saltykov-Shchedrin, and Plekhanov. Beginning with Belinsky, all of the best representatives of the revolutionary-democratic Russian intelligentsia repudiated so-called "pure art" and "art for art's sake." They were heralds of art for the people, of art of high ideological and social significance. Art cannot separate itself from the fate of the people. . . .

V. I. Lenin was the first to formulate with utmost precision the attitude of advanced social thought toward literature and art. I remind you of Lenin's well-known article, "Party Organization and Party Literature," written at the end of 1905, in which he showed with characteristic force that literature cannot be non-Party, that it must be an important component part of the general proletarian cause. In this article Lenin lays the foundations on which the development of our Soviet literature is based. He wrote as follows:

"Literature must become Party. As a counterpoise to bourgeois morals, to the bourgeois commercial press, to bourgeois literary careerism and individualism, to 'manorial anarchism' and the pursuit of gain, the socialist proletariat must promote and develop the principle of *Party literature*

FROM: Zhdanov, Report to the Leningrad Branch of the Union of Soviet Writers and the Leningrad City Committee of the Communist Party, August 21, 1946 (English translation in George S. Counts and Nucia Lodge, *The Country of the Blind: the Soviet System of Mind Control*, Boston, Houghton Mifflin, 1949, pp. 86-90, 95-96; reprinted by permission of the publisher).

and bring this principle to life in the most complete and integral form possible. . . ."

Leninism proceeds from the fact that our literature cannot be politically indifferent, cannot be "art for art's sake." On the contrary, it is called upon to play an important leading role in social life.

From this position issues the Leninist principle of partisanship in literature—a most important contribution of V. I. Lenin to the science of literature. . . .

Leninism recognizes the tremendous socially-transforming significance of our literature. For our Soviet literature to permit a lowering of its vast educational role would mean a development backward, a return "to the stone age."

Comrade Stalin called our writers engineers of human souls. This definition has profound meaning. It speaks of the enormous responsibility of Soviet writers for the education of the people and for the education of Soviet youth. It says that wastage in literary work is intolerable. . . .

Recently large gaps and weaknesses have been exposed on the ideological front. It suffices to remind you of the backwardness of our cinema, of the littering of our theatrical-dramatic repertoire with inferior productions, not to mention what happened in the journals *Zvezda* ["star"] and *Leningrad.* The Central Committee was compelled to interfere and introduce decisive corrections. It had no right to soften its blow against those who forget their obligations to the people and for the education of the young. If we want to turn the attention of our active members to questions of ideological work and bring order here, if we want to give clear direction in this work, we must be quick, as befits Soviet people and Bolsheviks, to criticize mistakes and weaknesses in ideological work. Only then will we be able to correct matters. . . .

Our successes within our country as well as in the international arena do not please the bourgeois world. As a result of the second world war the positions of socialism have been strengthened. The question of socialism has been placed on the order of the day in many countries of Europe. This is unpleasant to imperialists of all colors. They are afraid of socialism. They fear socialism and our socialist country, which is a model for all progressive mankind. Imperialists and their ideological servants, their writers and journalists, their politicians and diplomats, strive in every way to defame our country, to present it in a wrong light, to slander socialism. Under these conditions the task of Soviet literature is not only to reply, blow for blow, to all this base calumny and to the assaults on our Soviet culture and on socialism, but also to lash out boldly and attack bourgeois culture which is in a state of emaciation and depravity.

However outwardly beautiful the form that clothes the creative work of the fashionable contemporary bourgeois West-European and American writers, and also film and theatrical producers, still they can neither redeem nor lift up their bourgeois culture. That culture is putrid and baneful in its moral foundations. It has been put at the service of private capitalist property, at the service of the egoistic and selfish interests of the highest stratum of bourgeois society. The entire host of bourgeois writers, of film and theatrical producers, is striving to divert the attention of the advanced strata of society from acute questions of the political and social struggle and to shift attention into the channel of vulgar and ideologically empty literature and art, crowded with gangsters, chorus girls, praise of adultery, and the affairs of adventurers and rogues of every kind.

Is the role of worshipers or pupils of bourgeois culture becoming to us, Soviet patriots and representatives of the most advanced Soviet culture? Certainly our literature, which reflects a social order higher than any bourgeois-democratic order and a culture many times higher than bourgeois culture, has the right to teach others this new universal morality. Where will you find such people and such a country as ours? Where will you find the magnificent qualities which our people displayed in the Great Patriotic War and which they display in their daily work as they pass to the peaceful restoration and development of economy and culture? Every day our people rise higher and ever higher. Today we are not what we were yesterday, and tomorrow we shall not be as we are today. Already we are not the same Russians we were before 1917, our Russia is different, our character is not the same. We have changed and grown along with the great reforms which have profoundly changed the face of our country.

To reveal these new high qualities of Soviet persons, not only to reveal our people in their today, but also to give a glimpse of them in their tomorrow, to help light the way ahead with a searchlight—such is the task of every conscientious Soviet writer. The writer cannot trudge along at the tail of events; he must march in the front ranks of the people, pointing out to them the road of their development. Guided by the method of socialist realism, studying conscientiously and attentively our reality, striving to penetrate more deeply into the essence of the processes of our development, the writer must educate the people and arm them ideologically. While selecting the best sentiments and qualities of Soviet man and revealing his tomorrow, we must at the same time show our people what they must not be and scourge the vestiges of yesterday, vestiges which hamper the Soviet people in their forward march. Soviet writers must assist the people, the state, and the Party in the education of our youth to be cheerful, confident of their own strength, and fearful of no difficulties. . . .

The "People's Democracies"

Between 1945 and 1947 the local Communist parties were given positions of decisive political influence throughout Soviet-occupied Eastern Europe, although there were no mass upheavals and usually no overt overthrow of governments. Since the resulting regimes did not conform to the Soviet political pattern they were something of a theoretical embarrassment. The Hungarian-born Soviet economist Eugene Varga expounded the official explanation of these satellite states as transitional societies whose socialist direction was assured by the new quality of their governments.

One of the most important political results of the Second World War is the emergence of democratic states of a new type: Yugoslavia, Bulgaria, Poland, Czechoslovakia and, also, Albania. We understand by a "democracy of a new type" a state of affairs in a country where feudal remnants—large-scale landownership—have been eliminated, where the system of private ownership of the means of production still exists but large enterprises in the spheres of industry, transport and credit are in state hands, while the state itself and its apparatus of coercion serve not the interests of a monopolistic bourgeoisie but the interests of the working people in town and countryside.

The social structure of these states differs from all those hitherto known to us; it is something totally new in the history of mankind. It is neither a bourgeois dictatorship nor a proletarian dictatorship. The old state apparatus has not been smashed, as in the Soviet Union, but re-organized by means of a continuous inclusion in it of the supporters of the new regime. They are not capitalist states in the ordinary sense of the word. Neither, however, are they Socialist states. The basis for their transition to Socialism is given by the nationalization of the most important means of production and by the essential character of the state. They may, with the maintenance of the present state apparatus, gradually pass over to Socialism, developing to an ever-increasing extent the socialist sector which already exists side by side with the simple commodity sector (peasant and artisan) and the capitalist sector, which has lost its dominant position. . . .

The change in the character of the state—its transformation from a weapon of domination in the hands of the propertied classes into the state of the working people—this is what determines the real significance of the transfer of a decisive part of the means of production into the hands of the state in the countries of a democracy of a new type.

The change in the character of the state explains also why the influence of nationalization on the distribution of the national revenue is totally different in the democratic states of a new type from that in the bourgeois-democratic countries such as Great Britain.

FROM: Varga, "Democracy of a New Type" (English translation in *The Labour Monthly*, August-September, 1947; reprinted by permission).

Nationalization in the new democratic states signifies a special sort of economic revolution. The property of traitors to the country, of fascist capitalists, was confiscated without compensation. Other big capitalists received compensation, but their income after compensation was only a small part of the surplus value which they previously appropriated. . . .

The second important feature of the economies of the countries of democracy of a new type is the complete and final elimination of large-scale landlordism, of this feudal survival inside the capitalist system of economy. The social and political power of the big landowners, dating back a thousand years, has been destroyed. The big landed properties were confiscated by the state and distributed among peasants having little land and landless agricultural laborers. The number of peasants households (i.e., private owners of land) increased very considerably in these countries.

The division of the lands among many hundreds of thousands of peasants who had little or no land has converted the overwhelming majority of these peasants into loyal supporters of the new regime. The mistake made by the Hungarian Communists in 1919, when they wanted to leap over an essential historical stage by converting the confiscated large landed properties into state farms, instead of dividing them up among the peasants and so satisfying the land hunger, has nowhere been repeated.

The cultivation of land by the peasants using their own resources and giving them the opportunity of selling their produce on the market (in some countries only after fulfilling tax payments and deliveries to the state) make possible the preservation or re-emergence of commodity capitalist relations in the economy of the country. As Lenin pointed out, "Small-scale production engenders capitalism and the bourgeoisie continuously, daily, hourly, spontaneously and on a mass scale."

Thus, the social order in the states of democracy of a new type is not a socialist order, but a peculiar, new, transitional form. The contradiction between the productive forces and relations of production becomes mitigated in proportion as the relative weight of the socialist sector increases. . . .

As regards the class struggle, however, there exists a difference in principle between the states of democracy of a new type and the old bourgeois countries. In the old bourgeois countries the state is a weapon of domination in the hands of the propertied classes. The entire state apparatus—officials, judges, police and as a last resort, the standing army—is on the side of the propertied classes.

The opposite is to be seen in the countries of new democracy. Here the state protects the interests of the working people against those who live by appropriating surplus value. When conflicts arise the armed forces of the State are to be found, not on the side of the capitalists, but on the side of the workers. . . .

In this connection an important theoretical question arises: the idea was widely held in the Communist parties that the political domination of the working people, as is the case in the Soviet Union, could only be realized in the form of soviet power. This is not correct, nor is it an expression of Lenin's opinion. . . .

The rise of the states of new democracy shows clearly that it is possible to have political rule by the working people even while the outward forms of parliamentary democracy are still maintained. . . .

It is equally understandable that these countries maintain close, friendly relations with the Soviet Union. This is so not only because it was precisely the victorious troops of the Soviet Union that liberated their countries (Yugoslavia being, in part, an exception) from German occupation, and not only because they are all Slav states, but primarily because the present social order brings them close to the Soviet Union, because of all the great powers the Soviet Union alone is interested in the maintenance and further progressive development of the social order and political regime existing in these countries and can afford them diplomatic support against the reactionary offensive from outside.

The Soviet Union is at the same time interested in the maintenance by these countries of the existing regime and their further development in a progressive direction. The present regime in these countries provides the guarantee that they will not, in the future, again voluntarily serve as a *place d'armes* for any power which tries to attack the Soviet Union. . . .

The "Cold War" and the Cominform

By 1947 the Communist international line had become aggressively anti-Western. A new international Communist center, the so-called "Communist Information Bureau," was organized to link the Communist parties of the Soviet Union and the East European states together with the two powerful Western Communist parties, the French and Italian. Speaking at the founding conference of the Cominform, Zhdanov recast the Communist view of World War II and represented the current world situation as a bitter contest between the "socialist camp" and "American imperialism."

The end of the Second World War brought with it big changes in the world situation. The military defeat of the bloc of fascist states, the character of the war as a war of liberation from fascism, and the decisive role played by the Soviet Union in the vanquishing of the fascist aggressors sharply altered the alignment of forces between the two systems—the Socialist and the Capitalist—in favour of Socialism.

What is the essential nature of these changes?

The principal outcome of World War II was the military defeat of Germany and Japan—the two most militaristic and aggressive of the capitalist countries. The reactionary imperialist elements all over the world, notably in Britain, America and France, had reposed great hopes in Germany and Japan, and chiefly in Hitler Germany: firstly as in a force most capable of inflicting a blow on the Soviet Union in order to, if not having it destroyed altogether, weaken it at least and undermine its influence; secondly, as in a force capable of smashing the revolutionary labour and democratic

FROM: Zhdanov, Report on the International Situation, at the Founding Conference of the Communist Information Bureau in Poland, September, 1947 (English translation in *The Strategy and Tactics of World Communism,* pp. 212-16, 219, 222-24, 228-29).

movement in Germany herself and in all countries singled out for Nazi aggression, and thereby strengthening capitalism generally. This was the chief reason for the pre-war policy of "appeasement" and encouragement of fascist aggression, the so-called Munich policy consistently pursued by the imperialist ruling circles of Britain, France, and the United States.

But the hopes reposed by the British, French, and American imperialists in the Hitlerites were not realized. The Hitlerites proved to be weaker, and the Soviet Union and the freedom-loving nations stronger than the Munichists had anticipated. As the result of World War II the major forces of bellicose international fascist reaction had been smashed and put out of commission for a long time to come.

This was accompanied by another serious loss to the world capitalist system generally. Whereas the principal result of World War I had been that the united imperialist front was breached and that Russia dropped out of the world capitalist system, and whereas, as a consequence of the triumph of the Socialist system in the U.S.S.R., capitalism ceased to be an integral, world wide economic system, World War II and the defeat of fascism, the weakening of the world position of capitalism and the enhanced strength of the anti-fascist movement resulted in a number of countries in Central and Southeastern Europe dropping out of the imperialist system. In these countries new, popular, democratic regimes arose. . . .

The war immensely enhanced the international significance and prestige of the U.S.S.R. The U.S.S.R. was the leading force and the guiding spirit in the military defeat of Germany and Japan. The progressive democratic forces of the whole world rallied around the Soviet Union. The socialist state successfully stood the strenuous test of the war and emerged victorious from the mortal struggle with a most powerful enemy. Instead of being enfeebled, the U.S.S.R. became stronger. . . .

World War II aggravated the crisis of the colonial system, as expressed in the rise of a powerful movement for national liberation in the colonies and dependencies. This has placed the rear of the capitalist system in jeopardy. The peoples of the colonies no longer wish to live in the old way. The ruling classes of the metropolitan countries can no longer govern the colonies on the old lines. Attempts to crush the national liberation movement by military force now increasingly encounter armed resistance on the part of the colonial peoples and lead to protracted colonial wars (Holland-Indonesia, France-Viet Nam). . . .

But America's aspirations to world supremacy encounter an obstacle in the U.S.S.R., the stronghold of anti-imperialist and anti-fascist policy, and its growing international influence, in the new democracies, which have escaped from the control of Britain and American imperialism, and in the workers of all countries, including America itself, who do not want a new war for the supremacy of their oppressors. Accordingly, the new expansionist and reactionary policy of the United States envisages a struggle against the U.S.S.R., against the labour movement in all countries, including the United States, and against the emancipationist, anti-imperialist forces in all countries.

Alarmed by the achievements of Socialism in the U.S.S.R., by the achievements of the new democracies, and by the post-war growth of the labour and democratic movement in all countries, the American reactionaries are disposed to take upon themselves the mission of "saviours" of the capitalist system from Communism.

The frank expansionist program of the United States is therefore highly reminiscent of the reckless program, which failed so ignominiously, of the fascist aggressors, who, as we know, also made a bid for world supremacy.

Just as the Hitlerites, when they were making their preparations for piratical aggression, adopted the camouflage of anti-Communism in order to make it possible to oppress and enslave all peoples and primarily and chiefly their own people, America's present-day ruling circles mask their expansionist policy, and even their offensive against the vital interests of their weaker imperialist rival, Great Britain, by fictious considerations of defense against Communism. The feverish piling up of armaments, the construction of new military bases and the creation of bridgeheads for the American armed forces in all parts of the world is justified on the false and pharisaical grounds of "defence" against an imaginary threat of war on the part of the U.S.S.R. . . .

Soviet foreign policy proceeds from the fact of the co-existence for a long period of the two systems—capitalism and socialism. From this it follows that co-operation between the U.S.S.R. and countries with other systems is possible, provided that the principle of reciprocity is observed and that obligations once assumed are honoured. Everyone knows that the U.S.S.R. has always honoured the obligations it has assumed. The Soviet Union has demonstrated its will and desire for co-operation. . . .

In their ideological struggle against the USSR, the American imperialists, who have no great insight into political questions, demonstrate their ignorance by laying primary stress on the allegation that the Soviet Union is undemocratic and totalitarian, while the United States and Great Britain and the whole capitalist world are democratic. On this platform of ideological struggle—on this defence of bourgeois pseudo-democracy and condemnation of Communism as totalitarian—are united all the enemies of the working class without exception, from the capitalist magnates to the Right Socialist leaders, who seize with the greatest eagerness on any slanderous imputations against the USSR suggested to them by their imperialist masters. The pith and substance of this fraudulent propaganda is the claim that the earmark of true democracy is the existence of a plurality of parties and of an organized opposition minority. On these grounds the British Labourites, who spare no effort in their fight against Communism, would like to discover antagonistic classes and a corresponding struggle of parties in the USSR. Political ignoramuses that they are, they cannot understand that capitalists and landlords, antagonistic classes, and hence a plurality of parties, have long ceased to exist in the USSR. They would like to have in the USSR the bourgeois parties which are so dear to their hearts, including pseudo-socialistic parties, as an agency of imperialism. But to their bitter regret these parties of the exploiting bourgeoisie have been doomed by history to disappear from the scene. . . .

One of the lines taken by the ideological campaign that goes hand in hand with the plans for the enslavement of Europe is an attack on the principle of national sovereignty, an appeal for the renouncement of the sovereign rights of nations, to which is opposed the idea of a world government. The purpose of this campaign is to mask the unbridled expansion of American imperialism which is ruthlessly violating the sovereign rights of nations, to represent the United States as a champion of universal laws, and those who resist American penetration as believers in obsolete and selfish nationalism. The idea of a world government has been taken up by bourgeois intellectual cranks and pacifists, and is being exploited not only as a means of pressure, with the purpose of ideologically disarming the nations that defend their independence against the encroachments of American imperialism, but also as a slogan specially directed against the Soviet Union, which indefatigably and consistently upholds the principle of real equality and protection of the sovereign rights of all nations, big and small. Under present conditions imperialist countries like the USA, Great Britain and the states closely associated with them become dangerous enemies of national independence and the self-determination of nations, while the Soviet Union and the new democracies are a reliable bulwark against encroachments on the equality and self-determination of nations. . . .

The Truman doctrine, which provides for the rendering of American assistance to all reactionary regimes which actively oppose the democratic peoples, bears a frankly aggressive character. . . .

The vague and deliberately guarded formulations of the Marshall Plan amount in essence to a scheme to create a bloc of states bound by obligations to the United States, and to grant American credits to European countries as a recompense for their renunciation of economic, and then of political, independence. Moreover, the cornerstone of the Marshall Plan is the restoration of the industrial areas of

Western Germany controlled by the American monopolies. . . .

The dissolution of the Comintern, which conformed to the demands of the development of the labour movement in the new historical situation, played a positive role. The dissolution of the Comintern once and for all disposed of the slanderous allegation of the enemies of Communism and the labour movement that Moscow was interfering in the internal affairs of other states, and that the Communist Parties in the various countries were acting not in the interests of their nations, but on orders from outside. . . .

But the present position of the Communist Parties has its shortcomings. Some comrades understood the dissolution of the Comintern to imply the elimination of all ties, of all contact, between the fraternal Communist Parties. But experience has shown that such mutual isolation of the Communist Parties is wrong, harmful and, in point of fact, unnatural. . . .

Party Control of Science—Genetics

Since the 1930's the conventional study of genetics in the USSR had been challenged by a pseudo-scientific quack, Trofim D. Lysenko, who claimed to speak in the name of Marxism. In 1948 Lysenko's "Michurinist" doctrine of the inheritance of acquired characteristics received party sanction, and biologists who refused to accept this were summarily purged on grounds of "reactionary bourgeois idealism."

The Session of the V. I. Lenin All-Union Academy of Agricultural Sciences (LAAAS) has placed a number of important problems before Soviet biological science, whose solution must contribute to the great work of socialistic construction. The Session of the LAAAS has revealed the reac-

FROM: Resolution of the Presidium of the Academy of Sciences of the USSR, August 26, 1948, "On the Question of the Status and Problems of Biological Science in the Institutes and Institutions of the Academy of Sciences of the USSR" (English translation in Conway Zirkle, ed., *Death of a Science in Russia*, Philadelphia, University of Pennsylvania Press, 1949, pp. 285-86, 288; reprinted by permission of the publisher).

tionary, anti-national nature of the Weismann-Morgan-Mendel movement in biological science,* and has exposed its actual bearers. The destruction of the anti-Michurinist movement has opened new possibilities for the creative development of all branches of advanced biological science.

The materials of the LAAAS Session have shown, with all transparency, that there has been in progress a struggle between two diametrically opposite, according to their ideological and theoretical concepts, movements in biological science: the struggle of a progressive, materialistic, Michurinist movement against a reactionary, idealistic, Weismannist-Morganist movement.

The Michurinist movement, having creatively enriched the theory of evolution and revealed the laws of development of living nature, has through its methods of controlled alteration of the nature of plants and animals made an outstanding contribution to the practice of socialistic agriculture. The Weismannist-Morganist movement, maintaining the independence of hereditary changes of an organism from its characteristics of form and its conditions of life, has supported the idealistic and metaphysical views, torn apart from life; has disarmed practical workers in agriculture from their goal of improving existing and creating new varieties of plants and animal breeds; and has occupied itself with fruitless experiments.

The Academy of Sciences not only failed to take part in the struggle against the reactionary bourgeois movement in biological science, but actually supported representatives of formal-genetic pseudoscience in the Institute of Cytology, Histology, and Embryology; in the Institute of Morphological Evolution; in the Institute of Plant Physiology; in the Main Botanical Gardens; and in other biological institutions of the Academy of Sciences.

The Praesidium of the Academy of Sciences, USSR, admits that its work in directing the Academy's biological institutes was unsatisfactory. . . .

The brilliant transformer of nature, I. V. Michurin, created

* I.e., the standard conception of inheritance through the genes—Ed.

by his efforts a new epoch in the development of Darwinism. The teaching of I. V. Michurin is founded on the great creative force of Marxist-Leninist philosophy. Michurinist teaching sets for itself the most important task of controlling organic nature; of creating new forms of plants and animals necessary for a socialistic society.

Czarist Russia was incapable of evaluating the significance and transforming force of I. V. Michurin's scientific creative genius.

Michurin was discovered for our people and for advanced science through the genius of Lenin and Stalin. In an epoch of Socialism, Michurin's teaching has proved to be a powerful lever in the matter of the transformation of nature. It has received wide opportunities for its development, and popular acclaim.

If in its old form Darwinism set before itself only the problem of explanation of the evolutionary process, then Michurin's teaching, receiving further development through the works of T. D. Lysenko, has set and solves the problem of controlled alteration of hereditary characteristics of plants and animals, has set and solves the problem of controlling the process of evolution.

T. D. Lysenko and his adherents and students have made an essential contribution to Michurinist biological science, to the goal of the development of socialistic agricultural economy, to the concern of the struggle for abundant yields of agricultural crops and productivity of animal husbandry.

The Praesidium of the Academy of Sciences, USSR, obliges the Division of Biological Sciences, biologists, and all naturalists working in the Academy of Sciences to reorganize their work radically; to assume the leadership in the struggle against idealistic and reactionary teachings in science; against toadyism and servility to foreign pseudoscience. The natural-history scientific institutes of the Academy of Sciences must fight actively for a continual progress of native biological science and, in the first place, for the further development of the teachings established by I. V. Michurin, V. V. Dokuchayev, and V. R. Williams, continued and developed by T. D. Lysenko. . . .

The Communist Coup in Czechoslovakia

Increasing East-West tension was reflected in the breakdown of the last case of Communist—non-Communist cooperation, when the Communists took over full power in Czechoslovakia in February, 1948. Communist moves to cement their control over the police provoked the protest resignations of the anti-Communist cabinet ministers, and the Communists took advantage of this to form a new government which, with the support of Social-Democrats manipulated by crypto-Communists in their leadership, was able to command a parliamentary majority. The new regime immediately began to destroy all organized opposition and complete the nationalization of the economy. When the Communist premier Gottwald spoke in justification of the coup shortly afterwards, he illustrated the new Communist appeal to all the "people" against the "reactionaries," whom he identified with the enemies of the nation. At the same time he made it clear that all political organizations in the country would be "regenerated"—i.e., converted into auxiliaries of the Communist dictatorship. Gottwald's report was approved unanimously by the now rubber-stamp National Assembly.

Honourable Members of the Constituent National Assembly! On February 20th, 1948, the members of the government representing the National Socialist, the Catholic People's and the Slovak Democratic Parties handed in their resignations. Thereby an open government *crisis was provoked.* On the 25th of February, 1948, the President of the Republic accepted the resignations of these members of the government and sanctioned our proposals for the reconstruction of the government. Thus *the government crisis was overcome.* Today the newly formed government comes before the Constituent National Assembly with a declaration of its programme. By approving of this government declaration, the Constituent National Assembly will have confirmed the solution of the government crisis also in *a parliamentary manner.* . . .

FROM: Gottwald, "Program of Action of the New Czechoslovak Government" (Speech to the Constituent National Assembly, March 10, 1948; English translation in Gottwald, *Selected Speeches and Articles,* 1929-53, Prague, Orbis, 1954, pp. 158, 160, 162-66, 171-73).

During the occupation . . . it became more and more clear that, after the Germans, their Czech and Slovak helpmates had also to be chased from power, and that their power must be gripped at the roots, which were their great possessions, amassed through long years of exploitation of the people. In short, it had become clear that *in the liberated Republic it was the people that must wield the decisive power. Not on paper, but in fact.*

And so, after the liberation of Czechoslovakia by the glorious Soviet Army, we nationalized banking and the heavy and big industries; we transferred the Germans from our country and delivered the soil, the banks and the factories, which had formerly belonged to them, not into the hands of Czech and Slovak capitalists, but into the hands of Czech and Slovak peasants, workers and tradesmen, into the hands of the nation; we did away with the bureaucratic police-state system, and by the setting up of National Committees we placed our public administration in the hands of the people; we did not allow the revival of the pre-Munich reactionary political parties, which were simply the tools of the Czech and Slovak bourgeoisie; and the Government of the National Front was formed, as the executive of the union of workers, peasants, tradesmen, and the intelligentsia. By these various means the former ruling class was ousted from political power, and was hit in its weakest spot, its property. *And in the new people's democracy the principle that the people is the source of all power began to be put into practice.* . . .

Reactionaries who had misused their economic position to enrich themselves once again and who had gained complete control in several parties of the former National Front so that by their help they directly entered the government—these reactionaries decided on a frontal attack upon the people's democratic regime. The *immediate* aim of reaction was to bring about a realignment of forces in the government and in the whole state before the elections, because they feared defeat in the elections. The *ultimate* aim of reaction was, however, completely to overthrow the people's democratic order, to take from the people all that the liberation and national revolution had brought them, to return to former owners what had been nationalized, and to reinstate the absolute power of the big and powerful masters. As regards *foreign policy,* reaction wanted to separate us from the Soviet Union and our other allies and link up the Republic once more with those who have Munich on their conscience. . . .

On the surface, it was just a case of eight officials of the National Security Corps in Prague being removed from their jobs. In reality, the attack of reaction was being concentrated against the whole of the state security service. These gentlemen reckoned on getting the national Security Corps again into reactionary hands, again under reactionary leadership and, as a result, on being able to use the Security Corps against the people as it was used in the unhappy time before Munich. . . .

The overwhelming majority of the people understood clearly that here it was a question of a dangerous attempt to overthrow the people's democratic regime and to bring to nothing all that the people had gained from the liberation. That is why such a storm of anger and resistance was raised by the people, which swept through the Republic from the Bohemian Forest to the Tatras between February 20th and 25th, and which tumbled down the sinister plans of reaction like a house of cards.

I am not exaggerating if I say that in these critical days our working people of town and country passed a new test of their political maturity, and that they came out of it splendidly—indeed, more than splendidly. I consider it my duty to express, also from the tribune of the Constituent National Assembly, to our working people in town and country and to their real political representatives, my great admiration and great thankfulness for their determined and truly statesmanlike behaviour in this crisis. You, millions and millions of common people of town and countryside, *You have saved our country from another battle of Lipany and therefore from another White Mountain defeat.* This latter-day Barons' League has been crushed, and in all affairs of the nation and state, it is the descendants of the real Taborites, the successors of Jan Hus, Jan Žižka of Trocnov, Prokop the Great and Roháč of Duba who will have the decisive say.*

In this way, as a result of the too conspicuous and insolent behaviour of the counter-revolution, its plot was nipped in the bud, thanks to the preparedness and vigilance of our people and, last but not least, thanks to the vigilance and foresight of their leading party, the Communist Party of Czechoslovakia. At the time when the resignation of the ministers representing the parties mentioned above was announced, we said clearly and unambiguously to everybody concerned, first of all, that it was not possible for those ministers who resigned to return to the government; secondly, that it was impossible to have discussions on the reconstruction of the government with those cliques which pretended to be the legitimate leaders of their parties in whose name they had acted up till then and whose confidence they had so grossly betrayed. Thirdly, we said that we would discuss the completing of the government with those representatives of the parties of the former National Front who had remained true to the original spirit and programme of the National Front. And finally we said that there must be included in the government representatives of so important an organization as is the Revolutionary Trade Union Movement.

It was on this basis that the completion and reconstruction of the government came about. The completed and reconstructed Cabinet is a government of the *regenerated* National Front. In the government, all the *regenerated* political parties are directly represented, as well as our greatest organization, the Revolutionary Trade Union Movement. In this sense the government of the regenerated National Front is the executive body of the union of workers, farmers, tradesmen and intelligentsia. And in this, we return to the original idea and spirit of the National Front as it was created in the Resistance, in the Slovak and the Prague uprisings, and in the glorious days of liberation.

* References to the Czech national heroes of the Hussite Wars of the fourteenth century, and to the disasters of the Thirty Years War—Ed.

The completion and reconstruction of the government was carried out *in a strictly constitutional, democratic and parliamentary manner*. Every one who has eyes to see and ears to hear must admit this. The Constitution and custom lay down that the President of the Republic nominates new members of the government on the proposal of the Prime Minister, to replace those who have resigned. That is what happened. The Constitution further lays down that every government, including the present one, must have the confidence of Parliament. The present government of the regenerated National Front is asking the Constituent National Assembly for this confidence. It is up to you to grant it or withhold it. I am sure that the vast majority of members of this house *will vote their confidence in the government*. They will express it all the more when they fairly judge its programme. . . .

I should like to emphasize that the following measures will have to be taken before the elections:

A state organization set up for all *domestic wholesale trade*, and a state organization for *export and import trade*.

The *nationalization* of all capitalist enterprises employing more than 50 persons, and the complete nationalization of certain branches in which the public interest demands this change.

These measures are necessary first and foremost on *economic* grounds. They will ensure that tens of milliards of crowns' worth of values which were previously drained away from the national income and misused partly for purposes harmful to the nation are preserved for the nation, for the community. These measures are also necessary for reasons of *state policy*. The sector in which further nationalization is to be introduced was and is a hot-bed of subversive intrigues, and it is here that the roots of the government crisis of last February are to be found. These roots of anti-state and anti-popular plotting must be torn out. And they *will* be torn out!

Finally, we must also draw the political conclusions from the February crisis. I have already said that certain parties in the former National Front fell completely into the hands of reaction and were its tools. I have said that the reconstructed government is an expression of the *regenerated* National Front. To this I must expressly add that the component parts of the regenerated National Front can only be *regenerated* political parties and non-party organizations. The agents of reaction must be *unconditionally* removed from these parties and organizations! We are under an obligation to our people in town and country to put this into effect. We are under an obligation to the nation and to the Republic to put this into effect. We are in duty bound to do so if we want to guarantee a peaceful and free development, as well as the independence of our Republic.

This purge of our public life is now going on. It is being carried out by the Action Committees of the National Front which have spontaneously arisen. This purge must not take the form of political revenge; still less must it be a series of campaigns to settle personal accounts. The Central Committee of the National Front has given clear directions to this effect, and the government will co-operate with it in seeing that they are carried out. In a task of this kind it is not possible to prevent a certain amount of encroachments and misunderstandings. I therefore solemnly declare that where such have occurred, they will be put right again. But I declare equally solemnly: We shall not stop half-way! The infiltration of agents of reaction into leading positions in our public life must be stopped and any repetition of their penetration prevented. Our common people do not want February 1948 to be repeated some months later.

The February storm has also cleared the horizon as far as our *foreign policy* is concerned. The lengths to which our reactionaries went in this direction, misusing as they did freedom of speech and of the printed word, exceeded all bounds. By systematic incitement against our allies, they undermined our international position and so threatened the security, indeed the very foundations of the existence of our Republic. This state of affairs has now been ended. It can no longer appear that the foreign policy of the Republic is falling between two chairs. Let it be said to all sides that Czechoslovakia is and will remain a true and dependable member of the Slav family, and that she also feels herself to be an ally of the other People's Democracies. This, however, in no way prevents us from wanting to do everything possible on our side to preserve good relations with all other countries, but this naturally must be a matter of reciprocity. We do not ask anything of them but honest business dealings and non-intervention in our internal affairs. I think this is a reasonably modest wish! . . .

The Soviet-Yugoslav Break

In June, 1948, the solid front of Communist states was broken by the expulsion of Yugoslavia from the Cominform. By resisting Soviet control the Yugoslav Communists incurred charges of un-Marxist deviation, and despite their professions of orthodoxy were read out of the movement. Tito's position, however, was geographically and politically strong enough for him to hold out against Soviet pressure.

a) The Cominform Resolution

. . . The leaders of the Communist Party of Yugoslavia have taken a stand unworthy of Communists, and have begun to identify the foreign policy of the Soviet Union with the foreign policy of the imperialist powers, behaving toward the Soviet Union in the same manner as they behave to the bourgeois states. Precisely because of this anti-Soviet stand, slanderous propaganda about the "degeneration" of the CPSU(B), about the "degeneration" of the USSR, and so on, borrowed from the arsenal of counter-revolutionary Trotskyism, is current within the Central Committee of the Communist Party of Yugoslavia.

The Information Bureau denounces this anti-Soviet attitude of the leaders of the Communist Party of Yugoslavia, as being incompatible with Marxism-Leninism and only appropriate to nationalists.

FROM: Resolution of the Communist Information Bureau, June 28, 1948, "Concerning the Situation in the Communist Party of Yugoslavia" (English translation in *The Soviet-Yugoslav Dispute*, London, Royal Institute of International Affairs, 1948, pp. 62-63, 68-70).

In home policy, the leaders of the Communist Party of Yugoslavia are departing from the positions of the working class and are breaking with the Marxist theory of classes and class struggle. They deny that there is a growth of capitalist elements in their country, and consequently, a sharpening of the class struggle in the countryside. This denial is the direct result of the opportunist tenet that the class struggle does not become sharper during the period of transition from capitalism to socialism, as Marxism-Leninism teaches, but dies down, as was affirmed by opportunists of the Bukharin type, who propagated the theory of the peaceful growing over of capitalism into socialism.

The Yugoslav leaders are pursuing an incorrect policy in the countryside by ignoring the class differentiation in the countryside and by regarding the individual peasantry as a single entity, contrary to the Marxist-Leninist doctrine of classes and class struggle, contrary to the well-known Lenin thesis that small individual farming gives birth to capitalism and the bourgeoisie continually, daily, hourly, spontaneously and on a mass scale. Moreover, the political situation in the Yugoslav countryside gives no grounds for smugness and complacency. In the conditions obtaining in Yugoslavia, where individual peasant farming predominates, where the land is not nationalized, where there is private property in land, and where land can be bought and sold, where much of the land is concentrated in the hands of kulaks, and where hired labour is employed—in such conditions there can be no question of educating the Party in the spirit of glossing over the class struggle and of reconciling class contradictions without by so doing disarming the Party itself in face of the difficulties connected with the construction of socialism. . . .

. . . The Information Bureau unanimously concludes that by their anti-Party and anti-Soviet views, incompatible with Marxism-Leninism, by their whole attitude and their refusal to attend the meeting of the Information Bureau, the leaders of the Communist Party of Yugoslavia have placed themselves in opposition to the Communist Parties affiliated to the Information Bureau, have taken the path of seceding from the united Socialist front against imperialism, have taken the path of betraying the cause of international solidarity of the working people, and have taken up a position of nationalism.

The Information Bureau condemns this anti-Party policy and attitude of the Central Committee of the Communist Party of Yugoslavia.

The Information Bureau considers that, in view of all this, the Central Committee of the Communist Party of Yugoslavia has placed itself and the Yugoslav Party outside the family of the fraternal Communist Parties, outside the united Communist front and consequently outside the ranks of the Information Bureau.

The Information Bureau considers that the basis of these mistakes made by the leadership of the Communist Party of Yugoslavia lies in the undoubted fact that nationalist elements, which previously existed in a disguised form, managed in the course of the past five or six months to reach a dominant position in the leadership of the Communist Party of Yugoslavia, and that consequently the leadership of the Yugoslav Communist Party has broken with the international traditions of the Communist Party of Yugoslavia and has taken the road of nationalism.

Considerably overestimating the internal, national forces of Yugoslavia and their influence, the Yugoslav leaders think that they can maintain Yugoslavia's independence and build socialism without the support of the Communist Parties of other countries, without the support of the people's democracies, without the support of the Soviet Union. They think that the new Yugoslavia can do without the help of these revolutionary forces.

Showing their poor understanding of the international situation and their intimidation by the blackmailing threats of the imperialists, the Yugoslav leaders think that by making concessions they can curry favor with the Imperialist states. They think they will be able to bargain with them for Yugoslavia's independence and, gradually, get the people of Yugoslavia orientated on these states, that is, on capitalism. In this they proceed tacitly from the well-known bourgeois-nationalist thesis that "capitalist states are a lesser danger to the independence of Yugoslavia than the Soviet Union."

The Yugoslav leaders evidently do not understand or, probably, pretend they do not understand, that such a nationalist line can only lead to Yugoslavia's degeneration into an ordinary bourgeois republic, to the loss of its independence and to its transformation into a colony of the imperialist countries.

The Information Bureau does not doubt that inside the Communist Party of Yugoslavia there are sufficient healthy elements, loyal to Marxism-Leninism, to the international traditions of the Yugoslav Communist Party and to the united socialist front.

Their task is to compel their present leaders to recognize their mistakes openly and honestly and to rectify them; to break with nationalism, return to internationalism; and in every way to consolidate the united socialist front against imperialism.

Should the present leaders of the Yugoslav Communist Party prove incapable of doing this, their job is to replace them and to advance a new internationalist leadership of the Party.

The Information Bureau does not doubt that the Communist Party of Yugoslavia will be able to fulfill this honourable task.

b) *The Yugoslav Reply*

In connection with the publication of the Resolution of the Information Bureau, the Central Committee of the Communist Party of Yugoslavia makes the following statement:

1. The criticism contained in the Resolution is based on inaccurate and unfounded assertions and represents an attempt to destroy the prestige of the CPY both abroad and in the country, to arouse confusion amongst the masses in the country and in the international workers' movement, to

FROM: Statement of the Central Committee of the Communist Party of Yugoslavia on the Resolution of the Communist Information Bureau on the Situation in the Communist Party of Yugoslavia, June 29, 1948 (*The Soviet-Yugoslav Dispute*, pp. 73-75, 78-79).

weaken the unity within the CPY and its leading role. . . .

2. The Resolution maintains, without citing any proof, that the leadership of the CPY carried out a hostile policy towards the USSR. The statement that Soviet military specialists in Yugoslavia have been treated with scant respect, and that Soviet civilian citizens have been under the surveillance of state security agents does not in the least correspond to the truth. . . .

On the contrary, it is correct, as stated in the letter to the CC of the CPSU of 13 April, and based on numerous reports of members of the CPY to their Party organizations as well as on statements of other citizens of our country, that from the liberation up to date the Soviet intelligence service sought to enroll them. The CC of the CPY considered and considers that such an attitude towards a country where the communists are the ruling party and which is advancing toward socialism is impermissible. . . .

4. The CC of the CPY cannot but reject with deep indignation the assertions that the leading ranks in the CPY are deviating to the course of a kulak party, to the path of the liquidation of the Communist Party of Yugoslavia, that there is no democracy in the Party, that methods of military leadership are fostered within the Party, that the most basic rights of Party members are trampled upon by the Party and that the mildest criticism of irregularities in the Party is answered by sharp reprisals, etc. Could the members of the Party who dauntlessly faced death in thousands of battles, tolerate in the Party a state of affairs unworthy of both men and communists? The assertion that criticism is not allowed in the Party and similar statements are a terrible insult to every member of our Party, a degradation of the heroic and glorious past of the Party and its present heroic struggle for the reconstruction and development of the country. . . .

8. . . . The Information Bureau has committed a breach of the principles on which it was based and which provide for the voluntary adoption of conclusions by every Party. The Information Bureau, however, not only forces the leaders of the CPY to admit errors which they did not commit but also calls members of the CPY to rebellion within the Party, to

shatter the unity of the Party. The CC of the CPY can never agree to a discussion about its policy on the basis of inventions and uncomradely behaviour without mutual confidence. Such a basis is not one of principle and in this and only in this sense the CC of the CPY considered that it was not on an equal footing in the discussion and that it could not accept discussion on that basis. Further, in connection with the above, the CC of the CPY resolutely rejects the accusation that the CPY has passed on to positions of nationalism. By its entire internal and foreign policy, and especially by its struggle during the national liberation war and the proper solution of the national question in Yugoslavia, the CPY has given proof of the exact opposite.

By the above-mentioned unjust charges, the greatest historical injustice has been done to our Party, our working class and working masses, the peoples in Yugoslavia in general and their unselfish and heroic struggle. . . .

The CC of the CPY calls upon the Party membership to close their ranks in the struggle for the realization of the Party line and for even greater strengthening of Party unity, while it calls upon the working class and other working masses, gathered in the People's Front, to continue to work even more persistently on the building of our socialist homeland. This is the only way, the only method to prove in full and by deeds the unjustness of the above-mentioned charges.

National Communism in Poland—the Fall of Gomulka

The Soviet-Yugoslav break was quickly followed by political crises in the other East-European satellite states, as the Russians moved to crush potential independent-mindedness among the local Communist leaders. The first blow came in Poland, where the nationalist tendency represented by Wladyslaw Gomulka, General Secretary of the "Polish Work-

FROM: Gomulka, Speeches at the Plenum of the Central Committee of the Polish Workers' [Communist] Party, September, 1948 (in *New Roads*, September-October, 1948, pp. 40-42, 50, 141-144; editor's translation with the assistance of Yvonne Starcheska).

ers' Party" (as the Communists were known), was particularly strong. At a session of the Central Committee of the party in September, 1948, Gomulka was attacked for his "rightist-nationalist deviation," his alleged compromises with non-Communist groups during the German occupation of Poland, and his resistance to Soviet-sponsored policies such as collectivization of the peasant. At first Gomulka tried to qualify his admission of the charges, but in the end he confessed to them almost completely. He was removed from the post of General Secretary, and the Stalinists under Boleslaw Bierut proceeded to subordinate Poland completely to the Soviet pattern and Soviet policies.

Today's plenum is being held under the banner of struggle with the right-nationalist deviation in the leadership of the party, and under the banner of self-criticism by those comrades who in their political consciousness acknowledge the commission of the mistakes which contributed to the occurrence of this deviation. I wish to speak, comrades, about my own mistakes which I made in the period just past, mistakes which must be assessed not only as to their content, but also in the light of the fact that I committed them at a time when I held the position of General Secretary of the Party. . . .

The draft resolution which the comrade has proposed states that "The Yugoslav events became the stimulus for Comrade Wieslaw's* move in June. As I look within myself it is difficult for me to say that this is not so, at least in my subconscious. The Yugoslav affair, the conflict which occurred between the CPSU and the CPY, struck me like a bolt from the blue. I was frightened by this conflict. My position in the period when the Yugoslav crisis was coming to a head expressed an indubitably conciliatory attitude toward the leadership of the CPY; it also included some distrust and criticism in regard to the tactical forms introduced by the CPSU into the struggle with the leadership of the CPY. When today I ask myself the question, Comrades, whether there was another way of reacting to the erroneous nationalistic and anti-Marxist attitude and policy of the leadership of the

* "Wieslaw" was Gomulka's underground pseudonym—Ed.

CPY, I must admit that I still cannot find in myself a definite answer. In regard to the actual facts in Yugoslavia all speculations on this subject are equally unrealistic and abstract.

Apart from the question of the collectivization of the peasants' farms, of which I will speak later, the resolution of the Information Bureau [Cominform] on the question of the CPY from the first moment evoked no reservations in me. I considered it correct and I still do. . . .

As we face the new tasks which stand before the Party, unity of the party ranks is a fundamental condition for the accomplishment of these tasks. Such unity is assured by the firm and united stand of the whole Central Committee. I share this position with you, Comrades, and I thank you for the confidence bestowed on me in the position of General Secretary of the Party. . . .

Comrades, if you had not undertaken these three days of criticism, it would be hard for me to overcome that whole complex of false views which I represented. They were overcome by way of struggle. They were overcome by the determined position of my comrades in regard to me, in regard to my deviation. After all, the CPY is perhaps the most glaring case of rightist and nationalist deviation in the workers' movement. I have realized that with this kind of thing, with this kind of ideological deviation, we cannot allow any conciliation. It cannot be settled by any kind of compromise. Any compromise in this matter would be harmful. I criticized the methods which were used in regard to the CPY; I felt that they were severe. I felt that we should talk things over with the leadership of the CPY, send a delegation, explain the matter, plead with them, and perhaps make some concessions. Now I have realized that such methods would not have the effect of correcting the situation, but the opposite—they would have prolonged the process of rotting which has already been going on for a long time in the Yugoslav Party. But today I really affirm with conviction that I have no reservations about the resolution of the Information Bureau nor about the methods used by the CPSU and the Information Bureau; I consider these methods proper. . . .

I realize, comrades, that my position was an expression of disbelief in the revolutionary forces of the working class, that its sources went deep, that it is one further expression of the right deviation, that it is an expression of the Social-Democratic, opportunistic tendencies which developed in me to the greatest degree just at that time of crisis, at that turning point in history.

My actual attitude regarding the issue of group, collective work on the farms expressed what the resolution of the Political Bureau defines as an orientation toward automatism,* since I had no other conception. To that conception of the road to socialism I could not counterpose any other conception. I recoiled and shielded myself from the conception of the reconstruction of the village on the basis of collective farms, by rejecting it as premature for our conditions. Therefore automatism was actually manifested in my attitude, leaving agriculture to develop by itself—let it develop spontaneously in any way it will. Now I realize that such automatism would lead to the steady growth of the capitalist sector in our economy. I realize now that such automatism would quickly lead to the growth of the class of rich farmers and capitalism in the village, that leaving the village on the path of automatic development would lead to ideological distortions in our Party, would simply lead to our Party failing to promote or even have any other conception—it would actually rest on the basis of the conception of capitalist enterprise in the agricultural, peasant sector. I realize that this automatism would consequently lead in practice to the restoration of capitalistic relationships not only in the agricultural sector but equally in the sector of industry, in the urban sector. Therefore I also understand now that it was right and necessary to put forth the perspective of collective farming, without waiting for the maturation of the base of production, the technical cadres or the cadres of specialists, either here or anywhere else. This had to be affirmed, comrades, in order to realize just what is our Polish road to socialism of which we have spoken so often. I am not quite prepared today—these matters do not seem clear enough to me—to indicate

* I.e., letting nature take its course—Ed.

the elements of the Polish road to socialism. It seems to me that it would be incorrect to assert that in general there is no Polish road, that there is only one mold, one such method. After all, conditions are different; at present we are living in another period of history; collectivization was carried out in the Soviet Union in another period of history, under other conditions, in another situation with another pattern of class forces—and we will carry out the reconstruction of the village under other conditions. So therefore there must be some elements of a Polish road to socialism.

On this question we have not undertaken any basic discussion. I do not intend to insist that I have always formulated that issue correctly. If a position were not taken on the question of the socialization of agriculture, only automatism would be possible, and automatism cannot constitute the Polish road. Comrades, I now realize that my vacillations in the face of the class struggle in the village were incorrect, that they stemmed from a whole complex which was implanted in me and which in one form or another I may still have. I am aware that without class struggle further development on the road to socialism would be impossible. And without further development we would be forced to fall back, to retreat. The matter does not depend on whether we want class war or not. We do not want nor do we provoke any struggle in the sense of a useless struggle. The struggle which faces us and which we must carry through is a historical necessity, a normal historical necessity without which it is impossible to go forward, without which there is no development, no progress.

I understand that the tendencies toward separating our Polish road from the Soviet experience and practice are completely false. Without studying this practice, without an intimate connection between our road and the Soviet road there is no question that we would fall into new error in this sector.

Nowhere in the world outside the Soviet Union has socialism been built, and nowhere in the world has any party had, nor can it have, such practice and such experience as the CPSU. Therefore it would also be entirely false even to think that there is some wholly different conception, some other means of solving the problem of agricultural production, the problems of building socialism. I also understand that the distinctiveness of our road does not mean its absolute differentiation from the Soviet road. I have been helped to understand this problem by my comrades' severe criticism and their indication of the necessity of the class struggle which we must carry through, for which we must mobilize the Party, mobilize the working class and the masses of the poor peasantry. In reaching the correct position on this question I was aided by my comrades' criticism.

Please, comrades, it is clear that the core of the right-nationalist complex of which I speak was of necessity my attitude toward the Soviet Union, toward the CPSU. I have examined myself more than once from this point of view, and I admit that in actual practice my attitude reduced not so much to the party relationship between the CPSU and the PPR [Polish Worker's Party], but rather to the governmental relationship between Poland and the USSR, a good, friendly relationship of allies, but only the governmental and not the party relationship. I never conceived that Poland could step forward on the road to socialism, that it could assure the development of its people and its government, its independence, its sovereignty, without the support of the Soviet Union. I understood these things, although it was difficult for me—as I often appreciated intellectually—to demonstrate my attitude toward the Soviet Union in practice, particularly on the ideological and party plane.

I will do everything possible to root out my underestimation of the actual role of the USSR, an underestimation which was an expression of tendencies of nationalistic provincialism. I want to demonstrate this in practice, and not only in words, so that in this way I will contribute to the realization of the goals and intentions which have inspired me. . . .

The "Dictatorship of the Proletariat" in Eastern Europe

By 1949 one-party Communist dictatorship without qualification was the rule throughout Soviet-dominated Eastern

Europe. The Hungarian party theoretician Jozsef Revai spoke frankly of the means by which this was accomplished.

I want to speak about the problem of the dictatorship of the proletariat. . . . Comrades, we are not speaking about a plain theoretical statement, but about a really practical problem. If we make it known within the party, in the working class, that the People's Democracy is the dictatorship of the proletariat, then this becomes and should become a further resource of the effort to build socialism, of the struggle against class enemies, and of the defense against the imperialists. . . .

It is obvious that our People's Democracy has not been from the beginning a dictatorship of the proletariat, but became so during the struggle.

The development of our democracy is nothing else than a struggle which began with the goals of destroying fascism, of realizing our national independence, and of steadily executing civic democratic tasks, and which was transformed subsequently into a fight against the big fortunes, and then against the whole bourgeoisie; in a fight against capitalism, aiming first at the expulsion of capitalistic elements and of the capitalistic class, and then at their liquidation. Our transformation began as an anti-Fascist, national, civic democratic one, and it became deeper and larger and developed during the struggle into a socialistic transformation. . . .

Do you think, Comrades, that our transformation, in its first phase, before it became a socialistic transformation, was anything else than a bourgeois-democratic transformation? By no means. You know very well that the working class was represented in the government and in the apparatus of power. We were a minority in Parliament and in the government, but at the same time we represented the leading force. We had decisive control over the police forces. Our force, the

FROM: Revai, "On the Character of Our People's Democracy" (1949; English translation in Robert A. Goldwin and Marvin Zetterbaum, eds., *Readings in Russian Foreign Policy*, Chicago, American Foundation for Political Education, 1953, Vol. II, pp. 186-190, 193; reprinted by permission of the publisher).

force of our party and the working class, was multiplied by the fact that the Soviet Union, and the Soviet Army, were always there to support us with their assistance. In the first phase of our transformation, when we struggled directly and apparently *only* for a steadfast achievement of bourgeois-democratic tasks, we fought as well for the establishment and assurance of the conditions which made possible the Socialist transformation. The change in the development of our People's Democracy into the dictatorship of the proletariat began with the destruction of the right wing of the Smallholders' Party, with the liquidation of the conspiracy and the fall of Ferenc Nagy.* Then the kulak became an enemy, then the leading role of our party and the working class was strengthened. But the struggle for the transformation of Hungary along anti-capitalistic and Socialistic lines was initiated long before, when in the spring of 1946 the Left Wing Bloc, under the leadership of the Communist Party, succeeded in the fight for the nationalization of heavy industry; when, in the fall of 1946, the Third Congress of our party announced the watchword: "We are constructing the country, not for the capitalists, but for the people.". . .

We must ask the question, whether we were able to see clearly, whether we were aware, during the struggle, of the nature and direction of the changes occurring in our people's democracy, in the character of our state. No, comrades, we did not see it clearly. At most we were feeling our way in the right direction. The party didn't possess a unified, clarified, elaborated attitude in respect to the character of the People's Democracy and its future development. We must point this out, exercising self-criticism. And we must emphasize the fact that we received the decisive stimulation and assistance for the clarification of our future development from the Communist Party of the Soviet Union (Bolshevik), from the teachings of Comrade Stalin. The two sessions of the Cominform, the first in the fall of 1947, the second in the summer of 1948, were of fundamental help for us. The

* Ferenc Nagy: Small-Holder Prime Minister of Hungary, 1946-47—Ed.

first taught us that a People's Democracy couldn't halt at any but the final stage of its destruction of the capitalistic elements, and the second showed us that the socialistic transformation couldn't be limited to the towns, but had to be extended to the rural districts and that as regards the fundamental questions of the transformation into socialism, the Soviet Union is our model and that the way of the People's Democracies differs only in certain external forms, and not in essence, from the way of the Soviet Union. . . .

. . . We must liquidate the concept that the working class shares its power with other classes. In this concept we find remnants of a viewpoint according to which a People's Democracy is some quite specific kind of state which differs from the Soviet's not only in its form, but also in its essence and functions.

However, the fact that power is exclusively possessed by the working class isn't to be chattered about everywhere. We do not intend to mislead the peasantry but equally don't wish to strengthen reactionary elements. Toward the peasantry, we should stress—what is true—that in important fields even the dictatorship of the proletariat includes the working peasantry in wielding power, that the dictatorship of the proletariat is being built upon the close alliance of the working class and the peasantry; of course, not upon any kind of alliance, but upon one building Socialism.

I shall mention briefly what consequences should be drawn from the realization that our People's Democracy is a variation of the dictatorship of the proletariat.

To begin with, the power in possession of the working class must, in the interest of the shaping of Socialism, the oppressing of class enemies and the defense against imperialism be still more decidedly and severely exercised than it has been up to now. "Dictatorship" also means the exercising of force in oppressing enemies. The realization that the Peoples' Democracy is a variation of the dictatorship of the proletariat arms us with the knowledge that, in fighting this class enemy, those organs destined to apply this force must be rendered more effective and unified than they are. . . .

The Campaign against "Cosmopolitanism"

A new wave of ideological tightening-up swept the Soviet Union in 1949. Historians and literary critics in particular were attacked for the "denationalized cosmopolitanism" which failed to assert the superiority of Russian culture and facilitated contamination by "imperialist" influences. History was reduced to a device for national glorification of Russia. The campaign had a marked anti-Jewish aspect; Yiddish-language culture in the USSR was virtually obliterated, while the other minorities were forced to acknowledge the past and present virtues of Great-Russian domination.

Historical science plays a great role in the cause of educating and uplifting the mass of the people, and it is the strongest instrument of class struggle on the ideological front. The exploiting classes have always tried and are trying to utilize historical science for the purpose of making their class domination eternal. In the interests of the ruling classes bourgeois historians falsify history. Only in the Soviet socialist society has history been transformed into a genuine science, which, using the sole scientific method of historical materialism, studies the laws of the development of human society and in the first instance the history of its productive forces and productive relations, the history of the toiling mass of the people.

Soviet historical science not only explains the past, but also gives the key to the correct understanding of contemporary political events and aids in understanding the perspectives of the development of society, nations, and states.

The creators of Soviet historical science, the teachers and educators of the Soviet cadres of historians, are Lenin and Stalin. In the works of Lenin and Stalin the foundations of historical science are laid down, the classical evaluations of the most important questions of world history are given, the most important questions of modern and contemporary

FROM: Editorial, "On the Tasks of Soviet Historians in the Struggle with Manifestations of Bourgeois Ideology," *Questions of History*, No. 2, 1949 (pp. 3-6, 13; editor's translation. This number did not appear until July, 1949).

history and especially of the history of the peoples of the U.S.S.R. are worked out. Lenin and Stalin are the foundation-layers of the study of the Soviet period of the history of our country. . . .

A bunch of nationless cosmopolitans have been preaching a national nihilism hostile to our world view. Defending the anti-scientific and reactionary idea of a "single world stream" of the development of culture, the cosmopolitans declared that such concepts as national culture, national traditions, national priority in scientific and technical discoveries, were antiquated and outlived. They denied and bemoaned the national forms of socialist culture, and refused to admit that the best traditions and cultural achievements of the peoples of the U.S.S.R.—above all, the traditions and cultural achievements of the Russian people—provided the basis for Soviet socialist culture. The nationless cosmopolitans have slandered the great Russian people and have propagated a false assertion about its centuries-old backwardness, about the foreign origin of Russian culture and about the absence of national traditions among the Russian people. They have denied and discredited the best achievements of Soviet culture and have tried to deprecate it in favor of the corrupt culture of the bourgeois West.

In this manner nationless cosmopolitanism is closely bound up with subservience toward things foreign. The preaching of cosmopolitan ideas is harmful and dangerous because they are aimed against Soviet patriotism, they undermine the cause of educating the Soviet people in a spirit of patrotic pride in our socialist motherland, in the great Soviet people. Therefore, it is a matter of special importance and immediacy to uproot all manifestations of cosmopolitanism from our literature, art and science.

Bourgeois cosmopolitanism, moreover, represents a special danger because at the present time it is an ideological weapon of the struggle of international reaction against socialism and democracy, an ideological cover for the efforts of the American imperialists to establish world domination.

The events of the last few years show what a dangerous enemy cosmopolitanism is of the freedom and independence of nations. Screening themselves with ideas about the "world economy," a "world state," and "world government," and proclaiming the idea of getting rid of national sovereignty supposedly as antiquated, the cunning businessmen and politicians of Wall Street are operating in the countries of Europe and Asia to suppress the national independence of the nations and prepare war against the Soviet Union and the countries of People's Democracy. . . .

Since it is a manifestation of bourgeois ideology, cosmopolitanism does not at all stand in contrast to its other forms, but finds in them—in bourgeois objectivism and bourgeois nationalism, in Kadet liberalism and social-reformism—its allies, and a nutritious milieu and the basis for its development. The bourgeois objectivist castrates the historical process of its class content, extols the reactionary sides of the historical past, worships the old conservative principles, and hates the new revolutionary principles. The bourgeois cosmopolitan castrates the historical process not only of its class content, but also of its national form. To the clear Marxist-Leninist class analysis of the historical process, which teaches about national factors as well as social-economic ones, he counterposes flimsy idealistic schemes of cultural borrowing and the affiliation of ideas as the foundation of the historical process.

This is why we must not weaken our struggle against other forms of the manifestation of bourgeois ideology.

Individual manifestations of the conceptions of bourgeois cosmopolitanism take place even in Soviet historical science.

In their time cosmopolitan ideas were implanted by M. N. Pokrovsky* and his anti-historical "school." Replacing historical materialism with vulgar sociologism, the "school" of Pokrovsky falsified and distorted historical events, blackened the great past of the peoples of our country, and ridiculed the national traditions of the Russian people. The party destroyed the Pokrovsky movement, but some notions of this "school" have been current in historical science to the present time. The manifestation of cosmopolitan ideas has

* Pokrovsky: the leading Soviet historian until his death in 1932. In 1936 he was posthumously condemned for his ultra-materialist and antinationalist views—Ed.

also been facilitated by the as yet not completely outlived influence of the traditions of the old, pre-revolutionary aristocratic and bourgeois historiography, which, as is known, cultivated all kinds of cosmopolitan "theories." Finally, cosmopolitan conceptions penetrate our historical science from the bourgeois-imperialist encirclement, for cosmopolitanism is one of the ideological instruments directed from Wall Street and its agencies and aimed at weakening Soviet patriotism, at weakening the will of the Soviet people to struggle for communism.

Such are the roots of bourgeois cosmopolitanism manifested in the field of historical science by a bunch of nationless cosmopolitans who are divorced from the people and their strivings.

The nationless cosmopolitans of our day distort the history of the heroic struggle of the Russian people against their oppressors and foreign usurpers, they deprecate the leading role of the Russian proletariat in the history of the revolutionary struggle of the whole world as well as of Russia, they shade over the socialist character and international significance of the Great October Socialist Revolution, they falsify and distort the world-historical role of the Russian people in the construction of a socialist society and in the victory over the enemy of mankind—German fascism—in the Great Patriotic War. . . .

Soviet historians must be impassioned, militant Bolshevik propagandists, they must pose the substantive problems of history and boldly work them out. The Soviet historical front must not resemble a quiet creek or a rear-area bivouac. Soviet historians have all the foundations for fulfilling those present tasks which our party, the government and Comrade Stalin personally have set before us.

Soviet historians must march in the front ranks of the fighters against the bourgeois ideology of Anglo-American imperialism, to expose Anglo-American imperialism and its reactionary essence, to expose social-reformism, which falsifies and adapts history in the interests of its bosses, the imperialists.

With the active participation of the whole army of Soviet

historians the journal "Problems of History" must become a militant organ, directing the development of Soviet historical thought, generalizing its achievements, and organizing the Soviet historians, educated and led by the party of Lenin-Stalin, for the struggle to build a communist society.

The Purge of "Titoists" in Eastern Europe

Between 1949 and 1952 the Stalinist leaders of the East-European Communist parties took violent measures to liquidate national Communist deviators. Gomulka was ousted from the Polish Central Committee in 1949, and jailed from 1951 to 1956. In Hungary and Bulgaria in 1949 (and in Czechoslovakia in 1952) show trials of former Communist leaders were staged on the model of the Moscow trials of 1936-38. The indictment of László Rajk, formerly Minister of the Interior and Minister of Foreign Affairs in Hungary, is a vivid example of the fabricated charges of espionage and plotting on the basis of which the national Communists were executed. In most cases (including Rajk) the victims were posthumously "rehabilitated" in 1956.

At the end of May, 1945, László Rajk returned to Hungary. He succeeded in concealing his past and playing the part of a much-persecuted communist, steeled in the Spanish struggle. He rose to be the secretary of the Greater Budapest district of the Hungarian Communist Party, a member of the National Assembly, Minister of Home Affairs and finally Minister of Foreign Affairs. Naturally he continued his old activities. About this he admitted in his statement: "I regularly and constantly informed the American intelligence agents of every question that cropped up in the Ministry of Home Affairs and later in the Ministry of Foreign Affairs."

American intelligence in Hungary gave increasing prominence to the Yugoslav spies of the foreign espionage services, the envoys of Tito. Foully abusing the fraternal sympathy

FROM: Indictment of László Rajk, September, 1949 (English translation in *Hungary: László Rajk and his Accomplices before the People's Court, Budapest,* 1949; extracts reprinted in *Documents on International Affairs,* 1949-50, pp. 390-91, 395).

of Hungarian democracy with the working people of Yugoslavia, Tito's diplomatic representatives and other official envoys built up their net of espionage with the greatest effrontery from the moment they first set foot on Hungarian soil at the beginning of 1945. First of all they recruited László Rajk for their service, as they were acquainted with his past as police informer and spy. . . .

László Rajk, as cabinet minister and member of the National Assembly, that is, as a public servant, grossly abusing his official position, gave secrets to foreign powers which seriously endangered the interests of the Hungarian state; by so doing he committed the crimes of espionage and sedition.

The coming into prominence of the Yugoslav spies was connected with the fact that American spies, *agents provocateurs,* and Trotskyists like Rajk himself had come into power in liberated Yugoslavia. The Gestapo had sent, from French internment camps alone, 150 of these people to Yugoslavia for espionage work at the same time as Rajk himself had been sent home. These spies formed the bulk of the circle around Tito and they systematically forced back the honest elements among the Yugoslav partisans, those who were true to their people. Encouraged by this success, the American imperialists set themselves no smaller target than, with the assistance of Tito and company, to attempt to bring the countries of the people's democracies over to their side. Rajk said of this: "Rankovich, Yugoslav Minister of Home Affairs, told me squarely that the people's democracies must unite under the leadership of Yugoslavia and Tito.". . .

About Hungary Rajk said in his statement: "Very soon after this Tito was to begin an intensive campaign against the leaders of the Hungarian government and state. They were to accuse Rakosi* of revisionism** and say that under his leadership the Hungarian government attempted to annex territories peopled by Hungarians. Having thus created differences between the Hungarian and Yugoslav people they

* Mátyás Rákosi: deputy premier and actual dictator of Hungary, 1947-53 and 1955-56—Ed.

** Evidently in the sense of "revising" the country's boundaries —Ed.

were at the appropriate moment to raise the issue in the Yugoslav Parliament. This action was to be followed by frontier incidents for which Yugoslavia would make Hungary responsible."

According to the plan proposed by Rankovich, these frontier incidents would serve the purpose of giving a formal pretext to Yugoslavia for violent military intervention against Hungary, for the armed occupation of part of Hungarian territory. This intervention was to take place at a time when the Soviet Union would be occupied by being involved in some sort of international complication. Part of the armed military action would be for sections of the Yugoslav Army to be sent across the frontier wearing Hungarian uniforms. The plan also provided for the invasion of Hungary by gendarmes, arrow-cross men and Horthyists* in Hungarian uniform—all collected in the British and American occupation zones and passing through Yugoslav territory.

The plan involved the physical liquidation of some of the ministers of the Hungarian government, first of all, of Mátyás Rákosi, [Minister of Defense] Mihaly Farkas and Ernö Gerö [president of the economic council].

The Titoist Critique of Stalinism—Djilas

To defend themselves against Cominform denunciations the Yugoslav Communist leaders sought Marxist arguments against the USSR, and found them readily. Vice premier Milovan Djilas took the leading role in stating the theoretcal case against the "bureaucratic" and "imperialist" distortion of socialism under Stalin.

. . . Taking as a point of departure the economic laws of development toward communism, Marx and Lenin foresaw two dangers threatening the triumphant working class in socialism: from the overthrown bourgeoisie on the one hand

FROM: Djilas, *On New Roads of Socialism* (Speech at a pre-election rally of Belgrade students, March, 1950; English edition, Belgrade, Jugoslovenska Knjiga, 1950, pp. 8-12, 17-18).

* Arrow Cross: pre-1945 Hungarian fascist organization; Admiral Nicholas Horthy: Regent of Hungary, 1920-1945—Ed.

and its own bureaucracy on the other. It was not accidental that Marx asked that civil service employees be elected and that only for a certain period of time after which they were to go into production. Engels and Lenin emphasized often that with the change in economic relations, that is, with the liquidation of private capitalist ownership over the means of production, changes in political relationships do not come about immediately, easily and automatically. The development of dictatorship of the proletariat, socialist democracy, can therefore go in two directions: in the direction of its own disappearance to the extent that socialism itself strengthens, or in the direction of strengthening and transformation of bureaucracy into a privileged caste which lives at the expense of society as a whole. . . .

The development of production forces in the Soviet Union has reached a point where social relations no longer correspond to it. Neither does the method of management of the process of production itself or the method of distribution of the goods produced. The classic antagonism between productive forces and relationships in production has arisen. But this antagonism in the Soviet Union is not the same as that in earlier class social formations, for the relationships of property are different than they were then. Although we have there the existence of capitalist, and even pre-capitalist remnants, they do not play an essential role in social development, for property relationships have been destroyed and it is on these that remnants could base their further development. This is therefore a new historical phenomenon in which new, socialist relationships of ownership and new development of production forces no longer suit the method of management of that property itself and the production forces themselves.

Let us see the forms in which this process appears: introduction of unequal relations and exploitation of other socialist countries; un-Marxist treatment of the role of the leader which often takes the shape of even vulgar, historical falsifications and idolatries similar to those in absolute monarchies; differences in pay which are greater than in bourgeois bureaucracies themselves, ranging from 400 to 15,000 rubles; ideological promotion of Great-Russian nationalism and underestimation and subordination of the role, culture and history of other peoples; a policy of division of spheres of influence with the capitalist states; monopolization of the interpretation of Marxist ideology and the tactics of the international working class movement; introduction of lying and slandering methods into the working-class movement; neglect of study of Marx, Engels and Lenin, and especially their premises about the laws of the transition period and communist society; underestimation of the role of consciousness—especially the consciousness of the masses—in the struggle for a new society; tendencies toward actual liquidation of socialist democracy and transforming it into a mere form; rendering impossible a struggle of opinions and putting brakes on the initiative of the masses, that is, the basic productive forces, and by that very fact productive forces in general; revision of the philosophical foundations of Marxism, etc., etc. Seeing all this, drawing conclusions from the conflict between the Central Committee of the Communist Party of the Soviet Union and the Soviet Government and the Central Committee of the Yugoslav Communist Party and the Yugoslav Government and seeking theoretical explanations both of the phenomenon and practice, many comrades pose the question: whence such phenomena, in every way characteristic of class formations; what do they mean and why must they exist in socialism? Further, where, actually, are the roots of these phenomena? Is what is taking place in the Soviet Union some new kind of class society, is it state capitalism, or "deviations" within socialism itself?

. . . The basis which is the point of departure (socialist revolution and dictatorship of the proletariat, nationalization of capitalist property and struggle for socialist construction) is the same here and in the USSR. Both here and there, these bases are progressive as beginnings. But the tendencies of development, which came about as the result of different general historic conditions and dissimilar conditions in both countries, are unlike. There we see the creation of a privileged bureaucratic stratum, bureaucratic centralism, temporary transformation of the state into "a force above society." (Some of the reasons for this are the fact that the USSR was for a long time the only socialist country, that it was backward, surrounded by capitalism, that the masses had a relatively weak conscious role in the struggle for socialist building and that there were relatively weak foreign and internal revolutionary forces.) Here, in our country, there is also a tendency toward domination by bureaucracy for, as we see in Marx, it is a law that this becomes a danger, a necessarily conditioned phenomenon, a necessary remnant of the old class society in the struggle for the creation of a new classless society. But here, these tendencies will not and cannot win, because historical conditions are different, because the relationship of forces, which changes in struggle every day, is different, because the tendencies of development are different—toward accelerating the decrease of the role of bureaucracy, toward giving greater initiative to the masses and actual power (to put it that way) to the direct producers in the process of production. . . .

. . . Bureaucratic elements in the USSR who have frozen their privileged position, are attempting to find the solution to the internal crisis in the outside world, that is, to hush it temporarily by foreign successes, by exploitation and subordination of other socialist countries. And since methods of exploitation and subordination of peoples in the contemporary world, which is divided and in which the world market is still dominated by capitalism, can only be capitalistic, they inevitably appear as a struggle for spheres of influence and as a brake to the further development of socialism, as a struggle for the victory of socialism, only there, to that extent and in that form that suits the narrow, hegemonistic interests of that privileged stratum. That is why what is directly advantageous to that stratum becomes, for it, theoretically true and justified. Thence the ever broader and more ruthless orientation toward Great-Russian nationalism, the backwardness of the masses and their obscure instincts, inherited from the past, which were always stimulated and appealed to by the bourgeoisie. But this has a new, different character here—the character of bureaucratic, imperialist expansion and domination by the bureaucracy of one nation over other nations. Reliance on historic nationalistic backwardness, in the given conditions, is possible only for the biggest nation where these remnants are the strongest precisely because it has long been the ruling nation. Thence subjective idealism—despite its materialistic and dialectic phraseology—in the philosophy and science of the USSR, which is unfolding on the basis of untrue and undialectic proclamations to the effect that there are no more internal contradictions there. It is on this erroneous basis that their scientific methodology and practice is founded and it must substitute apologetics for scientific work, and routine for revolutionary practice. . . .

Yugoslav Socialism—Tito on Workers' Control of Industry

To buttress their theoretical defenses against the Soviet bloc, the Yugoslav Communists undertook reforms in the direction of the Marxist ideal which they charged Stalin had abandoned. Among these were the diminution of direct party control, a measure of intellectual freedom, administrative decentralization, and the forms of workers' control of industry such as the Russians had discussed and experimented with immediately after the revolution. In 1950, when the law on workers' control was being considered, Tito spoke in praise of it as a higher form of socialism.

The Federal Assembly is today considering the draft of one of the most important bills in socialist Yugoslavia—the bill on management of state economic enterprises and higher economic associations by the workers. The adoption of this bill will be the most significant historic act of the Federal Assembly next to the Law on Nationalization of the Means of Production. When the state took over the means of production, that still did not mean fulfillment of the action slogan of the working-class movement—"the factories for the workers." The mottoes "the factories for the workers" and "the land for the peasants" are not abstract propaganda slogans, but mottoes which have deep meaning. They contain the

FROM: Tito, *Workers Manage Factories in Yugoslavia* (Speech to the Yugoslav Federal Assembly, April, 1950; English edition, Belgrade, Yugostampa, 1950, pp. 9, 13, 22, 24-25, 29-30, 36, 41-42).

entire program of socialist relations in production, in regard to social ownership, in regard to the rights and duties of working people. Therefore, they can be and they must be realized in practice if we are really to build socialism. . . .

Today, the Soviet leaders and all the servile leaders of other communist parties are disputing our revolution, our hard struggle. They are not only trying to deny that we are Marxists and that we are building socialism, but they also say that we are fascists. There is no length to which they have not gone in blackening our name. This is simply the most ordinary kind of unethical propaganda worthy of fascist mouthpieces of the type of Goebbels and others. . . .

. . . The essence of our road to socialism . . . can be defined in a few words: our road to socialism consists in the application of Marxist science to the given stage, in the closest possible harmony with the specific conditions existing in our country. For us, that science is not a dogma but a means of leadership, a means for orientation in every concrete situation, regardless of how complicated it may be. We are endeavoring to introduce the spirit of that science into everything we do, for we are deeply convinced that this is correct. It has turned out in practice that the principles of this science are correct, thanks to the brilliant scientific forecasts of our great teachers. And in the present stage of international development, they are fully valid. Any departure from these principles under any excuse whatsoever would mean revision and betrayal of not only the working class but all progressive mankind. . . .

How do things look in the Soviet Union thirty-one years after the October Revolution? The October Revolution made it possible for the state to take the means of production into its hands. But these means are still, after 31 years, in the hands of the state. Has the slogan "the factories for the workers" been put into practice? Of course not. The workers still do not have any say in the management of the factories. They are managed by directors who are appointed by the state, that is, by civil service employees. The workers only have the possibility and the right to work but this is not very different from the role of the workers in capitalist countries.

The only difference for workers is that there is no unemployment in the Soviet Union, and that is all. Therefore, the leaders of the Soviet Union have not, so far, put through one of the most characteristic measures of a socialist state, that of turning over the factories and other economic enterprises to the workers so that they may manage them. . . .

. . . After the Second World War, when a whole series of new socialist states emerged in the proximity of the Soviet Union, there could no longer be any question of the capitalist encirclement of the Soviet Union. To say that the functions of the state as an armed force, not only of the army but also the so-called punitive organs, are directed only outwards means talking with no connection with reality, just as it has no connection with the present situation in the Soviet Union. What is the tremendous bureaucratic, centralistic apparatus doing? Are its functions directed outwards? Who deports millions of citizens of various nationalities to Siberia and the Far North? Can anyone claim that these are measures against the class enemy, can anyone say that whole nations are a class to be destroyed? Who is obstructing the struggle of opinions in the Soviet Union? Is not all this being done by one of the most centralized, most bureaucratic state apparatuses, which bears no resemblance whatsoever to a state machine that is withering away? Stalin is right in one thing here if it is applied to the present period and that is that this state machine really has functions regarding the outside world. But this must be added, too—that these functions are aimed where they are necessary and where they are not. They are directed at interfering in the internal affairs of other countries and against the will of people of those countries. Therefore, these are least of all the functions of a socialist state that is withering away but rather resemble the functions of an imperialist state machine which is fighting for spheres of influence and the subjugation of other peoples. . . .

By turning over the factories, mines, etc., to the workers to manage, we will make it impossible for an infectious disease to take hold there, a disease bearing the name of bureaucracy. This disease is unbelievably easily and rapidly carried over from boureois society and it is dangerous in the transition period. Like a polyp with thousands of tentacles it obstructs and impedes the correct and rapid process of development. Bureaucracy is among the biggest enemies of socialism precisely because it insinuates itself unnoticed into all the pores of social activity and people are not conscious of it in the beginning. It would be erroneous to think that bureaucracy has not taken root in our country, too. It has begun worming its way into various institutions, into the state apparatus and into the economy, but we are conscious of that and have already undertaken a whole series of measures to render it impossible. It is not enough simply to undertake periodical drives against it but to wage incessant struggle and to educate people. . . .

From now on, the state ownership of the means of production—factories, mines, railways—is passing gradually on to a higher form of socialist ownership. State ownership is the lowest form of social ownership and not the highest, as the leaders of the USSR consider it to be. Therein lies our road to socialism and that is the only right road as regards the withering away of state functions in the economy. Let the Cominformists remember that their slanderous hue and cry cannot obscure the correctness of our building of socialism.

On the other hand, this bill on the participation of working collectives, of our working people, in the management of the economy of our country is the best answer to the question of where there is true democracy—here in our country, or in the much praised and lauded western democracy. In our country, democracy is based on a material basis for the broadest masses of working people. It is felt by the masses, they are making use of it to build a better and happier future for all the working people of our country. . . .

Stalin on Language and Society

In 1950 the party line on the subject of linguistics changed in a way paralleling other fields of thought, as extreme Marxist notions were replaced by conservative ideas bearing the Marxist label. Stalin intervened to dismiss the class theory of language promoted by the late N. Y. Marr. In so doing Stalin further revised his conception of Marxism, by suggesting that the political and ideological "superstructure" of society enjoyed a measure of independence from the economic "base," and that governments could bring about decisive changes without revolution.

The base is the economic structure of society at a given stage of its development. The superstructure consists of the political, legal, religious, artistic, and philosophical views of society and the political, legal, and other institutions corresponding to them.

Every base has its own superstructure corresponding to it. The base of the feudal system has its superstructure—its political, legal, and other views and the corresponding institutions; the capitalist base has its own superstructure, and so has the socialist base. If the base changes or is eliminated, then following this its superstructure changes or is eliminated; if a new base arises, then following this a superstructure arises corresponding to it.

In this respect language radically differs from superstructure. Take, for example, Russian society and the Russian language. During the past thirty years the old, capitalist base was eliminated in Russia and a new, socialist base was built. Correspondingly, the superstructure on the capitalist base was eliminated and a new superstructure created corresponding to the socialist base. The old political, legal, and other institutions were consequently supplanted by new, socialist institutions. But in spite of this the Russian language has remained essentially what it was before the October Revolution.

What has changed in the Russian language in this period? To a certain extent the vocabulary of the Russian language has changed, in the sense that it has been supplemented by a large number of new words and expressions, which have arisen in connection with the rise of a new socialist produc-

FROM: Stalin, *Marxism and Linguistics* (1950; English translation, New York, International Publishers, 1951, pp. 9-10, 27-28; reprinted by permission of the publisher).

tion, of a new state—a new socialist culture, a new public spirit and ethics, and lastly, in connection with the development of technology and science; a number of words and expressions have changed their meaning; a number of obsolete words have fallen out of the vocabulary. As to the basic vocabulary and grammatical structure of the Russian language, which constitute the foundation of the language, they, after the elimination of the capitalist base, far from having been eliminated and supplanted by a new basic vocabulary and a new grammatical system of the language, have been preserved in their entirety and have not undergone any serious changes—have been preserved precisely as the foundation of modern Russian.

Further, the superstructure is a product of the base; but this does not mean that it merely reflects the base, that it is passive, neutral, indifferent to the fate of its base, to the fate of the classes, to the character of the system. On the contrary, no sooner does it arise than it becomes an exceedingly active force, actively assisting its base to take shape and consolidate itself, and doing everything it can to help the new system finish off and eliminate the old base and the old classes.

It cannot be otherwise. The base creates the superstructure precisely in order that it may serve it, that it may actively help it to take shape and consolidate itself, that it may actively strive for the elimination of the old, moribund base and its old superstructure. The superstructure has only to renounce its role of auxiliary, it has only to pass from a position of active defense of its base to one of indifference toward it, to adopt the same attitude to all classes, and it loses its virtue and ceases to be a superstructure. . . .

Marxism holds that the transition of a language from an old quality to a new does not take place by way of an explosion, by the destruction of an existing language and the creation of a new one, but by the gradual accumulation of the elements of the new quality, and, hence, by the gradual dying away of the elements of the old quality.

It should be said in general for the benefit of comrades who have an infatuation for such explosions that the law of transition from an old quality to a new by means of an explosion is inapplicable not only to the history of the development of languages; it is not always applicable to some other social phenomena of a basal or superstructural character. It is compulsory for a society which has no hostile classes. In a period of eight to ten years we effected a transition in the agriculture of our country from the bourgeois individual-peasant system to the socialist, collective-farm system. This was a revolution which eliminated the old bourgeois economic system in the countryside and created a new, socialist system. But this revolution did not take place by means of an explosion, that is, by the overthrow of the existing power and the creation of a new power, but by a gradual transition from the old bourgeois system of the countryside to a new system. And we succeeded in doing this because it was a revolution from above, because the revolution was accomplished on the initiative of the existing power with the support of the overwhelming mass of the peasantry. . . .

Stalin on Economic Laws

In his last theoretical pronouncement Stalin tried to rehabilitate the notion of fixed economic laws, though actually he was unable to distinguish clearly between deterministic economic influences and deliberate policies. He then went on to argue on Marxist grounds that the Soviet Union could avoid involvement in war.

. . . Some comrades deny the objective character of laws of science, and of the laws of political economy particularly, under socialism. They deny that the laws of political economy reflect law-governed processes which operate independently of the will of man. They believe that in view of the specific role assigned to the Soviet state by history, the Soviet state and its leaders can abolish existing laws of political economy and can "form," "create," new laws.

These comrades are profoundly mistaken. It is evident

FROM: Stalin, *Economic Problems of Socialism in the USSR* (English edition, Moscow, Foreign Languages Publishing House, 1952, pp. 5-6, 9-11, 39-41).

that they confuse laws of science, which reflect objective processes in nature or society, processes which take place independently of the will of man, with the laws which are issued by governments, which are made by the will of man, and which have only juridical validity. But they must not be confused.

Marxism regards laws of science—whether they be laws of natural science or laws of political economy—as the reflection of objective processes which take place independently of the will of man. Man may discover these laws, get to know them, study them, reckon with them in his activities and utilize them in the interests of society, but he cannot change or abolish them. Still less can he form or create new laws of science. . . .

It is said that economic laws are elemental in character, that their action is inavertible and that society is powerless against them. That is not true. It is making a fetish of laws, and oneself the slave of laws. It has been demonstrated that society is not powerless against laws, that, having come to know economic laws and relying upon them, society can restrict their sphere of action, utilize them in the interests of society and "harness" them, just as in the case of the forces of nature and their laws, just as in the case of the overflow of big rivers . . .

. . . Relying on the economic law that the relations of production must necessarily conform with the character of the productive forces, the Soviet government socialized the means of production, made them the property of the whole people, and thereby abolished the exploiting system and created socialist forms of economy. Had it not been for this law, and had the Soviet government not relied upon it, it could not have accomplished its mission.

The economic law that the relations of production must necessarily conform with the character of the productive forces has long been forcing its way to the forefront in the capitalist countries. If it has failed so far to force its way into the open, it is because it is encountering powerful resistance on the part of obsolescent forces of society. Here we have another distinguishing feature of economic laws.

Unlike the laws of natural science, where the discovery and application of a new law proceeds more or less smoothly, the discovery and application of a new law in the economic field, affecting as it does the interests of obsolescent forces of society, meets with the most powerful resistance on their part. A force, a social force, capable of overcoming this resistance, is therefore necessary. In our country, such a force was the alliance of the working class and the peasantry, who represented the overwhelming majority of society. There is no such force yet in other, capitalist countries. This explains the secret why the Soviet government was able to smash the old forces of society, and why in our country the economic law that the relations of production must necessarily conform with the character of the productive forces received full scope.

It is said that the necessity for balanced (proportionate) development of the national economy in our country enables the Soviet government to abolish existing economic laws and to create new ones. That is absolutely untrue. Our yearly and five-yearly plans must not be confused with the objective economic law of balanced, proportionate development of the national economy. The law of balanced development of the national economy arose in opposition to the law of competition and anarchy of production under capitalism. It arose from the socialization of the means of production, after the law of competition and anarchy of production had lost its validity. It became operative because a socialist economy can be conducted only on the basis of the economic law of balanced development of the national economy. That means that the law of balanced development of the national economy makes it *possible* for our planning bodies to plan social production correctly. But *possibility* must not be confused with *actuality*. They are two different things. In order to turn the possibility into actuality, it is necessary to study this economic law, to master it, to learn to apply it with full understanding, and to compile such plans as fully reflect the requirements of this law. It cannot be said that the requirements of this economic law are fully reflected by our yearly and five-yearly plans. . . .

It is said that the contradictions between capitalism and socialism are stronger than the contradictions among the capitalist countries. Theoretically, of course, that is true. It is not only true now, today; it was true before the Second World War. And it was more or less realized by the leaders of the capitalist countries. Yet the Second World War began not as a war with the U.S.S.R., but as a war between capitalist countries. Why? Firstly, because war with the U.S.S.R., as a socialist land, is more dangerous to capitalism than war between capitalist countries; for whereas war between capitalist countries puts in question only the supremacy of certain capitalist countries over others, war with the U.S.S.R. must certainly put in question the existence of capitalism itself. Secondly, because the capitalists, although they clamour, for "propaganda" purposes, about the aggressiveness of the Soviet Union, do not themselves believe that it is aggressive, because they are aware of the Soviet Union's peaceful policy and know that it will not itself attack capitalist countries. . . .

. . . When the United States and Berlin assisted Germany's economic recovery, they did so with a view to setting a recovered Germany against the Soviet Union, to utilizing her against the land of socialism. But Germany directed her forces in the first place against the Anglo-French-American bloc. And when Hitler Germany declared war on the Soviet Union, the Anglo-French-American bloc, far from joining with Hitler Germany, was compelled to enter into a coalition with the U.S.S.R. against Hitler Germany.

Consequently, the struggle of the capitalist countries for markets and their desire to crush their competitors proved in practice to be stronger than the contradictions between the capitalist camp and the socialist camp.

What guarantee is there, then, that Germany and Japan will not rise to their feet again, will not attempt to break out of American bondage and live their own independent lives? I think there is no such guarantee.

But it follows from this that the inevitability of wars between capitalist countries remains in force.

It is said that Lenin's thesis that imperialism inevitably

generates war must now be regarded as obsolete, since powerful popular forces have come forward today in defence of peace and against another world war. That is not true.

The object of the present-day peace movement is to rouse the masses of the people to fight for the preservation of peace and for the prevention of another world war. Consequently, the aim of this movement is not to overthrow capitalism and establish socialism—it confines itself to the democratic aim of preserving peace. In this respect, the present-day peace movement differs from the movement of the time of the First World War for the conversion of the imperialist war into civil war, since the latter movement went farther and pursued socialist aims.

It is possible that in a definite conjuncture of circumstances the fight for peace will develop here or there into a fight for socialism. But then it will no longer be the present-day peace movement; it will be a movement for the overthrow of capitalism. . . .

The Limits of Stalinism—Malenkov on Imperfections in the Party

At the Nineteenth Party Congress in October, 1952, Georgi Malenkov emerged as Stalin's successor-designate by delivering the political report of the Central Committee. Together with the usual glorification of Soviet achievements Malenkov made some sharp criticisms of inadequacies in the party's control work. This was followed by a typical example of the adulation of Stalin.

. . . The Soviet people's historic victory in the great patriotic war, the fulfillment of the Fourth Five-Year Plan ahead of schedule, the further development of the national economy, the improvement in the living and cultural standards of the Soviet people, the strengthening of the moral-

FROM: Malenkov, Report of the Central Committee, to the Nineteenth Party Congress, October, 1952 (English translation in Leo Gruliow, ed., *Current Soviet Policies*, New York, Praeger, 1953, pp. 116-120, 123; reprinted by permission of the publisher).

political unity of Soviet society and of the friendship of peoples of our country, and the rallying of all the forces of the camp of peace and democracy around the Soviet Union—these are the principal results confirming the correctness of our party's policy. . . .

However, it would be a mistake not to see that the level of Party political work still lags behind the demands of life, the tasks put forward by the Party. It must be admitted that there are defects and errors in the work of the Party organizations and that there are still many negative and at times even unhealthy phenomena in the life of our Party organizations, which must be recognized, seen and brought to light in order to overcome and eliminate them and secure further progress. . . .

The role of criticism and self-criticism in the life of the Party and state is still underestimated in the party organizations; persecution and victimization for criticism occur. One can still meet officials who never stop shouting about their devotion to the party but actually tolerate no criticism from below, stifle it and take revenge on those who criticize them. . . .

Among our cadres there are many officials who react in a formal manner to decisions of the party and government, who do not display activeness or persistence in the struggle to carry them out and who are not concerned that things are going badly in their work and that harm is being done to the interests of the country. A formal attitude toward decisions of the party and government and a passive attitude toward fulfilling them are vices which must be eradicated in the most merciless fashion. The party does not need hardened and indifferent bureaucrats who prefer their own peace of mind to the interests of work, but tireless and selfless fighters for fulfillment of the directives of the party and government who place the interests of the state above all else.

One of the most dangerous and vicious violations of party and state discipline is the concealment by certain officials of the truth about the state of affairs in enterprises and institutions in their charge, the embellishment of results in the work. . . .

One of the most widespread and deep-rooted defects in the practical work of Soviet, economic and Party organizations is poor organization of the factual fulfillment of directives from the center and of their own decisions, and absence of proper check on their execution. Our organizations and institutions issue far more decisions, directives and orders than required, but take little care to see whether or how they are being carried out. After all, the essence of the job is to carry them out correctly and not bureaucratically. An unconscientious, irresponsible attitude toward carrying out directives from the executive bodies is a most dangerous and vicious manifestation of bureaucracy. Experience shows that even good officials begin to grow spoiled and bureaucratic when left to themselves with no control or check on their activities. . . .

Ideological work is a paramount duty of the party and underestimation of it may do irreparable damage to the interests of the party and the state. We must always remember that any weakening of the influence of the socialist ideology signifies a strengthening of the influence of bourgeois ideology.

In our Soviet society there is not and cannot be any class basis for acceptance of bourgeois ideology. The socialist ideology reigns in our country; its indestructible foundation is Marxism-Leninism. But remnants of the bourgeois ideology, survivals of private-property mentality and morality are still with us. These survivals do not wither away by themselves. They are still very tenacious. They can grow, and a vigorous struggle must be waged against them. Nor are we guaranteed against the infiltration of alien views, ideas and sentiments from outside, from the capitalist states, and from inside, from the remnants of groups hostile to the Soviet regime and not yet completely destroyed by the party. It must not be forgotten that enemies of the Soviet state are trying to spread, fan and inflame all sorts of unhealthy sentiments, are trying to corrupt unstable elements of our society ideologically. . . .

Comrade Stalin's writings are a vivid indication of the outstanding importance our party attaches to theory. Revolutionary theory was, is and will remain the unfailing beacon which illumines the path of advance of our party and our people to the complete triumph of communism.

Comrade Stalin is constantly advancing Marxist theory. . . .

. . . Comrade Stalin's discoveries in the field of theory have world-historic importance and arm all peoples with knowledge of the ways of revolutionary transformation of society and with our party's wealth of experience in the struggle for communism.

The immense significance of Comrade Stalin's works of theory is that they warn us against skimming the surface, they penetrate the heart of phenomena, the very essence of the society's development, teach us to perceive in embryo the factors which will determine the course of events, which makes possible Marxist prognosis. . . .

Chapter Seven: Communism Since Stalin

Communism since 1953 has been stable. Its spread to new regions has for the time being stopped, and on the whole its international aggressiveness has moderated. Within its own orbit communism has proved capable of making the transition from the harsh but formative despotism of Stalin to a more moderate bureaucratic routine, although it faces a permanent dilemma between the pressure to alleviate popular discontent through reform, and the need to maintain the basic organizational and doctrinal controls. 1956 was the critical year, when reform almost got out of hand.

In the countries where it is in power communism is solving the problems of backwardness which contributed to its initial success. The Soviet Union now sets itself the goal of realizing Marx's ideal state of "communism," but in practice this mainly means catching up with the standard of living under American capitalism. At this point it is impossible to predict whether the political structure of communism will prove indefinitely viable, drive the world into war, or break down under the weight of its own internal contradictions.

The Death of Stalin and Collective Leadership

Immediately after Stalin's death on March 5, 1953, the Communist leadership was reorganized to forestall Malenkov as a strong individual successor. Malenkov received the post of premier, but the party Secretariat was taken over by Nikita Khrushchev. The party Presidium (as the Politbureau had been renamed) became for the time being a real collective leadership. Praise of Stalin quickly gave way to enunciation of the new principle and criticism of the domineering individual, which *Pravda* made explicit in April, 1953.

. . . The party committees are organs of political leadership. They cannot apply methods inherent in administrative-managerial agencies in their practical work. There were cases of this during the war. Wartime circumstances caused certain particular features in the methods of leadership which were to some extent justified for those conditions. But this led to serious shortcomings in the practical work of party organizations.

This is why in many very important cases of party work in the postwar period the party has set the task of raising the level of party leadership, of putting an end to such phenomena as the application in party organizations of administrative methods of leadership, which lead to bureaucratization of party work.

One of the fundamental principles of party leadership is collectivity in deciding all important problems of party work. It is impossible to provide genuine leadership if inner party democracy is violated in the party organization, if genuine collective leadership and widely developed criticism and self-criticism are lacking. Collectiveness and the collegium principle represent a very great force in party leadership. . . .

The principle of collectivity in work means, above all, that decisions adopted by party committees on all cardinal questions are the fruit of collective discussion. No matter how experienced leaders may be, no matter what their knowledge and ability, they do not possess and they cannot replace the initiative and experience of a whole collective. In any collegium, in any directing collective, there are people who possess diverse experience, without relying upon which the leaders cannot make correct decisions and exercise qualified leadership.

Individual decisions are always or almost always one-sided decisions. Hence, the very important requirement that decisions must rest on the experience of many, must be the fruit of collective effort. If this is not so, if decisions are adopted individually, serious errors can occur in work. Insofar as each person is able to correct the errors of individual persons and

FROM: Slepov, "Collectivity Is the Highest Principle of Party Leadership" (*Pravda*, April 16, 1953; English translation in *The Current Digest of the Soviet Press*, V: 13 (May 9, 1953), pp. 3, 30; this and subsequent selections reprinted by permission).

insofar as party agencies in the course of practice reckon with these corrections, the decisions which result are more correct. . . .

Leaders cannot consider criticism of themselves as a personal affront. They must be able to accept criticism courageously and show readiness to bend their will to the will of the collective. Without such courage, without the ability to overcome one's own vanity and to bend one's own will to the will of the collective, there can be no collective leadership, no collective. . . .

For correct training of cadres it is important that they be placed under the supervision of the party masses, that officials display readiness not only to teach the masses but to learn from the masses as well. Collectivity in work is called upon to play an important role in this connection. Where the collective principle is violated the necessary conditions for criticism and self-criticism are absent, the sense of responsibility is blunted and officials are infected by dangerous conceit and smugness. It is precisely in such a situation that some workers begin to behave as if they know everything, as if only they can say anything that makes sense, and as if the role of others is only to support their opinion.

Such a situation prepares the ground for unprincipled, alien habits of kowtowing and flattery. There are cases in which the head of a party committee behaves incorrectly and the party committee members accept this and, in order not to mar relations with the committee head, tolerate unprincipled behavior, do not think it necessary or possible to voice objections and even orient themselves to his views and defer to him in everything. Actually, the function of collective leadership is to correct and criticize one another. Where there is an intolerable atmosphere of kowtowing, which excludes businesslike, critical discussion of problems, where criticisms of comrades who are officials are not expressed, there are, as a rule, serious shortcomings in work.

It is necessary in discussing and solving problems to know how to combine the collective principle with personal responsibility in carrying matters through. Just as collectivity is essential in discussing basic problems, so individual responsibility is essential in carrying matters through in order to prevent evasion of responsibility for implementing resolutions. . . .

The method of collective leadership is the basic principle of party leadership, violation of which in party work cannot be viewed otherwise than as a manifestation of bureaucratic habits, which freeze the initiative and self-reliance of party organizations and party members. Strictest observance of this highest principle is the guarantee of correct leadership and a primary requisite for a further advance in party work for successful progress along the path of building communism in our country.

The Purge of Beria

In June 1953, the Soviet Minister of Internal Affairs, Lavrenty Beria, was removed and arrested on the not implausible charge that he planned to use the police to put himself in power and eliminate the collective leadership. In elaborating the case against Beria, however, the Soviet leaders revealed that they still had the habit of rewriting history in order to create an individual scapegoat.

Beria, a now exposed enemy of the people, through various careerist machinations wormed his way into a position of confidence, and threaded his way to the leadership. Whereas in the past his criminal anti-Party and anti-state work was carefully concealed and masked, Beria has lately become insolent and let himself go, exposing his real countenance, the countenance of a vicious enemy of the Party and the Soviet people. This intensification of Beria's criminal work is explained by the general intensification of subversive anti-Soviet activities by the international forces of reaction, hostile to our state. As international imperialism becomes more active, so also do its agents.

Beria began his foul machinations for the purpose of seiz-

FROM: *Pravda* Editorial on the Dismissal of Beria, July 10, 1953 (English translation in *Soviet News,* July 16, 1953, reprinted in *Documents on International Affairs,* 1953, pp. 19-20).

ing power with his attempts to place the Ministry of Internal Affairs [MVD] above the Party and the government, and by using the MVD organs in the centre and in the localities against the Party and its leadership, against the government of the U.S.S.R., promoting workers in the Ministry of Internal Affairs on the basis of their personal devotion to him.

As has now been established, Beria used all sorts of invented pretexts for interfering in every way with the solution of the most important, urgent problems in agriculture. This was done in order to undermine the collective farms and to create food supply difficulties in the country.

In various treacherous ways Beria tried to undermine the friendship of the peoples of the U.S.S.R., the very basis of the multi-national socialist state and the main condition for all the successes of the fraternal Soviet republics, tried to sow discord among the peoples of the U.S.S.R., to intensify the activity of bourgeois nationalist elements in the union republics. . . .

. . . This adventurer and hireling of foreign imperialist forces was hatching plans to seize the leadership of the Party and the country, with the real object of destroying our Communist Party and substituting for the policy worked out by the Party over many years, a policy of capitulation which in the final analysis would have led to the restoration of capitalism.

Thanks to the timely and determined measures taken by the Presidium of the Central Committee of the C.P.S.U., approved unanimously and fully by a plenary meeting of the Central Committee of the Party, Beria's criminal designs against the Party and the state were exposed. The ending of Beria's criminal adventure shows again and again that any anti-Soviet plans of foreign imperialist forces have crashed and will crash against the unbreakable might and great unity of the Party, the government and the Soviet people.

At the same time, the political lessons and necessary conclusions must be drawn from the Beria case.

The strength of our leadership lies in its collective nature and its solid and monolithic unity. Collective leadership is the highest principle of leadership in our Party. This principle accords entirely with Marx's well-known thesis that the cult of personality is harmful and impermissible. . . .

Any official, no matter what post he occupies, must be subject to the unrelaxed supervision of the Party. The Party organizations must regularly check the work of all organizations and departments, the activities of all leading workers. It is also necessary to exercise systematic and unrelaxed supervision over the work of the organs of the Ministry of Internal Affairs. This is not only the right, it is the direct duty of Party organizations.

The "New Course" in Eastern Europe—Imre Nagy

In the months following Stalin's death the Soviet leaders took a series of steps to alleviate the most oppressive rigors of the regime, with respect both to economic policy and police controls. This relaxation was quickly echoed in Eastern Europe: hopes of reform set off a wave of demonstrations in Soviet-occupied East Germany, while in Hungary the moderate national-Communist Imre Nagy became premier and announced drastic reforms that harked back to Bukharin's Right Opposition.

Our advancement along the road of People's Democracy, of socialist industrialization, towards Socialism must be such as would bring with it the steady improvement of the living standard and the social and cultural conditions of the working people, first of all, of the working class, the main army of socialist construction. This should clearly outline one of the important tasks of the economic policy of the government, a substantial all-round reduction, in accordance with the capacity of the country, of the pace of development of our national economy and of the investments. Bearing this in mind, the government will revise the plan of national economy in the spheres of both production and investments and will make proposals for an appropriate reduction in it.

FROM: Nagy, Speech to the Hungarian National Assembly, July 4, 1953 (English translation in the *Hungarian Bulletin,* 1953; extracts reprinted in *Documents on International Affairs, 1953,* pp. 177-81).

The trend of development in the national economy must be also modified. There is no reason whatever for any excessive industrialization or any efforts to achieve industrial autarchy, especially if the necessary sources of basic materials are wanting. . . .

The course of economic policy must be altered also with regard to the two main branches of national economy—industry and agriculture. With an excessive industrialization, particularly the too rapid development of heavy industry and the large scale investments involved, the material resources of the country were insufficient to provide for the development of agriculture. As a result of this, with the too rapid development of industry and, first of all the almost solely, of heavy industry, agricultural production was brought to a standstill and could not secure the satisfaction of either the raw material requirements of a rapidly growing industry, or of the food requirements of the steadily increasing number of industrial workers and of the population as a whole. The Government considers it as one of its most important tasks to increase substantially the investments in agriculture, simultaneously with a cut in industrial investments, in order to bring about the earliest and biggest possible boom in production. . . .

. . . The government believes that it is right and necessary to slow down the pace of the farmers' cooperative movement, and in order to secure a strict compliance with the voluntary principle, it will make it possible for cooperative farm members, who wish to return to individual farming because they believe that is their way to prosperity, to withdraw from the farmers' cooperative. Moreover, it will permit the winding up of cooperative farms, where the majority of the membership wishes it. . . .

During recent years the state extended its economic activity to certain fields where private initiative and enterprise might still have an important role and might better promote the satisfaction of the needs of the population. Retail trade and crafts are these fields. Although handicrafts cooperatives show considerable development, they cannot make up for the shortage experienced in handicrafts production.

This fact encourages the government to allow private enterprise and to issue trade licenses according to legal provisions to those who are entitled to such, and at the same time to grant them the conditions required for their trade, such as a supply of materials, credit, etc. . . .

Greater tolerance is to be shown in religious questions. The employment of administrative measures in this field—which, as a matter of fact, has occurred occasionally—is impermissible. In this question the government espouses the principle of tolerance, of action through enlightenment and education. The government condemns and will not permit administrative and other coercive measures. . . .

The consolidation of legality is one of the most urgent tasks of the government. By applying strict measures and, if this is of no avail, with strict punishment, getting rid of mistakes and slackness, it must be achieved in a short time that our judicial and police organs and local Councils be firm pillars and guarantees of the people's State, of legality and of law and order. . . .

. . . The government will move a bill which will provide for the release of all those people whose offense is not of such a grave nature that their discharge might jeopardize either the security of the state or public order. At the same time, the institution of internment will be abolished and the internment camps wound up. By this measure the government's intention is to make it possible for those granted amnesty and the internees to return to their homes, rejoin their family, to return to the community and through their work to become useful members in it. The government also wishes to settle the issue of resettled people, enabling them to choose their residence in compliance with legal provisions applying to all citizens.

The institution of police-courts, which means, in fact, that the investigating authorities themselves pass judgments, is incompatible with the fundamental principles of people's democratic administration of justice. The government will introduce legislation providing for the abolition of this relic of the past.

The "New Course" in the USSR—Malenkov on Agriculture and Coexistence

Under Malenkov's leadership the Soviet government relaxed its industrialization drive and gave long-overdue attention to agriculture and higher living standards. At the same time efforts were made to alleviate international tension; Soviet initiative was apparently responsible for the conclusion of the Korean War. Malenkov expounded these moderated domestic and foreign policies in a speech to the Supreme Soviet in August, 1953.

. . . The urgent task is to secure in the next two or three years, by generally improving agriculture and further consolidating the collective farms organizationally and economically, the creation in our country of an abundance of food for the population and of raw materials for the light industries.

For the successful accomplishment of this task, the Government and the Central Committee of the Party consider it necessary to carry out a number of major measures to ensure the further swift progress of agriculture—measures, in the first place, which will provide a greater economic incentive to collective farms and collective farmers in developing lagging branches of agriculture. . . .

In addition to providing a greater material incentive to collective farmers to develop the common enterprises of their collective farms, the Government and the Central Committee of the Party have decided thoroughly to correct and revise the wrong attitude which has arisen towards the personal subsidiary husbandry of the collective farmer [the private plot]. . . .

Owing to the defects in our policy of taxing the personal subsidiary husbandry of the collective farmer, the latter's income from his personal subsidiary husbandry has diminished of late years, and there has also been a reduction in the amount of livestock, especially cows, in the personal posses-

FROM: Malenkov, Speech to the Supreme Soviet of the USSR, August 8, 1953 (English translation in *Soviet News,* August 15, 1953, supplement; reprinted in *Documents on International Affairs,* 1953, pp. 22-25, 30).

sion of the collective farmers, which runs counter to our Party's policy in collective farming.

Accordingly, the Government and the Central Committee of the Party deem it necessary substantially to reduce the obligatory delivery quotas levied on the personal subsidiary husbandry of the collective farmers, and have decided, as Minister of Finance Comrade Zverev has already informed you, to change the system of levying the agricultural tax on collective farmers. The monetary tax payable by them is to be reduced by an average of about one-half, and also arrears in agricultural taxes incurred in past years are to be cancelled. . . .

. . . Desirous of promoting peaceful cooperation with all countries, the Soviet Government attaches particular importance to strengthening the Soviet Union's relations with its neighbours. To elevate these relations to the level of genuine good-neighbourliness is the aim for which we are striving and will continue to strive.

The Soviet Union has no territorial claims on any country, and none, in particular, on any of its neighbours. Respect for the national liberty and sovereignty of all countries, big and small, is an inviolable principle of our foreign policy. It goes without saying that the fact that our social and economic system differs from that of some of our neighbours cannot be an obstacle to the furtherance of friendly relations with them. The Soviet Government has, on its part, taken measures to promote neighbourly friendship with such countries, and everything now depends on the readiness of their governments actively to co-operate in establishing the friendship in fact, and not only in word, friendship which presumes mutual concern for safeguarding the peace and security of our countries. . . .

The active and persistent efforts for peace of the Soviet Union and the entire democratic peace camp have yielded definite results. A change in the international atmosphere is to be observed. After a long period of mounting tension, one feels for the first time since the war a certain easing of the international situation. Hundreds of millions of people are becoming increasingly hopeful that a way can be found of settling disputes and outstanding issues. This is a reflection of the deep desire of the peoples for stable and prolonged peace.

We cannot, however, close our eyes to the fact that there are forces which are working against the policy of relaxing international tension and trying to frustrate it at any cost. That is why the Korean armistice negotiations were so protracted, why strategic bridgeheads are being built in West Germany and Japan, why provocations are instigated against the countries of the democratic camp, and why the policy of atomic blackmail is persisted in.

The aggressive elements are stubbornly working against relaxation of international tension because they fear that if developments take this course they will have to curtail armaments programmes, which are a source of huge profits to the munitions manufacturers and which create artificial employment for industry. They fear for their fabulous profits. These elements are afraid that if international tension is lessened, more millions upon millions of people will realize that the North Atlantic bloc, which was ostensibly established for defence, actually constitutes the principal danger to peace. The aggressive elements are also aware that if now, at the time of international tension, the North Atlantic bloc is torn by internal conflicts and contradictions, it may fall to pieces altogether if that tension is relaxed. . . .

Soviet foreign policy is clear.

The Soviet Union will consistently and firmly pursue a policy of preserving and consolidating peace, will promote co-operation and business relations with all states which have a like desire, and strengthen the ties of brotherly friendship and solidarity with the great Chinese people, with all the People's Democracies.

We firmly stand by the belief that there are no disputed or outstanding issues today which cannot be settled peacefully by mutual agreement between the parties concerned.

This also relates to disputed issues between the United States of America and the Soviet Union. We stand, as we have always stood, for the peaceful co-existence of the two systems. We hold that there are no objective reasons for clashes between the United States of America and the Soviet Union. The security of the two states and of the world, and the development of trade between the United States of America and the Soviet Union, can be ensured on the basis of normal relations between the two countries. . . .

The Fall of Malenkov and the Renewed Stress on Industrialization

By the beginning of 1955 a serious division had developed within the Soviet collective leadership on the issue of heavy industry versus consumer goods. The rising party theorist Dimitri Shepilov attacked the emphasis on consumer goods in harsh terms, and in February, 1955, Malenkov was forced to confess his errors and resign as premier. He was replaced by Nikolai Bulganin, who for a time appeared to share power with party secretary Khrushchev as the collective leadership became a diarchy.

a) Shepilov's Attack on the Consumer Goods Line

Views utterly alien to Marxist-Leninist political economy and to the general line of the Communist Party on some fundamental questions of development of the socialist economy have begun to take shape of late among some economists and teachers in our higher educational institutions. . . .

. . . Preponderant development of production of means of production, advancing faster than production of consumers' goods under capitalism, is the rule for the capitalist mode of production.

A completely different pattern is inherent in the socialist mode of production. Here the goal of production is man and his needs. Hence, say these economists, preponderant development of production of the means of production, of heavy industry, cannot be the law of the socialist mode of production, for, if it were, it is alleged, the contradiction between

FROM: Shepilov, "The Party General Line and Vulgarizers of Marxism" (*Pravda*, January 24, 1955; English translation in *The Current Digest of the Soviet Press*, VI: 52 (Feb. 9, 1955), pp. 4, 6).

production and consumption would inevitably arise and grow constantly stronger. Preponderant development of production of the means of production, of heavy industry, has been an economic necessity only, if you please, in the early stages of development of Soviet society, when our country was backward. But, now that we have created a mighty industry, the situation has changed radically. Production under socialism is production for consumption. Faster production of means of production, of heavy industry, they say, contradicts the basic economic law of socialism. Hence the far-reaching conclusion: The policy, pursued by the party, of forced development of branches of heavy industry has allegedly entered into conflict with the basic economic law of socialism, since forced development of branches of heavy industry retards public consumption.

Grossly distorting the essence of party and government decisions to increase production of consumers' goods, the authors of this conception assert that since 1953 the Soviet land has entered a new stage of economic development, the essence of which is allegedly a radical change in the party's economic policy. While the party used to put the emphasis on developing *heavy* industry, now, if you please, the center of gravity has shifted to developing *light* industry, to production of consumers' goods. Trying to present their imaginary formulae as requirements of the basic economic law of socialism, these economists propose setting an identical rate of development for heavy and light industry or even providing for preponderant development of light industry as compared with heavy industry throughout the entire period of completion of the building of socialism and gradual transition from socialism to communism.

If views of this kind were to become widespread, it would cause great harm to the entire cause of communist construction. It would lead to complete disorientation of our cadres on basic questions of the party's economic policy. In practice it would mean that development of our heavy industry, which is the backbone of the socialist economy, would take a descending line, leading to decline in all branches of the national economy, not to a rise but a drop in the working people's living standards, to undermining the economic power of the Soviet land and its defense capacity.

The rightist restorationists,* in their day, pressed the party along this path, as we know. But the party rejected these formulae of surrender. Guided by the Marxist-Leninist economic theory, the party spurred the production of means of production, heavy industry, at forced pace, and on this basis ensured powerful development of the national economy, for heavy industry was, is and will be the granite foundation of all branches of the socialist economy, the cornerstone of the might of the Soviet country and of its people's well-being. . . .

The Soviet people's entire great creative activity is going on in an international situation which obligates Soviet people to display great vigilance. The forces of imperialist reaction, armed to the teeth and arming even more, are nurturing plans for another world war. In this situation a consistent and resolute struggle for world peace and every possible strengthening of the might of the Soviet country and its defense capacity are the first, sacred, patriotic and international duty of the Soviet people.

A major prerequisite for successful solution of these tasks is the struggle for the purity of Marxist-Leninist theory, since any waverings in matters of theory, particularly revisions of the basic theses of Marxist-Leninist economics, can harm our practical work. Marxist-Leninist theory is a powerful projector which illumines for us the path to creating a new society and provides clear guidance in the work and certainty in the victory of our cause.

Under the great banner of Marx-Engels-Lenin-Stalin the Soviet people have built socialist society. Under this all-conquering banner our people, guided by the party of Communists, are proceeding confidently toward their sacred goal —communism.

b) Malenkov's Statement of Resignation

To the chairman of the joint meeting of the Soviet of the Union and the Soviet of Nationalities:

* I.e., Bukharin and the Right Opposition—Ed.

I ask you to bring to the notice of the Supreme Soviet of the U.S.S.R. my request to be relieved from the post of chairman of the Council of Ministers of the U.S.S.R. My request is due to business considerations on the necessity of strengthening the leadership of the Council of Ministers and the need to have at the post of chairman of the Council of Ministers another comrade with greater experience in state work.

I clearly see that the carrying out of the complicated and responsible duties of chairman of the Council of Ministers is being negatively affected by my insufficient experience in local work, and the fact that I did not have occasion, in a ministry or some economic organ, to effect direct guidance of individual branches of national economy.

I also consider myself bound to say in the present statement that now, when the Communist Party of the Soviet Union and the workers of our country are concentrating special efforts for the most rapid development of agriculture, I see particularly clearly my guilt and responsibility for the unsatisfactory state of affairs which has arisen in agriculture, because for several years past I have been entrusted with the duty of controlling and guiding the work of central agricultural organs and the work of local party and administrative organizations in the sphere of agriculture.

The Communist Party, on the initiative and under the guidance of the Central Committee of the C.P.S.U., has already worked out and is implementing a series of large-scale measures for overcoming the lagging behind in agriculture.

Among such important measures is, undoubtedly, the reform of agricultural taxation, regarding which I think it opportune to say it was carried out on the initiative of and in accordance with the proposals of the Central Committee of the C.P.S.U.

It is now evident what important role this reform played in the task of developing agriculture.

FROM: Malenkov, Statement to the Supreme Soviet on his resignation from the post of Chairman of the Council of Ministers of the U.S.S.R., February 8, 1955 (English translation in *Current History*, March, 1955, p. 185-186).

Now, as is known, on the initiative and under the guidance of the Central Committee of the C.P.S.U., a general program has been worked out for overcoming the lagging behind in agriculture and for its most rapid development.

This program is based on the only correct foundation: The further development, by every means, of heavy industry, and only its implementation will create the necessary conditions for a real upsurge in the production of all essential commodities for popular consumption.

It is to be expected that various bourgeois hysterical viragos will busy themselves with slanderous inventions in connection with my present statement, and the fact itself of my release from the post of chairman of the U.S.S.R. Council of Ministers, but we, Communists and Soviet people, will ignore this lying and slander.

The interest of the motherland, the people and the Communist Party stand above everything for every one of us.

Expressing the request of my release from the post of chairman of the U.S.S.R. Council of Ministers, I wish to assure the U.S.S.R. Supreme Soviet that, in the new sphere entrusted to me, I will, under the guidance of the Central Committee of the C.P.S.U., monolithic in its unity and solidarity, and the Soviet government, perform in the most conscientious manner my duty and the functions which will be entrusted to me. . . .

Khrushchev and Tito

In May, 1955, Khrushchev went to Belgrade to apologize for Yugoslavia's expulsion from the Soviet bloc and restore close relations. The Cominform was dissolved, but Tito was careful to avoid Soviet control, and after he took an independent position on the Hungarian uprising of 1956, he was once again repudiated by the Russians.

Dear Comrade Tito, dear comrades, members of the government and leaders of the Union of Communists of Yugoslavia, dear comrades and citizens.

FROM: Khrushchev, Speech on Arrival at Belgrade, May 26, 1955 (English translation in *Soviet News,* May 27, 1955; reprinted in *Documents on International Affairs,* 1955, pp. 265-66).

In the name of the Presidium of the Supreme Soviet of the U.S.S.R., of the government of the Soviet Union and of the Central Committee of the Communist Party of the Soviet Union, on behalf of the Soviet people, I extend cordial greetings to you and to the working people of the glorious capital of Yugoslavia, Belgrade, to all the fraternal peoples of Yugoslavia. . . .

The peoples of our countries are bound by ties of an age-old fraternal friendship and joint struggle against common enemies. This friendship and militant co-operation had been especially strengthened in the hard trials of the struggle against the fascist invaders, in the years of the Second World War. . . .

It will be remembered that those years witnessed the development of the best relations between the peoples of the Soviet Union and Yugoslavia, between our states and our Parties. But those good relations were disturbed in the years that followed.

We sincerely regret that, and we resolutely sweep aside all the bitterness of that period.

On our part, we have no doubt about the part played in provoking that bitterness in the relations between Yugoslavia and the U.S.S.R. by Beria, Abakumov* and other exposed enemies of the people. We have thoroughly investigated the materials upon which the grave accusations against and insults to the leaders of Yugoslavia were based at that time. Facts indicate that those materials were fabricated by the enemies of the people, the contemptible agents of imperialism who had fraudulently wormed their way into the ranks of our Party. . . .

True to the teachings of the founder of the Soviet state, Vladimir Ilich Lenin, the government of the Soviet Union bases its relations with other countries, big and small, on the principles of the peaceful co-existence of states, on the principles of equality, non-interference, respect for sovereignty and national independence, on the principles of non-aggres-

* V. S. Abakumov: Beria's deputy for state security; tried and shot in December, 1954—Ed.

sion and recognition that any encroachments by states upon the territorial integrity of other states are impermissible.

We hope that the relations between our countries will in the future too develop on the basis of these principles, for the good of our peoples. And that will be another major contribution to the efforts to ease international tension, to sustain and strengthen general peace.

We fully appreciate Yugoslavia's desire to promote relations with all states, in the West and in the East. We believe that greater friendship and contact between our countries will help to improve relations between all countries, irrespective of social system, and to advance the cause of general peace.

"De-Stalinization"

In February, 1956, Khrushchev spoke at a closed session of the Twentieth Party Congress to attack some of the abuses of Stalin's rule, particularly the Great Purge of 1937-38 and the personal glorification of the dictator. The speech was read to party meetings throughout the Soviet Union, though never officially published; the text was obtained by the United States Department of State through an East European source.

At the present we are concerned with a question which has immense importance for the party now and for the future —[we are concerned] with how the cult of the person of Stalin has been gradually growing, the cult which became at a certain specific stage the source of a whole series of exceedingly serious and grave perversions of party principles, of party democracy, of revolutionary legality. . . .

When we analyze the practice of Stalin in regard to the direction of the party and of the country, when we pause to consider everything which Stalin perpetrated, we must be convinced that Lenin's fears were justified. The negative characteristics of Stalin, which, in Lenin's time, were only incipient, transformed themselves during the last years into

FROM: Khrushchev, Secret Speech on the "Cult of the Individual," delivered at the Twentieth Congress of the Communist Party of the Soviet Union, February 25, 1956 (*The Anti-Stalin Campaign*, pp. 3, 9-13, 22-23, 39-40, 62-63, 81-82, 87-89).

a grave abuse of power by Stalin, which caused untold harm to our Party.

We have to consider seriously and analyze correctly this matter in order that we may preclude any possibility of a repetition in any form whatever of what took place during the life of Stalin, who absolutely did not tolerate collegiality in leadership and in work, and who practiced brutal violence, not only toward everything which opposed him, but also toward that which seemed to his capricious and despotic character, contrary to his concepts.

Stalin acted not through persuasion, explanation, and patient co-operation with people, but by imposing his concepts and demanding absolute submission to his opinion. Whoever opposed this concept or tried to prove his viewpoint, and the correctness of his position, was doomed to removal from the leading collective and to subsequent moral and physical annihilation. This was especially true during the period following the XVIIth Party Congress [1934], when many prominent party leaders and rank-and-file party workers, honest and dedicated to the cause of Communism, fell victim to Stalin's despotism.

We must affirm that the party had fought a serious fight against the Trotskyites, rightists and bourgeois nationalists, and that it disarmed ideologically all the enemies of Leninism. This ideological fight was carried on successfully, as a result of which the Party became strengthened and tempered. Here Stalin played a positive role. . . .

Worth noting is the fact that even during the progress of the furious ideological fight against the Trotskyites, the Zinovievites, the Bukharinites and others, extreme repressive measures were not used against them. The fight was on ideological grounds. But some years later when socialism in our country was fundamentally constructed, when the exploiting classes were generally liquidated, when the Soviet social structure had radically changed, when the social basis for political movements and groups hostile to the party had violently contracted, when the ideological opponents of the party were long since defeated politically—then the repression directed against them began.

It was precisely during this period (1935-1937-1938) that the practice of mass repression through the government apparatus was born, first against the enemies of Leninism—Trotskyites, Zinovievites, Bukharinites, long since politically defeated by the party, and subsequently also against many honest Communists, against those party cadres who had borne the heavy load of the Civil War and the first and most difficult years of industrialization and collectivization, who actively fought against the Trotskyites and the rightists for the Leninist Party line.

Stalin originated the concept "enemy of the people." This term automatically rendered it unnecessary that the ideological errors of a man or men engaged in a controversy be proven; this term made possible the usage of the most cruel repression, violating all norms of revolutionary legality, against anyone who in any way disagreed with Stalin, against those who were only suspected of hostile intent, against those who had bad reputations. This concept, "enemy of the people," actually eliminated the possibility of any kind of ideological fight or the making of one's views known on this or that issue, even those of a practical character. In the main, and in actuality, the only proof of guilt used, against all norms of current legal science, was the "confession" of the accused himself; and, as subsequent probing proved, "confessions" were acquired through physical pressures against the accused.

This led to glaring violations of revolutionary legality, and to the fact that many entirely innocent persons, who in the past had defended the party line, became victims.

We must assert that in regard to those persons who in their time had opposed the party line, there were often no sufficiently serious reasons for their physical annihilation. The formula, "enemy of the people," was specifically introduced for the purpose of physically annihilating such individuals. . . .

. . . Many party, soviet and economic activists who were branded in 1937-1938 as "enemies" were actually never enemies, spies, wreckers, etc., but were always honest Communists; they were only so stigmatized, and often, no longer able to bear barbaric tortures, they charged themselves (at the order of the investigative judges—falsifiers) with all kinds of grave and unlikely crimes. The commission [for investigation of the purge] has presented to the Central Committee Presidium lengthy and documented materials pertaining to mass repressions against the delegates to the XVIIth Party Congress and against members of the Central Committee elected at that Congress. These materials have been studied by the Presidium of the Central Committee.

It was determined that of the 139 members and candidates of the Party's Central Committee who were elected at the XVIIth Congress, 98 persons, i.e., 70 percent, were arrested and shot (mostly in 1937-1938). (*Indignation in the hall*) . . . The same fate met not only the Central Committee members but also the majority of the delegates to the XVIIth Party Congress. Of 1966 delegates with either voting or advisory rights, 1,108 persons were arrested on charges of anti-revolutionary crimes, i.e., decidedly more than a majority. This very fact shows how absurd, wild and contrary to common sense were the charges of counterrevolutionary crimes made out, as we now see, against a majority of participants at the XVIIth Party Congress. (*Indignation in the hall*) . . .

We have examined the cases and have rehabilitated Kossior, Rudzutak, Postyshev, Kosarev and others.* For what causes were they arrested and sentenced? The review of evidence shows that there was no reason for this. They, like many others, were arrested without the Prosecutor's knowledge. In such a situation there is no need for any sanction, for what sort of a sanction could there be when Stalin decided everything? He was the chief prosecutor in these cases. Stalin not only agreed to, but on his own initiative issued, arrest orders. We must say this so that the delegates to the Congress can clearly undertake and themselves assess this and draw the proper conclusions.

Facts prove that many abuses were made on Stalin's orders without reckoning with any norms of party and Soviet legal-

* S. V. Kossior: Politburo member; Y. E. Rudzutak and P. P. Postyshev, Politburo alternates; A. V. Kosarev, member of the Central Committee; all secretly purged, 1937-38—Ed.

ity. Stalin was a very distrustful man, sickly suspicious; we knew this from our work with him. He could look at a man and say: "Why are your eyes so shifty today?" or "Why are you turning so much today and avoiding to look me directly in the eyes?" The sickly suspicion created in him a general distrust even toward eminent party workers whom he had known for years. Everywhere and in everything he saw "enemies," "two-facers" and "spies."

Possessing unlimited power he indulged in great willfulness and choked a person morally and physically. A situation was created where one could not express one's own will.

When Stalin said that one or another should be arrested, it was necessary to accept on faith that he was an "enemy of the people." Meanwhile, Beria's gang, which ran the organs of state security, outdid itself in proving the guilt of the arrested and the truth of materials which it falsified. And what proofs were offered? The confessions of the arrested, and the investigative judges accepted these "confessions." And how is it possible that a person confesses to crimes which he has not committed? Only in one way—because of application of physical methods of pressuring him, tortures, bringing him to a state of unconsciousness, deprivation of his judgment, taking away of his human dignity. In this manner were "confessions" acquired. . . .

The willfulness of Stalin showed itself not only in decisions concerning the internal life of the country but also in the international relations of the Soviet Union.

The July Plenum of the Central Committee studied in detail the reasons for the development of conflict with Yugoslavia. It was a shameful role which Stalin played here. The "Yugoslav Affair" contained no problems which could not have been solved through party discussions among comrades. There was no significant basis for the development of this "affair"; it was completely possible to have prevented the rupture of relations with that country. This does not mean, however, that the Yugoslav leaders did not make mistakes or did not have shortcomings. But these mistakes and shortcomings were magnified in a monstrous manner by Stalin, which resulted in a break of relations with a friendly country.

I recall the first days when the conflict between the Soviet Union and Yugoslavia began artificially to be blown up. Once, when I came from Kiev to Moscow, I was invited to visit Stalin who, pointing to the copy of a letter lately sent to Tito, asked me, "Have you read this?" Not waiting for my reply he answered, "I will shake my little finger—and there will be no more Tito. He will fall." . . .

But this did not happen to Tito. No matter how much or how little Stalin shook, not only his little finger but everything else that he could shake, Tito did not fall. Why? The reason was that, in this case of disagreement with the Yugoslav comrades, Tito had behind him a state and a people who had gone through a severe school of fighting for liberty and independence, a people which gave support to its leaders.

You see to what Stalin's mania for greatness led. He had completely lost consciousness of reality; he demonstrated his suspicion and haughtiness not only in relation to individuals in the USSR, but in relation to whole parties and nations. . . .

Some comrades may ask us: Where were the members of the Political Bureau of the Central Committee? Why did they not assert themselves against the cult of the individual in time? And why is this being done only now?

First of all we have to consider the fact that the members of the Political Bureau viewed these matters in a different way at different times. Initially, many of them backed Stalin actively because Stalin was one of the strongest Marxists and his logic, his strength and his will greatly influenced the cadres and party work. . . .

Later, however, Stalin, abusing his power more and more, began to fight eminent party and government leaders and to use terroristic methods against honest Soviet people. As we have already shown, Stalin thus handled such eminent party and government leaders as Kossior, Rudzutak, Eikhe, Postyshev and many others.

Attempts to oppose groundless suspicions and charges resulted in the opponent falling victim of the repression. This characterized the fall of Comrade Postyshev.

In one of his speeches Stalin expressed his dissatisfaction with Postyshev and asked him, "What are you actually?"

Postyshev answered clearly, "I am a Bolshevik, Comrade Stalin, a Bolshevik."

This assertion was at first considered to show a lack of respect for Stalin; later it was considered a harmful act and consequently resulted in Postyshev's annihilation and branding without any reason as a "people's enemy."

In the situation which then prevailed I have talked often with Nikolai Alexandrovich Bulganin; once when we two were traveling in a car, he said, "It has happened sometimes that a man goes to Stalin on his invitation as a friend. And when he sits with Stalin, he does not know where he will be sent next, home or to jail."

It is clear that such conditions put every member of the Political Bureau in a very difficult situation. And when we also consider the fact that in the last years the Central Committee plenary sessions were not convened and that the sessions of the Political Bureau occurred only occasionally, from time to time, then we will understand how difficult it was for any member of the Political Bureau to take a stand against one or another injust or improper procedure, against serious errors and shortcomings in the practices of leadership. . . .

Comrades: We must abolish the cult of the individual decisively, once and for all; we must draw the proper conclusions concerning both ideological-theoretical and practical work.

It is necessary for this purpose: . . . to return to and actually practice in all our ideological work the most important theses of Marxist-Leninist science about the people as the creator of history and as the creator of all material and spiritual good of humanity, about the decisive role of the Marxist Party in the revolutionary fight for the transformation of society, about the victory of Communism.

In this connection we will be forced to do much work in order to examine critically from the Marxist-Leninist viewpoint and to correct the widely spread erroneous views connected with the cult of the individual in the sphere of history, philosophy, economy and of other sciences, as well as in literature and the fine arts. . . .

[It is necessary] to restore completely the Leninist principles of Soviet socialist democracy, expressed in the Constitution of the Soviet Union, to fight willfulness of individuals abusing their power. The evil caused by acts violating revolutionary socialist legality, which have accumulated during a long time as a result of the negative influence of the cult of the individual, has to be completely corrected. Comrades! The XXth Congress of the Communist Party of the Soviet Union has manifested with a new strength the unshakable unity of our party, its cohesiveness around the Central Committee, its resolute will to accomplish the great task of building Communism. (*Tumultuous applause*) And the fact that we present in all their ramifications the basic problems of overcoming the cult of the individual which is alien to Marxism-Leninism, as well as the problem of liquidating its burdensome consequences, is an evidence of the great moral and political strength of our party. (*Prolonged applause*)

We are absolutely certain that our party, armed with the historical resolutions of the XXth Congress, will lead the Soviet people along the Leninist path to new successes, to new victories. (*Tumultuous, prolonged applause*)

Long live the victorious banner of our party—Leninism! (*Tumultuous, prolonged applause ending in ovation. All rise.*)

Togliatti on De-Stalinization

The publication of Khrushchev's criticism of Stalin produced a major crisis in the Communist parties outside Russia. The East European satellites were in ferment, while many Western Communist leaders expressed grave misgivings or actually quit the movement. Palmiro Togliatti, head of the Communist Party of Italy, raised broad questions of the defects which permitted Stalinism, and considered the possibility of decentralizing the Communist movement.

. . . We must admit openly and without hesitation that

while the XXth Congress greatly aided the proper understanding and solution of many serious and new problems confronting the democratic and socialist movement, and while it marks a most important milestone in the evolution of Soviet society, it is not possible, however, to consider satisfactory the position which was taken at the Congress and which today is being fully developed in the Soviet press regarding the errors of Stalin and the causes and conditions which made them possible.

The basic cause of everything allegedly lies in the "personality cult," and in the cult of one person with specific and serious faults who lacked modesty, leaned toward personal power, who at times erred because of incompetence, was not loyal in his relations with the other leaders, who had a megalomania for self-aggrandizement and excessive self-love, was suspicious in the extreme, and at the end through the exercise of personal power reached the point where he detached himself from the people, neglected his work, and even submitted to an obvious form of persecution mania. . . .

. . . As long as we confine ourselves, in substance, to denouncing the personal faults of Stalin as the cause of everything we remain within the realm of the "personality cult." First, all that was good was attributed to the superhuman, positive qualities of one man: now all that is evil is attributed to his equally exceptional and even astonishing faults. In the one case, as well as in the other, we are outside the criterion of judgment intrinsic in Marxism. The true problems are evaded, which are why and how Soviet society could reach and did reach certain forms alien to the democratic way and to the legality which it had set for itself, even to the point of degeneration. . . .

We are reminded, first of all, that Lenin, in his last speeches and writings, stressed the danger of bureaucracy which threatened the new society. It seems to us that undoubtedly Stalin's errors were tied in with an excessive increase in the bureaucratic apparatus in Soviet economic

FROM: Togliatti Interview, "Nine Questions on Stalinism," *Nuovi Argomenti,* June 16, 1956 (English translation in *The Anti-Stalin Campaign,* pp. 119-25, 138-39; reprinted by permission of the publisher).

and political life, and perhaps, above all in party life. And here it is extremely difficult to distinguish between cause and effect. The one gradually became the expression of the other. Is this excessive bureaucratic burden also a traditional outgrowth of political and organizational forms and customs of Old Russia? . . .

The first years after the revolution were hard and terrible years marked by superhuman difficulties, foreign intervention, war, and civil war. A maximum of power centralization was required along with severe repressive measures to crush the counter-revolution. . . . At this time the fight erupted between groups who were at odds over the possibilities of socialist economic development, and this naturally had a widespread influence on all of Soviet life. This struggle also had all the elements of a real battle, which was decisive in determining who would assume power, and which had to be won at any price.

And it was in this period that Stalin assumed a positive role, and the sound forces of the party rallied and united around him. Now it can be observed that these forces rallied around Stalin and, guided by him, accepted such modifications in the function of the party and of its directing organisms, i.e., the new functioning of the apparatus controlled from above, as a result of which either they could not offer opposition when the evils began to appear, or else at the outset they did not fully understand that they were evils.

Perhaps we are not in error in asserting that the damaging restrictions placed on the democratic regime and the gradual emergence of bureaucratic organizational forms stemmed from the party.

More important it seems to me should be a close examination of that which followed, when the first Five-Year Plan was carried out, and agricultural collectivization was realized. Here we are dealing with fundamental questions. The successes attained were great, in fact, superlative. . . .

In the exaltation of the achievements there prevailed, particularly in the then current propaganda but also in the general political line, a tendency to exaggerate, to consider all problems already solved and objective contradictions, difficulties, and differences, which are always inherent in the development of a society, as having been overcome. . . .

When reality came into play and difficulties came to light as the result of the imbalance and contrasts which still existed everywhere, there occurred little by little, until at last it was the main force, the tendency to consider that, always and in every case, every evil, every obstacle in the application of the plan, every difficulty in supplying provisions, in delivering raw materials, in the development of the various sectors of industry or agriculture, etc.—all was due to sabotage, to the work of class enemies, counter-revolutionary groups operating clandestinely, etc. It is not that these things did not exist; they did indeed exist. The Soviet Union was surrounded by merciless enemies who were ready to resort to any means to damage and to check its rise. But this erroneous trend in judging the objective situation caused a loss of the sense of limits, made them lose the idea of the borderline between good and evil, friend and enemy, incapacity or weakness and conscious hostility and betrayal, contrasts and difficulties which come from things and from the hostile action of one who has sworn to ruin you. Stalin gave a pseudo-scientific formulation to this fearful confusion through his erroneous thesis of the inherent increase in enemies and in the sharpening of the class struggle with the progress of building socialism. This made permanent and aggravated the confusion itself and was the origin of the unheard-of violations of socialist legality which have been denounced publicly today. . . .

What the CPSU has done remains, as I said, as the first great model of building a socialist society for which the way was opened by a deep, decisive revolutionary breach. Today, the front of socialist construction in countries where the Communists are the leading party has been so broadened (amounting to a third of the human race) that even for this part the Soviet model cannot and must not any longer be obligatory. In every country governed by the Communists, the objective and subjective conditions, traditions, the organizational forms of the movement can and must assert their influence in different ways. In the rest of the world there are countries where we wish to start socialism although the Communists are not the leading party. In still other countries, the march toward socialism is an objective for which there is a concentration of efforts coming from various movements, which, however, have not yet reached either an agreement or a reciprocal understanding. The whole system becomes polycentric, and even in the Communist movement itself we cannot speak of a single guide but rather of a progress which is achieved by following paths which are often different. One general problem, common to the entire movement, has arisen from the criticisms of Stalin—the problem of the perils of bureaucratic degeneration, of stifling democratic life, of the confusion between the constructive revolutionary force and the destruction of revolutionary legality, of separation of the economic and political leadership from the life, criticism, and creative activity of the masses. We shall welcome a contest among the Communist parties in power to find the best way to avoid this peril once and for all. It will be up to us to work out our own method and life in order that we, too, may be protected against the evils of stagnation and bureaucratization, in order that we may learn to solve together the problems of freedom for the working masses and of social justice, and hence gain for ourselves ever increasing prestige and membership among the masses.

The "October Revolution" in Poland

In June, 1956, while hopes for reform were sweeping Eastern Europe, Poland was shaken by a workers' uprising in the city of Poznan. The Stalinists lost their hold on the Polish "United Workers' Party," and in October Gomulka was reinstated as Secretary General in defiance of the Russians. Gomulka then addressed his Central Committee on the nation's economic straits and the need for a more gradual, humane, and national road to socialism.

FROM: Gomulka, Speech to the Central Committee of the Polish United Workers' [Communist] Party, October 20, 1956 (English translation in Paul Zinner, ed., *National Communism and Popular Revolt in Eastern Europe,* New York, Columbia University Press, 1956, pp. 197, 206-7, 209-10, 212, 222, 226-28, 230-33, 235-36, 238; this and following selections reprinted by permission of the publisher).

When I addressed the November Plenum of the Central Committee of the Polish United Workers' Party seven years ago, I thought that it was my last speech to the members of the Central Committee. Although only seven years have elapsed since that time, or eight years since the August Plenum, where an abrupt change occurred in the party's policy, these years constitute a closed historic period. I am deeply convinced that that period has gone into the irrevocable past. There has been much evil in those years. The legacy that that period left the party, the working class, and the nation is more than alarming in certain spheres of life. . . .

The working class recently gave a painful lesson to the party leadership and the Government. When seizing the weapon of strike and going out to demonstrate in the streets on the black Thursday last June, the Poznan workers shouted in a powerful voice: Enough! This cannot go on any longer! Turn back from the false road. . . .

The Poznan workers did not protest against People's Poland, against socialism when they went out into the streets of the city. They protested against the evil which was widespread in our social system and which was painfully felt also by them, against the distortions of the fundamental principles of socialism, which is their idea. . . .

The clumsy attempt to present the painful Poznan tragedy as the work of imperialist agents and provocateurs was very naïve politically. Agents and provocateurs can be and act anywhere, but never and nowhere can they determine the attitude of the working class. . . .

Among the charges which were raised against me in the past was that my attitude in different matters stemmed from an alleged lack of faith in the working class. This is not true. I have never lost faith in the wisdom, common sense, selflessness, and revolutionary attitude of the working class. In these values of the working class I believe also today. I am convinced that the Poznan workers would not have gone on strike, that they would not have demonstrated in the streets, that no men would have been found among them who even resorted to arms, that our fraternal, workers' blood would not have been shed there had the party, that is the leadership of the party, presented the whole truth to them. It was necessary to recognize without any delays the just claims of the workers; it was necessary to say what can be done today and what cannot be done; it was necessary to tell them the truth about the past and the present. There is no escaping from truth. If you cover it up, it will rise as an awful specter, frightening, alarming, and madly raging. . . .

The loss of the credit of confidence of the working class means the loss of the moral basis of power.

It is possible to govern the country even in such conditions. But then this will be bad government, for it must be based on bureaucracy, on infringing the rule of law, on violence. The essence of the dictatorship of the proletariat, as the broadest democracy for the working class and the working masses, becomes in such conditions deprived of its meaning. . . .

. . . We must tell the working class the painful truth. We cannot afford at the present moment any considerable increase of wages, for the string has already been stretched so tight that it can break. . . .

The road to setting up a vast network of cooperative farms in Poland's countryside is a long one. A quantitative development of producer cooperation cannot be planned because, on the basis of voluntary entry in a cooperative, this would amount to planning the growth in human consciousness, and that cannot be planned. The consciousness of the masses is shaped by their experience in life. It is shaped by facts. There are not a few facts in our present state of cooperative farming which repel the peasant masses from the cooperative farms. Such facts must be liquidated. . . .

What is immutable in socialism can be reduced to the abolition of the exploitation of man by man. The roads of achieving this goal can be and are different. They are determined by various circumstances of time and place. The model of socialism can also vary. It can be such as that created in the Soviet Union; it can be shaped in a manner as we see it in Yugoslavia; it can be different still.

Only by way of the experience and achievements of various countries building socialism can the best model of socialism under given conditions arise. . . .

. . . The mapping out of the Russian road to socialism passed gradually from the hands of the Central Committee into the hands of an ever smaller group of people, and finally became the monopoly of Stalin. This monopoly also encompassed the theory of scientific socialism.

The cult of personality is a specific system of exercising power, a specific road of advancing in the direction of socialism, while applying methods contrary to socialist humanism, to the socialist conception of the freedom of man, to the socialist conception of legality. . . .

The cult of personality cannot be confined solely to the person of Stalin. The cult of personality is a certain system which prevailed in the Soviet Union and which was grafted to probably all Communist Parties, as well as to a number of countries of the socialist camp, including Poland.

The essence of this system consisted in the fact that an individual, hierarchic ladder of cults was created. Each such cult comprised a given area in which it functioned. In the bloc of socialist states it was Stalin who stood at the top of this hierarchic ladder of cults. All those who stood on lower rungs of the ladder bowed their heads before him. Those who bowed their heads were not only the other leaders of the Communist Party of the Soviet Union and the leaders of the Soviet Union, but also the leaders of Communist and Workers Parties of the countries of the socialist camp. The latter, that is the First Secretaries of the Central Committees of the Parties of the various countries who sat on the second rung of the ladder of the cult of personality, in turn donned the robes of infallibility and wisdom. But their cult radiated only on the territory of the countries where they stood at the top of the national cult ladder. This cult could be called only a reflected brilliance, a borrowed light. It shone as the moon does. Nonetheless it was all-powerful in the sphere of its action. Thus in each country there was a ladder of cults from top to bottom. . . .

That system violated the democratic principles and the rule of law. Under that system, the characters and consciences of men were broken, people were trampled underfoot and their honor was besmirched. Slandering, falsehood, and lies, even provocations, served as instruments in the exercise of authority.

In Poland, too, tragic events occurred when innocent people were sent to their death. Many others were imprisoned, often for many years, although innocent, including Communists. Many people were submitted to bestial tortures. Terror and demoralization were spread. On the soil of the cult of personality, phenomena arose which violated and even nullified the most profound meaning of the people's power.

We have put an end to this system, or we are putting an end to it once and for all. Great appreciation should be expressed to the 20th Congress of the CPSU which so greatly helped us in the liquidation of this system. . . .

The road of democratization is the only road leading to the construction of the best model of socialism in our conditions. We shall not deviate from this road and we shall defend ourselves with all our might not to be pushed off this road. And we shall not allow anyone to use the process of democratization to undermine socialism. Our party is taking its place at the head of the process of democratization and only the party, acting in conjunction with the other parties of the National Front, can guide this process in a way that will truly lead to the democratization of relations in all the spheres of our life, to the strengthening of the foundations of our system, and not to their weakening.

The party and all the people who saw the evil that existed in the past and who sincerely desire to remove all that is left of the past evil in our life today in order to strengthen the foundations of our system should give a determined rebuff to all persuasions and all voices which strive to weaken our friendship with the Soviet Union.

If in the past not everything in the relations between our party and the CPSU and between Poland and the Soviet Union shaped up in the manner it should have in our view, then today this belongs to the irrevocable past. . . .

Among the many ailments of the past period was also the fact that the Sejm [Parliament] did not fulfill its constitutional task in state life. We are now facing elections to the new Sejm which ought to occupy in our political and state life the place assigned to it by the Constitution. The elevation of the role of the Sejm to that of the supreme organ of state power will probably be of the greatest importance in our democratization program. . . .

Postulating the principle of the freedom of criticism in all its forms, including criticism in the press, we have the right to demand that each criticism should be creative and just, that it should help to overcome the difficulties of the present period instead of increasing them or sometimes even treating demagogically certain phenomena and problems.

We have the right to demand from our youth, especially from university students, that they should keep their ardor in the search for roads leading to the improvement of our present reality, within the framework of the decisions which will be adopted by the present Plenum. . . .

. . . Our party should say clearly to the young people: march in the vanguard of this great and momentous process of democratization but always look up to your leadership, to the leadership of all People's Poland—to the party of the working class, to the Polish United Workers Party.

The Hungarian Revolution

Firing on demonstrators in Budapest by the political police on October 23, 1956, served as the signal for a nation-wide popular uprising against the Soviet-sponsored regime in Hungary. While revolutionary workers' councils took power in some localities, the government was turned over once again to Imre Nagy, in the hope of appeasing the populace. Nagy promised reform, ended one-party Communist rule by forming a coalition government, and took the fatal step of repudiating Hungary's treaty ties with the USSR. The new party secretary Janos Kadar meanwhile announced formation of a new Communist party frankly espousing national communism. On November 4 the experiment in liberal Communist rule was rudely terminated by Soviet military intervention, aided by Kadar and others who betrayed the revolutionary regime. Resistance, in some cases even in the name of communism, went vainly on for some days after the Russians overthrew Nagy, but effective force was lacking to prevent the restoration of the Communist dictatorship under Kadar.

The Hungarian revolution is notable as the event where the forces and circumstances—armed uprising by intellectuals and workers—most nearly approximated the Bolshevik Revolution in Russia. It is appropriately ironic that this movement was directed against the power of the imperialism which that revolution in Russia had brought into being.

a) Demands of a Workers' Council

End the massacre of Hungarians in Budapest! Do not believe deceptions! Let them withdraw Soviet troops from Hungary! Strike! . . .

We have had enough—enough of the autocracy of certain leaders. We too want socialism but according to our own special Hungarian conditions, which reflect the interests of the Hungarian working class and the Hungarian nation, and our most sacred national sentiments.

We demand that all persons who compromised themselves by the cult of personality be eliminated immediately. . . .

We demand that those Communists and non-Communists be given the most important positions in government and party life who, in following the principles of proletarian internationalism, honor above all else our Hungarian national traditions and our thousand-year history.

We demand the revision of the institutions of the state security authority and the elimination immediately of all leaders and functionaries who are compromised. . . .

We demand a public trial of Mihaly Farkas* before an independent court, regardless whether this trial may reflect on individuals currently holding important office.

With regard to the grave errors committed in the field of planned economy we demand the immediate dismissal of the responsible leaders of the planning offices.

FROM: Resolution of the Workers' Council of Miskolc and Borsod County, Hungary, October 25, 1956 (Broadcast by Radio Free Miskolc; English translation in M. J. Lasky, ed., *The Hungarian Revolution: A White Book,* New York, Praeger, 1957, p. 80; this and following selections reprinted by permission of the publisher).

* Because of his responsibility for the purge of Rajk—Ed.

We demand an increase of real wages.

We believe our demands will be realized when our parliament ceases to be an electoral machine, and the members of parliament cease being yes-men.

We demand that March 15th be proclaimed a national holiday, and we also demand that October 6th be a national memorial day.*. . .

b) The Workers' Council Movement

The Trade Union Council Presidium recommends that workers and employees embark on the introduction of worker-management in factories, workshops, mines and everywhere else. They should elect Workers' Councils. . . .

The tasks of the Workers' Councils: A Workers' Council shall decide all questions connected with production, administration and management of the plant. Therefore: (a) it should elect from among its own members a council of 5—15 members, which in accordance with direct instructions of the Workers' Council, shall decide questions connected with the management of the factory—it will hire and fire workers, economic and technical leaders; (b) it will draw up the factory's production plan and define tasks connected with technical development; (c) the Workers' Council will choose the wage-system best suited to conditions peculiar to the factory, decide on the introduction of that system as well as on the development of social and cultural amenities in the factory; (d) the Workers' Council will decide on investments and the utilisation of profits; (e) the Workers' Council will determine the working conditions of the mine, factory, etc.; (f) the Workers' Council will be responsible to all the workers and to the State for correct management.

FROM: Recommendation of the Presidium of the National Trade Union Council of Hungary, on the establishment of Workers' Councils, October 27, 1956 (Broadcast by Radio Kossuth; English translation in Lasky, *The Hungarian Revolution*, pp. 100-01).

* March 15: the pre-Communist national holiday, anniversary of the Revolution of 1848; October 6: date of the reinterrment of Rajk after his posthumous rehabilitation, 1956—Ed.

At present the principal task of the Workers' Councils is to effect and ensure order, discipline and production. With the help of all the workers, their electors, the Workers' Council should defend the factory, the source of their livelihood.

On this basis of the aforesaid, the Presidium of the Trade Union Council recommends the setting up of Workers' Councils.

c) *The Nagy Government*

During the course of the past week bloody events took place with tragic rapidity. The fatal consequences of the terrible mistakes and crimes of these past 10 years unfold before us in these painful events which we are witnessing and in which we are participating. During the course of 1,000 years of history, destiny was not sparing in scourging our people and nation. But such a thing has never before afflicted our country.

The government condemns the viewpoints according to which the present formidable movement is a counterrevolution. Without doubt, as always happens at times of great popular movements, this movement too was used by criminal elements to compromise it and commit common criminal acts. It is also a fact that reactionary and counterrevolutionary elements had penetrated into the movement with the aim of overthrowing the popular democratic regime.

But it is also indisputable that in these stirrings a great national and democratic movement, embracing and unifying all our people, developed with elemental force. This movement aims at guaranteeing our national freedom, independence, and sovereignty, of advancing our society, our economic and political system on the way of democracy—for this is the only foundation for socialism in our country. This great movement exploded because of the grave crimes committed during the past historic period.

The situation was further aggravated by the fact that up

FROM: Imre Nagy, Radio Address Announcing the Formation and the Program of a New Government, October 28, 1956 (Zinner, *National Communism*, pp. 428-32).

to the very last, the [party] leadership had not decided to break finally with the old and criminal policy. It is this above all which led to the tragic fratricidal fight in which so many patriots died on both sides. In the course of these battles was born the government of democratic national unity, independence, and socialism which will become the true expression of the will of the people. This is the firm resolution of the government. . . .

The government wishes to rest in the first place on the support of the fighting Hungarian working class, but also, of course, on the support of the entire Hungarian working population. We have decided to work out a broad program, in the framework of which we wish to settle old and justified demands and rectify damages to the satisfaction of the working class, among other things on the question of wages and work norms, the raising of minimum pay in the lowest wage brackets and of the smallest pensions, taking into account the number of years worked, and the raising of family allowances. . . .

The Hungarian Government has come to an agreement with the Soviet Government that the Soviet forces shall withdraw immediately from Budapest and that simultaneously with the formation of our new Army they shall evacuate the city's territory. The Hungarian Government will initiate negotiations in order to settle relations between the Hungarian People's Republic and the Soviet Union, among other things with regard to the withdrawal of Soviet forces stationed in Hungary, in the spirit of Soviet-Hungarian friendship and the principle of the mutual equality and the national independence of socialist countries.

After the reestablishment of order we shall organize a new and unified state police force and we shall dissolve the organs of state security. No one who took part in the armed fighting need fear further reprisals. The government will put proposals before the National Assembly for the restoration of the emblem of Kossuth as the national emblem and the observance of March 15 once again as a national holiday.

People of Hungary!

In these hours of bitterness and strife one is prone to see only the dark side of the past twelve years. We must not let our views become clouded. These twelve years contain lasting, ineradicable, historic achievements which you, Hungarian workers, peasants, and intellectuals, under the leadership of the Hungarian Workers Party brought into being by virtue of hard labor and sacrifice. Our renascent popular democracy relies on the strength and self-sacrifice which you have displayed in our founding labors and which constitute the best guarantee of our country's happier future.

d) A National-Communist Party

Hungarian workers, peasants, and intellectuals! In a fateful hour we appeal to those who, inspired by loyalty to the people and the country and the pure ideals of socialism, were led to a party which later degenerated to a medium of despotism and national slavery through the blind and criminal policy of the Hungarian representatives of Stalinism—Rakosi and his clique. This adventurous policy unscrupulously frittered away the moral and ideological heritage which you acquired in the old days through honest struggle and blood sacrifice in the fight for our national independence and our democratic progress. Rakosi and his gang gravely violated our national decency and pride when they disregarded the sovereignty and freedom of our nation and wasted our national wealth in a lighthearted manner. In a glorious uprising, our people have shaken off the Rakosi regime. They have achieved freedom for the people and independence for the country, without which there can be no socialism.

We can safely say that the ideological and organizational leaders who prepared this uprising were recruited from among your ranks. Hungarian Communist writers, journalists, university students, the youth of the Petöfi Circle,* thousands

FROM: Kadar, Radio Address, November 1, 1956 (Zinner, *National Communism*, pp. 464-66).

* Petöfi Circle: a national-Communist intellectual group, named after the nineteen-century Hungarian poet Alexander Petöfi, active in pressing demands for reform—Ed.

and thousands of workers and peasants, and veteran fighters who had been imprisoned on false charges fought in the front line against the Rakosiite despotism and political hooliganism. We are proud that you, permeated by true patriotism and loyalty to socialism, honestly stood your ground in the armed uprising and led it.

We are talking to you frankly. The uprising of the people has come to a crossroads. The Hungarian democratic parties will either have enough strength to stabilize our achievements or we must face an open counterrevolution. The blood of Hungarian youth, soldiers, workers, and peasants was not shed in order that Rakosiite despotism might be replaced by the reign of the counterrevolution. . . .

In these momentous hours the Communists who fought against the despotism of Rakosi have decided, in accordance with the wish of many true patriots and socialists, to form a new party. The new party will break away from the crimes of the past once and for all. It will defend the honor and independence of our country against anyone. On this basis, the basis of national independence, it will build fraternal relations with any progressive socialist movement and party in the world.

On this basis, the basis of national independence, does it desire friendly relations with every country, far and near, and in the first place with the neighboring socialist countries. It defends and will defend the achievements of the Hungarian Republic—the land reform, the nationalization of factories, mines, and banks, and the indisputable social and cultural gains of our people.

It defends and will defend the cause of democracy and socialism, whose realization it seeks not through servile copying of foreign examples, but on a road suitable to the historic and economic characteristics of our country, relying on the teachings of Marxism-Leninism, on scientific socialism free of Stalinism and any kind of dogmatism, and on the revolutionary and progressive traditions of Hungarian history and culture. . . .

e) Soviet Intervention

This is Imre Nagy, Premier, speaking. In the early hours of this morning, the Soviet troops launched an attack against our capital city with the obvious intention of overthrowing the lawful, democratic, Hungarian Government. Our troops are fighting. The government is in its place. I inform the people of the country and world public opinion of this.

f) Kadar's Pro-Soviet Regime

The Hungarian Revolutionary Worker-Peasant Government has been formed. The mass movement which started on October 23 in our country had the noble aims of remedying anti-party and anti-democratic crimes committed by Rakosi and his associates and defending national independence and sovereignty. Through the weakness of the Imre Nagy government and through the increased influence of counterrevolutionary elements who edged their way into the movement, socialist achievements, our people's state, our worker-peasant power, and the existence of our country have become endangered.

This has prompted us, Hungarian patriots, to form the Hungarian Revolutionary Worker-Peasant Government. . . .

With growing impudence the counterrevolutionaries are ruthlessly persecuting the followers of democracy. Arrow Cross members and other beasts are murdering the honest patriots, our best comrades. We know that many questions are still awaiting solution in our country and that we have to cope with many difficulties. The life of the workers is still far from what it should be in a country building socialism. Simultaneously, with the progress attained during the past twelve years, the clique of Rakosi and Gero has committed many grave mistakes and gravely violated legality. . . .

Making use of the mistakes committed during the building

FROM: Imre Nagy, Radio Announcement of November 4, 1956 (Zinner, *National Communism*, p. 472).

FROM: Kadar, "Appeal to the Hungarian People," November 4, 1956 (Zinner, *National Communism*, pp. 474-76, 478).

of our people's democratic system, the reactionary elements have misled many honest workers and particularly the major part of the youth, who joined the movement with honest and patriotic intentions. . . .

. . . By utilizing the weakness of Imre Nagy's government, counterrevolutionary forces are indulging in excesses, murdering and looting in the country, and it is to be feared that they will gain the upper hand. We see with deep sadness and a heavy heart into what a terrible situation our beloved Fatherland has been driven by those counterrevolutionary elements, and often even by well-meaning progressive people, who willy-nilly abused the slogans of freedom and democracy and thus opened the way to reaction.

Hungarians, brethren, patriots, soldiers, citizens!

We must put an end to the excesses of the counterrevolutionary elements. The hour of action has struck. We will defend the power of the workers and peasants and the achievements of the people's democracy. We will create order, security, and calm in our country. The interest of the people and the country is that they should have a strong government, a government capable of leading the country out of its grave situation. It is for this reason that we formed the Hungarian Revolutionary Worker-Peasant Government. . . .

The Hungarian Revolutionary Worker-Peasant Government, in the interest of our people, working class, and country, requested the command of the Soviet Army to help our nation in smashing the sinister forces of reaction and restoring order and calm in the country. . . .

g) *Communist Resistance to Kadar*

We have very little to say to the Soviet masters. They have convinced not only the whole world, but also all Communists, that they do not care for Communism, that they simply prostituted Communism . . . to Russian imperialism.

We also want to speak of the traitors . . . the Janos Kadars, who play the dirty role of colonial governors. . . .

FROM: Broadcast by Free Radio Rajk, Hungary, November 5, 1956 (English translation in Lasky, *The Hungarian Revolution*, p. 250).

We send them the message that we consider them all traitors to Communism. . . . [Kadar's] crime and that of his accomplices is clear and the sentence has already been pronounced. We Hungarian Communists will see to it that the sentence is carried out. . . .

The Disintegration of the American Communist Party

The events of 1956, beginning with the repudiation of the Stalin cult in the USSR and ending with the Soviet intervention in Hungary, dealt a crushing blow to what was left of the Communist movement in North-West Europe and the United States. Bitter dissension broke out among the American Communist leadership over the issue of independence from Moscow, and in the fall of 1957 the anti-Moscow leaders followed the majority of the rank and file in breaking with the party. Most prominent among the dissenters were John Gates and Joseph Clark, respectively editor-in-chief and foreign editor of the *Daily Worker*. Clark's statement of resignation was a soul-searching analysis of the failure of American communism.

Editor, *Daily Worker:*

Regretfully, this will be the last time I speak my piece as an editor of the *Daily Worker* and member of the Communist Party. After 28 years of association I am resigning from both because I find it is no longer possible to serve the cause of American socialism through them.

I continue to adhere as strongly as ever to the ideal which brought me into the Communist movement—a world free from poverty, racism, injustice and war. This has become a categorical imperative in the atomic age. Unless the exploitation of man by man is ended it is impossible to conceive of humanity living in both peace and freedom.

It is a grievous comment on the situation in our country, as well as in the Communist Party, that I am the first to resign from the party by making it known through the *Daily Worker*. The most recent meeting of the party's National

FROM: Clark's Letter of Resignation (*The Daily Worker*, September 9, 1957).

Committee was told that at least 7,000 of the 17,000 reported members last year, have left the organization. About 60,000 quit in the previous decade. However, the great majority could not resign publicly because they were never able to declare their affiliation in the first place. This is because freedom of thought and association in our country has been infringed by legislation such as the Smith and McCarran acts.

Furthermore, many who resigned were concerned, as I am, lest opponents of democracy and socialism utilize their resignations to defame the high ideals for which they joined the Communist Party and to which we have devoted some of the best years of our lives. It is a source of pride to me that I have never concealed my views and aims. This includes that very first classification interview when I joined the ranks of the United States Army and served my country together with 15,000 other Communists in the armed forces.

Among those who left the party before me were the great majority of its workingclass and Negro members, active trade unionists, as well as writers, scientists, professional and also party organizers, Smith Act prisoners, *Daily Worker* editors and reporters.

Loss of membership is only one indication of the complete isolation of the Communist Party from the struggles of American labor. Having once been the major organization—in 1935-1945—to continue the century-old socialist tradition in this country, the reason for such total isolation today must go far deeper than the mistakes we made. Many of those mistakes have been catalogued by the self-criticism of the party during the past year. But fundamentally, the demise of the party is related to that of every other socialist movement in our country since the days of the first Marxists here. Not content with growing directly out of the struggles of the American people, and basing themselves on the specific conditions of American life, these movements have unwittingly tried to impose their dogmas on the struggles.

The party became a sect primarily because history rode roughshod over dogma. Since the trend is toward aggravation of this process the party has become a hindrance rather than a means for advancing socialism. . . .

. . . My view is that socialism can be served only by a complete break with Stalinism. The latter perverted socialism by substituting autocracy for democracy. But Marxists have always advocated socialist democracy, which they uphold as more libertarian than any yet attained.

It is my view that to advance the all-important goal of American-Soviet friendship one must win the people for strong opposition to the cold war diplomacy of John Foster Dulles. But to do this one must also take a critical view of what is wrong in the Soviet Union.

Are we helping socialism and the Soviet people if we seem to go along with Khrushchev when he proclaimed that Malenkov was responsible for the evil that Stalin wrought? I have no doubt that Malenkov, as well as Khrushchev, was implicated in those evils. But the roots of the evil require a better explanation than the "character" of Stalin or Khrushchev's latest gloss: "Malenkov not only did not restrain Stalin, he very skillfully took advantage of Stalin's weaknesses and habits in the last year of his life."

To support Khrushchev against Molotov and Malenkov, as the party and *Daily Worker* have done, is no service to socialism or the Soviet Union. Wrong though Molotov has been, the Soviet people face the perspective, and I think will succeed, in producing a new leadership, one which is not responsible for the crimes of Stalin as both Molotov and Khrushchev are. American socialists should be partisans of socialism everywhere.

But one cannot have an independent stance, or a scrupulous regard for truth, and support the "unity" of the Soviet Communist party behind Khrushchev, as the *Daily Worker* did editorially. Since there is no prospect that a common sense, Marxist view will prevail in this regard, party membership has become incompatible with a truly socialist position.

The only effective posture from which American Marxists can work for American-Soviet friendship—necessary if mankind is to survive in a time of hydrogen-headed ICBM weapons—is that of independence. The issue was posed directly at the last convention of the party by the letter of Jacques Duclos, who, for a second time, meddled in the affairs of the American Communist movement. The essence of the Duclos letter was rejected by the convention. But, unfortunately, it was not argued or specifically refuted in a way which would establish beyond a shadow of a doubt the independence of the American Communist Party and demolish the slanders of J. Edgar Hoover. I refer particularly to Duclos' declaration that proletarian internationalism "implies solidarity with the foreign policy of the Soviet Union."

History is replete with instances where the opposite is true. In 1939 internationalism required support for the anti-Hitler war, not the shameful neutrality of both the French and American Communist parties. And in 1956 proletarian internationalism required solidarity with the Hungarian workers opposing Soviet intervention. It demanded support for the Hungarian workers who formed a solid phalanx of workers councils and for their 100 percent solid general strike. It meant solidarity with the views expressed by Janos Kadar in his Nov. 1 radio address, when he was still with the Hungarian masses, and said: "Our people have proved with their blood their intention to support unflinchingly the Government's (Nagy's) efforts for the complete withdrawal of Soviet forces."

There is no prospect that party leaders will rebuff the Duclos argument quoted above, not in generalities, but with specific reference to the Duclos letter. All efforts that I made to get a specific refutation of the Duclos statement were rebuffed. Therefore to remain in the party tends to lend support to the disastrously un-Marxist policy which has time and again isolated us from the American workers, as in 1939.

Communism on a world scale has been the major current in our time through which socialist transformations have taken place. The successful revolutions in Russia, China and Yugoslavia, and the socialist transformation in Poland last October, have advanced socialism as an issue for our time. But these revolutions have created no guides or patterns for socialism in most Western countries, and certainly not for ours. Marxism realized its greatest triumph in the Russian and Chinese revolutions. It also reached its most serious crisis as a result of Stalinist perversion of the Communist movement. Within the Communist countries there is great hope for socialism in the complete elimination of Stalinism which deprived socialism of its humanism and high moral principles and which replaced scientific method with a religious-type dogma.

Within our own country communism has made an important contribution to the welfare of the people. A high-point was reached in the decade of 1935-1945. We were to some degree in the mainstream of American labor and of the country. Social security, the industrial organization of labor, the development of a popular folk culture, integration of the Negro people, were important achievements of American democracy to which we contributed. But that is past and no movement can live in the past. Even during the period of our greatest success we were never a mass party and we were never able to bring socialism into the arena of American political thought and action.

It therefore seems to me that we are entering a period when all questions relating to socialism and America are up for reconsideration. Certainly no organization exists today as a proper vehicle for socialism. No fixed dogma can guide our study. Our starting point must be American reality, as it is today, not as it was a century ago when Marx studied it. We must begin from facts. This is a virtue of Marxism we have often forgotten. And we must above all maintain the moral and humanist essence of socialism.

The very best friends I have, some of whom are still in the party, may justly ask why I take this step now. Why didn't I resign at the time of the Khrushchev revelations on Stalin, or during the Hungarian uprising? The reason is that I had hopes for the cause of those opposing Stalinism within the party. The *Daily Worker* opened its pages to free debate unparalleled in any other American newspaper. But nevertheless, the hope I had for the party died. The hope I have for socialism remains as it has for 28 years. The discussion, the ferment and debate about these questions will bear fruit. And out of the struggles and ranks of the American working-class will come the new organizations that will help us find a path to a free commonwealth of all who labor.

The striving for freedom, equality and justice has motivated and continues to motivate the majority of Communists everywhere. All can therefore find a way better to serve the American people in their quest for greater freedom, abundance and peaceful coexistence. I, for one, shall try to do so.

"Revisionism" in Poland

Following the "October Revolution" of 1956, Poland temporarily enjoyed considerable freedom of expression, and a notable intellectual ferment commenced. Many Polish Communists, particularly the intellectuals, reacted against the decade of Stalinist controls with sharp criticism of Communist dogmatism and demands for further freedom. Outstanding among these "revisionists" was the young philosopher Leszek Kolakowski, who managed to publish some of the most penetrating criticisms of Marxist doctrine, before Gomulka pressed the lid of orthodoxy on again.

. . . It is enough to believe in the inevitability of progress to believe simultaneously in the progressiveness of inevitability. It is enough to believe in Providence in order to bless the brick which hits one on the head. When the spirit of history assumes the difficult role of Divine Providence, it must accordingly demand humble gratitude for every blow it inflicts on its chosen. The demiurge of progress which guards the world demands the worship of his every creation and image. What could be easier than to prove that this or that national leader, this or that system of government, or of social relations, is the demiurge's anointed, even if its external appearance terrifies people with its simian hide? . . . How . . . is it possible to reconcile the conviction of the existence of historical necessity with the conviction that this necessity must be realized by brutal and terroristic means? How can this be reconciled with acceptance of any universal values, that is, with the conviction that certain actions are called for and

FROM: Kolakowski, "Responsibility and History" (September, 1957; English translation in *East Europe*, February, 1958, pp. 18-21; March, 1958, pp. 26-28).

others prohibited in all circumstances? Moral duty is the belief, perpetuated in a given social environment, that certain human actions are ends in themselves and not merely means to an end, and that other actions are counter-ends in themselves; that is, they are prohibited. If historical necessity is considered either as an unlimited process without a final end, or if an ultimate end is ascribed to it, though still unrealized and subject only to a promise of the future, and if, simultaneously, moral judgments are subject to the realization of that necessity, then there is nothing in contemporary life which can be considered an end in itself. In other words, moral values in the strict sense of the term cease to exist altogether. Can the view of the world of reality be reconciled with the view of the world of values? . . .

. . . The very nature of historical determinism is vague in character. I mean "determinism" as a doctrine, describing rules of social change which can be considered valid for the future. Marx's predictions referred to a change in economic structure and were formulated in those terms. Ordinary scientific criticism did not permit going into further details so happily indulged in by Fourier and the majority of the utopians. The details of Lenin's programs, formulated before the October Revolution, went considerably further. Yet, to this very day, we cannot positively decide which part of those programs was based on peculiarly Russian conditions, and which retained, or was intended to retain, universal validity for the period of transition from capitalism to Socialism. We can almost certainly take for granted Marx's fundamental assumption that the development of capitalist technology creates the tendency to endow the means of production with a collective ownership; and this assumption is confirmed, in general outline, by historical experience. However, in the course of how many revolutions won and lost, how many wars and crises, how many years and decades, according to what geographical and chronological circumstances, in the course of what progress and regress, and in what diverse forms, a Socialist way of life will be realized cannot be deduced authoritatively from a superficial knowledge of the "laws of history." These questions are answered by the experiences of everyday life, daily shocking us with new surprises like a virtuoso magician.

In general, these facts do not hinder philosophers of history. They are happy through the years in always writing the same epitaph for capitalist society, and in composing it on the basis of their belief in "scientific prognostication." The rest—the wars, revolutions, crises, decades of struggle and suffering—fall into the philosophic category of "accident" and so do not count. They are no longer subject to penetrating historiosophical analysis. . . .

The philosophy of history draws its strength not from itself but from the faith invested in it, and this faith is a part of political practice and has a semi-sacred character. Even the most tattered and patched-up cloak may look like a royal ceremonial gown if it is worn by a priest the people revere. Those who foretell the future from dreams will always be believed; the faithful never falter in their belief even when it is proved to them empirically that their dreams do not come true, because believers always have one or two examples illustrating the contrary, and sufficient to support their faith. And faith never requires proof, only examples and sanctions. . . .

. . . How can we free the morality of daily life from the nightmare of the philosophy of history and from those pseudo-dialectics which, by transforming morality into an instrument of history, in fact make history the pretext for disgraceful behavior? . . .

The danger is based on a complete substitution of criteria of usefulness, which the demiurge of history derives from our actions, for moral criteria. The greater the degree of certainty we have concerning the demiurge's intentions, the greater the threat. The sectarian spirit is the natural enemy of the skeptical spirit, and skepticism is the best possible antidote, however difficult to apply generally, against the insane fanaticism of visionaries. This centuries-old truth should be refurbished from time to time whenever historical experiences which demonstrate this truth with particular clarity recur. When one achieves an absolute and unshakeable certainty that the kingdom of heaven is around the corner, that the "Third Order," of which Joachim of Floris* wrote, is nearing its triumph and simultaneously approaching the final establishment of a new historical era, the ultimate one which "really" gives happiness and is "really" different from all the others, the only one to scotch the serpent's head and put an end to human suffering, when therefore we are hypnotized by boundless conviction that we are on the threshold of some kind of second coming, it is no wonder that this single messianic hope will become the sole law of life, the only source of moral precept, and the only measure of virtue. A consistent messianist must be convinced that he cannot hesitate to do anything that might help to bring about the new era. Morality, then, speaks in the language of the Apocalypse. It sees "a new heaven and a new earth" and knows simultaneously that before the far side is reached the four angles will destroy a third of mankind, burning stars will fall, the abyss will open, the seven vessels of God's wrath will be poured over the world, and glory will illuminate the victor who crushes the heathen with an iron rod. The historiosophy of the Apocalypse, of Joachim of Floris and of Thomas Munzer,** has been revived to some extent in the Communist movement. Although in this latter case it was supported by an honest and prolific effort of scientific analysis, it acted like a messianic vision in the operations of the mass movement. Probably it could not have been different, but awareness of this cannot provide us with a sense of security precisely because we want to prove that out of more or less reliable knowledge of historical necessities, we still cannot deduce the rules of our conduct.

In any case we take note of one of many practical lessons, which states that one needs a certain skepticism in the face

* Joachim of Floris: Heretical Italian monk of the twelfth century, who prophesied the coming of a new "age of the Holy Spirit," to succeed those of the "Father" and the "Son."—Ed.

** Thomas Munzer: Anabaptist leader of the German peasants' revolt of 1524-25—Ed.

with excessive certainty. Experience shows that, as Marx wrote, it is still easy to enslave people by an independent historical process. . . .

Nobody is free from positive or negative responsibility because his individual actions constitute only a fragment of a specific historical process. . . . If a social system exists which needs criminals for some of its tasks, one may be sure that these criminals will be found, but it does not follow that as a result of this certainty every individual criminal is freed from responsibility. In order to take upon oneself the role of such an instrument of the system, one must intrinsically be a criminal, one must voluntarily commit a specific act subject to moral judgment. We therefore support the doctrine of the total responsibility of the individual for his own deeds, and the amorality of the historical process. . . .

It is not true that the philosophy of history determines our main choices in life. Our moral sensibility does this. We are not Communists because we have recognized Communism as historical necessity; we are Communists because we have joined the side of the oppressed against their masters, the side of the persecuted against their persecutors. Although we know that the correct theoretical division of society is not into "rich" and "poor," not into "persecuted" and "persecutors," when we must make a *practical* choice apart from the theory, that is, a fundamental option, we are then morally motivated, and not motivated by theoretical considerations. It cannot be otherwise because even the most convincing theory is not by itself capable of making us lift a finger. A practical choice is a choice of values; that is, a moral act which is something for which everyone bears his own personal responsibility.

The Liberal Communist Protest—Djilas

Following the initial reforms after Yugoslavia's break with the Cominform, Djilas went on to argue for further democratization. Tito and the rest of the Yugoslav Communist leadership turned against his "reactionary deviation" in 1954 and ousted him from the party and the government. Subsequently he was tried and jailed, but nevertheless he succeeded in sending abroad a manuscript in which he analyzed the degeneration of the Communist movement.

All so-called *bourgeois* revolutions, whether achieved from below, i.e., with participation of the masses as in France, or from above, i.e., by *coup d'état* as in Germany under Bismarck, had to end up in political democracy. That is understandable. Their task was chiefly to destroy the old despotic political system, and to permit the establishment of political relationships which would be adequate for already existing economic and other needs, particularly those concerning the free production of goods.

The case is entirely different with contemporary Communist revolutions. These revolutions did not occur because new, let us say socialist, relationships were already existing in the economy, or because capitalism was "overdeveloped." On the contrary. They did occur because capitalism was not fully developed and because it was not able to carry out the industrial transformation of the country.

In France, capitalism had already prevailed in the economy, in social relationships, and even in the public conscience prior to inception of the revolution. The case is hardly comparable with socialism in Russia, China, or Yugoslavia. . . .

This leads to an apparent contradiction. If the conditions for a new society were not sufficiently prevalent, then who needed the revolution? Moreover, how was the revolution possible? How could it survive in view of the fact that the new social relationships were not yet in the formative process in the old society?

No revolution or party had ever before set itself to the task of building social relationships or a new society. But this was the primary objective of the Communist revolution.

Communist leaders, though no better acquainted than others with the laws which govern society, discovered that

FROM: Djilas, *The New Class: An Analysis of the Communist System* (New York, Praeger, 1957, pp. 19-23, 27-28, 38-39, 101-2, 153, 155, 162-63; reprinted by permission of the publisher).

in the country in which their revolution was possible, industrialization was also possible, particularly when it involved a transformation of society in keeping with their ideological hypothesis. Experience—the success of revolution under "unfavorable" conditions—confirmed this for them; the "building of socialism" did likewise. This strengthened their illusion that they knew the laws of social development. In fact, they were in the position of making a blueprint for a new society, and then of starting to build it, making corrections here and leaving out something there, all the while adhering closely to their plans.

Industrialization, as an inevitable, legitimate necessity of society, and the Communist way of accomplishing it, joined forces in the countries of Communist revolutions. . . .

. . . In Communist revolutions, force and violence are a condition for further development and even progress. In the words of earlier revolutionaries, force and violence were only a necessary evil and a means to an end. In the words of Communists, force and violence are elevated to the lofty position of a cult and an ultimate goal. In the past, the classes and forces which made up a new society already existed before the revolution erupted. The Communist revolutions are the first which have had to create a new society and new social forces. . . .

War, or more precisely, national collapse of the state organization, was unnecessary for past revolutions, at least for the larger ones. Until now, however, this has been a basic condition for the victory of Communist revolutions. This is even valid for China; true, there the revolution began prior to the Japanese invasion, but it continued for an entire decade to spread and finally to emerge victorious with the end of the war. The Spanish revolution of 1936, which could have been an exception, did not have time to transform itself into a purely Communist revolution, and, therefore, never emerged victorious.

The reason war was necessary for the Communist revolution, or the downfall of the state machinery, must be sought in the immaturity of the economy and society. In a serious collapse of a system, and particularly in a war which has been unsuccessful for the existing ruling circles and state system, a small but well-organized and disciplined group is inevitably able to take authority in its hands. . . .

. . . The masses of a nation also participated in a Communist revolution; however, the fruits of revolution do not fall to them, but to the bureaucracy. For the bureaucracy is nothing else but the party which carried out the revolution. . . .

. . . Revolutionaries who accepted the ideas and slogans of the revolution literally, naïvely believing in their materialization, are usually liquidated. The group which understood that revolution would secure authority, on a social-political-Communist basis, as an instrument of future industrial transformation, emerges victorious. . . .

This new class, the bureaucracy, or more accurately the political bureaucracy, has all the characteristics of earlier ones as well as some new characteristics of its own. . . .

. . . In spite of its illusions, it represented an objective tendency toward industrialization. Its practical bent emanated from this tendency. The promise of an ideal world increased the faith in the ranks of the new class and sowed illusions among the masses. At the same time it inspired gigantic physical undertakings.

Because this new class had not been formed as a part of the economic and social life before it came to power, it could only be created in an organization of a special type, distinguished by a special discipline based on identical philosophic and ideological views of its members. A unity of belief and iron discipline was necessary to overcome its weaknesses.

The roots of the new class were implanted in a special party, of the Bolshevik type. Lenin was right in his view that his party was an exception in the history of human society, although he did not suspect that it would be the beginning of a new class.

To be more precise, the initiators of the new class are not found in the party of the Bolshevik type as a whole but in that stratum of professional revolutionaries who made up its core even before it attained power. It was not by accident that Lenin asserted after the failure of the 1905 revolution that only professional revolutionaries—men whose sole profession was revolutionary work—could build a new party of the Bolshevik type. It was still less accidental that even Stalin, the future creator of a new class, was the most outstanding example of such a professional revolutionary. The new ruling class has been gradually developing from this very narrow stratum of revolutionaries. . . .

. . . The new class may be said to be made up of those who have special privileges and economic preference because of the administrative monopoly they hold. . . .

National feelings and national interest . . . do not lie at the basis of the conflict between the Communist national bureaucracies. The motive is quite different: it is supremacy in one's own zone, in the sphere which is under one's administration. The struggle over the reputation and powers of one's own republic does not go much further than a desire to strengthen one's own power. The national Communist state units have no significance other than that they are administrative divisions, on the basis of language. . . .

Just as personality, various social classes, and ideas still live, so do the nations still live; they function; they struggle against despotism; and they preserve their distinctive features undestroyed. If their consciences and souls are smothered, they are not broken. Though they are under subjugation, they have not yielded. The force activating them today is more than the old or bourgeois nationalism; it is an imperishable desire to be their own masters, and, by their own free development, to attain an increasingly fuller fellowship with the rest of the human race in its eternal existence. . . .

History does not have many movements that, like Communism, began their climb with such high moral principles and with such devoted, enthusiastic, and clever fighters, attached to each other not only by ideas and suffering, but also by selfless love, comradeship, solidarity, and that warm and direct sincerity that can be produced only by battles in which men are doomed either to win or die. . . .

. . . During the climb to power, intolerance, servility, incomplete thinking, control of personal life—which once was comradely aid but is now a form of oligarchic management

—hierarchical rigidity and introversion, the nominal and neglected role of women, opportunism, self-centeredness, and outrage repress the once-existent high principles. The wonderful human characteristics of an isolated movement are slowly transformed into the intolerant and Pharisaical morals of a privileged caste. Thus, politicking and servility replace the former straightforwardness of the revolution. Where the former heroes who were ready to sacrifice everything, including life, for others and for an idea, for the good of the people, have not been killed or pushed aside, they become self-centered cowards without ideas or comrades, willing to renounce everything—honor, name, truth, and morals—in order to keep their place in the ruling class and the hierarchical circle. The world has seen few heroes as ready to sacrifice and suffer as the Communists were on the eve of and during the revolution. It has probably never seen such characterless wretches and stupid defenders of arid formulas as they become after attaining power. . . .

Throughout history there have been no ideal ends which were attained with non-ideal, inhumane means, just as there has been no free society which was built by slaves. Nothing so well reveals the reality and greatness of ends as the methods used to attain them. . . .

No regime in history which was democratic—or relatively democratic while it lasted—was predominantly established on the aspiration for ideal ends, but rather on the small everyday means in sight. Along with this, each such regime achieved, more or less spontaneously, great ends. On the other hand, every despotism tried to justify itself by its ideal aims. Not a single one achieved great ends.

Absolute brutality, or the use of any means, is in accord with the grandiosity, even with the unreality, of Communist aims.

By revolutionary means, contemporary Communism has succeeded in demolishing one form of society and despotically setting up another. At first it was guided by the most beautiful, primordial human ideas of equality and brotherhood; only later did it conceal behind these ideas the establishment of its domination by whatever means. . . .

The "Anti-Party Group"

In June, 1957, the final stage in the succession to Stalin was reached when Khrushchev's colleagues in the party Presidium, alarmed over his power and perhaps genuinely opposed to some of his economic policies, attempted to remove him from the Secretariat. Khrushchev successfully appealed to the Central Committee, which was made up largely of party secretaries loyal to him, and had his opponents denounced for the old familiar sin of factionalism. Malenkov, Molotov, Kaganovich and Shepilov were removed from all their party and government offices, and were followed the next year by Bulganin. Khrushchev then assumed the premiership in addition to his post as First Secretary of the party, and emerged as the unchallenged individual leader of the USSR.

At its meetings of June 22 to June 29, 1957, the plenary session of the Party Central Committee considered the question of the anti-Party group of Malenkov, Kaganovich and Molotov which had formed within the Presidium of the Party Central Committee.

At a time when the Party, led by the Central Committee and supported by the people as a whole, is doing tremendous work to carry out the historic decisions of the 20th Congress—intended to develop the national economy further and steadily raise the living standard of the Soviet people, to re-establish Leninist norms of inner-Party life, to eliminate violations of revolutionary legality, to expand the Party's ties with the masses, to develop Soviet socialist democracy, to strengthen the friendship of the Soviet peoples, to pursue a correct nationality policy and, in the sphere of foreign policy, to relax international tension in order to secure a lasting peace—and when notable progress, well known to every Soviet citizen, has been made in all these fields, the anti-Party group of Malenkov, Kaganovich and Molotov came out against the Party line.

FROM: Resolution of the Central Committee of the CPSU, "On the Anti-Party Group of G. M. Malenkov, L. M. Kaganovich, and V. M. Molotov," June 29, 1957 (English translation in *The Current Digest of the Soviet Press,* IX: 23, July 17, 1957, pp. 5-7).

Seeking to change the Party's political line, this group used anti-Party, factional methods in an attempt to change the composition of the Party's leading bodies, elected by the plenary session of the Party Central Committee. . . .

This group persistently opposed and sought to frustrate so vastly important a measure as the reorganization of industrial management and the setting up of economic councils in the economic regions, a measure approved by the entire Party and the people. They refused to understand that at the present stage, when progress in socialist industry has assumed a tremendous scale and continues to grow rapidly, with the development of heavy industry receiving priority, it was essential to find new, more perfect forms of industrial management which would uncover great reserves and assure an even more powerful rise in Soviet industry. This group went so far as to continue its struggle against the reorganization of industrial management, even after the approval of these measures in the course of the nationwide discussion and the subsequent adoption of the law at a session of the U.S.S.R. Supreme Soviet.

With regard to agricultural questions, the members of this group failed to understand the new and vital tasks. They did not acknowledge the need to increase material incentives for the collective farm peasantry in increasing the output of agricultural products. They opposed abolition of the old bureaucratic system of planning on the collective farms and the introduction of the new system of planning which unleashes the initiative of the collective farms in managing their own affairs—a measure which has already yielded positive results. They have become so divorced from life that they cannot understand the real opportunity which makes it possible to abolish obligatory deliveries of farm products from collective farm households at the end of this year. Implementation of this measure, which is of vital importance for the millions of working people of the land of the Soviets, has been made possible by substantial progress of communal animal husbandry on the collective farms and by the development of the state farms. Instead of supporting this pressing measure, the members of the anti-Party group opposed it.

They waged an entirely unwarranted struggle against the Party's appeal—actively supported by the collective farms, provinces and republics—to overtake the U.S.A. in per capita output of milk, butter and meat in the next few years. Thereby the members of the anti-Party group demonstrated lordly indifference to the vital life interests of the broad masses of the people and lack of faith in the enormous potentialities inherent in the socialist economy, in the nation-wide movement now going on for a faster increase in milk and meat production.

It cannot be considered accidental that Comrade Molotov, a participant in the anti-Party group, manifesting conservatism and a stagnant attitude, not only failed to realize the need for developing the virgin lands but even opposed the plowing up of 35,000,000 hectares of virgin land, which has been of such tremendous importance in our country's economy.

Comrades Malenkov, Kaganovich and Molotov stubbornly opposed those measures which the Central Committee and our entire party carried out to eliminate the consequences of the cult of the individual leader, to eliminate the violations of revolutionary law which had occurred and to create conditions which would preclude their recurrence.

Whereas the workers, collective farmers, our glorious youth, our engineers and technicians, scientists, writers, the entire intelligentsia, unanimously supported the measures promulgated by the Party in accordance with the decisions of the 20th Party Congress, whereas the entire Soviet people joined the active struggle to carry out these measures, and whereas our country is experiencing a mighty increase in the active part played by the people and a fresh surge of new creative forces, the participants in the anti-Party group remained deaf to this creative movement of the masses.

In the sphere of foreign policy, this group, in particular Comrade Molotov, showed stagnation and hampered in every way implementation of new and pressing measures intended to alleviate international tension and strengthen world peace. As Minister of Foreign Affairs, Comrade Molotov for a long time not only failed to take any measures through the Ministry of Foreign Affairs to improve relations between the

U.S.S.R. and Yugoslavia but repeatedly came out against those measures which the Presidium of the Central Committee carried out to improve relations with Yugoslavia. Comrade Molotov's erroneous stand on the Yugoslav question was unanimously condemned by the July, 1955, plenary session of the Party Central Committee as "not corresponding to the interests of the Soviet state and the socialist camp and not conforming to the principles of Leninist policy.". . .

Seeing that their erroneous statements and actions were constantly rebuffed in the Presidium of the Central Committee, which has been consistently carrying out the line of the 20th Party Congress, Comrades Molotov, Kaganovich and Malenkov embarked on a group struggle against the Party leadership. Reaching agreement among themselves on an anti-Party basis, they set out to change the policy of the Party, to return the Party to those erroneous methods of leadership which were condemned by the 20th Party Congress. They resorted to methods of intrigue and reached a secret agreement against the Central Committee. The facts revealed at the Plenary session of the Central Committee show that Comrades Malenkov, Kaganovich and Molotov, as well as Comrade Shepilov, who joined them, having embarked on the path of factional struggle, violated the Party Statutes and the "On Party Unity" decision of the Tenth Party Congress, drafted by Lenin. . . .

. . . Guided by the interests of comprehensively strengthening the Leninist unity of the Party, the plenary session of the Party Central Committee resolves:

1. To condemn as incompatible with the Leninist principles of our party the factional activities of the anti-Party group of Malenkov, Kaganovich and Molotov, and of Shepilov, who joined them.

2. To exclude Comrades Malenkov, Kaganovich and Molotov from membership in the Presidium of the Central Committee and from the Central Committee; to remove Comrade Shepilov from the post of Secretary of the Central Committee and to exclude him from the list of candidates for membership in the Presidium of the Central Committee and from membership in the Central Committee. . . .

Khrushchev on the Arts

Following the "thaw" or relaxation of ideological controls in 1956, Khrushchev reaffirmed the primacy of the party in cultural life.

. . . Why does the party pay so much attention to questions of literature and the arts? Because literature and the arts have an exceptionally important role in our party's ideological work, in the communist education of the working people. . . .

The main line of development is that literature and the arts must always be inseparably linked with the people's life, must truthfully portray the wealth and variety of our socialist reality and vividly and convincingly show the Soviet people's great work of transformation, the nobility of their aims and aspirations and their lofty moral qualities. The highest social purpose of literature and the arts is to arouse the people to a struggle for new victories in the building of communism.

It must be admitted, comrades, that some of our writers and workers in the arts continue to lose their foothold and to stray from the right road. These people treat the tasks of literature and the arts erroneously and in a distorted way. They try to present matters as if the duty of literature and the arts were to find only the faults, to speak primarily of life's negative aspects, of lack of harmony, and to keep silent about all that is favorable. Yet it is the positive, the new and the progressive in life that is most important in the tempestuously developing reality of a socialist society. . . .

Unfortunately, there are among our workers in literature and the arts advocates of "creative freedom" who desire us to pass by, not to notice, not to subject to principled appraisal and not to criticize works that portray the life of Soviet society in a distorted fashion. It appears to these people that the guidance of literature and the arts by the party and the

FROM: Khrushchev, "For a Close Tie between Literature and Art and the Life of the People" (August, 1957; English translation in *The Current Digest of the Soviet Press,* IX: 35, October 9, 1957, pp. 7-9).

state is oppressive. They sometimes oppose this guidance openly; more often, however, they conceal their feelings and desires behind talk of excessive tutelage, the fettering of initiative, etc.

We assert openly that such views run counter to the Leninist principles of the party's and state's attitude to questions of literature and the arts. . . .

The whole history of the development of Soviet society is convincing proof that guidance by the party and the state, their attention to artistic creation and their concern for writers, artists, sculptors and composers, has ensured outstanding successes of literature and the arts, the flowering of the socialist culture of all the peoples of the U.S.S.R. The party's decisions on ideological questions have defined the major tasks and the basic principles of the Party's policy in the sphere of art and literature, and they retain their force to this day. One of the primary principles is that Soviet literature and art must be indissolubly linked with the policy of the Communist Party, which constitutes the vital foundations of the Soviet system. . . .

The party has resolutely condemned the errors that were committed in all spheres of life, including ideological work, during the period of the cult of the individual, and it is consistently rectifying them. However, at the same time the party vigorously opposes those who try to make use of these past errors to resist the guidance of literature and the arts by the Party and the state. . . .

The development of literature and art is proceeding in conditions of ideological battle against the influence of bourgeois culture, which is alien to us—against obsolete concepts and views and for the affirmation of our Communist ideology.

We would not be Marxist-Leninists if we held aloof, if we remained passive and indifferent to attempts to insinuate into our literature and art bourgeois views that are alien to the spirit of the Soviet people. We must look at things soberly and take cognizance of the fact that enemies exist, and that they are trying to utilize the ideological front to weaken the forces of socialism. In such a situation our ideological weapons must be in good order and must operate unfailingly. The lesson of the Hungarian events in which the counterrevolution used certain writers for its dirty ends, reminds us what political complacency, lack of principle and weakness of will in regard to the machinations of forces hostile to socialism may lead to. It must be clear to everyone that in the present conditions, when a sharp conflict between the forces of socialism and the forces of imperialist reaction is under way, we must keep our powder dry.

The Reaffirmation of International Communist Solidarity

In November, 1957, a world-wide conference of Communist parties (excepting only Yugoslavia) was held in Moscow to repair the damage done to Communist discipline by de-Stalinization and the Polish and Hungarian revolutions. While some flexibility of tactics was admitted, the aim of Communist dictatorship was made clear, and unyielding doctrinal orthodoxy was demanded.

The Communist and Workers' Parties taking part in this conference declare that the Leninist principle of peaceful coexistence of the two systems, which has been further developed in contemporary circumstances in the decisions of the 20th Party Congress, is the firm foundation of the foreign policy of the socialist countries and the reliable foundation of peace and friendship among the peoples. The five principles advanced jointly by the Chinese People's Republic and the Republic of India and the program adopted by the Bandung conference of African and Asian countries correspond to the interests of peaceful coexistence. The struggle for peace and peaceful coexistence have now become the demands of the broadest masses in all countries of the world.

The Communist Parties regard the struggle for peace as their foremost task. Together with all peace-loving forces, they will do all in their power to prevent war.

The conference considers that strengthening of the unity

FROM: Declaration of the Conference of Representatives of Communist and Workers' Parties of Socialist Countries, Moscow, November, 1957 (English translation in *The Current Digest of the Soviet Press,* IX: 47, January 1, 1958, pp. 4-7).

and fraternal cooperation of the socialist states and of the Communist and Workers' Parties of all countries and closing of the ranks of the international working class, national-liberation and democratic movements take on special importance in the present situation. . . .

Intensification of the struggle against opportunist trends in the workers' and Communist movement is of great importance at the present stage. The conference stresses the necessity of resolutely overcoming revisionism and dogmatism in the ranks of the Communist and Workers' Parties. Revisionism and dogmatism in the workers' and Communist movement are today, as they have been in the past, of an international nature. Dogmatism and sectarianism hinder the development of Marxist-Leninist theory and its creative application in specific changing conditions, replace study of the specific situation with quotations and pedantry, and lead to the Party's isolation from the masses. A party that has locked itself up in sectarianism and that has lost contact with the broad masses can by no means bring victory to the cause of the working class.

In condemning dogmatism, the Communist Parties consider the main danger in present-day conditions to be revisionism or, in other words, right-wing opportunism, as a manifestation of bourgeois ideology that paralyzes the revolutionary energy of the working class and demands the preservation or restoration of capitalism. However, dogmatism and sectarianism can also be the main danger at different stages of development of one party or another. Each Communist Party determines what danger is the main danger to it at a given time. . . .

Present-day revisionism seeks to defame the great teaching of Marxism-Leninism, declares that it is "obsolete" and that it has allegedly lost its importance for social development. The revisionists are trying to destroy the revolutionary soul of Marxism, to undermine the faith of the working class and the working people in socialism. They deny the historical necessity of a proletarian revolution and the dictatorship of the proletariat during the period of transition from capitalism to socialism, deny the leading role of the Marxist-Leninist party, deny the principles of proletarian internationalism, demand abandonment of the Leninist principles of Party organization and, above all, of democratic centralism and demand that the Communist Party be transformed from a militant revolutionary organization into a kind of debating club.

The entire experience of the international Communist movement teaches that resolute defense by the Communist and Workers' Parties of the Marxist-Leninist unity of their ranks and the banning of factions and groups that undermine its unity are a necessary guarantee of the successful accomplishment of the tasks of the socialist revolution and the building of socialism and communism. . . .

The forms of the transition of different countries from capitalism to socialism may vary. The working class and its vanguard—the Marxist-Leninist party—seek to bring about socialist revolution by peaceful means. Realization of this possibility would accord with the interests of the working class and of all the people and with the over-all national interests of the country.

In present-day conditions in a number of capitalist countries the working class, headed by the vanguard, has the possibility—on the basis of a workers' and people's front or of other possible forms of agreement and political cooperation among the different parties and public organizations—to unite the majority of the people, win state power without civil war and ensure the transfer of the basic means of production to the hands of the people. Relying on the majority of the people and decisively rebuffing the opportunist elements incapable of relinquishing a policy of compromise with the capitalists and landlords, the working class can defeat the reactionary, antipopular forces, win a firm majority in parliament, transform the parliament from an instrument serving the class interests of the bourgeoisie into an instrument serving the working people, develop a broad mass struggle outside the parliament, break the resistance of the reactionary forces and create the necessary conditions for bringing about the socialist revolution peacefully. All this will be possible only by extensive, steady development of the class struggle of the workers, peasant masses and middle urban strata against big monopoly capital, against reaction, for profound social reforms, for peace and socialism.

In conditions in which the exploiting classes resort to violence against the people, it is necessary to bear in mind another possibility—nonpeaceful transition to socialism. Leninism teaches and history confirms that the ruling classes never relinquish power voluntarily. In these conditions the severity and forms of the class struggle will depend not so much on the proletariat as on the resistance of the reactionary circles to the will of the overwhelming majority of the people, on the use of force by these circles at one or another stage of the struggle for socialism.

In each country the real possibility of one or another means of transition to socialism depends on the specific historical conditions.

The Communist Parties stand for the establishment of cooperation with socialist parties both in the struggle for improving the working people's living conditions, for extending and preserving their democratic rights, for winning and defending national independence and for peace among peoples and in the struggle for winning power and building socialism. Although the right-wing leaders of the socialist parties are trying in every way to impede this cooperation, there are increasing opportunities for cooperation between the Communists and the socialists on many questions. The ideological differences between the Communist and socialist parties should not keep them from establishing unity of action on the many current problems that today confront the workers' movement. . . .

The participants in the conference unanimously express their firm confidence that, by rallying their ranks and thereby rallying the working class and the peoples of all countries, the Communist and Workers' Parties will undoubtedly surmount all obstacles on the path of progress and hasten great new victories for the cause of peace, democracy and socialism on a world scale.

Khrushchev on the "Transition to Communism"

At the Twenty-First Party Congress in January, 1959, Khrushchev staked his claim to be a major Communist theorist in a long discussion of the conditions and features of the anticipated transition to the higher social stage of "communism." As his definitions showed, this was but the latest in a long series of efforts to square the Marxian ideal of anarchistic equalitarianism with the realities of bureaucratic industrialism in a world of competitive power politics.

. . . Comrades, under the leadership of the party the Soviet people have reached such heights, have performed such giant transformations in all fields of economy and public political life, as enable our country now to enter a new, most important period of its development—the period of all-out building of a communist society.

The main tasks of this period are the creation of the material-technical basis of communism, a further consolidation of the economic and defense might of the USSR, and at the same time an increasingly full satisfaction of the growing material and spiritual needs of the people. A practical solution must be found for the historic task of catching up with and outstripping the most developed capitalist countries in per capita output. The fulfillment of these tasks will demand a stretch of time going beyond the limits of the seven-year plan. . . .

Our foreign enemies allege that in drawing up the Soviet seven-year plan the main stress has been placed on heavy industry, which will demand sacrifices on the part of the population. It is true that large capital investment in the development of heavy industry is envisaged in our plan. How could it be otherwise? In order to have a sufficient amount of consumer goods we need to increase the means of production. It is necessary to produce metal, to create machines, to put into operation automatic lines which will work for man in order to meet his needs. . . .

In the years of the first five-year plan, when the life and death of the Soviet country—the world's only country of

FROM: Khrushchev, Political Report to the Twenty-First Congress of the CPSU, January, 1959 (English translation in U. S. Government, Foreign Broadcast Information Service, *Daily Report—Supplement: USSR and Eastern Europe,* no. 3, 1959, pp. 95, 128-30, 132-34, 147, 167, 173-74, 176, 178, 180-81, 183).

socialism, surrounded by capitalist countries—was at stake, the Soviet people exerted all their strength, made conscious sacrifices in order to get out of the century-old backwardness and to create a powerful socialist economy. Even then, the party and the state did everything possible to improve the material situation of the working people.

Now we have a different level of development, different possibilities, different strength. We firmly put forward the task of advancing considerably the welfare of the Soviet people. . . .

Comrades, the transition to communism demands not only a developed material-technical base but also a high level of consciousness in all citizens. The higher the consciousness of the masses the more successful will be the implementation of the plans for communist construction. That is why exceptional importance is now being assumed by the problem of the communist training of the working people, especially that of the younger generation. The whole ideological work of our party and state is called upon to develop new qualities in Soviet people—to educate them in the spirit of collectivism and love of work, socialist internationalism and patriotism, high moral principles of the new society, in the spirit of Marxism-Leninism.

In order to achieve communism—the most just and perfect society where the best moral traits of free men will be fully disclosed—we must even now educate future man. One must develop in the Soviet people an irreconcilable attitude toward its enemies, recognition of duty to society, active participation in work for the benefit of society, voluntary adherence to the basic rules of the human community, comradely mutual help, honesty and truthfulness, intolerance toward those who disturb public order. . . .

The spirit of individualism, personal gain, greed for profits, hostility and confusion—such is the essence of bourgeois morality. Exploitation of man by man, on which bourgeois society is built, represents the grossest violation of morals. It is not for nothing that the morals of the exploiting classes are characterized by the cruel formula, dog eat dog.

Socialism affirms a socialist morality—a morality of collaboration and collectivism, friendship and mutual help. Here solicitude for the general welfare of the people, for the all-sided development of the individual under collectivist conditions where man is not enemy of man but a friend and brother, is put in the foreground. . . .

The great moral influence of the ideas of communism in socialist countries is vividly manifested in the active participation of millions of people in the building of the new life. It is beyond the ability of bourgeois politicians to understand the patriotism and labor enthusiasm of the Soviet people, who place the interests of society higher than private interests, conscious of the fact that the welfare and happiness of people under socialism are secured by society as a whole.

Take, for example, a fact such as the measure with regard to state loans, brought about at the initiative of the working people. Millions of Soviet people voluntarily expressed themselves in favor of the postponement for 20 to 25 years of repayments under the old state loans. This fact reveals to us such new human traits, such moral qualities in our people as are inconceivable under conditions of a regime of exploitation. . . .

The assertion of communist views and norms of behavior is being achieved in the struggle against the remnants of capitalism. It is not too rare that we find people who have an unconscientious attitude toward social work, who engage in speculation, violate discipline and the social order. One cannot calmly wait for these remnants of capitalism to disappear by themselves; it is imperative to wage a determined struggle against them and to direct public opinion against any manifestation of bourgeois views and morals and against antisocial elements. . . .

Some workers underestimate the evil of the bourgeois influence upon the Soviet youth and consider that bourgeois ideas are far from us and that our youth is beyond their reach. But this is an error. We cannot ignore the possibility of bourgeois influence and are obliged to wage a struggle against it, against the penetration among the Soviet people, and, particularly among the young, of alien views and morals.

A special role in the communist education of the growing

generation belongs to the school. The Soviet school has trained tens of millions of educated citizens, builders of socialism; it has helped to raise wonderful cadres of engineers, technicians, agronomists, teachers, doctors, and other specialists with secondary and higher qualifications.

The positive role of the school in the training and education of the young generation is well known. However, in spite of all successes, the Soviet school still lags behind the requirements of communist construction work and has serious shortcomings. . . .

The close tie of education with life, production, and the practice of communist construction work must become the main principle for the study of the foundations of the sciences in schools and the basis of the education of the growing generation in the spirit of communist morality. The link of education with productive labor does not diminish but, on the contrary, strengthens the significance of the knowledge acquired. . . .

What new things in the international arena will be introduced by the fulfillment of the economic plans of the Soviet Union and of all socialist countries of Europe and Asia? As a result of these, real possibilities will be created for doing away with war as a means of solving international issues. Indeed, when the USSR becomes the world's foremost industrial power, when the Chinese People's Republic becomes a mighty industrial power, when all socialist countries taken together will produce more than half the world's industrial output, then the international situation will change radically. . . .

Based on the might of the camp of socialism, peaceloving peoples will then be able to force the bellicose imperialist circles to renounce plans for another world war. . . .

. . . The development of Soviet society confirmed the Marxist-Leninist foresight about the two phases of communism. Having built a socialist society, the Soviet people have entered the new stage of historic development in which socialism develops into communism. The theory of Marxism-Leninism and the practical experience of the building of socialist society provide ground for drawing some important conclusions on the nature of the progression of society toward communism.

The transition from the socialist phase of development to a higher phase is, first of all, a natural historic process which cannot be intentionally violated or bypassed. The Marxist-Leninist party considers the setting up of a communist society its final aim. But society cannot switch over to communism from capitalism without passing through the socialist phase of development. From capitalism, Lenin said, mankind can switch over directly only to socialism, that is, to communal ownership of production means and distribution of products to individuals in accordance to their work. Our party looks farther ahead. Socialism must inevitably develop gradually into communism, on the banner of which is written: From each according to his abilities, to each according to his needs. . . .

Under the conditions of socialism class inequality is excluded, and there remains only inequality of portions received in the distribution of goods. Insofar as people have different qualifications, are unequally gifted, have unequal ability to work, and have families of different sizes, it is natural that, given equal remuneration for equal toil, they should be getting unequal incomes. Yet such order is inevitable for the first phase of the communist society. . . .

. . . One cannot fail to see that equalization would lead to unjust distribution. Both the good and bad workers would receive the same. This is advantageous only for idlers. Thus, the material incentive of people to work better, to increase labor productivity, to produce more, would be undermined. Equalization would mean not a transition to communism but the discrediting of communism. . . .

The necessity of regulating the distribution of products among members of society will disappear only under communism, when productive forces will be developed so far that there will be plenty of all necessary consumer goods, and when everybody will, voluntarily and independently of the amount of material value received, work to his full capability, realizing that this is necessary for society.

Naturally in a communist society there will be planned

and organized distribution of work according to various branches of production, and social regulation of working time, with special reference to the specific characteristic of production processes. Machine production has a definite rhythm which is impossible to maintain without corresponding planning of human work.

Some people have a vulgar concept of communist society as a formless and unorganized, anarchistic mass of people. No, this will be a highly organized and harmonious fraternity of working people. In order to control machinery, everybody will have to fulfill within a definite time and in a definite order his function of work and his social duty. The highly mechanized and automated production of the future will not demand many hours of work by an individual. There will be much free time to be occupied by sciences, art, literature, sports and so forth. . . .

. . . The question of the dying off of the state, if it is to be understood dialectically, is a question of the development of a socialist state system into communist public self-government.

Under communism certain public functions will remain, analogous to present state functions. But the nature and means of implementing them will be different than at the present stage of development. The main orientation in the development of the socialist state is the all-out development of democracy, the inclusion of the widest strata of the population in the management of all the affairs of the country, the inclusion of all citizens in the management of economic and cultural construction. . . .

The socialist society is creating voluntary organs for maintaining public order such as the people's militia, comrades courts, and similar organs. They will work in a new way and discharge public functions in a new manner. Voluntary detachments of the people's militia must take it upon themselves to maintain public order in their own localities and see to it that the rights and interests of all citizens are maintained and safeguarded. . . .

It stands to reason that the transfer of certain functions from state bodies to public organizations in no way signifies a weakening of the part played by the socialist state in the construction of communism. The implementation by public organizations of several functions which at the moment belong to the state will broaden and strengthen the political foundation of the socialist society and will lead to the further development of socialist democracy. . . .

Leninism teaches that the withering away of the state will take place at the time of complete victory of communism. In the present circumstances, to weaken the socialist state means to help our enemies. If the imperialists cannot at present destroy us, the revisionists are in actual fact suggesting that we ourselves should disarm, destroy state organs which insure the defense of the country, and thus place ourselves at the mercy of our enemies. The functions of the defense of the socialist fatherland at present carried out by the state can wither away only when the danger of attack by imperialists upon our country and our allied countries is fully eliminated. . . .

No forces exist at present in the world capable of restoring capitalism in our country and of shattering the socialist camp. The danger of the restoration of capitalism in the Soviet Union has been excluded. This means that socialism has triumphed, triumphed fully and finally. (Prolonged stormy applause) Thus, it can be considered that the problem of building socialism in our country, of the complete and final victory, has been solved by the world-historic progress of social development. . . .

How will the development of socialist countries proceed toward communism? Can a situation be imagined in which one socialist country attains communism and carries out communist principles of production and distribution, while other countries still remain somewhere behind, in the first stage of building a socialist society? If one takes into account the laws of economic development of socialist systems of economy, such a prospect is hardly possible. It would be theoretically correct to assume that socialist countries, correctly using the opportunities inherent in the socialist order, will more or less simultaneously reach the highest phase of communist society. . . .

Peculiarities of the road involve taking into consideration the particular characteristics of the situation and the time in which one or another country develops. For example, some measures in building socialism which were used at the time in the Soviet Union cannot be mechanically applied in other countries. All socialist countries build socialism, but this is not done according to a standard pattern. The Communist Party of China is using many special forms in building socialism, and yet we have not and cannot have any differences with it. . . .

Why are there no differences between us and the Communist Party of China? Because the class approach and class understanding of both parties is the same. The Chinese Communist Party stands firmly on Marxist-Leninist class positions; it is waging a struggle against the imperialists and exploiters, a struggle for the reorganization of life on socialist principles. It observes the principle of international proletarian solidarity and is guided by the Marxist-Leninist theory. The main thing is the maintenance and strengthening of class solidarity in the struggle against capitalism, for the liberation of the working class, for the construction of socialism. . . .

Chapter Eight: Communism in the Far East

The history of communism in the Far East is largely the story of the most successful Asian Communist movement in the continent's most populous country, China. From the early 1920's Russia, the Communist International and the Chinese Communist Party were important factors in Chinese politics, whereas elsewhere in Asia communism was a negligible force until World War II. Chinese communism matured over more than two decades of regional rule and struggle with the nationalist government, until successive gains in the anti-Japanese war and the civil war brought it to power as a disciplined totalitarian movement.

The Chinese Communist victory was anomalous from the Marxist standpoint because it was not based on the working class and lacked a definite class struggle. The pattern, which the other Far-Eastern Communist movements have copied, was to bring all available social groups into a movement controlled by the disciplined Communist Party; to capitalize on nationalistic and anti-imperialist emotion; and to develop the "proletarian" base of the movement not by social selection but by intellectual "remolding" or conversion on the basis of Marxist-Leninist ideology (irrelevant as it was). It is in the Far East that communism comes closest to being a religion—with salvation, one might say, based on faith.

The successes of communism in the Far East have had a major effect on the nature of the movement as a whole. It is no longer centered on one nation, but has become bi-polar; in political and ideological influence China is nearly on a par with the USSR, and may be expected to play an increasingly powerful role.

The Founding of the Chinese Communist Party

Marxism had virtually no following in China until the Russian Revolution dramatized its anti-imperialist appeal. A small Communist Party, drawing its members mostly from the intellectuals, was organized in 1921 under the leadership of Ch'en Tu-hsiu, a university dean. The party's plan, as put forth in the manifesto of 1922, was to press for completion of the "bourgeois-democratic revolution" in alliance with the Nationalist Party (the "Kuomintang," the party of Sun Yat-sen and later of Chiang Kai-shek, which at that time held power only in the region of Canton).

. . . The revolution of 1911 had two historical tasks: first, the overthrow of the Manchu dynasty and, second, the liberation of China from foreign oppression and the transformation of China into an independent state. In this second objective the 1911 revolution aimed to create, within a framework of racial and national independence, favourable conditions for the industrial development of China. The 1911 revolution expressed the transition from the political system of feudalism to a democratic regime, from manual labour and an artisan economy to capitalist production. . . .

The result of the revolution's defeat has been a strengthening of the world imperialist yoke in China and of the reactionary regime of her own militarists. The so-called republican rule is in the hands of militarists who, under conditions of a semi-feudal economy, use it to join their own actions with those of the world imperialists, who are concluding an agreement with the Chinese military clique regarding loans for their military needs and for the state's self-preservation. The foreign states are making use of the opportunity to invest their capital in China, thus acquiring, by means of a system of financial enslavement, "spheres of influence" in China and special rights and privileges. . . .

FROM: Manifesto of the Chinese Communist Party, "On the Current Situation," June 10, 1922 (English translation in Conrad Brandt, Benjamin Schwartz, and John K. Fairbank, *A Documentary History of Chinese Communism*, Cambridge, Mass., Harvard University Press, 1952, pp. 55-58, 62; this and subsequent selections reprinted by permission of the publisher).

The socio-economic conditions in China affect the middle, intermediary classes with particular force. The owners of small enterprises are being deprived of property; artisans fill the ranks of the army of the unemployed; peasants sell their land to landlords for absurd sums of money because they are unable to conduct their own economy, owing to the continuously rising cost of living.

These conditions will remain unchanged so long as power remains in the hands of the feudal-lord government, in the hands of militarists; so long as power is not seized from their hands; and so long as a democratic government is not established.

Democratic government means a democratic party government. We have in mind the creation of power on the basis of a total reorganization of the entire political system of administration. Basically, this demand entails the overthrow of the authority of the reactionary, counterrevolutionary elements and groups by revolutionary methods, by a democratic party, or by a bloc of democratic groupings which will organize power to conform to the historical requirements of their own country and with consideration for the realities of the new international environment. . . .

The postulate must be clear to everyone that the political struggle is not a struggle between individuals for power, but a manifestation and expression of class struggle—the social struggle of the proletariat against the bourgeoisie in the period of revolution and, in the period of bourgeois revolution, the struggle of the bourgeoisie against the feudal lords and the system of feudal economy. The postulate must also be clear that only such freedom is precious as is achieved in the process of hard struggle and at the price of human blood, in distinction from those methods of struggle which are used by our class enemies.

The struggle for democracy is a struggle of one class, a struggle which aims to overthrow the dominance of another class; it is the replacement of one system by another, and in no event can it be regarded as a struggle of one individual or one group for the overthrow of another individual or group.

A real democratic party must possess two characteristic

elements: (1) its principles must be correlated with the concepts of democracy; and (2) its actions must consist in an active struggle against feudalism in the form of the military. Of all the political parties existing in China, only the Kuomintang can be characterized as a revolutionary party, yet it possesses only a relative amount of democratic and revolutionary spirit. The programme of this party has not yet been fully elaborated. But its three principles, "of the people, for the people, and by the people" . . . in conjunction with plans for the industrial development of China . . . reflect the democratic spirit of the Kuomintang. . . .

For all of us, the only way by which we can liberate ourselves from the hard yoke of the military is to join the democratic struggle against the relics of the past—a struggle for freedom and peace. The government opposition game, played by the bourgeoisie, the intelligentsia, and the politicians, cannot be trusted. We all want peace, but real peace rather than false peace. We welcome a war to achieve the triumph of democracy, to overthrow the military and the militarists and to liberate the Chinese people.

The Chinese Communist Party, as the vanguard of the proletariat, struggles for working-class liberation and for the proletarian revolution. Until such time as the Chinese proletariat is able to seize power in its own hands, considering the present political and economic conditions of China's development and all the historical processes now going on in China, the proletariat's urgent task is to act jointly with the democratic party to establish a united front of democratic revolution to struggle for the overthrow of the military and for the organization of a real democratic government. . . .

The Comintern and Chinese Communism

The Russian leaders of the Communist International found the Chinese Communists fully prepared to abide by their decisions. Moscow's policy was to build an alliance with Chiang and the Kuomintang, both through direct assistance and by forcing the Chinese Communists to continue the alliance with the Kuomintang even after they became restive about it. This line was affirmed by the Comintern Executive in 1926.

. . . During the last two years, imperialism has suffered a heavy defeat in China, the effects of which will contribute considerably to the aggravation of the crisis of world capitalism. . . .

The further victories of the revolutionary armies of Canton, supported by the broad masses of the Chinese people, will lead to victory over the imperialists, to the achievement of the independence of China, and to its revolutionary unification, which will consequently increase in numerous ways its power of resistance to imperialism. . . .

To overthrow the militarists completely, the economic and political struggle of the peasantry, which constitutes the overwhelming majority of the population, must be developed as a part of the anti-imperialist struggle. The fear that the aggravation of the class struggle in the countryside will weaken the anti-imperialist front is baseless. . . . The refusal to assign the agrarian revolution a prominent place in the national-liberation movement, for fear of alienating the dubious and indecisive co-operation of a section of the capitalist class, is wrong. This is not the revolutionary policy of the proletariat. The Communist Party must be free from such mistakes. . . .

The supreme necessity of winning influence over the peasantry determines the relation of the Communist Party to the Kuomintang and to the Canton government likewise. The machinery of the national-revolutionary government provides a very effective way to reach the peasantry. The Communist Party must use this machinery.

In the newly liberated provinces (local) governments of

FROM: "Theses on the Chinese Situation and Plan of Action for the Chinese Communists," adopted at the Seventh Plenum of the Executive Committee of the Communist International, November–December, 1926 (English translation in Xenia J. Eudin and Robert C. North, *Soviet Russia and the East, 1920-1927: A Documentary Survey*, Stanford, Calif., Stanford University Press, 1957, pp. 356, 359-62; reprinted by permission of the publisher; copyright 1957 by the Board of Trustees of Leland Stanford Junior University).

the type of the Canton government will be set up. The Communists and their revolutionary allies must penetrate the new governments, so as to give practical expression to their agrarian program by using the governmental machinery to confiscate land, reduce taxes, invest real power in the peasant committees. . . .

For this reason and many other equally important reasons, the point of view that the Communist Party must leave the Kuomintang is incorrect. The whole process of development of the Chinese revolution, its character and its prospects, demand that the Communists stay in the Kuomintang and intensify their work in it. . . .

The Communist Party of China must strive to develop the Kuomintang into a real people's party—a solid revolutionary bloc of the proletariat, the peasantry, the urban petty bourgeoisie and the other oppressed and exploited strata—a party dedicated to a decisive struggle against imperialism and its agents. . . .

. . . The Canton government, in spite of its bourgeois-democratic character, essentially and objectively contains the germs of a revolutionary petty bourgeois state—a democratic dictatorship of the revolutionary bloc of the proletariat, peasantry, and the urban petty bourgeoisie. The petty-bourgeois democratic movement becomes revolutionary in China because it is an anti-imperialist movement. The Canton government is revolutionary primarily because it is anti-imperialist. Being primarily anti-imperialist, the Chinese revolution and the government created by it must strike at the root of imperialist power in China. Repudiation of unequal treaties and abolition of territorial concessions will not be sufficient to weaken the position of imperialism. The blow must be dealt at the economic basis of imperialist power; the revolutionary government must gradually confiscate the railways, concessions, factories, mines, banks, and other business enterprises owned by foreign capital. By so doing it will immediately outstrip the narrow boundary of bourgeois democracy and enter into the state of transition to revolutionary dictatorship. . . .

The 1927 Debacle of Chinese Communism

In the course of taking over central authority in China in 1926-27, Chiang Kai-shek broke with the Communists and almost destroyed the movement. Belatedly Moscow ordered revolutionary action and blamed the Chinese Communist leaders for maintaining the alliance with Chiang too long. The Chinese Central Committee displayed its subservience by acknowledging the blame and dropping its leader, Ch'en Tu-hsiu.

. . . In the recent resolution of the Executive Committee of the Communist International it was pointed out that the leadership of our Party had committed grave errors of opportunism. The Executive Committee of the Communist International called on the entire Party to criticize itself thoroughly and correct such mistakes. The mistakes mentioned here are neither individual nor incidental but rather result from the grievously erroneous opportunist line carried out by the leadership of our Party. . . .

The Chinese Communist Party should spread and encourage the class struggle of the proletariat and help every workers' struggle against the bourgeoisie. The Communist International has repeatedly instructed the Chinese Communist Party to fight for the improvement of the material conditions of the working masses, and for the betterment of living conditions in the factories and in society, for the immediate abolition of the laws which oppress the workers, and for the realization of such rights as the eight-hour working day, increase of wages, and recognition of workers' rights to organize unions and to strike. At the same time, the Communist International points out that it is necessary to arm the workers speedily, boldly, and resolutely, especially those elements which are most class-conscious and best organized. This course is considered absolutely essential by the Communist International. Such directives of the Communist International are in keeping with the struggle of the workers themselves in

FROM: Circular Letter of the Central Committee of the Chinese Communist Party, to All Party Members, August 7, 1927 (Brandt, Schwartz, Fairbank, pp. 102-3, 106-7, 109-10, 116-17).

the industrial areas and the actions of the rank and file Party members. But the leading organ of our Party has developed a different course. It has simply hindered and minimized the class struggle and the revolutionary actions of the workers. Instead of spreading and promoting strike movements, the Central Committee, together with the leaders of the Kuomintang, decided on an arbitrary method of mediation and ruled that the final authority belonged to the government. Under the government of a coalition of classes, led at this first stage by the bourgeoisie, this kind of policy actually served merely to protect the interests of the bourgeoisie and greatly obstructed the workers' movement. . . .

The question of agrarian revolution is the crux of the bourgeois-democratic revolution in China. The Communist International has repeatedly explained itself concerning this question. . . . Agrarian revolution consists of confiscation and nationalization of land—this is the major content of the internal social economy in the new stage of the Chinese revolution. The main thing at present is to employ the "mass-type" revolutionary methods to solve the land problem [and allow] the tens of millions of peasants to solve this problem by rising from below. The Central Committee should be the vanguard of this movement and direct it. In the government, the Communist Party should carry out such a policy so that the government itself will act to support the agrarian revolution. Only thus can the present government be turned into the centre of political organization of the workers' and peasants' movement, and the organ of the dictatorship of the workers and peasants. . . .

The relation between the Party and the Communist International was also not in accordance with accepted organizational procedure. There has never been a case in the history of the Communist International where the instructions and resolutions were actually rejected in such a critical situation. This was no longer merely a simple breach of discipline, but a criminal act against the Chinese and international Communist movement. The Chinese revolution does not merely have a national significance, but also forms a major sector in the world revolution. The fate of the world revolution will be decided by the fate of the Chinese revolution. The Chinese Communist Party not only carried out an erroneous policy, a policy that brought the revolution to defeat, that voluntarily liquidated the revolution and capitulated to the enemy, but also would not admit its errors or obey the instructions of the Communist International. . . .

The Communist International has severely criticized the opportunist line of the Central Committee, which has in reality betrayed the [Chinese] revolution. We agree that this criticism is entirely just and that the policy of the Executive Committee of the Communist International regarding the Chinese problem is entirely correct. We welcome the recent instructions of the Communist International which have made possible the unmasking of the past mistakes of the [Party] leadership and have saved our Party [from destruction]. We positively agree that, in the past, the leadership of the Central Committee carried out an opportunist, unrevolutionary policy and that it is necessary to carry out a thorough revision of our policy on the basis of the lessons of the past. . . .

Mao Tse-tung on the Peasant Movement

Mao Tse-tung, born in 1893 to a family of the petty gentry and a secondary leader of the Chinese Communist Party since its founding, began in 1927 to organize peasant uprisings in south-central China. He developed an army that was able to maintain control over certain mountainous areas. After Chiang Kai-shek smashed the Communists in the coastal cities, Mao commanded the only effective Communist power, and over Moscow's objections assumed de facto leadership of the party.

The phenomenon that within a country one or several small areas under Red political power came into existence amid the

FROM: Mao, "The Struggle in the Chingkang Mountains" (Report to the Central Committee of the Chinese Communist Party, November, 1928; English translation in Mao, *Selected Works*, New York, International Publishers, 1954, Vol. I, pp. 71, 79-83, 99; reprinted by permission of the publisher).

encirclement of White political power is one which, of all the countries in the world today, occurs only in China. Upon analysis we find that one of the reasons for its occurrence lies in the incessant splits and wars within China's comprador class* and landed gentry. So long as splits and wars continue within these classes, the workers' and peasants' armed independent regime can also continue to exist and develop. In addition to this, the existence and development of such an armed independent regime require the following conditions: (1) a sound mass basis, (2) a first-rate party organization, (3) a Red Army of adequate strength, (4) a terrain favourable to military operations, and (5) economic strength sufficient for self-support. . . .

Since the struggle in the border area is exclusively military, both the party and the masses have to be placed on a war footing. How to deal with the enemy and how to fight have become the central problems in our daily life. An independent regime must be an armed one. Wherever there are no armed forces, or the armed forces are inadequate, or the tactics for dealing with the enemy are wrong, the enemy will immediately come into occupation. As the struggle is getting fiercer every day, our problems have also become extremely complicated and serious. . . .

After receiving some political education, the Red Army soldiers have all become class-conscious and acquired a general knowledge about redistributing land, establishing political power, arming the workers and peasants, etc.; and they all know that they are fighting for themselves and for the working class and the peasantry. Hence they can endure the bitter struggle without complaint. Each company, battalion or regiment has its soldiers' council which represents the interests of the soldiers and carries out political and mass work. . . .

Apart from the role played by the party, the reason why the Red Army can sustain itself without collapse in spite of such a poor standard of material life and such incessant engagements, is its practice of democracy. The officers do not beat

* Compradors: Chinese agents of foreign businesses—Ed.

the men; officers and men receive equal treatment; soldiers enjoy freedom of assembly and speech; cumbersome formalities and ceremonies are done away with; and the account books are open to the inspection of all. All these measures are very satisfactory to the soldiers. The newly captured soldiers in particular feel that our army and the Kuomintang's army are worlds apart. They feel that, though in material life they are worse off in the Red Army than in the White army, spiritually they are liberated. The fact that the same soldier who was not brave in the enemy army yesterday becomes very brave in the Red Army today shows precisely the impact of democracy. The Red Army is like a furnace in which all captured soldiers are melted down and transformed the moment they come over. In China not only the people need democracy but the army needs it too. The democratic system in an army is an important weapon for destroying the feudal mercenary army. . . .

A programme for a thorough democratic revolution in China includes, externally, the overthrow of imperialism so as to achieve complete national liberation, and, internally, the clean-up of the influence of the comprador class in the cities, the completion of the agrarian revolution, the elimination of feudal relations in the villages, and the overthrow of the government of the warlords. We must go through such a democratic revolution before we can lay a real foundation for passing on to socialism. Having fought in various places in the past year, we are keenly aware that the revolutionary upsurge in the country as a whole is subsiding. While Red political power has been established in a few small areas, the people of the country as a whole still do not possess basic democratic rights; the workers and the peasants and even the bourgeois democrats have no rights of speech and assembly, and joining the Communist Party constitutes the greatest crime. Wherever the Red Army goes, it finds the masses cold and reserved; only after propaganda and agitation do they slowly rouse themselves. We have to fight the enemy forces hard whoever they are, and scarcely any mutiny or uprising has taken place within the enemy forces. The same is true even of the Sixth Army, which recruited the greatest number of "rebels" after the Incident of May 21.* We have an acute sense of loneliness and are every moment longing for the end of such a lonely life. To turn the revolution into a seething, surging tide all over the country, it is necessary to launch a political and economic struggle for democracy involving also the urban petty bourgeoisie. . . .

Ch'en Tu-hsiu on Stalin's Errors

After he was ousted from the Chinese Communist leadership as a scapegoat for the 1927 defeat, Ch'en Tu-hsiu participated in an ineffectual attempt to organize a Trotskyist opposition group. He distributed a statement to the party blaming Moscow for the setback and abjectly confessing his own error in following the "opportunistic" instructions of the International.

. . . Since the time when I followed the appeal to organize a Chinese Communist Party in 1920, I have sincerely carried out to the utmost the opportunistic policy of the leaders of the International, Stalin, Zinoviev, Bukharin, and the others, who led the Chinese Revolution to a shameful and terrible defeat. Although I worked hard day and night, my mistakes nevertheless outweighed my merits. . . .

I categorically hold that the objective causes of the defeat of the late Chinese revolution have secondary significance, and that the chief cause of the defeat was the error of opportunism, i.e., the falseness of our whole policy in relation to the bourgeois Kuomintang. . . .

Under the direction of such a consistently opportunistic policy how could the Chinese proletariat and the Communist Party clearly see their own future? How could they have their own independent policy? They just capitulated step by step before the bourgeoisie and submitted to it. And then when it

FROM: Ch'en, "Open Letter to All Members of the Chinese Communist Party," December 10, 1929 (editor's translation from excerpts of Russian version in *The Bulletin of the Opposition*, Paris, no. 15-16, September-October, 1930, pp. 20-23).

* May 21, 1927: occasion of military repression of the labor and peasant movement in the province of Hunan—Ed.

suddenly began to exterminate us, we definitely did not know what to do. . . .

If we had the forces to rearrange the old committee and reorganize the Kuomintang, why could we not organize soviets? Why did we have to send our worker and peasant leaders into the bourgeois Kuomintang, which at that time was exterminating workers and peasants? Or why did we have to embellish this Kuomintang with our leaders? . . .

Once the party had consistently made such radical mistakes, other subordinate mistakes, large and small, inevitably had to issue from them. I, whose understanding was not sufficiently clear, whose opinion was not sufficiently resolute, deeply mired in the atmosphere of opportunism [*sic*], sincerely supported the opportunistic policy of the Third International. I unconsciously became an instrument of the narrow Stalin faction; I did not have an opportunity to develop; I could not save the party; I could not save the revolution. . . .

We must openly and objectively admit that the whole past and present opportunistic policy came and now comes from the Third International. The Comintern must bear the responsibility. The Chinese party, which had scarcely emerged from infancy, did not have the capacity to create a theory for itself and then establish a policy. But the leading organ of the Chinese party must bear responsibility for the fact that it blindly carried out the opportunistic policy of the Third International. . . .

I am deeply convinced that if I or the other responsible comrades had at that time a clear enough understanding of the errors of the opportunistic policy and sufficiently strong arguments against it to mobilize the whole party by means of a burning controversy, as Trotsky did—the result of this would have been a great help to the revolution, which would have been protected from such a shameful smash-up even if we were expelled from the International and a split came about in the party. . . .

After the time of the conference of August 7 the Central Committee did not allow me to participate in any of its sessions and did not give me any work. However, on October 6 of that year (1927), forty days before my expulsion, they suddenly wrote me a letter announcing, "The Central Committee has decided to propose that you undertake publishing work for the Central Committee on the basis of the party's political line and in the course of a week write an article *against the opposition.*" Since I was then criticizing the Central Committee precisely for the policy of opportunism and putschism, they were trying to create some sort of grounds for expelling me from the party. Then I openly realized that Trotsky's opinion coincided with Marxism and Leninism. How could I speak false words opposing my real opinion? . . .

I clearly understood why they were falsely accusing me of being a counter-revolutionary. This is a weapon recently fashioned by Chinese politicians for the struggle with those who do not join them. . . .

Dear comrades! The party's present errors do not refer to particular problems; they reveal, as in the past, the whole opportunistic policy which Stalin has conducted in China. Responsible functionaries of the Central Committee of the Chinese Communist Party who have agreed to become Stalin's phonographs have since lost whatever political conscience they had, they have gotten worse and worse and can no longer be saved. . . .

Every member of our party is responsible for the salvation of the party. We must turn back to the spirit and policy of Bolshevism, unite with strength and a united spirit, and work undeviatingly on the side of the international opposition led by Comrade Trotsky, i.e., to struggle under the banner of real Marxism and Leninism, resolutely, firmly, and to the end, against the opportunism of the Comintern and the Central Committee of the Chinese Communist Party. . . .

The Proletarian Line—Li Li-san

Pursuant to the aggressive line adopted by the Communist International in 1928, the Chinese Communist Party was placed under the leadership of Li Li-san, a doctrinaire adherent of immediate proletarian revolution. Li attacked the peasant emphasis of Mao Tse-tung and stressed the key importance of Communist success in the cities, in conjunction with the world revolution which he expected momentarily. Despite its Marxist rigor, however, Li's effort to promote insurrection by the workers was a complete failure, and Moscow soon removed him from the Chinese leadership. Li lived in Russia until 1945, when he returned to China apparently to promote Soviet influence. In 1949 he became Minister of Labor in the new Communist government.

. . . The major signs of the revolutionary rising tide are the heightened political struggle of the revolutionary vanguard and of the general and even the backward masses, and the outbreak of great political strikes in the major cities. But serious rightist or even liquidationist concepts will inevitably result if [one] considers only the superficial unevenness in the development [of the revolution] in the cities and countryside, and neglects [to consider] the workers' struggle, the sharpening of class antagonisms, the rapid growth of revolutionary spirit and determination on the part of the broad masses, and the bankruptcy of the ruling power of the ruling class; that is, the conditions under which every incident may lead to the outbreak of a great revolutionary struggle. The major reason why the workers' strike movement has not yet turned into a revolutionary rising tide decidedly does not lie in a lag of revolutionary consciousness on the part of the workers, nor in their lack of desire for revolution; rather it lies in the fact that the ruling class, about to collapse, is waging a last-ditch battle in the cities, using all possible methods —white terror and trickery—to suppress the workers' struggle. Thus the urban struggle is more intense and cruel than that in the countryside; this is why we must redouble our efforts in city work for the ultimate victory in the revolution. But the major handicaps in our present work are rightist ideas of doubt and pessimism regarding the workers' struggle. The elimination of such waverings is the major prerequisite for speeding the arrival of the rising tide in the workers' struggles. . . .

FROM: Li, Resolution, "The New Revolutionary Rising Tide and Preliminary Successes in One or More Provinces," adopted by the Politbureau of the Chinese Communist Party, June 11, 1930 (Brandt, Schwartz, Fairbank, pp. 188, 190-91, 193-94).

. . . Preliminary successes in one or more provinces are the beginning of national victory, a step towards more intensive struggle in the national revolution. There can never be any "local regimes" or "regional governments"; every provincial [party headquarters] should actively prepare for successful insurrection in that province in co-ordination with the general situation. Thus, in preparing for preliminary successes in one or more provinces, special attention must be paid to heightening [our] national activities, as well as to their co-ordination with the struggle of the international proletariat. Especially more propaganda about the Chinese revolution [must be spread] among the international proletariat.

The great struggle of the proletariat is the decisive force in the winning of preliminary successes in one or more provinces. Without an upsurge of strikes of the working class, without armed insurrection in key cities, there can be no successes in one or more provinces. It is a highly erroneous concept to pay no special attention to urban work, and to plan "to use village [forces] to besiege the cities" and "to rely on the Red Army alone to occupy the cities." Henceforth, the organization of political strikes and their expansion into a general strike, as well as the strengthening of the organization and training of the workers' militia to set up a central force for armed insurrections, are the major tactics in preparing for preliminary successes in one or more provinces. Particular attention should be directed to [the fact that] the ruling class will [stage] a final struggle in the cities. This cruel struggle will be even fiercer that that in the rural areas; therefore, [we] must redouble our efforts in urban work, set up strong bases in the key cities—especially among workers of important industries—awaken the will of the broad masses to struggle to the death. These are the most grave tasks for the present and the tactical problems that must be solved first.

In view of the present objective economic and political conditions of China, a rising tide of proletarian struggles unaccompanied by peasant uprisings, soldiers' mutinies, powerful assaults by the Red Army, and a [whole] combination of various revolutionary forces, also will not lead the revolution to victory. Also it will be unattainable if one of the above four revolutionary forces is lacking. The liquidationists who look down on the peasantry and [want to] liquidate the Red Army, are undoubtedly [spreading] reactionary ideas, attempting to weaken the ally of the proletariat and to destroy the fighting power of the revolution. The great revolutionary role of the peasantry has even a higher significance in China; the birth of the Red Army in the agrarian revolution is a special feature of China, which can never be understood by the Trotskyite liquidationists. It is also entirely false to adopt a wait-and-see attitude, maintaining that the present workers' struggle in the cities has not [yet] reached the rising tide [stage] and that a conservative policy should be adopted in the rural areas, and the expansion of the Red Army should be stopped. Granted that the workers' struggle has not yet reached a revolutionary high tide, and peasant uprisings, soldiers' mutinies, and the Red Army's expansion are still inadequate; still we should specially emphasize the intensifying of the workers' struggle while working for the development of peasant uprisings, the outbreak of soldiers' mutinies, and the vigorous expansion of the Red Army. . . .

Another factor decisive for the victory and transformation of the revolution is the mighty support from the already successful proletariat of the Soviet Union, and especially the outbreak of proletarian revolutions in capitalist countries. Because of China's semi-colonial nature, the victory of socialism in the Chinese revolution will be inseparable from the world revolution. The unprecedently fierce struggle of the Chinese revolution against the imperialists will inevitably heighten the world revolutionary upsurge; on the other hand, without a revolutionary rising tide of the world proletariat, it would be difficult to assure the continued success of the Chinese revolution. Therefore, it is at present our grave duty—and one of the main factors in the preparation for the victory and transformation of the revolution—that [we should] intensify propaganda for the Chinese revolution among the world proletariat, and, in particular, strengthen the alliance [with the latter] in the struggle. . . .

The Moscow Orientation—Wang Ming

After Li Li-san's failure Moscow vainly backed a group of Russian-trained Chinese Communist leaders under Wang Ming (Ch'en Shao-yü), who endeavored to apply Soviet experience to China point by point. Meanwhile Mao Tse-tung and the peasant army, under heavy pressure from the Nationalist government, carried out the "long march" and relocated the Communist regime at Yenan in northwest China. In 1935 Mao demonstrated his domination of the party and his independence from Moscow by having the Wang group censured for its "left" deviation. Wang was dropped from the Central Committee during the "thought-reform" movement of 1942; he was reinstated in 1945, but has not had appreciable influence.

. . . After the Manchurian events, in September, 1931,* and the creation of the central soviet government,** our general line was concretized to form the following three-fold slogan:

1. National revolutionary war of the armed nation against Japanese and other imperialisms to defend the integrity, independence and unity of China;

2. Overthrow of the Kuomintang as the government of national betrayal and national disgrace, as a condition of the successful carrying out of the national-revolutionary war;

3. Only the Soviet government and the Red Army of China can consistently carry out and lead the national-revolutionary war against Japanese and other imperialisms and achieve full national liberation. . . .

The economic policy of the Chinese Soviet Republic at the present stage of development of the Chinese revolution must

FROM: Wang, "Revolution, War, and Intervention in China, and the Tasks of the Communist Party" (Speech to The Thirteenth Plenum of The Executive Committee of The Communist International, December, 1933; English translation in *Revolutionary China Today,* New York, Workers Library Publishers, 1934, pp. 33, 35-36, 40-41, 52, 54).

* The Japanese seizure of Manchuria—Ed.
** I.e., in Mao's guerrilla territory—Ed.

be an economic policy of the democratic dictatorship of the proletariat and the peasantry in the form of Soviets, that is, an economic policy of the transition period from the completion of the tasks of the bourgeois-democratic revolution to the socialist path of development of China. Because its territories are scattered and the present Soviet districts are economically backward, likewise because the state of war has been so continuous and lengthy, the Chinese Soviet government, in carrying out its economic policy, must necessarily encounter difficulties and complications.

Therefore, although the First All-China Congress of Soviets adopted the main laws and basic principles of economic policy, this matter was nevertheless not clear to all party members and soviet workers. This gave rise in the soviet districts now to Right, now to "Left" errors in economic matters committed by many party, soviet and trade union workers. This is the very reason why the [Central Committee] of the party took the economic policy seriously in hand both theoretically and practically. The [Central Committee] placed before the party a clear and precise theoretical line. It stated that the starting point of the economic policy of the Chinese Soviet Republic at the present moment ought to be determined by the following considerations:

a. The character of the revolution at the given stage, that is, the fact that it is a bourgeois-democratic revolution;

b. The present stage of the Soviet Republic, that is, a state of prolonged and continuous civil war, of economic backwardness and scattered disposition of the present territories, and

c. The prospects of the revolution, that is, the struggle for the noncapitalist path of further development. . . .

One of the principal reasons which go to explain the successes of our Red Army and of the Soviet government in the struggle against the fifth Kuomintang expedition was the victorious completion in four years of the first Five-Year Plan in the U.S.S.R. and the recital of its results in the report of Comrade Stalin. Our party has popularized far and wide Comrade Stalin's report delivered at the January Plenum of the [Central Committee] and the [Central Control Commission] of the C.P.S.U., especially the part which directly deals with China. For instance the place where Comrade Stalin, in speaking of the harm caused by relegating the tasks of industrialization to the rear, directly declared:

"Our position would then have been more or less analogous to the present position of China, which has no heavy industry, has no war industry of its own and is pecked at by everybody who cares to do so."

Our party, availing itself of these words of Comrade Stalin and of the triumph of the first Five-Year Plan, declares resolutely and firmly before all China, before the whole world, that only the Chinese Bolsheviks and the Chinese Soviet Republic which they head can change China from a country without a war industry, incapable of defending itself, an object of military operations by foreign enemies, into a country having its own heavy and war industries, capable of defending itself and powerful enough to repulse all attacks from without. Only the Chinese Bolsheviks and the Chinese Soviet Republic they head can change China from a country economically backward, politically dependent and colonial into a country economically developed and politically independent. . . .

Weak points and mistakes in our party and mass work in non-Soviet China there have been many and some of them not minor ones, either. In the main they find expression in the following: Inability so far to create an organized proletarian framework in the widely developing anti-imperialist movement. This is due to poor work and poor organization of the party and Red trade unions in a number of important cities (Wuhan, Canton, Kiu Kiang, etc.). Another fault is the still inadequate work in the yellow and Kuomintang trade unions in non-Soviet China. A further cause is the impermissibly poor and unsystematic work of a number of party organizations among the armed forces of the enemy, under the strained conditions of revolution and war. Then there is the very small amount of work done among the masses of the peasants and starving, the neglectful attitude toward the mass struggle of the city poor and intelligentsia, the failure to appreciate the importance of working among the toiling women and youth, and finally shortcomings and weak spots in the struggle for the elementary rules of secrecy and against acts of provocation. . . .

The present-day international and internal situation of China is doubtless still more favorable than before for the further development and the victory of the Soviet revolution in China. We have shown above that in the near future two perspectives are possible: either the decisive victory of the Soviet revolution in China will prevent the outbreak of a world imperialist war for the Pacific and a war of the imperialists against the U.S.S.R.; or an imperialist war, primarily *a war of the Japanese and other imperialists against the Soviet Union will precede the decisive victory of the Soviet revolution in China. The endless and open acts of provocation, intrigues and even military feelers of the Japanese militarists in Manchuria on the Chinese Eastern Railway, at the borders of the Mongolian People's Republic and at the Soviet Far Eastern borders speak with sufficient eloquence of the nearness of the anti-Soviet war and of the possibility of its outbreak at any moment. In either event we, the* [*Communist Party of China*] *consider the following to be our basic task: A struggle for the decisive victory of the Soviet revolution in all China,* or in other words, in the words of Comrade Molotov, "the complete defeat of the enemy and the victory of the Red Army." In our opinion these words suit not only the tasks of the C.P.S.U. in case of an attack by the Japanese or other imperialists upon the U.S.S.R. but they also fit the basic tasks of the C.P.C. in the very near future. . . .

Mao on the Anti-Japanese "United Front"

When the Japanese invaded China in 1937, Mao announced a moderation of the Communist program, and the Communist-Kuomintang conflict was more or less restrained.

. . . To resist Japan we need a strengthened united front which means the mobilization of the people of the whole country to participate in the united front. To resist Japan we need a solid united front, which means the necessity of common policies. Common policies should be the guiding principle of the united front. They will also serve as a binding force of the united front, binding tightly, as with a cord, all the organizations and individuals from all the parties, groups, classes and armies that participate in it. Only thus can solidarity be achieved. We are opposed to the old form of control because it is unsuitable to the national revolutionary war. We welcome the establishment of a new system of control to replace the old, that is, by promulgating common policies to set up a revolutionary order. For only thus can the needs of the war of resistance be met.

What should our common policies be? They are the Three People's Principles of Dr. Sun Yat-sen and the Ten Great Policies for Anti-Japanese Resistance and National Salvation announced by the Chinese Communist Party. . . .

Communism is to be implemented in a future stage of the revolutionary development. Communists do not wishfully envisage the realization of Communism at present, but are striving for the realization of the historically determined principles of national revolution and democratic revolution. This is the basic reason why the Chinese Communist Party has raised the slogans of an anti-Japanese national united front and a united democratic republic. As to the implementation of the Three People's Principles, the Chinese Communist Party agreed to it during the first united front formed ten years ago at the First National Congress of the Kuomintang, and they were indeed carried out on a national scale between 1925 and 1927 by every faithful Communist and every faithful Kuomintang member. Unfortunately in 1927 the united front was shattered, resulting in the suspension of the Three People's Principles during the past decade. However, as far as the Chinese Communist Party is concerned, all the policies carried out by it during the last ten years have been in harmony with the revolutionary spirit of Dr. Sun Yat-sen's

FROM: Mao, "Urgent Tasks of the Chinese Revolution since the Formation of the Kuomintang–Chinese Communist Party United Front" (September, 1937; Brandt, Schwartz, Fairbank, pp. 252-54, 257).

Three People's Principles and the three great policies. The Chinese Communist Party has never ceased its firm resistance to imperialism; this is the principle of nationalism. The Soviet system of people's representative councils is nothing else than the principle of democracy, and the agrarian revolution is without a doubt the principle of people's livelihood. Why, then, has the Chinese Communist Party announced the abolition of the Soviet and the cessation of land confiscation? This we have explained before. It is not that these measures are undesirable, but that armed invasion by Japanese imperialists has brought about changes in class relations in China, thus making imperative and making possible the alliance of all classes in the fight against Japanese imperialism. Furthermore, a democratic united front is being formed internationally, to fight against the danger of fascism. Therefore, the formation of a national, democratic united front in China is today a necessity in China. . . .

Our race and nation now stand at a critical hour of survival. May the Kuomintang and the Chinese Communist Party work in close harmony! May all our fellow countrymen who do not want to be slaves rally together on the foundation of Kuomintang-Chinese Communist Party solidarity! The realization of all necessary reforms in order to overcome numerous difficulties—such is the urgent task now facing us in the Chinese revolution. The accomplishment of this task will certainly bring about the defeat of Japanese imperialism. If we devote our efforts [to this task] our future is indeed bright. . . .

Liu Shao-ch'i on Party Discipline

At Yenan the Chinese Communist party began to refashion itself on Stalinist lines. Liu Shao-ch'i, a party secretary since 1931 (and Mao's successor as Chairman of the Republic in 1959), took a leading role in setting the standards of monolithic organization and complete doctrinal control.

A Communist Party member must not only clearly determine his Communist philosophy of life and his world view,

FROM: Liu, "On the Training of a Communist Party Member" (August, 1939; Brandt, Schwartz, Fairbank, pp. 336, 343-44).

but must also explicitly determine the correct relationship between his individual interests and the interests of the party. The Marxist principle is that the interests of the individual are subordinate to the interests of the party, the interest of the part is subordinate to the interest of the whole, the short-range interest is subordinate to the long-range, and the national interest is subordinate to the international.

The Communist Party is a political party representing the proletariat. The Communist Party has no interest or aim aside from the interest of the liberation of the proletariat. However, the final liberation of the proletariat must also be the final liberation of all mankind. . . .

. . . Therefore, the individual interests of the party member are subordinate to the interests of the party, which means subordinate to the interests of class and national liberation, of Communism and of social progress. . . .

. . . Fundamentally, it is in the struggle against various dark forces within and without the party that we reform the world and mankind, and at the same time reform our party and ourselves. The intra-party struggle is a reflection of the class struggle outside the party. In the class struggle outside the party—in the revolutionary struggle of the broad masses—the party is tempered, developed, and strengthened; at the same time, the party achieves consolidation and unity in the intra-party struggle and gives planned, correct, powerful leadership to the revolutionary struggle of the broad masses. It is therefore fundamentally incorrect and of benefit to the enemy to adopt the attitude of liberalism towards various errors, defects, and undesirable phenomena in the party, to attempt to blot out divergencies in principle in the party, to evade the intra-party struggle, to conceal the party's internal contradictions or to exhibit negligence; because they are in contradiction to the rules of development of the class struggle and to our basic viewpoint of reforming the world and mankind through struggle. It is therefore also incorrect to separate the intra-party struggle from the class struggle outside the party—from the revolutionary movement of the broad masses—and transform it into empty talk; because the party cannot be tempered, developed, or strengthened if it is separated from the revolutionary struggle of the broad masses. Yet it is also incorrect to carry things to the other extreme and adopt a categorical attitude towards all comrades who have errors or defects [which are] not incurable, to carry on the intra-party struggle mechanically, or to subjectively manufacture intra-party struggles within the party. Because this is also injurious to the party, it gives the enemy an opportunity to mount an attack on our party. This also runs completely counter to the rules of the party's development. Loyal comrades in the party who have committed errors should not be utterly denounced from the start; instead they should be persuaded, educated, and tempered with a friendly, sympathetic attitude, and only when absolutely necessary should they be publicly attacked and expelled. Of course, we cannot allow anyone to harm the party's interests, and we must take precautions lest opportunists, spies, Trotskyites, and two-faced elements take advantage of every opportunity to harm the party's interests. . . .

In general, our ideological training is our fundamental training to become loyal, pure, progressive, model party members and cadres. We should: (1) from the learning of Marxism-Leninism and the actuality of the revolution, establish our own Communist philosophy of life and world view, establish our own determined party and class stand; (2) on the basis of Communism's philosophy of life and world view, and a determined party standpoint, examine all of our own thoughts and actions, correct all our incorrect thoughts, and at the same time observe problems as well as other comrades from this position; (3) make constant use of appropriate forms and attitudes in struggling with the various incorrect ideological concepts in the party, especially the ideologies influencing the present revolutionary struggle; (4) hold ourselves strictly in check in thought, speech, and action; primarily by the adoption of strict standpoints and principles in regulating [ourselves] in political thought, speech, and action which are related to the present revolutionary struggle. In this regard, even petty matters (such as individual life and attitude) deserve our attention. But aside from questions of principle and vital political questions, we should not be excessively strict with our comrades, and should not meticulously find fault with them in petty matters. . . .

Mao on the "New Democracy"

In 1940 Mao stated a new theory of the Chinese revolution—a "bourgeois democratic" revolution carried through by the Communists in alliance with the international "proletarian" revolution. However, the "proletarian" leadership which Mao claimed for the movement existed only in the labeling of the Communist Party as such, since at this time the party had no contact with the urban working class. The "new democracy," with its stress on Communist leadership of a multi-class coalition, became the basic doctrinal foundation of the Chinese Communist state.

. . . The historical characteristic of the Chinese revolution is that it is divided into two steps, that of democracy and that of socialism. The first step is not democracy in the general sense, but a new and specific kind, of a Chinese type—i.e., new democracy. . . .

Evidently, if the nature of the present Chinese society is colonial, semi-colonial, and semi-feudal, then the progress of the Chinese revolution must be in two steps. The first step is to turn the colonial, semi-colonial, and semi-feudal society into an independent democratic society; the second step is to push the revolution forward to build up a socialist society. The present phase of the Chinese revolution carried out by us is the first step.

The beginning of the first step of the Chinese revolution can be traced back to the Opium War when the Chinese society began to change from a feudal society to a semi-colonial, semi-feudal society. . . .

But a change took place in the Chinese bourgeois-democratic revolution after the outbreak of the first imperialist World War and the establishment of a socialist state on one-sixth of the land surface of the globe, i.e., after the Russian revolution of 1917.

FROM: Mao, "On the New Democracy" (January 1940; Brandt, Schwartz, Fairbank, pp. 264-68, 270-73, 275).

Before that time, the Chinese bourgeois-democratic revolution was within the orbit of the old bourgeois-democratic world revolution and was a part of it.

From then on, the Chinese bourgeois-democratic revolution changed and came within the orbit of the new bourgeois-democratic revolution. From the standpoint of the revolutionary front, it is a part of the world proletarian-socialist revolution. . . .

As to the first stage or the first step in this colonial and semi-colonial revolution—according to its social nature, it is fundamentally still a bourgeois-democratic revolution in which the objective requirement is still basically to clear away the obstacles in the way of capitalist development; nevertheless, this revolution is no longer the old type led solely by the bourgeoisie for the building of capitalist society and a state of the bourgeois dictatorship, but a new type of revolution wholly or partly led by the proletariat, the first stage of which aims at the setting up of a new democratic society, a new state of the joint dictatorship of all revolutionary classes. The fundamental character of this revolution will not change until the [arrival of the stage of] socialist revolution, even though, during its progress, it may pass through a number of stages in accordance with the possible changes in the conditions of enemies and allies.

This kind of revolution, because it is a great blow to the imperialists, is bound to be opposed and not tolerated by the imperialists; on the other hand, it is permitted by the socialist country and socialistic international proletariat.

Therefore, it is inevitable that this revolution will become a part of the proletarian-socialist world revolution. . . .

Today those who are capable of leading the people to defeat Japanese imperialism and put democracy into practice are the saviours of the people. If the Chinese bourgeoisie is capable of fulfilling this duty, it certainly deserves every praise. Otherwise, the responsibility on the whole cannot but fall on the shoulders of the proletariat.

Therefore, no matter what the circumstances, the Chinese proletariat, peasantry, intelligentsia, and other petty-bourgeois elements are the main force upon which the fate of China depends. These classes either have awakened or are awakening, and are bound to be the basic parts of the state and government framework in the democratic Republic of China. The democratic Republic of China which we are aiming to construct now can only take the form of dictatorship of all anti-imperialist and anti-feudal people, i.e., a new democratic republic. In other words, a republic of the Three People's Principles in the true revolutionary sense as put forward by Dr. Sun Yat-sen including the Three Great Policies.

Such a new democratic republic differs, on the one hand, from the old, western-type bourgeois-democratic republics that are under the dictatorship of the bourgeoisie; that kind of republic is out of date; it differs, on the other hand, from the newest, Soviet-style republic, which is under proletarian dictatorship. This kind of republic has already arisen in the Soviet Union and will be established in every country. It will no doubt be the final form of control for the completion of the nation and of government power in all progressive countries. Nevertheless, in a certain historical period, the Soviet-style republic cannot be fittingly put into practice in colonial and semi-colonial countries, the state form of which must be of a third form, namely, that of the new democratic republic. Being the state form of a certain historical period, it is a transitional form; but it is all the same an inevitable and necessary form of state.

Hence the forms of state in the world can be fundamentally classified, according to their social nature, into the following three categories:

(1) Republics of a bourgeois dictatorship.

(2) Republics of a proletarian dictatorship.

(3) Republics of a joint dictatorship of several revolutionary classes. . . .

In such a republic as that mentioned above, our economy must be the economy of the new democracy, just as the politics is the politics of the new democracy.

Big banks, big industries, and big business shall be owned by this republic. "In order that private capital may not manipulate the livelihood of the people, all native-owned or foreign-owned enterprises, either monopolist or of a dimension too large for private efforts to manage such as banks, railroads, airlines, etc., will be managed and controlled by the state. This is the essence of restriction of capital." This was a slogan statement made by the Kuomintang in the declaration of its First National Congress. This is the correct course for the economic constitution of the new democratic republic; at the same time, however, the state will not confiscate other capitalist private property and will not forbid the development of capitalist production that "cannot manipulate the people's livelihood." This is because the Chinese economy is still in a very backward state.

It will adopt certain necessary measures to confiscate the land of big landlords and distribute it among peasants without any, or with very little, land, in order to realize Dr. Sun's slogan, "The tiller should own his land," and to liquidate the feudal relations in rural areas. This is not to build up socialist agriculture, but to turn the land into the private property of the peasants. The rich peasant economy will also be allowed to exist in the rural areas. This is the policy of "the equalization of landownership," the correct slogan of which is, "The tiller should own his land.". . .

. . . The Chinese revolution is in essence a revolution of the peasantry; the present war of resistance is in essence a war of resistance of the peasantry. The politics of new democracy is in essence [the politics of] the transfer of power to the peasantry. The new, genuine Three People's Principles are in their essence the principles of a peasant revolution. The content of popular culture is in essence [the question of] the elevation of the cultural [level] among the peasantry. The anti-Japanese war is in essence a peasant war. . . . Therefore, the peasant question becomes the fundamental question of the Chinese revolution, and the force of the peasantry is the main force of the Chinese revolution. Besides the peasantry, the second [largest] section of the Chinese population consists of workers. China has several millions of industrial workers. Without them, China would not be able to live on, for it is they who are the producers in the industrial economy. Without the workers, the [Chinese] revolution would not be able to succeed, for it is they who are the leaders of the revolution and have the highest revolutionary spirit. Under these conditions the revolutionary, new or genuine Three People's Principles must adopt the policy of [aiding] the workers and peasants. If there is such a Three People's Principles which does not adopt this policy, does not truly protect and assist them, does not endeavour to "awaken the people," then it is bound to decay. . . .

The culture of the new democracy is the anti-imperialist and anti-feudal culture of the masses, or, in terms of present-day China, the culture of the anti-Japanese united front. It can only be led by the cultural thought of the proletariat, i.e., Communist thought; it cannot be led by the thought of any other class. The culture of the new democracy, in short, is "the proletarian-led anti-imperialist and anti-feudal culture of the masses.". . .

. . . The essence of the new culture is still that of the new democracy, not of socialism. But undoubtedly we should now expand the propaganda of Communist thought and speed up the study of Marxist-Leninist teachings; for, without the two, not only the guiding of the Chinese revolution to the future socialist stage, but the very success of the democratic revolution of the present day itself, will be impossible. However, it still holds true that the fundamental nature of our national culture at present is not that of socialism but that of new democracy, because it is the anti-imperialist and anti-feudal culture of the people, not the anti-capitalist culture of the proletariat. . . . China should absorb on a great scale the progressive culture of foreign countries as a raw material for her own cultural food. Such absorption was not sufficient in the past. This refers not only to the socialist and new democratic culture, but also to the ancient cultures of foreign countries, which are useful to us; for instance, the cultural heritage of the capitalist countries in their earlier period of growth. These foreign materials we must treat as we treat our food. We submit our food to the mouth for chewing and to the stomach and intestines for digestion, add to it saliva, pepsin, and other secretions of the intestines to separate it into the essence and the residue, and then absorb the essence of our nourishment and pass off the residue. It should never be indiscriminately and uncritically absorbed. The thesis of "wholesome Westernization" is a mistaken viewpoint. To absorb blindly foreign materials has done China much harm. The same attitude is necessary for the Chinese Communists in the application of Marxism to China. We must unify appropriately the general truth of Marxism and the concrete actuality of the Chinese revolution, i.e., we must adopt the national form before we can make Marxism useful and not apply it subjectively and dogmatically. Subjective and formal Marxists are only playing with Marxism and the Chinese revolution, and there is no place for them in the revolutionary ranks of China. Chinese culture must have its own form, i.e., a national form. A national form and a new democratic content—this is our new culture of today. . . .

The combination of new democratic politics, new democratic economics, and new democratic culture is the Republic of New Democracy. It is truly a republic in name and in reality. And that is the New China we aim to build.

The New China stands before every one of us. We should be ready to receive it.

The mast of the ship New China is appearing on the horizon. We should clap our hands to welcome it.

Raise both your hands! The New China is ours! . . .

The "Thought Reform" Movement

From 1942 to 1944 the so-called "thought-reform" movement was conducted at Yenan. In the course of this the principles and practice of mass manipulation and party control over thought and culture were firmly established in the Chinese Communist movement.

a) Mao on Literature and Art

. . . The various fronts of our struggle for the liberation of the Chinese people may be grouped into two: the civil and the martial; they are the cultural front and the military front.

FROM: Mao, Speeches at the Forum on Literature and Art, Yenan, May 2 and 23, 1942 (Brandt, Schwartz, Fairbank, pp. 408, 414-15, 417-18).

We must rely on armed troops to conquer the enemy, but this in itself is not enough. A cultural army is also indispensable for uniting ourselves and conquering the enemy. This cultural army has materialized in China since May Fourth,* it has helped the Chinese revolution, and has caused a gradual decrease in the territory dominated by a feudalistic and slavish culture which has yielded to imperialistic encroachments. . . .

The purpose of our meeting today is to make literature and art become a constructive part of the whole revolutionary machine; to use it as a powerful weapon for uniting and educating the people and for crushing and destroying the enemy, as well as to help the people wage the struggle against the enemy with one heart and one mind. . . .

. . . In the world of today, all culture or literature and art belong to some one definite class, some one definite party, i.e., some one definite political line. Art for art's sake, art which transcends class or party, art which stands as a bystander to, or independent of, politics, does not in actual fact exist. Since art is subordinate to class and party in a society which has classes and parties, it must undoubtedly follow the political demands of those classes and parties. . . . If it deviates from these, it will deviate from the basic needs of the masses. Proletarian literature and art are one part of the entire proletarian revolutionary cause: as Lenin says, "a screw in the whole machine." Therefore, the literary and artistic work of the Party has a definite and set position in the Party's entire revolutionary work. . . .

Under the great principle of unity in the war of resistance we must allow the inclusion of literary and artistic works representing every kind and sort of political attitude. However, our criticism will be firm upon our principle and standpoint. We must give severe judgment to all works of literature and art that are anti-national, anti-scientific, anti-masses, and anti-Communistic in viewpoint, because these so-called works

* May 4, 1919: occasion of student demonstrations against Japan and the Far-Eastern provisions of the Treaty of Versailles, which launched the "May Fourth Movement" of nationalistic intellectual revival—Ed.

of literature and art, their motivation and effect, all harm the unity of the war effort.

According to artistic standards, everything having comparatively high artistic quality is good or comparatively good; and everything having comparatively low artistic quality is bad or comparatively bad. This sort of distinction, naturally, also requires a glance at the social application. There are almost no writers or artists who do not consider their own works to be excellent. Our criticism ought to allow the free competition of every kind and sort of work of art, but if we supply correct criticism according to scientific standards of art, we can make comparatively low-grade art gradually become elevated to a high-grade art, and make art which is not suitable to the needs of the mass struggle (even though it may be very high-grade art) change into an art which does meet these needs. This also is absolutely necessary.

There is a political standard, there is an artistic standard; what is the relationship between the two? Politics is not synonymous with art, nor is a general view of the world synonymous with the methodological theories of artistic creation. We not only do not recognize abstract and eternal political standards, but also do not recognize such standards for art. Every class society and every separate class within that society has different political and artistic standards. But no matter what kind of class society or what kind of separate class within that class society it may be, it always puts the political standard first and artistic standard second. The bourgeois class always rejects the proletarian works of literature and art, no matter how high their standards may be. The proletarian classes must . . . reject the reactionary political nature of the bourgeois works of literature and art, and assimilate their art only in a critical manner. It is possible for some things [which are] politically, basically reactionary to have a certain artistry, for example the fascist literature and art. However, the more artistic a work which is reactionary in content, the more harmful does it become to the people and the more it ought to be rejected. The common characteristics in the literature and art of the exploiting classes in their period of decline are the inconsistencies between their reactionary political content and their artistic form. Our demand, then, is a unity of politics and art, a unity of content and form, and a unity of revolutionary political content and an artistic form of as high a standard as possible. Works of art which are deficient in artistry, no matter how advanced they are politically, will not have any force. For this reason, we oppose works of art whose content is harmful and also oppose the so-called "slogan type" tendency which only considers the content and not the form. We must carry on this twofold struggle in the problem of literature and art. . . .

b) *Leadership and the Masses*

If any work or mission lacks a general, universal slogan, the broad masses cannot be moved to action, but if there is nothing more than a general slogan and the leaders do not make a concrete, direct and thorough application of it with those from a particular unit who have been rallied around the slogan, [if the leaders] fail to break through at some point and gain experience, or fail to use acquired experience in later guiding other units, there is then no way for the leaders to test the correctness of the general slogan and there is no way for them to carry out its contents; there is then the danger that the general slogan will have no effect. . . .

The experience of the reform movement of 1941 has also proved that in the process of reform, the reforms of each concrete unit must produce a leading nucleus of minority activists who are the core of the administrative leadership of that unit and it must also bring this leading nucleus into close union with the broad masses engaged in study; in this way only can reform fulfill its mission. If there is only a positive spirit on the part of the leading nuclei, it (the reform) becomes an empty flurry of activity on the part of a minority;

FROM: Resolution of the Central Committee of the Chinese Communist Party "On Methods of Leadership," June 1, 1943 (English translation in Boyd Compton, *Mao's China: Party Reform Documents, 1942-44,* Seattle, University of Washington Press, 1952, pp. 176-79, 183; reprinted by permission of the publisher).

yet if there is only a positive spirit on the part of the broad masses, with no powerful leading nucleus to organize the positive spirit of the masses properly, the masses' spirit then cannot endure, nor can it move in a correct direction or be elevated to a high standard.

In all our Party's actual work, correct leadership must come from the masses and go to the masses. This means taking the views of the masses (unintegrated, unrelated views) and subjecting them to concentration (they are transformed through research into concentrated systematized views), then going to the masses with propaganda and explanation in order to transform the views of the masses, and seeing that these [views] are maintained by the masses and carried over into their activities. It also means an examination of mass activities to ascertain the correctness of these views. Then again, there is concentration from the masses and maintenance among the masses. Thus the process is repeated indefinitely, each time more correctly, vitally, and fruitfully. This is the epistemology and methodology of Marxism-Leninism. . . .

. . . Comrades in all areas should reflect carefully and develop their own creative abilities. The more bitter the struggle becomes, the more necessary is the demand for close union between men of the Communist Party and the broad masses, the more necessary to Communist Party members is the close union between general slogans and particular guidance, and [the more necessary] is the thorough disruption of subjectivistic and bureaucratic methods of leadership. All leading comrades of our Party must forthwith adopt scientific methods of leadership and oppose them to subjective and bureaucratic methods of leadership, overcoming the latter with the former. Subjectivists and bureaucratists who do not understand the principles of uniting leadership with the masses and combining the general and the particular, greatly hamper the development of Party work. We must therefore oppose subjectivistic and bureaucratic methods of leadership, and universally and profoundly promote methods of leadership which are scientific.

Mao's War Aims

By the end of World War II the Communist position in China was greatly strengthened, thanks to the widespread peasant guerilla movement which the Communist Party had built behind the Japanese lines in North China. This made the party a major contender for power. In April, 1945, Mao outlined the coalition regime which he expected for China after the defeat of Japan, but he made it clear that it would be led by the Communists and exclude the Kuomintang. It was, in effect, to be the application of his "New Democracy."

. . . A decisive victory has been scored in the sacred and just war against fascist aggressors throughout the world; the time is near for the Chinese people to defeat the Japanese invaders in collaboration with our Allies; but China, still hard pressed by the Japanese invaders, is not yet united and a grave crisis still exists in China. In such circumstances, what should we do? Indubitably, what China urgently needs is the establishment, through uniting all political parties and groups and non-partisan leaders, of a democratic, provisional coalition government, so that democratic reforms may be instituted, the present crisis overcome, all anti-Japanese forces mobilized and united for the defeat of the Japanese invaders in effective collaboration with our Allies, and the Chinese people liberated from the hands of the Japanese. This being done, the National Assembly, on a broad democratic basis, will have to be summoned to establish a regular democratic government, of a similar coalition nature, embracing more broadly all parties and groups and non-partisan representatives. This government will then lead the liberated people of the entire nation to build an independent, free, democratic, unified, prosperous, and strong new nation, in short, to build a new China after defeating the aggressors through unity and democracy. . . .

The leading ruling clique in the Kuomintang has persisted in maintaining a dictatorial rule and carried out a passive

FROM: Mao, "On Coalition Government" (April, 1945; Brandt, Schwartz, Fairbank, pp. 295-96, 299-302, 305-06, 311-14).

policy against Japan while it has upheld a policy of opposing the people within the country. In this way, the Kuomintang armies have shrunk to half their former size and the major part of them has almost lost its combat ability; in this way, a deep chasm exists between the Kuomintang government and the people, and a serious crisis of poverty, discontent, and revolts among the people is engendered; thus the ruling clique of the Kuomintang has not only greatly reduced its role in the war against Japan, but, moreover, has become an obstacle to the mobilization and unification of all the anti-Japanese forces in the country.

Why did this serious situation come into existence under the leadership of the major ruling clique of the Kuomintang? Because this ruling clique represents the interests of China's big landlords, big bankers, and the big compradore class. This reactionary and extremely small stratum monopolizes all the important organs of military, political, economic, and cultural bodies under the Kuomintang government. They place the preservation of their own vested interests in the first place and interests of the war against Japan in the second place. . . .

Up to the present, the main ruling clique in the Kuomintang has persisted in its reactionary policy of dictatorship and civil war. There are many indications that they have prepared, and particularly at present, are preparing to start civil war once the Japanese aggressors are sufficiently driven out of China by the troops of a certain ally. They also hope that some Allied generals will pursue the same duties in China as General Scobie did in Greece.* They cheered the slaughter of the Greeks by Scobie and the reactionary Greek government. . . .

Under the over-all premise of annihilating the Japanese aggressors and of building a new China, the fundamental views of us Chinese Communist Party members are, at the present stage, identical with those held by the overwhelming majority of the Chinese populace. These are, firstly, that China should not have a feudalistic, fascist, anti-popular sys-

* Reference to British intervention on the side of the Royal Greek Government against the Communist-led resistance movement, December, 1944—Ed.

tem of government exclusively controlled by big landowners and big bourgeoisie, because such a system has been proved to be entirely bankrupt by the chief ruling cliques of the Kuomintang in their eighteen years' rule. Secondly, China cannot, and therefore should not, attempt to build a state along the old-type democratic lines entirely ruled by the liberal bourgeois dictatorship. For in China, the liberal bourgeoisie has so far proved itself to be weak economically and politically, while on the other hand there has been born in China a politically powerful new factor that leads the broad masses of the peasant class, the petty bourgeoisie, the intellectuals, and other democratic elements—the awakened Chinese proletariat and its leader, the Chinese Communist Party. Thirdly, in the present stage, while the task of the Chinese people is still to oppose imperialistic and feudal oppression, while the requisite social and economic conditions are still lacking in China, the Chinese people cannot, and therefore should not, attempt to build a socialist state system.

Then, what is our proposal? We want to build, after annihilating the Japanese aggressors, a system of government based on the support of the overwhelming majority of the people, on the united front and the coalition of democratic alliance. We call this the New Democratic system of government. . . .

Some people wonder if the Communists, once in power, will establish a dictatorship by the proletariat and a one-party system, as they have done in Russia. Our answer is that a New Democratic state of a union of several democratic classes is different in principle from a socialist state of a proletarian dictatorship. China, throughout the period of her New Democratic system, cannot and should not have a system of government of the character of a one-class dictatorship or a one-party autocracy. We have no reason not to co-operate with political parties, social groups, or individuals outside the Communist Party, who adopt a co-operative, but not a hostile, attitude. Russian history has created the Russian system. . . . Chinese history will create the Chinese system. A special type, a New Democratic type of state with a union of several democratic classes will be produced, which will be entirely necessary and rational to us and different from the Russian system. . . .

Generally speaking, a China without independence, freedom, democracy, and unity cannot be an industrial China. Independence can be gained through the annihilation of the Japanese aggressors; freedom, democracy, and unity can be attained by abolishing the Kuomintang one-party dictatorship, setting up a democratic coalition government, realizing the people's freedom, the people's unity, and the people's army, instituting land reforms, and liberating the peasants. Without independence, freedom, democracy, and unity, there cannot be a truly large-scale national industry. And without an industry, there will be no consolidated national defence, no well-being for the people, no prosperity and strength for the nation. . . .

Under the New Democratic system of government, a policy of readjusting the relations between capital and labour will be adopted. On the one hand, the interests of workers will be protected. An eight to ten-hour-day system, according to varying circumstances, will be adopted, as well as suitable relief for the unemployed, social security, and the rights of labour unions. On the other hand, reasonable profits of state, private, and co-operative enterprises will be guaranteed. In general, this will enable both labour and capital to work jointly for the development of industrial production.

Large amounts of capital will be needed for the development of industries. Where will it come from? It can only come from two sources: mainly from dependence on the accumulated capital of the Chinese people, and at the same time from borrowing foreign aid. We welcome foreign investments if such are beneficial to China's economy and are made in observance of China's laws. . . .

The basic principles in the Chinese Communist Party's foreign policy are the establishment and consolidation of friendly relations with all nations on the basis of the thorough annihilation of the Japanese aggressors, the maintenance of world peace, mutual respect for national independence and equality, and the mutual promotion of national and popular interests and friendship, as well as the solution of all war-time and post-war problems such as the co-ordination of action in the war, peace conferences, trade, foreign investments, etc. . . .

We maintain that the Kuomintang government must end its hostile attitude towards the Soviet Union and immediately improve the Sino-Soviet relationship. The Soviet Union was the first nation to abrogate the unequal treaties and to sign equal new treaties with China. During the First Kuomintang National Congress, summoned by Dr. Sun Yat-sen himself in 1924, and the subsequent Northern Expedition, the Soviet Union was the only nation that assisted the Chinese war of liberation. After the war of resistance broke out on July 7, 1937, the Soviet Union was again the first to come to the aid of China in her fight against the Japanese aggressors. The Chinese people express their thankfulness to the Soviet government and its people for this help. We believe that the final, thorough solution of Pacific problems is impossible without participation of the Soviet Union.

We believe that the great efforts, sympathy, and help to China by both the governments and peoples of the two great nations, Great Britain and the United States, especially the latter, in the common cause of fighting the Japanese aggressors, deserve our thanks.

But we request the governments of all Allies, especially the British and the United States governments, to pay serious attention to the voice of the overwhelming majority of the Chinese people, so that their foreign policy may not go against the will of the Chinese people, and so as to avoid impairing our friendship or losing the friendship of the Chinese people. We believe that any foreign government that helps the Chinese reactionaries to stop the Chinese people's pursuit of democracy will be committing a grave error. . . .

The Chinese Civil War

Civil war between the Communists and the Kuomintang broke out again in 1946 despite American mediation, and continued until the Kuomintang forces collapsed in the first half of 1949. Late in 1947 Mao put forth an analysis of Communist strength and expressed confidence of victory despite American support of Chiang. However, Mao indicated that success involved new problems of tightening and purifying the Communist movement.

The revolutionary war of the Chinese people has now reached a turning point. That is, the Chinese People's Liberation Army (PLA) has repelled the attacks of the millions of reactionary troops of Chiang Kai-shek, the running dog of America; and has enabled itself to go over to the offensive. . . .

. . . Our enemy's superiority in military strength was only a temporary phenomenon, a factor playing only a temporary role; the aid of American imperialism was likewise a factor playing only a temporary role; while the anti-popular nature of Chiang Kai-shek's war and the support or opposition of the people are factors playing a constant role; and in these respects the PLA held superiority. The war of the PLA is a patriotic, just and revolutionary war which must of necessity obtain the support of the people throughout the country. This is the political basis for the victory over Chiang Kai-shek. The experience of eighteen months of war fully bears out our judgment. . . .

At present, the rear areas of the PLA are much more consolidated than they were eighteen months ago. That is the outcome of our Party's firmly siding with the peasants in reforming the agrarian system. During the anti-Japanese war, for the sake of establishing an anti-Japanese united front with the KMT and uniting all people who at the time were still capable of resisting Japan, our party on its own initiative changed from the policy before the anti-Japanese war of confiscating landlords' lands and distributing them to the peasants to that of reducing rents and interests—this was entirely necessary. After the Japanese surrender, the peasants urgently demanded land and we therefore made a timely decision to change the agrarian policy of reducing rents and interest to

FROM: Mao, "The Present Situation and Our Tasks" (December, 1947; English translation by the New China News Agency, reprinted in H. Arthur Steiner, ed., *Maoism: A Sourcebook—Selections from the Writings of Mao Tse-tung*, Los Angeles, editor's mimeographed edition, 1952, pp. 85, 87, 89-92, 95-96).

one of confiscating the lands of the landlord class and distributing them to the peasants. . . .

The Basic Program on Chinese Agrarian Law stipulates that under the principle of eliminating the agrarian system of feudal and semi-feudal exploitation and carrying out the agrarian system of land to the tillers, the land shall be equally distributed according to population. . . . Poor peasants' leagues and their elected committees, comprising the masses of poor peasants and farm laborers, must be organized in the villages. These shall be the legal organs for carrying out agrarian reform, and the poor peasants' leagues should become the backbone leading all rural struggles. Our line is to rely on poor peasants and solidly unite with middle peasants to destroy the feudal and semi-feudal exploitation system of the landlord class and old-type rich peasants. . . .

For the sake of resolutely and thoroughly carrying out agrarian reform and consolidating the rear areas of the PLA, it is necessary to reorganize and purify the ranks of the party. The movement for the reformation of ideology and style of work within our party during the period of the anti-Japanese war in general attained success. This success lay, in the main, in the fact that our party's leading organs as well as many cadres have gone a step further in their grasp of such a basic orientation as the integration of the universal truth of Marxism-Leninism with the concrete practice of the Chinese revolution.

In this respect, our party has taken a great stride forward in comparison with the several historical periods prior to the anti-Japanese war. However, the question of impure composition and working style of the party's local organizations, and especially of the party's primary rural organizations, was not solved. During the eleven years from 1937 to 1947, our party organization developed from several tens of thousands of party members to 2,700,000 party members. This is a huge leap forward. It has made our party an unprecedentedly powerful party. It provided us with the possibilities of defeating Japanese imperialism and repelling the offensives of Chiang Kai-shek, and leading the Liberated Areas of more than 100,000,000 population and a PLA 2,000,000 strong.

But along with this came defects. That is, many landlord, rich peasant and *lumpen*-proletarian* elements took this opportunity to slip into our party. They dominate many party, government and mass organizations in the rural areas; lord it over, bully and oppress the people, and distort the Party's policies, causing these organizations to become alienated from the masses of the people and preventing agrarian reform from being thorough.

Such serious conditions place before us the task of reorganizing and purifying the ranks of the party. If this task is not solved we cannot make progress in the rural areas. . . .

Without the broadest united front, comprising the overwhelming majority of the entire national population, the victory of the Chinese New Democratic Revolution is impossible. But this is not all. This united front must also be under the firm leadership of the Chinese Communist Party. Without the firm leadership of the Chinese Communist Party, no revolutionary united front can be victorious. . . .

. . . Reliance on American imperialism is a common characteristic of reactionary forces in various countries throughout the world following the conclusion of World War II.

This fact reflects the seriousness of the blow dealt to world capitalism by World War II, the feebleness of the reactionary forces in the various countries and their psychological panic and loss of confidence. It reflects the powerful might of the revolutionary forces of the whole world which causes the reactionaries of various countries to feel that there is no way out except to rely on the aid of American imperialism. But in reality is American imperialism after World War II as powerful as Chiang Kai-shek and the reactionaries of various countries imagine? . . .

. . . Crisis, like a volcano, is daily menacing American imperialism: American imperialism is sitting right on this volcano. This situation forced American imperialist elements to establish a plan for enslaving the world: to plunge like wild beasts into Europe, Asia and other places, muster the reac-

* "*Lumpen*-proletarian": from the German, "ragged proletarian" —Ed.

tionary forces of various countries—these dregs spat out by the people—to organize the imperialist, antidemocratic front against all democratic forces headed by the Soviet Union, and prepare war—scheming at some remote time in the future to unleash World War III and defeat the democratic forces. This is a wild plan. The democratic forces of the whole world must, and entirely can, defeat this plan. The strength of the world anti-imperialist camp exceeds that of the imperialist camp. The superiority is with us, not with the enemy. The anti-imperialist camp headed by the Soviet Union has already been formed. . . .

We are clearly aware of the fact that there will be all kinds of obstructions and difficulties in our path of advance. We should prepare to cope with the greatest degree of resistance and struggle on the part of all foreign and domestic enemies. Only if we are able to grasp the science of Marxism-Leninism, have faith in the masses, stand closely together with the masses and lead them forward will we be entirely capable of surmounting any obstacle and conquering any difficulty and will our strength be matchless. This is the historic era in which capitalism and imperialism of the whole world are moving toward their doom, in which Socialism and Democracy of the whole world are moving toward victory. The light of dawn is just before us. We should put forth our efforts.

Communist Victory in China

By the middle of 1949 Communist control was extended to the whole of mainland China, as Chiang Kai-shek took refuge in Formosa. Mao announced the main policies which he intended to pursue—dictatorship and "re-education," to mobilize the whole population in building up the country and fighting the enemies of communism.

. . . The experience of several decades, amassed by the Chinese people, tells us to carry out the people's democratic

FROM: Mao, "On the People's Democratic Dictatorship" (July, 1949; Brandt, Schwartz, Fairbank, pp. 456-61).

dictatorship. That is, the right of reactionaries to voice their opinions must be abolished and only the people are allowed to have the right of voicing their opinions.

Who are the "people"? At the present stage in China, they are the working class, the peasant class, the petty bourgeoisie, and national bourgeoisie. Under the leadership of the working class and the Communist Party, these classes unite together to form their own state and elect their own government [so as to] carry out a dictatorship over the lackeys of imperialism—the landlord class, the bureaucratic capitalist class, and the Kuomintang reactionaries and their henchmen representing these classes—to suppress them, allowing them only to behave properly and not to talk and act wildly. If they talk and act wildly their [action] will be prohibited and punished immediately. The democratic system is to be carried out within the ranks of the people, giving them freedom of speech, assembly, and association. The right to vote is given only to the people and not to the reactionaries. These two aspects, namely, democracy among the people and dictatorship over the reactionaries, combine to form the people's democratic dictatorship.

Why should it be done this way? Everybody clearly knows that otherwise the revolution would fail, and the people would meet with woe and the State would perish.

"Don't you want to eliminate state authority?" Yes, but we do not want it at present, we cannot want it at present. Why? Because imperialism still exists, the domestic reactionaries still exist, and classes in the country still exist. Our present task is to strengthen the apparatus of the people's state, which refers mainly to the people's army, people's police, and people's courts, for the defence of the country, and the protection of the people's interests; and with this as a condition, to enable China to advance steadily, under the leadership of the working class and the Communist Party, from an agricultural to an industrial country, and from a New Democratic to a Socialist and Communist society, to eliminate classes and to realize the state of universal fraternity. The army, police, and courts of the state are instruments by which classes oppress classes. To the hostile classes the state apparatus is the instrument of oppression. It is violent, and not "benevolent." "You are not benevolent." Just so. We decidedly will not exercise benevolence towards the reactionary acts of the reactionaries and reactionary classes. Our benevolence applies only to the people, and not to the reactionary acts of the reactionaries and reactionary classes outside the people.

The function of the people's state is to protect the people. Only when there is the people's state, is it possible for the people to use democratic methods on a nationwide and all-round scale to educate and reform themselves, to free themselves from the influence of reactionaries at home and abroad (this influence is at present still very great and will exist for a long time and cannot be eliminated quickly), to unlearn the bad habits and ideas acquired from the old society and not to let themselves travel on the erroneous path pointed out by the reactionaries, but to continue to advance and develop towards a Socialist and Communist society accomplishing the historic mission of completely eliminating classes and advancing towards a universal fraternity.

The methods we use in this field are democratic; that is, methods of persuasion and not coercion. When people break the law they will be punished, imprisoned, or even sentenced to death. But these are individual cases and are different in principle from the dictatorship over the reactionary class as a class.

After their political regime is overthrown the reactionary classes and the reactionary clique will also be given land and work and a means of living; they will be allowed to re-educate themselves into new persons through work, provided they do not rebel, disrupt, or sabotage. If they are unwilling to work, the people's state will compel them to work. Propaganda and educational work will also be carried out among them, and, moreover, with care and adequacy, as we did among captured officers. This can also be called "benevolent administration," but we shall never forgive their reactionary acts and will never let their reactionary activity have the possibility of a free development.

Such re-education of the reactionary classes can only be carried out in the state of the people's democratic dictatorship. If this work is well done the main exploiting classes of China—the landlord and bureaucratic capitalist classes—will be finally eliminated. [Of the exploiting classes] there remain the national bourgeoisie, among many of whom appropriate educational work can be carried out at the present stage. When socialism is realized, that is, when the nationalization of private enterprises has been carried out, they can be further educated and reformed. The people have in their hands a powerful state apparatus and are not afraid of the rebellion of the national bourgeois class.

The grave problem is that of educating the peasants. The peasants' economy is scattered. Judging by the experience of the Soviet Union, it requires a very long time and careful work to attain the socialization of agriculture. Without the socialization of agriculture, there will be no complete and consolidated socialism. And to carry out the socialization of agriculture a powerful industry with state-owned enterprises as the main component must be developed. The state of the people's democratic dictatorship must step by step solve this problem. . . .

The people's democratic dictatorship needs the leadership of the working class, because only the working class is most far-sighted, just and unselfish and endowed with revolutionary thoroughness. The history of the entire revolution proves that without the leadership of the working class, the revolution is bound to fail, and with the leadership of the working class, the revolution is victorious. In the era of imperialism no other class in any country can lead any genuine revolution to victory. This is clearly proved by the fact that the Chinese national bourgeoisie had led the revolution many times and each time had failed.

The national bourgeoisie is of great importance at the present stage. Imperialism is still standing near us and this enemy is very fierce. A long time is required for China to realize true economic independence and become free from reliance on imperialist nations. Only when China's industries are developed, and she no longer depends economically on powerful nations, can there be real independence. The proportion of China's modern industry in the entire national economy is still very small. There are still no reliable figures at present, but according to certain data it is estimated that modern industry only occupies about ten per cent of the total productive output in the national economy of the whole country. To cope with imperialist oppression, and to raise our backward economic status one step higher, China must utilize all urban and rural factors of capitalism which are beneficial and not detrimental to the national economy and the people's livelihood, and unite with the national bourgeoisie in a common struggle. Our present policy is to restrict capitalism and not to eliminate it. . . .

We must overcome difficulties, and must master what we do not know. We must learn economic work from all who know the ropes (no matter who they are). We must acknowledge them as our teachers, and learn from them respectfully and earnestly. We must acknowledge our ignorance, and not pretend to know what we do not know, nor put on bureaucratic airs. Stick to it, and eventually it will be mastered in a few months, one or two years, or three or five years. At first some of the Communists in the U.S.S.R. also did not know how to do economic work, and the imperialists also waited Union won. Under the leadership of Lenin and Stalin they for their failure. But the Communist Party of the Soviet not only could do revolutionary work but also reconstruction work. They have already built up a great and brilliant socialist state. The Communist Party of the U.S.S.R. is our best teacher from whom we must learn. We can rely wholly on the weapon of the people's democratic dictatorship to unite all people throughout the country, except the reactionaries, and advance steadily towards the goal. . . .

The Chinese People's Republic

The Communist government of China was officially proclaimed in effect on October 1, 1949, as the "Chinese People's Republic," with Mao as chief of state or "chairman" and Chou En-lai as premier. The legal basis of the regime was a provisional constitution known as the "Common Program," which remained in effect until the permanent constitution was adopted in 1954.

Preamble:

The great victories of the Chinese People's war of liberation and people's revolution have ended the era of the rule of imperialism, feudalism and bureaucratic capitalism in China. From the status of the oppressed, the Chinese people has become the master of a new society and a new state, and replaced the feudal, compradore, fascist, dictatorial Kuomintang reactionary rule with the republic of the people's democratic dictatorship. The Chinese people's democratic dictatorship is the state power of the people's democratic united front of the Chinese working class, peasantry, petty bourgeoisie, national bourgeoisie and patriotic democratic elements based on the alliance of workers and peasants and led by the working class. The Chinese People's Political Consultative Conference composed of the representatives of the Communist Party of China, all democratic parties and groups, people's organizations, all areas, People's Liberation Army, all national minorities, overseas Chinese and patriotic democratic elements is the form of organization of the Chinese people's democratic united front. The Chinese People's PCC, representing the will of the people throughout the country, proclaims the establishment of the People's Republic of China and organizes the people's own central government. The Chinese People's PCC unanimously agrees that the New Democracy, namely the people's democracy, shall be the political foundation for national construction of the People's Republic of China. . . .

Organs of State Power:

Article 12:

The state power of the People's Republic of China belongs to the people. All levels of the people's congress and all

FROM: "Common Program of the Chinese People's Republic" (September 29, 1949; English translation in *Current Background* [American Consulate General, Hong Kong], no. 9, September 21, 1950, pp. 1, 3-5).

levels of the people's government are the organs for exercising state power by the people. All levels of the people's congress shall be elected through universal suffrage by the people. All levels of the people's congress shall elect the respective levels of the people's government. The various levels of the people's government shall be the organs for exercising state power at their respective levels when their respective people's congresses are not in session. The All-China People's Congress is the supreme organ of state power. The Central People's Government shall be the supreme organ for exercising state power when the All-China People's Congress is not in session.

Article 13:

The Chinese People's PCC is the form of organization of the people's democratic united front. It shall be composed of the representatives of the working class, the peasantry, revolutionary service men, intellectuals, the petty bourgeoisie, the national bourgeoisie, national minorities, overseas Chinese, and patriotic democratic elements.

Pending the convocation of the All-China People's Congress, elected through universal suffrage, the plenary session of the Chinese People's PCC shall exercise the functions and powers of the All-China People's Congress, enact the statute of the Central People's Government of the People's Republic of China, elect the Central People's Government Council of the People's Republic of China, and vest it with the authority of exercising state power. . . .

Article 15:

All levels of organs of state power shall put into practice democratic centralism. Its main principles are: The people's congress is responsible and accountable to the people. The people's government council is responsible and accountable to the people's congress. Within the people's congress and the people's government council, the minority shall abide by the decisions of the majority. The appointment of the people's governments of various levels shall be confirmed by the people's government of the higher level. The people's government of the lower level shall obey the people's government of the higher level and all local people's governments throughout the country shall obey the Central People's Government. . . .

Article 17:

All laws, decrees and judicial systems of the Kuomintang reactionary government oppressing the people are abolished and laws and decrees protecting the people shall be enacted and the people's judicial system shall be set up.

Article 18:

All state organs must enforce a revolutionary working style of honesty, simplicity and service to the people; must severely punish graft, forbid extravagance and oppose the bureaucratic working style of estrangement from the masses of the people.

Article 19:

People's supervisory organs shall be set up on the people's governments of county and municipal level and above to supervise the execution of duties by the various levels of state organs and public functionaries, and indict organs and functionaries who violate the law or are derelict in the performance of their duties. . . .

The Sino-Soviet Alliance

While Soviet aid to the Chinese Communists during the civil war was not conspicuous and probably not decisive, the Chinese Communists never faltered in their professions of solidarity with the USSR. The USSR maintained relations with the nationalist government of China until 1949, but then quickly recognized the new Communist republic. A formal treaty of alliance was concluded in Moscow early in 1950.

The new Treaty of Friendship, Alliance and Mutual Assistance, the Agreement on the Chinese Changchun [South-

FROM: Chou En-lai, Speech on the Signing of the Sino-Soviet Agreements of Feb. 14, 1950 (English translation in *People's China,* March 1, 1950, pp. 28-29.)

Manchurian] Railway, Port Arthur and Dairen, the Agreement on granting credit to China have been signed today between the People's Republic of China and the Union of Soviet Socialist Republics and notes have been exchanged. The conclusion of the above treaty and agreements is based on the vital interests of the great peoples of China and the Soviet Union and indicates fraternal friendship and eternal co-operation between China and the Soviet Union. The conclusion of the treaty and agreements is a special expression of fervent assistance to the revolutionary cause of the Chinese people on the part of the Soviet Union directed by the policy of Generalissimo Stalin. There is no doubt that this close and sincere co-operation between China and the Soviet Union is of extremely profound historical importance and will inevitably have immense influence upon and consequences for the cause of peace and justice for the peoples of the East and the whole world.

The great friendship between our two powers has been built up since the October Socialist Revolution. However, imperialism and the counter-revolutionary government of China hampered further co-operation between us. The victory of the Chinese people has brought about radical changes in the situation. The Chinese people, under the leadership of Chairman Mao Tse-tung, have set up the People's Republic of China and have formed a state having unprecedented unity and this has made sincere co-operation possible between our two great states. Thanks to the meetings and the exchange of opinions between Generalissimo Stalin and Chairman Mao Tse-tung, this possibility became a reality and the friendship, alliance and mutual assistance between China and the Soviet Union are sealed now with the signed treaty. The imperialist bloc headed by American imperialism has resorted to all kinds of provocative methods attempting to frustrate the friendship between our two nations but these ignominious attempts have utterly failed.

The significance of the treaty and agreements between China and the Soviet Union is of particular importance for the new-born People's Republic of China. This treaty and these agreements will help the Chinese people to realize that they are not alone, and will help in the restoration and development of Chinese economy. . . .

Permit me on behalf of the Chinese people to express gratitude to Generalissimo Stalin and the Soviet Government for this great friendship. . . .

Long live permanent friendship and eternal co-operation between China and the Soviet Union! . . .

Land Reform

The breakup of landlords' holdings, already accomplished in the former Communist guerilla areas, was extended by stages to the rest of China after the new Communist government was established. The landlord class was eliminated, with a large though indeterminate number of executions.

Agrarian reform must be carried out under guidance, in a planned and orderly way, in complete accordance with the laws and decrees promulgated by the Central People's Government and the people's governments at various levels, and the principles, policies and steps decided by them. Because our future agrarian reform is on the biggest scale in history, only in this way can it conform with the interests of the great majority of the people. . . .

The essential content of agrarian reform is the confiscation of the land of the landlord class for distribution to the landless peasants and land-poor peasants. Thus landlords as a class are abolished from society and the land ownership system of feudal exploitation is transformed into a system of peasant land ownership. Such a reform is indeed the greatest and most thorough reform in thousands of years of Chinese history.

Why should such a reform be made? In a few words, because the original land system of China is extremely irrational. In general the old land situation in China is roughly as follows:

FROM: Liu Shao-ch'i, "On the Agrarian Reform Law" (Speech at the Second Session of the National Committee of the People's Political Consultative Conference, June, 1950; English translation in *People's China*, July 16, 1950, pp. 5-8, 28-31).

Landlords and rich peasants, who constitute less than 10 per cent of the rural population, possess approximately from 70 to 80 per cent of the land and brutally exploit the peasants by means of this land. . . .

This lies at the root of our nation having become the object of aggression and oppression and having become poor and backward. This is also the basic obstacle to the achievement of democracy, industrialization, independence, unification and prosperity in our country. Unless we change this situation, the victory of the Chinese people's revolution cannot be consolidated, the productive forces in the rural areas cannot be set free, the industrialization of New China cannot be realized and the people cannot enjoy the fundamental gains of the victory of the revolution. . . .

We can see from the basic reason and aim of agrarian reform that the historical crimes committed by the landlord class in the past are rooted in the former social system. Landlords in general will only be deprived of their feudal land holdings and abolished as a social class, but they will not be physically eliminated. The smallest minority, those on whom the people's courts should pass sentences of death or imprisonment, are certain landlords guilty of heinous crimes—rural despots whose crimes are gross and whose iniquities are extreme and those criminal elements who persistently resist agrarian reform. Therefore, it is stipulated in the Draft Agrarian Reform Law that after the landlords' land and other means of production have been confiscated, the landlords will still be allocated one share of the land and the other means of production so that they can also make a living by their own labour, and reform themselves through labour. After undergoing long-term reform through labour, it is possible for landlords to become new men.

This view of the basic reason for and aim of agrarian reform is different from the view that agrarian reform is only designed to relieve the poor people. The Communist Party has always been fighting for the interests of the labouring poor, but the ideas of Communists have always been different from those of philanthropists. The results of agrarian reform are beneficial to the impoverished labouring peasants. They can help peasants partly solve the question of their poverty. But the basic aim of agrarian reform is not purely one of relieving poor peasants. It is designed to set free the rural productive forces, that is, to free rural labourers, land and other means of production from the shackles of the feudal ownership system of the landlord class, in order to develop agricultural production and to clear the path for the industrialization of China. The question of poverty among the peasantry can be finally solved only if agricultural production can be greatly developed, if the industrialization of New China can be realized, if the living standards of the people throughout the country can be raised and if China finally proceeds upon the road of Socialist development. By merely carrying out agrarian reform, part, but not all, of the problem of the peasants' poverty can be solved. . . .

Rich peasant economy should not be destroyed. This is because the existence of a rich peasant economy and its development within certain limits is advantageous to the development of the people's economy in our country. It is, therefore, also beneficial to the broad peasant masses. . . .

If the people's government carry out a policy of preserving the rich peasant economy, the rich peasants can be won over to a neutral attitude in general, and better protection can then be given to the middle peasants, thus eliminating certain unnecessary misgivings of the peasants during the development of production. Therefore, in the present situation, the adoption of a policy which will preserve the rich peasant economy in the coming agrarian reform is necessary both politically and economically. . . .

The purity of the leadership of the peasant associations at all levels should be guarded. The masses should be mobilized to re-elect the leadership where there is impurity. Here, the term "purity" does not mean the adoption of a closed-door attitude toward such farm labourers, poor peasants or middle peasants as may have committed certain errors or the exclusion of them from participation in the associations. On the contrary, they should be welcomed into the associations, educated and brought into unity. The term "purity" here means to prevent landlords, rich peasants and their agents from joining the peasants' associations and, still more important, from taking leading positions in them. . . .

Only those landlords, secret agents and counter-revolutionary elements who conspire to organize resistance and carry out subversive activities should be ruthlessly suppressed and all their resistance smashed in good time. . . .

People's courts should be set up to suppress and punish the resistance and subversive activities of despots, secret agents, counter-revolutionary elements and the landlord class in good time and to handle the charges made by the peasants against these elements during the agrarian reform. . . .

National Minorities in China—Tibet

In 1951, Chinese Communist forces entered Tibet, which in the past had usually been under Chinese suzerainty. An agreement was concluded by which Tibet was promised internal autonomy. The agreement broke down in 1959, as Communist moves toward socialism and tighter control precipitated an abortive Tibetan uprising.

1. The Tibetan people shall unite and drive out imperialist aggressive forces from Tibet so that the Tibetan people shall return to the big family of the motherland—the People's Republic of China.

2. The local government of Tibet shall actively assist the People's Liberation Army to enter Tibet and consolidate the national defences.

3. In accordance with the policy towards nationalities laid down in the Common Programme of the Chinese People's Political Consultative Conference, the Tibetan people have the right of exercising regional autonomy under the unified leadership of the Central People's Government.

4. The central authorities will not alter the existing political system in Tibet. The central authorities also will not alter

FROM: Agreement between the Chinese Central People's Government and the Tibetan Government on the Administration of Tibet, May 23, 1951 (English translation by New China News Agency; reprinted in *Documents on International Affairs*, 1951, pp. 577-78).

the established status, functions and powers of the Dalai Lama. Officials of various ranks shall hold office as usual.

5. The established status, functions and powers of the Panchen Ngoerhtehni* shall be maintained.

6. By the established status, functions and powers of the Dalai Lama and of the Panchen Ngoerhtehni are meant the status, functions and powers of the Thirteenth Dalai Lama and of the Ninth Panchen Ngoerhtehni when they were in friendly and amicable relations with each other.

7. The policy of freedom of religious belief laid down in the Common Programme of the Chinese People's Political Consultative Conference shall be carried out.

The religious beliefs, customs and habits of the Tibetan people shall be respected, and lama monasteries shall be protected. The central authorities will not effect a change in the income of the monasteries.

8. Tibetan troops shall be reorganised step by step into the People's Liberation Army and become a part of the national defence forces of the People's Republic of China.

9. The spoken and written language and school education, etc., of the Tibetan nationality shall be developed step by step in accordance with the actual conditions in Tibet.

10. Tibetan agriculture, livestock raising, industry and commerce shall be developed step by step, and the people's livelihood shall be improved step by step in accordance with the actual conditions in Tibet.

11. In matters related to various reforms in Tibet, there will be no compulsion on the part of the central authorities. The local government of Tibet should carry out reforms of its own accord, and when the people raise demands for reform, they shall be solved by means of consultation with the leading personnel of Tibet.

12. Insofar as former pro-imperialist and pro-Kuomintang officials resolutely sever relations with imperialism and with the Kuomintang and do not engage in sabotage or resistance, they may continue to hold office irrespective of their past.

* The Panchen Lama, Tibetan spiritual leader, who had been at odds with the Dalai Lama, the theocratic head of the Tibetan government—Ed.

13. The People's Liberation Army entering Tibet shall abide by all the above mentioned policies and shall also be fair in all buying and selling and shall not arbitrarily take a needle or thread from the people.

14. The Central People's Government shall have the centralised handling of all external affairs of the area of Tibet; and there will be peaceful co-existence with neighbouring countries and the establishment and development of fair commercial and trading relations with them on the basis of equality, mutual benefit and mutual respect for territory and sovereignty.

15. In order to ensure the implementation of this agreement, the Central People's Government shall set up a military and administrative committee and a military area headquarters in Tibet, and apart from the personnel sent there by the Central People's Government shall absorb as many local Tibetan personnel as possible to take part in the work. . . .

The Korean War and Industrialization

The anti-imperialist sentiments of the Chinese Communists were charged with new intensity with Chinese involvement in the Korean War. In February, 1953, Chou En-lai spoke to the People's Political Consultative Council (the provisional legislative body) to report on the government's political and military strength, and to call for a major industrialization effort in the Five-Year Plan which was just beginning.

Under the leadership of the Communist Party of China, the Chinese people have become further organized, on a nationwide scale, through the trade unions, peasant associations, the New Democratic Youth League, the women's federations, the students' federation, the industrialists and merchants' associations, the Sino-Soviet Friendship Association, and the people's organizations in the spheres of literature, arts and sciences. By relying on the strength of the broad masses of the people, we have, during the past 3 years, carried out such

FROM: Chou, Political Report to the Fourth Session of the First National Committee of the PPCC, February, 1953 (*Current Background*, No. 228, February 8, 1953, pp. 3-4, 9-10).

great struggles as land reform, the suppression of counter-revolutionaries, the movement to resist American aggression and aid Korea, the "3-anti" movement (against corruption, waste and bureaucratism) and the "5-anti" movement (against bribery, tax evasion, fraud, theft of state property, and theft of state economic secrets) and the ideological re-moulding of intellectuals.

Educated by these struggles, the Chinese people have raised their political consciousness to a level never known before. In this respect, the most striking achievements are: the drawing of a sharp distinction between ourselves and the enemy by the masses of the people in our country; the destruction of the remaining influence of the domestic counter-revolutionaries and the imperialists; the repudiation of decadent capitalist ideology and the further consolidation of the leading role of the working class and of socialist ideology. All this has strengthened our people's democratic united front more than ever, welding hundreds of millions of people into an organized and conscious force. Throughout the past year, all groups of the people in our country have taken up the study of the "Selected Works of Mao Tse-tung" and the Common Program. More recently, they have embarked on the study of Comrade Stalin's "Economic Problems of Socialism in the USSR" and Comrade Malenkov's report to the 19th Congress of the CPSU. These studies will arm us and enable us to work and remould ourselves better and more consciously.

Since the return of the Tibetan people to the great family of the motherland, solidarity between the Han [Chinese] and Tibetan people has made immense progress. National autonomous areas are being built up step by step in the areas inhabited by the minority nationalities. Patriotism and political consciousness are growing daily among the peoples of all nationalities. Fraternal relations of equality, cooperation, friendliness and solidarity among all these nationalities are being increasingly consolidated. United within one big family in our great motherland, these nationalities have embarked on developments of historic importance in their political, economic and cultural life.

All these achievements show that the leading position of the working class of our country has been strengthened economically, politically and ideologically; that our economy, which was disrupted by prolonged wars, has been rehabilitated and that a solid foundation has been built for the people's democratic dictatorship. This has created favorable conditions for our long-term, planned, large-scale national construction.

It must be pointed out that these successes were attained mainly in the process of the great struggle to resist American aggression and aid Korea. Two and a half years ago, the American imperialists launched their heinous war of aggression against our neighbor, Korea, crossed the 38th Parallel and pushed to the bank of the Yalu and Tumen Rivers along the borders of our country. At the same time, they occupied our territory of Taiwan. In order to preserve peace in the Far East and the World, to safeguard the security of our country and to support the just struggle of the Korean people against aggression, the Chinese people resolutely started their great campaign to resist American aggression and aid Korea. Hundreds of thousands of the finest sons and daughters of the Chinese people joined the Chinese People's Volunteers and have fought shoulder to shoulder with the Korean People's Army, repelling the U.S. imperialist aggression and forcing the enemy back to the 38th Parallel, thereby upsetting the timetable of the American imperialists for a war of world-wide aggression, increasing the internal contradictions within the camp of imperialism and placing increasingly serious difficulties in the way of the frantic scheme of the American imperialists to attack the camp of peace and democracy and extend aggression. This armed struggle against aggression by the Chinese people has not, as the imperialists imagined, caused any halt or interruption in the social transformation and economic rehabilitation of China. On the contrary, it has greatly stimulated the Chinese people's great spirit of patriotism and internationalism, infinitely strengthened their moral and political unity, conspicuously elevated the international status of our country, powerfully expanded the world movement against war and in defence of peace and reinforced the strength and influence of the world camp of peace and democracy headed by the Soviet Union. This great struggle to resist American aggression and aid Korea has been a tremendous driving force in every aspect of our work of national transformation and rehabilitation. The people of our country have everywhere ardently joined in the struggle by signing patriotic pacts increasing production and practising economy. In the course of this struggle, they have resolutely rooted out any pro-America, worship-America or fear-America ideology which had been left among a section of the people as the residue of reactionary Kuomintang indoctrination. The people of our country have answered the American imperialist war schemes by enthusiastic participation in the campaign for signatures for world peace. They have defeated American germ warfare by their patriotic mass sanitation movement. The campaign to resist American aggression and aid Korea has, in fact, guaranteed and accelerated the early and successful completion of our work of social transformation and economic rehabilitation. . . .

. . . In 1953, the first year of the first five-year plan, our industry and agriculture will register a marked rise in output compared with 1952. . . .

Our planned national construction is on a grand scale from the very beginning; the tasks before us are both immense and glorious and fraught with many difficulties. Our weightiest and central task throughout this year is therefore to mobilize the working class and all the other people of the whole country to concentrate their efforts in overcoming difficulties and to exert themselves to fulfill and overfulfill the plan of construction for 1953. To complete this complex and arduous task, we must develop intensive, precise work at every link in the process. We must guarantee the income of the state and ensure that our plans of economic construction, national defence and social and cultural development are not affected by any shortage of funds. . . .

We must rally all industrialists and merchants whose enterprises are beneficial to the national interests and the people's livelihood, and enable them to develop their initiative under the leadership of the state economy and the unified national plan. We must make a serious study of advanced Soviet experience, propagate the application of advanced experience, organize patriotic emulation and economy campaigns on the broadest mass base and gradually lift the living standards of the workers and peasants by raising the level of industrial and agricultural production.

We must make all working comrades understand that we are facing new things and new tasks, that we can overcome difficulties, fulfill our tasks, master our work and make fewer errors only by setting ourselves firmly against arrogance and complacency, by making every effort to learn humbly and by correcting our mistakes and shortcomings. We must strengthen our state discipline, oppose bureaucratism and commandism, mete out punishment to law-breakers and keep a strict watch against sabotage and destruction by vicious elements. It is our belief that under the correct leadership of Chairman Mao Tse-tung and the Chinese Communist Party and with the assistance of advanced Soviet technique and the Soviet experts, the intelligent, industrious workers, peasants and intellectuals of China will certainly be able to bring their great initiative and creativeness into play and to carry out every concrete task and plan. . . .

The Collectivization of the Chinese Peasants

Late in 1953 the Chinese Communist leadership ordered the general collectivization of the nation's agriculture. With an eye to Russian experience, the decision cautioned against the use of violence, but the organization of "cooperatives" was rapidly pushed. By 1957 it was substantially complete.

The general line of the party during the transition period is to gradually bring into realization socialist industrialization of the state and to effect, step by step, socialist reform of agriculture, handicraft industry and capitalist industry and commerce. According to the general line of the party, the

FROM: Decision of the Central Committee of the Chinese Communist Party on the Development of Agricultural Producer Cooperatives, December 16, 1953 (*Current Background,* No. 278, February 15, 1954, pp. 1-2, 4, 13).

national economic construction would not only bring our industrial economy to a high point but our agricultural economy to a relatively high level. However, the isolated, scattered, conservative and backward individual economy limits the development of the productive forces of agriculture and an ever greater contradiction between individual economy and socialist industrialization is making itself increasingly felt. It has become more and more evident that the small-scale agricultural production cannot satisfy the demand of the broad peasantry to improve their living conditions, nor can it meet the increasing need of the entire national economy. To further raise the productive forces of agriculture, the most fundamental task of the party in its rural work would be to educate the peasants through measures most acceptable and understandable to them and stimulate them to gradually get organized and carry out the socialist reform of agriculture. This will make it possible for our agriculture to change from a state of backward individual economy into one of advanced cooperative economy aiming at large-scale production, for the contradiction between the two types of economy, industrial and agricultural, to be gradually overcome, and for the peasants to gradually but completely free themselves from the state of poverty and, instead, enjoy a happy and prosperous life.

According to the nation's experiences, the concrete way for the gradual organization of China's peasants is to organize them through temporary mutual-aid teams which operate a simple form of collective labor, and year-round mutual-aid teams which have certain division of labor among their members on the basis of collective labor and with a small amount of property owned in common; then through agricultural cooperatives in which the members pool their land as shares and there is unified management and more property owned in common; and finally to agricultural cooperatives of a higher form (or collective farms) with collective peasant ownership which is entirely socialist in character. This is the path laid down by the party for the gradual, step-by-step socialist transformation of agriculture. . . .

There inevitably will grow in rural villages a conflict between socialism and capitalism as the two develop. The conflict will become more and more evident as the agricultural economy restores and gradually improves. The party's policy is to actively and carefully channel the peasants' activeness in individual economy to mutual aid and cooperation through numerous, concrete, appropriate and varied forms, so as to overcome the spontaneous tendency toward capitalism and gradually lead them to socialism. . . .

Cooperative farming must in all cases be developed along the basic principle of voluntariness. To carry out socialist reform in small peasant economy, we must not resort to the simple method of calling upon the masses to start it, nor should we command the poor peasants and middle peasants to join the cooperatives, nor could we use the means of depriving the peasants of their production materials by turning them into common property. If we should resort to such means, it would be a criminal act of sabotaging the workers' and peasants' alliance and also the poor peasants' and middle peasants' alliance, hence a criminal act against agricultural cooperation. . . .

The Central Committee of the party has repeatedly pointed out that the party must give active leadership and bring about steady progress in the mutual-aid and cooperation movement and the socialist transformation of agriculture. By active leadership is meant that the party leadership must not lag behind the demand of the masses and the requirements of national construction. By steady progress is meant that the party leadership should not exceed the degree of mass consciousness and disregard the possible conditions. For this reason, the leadership organs at all levels must fully grasp the objective conditions of the time and place and in no way commit the error of subjectivism nor the error of commandism. . . .

China and Coexistence

Following the armistice which concluded the Korean War in 1953, Chinese Communist foreign policy began to emphasize accommodations with non-Communist Asian states. An agreement with India in 1954 stated "five principles" of coexistence, which the Chinese proclaimed as the basis of their policy. In 1955 China participated in the Bandung Conference of Asian and African states, at which Chou En-lai proclaimed the community of interest of these countries against the Western colonial powers and sought to allay fears about Chinese expansion.

a) The "Five Principles" of Coexistence

. . . Recently India and China have come to an agreement in which they have laid down certain principles which should guide relations between the two countries. These principles are: (1) mutual respect for each other's territorial integrity and sovereignty, (2) non-aggression, (3) non-interference in each other's internal affairs, (4) equality and mutual benefit and (5) peaceful co-existence. The Prime Ministers reaffirmed these principles and felt that they should be applied in their relations with other countries in Asia as well as in other parts of the world. If these principles are applied not only between various countries, but also in international relations generally, they would form a solid foundation for peace and security, and the fears and apprehensions that exist today would give place to a feeling of confidence.

The Prime Ministers recognized that different social and political systems exist in various parts of Asia and the world. If, however, the above-mentioned principles are accepted and acted upon and there is no interference by any one country with another, these differences should not come in the way of peace or create conflicts. With assurance of the territorial integrity and sovereignty of each country and of non-aggression, there would be peaceful co-existence and friendly relations between the countries concerned. This would lessen the tensions that exist in the world today and help in creating a climate of peace. . . .

FROM: Communiqué on Talks between Jawaharlal Nehru and Chou En-lai, June 28, 1954 (*India News*, July 3, 1954; reprinted in *Documents on International Affairs, 1954*, pp. 313-314).

b) *The Bandung Conference*

The Chinese Delegation has come here to seek unity and not to quarrel. We Communists do not hide the fact that we believe in communism and that we consider the socialist system a good system. There is no need at this Conference to publicize one's ideology and the political system of one's country, although differences do exist among us.

The Chinese Delegation has come here to seek common ground, and not to create divergence. Is there any basis for seeking common ground among us? Yes, there is. The overwhelming majority of the Asian and African countries and peoples have suffered and are still suffering from the calamities of colonialism. This is acknowledged by all of us. If we seek common ground in doing away with the sufferings and calamities under colonialism, it will be very easy for us to have mutual understanding and respect, mutual sympathy and support, instead of mutual suspicion and fear, mutual exclusion and antagonism. . . .

Now first of all I would like to talk about the question of different ideologies and social systems. We have to admit that among our Asian and African countries, we do have different ideologies and different social systems. But this does not prevent us from seeking common ground and being united. Many independent countries have appeared since the Second World War. One group of them are countries led by the Communist parties; another group of them are countries led by nationalists. There are not many countries in the first group. But what some people dislike is the fact that the 600 million Chinese people have chosen a political system which is socialist in nature and led by the Chinese Communist Party and that the Chinese people are no longer under the rule of imperialism. The countries in the second group are greater in number, such as India, Burma, Indonesia and many other countries in Asia and Africa. Out of the colonial rule

FROM: Chou, Speech to the Bandung Conference, April 19, 1955 (in *Asia-Africa Speaks from Bandung*, Jakarta, 1955; reprinted in *Documents on International Affairs*, 1955, pp. 409-11).

both of these groups of countries have become independent and are still continuing their struggle for complete independence. Is there any reason why we cannot understand and respect each other and give support and sympathy to each other? There is every reason to make the five principles the basis for establishing friendly co-operation and good neighbourly relations among us. We Asian and African countries, with China included, are all backward economically and culturally. If our Asian-African Conference does not exclude anybody, why couldn't we understand each other and enter into friendly cooperation?

Secondly, I would like to talk about the question as to whether there is freedom of religious belief. Freedom of religious belief is a principle recognized by all modern nations. We Communists are atheists, but we respect all those who have religious belief. We hope that those who have religious belief will also respect those without. China is a country where there is freedom of religious belief. There are in China, not only seven million Communists, but also tens of millions of Islamists and Buddhists and millions of Christians and Catholics. Here in the Chinese Delegation, there is a pious Imam of the Islamic faith. Such a situation is no obstacle to the internal unity of China. Why should it be impossible in the community of Asian and African countries to unite those with religious belief and those without? The days of instigating religious strife should have passed, because those who profit from instigating such strife are not those among us.

Thirdly, I would like to talk about the question of the so-called subversive activities. The struggle of the Chinese people against colonialism lasted for more than a hundred years. The national and democratic revolutionary struggles led by the Chinese Communist Party finally achieved success only after a strenuous and difficult course of thirty years. It is impossible to relate all the sufferings of the Chinese people under the rule of imperialism, feudalism and Chiang Kai-shek. At last, the Chinese people have chosen their state system and the present government. It is by the efforts of the Chinese people that the Chinese revolution has won its victory. It is certainly not imported from without. The point cannot be denied even by those who do not like the victory of the Chinese Revolution. As a Chinese proverb says: "Do not do unto others what you yourself do not desire." We are against outside interference; how could we want to interfere in the internal affairs of others? . . .

The "Thaw" in China

Communist China reacted to de-Stalinization with a marked though temporary relaxation in ideological controls, and an invitation to free criticism. The public statement of the new line was made in May, 1956, by Lu Ting-yi, head of the propaganda department of the Communist Party.

If China is to become wealthy and powerful, apart from the need of consolidating the people's regime, developing the economic and educational enterprises and fortifying the national defense, it is also necessary to bring prosperous development to literature, the arts and scientific work. We cannot afford to go without any of these things.

To bring prosperous development to literature, the arts and scientific work, it is necessary to adopt the policy of "letting all flowers bloom together and all schools contend in airing their views." In literary and art work, if there is "only one flower in bloom," no matter how good the flower may be, it would not lead to prosperity. Take the instance of drama before us for illustration. Several years ago, there were people who were opposed to the Peking drama. At that time, the Party resolved to enforce the policy of "letting all flowers bloom together and the new emerge from the old" in the phase of drama. Everybody is now able to see that this policy is correct and tremendously successful. Because the different kinds of dramas are free to compete with and learn from each other, rapid progress has been made in the field of drama. . . .

We must be able to see also that although literature and arts and scientific research are closely related with class

FROM: Lu Ting-yi, "Let All Flowers Bloom Together, Let Diverse Schools of Thought Contend" (Speech of May 26, 1956; *Current Background,* No. 406, August 15, 1956, pp. 3-4, 6-8, 11, 15).

struggle, nonetheless they cannot be identified with politics in an absolute sense. Political struggle is an instrument for manifesting class struggle directly. In the case of literature and arts and social science, while they can also manifest class struggle directly, they can also manifest the latter in a more devious way. It is fallacious to entertain the rightist unilateral view of "literature and arts for the sake of literature and arts" and "science for the sake of science" on the ground that literature and arts and science bear no relations with politics. On the other hand, to identify literature and arts and science with politics would also lead to another one-sided view. This is the mistake of "leftist" simplicity.

The party's policy advocates freedom of independent thinking in the work of literature and art and in the work of scientific research, freedom of debate, freedom of creative work and freedom to criticize, freedom to express one's opinion, and freedom to maintain one's opinion and to reserve one's opinion. . . .

The people are both in agreement and disagreement among themselves. Our country has already had its Constitution, and it is the duty of the people to abide by it. On this the people throughout the country are in agreement. Love of motherland and support for socialism should be unanimous among the people throughout the country. There are also internal divergencies among the people. In ideology, there is the difference between materialism and idealism. This difference exists while there are classes and will also exist when classes are eliminated. It will exist even when communist society comes into being.

During the time when classes still exist, the contradiction between materialism and idealism manifests itself in the form of class contradiction. After the obliteration of classes, as long as the contradictions between subjectivism and objectivism, progression and retrogression, and social productivity and production relations continue to exist, then the contradiction between materialism and idealism will remain in existence in the socialist society and the communist society. . . .

In this struggle, the CCP Central Committee has taught us

the need for opposing the thoughts which hamper academic criticism and discussion. These thoughts find expressions in the bourgeois cult of the "famous people" on the ground that they are the authority and cannot be criticized. The adoption of the lordly attitude of the bourgeoisie to oppress the young Marxist academic workers; the habit of certain party members to look upon themselves as the "authority," their intolerance of criticisms made against them and their abstention from practicing self-criticism; the practice of restraint by certain Party members in criticizing others for fear of wrecking the united front and unity; the habit of certain party members to refrain from criticizing or even to shelter the mistakes of other people on account of personal friendship.

The CCP Central Committee has pointed out that it is necessary to support this principle: In academic criticism and discussion, nobody is in a privileged position. It is wrong for anybody to look upon himself as the "authority," to suppress criticism, to neglect the mistaken thoughts of the bourgeoisie or to adopt the attitude of liberalism or even surrenderism. . . .

(1) Natural sciences including medicine have no class character. They have their own laws of development. Their relation with social systems is only that under bad social systems, these sciences develop slowly and under better social systems they can develop quickly. These are questions which have already been solved theoretically. Therefore, it is erroneous to put on class labels such as "feudal," "capitalist," "socialist," "proletarian," or "bourgeois," to certain medical theories, or theories of biology or other natural sciences; for instance, to say that "Chinese traditional medicine is feudal," "Western medicine is capitalist," "Pavlov's theory is socialist," "Michurin's theory is socialist," or the "theory of heredity of Mendel-Morgan is capitalist." We must never believe in this fallacy. Some people fall victim to this fallacy because of their sectarian sentiment. Some fall victim to this fallacy unconsciously because they want to give undue stress to the need of learning advanced Soviet sciences. We must treat the different things according to their circumstances and cannot indulge in generality.

Simultaneously with pointing out the above mentioned error, we must also point out another kind of mistake. This is the negation of the Pavlov and Michurin theories as important theories. People also fall victim to this fallacy on different grounds. Some want to negate the Soviet scientific achievement because of their political anti-Soviet sentiment. Some are just unable to yield to the theories because they belong to another school of thought. The former involves the question of political viewpoint, while the latter involves the question of academic thought. We must treat them in a different way and cannot indulge in generality.

(2) The party makes only one demand of works of literature and art, that is, "to serve the workers, peasants and soldiers." Today, this means that they should serve all working people, including the intelligentsia. We regard socialist realism as the best method of creation. But it is by no means the only one. While serving the workers, peasants and soldiers, any author can use whatever method he thinks best to create and vie with the others. . . .

It is common for good men to commit mistakes. Nobody in the world can be completely free from mistakes. Such mistakes should be distinguished rigidly from counterrevolutionary utterances. Criticism of such mistakes should be well-intentioned, calm, and cool-headed reasoning by taking the whole matter into consideration, and should only proceed from unity with a view to reaching unity. Positive steps should be taken to help those who have committed mistakes so that their mistakes can be corrected. The criticized people have basically nothing to fear. . . .

Liu Shao-ch'i on the Transition to Socialism

The First Five-Year Plan of industrialization, extending from 1953 through 1957, brought China roughly to the economic level of Russia on the eve of World War I (in absolute though not per capita terms), but in the meantime agriculture was collectivized and industry was put on a semi-nationalized basis. This, as Liu Shao-ch'i explained in September, 1956, meant the end of the "bourgeois democratic" stage and the initiation of the dictatorship of the proletariat—so-called—and the transition to socialism.

What are the basic characteristics of the period of transition in our country?

First, our country is industrially backward. In order to build a socialist society, we must develop socialist industry, above all, heavy industry, so as to transform China from a backward agricultural country into an advanced industrial country. This, however, takes considerable time.

Second, in our country the allies of the working class consist not only of the peasantry and the urban petty-bourgeoisie, but also the national bourgeoisie. For this reason, in order to transform our old economy, we must use peaceful means of transformation not only in the case of agriculture and handicrafts, but also in the case of capitalist industry and commerce. This needs to be done step by step; this too needs time.

On the basis of the actual conditions of our country, the Central Committee has thus defined the party's general line in the period of transition: to bring about, step by step, socialist industrialization and to accomplish, step by step, the socialist transformation of agriculture, handicrafts and capitalist industry and commerce within a relatively long period. This general line of the party was first put forward in 1952, when the period of the rehabilitation of the national economy had come to an end. It was accepted by the National People's Congress in 1954, and written into the Constitution of the People's Republic of China as the fundamental task of the state in the transition period.

The party's general line in the transition period is a beacon that guides our work in every field. Any work, if it deviates from the general line, immediately lands itself in mistakes, either rightist or "leftist." In the last few years the tendency of deviating from the party's general line to the right has manifested itself mainly in being satisfied merely with what

FROM: Liu, Political Report to the Eighth National Congress of the Chinese Communist Party, 1st Session, September, 1956 (*Current Background,* No. 412, September 28, 1956, pp. 6-7, 19, 31-32, 34-36, 54-55).

has been achieved in the bourgeois-democratic revolution, in wanting to call a halt to the revolution, in not admitting the need for our revolution to pass on into socialism, in being unwilling to adopt a suitable policy to restrict capitalism in both town and countryside, in not believing that the party could lead the peasantry along the road to socialism, and in not believing that the party could lead the people of the whole country to build socialism in China. The tendency of deviating from the party's general line to the "left" has manifested itself mainly in demanding that socialism be achieved overnight, in demanding that some method of expropriation be used in our country to eliminate the national bourgeoisie as a class, or some methods be used to squeeze out capitalist industry and commerce and force them to go bankrupt, in not admitting that we should adopt measures for advancing, step by step, to socialism, and in not believing that we could attain the goal of socialist revolution by peaceful means. Our party resolutely repudiated as well as criticized these two deviations. It is quite obvious that had our party accepted any of these views, we would not be able to build socialism, or to be successfully building socialism as we are doing today. . . .

The Central Committee of the party holds that, in order to satisfy the needs of socialist expanded reproduction in our country, fulfill the task of socialist industrialization, strengthen international cooperation between the countries of the socialist camp, and help to promote a common economic upsurge in all the socialist countries, we should build, in the main, an integrated industrial system within the period of three five-year plans on the basis of our large population and rich resources. . . .

The people's democratic dictatorship in our country has gone through the period of bourgeois-democratic revolution and is passing through the period of the socialist revolution. Before the nation-wide victory of the bourgeois democratic revolution, the people's democratic dictatorship had already been established in the revolutionary bases.* This dictatorship was meant to fulfill the task of the bourgeois-democratic

* I.e., the guerrilla areas—Ed.

revolution because it only brought about changes in the feudal land system. It did not change the ownership of means of production by the national bourgeoisie, or individual ownership by the peasants. After the founding of the People's Republic of China, the people's democratic dictatorship began to shoulder the task of transition from capitalism to socialism. That is to say, it was to change the private ownership of the means of production by the bourgeoisie and the small producers into socialist, public ownership; and to eliminate in a thorough way the exploitation of man by man. Such state power, in its essence, can only be the dictatorship of the proletariat. Only when the proletariat, through its own vanguard, the Chinese Communist Party, has employed this weapon of state power without the slightest hindrance and closely rallied around itself all the working people and all other forces that are ready to accept socialism, jointly to implement the line of policy of the proletariat and, on the one hand, build the economic and cultural life along the road to socialism and, on the other, suppress the resistance of reactionary classes and cliques and guard against the intervention of foreign imperialism, will it be able to fulfill this serious and complex task. . . .

In recent years, most of the national bourgeoisie have experienced the profound change of socialist transformation. Our task shall be to continue and to improve our cooperation with them, with a view to giving full play to their abilities and expert knowledge, and helping them to further remould themselves. Such cooperation should, as in the past, be at once uniting with them and waging struggles against them. Class struggle will go on until socialist transformation is completed. Even after that, there will still be struggles between socialist and capitalist stands, viewpoints and methods over a long period of time. Our principal ways of conducting such struggles are education and persuasion. It is only for the few individuals who adopt a hostile attitude towards socialism and violate laws of the state, that compulsory methods of reform are adopted in accordance with the circumstances in each case. . . .

In keeping with the new situation in socialist transformation and socialist construction, an important task in the work of the state today is to extend democracy further and to carry on a struggle against bureaucracy.

In many of our state organs, there is a phenomenon of bureaucracy, characterized by armchair leadership which does not understand and which suppresses the opinions of subordinates and the masses, and pays little attention to the life of the masses. Such bureaucracy, which manifests itself in being isolated from the masses and from reality, seriously hinders the growth of democracy in national life, hampers the unfolding of popular initiative, and holds back the advance of the socialist cause. . . .

The struggle against bureaucracy will be a long one. But we firmly believe that, under our people's democracy, we shall be able gradually to eliminate the bureaucratic vices. This is because our state is poles apart from the exploiters' states, in which a minority of the people oppress the majority, and because our system, instead of protecting bureaucracy, is opposed to it. . . .

As at home the party relies on the support of the people, so, internationally, we rely on the support of the international proletariat and of the peoples of all countries. Without the great internationalist solidarity of the proletariat, the victory of our cause of socialism would be impossible, or it cannot be consolidated even if it has been won.

We must continue to strengthen our fraternal solidarity with the Communist parties and the workers' parties of all countries, we must continue to learn from the experience of the Communist Party of the Soviet Union and the Communist parties of all other countries in regard to revolution and construction. In our relations with all fraternal parties, we must show warmth and take a modest attitude towards them. We must resolutely oppose any dangerous inclination towards great nation chauvinism or bourgeois nationalism. . . .

Mao on Contradictions

In the first half of 1957 the "thaw" continued. Mao admitted the existence of conflicts—"contradictions"—within the Communist state, and stressed nonviolent ways of handling them. By "ideological remolding," people could be given the requisite "proletarian" quality.

Unification of the country, unity of the people and unity among our various nationalities—these are the basic guarantees for the sure triumph of our cause. However, this does not mean that there are no longer any contradictions in our society. It would be naïve to imagine that there are no more contradictions. To do so would be to fly in the face of objective reality. We are confronted by two types of social contradictions—contradictions between ourselves and the enemy and contradictions among the people. . . .

At this stage of building socialism, all classes, strata and social groups which approve, support and work for the cause of socialist construction belong to the category of the people, while those social forces and groups which resist the socialist revolution, and are hostile to and try to wreck socialist construction, are enemies of the people.

The contradictions between ourselves and our enemies are antagonistic ones. Within the ranks of the people, contradictions among the working people are non-antagonistic, while those between the exploiters and the exploited classes have, apart from their antagonistic aspect, a non-antagonistic aspect. . . . Our people's government is a government that truly represents the interests of the people and serves the people, yet certain contradictions do exist between the government and the masses. These include contradictions between the interests of the state, collective interests and individual interests; between democracy and centralism; between those in positions of leadership and the led, and contradictions arising from the bureaucratic practices of certain state functionaries in their relations with the masses. . . .

In our country, the contradiction between the working class and the national bourgeoisie is a contradiction among the

FROM: Mao, "On the Correct Handling of Contradictions Among the People," (Revised text of speech to the Eleventh Session of the Supreme State Conference, February 27, 1957; in *People's China*, July 1, 1957, supplement, pp. 3-7, 9, 11-12, 14-16, 18-19, 21).

people. The class struggle waged between the two is, by and large, a class struggle within the ranks of the people. . . . The contradiction between exploiter and exploited, which exists between the national bourgeoisie and the working class, is an antagonistic one. But, in the concrete conditions existing in China, such an antagonistic contradiction, if properly handled, can be transformed into a non-antagonistic one and resolved in a peaceful way. . . .

Our dictatorship is known as the people's democratic dictatorship, led by the working class and based on the worker-peasant alliance. That is to say, democracy operates within the ranks of the people, while the working class, uniting with all those enjoying civil rights, the peasantry in the first place, enforces dictatorship over the reactionary classes and elements and all those who resist socialist transformation and oppose socialist construction. By civil rights, we mean, politically, freedom and democratic rights.

But this freedom is freedom with leadership and this democracy is democracy under centralized guidance, not anarchy. Anarchy does not conform to the interests or wishes of the people.

Certain people in our country were delighted when the Hungarian events took place. They hoped that something similar would happen in China, that thousands upon thousands of people would demonstrate in the streets against the people's government. Such hopes ran counter to the interests of the masses and therefore could not possibly get their support. In Hungary, a section of the people, deceived by domestic and foreign counter-revolutionaries, made the mistake of resorting to acts of violence against the people's government, with the result that both the state and the people suffered for it. . . .

While we stand for freedom with leadership and democracy under centralized guidance, in no sense do we mean that coercive measures should be taken to settle ideological matters and questions involving the distinction between right and wrong among the people. Any attempt to deal with ideological matters or questions involving right and wrong by administrative orders or coercive measures will not only be ineffective but harmful. We cannot abolish religion by administrative orders; nor can we force people not to believe in it. We cannot compel people to give up idealism, any more than we can force them to believe in Marxism. In settling matters of an ideological nature or controversial issues among the people, we can only use democratic methods, methods of discussion, of criticism, of persuasion and education, not coercive, high-handed methods. . . .

In 1942 we worked out the formula "unity-criticism—unity" to describe this democratic method of resolving contradictions among the people. To elaborate, this means to start off with a desire for unity and resolve contradictions through criticism or struggle so as to achieve a new unity on a new basis. Our experience shows that this is a proper method of resolving contradictions among the people. . . .

Contradictions in a socialist society are fundamentally different from contradictions in old societies, such as capitalist society. Contradictions in capitalist society find expression in acute antagonisms and conflicts, in sharp class struggle, which cannot be resolved by the capitalist system itself and can only be resolved by socialist revolution. Contradictions in socialist society are, on the contrary, not antagonistic and can be resolved one after the other by the socialist system itself. . . .

After liberation, we rooted out a number of counter-revolutionaries. Some were sentenced to death because they had committed serious crimes. This was absolutely necessary; it was the demand of the people; it was done to free the masses from long years of oppression by counter-revolutionaries and all kinds of local tyrants; in other words, to set free the productive forces. If we had not done so, the masses would not have been able to lift their heads.

Since 1956, however, there has been a radical change in the situation. Taking the country as a whole, the main force of counter-revolution has been rooted out. . . .

Steps have been or are being taken to correct mistakes which have already been discovered in the work of suppressing counter-revolutionaries. Those not yet discovered will be corrected as soon as they come to light. Decisions on exoneration and rehabilitation should receive the same measure of publicity as the original mistaken decisions. . . .

The year 1956 saw the transformation of privately owned industrial and commercial enterprises into joint state-private enterprises as well as the organization of co-operatives in agriculture and handicrafts as part of the transformation of our social system. The speed and smoothness with which this was carried out are closely related to the fact that we treated the contradiction between the working class and the national bourgeoisie as a contradiction among the people. . . .

In building a socialist society, all need remoulding, the exploiters as well as the working people. Who says the working class doesn't need it? Of course, remoulding of the exploiters and that of the working people are two different types of remoulding. The two must not be confused. In the class struggle and the struggle against nature, the working class remoulds the whole of society, and at the same time remoulds itself. . . .

Our industrialists and business men can be thoroughly remoulded only in the course of work; they should work together with the staff and workers in the enterprises, and make the enterprises the chief centres for remoulding themselves. It is also important for them to change certain of their old views through study. Study for them should be optional. After they have attended study groups for some weeks, many industrialists and business men on returning to their enterprises find they speak more of a common language with the workers and the representatives of state shareholding, and so work better together. They know from personal experience that it is good for them to keep on studying and remoulding themselves. . . .

Our intellectuals have made some progress, but they should not be complacent. They must continue to remould themselves, gradually shed their bourgeois world outlook and acquire a proletarian, Communist world outlook so that they can fully meet the needs of the new society and closely unite with the workers and peasants. This change in world outlook is a fundamental one, and up till now it cannot yet be said that most of our intellectuals have accomplished it. We hope that they will continue making progress, and, in the course of work and study, gradually acquire a Communist world outlook, get a better grasp of Marxism-Leninism, and identify themselves with the workers and peasants. We hope they will not stop halfway, or, what is worse, slip back; for if they do they will find themselves in a blind alley. . . .

"Let a hundred flowers blossom," and "let a hundred schools of thought contend," "long-term co-existence and mutual supervision"—how did these slogans come to be put forward?

They were put forward in the light of the specific conditions existing in China, on the basis of the recognition that various kinds of contradictions still exist in a socialist society, and in response to the country's urgent need to speed up its economic and cultural development.

The policy of letting a hundred flowers blossom and a hundred schools of thought contend is designed to promote the flourishing of the arts and the progress of science; it is designed to enable a socialist culture to thrive in our land. Different forms and styles in art can develop freely and different schools in science can contend freely. We think that it is harmful to the growth of art and science if administrative measures are used to impose one particular style of art or school of thought and to ban another. Questions of right and wrong in the arts and sciences should be settled through free discussion in artistic and scientific circles and in the course of practical work in the arts and sciences. They should not be settled in summary fashion. A period of trial is often needed to determine whether something is right or wrong. In the past, new and correct things often failed at the outset to win recognition from the majority of people and had to develop by twists and turns in struggle. Correct and good things have often at first been looked upon not as fragrant flowers but as poisonous weeds. . . .

While criticizing doctrinairism, we should at the same time direct our attention to criticizing revisionism. Revisionism, or rightist opportunism, is a bourgeois trend of thought which is even more dangerous than doctrinarism. The revisionists, or right opportunists, pay lip-service to Marxism and also attack "doctrinairism." But the real target of their attack is actually the most fundamental elements of Marxism. They oppose or distort materialism and dialectics, oppose or try to weaken the people's democratic dictatorship and the leading role of the Communist Party, oppose or try to weaken socialist transformation and socialist construction. Even after the basic victory of the socialist revolution in our country, there are still a number of people who vainly hope for a restoration of the capitalist system. They wage a struggle against the working class on every front, including the ideological front. In this struggle, their right-hand men are the revisionists. . . .

In the political life of our country, how are our people to determine what is right and what is wrong in our words and actions? Basing ourselves on the principles of our Constitution, the will of the overwhelming majority of our people and the political programmes jointly proclaimed on various occasions by our political parties and groups, we believe that, broadly speaking, words and actions can be judged right if they:

(1) Help to unite the people of our various nationalities, and do not divide them;

(2) Are beneficial, not harmful, to socialist transformation and socialist construction;

(3) Help to consolidate, not undermine or weaken, the people's democratic dictatorship;

(4) Help to consolidate, not undermine or weaken, democratic centralism;

(5) Tend to strengthen, not to cast off or weaken, the leadership of the Communist Party;

(6) Are beneficial, not harmful, to international socialist solidarity and the solidarity of the peace-loving peoples of the world.

Of these six criteria, the most important are the socialist path and the leadership of the party. . . . Naturally, in judging the truthfulness of scientific theories or assessing the aesthetic value of works of art, other pertinent criteria are needed, but these six political criteria are also applicable to all activities in the arts or sciences. In a socialist country like ours, can there possibly be any useful scientific or artistic activity which runs counter to these political criteria? . . .

The Rectification Campaign

In the middle of 1957 the Chinese Communist line abruptly stiffened, as many of the "hundred flowers" were found to be "noxious weeds," and so-called "rightists" in the government and intellectual life were denounced in large numbers. In September, 1957, the new General Secretary of the Party, Teng Hsiao-p'ing, announced a systematic campaign to renew the discipline of the party and its control over the rest of the population. Among the defects which he catalogued was a deficiency of "proletarian" quality in the party and in the proletariat itself.

. . . The movement for rectifying the work style within the ranks of the people involves questions in two different social categories. For the bourgeoisie and the bourgeois intelligentsia it involves the acceptance of the socialist transformation. For the petty bourgeoisie (peasants and independent workers in urban and rural areas) and particularly for the well-to-do middle peasant, it is also a matter of accepting the socialist transformation. For the working class and the general ranks of the Communist Party it is a question of rectifying the work style. . . .

It is necessary to wage a resolute struggle against the enemy, to adopt methods of exposure, isolation and dispersal and, against certain persons, the methods of punishment and suppression. Within the ranks of the people the basic method to be applied is the method of education, the method of "rally—criticize—rally." It is also necessary to resort to legal punishment of violators of laws among the people. This punishment also has educational value. . . .

The movement has demonstrated the need for continuing the socialist re-education of the bourgeoisie and the bourgeois

FROM: Teng, "On the Movement to Rectify Work Style," Report to the Chinese Communist Party Central Committee, September 23, 1957 (*The Current Digest of the Soviet Press,* IX: 43, December 4, 1957, pp. 20-22).

intelligentsia, the petty bourgeoisie, particularly the middle peasants. Quite a number of these are drawn to capitalism. They are not pleased with socialism. The leadership of the proletariat and the Communist Party over them is still shaky. They represent the arena of the rightwing elements' activity. But the overwhelming majority of them can accept socialism if education and criticism are employed.

The movement has shown that it is absolutely essential to conduct a broad movement for socialist education among the working class, poor peasants and lower levels of the middle peasants in the countryside. They are the most decisive force for defending socialism. The conduct of socialist education among them would give them an even better weapon for waging the struggle. Moreover, there is a small segment of people among them with petty-bourgeois ideas who might fall under the influence of the bourgeoisie. However, if only they are told the facts and the truth is explained to them, they will easily grasp the essence of the situation.

The movement has shown that it is absolutely vital to conduct a large-scale movement to rectify the work style among the basic ranks of the Communist Party, the leading agencies and leading cadres of Party workers and workers in the government, in public organizations and enterprises at various levels. . . .

The party will pursue a consistent policy toward bourgeois elements. Toward the bourgeois industrialists and merchants the party follows a policy of redemption and will strive to see that they continue to serve socialism. A course of prolonged coexistence and mutual control will be practiced in regard to democratic parties and groups. In the realm of science and culture the party will stand by the policy of "let a hundred flowers bloom, a hundred schools of thought contend." The premise for such courses and political aims is socialism. The party is resolutely insisting that the bourgeois elements and the bourgeois intelligentsia should in the end be re-educated and gradually become one with the working class. Under no circumstances is it possible to allow the leading role of the party, the dictatorship of the proletariat and democratic centralism to be shaken. It is impossible to permit the basic political aims of the party to be shaken, i.e., the policy of liquidating counterrevolutionaries, the policy of collectivization, centralized purchasing and selling of farm products, etc. It is important to intensify Marxist-Leninist propaganda and political education. It is essential to criticize false ideologies. Poisonous weeds must be uprooted. We allow poisonous weeds to grow in order to educate the masses by negative examples, to root out poisonous weeds and use them for fertilizers, to steel the proletariat and the broad popular masses in battle. . . .

The bourgeois intelligentsia, in addition to the fact that a small segment of it adheres to right-wing views, also suffers from other seriously mistaken views, specifically individualism, liberalism, anarchism, leveling and nationalism. At this stage of ideological education, criticism and self-analysis is essential to eliminate these mistaken views through systematic criticism.

The ideological re-education of the intelligentsia will take a long time, possibly more than ten years. . . .

. . . As a result of collectivization the question of the ownership of the means of production has been essentially settled, but this does not mean that there are no problems in the countryside. Some of the peasants still lack a clear understanding of the relationship between the state, the cooperative and the family, and individualism and provincialism are still in existence among them and are expressed in the form of scorn for the state and the collective interests.

The overwhelming majority of the well-to-do middle peasants joined the cooperatives under the pressure of the general circumstances, but most of them vacillate in their ideological outlook. A small portion of those elements which resolutely supported capitalism, after being compelled to enter cooperatives, headed the movement for withdrawal from the cooperatives or engaged in activity outside the cooperatives designed to undermine the cooperatives. Counterrevolutionary elements, hostile elements and a segment of the landlords and kulaks also engaged in subversive activity at every opportunity.

Serious right-deviationist ideas were also found within the

party recently, ideas that the struggle between the two paths in the countryside was over and that the class line could not be further emphasized, that attention could be concentrated on production and that socialist education of the peasantry could be relaxed. Less attention was paid to the subversive activity of reactionary elements and these elements were not resolutely rebuffed in time. . . .

. . . The movement has shown that the old workers are a basic arm of the party and socialism. Among the new workers —nearly 65% of the workers at present—more than half are persons who come from the peasantry, students and the poor of the cities. They are largely contaminated by the ideology and work style of the petty bourgeosie. Three per cent of the new workers (5% in some organizations) are former landlords, kulaks, capitalists, police, soldiers of the reactionary army and declassified elements, among whom the ideology and depraved customs of the exploiting class have not been completely eradicated.

Therefore in rectifying the work style it is necessary to lead a movement for the broader and deeper socialist education of the working masses.

The leading position and the guiding role of the working class in the socialist revolution and socialist construction and the political tasks of the working masses under the dictatorship of the proletariat should be basic components of this education. It is essential that the working masses understand that, under the guidance of the Communist Party, they must constantly increase their awareness, strengthen their organization and discipline and consolidate the unity of the working class. . . .

The situation in the party derives from the following social and ideological factors: 1) The majority of party members are from nonproletarian classes; 2) party organizations have developed relatively rapidly, insufficient attention has been devoted to the quality of party membership and ideological and political work has lagged behind the growth of the party; 3) An even more important factor is that most persons joined the party after the victory of the revolution without having a true socialist world view and, after joining the party, they found themselves for a long time in a situation in which collaboration with the bourgeoisie existed in the country; thus they have not participated directly in a sharp class struggle with the bourgeoisie. Among the 1,880,000 Communist intelligentsia the majority have not been steeled in the work of production and have not had effective training in the class struggle. . . .

The "Great Leap Forward"

In January, 1958, the Chinese Communists began their Second Five Year Plan (roughly comparable in its targets to the first one in Russia), and in May Liu Shao-ch'i called upon the country to intensify its efforts toward rapid industrialization and cultural modernization. Hinting at differences within the party over the tempo of development, Liu placed great stress on the continuing rectification campaign and the enforcement of ideological discipline by the party, all in the name of overtaking the capitalist countries.

Liu's growing eminence in the Chinese Communist Party culminated in his appointment to succeed Mao Tse-tung as Chairman of the Republic in April, 1959.

. . . The spring of 1958 witnessed the beginning of a leap forward on every front in our socialist construction. Industry, agriculture and all other fields of activity are registering greater and more rapid growth. . . .

The upsurge in agriculture last winter and this spring gave a vigorous push to the new industrial upsurge of this year. The rapid development of industry in turn has prompted an even swifter growth of agriculture. . . .

The current mighty leap forward in socialist construction is the product not only of the successful development of the anti-rightist struggle and the rectification campaign but also of a correct implementation of the Party's general line—to build socialism by exerting our utmost efforts, and pressing

FROM: Liu, Report on the Work of the CCP Central Committee delivered to the Second Session of the Eighth National Congress of the Chinese Communist Party, May 5, 1958 (official translation reprinted in *Current Background*, no. 507, June 2, 1958, pp. 7-13, 19-21, 23-25).

ahead consistently to achieve greater, faster, better and more economical results.

Comrade Mao Tse-tung has often said that there are two ways of carrying on socialist transformation and construction: one will result in doing the work faster and better; the other slowly and not so well. Which way shall we take? This has been an issue. . . . The Central Committee of the Party and Comrade Mao Tse-tung have always taken a clear-cut stand, insisting that the way of working faster and better be adopted and the other way, of working slowly and not so well, be rejected. However, on this question some comrades still clung to such outmoded ideas as "keeping to the right is better than keeping to the left," "it is better to go slower than faster" or "it is better to take small steps than to go striding forward." The struggle between the two ways of dealing with this question was not fully decided until the launching of the rectification campaign and the anti-rightist struggle. . . .

The guiding lines and policies formulated by Comrade Mao Tse-tung have played a tremendous role in our work. In 1956, every phase of China's economy and culture made a mighty leap forward. . . .

There were individual defects in our work during the leap forward in 1956. . . . Some comrades at the time magnified these defects and underestimated the great achievements attained, and hence regarded the leap forward of 1956 as a "reckless advance." In a flurry of opposition to this so-called "reckless advance," some people even had misgivings about the principle of "achieving greater, faster, better, and more economical results" and the 40-Article Program for Agricultural Development. This damped the initiative of the masses and hampered progress on the production front in 1957, and particularly on the agricultural front. But the Party soon corrected this error. The third plenary session of the Central Committee of the Party held in September last year re-affirmed the need to adhere to the principle of achieving "greater, faster, better and more economical results," in building socialism. Following that, the Central Committee made public a revised version of the Draft Program for Agricultural Development and Comrade Mao Tse-tung issued a militant call to overtake and surpass Britain in the output of iron and steel and other major industrial products in 15 years. These correct directives of the Central Committee, combined with the initiative of the masses evoked by the rectification campaign and the anti-rightist struggle, gave rise to the all-round forward leap which is currently developing on an ever larger scale in our socialist construction. Many of those comrades who expressed misgivings about the principle of building socialism by achieving "greater, faster, better and more economical results" have learnt a lesson from all this. But some of them have not yet learnt anything. They say: "We'll settle accounts with you after the autumn harvest." Well, let them wait to settle accounts. They will lose out in the end! . . .

Now the people everywhere are full of confidence in the forward leap in production; they are determined to further speed up socialist construction. They are eager to remove the obstacles placed in their way by technological and cultural backwardness. In view of the basic victory of the socialist revolution already achieved on the economic, political and ideological fronts, the Central Committee of the Party and Comrade Mao Tse-tung consider that the time is ripe to set new revolutionary tasks before the Party and the people, that now is the time to call for a technological revolution and, along with it, a cultural revolution. . . .

In the light of the practical experience gained in the people's struggle and of the development of Comrade Mao Tse-tung's thinking in the past few years, the Central Committee of the Party is of the opinion that the following are the basic points of our general line, which is to build socialism by exerting our utmost efforts, and pressing ahead consistently to achieve greater, faster, better and more economical results:

To mobilize all positive factors and correctly handle contradictions among the people;

To consolidate and develop socialist ownership, i.e., ownership by the whole people and collective ownership, and consolidate the proletarian dictatorship and proletarian international solidarity;

To carry out a technological revolution and a cultural revolution step by step, while completing the socialist revolution on the economic, political and ideological fronts;

To develop industry and agriculture simultaneously while giving priority to heavy industry; and

With centralized leadership, overall planning, proper division of labor and coordination, to develop national and local industries, and large, small and medium-sized enterprises simultaneously.

Through all this we will build our country, in the shortest possible time, into a great socialist country with a modern industry, modern agriculture and modern science and culture. . . .

The central task of the rectification campaign is to handle correctly the contradictions among the people and improve human relations in socialist labor and all other group activities. We have in the main accomplished the socialist transformation of the means of production, which is the prerequisite for changing the relationships between men. . . . However, many of the administrative personnel and brain workers have not yet learnt to treat the masses on a footing of complete equality; they have not yet done away with some survivals of the working style of the Kuomintang and still have certain bureaucratic airs. This makes it difficult for them to gain the full confidence of the masses. This has also prevented part of the workers and peasants from taking the sort of attitude to socialist labor that befits the masters of the state and the enterprises. This state of affairs has been radically changed as a result of the rectification campaign. . . .

Of course, it is impossible to resolve all contradictions through one single rectification campaign. To build a socialist and Communist society, we must not only wipe out all the old systems of exploitation and oppression of man by man, but also utterly eliminate obsolete ideas and habits which are derived from and served these old systems; we must eliminate bourgeois ideology and foster proletarian ideology, that is to say, eventually eliminate all vestiges of the exploiting classes and exploiting systems from the minds of people. This is a much more difficult task than that of eliminating the exploiting classes economically. It can be accomplished only through a long process of education and complex struggle. As to other contradictions among the working people, such as those between the right and the wrong, between the advanced and the backward, they will always exist and must be resolved continually as they arise. Progress will be made in the process of resolving them. Therefore it is undoubtedly wrong to imagine that a single rectification campaign can settle all questions at a single stroke and that there will be no more twists and turns or up and down in the struggle. That is why from now on the method of the rectification campaign, the methods of criticism and self-criticism through full and frank airing of views, great debates and posters written in big characters must be made the regular method of reforming ideology and improving work. All-round rectification campaigns should be launched at set intervals to handle systematically the contradictions among the people and other contradictions that may have come to light at that time. . . .

As to the utterances and activities of those who aim to undermine socialism and restore capitalism, we have never sanctioned such utterances and activities, because they are not permitted under the socialist system. But we allow the anti-socialist poisonous weeds to grow and confront the people with contrasts, so that by way of comparison, the people can see clearly what they really are, and roused to indignation, rally together to uproot them. . . . To uproot poisonous weeds is a question between the enemy and ourselves. To let a hundred flowers blossom is a question among the people. These are two different kinds of contradictions and there are two different methods of handling them. The reactionary rightists of the bourgeoisie claimed to be one of the hundred socialist flowers. But that was simply a fraud. They can't be recognized as such. . . .

The guarantee of success in all our work of socialist construction is the Party's correct leadership. The Central Committee of the Party and local Party committees at all levels must be the leading core of the governments at all levels. In the past few years, the leadership of the Party concentrated its efforts mainly on the socialist revolution. While we shall continue to pay attention to this work, we now can and must concentrate greater efforts on socialist construction. Party committees at all levels must give the same resolute leadership to socialist construction and the technological and cultural revolutions as they have been giving the democratic and socialist revolutions. Both inside and outside the Party, there is a mistaken tendency among some people to think that the Party cannot lead construction work, or work in the fields of science and technology, culture and education. This must be thoroughly corrected. . . .

For more than a hundred years our country suffered from that oppression of foreign aggressors which made us backward in many respects. Although China has been liberated and has made rapid advances in every field, still the mentality of quite a few of our people still bears the imprint of the oppressed, their minds are still filled with all kinds of shibboleths, fears and feelings of inferiority. Instead of exerting their utmost efforts, they are apathetic, and instead of pressing ahead consistently, they are resigned to backwardness. The proletariat and the people's militants must rid themselves lock, stock and barrel of such states of mind; they should cultivate the noble way of firmly believing in the truth, resolutely relying on the masses and being fearless of any authority. We must remember that humility helps one to make progress whereas conceit makes one lag behind. But the practical humility we advocate has nothing to do with any sense of inferiority. We have a population of more than 600 million and our Party has ties of flesh and blood with this vast population. By relying on this great force we can, or soon can, do anything within the realms of human possibility. It is true that for the time being this population of 600 million and more is economically poor and culturally is like a clean sheet of white paper. But what does this matter to Marxist-Leninist revolutionaries? Comrade Mao Tse-tung has put it well: "In addition to other characteristics, our more than 600 million people are characterized by poverty and 'whiteness.' This appears to be a bad thing, but in fact it is a good thing. Poor people want to change, to work hard and make a revolution. A clean sheet of white paper has nothing written on it and is therefore well suited for writing the newest and most beautiful words on and for drawing the newest and most beautiful pictures." Isn't this a fact? Our 600 million and more people have already far surpassed the most advanced capitalist countries in the West in the speed of the upsurge of their revolutionary consciousness and of the victories of their revolutionary struggles and will definitely far surpass them too in the speed of economic and cultural growth. In history, it is always the newcomers who outstrip the old, always the new-born things, which for a time appear weak and small but represent what is progressive, that defeat the moribund things, which appear powerful but represent what is conservative. Within a very short historical period we shall certainly leave every capitalist country in the world far behind us. And so, shouldn't we have confidence in ourselves and discard everything that smacks of superstition, fear and feelings of inferiority?

The inevitable victory of our cause is also grounded in the fraternal aid of the countries in the socialist camp headed by the great Soviet Union—which is internationally the most important factor in our favor. We shall continue to draw on the advanced experience of the Soviet Union and other countries, continue to strengthen mutual assistance and cooperation with the other countries in the socialist camp and, shoulder to shoulder with our fraternal parties in all countries, raise still higher the banner of Marxism-Leninism and reinforce the militant solidarity of the international Communist movement. We resolutely support the peace proposals of the Soviet Union, the efforts of the peoples of all lands to safeguard peace, and all national movements which oppose aggression, defend their sovereign rights and seek independence. The struggles of the people of all countries support our cause and through our work we in turn support the people of all countries.

Comrades! Let us, on the basis of the Party's general line for socialist construction, strengthen ceaselessly the unity of the entire Party and unity between the Party and all the people. Let us strengthen ceaselessly our solidarity with the

Soviet Union and other countries in the socialist camp and with all the peoples of the world in the common cause of peace, democracy and socialism. Victory will surely be ours!

The Communes

To implement the "great leap forward" in the agricultural sphere the Chinese Communist leadership ordered the organization of the peasantry into communes, which were larger units than the earlier cooperatives, and much more fully collectivist (going considerably beyond the Russian collective farms in this respect). A resolution of the Central Committee formalizing the policy represented it as a spontaneous popular movement, but the role of the communes in improving both production and political control was stressed. It was also made clear that the communes did not correspond to the "communist" ideal of equality.

. . . The main basis for the development of people's communes is the overall and continuous leap forward in agricultural production in the whole country and the growing elevation of the political consciousness of the 500 million peasants. After the basic victory over the road of capitalism on the economic, political and ideological fronts, agricultural capital construction has been developed on an unprecedented scale, and we have basically built the new foundation for agricultural production to be developed under comparatively stable conditions, free from the menaces of flood and drought. With the overcoming of rightist conservatism, and the breaking down of conventions in agricultural technical measures, agricultural production is leaping forward at high speed, and the output of agricultural products is increasing by one hundred per cent, several hundred per cent, over one thousand per cent, and several thousand per cent. This has further promoted the ideological liberation of the people. Large-scale

FROM: Resolution of the Central Committee of the Chinese Communist Party, "On the Establishment of People's Communes in the Rural Areas," August 29, 1958 (English translation in *Survey of China Mainland Press*, U. S. Consulate-General, Hong Kong, No. 1853, September 15, 1958, pp. 1-2, 4).

agricultural capital construction and advanced agricultural technical measures demand the employment of more manpower. The development of industry in the rural areas also demands the transfer of a portion of manpower from the agricultural front. Thus the demand is more and more urgent for the mechanization and electrification of our countryside. In the struggle for agricultural capital construction and the quest for bumper harvests, the breaking down of boundaries between cooperatives, between *hsiang* [townships], and between *hsien* [counties] in order to carry out extensive cooperation, the "militarization" of organization, the placing of activities on a "combatant" basis, and the collectivization of daily living have become mass actions, and they have further raised the Communist consciousness of the 500 million peasants. Common mess halls, kindergartens, nurseries, tailoring teams, barbershops, public baths, "happiness homes" [old people's homes], agricultural middle schools, and schools for turning out red and expert personnel are leading the peasants to a collective life of greater happiness, and are further fostering and steeling the collectivism of the masses of the peasants. All these show that the simple agricultural producer cooperative with a few score or a few hundred households is no longer suited to the demand of the developing situation. Under the present circumstances, the establishment of people's communes which look after the overall development of agriculture, forestry, animal husbandry, sideline production, and fishery, and combine the activities of the workers, peasants, tradesmen, students and militiamen is a basic policy which must be adopted for the guidance of the peasants in the acceleration of socialist construction, the advanced building of socialism, and the gradual transition to communism.

According to present conditions, the scale of the organization of the people's commune should in general be fixed at one commune to a *hsiang* with about 2,000 households. . . .

The steps taken in the establishment of people's communes consist of the merger of small cooperatives into large cooperatives, and their change into communes. This is the common demand of the broad masses of the people today.

The poor peasants and the lower middle peasants resolutely support such a course. The majority of the upper middle peasants also support it. . . .

The merger into big cooperatives and change into communes must be closely combined with current production. The movement must not only affect production adversely, but must be made into a great force that promotes production to a greater leap forward. . . .

When the stage of the system of ownership by the whole people is reached, it is still socialist in nature, such as is the case with the state-owned industry, i.e., "from each according to his ability, to each according to his labor." After another period of many years, when social products have been greatly increased, the Communist ideological awakening and ethical standards of all the people have been greatly raised, universal education is practiced and elevated, the differences between workers and peasants, between urban and rural areas, and between mental and physical labor (all these differences having been left over from the old society had to be preserved during the period of socialism) are gradually wiped out, the remnants of the bourgeois state power which reflect these different cases of inequality have been gradually eliminated, and the function of the state is only to deal with aggression from enemies outside and plays no longer a role in domestic affairs, then and only then will our society enter the age of Communism, "from each according to his ability, to each according to his need" will be practiced.

After the establishment of the people's communes, there is also no need to hastily change the original system of distribution, to avoid unfavorable effects on production. We must start from concrete conditions. Where conditions are ripe, the wage systems may be taken up. Where conditions are not yet ripe, for the time being we may continue to adopt such systems as originally practiced, that of "the three contracts and one bonus award," or else we may adopt the system of fixing production quotas and paying wages on the basis of labor days. When the conditions are ripe, changes may then be instituted.

Though the people's communes still practice the system of

collective ownership, and the distribution system, whether it be the wage system or remuneration according to labor days, is still "to each according to his labor" and not "to each according to his need"; nevertheless the people's commune will be the best organizational form for the building of socialism and the gradual transition to communism. It will develop into the basic social unit of the future Communist society.

Our task at the present stage is the building of socialism. The establishment of people's communes is undertaken first of all for the acceleration of socialist construction, and the building of socialism is to actively make preparations for transition to communism. It appears now that the realization of communism in our country is no longer a thing of the distant future. We should actively employ the form of the people's commune to produce a concrete path for transition to communism.

North Korean Communism

After occupying northern Korea in 1945, the Russians created a "People's Democratic Republic of Korea" in their zone in 1948, with the Communist Kim Il Sung as premier. North Korean troops attacked the American-sponsored Republic of Korea in the South in June, 1950, and thus began the Korean War, which, after involving the United States and Communist China, dragged on until 1953. At the time of Chinese intervention in December, 1950, Premier Kim Il Sung expressed high hopes of victory and unification of all of Korea under his rule.

During the two past months of the sacred war for the liberation of our glorious motherland, the People's Army—the offspring of our motherland and of our people—was forced to make a temporary, strategic retreat under the weight of the offensive by superior forces of aggressors' troops of several imperialist states headed by the American imperialist interventionists. However, our retreat was a temporary one and

FROM: Kim Il Sung, Address to the Korean People on the Occasion of the Liberation of Pyongyang, December, 1950 (English translation in *The Current Digest of The Soviet Press,* II: 48, January 6, 1951, p. 3).

was carried out with the aim of delivering a crushing blow to the enemy, with the aim of routing, annihilating and expelling the enemy from our native soil, in order to obtain complete victory in the great liberation war.

The entire Korean people, who rose in the just struggle for the freedom, honor and independence of their motherland, never bowed before the enemy at the hardest moment of the retreat; on the contrary, they rallied even closer around the republic's government and by their practical efforts for the good of their country and people demonstrated their firm determination to attain conclusive victory over the enemy at any cost. This firm determination of the Korean people was manifested in the awesome partisan movement of the entire people, which spread all over the territory of South and North Korea under the enemy's temporary occupation, in the widespread activity of the underground agencies of the government and of the Workers' [Communist] Party, and in the patriotic, self-sacrificing work of helping the People's Army and the Chinese people's volunteer detachments.

The people's strength is inexhaustible. This inexhaustible strength is invincible. From the support of the great Soviet and Chinese peoples, from that of the people of the people's democracies and of the freedom-loving people of the entire world, the Korean people draw firm trust in victory and inexhaustible strength in their just struggle for the freedom, honor and independence of their motherland.

Dear warriors of the People's Army! Chinese people's volunteers and partisans! Dear fellow countrymen, brothers and sisters! The enemy is retreating in disorder, but he has not yet been completely routed. With mad fury, the enemy is striving to regroup and to achieve his perfidious aim at any cost. The road to conclusive victory lies before us. But we must remember that we shall still encounter all sorts of difficulties and obstacles along it. We can win the final victory only after a grim struggle, overcoming difficulties and accepting sacrifices. . . .

All the Korean people must rally still closer around the government of the Korean People's Democratic Republic and march boldly toward victory in the patriotic war of liberation.

Vengeance and death to the accursed enemies—the American interventionists and Syngman Rhee's band of traitors—who have caused great sufferings to our motherland and our people!

Glory to the valorous People's Army and to the heroic units of the Chinese people's volunteers, conducting the offensive and destroying the enemy!

Glory to the men and women partisans daringly operating in the enemy's rear!

Long live the united Korean people!

Long live the Korean People's Democratic Republic! . . .

Vietnamese Communism

In 1946 fighting began between French colonial forces and Indo-Chinese nationalists, who were under the Communist leadership of Ho Chi Minh. While the movement became increasingly Communistic, the nationalists conducted successful guerrilla warfare, until the Geneva agreement of 1954 ended the war and permitted the establishment of the Communist "Democratic Republic of Vietnam" in the northern part of the country. Meanwhile, the Communist movement had been reorganized in 1951 as the Viet-Nam Labor Party with a nationalistic program appealing to every class in the population.

Dear fellow countrymen and women!

The world of today is clearly divided into two camps:

There is the anti-democratic imperialist camp led by the American imperialists and composed of imperialist states and reactionary governments, lackeys of imperialism. They plan to seize the lands of other peoples in order to dominate the world; to suppress the national liberation movements of the peoples; to destroy world peace and democracy and to provoke a third world war which would plunge mankind into darkness and misery.

There is the anti-imperialist democratic camp headed by

FROM: "Manifesto of the Viet-Nam Lao Dong Party," February, 1951 (English translation in *People's China,* May 1, 1951, Supplement, pp. 2-3).

the Soviet Union and composed of the countries of socialism and People's Democracy, of the oppressed peoples, and of the working people and progressives in capitalist countries. This camp is striving to carry on the work of national liberation, for the defence of national independence and the maintenance of world peace and democracy; and it seeks to enhance the unity, progress and happiness of mankind.

That the democratic camp has become stronger than the imperialist camp is clearly shown by the fact that the Soviet Union is daily growing more prosperous and powerful; that the work of national construction is swiftly moving ahead in the People's Democracies; that the Chinese People's Revolution has been victorious; and that the Korean people are waging a successful struggle.

Our country and our people stand in the democratic camp.

The French colonialists stand in the imperialist camp. They want to plunder our land. In this they have the all-out assistance of the American imperialists. Our people, who definitely do not want to be enslaved, are determined to fight in defence of their land and homes. They are now preparing for an early general counter-offensive.

The forces of our resistance spring from the people. Over 90 per cent of our people are working people, that is, the workers, peasants and intellectual workers. Thus, the working people are the main driving force of our armed resistance and of our national construction.

The central task of the working class and the working people of Viet-Nam now is to unite the entire people, to carry the War of Resistance to complete victory, to build an independent, united, democratic, strong and prosperous Viet-Nam, and to fully realise People's Democracy so as to gradually advance towards socialism. In order to fulfill this task, the working class and the working people of Viet-Nam must have a vanguard army, a general staff, a powerful, clear-sighted, determined, pure and thoroughly revolutionary political party: the Viet-Nam Lao Dong Party.

The Viet-Nam Lao Dong Party will be composed of the most patriotic, the most enthusiastic, the most revolutionary workers, peasants and intellectual workers. It will be comprised of those who are determined to serve the Motherland, to serve the people, to serve labour, who place the overall interests of the country and the people above their own personal interests and who set the example in the War of Resistance and in national construction.

The theoretical foundation of the party is Marxism-Leninism.

The principle of organization of the party is democratic centralism.

The discipline of the party is a strict, voluntary discipline.

The policy of the party aims to serve the interests of the country and the people.

The law governing the development of the party is criticism and self-criticism.

The present main tasks of the Viet-Nam Lao Dong Party are: to unite and lead the working class, the working people and the whole Viet-Nam nation in their liberation struggle; to wipe out the aggressive French colonialists and defeat the American interventionists; and to lead the War of Resistance of the people of Viet-Nam to complete victory, thereby making Viet-Nam a genuinely independent and united country. . . .

The workers who are production fighters in enterprises shall have their living conditions improved and take part in the running of enterprises.

The peasants who are production fighters in the rural areas shall benefit from the reduction of land rent and interest rates, and from appropriate agrarian reforms.

The intellectual workers shall be encouraged and assisted to develop their abilities.

Small-scale traders and small workshop owners shall be assisted to develop their trade and handicrafts.

The national bourgeoisie shall be encouraged, assisted and guided in their undertakings in order to contribute to the development of the national economy.

The right of patriotic landlords to collect land rent in accordance with law shall be guaranteed.

National minorities shall be given every assistance and shall enjoy perfect equality of all rights and duties.

Effective help shall be extended to women so as to achieve equality between men and women.

Followers of all religions shall enjoy freedom of belief and worship.

Overseas citizens of Viet-Nam in foreign countries shall be given protection.

The lives and properties of foreign residents in Viet-Nam shall be protected. In particular, Chinese nationals, if they so desire, shall be allowed to enjoy the same rights and perform the same duties as citizens of Viet-Nam.

In the sphere of external affairs, the Viet-Nam Lao Dong Party recommends that the people of Viet-Nam closely unite with and help the peoples of Cambodia and Laos in their struggle for independence, and, jointly with them, liberate the whole of Indo-China; actively support the national liberation movements of oppressed peoples; closely unite with the Soviet Union, China and other People's Democracies; and closely ally themselves with the peoples of France and of the French colonies so as to contribute to the anti-imperialist struggle for the defence of world peace and democracy. . . .

All compatriots at home and abroad! Unite closely around the People's Government of the Viet-Nam Democratic Republic, the Viet-Nam Lao Dong Party and the leader of the people, of the working class and working people of Viet-Nam —President Ho Chi Minh!

The Viet-Nam Lao Dong Party earnestly requests other organisations sincerely to criticize Party cadres and rank and file members and the policy of the Party, so that it can make constant progress and act in accordance with the wishes of the people.

Confident in the efforts of all Party members, in the support of the workers and the response from the entire people, the Viet-Nam Lao Dong Party will certainly fulfill its tasks:

To lead the resistance to complete victory;

To develop the People's Democratic regime;

To contribute to the defense of world peace and democracy;

To march towards socialism.

Indian Communism

The Communist Party of India responded to independence in 1947 with vain efforts to enhance its power by violence. Repeated changes of leadership ended in 1951 with the ascendancy of Ajoy Ghosh and a policy of peaceful preparation of revolution in accordance with specifically Indian conditions. This line was expressed in a new party program and statement of policy, which included some frank comments about the peculiarities of Asian communism.

INDIA WILL STRIKE ITS OWN PATH TO FREEDOM & PEOPLE'S RULE.

The experience of the last four years has taught the people of our country that the present government, and the present system, cannot solve their main problems of life. It cannot give them land and bread, work and wages, peace and freedom. They are coming to realise the necessity of changing the present government, which mainly serves the interests of feudal landlords and big monopoly financiers and the hidden power behind them all, the vested interests of British imperialism.

The Communist Party has, therefore, adopted a programme, in which it says that it "regards as quite mature the task of replacing the present anti-democratic and anti-popular Government by a new Government of People's Democracy." . . .

Past Policies

There are a large number of people who think that [the present] government can be replaced by a People's Democratic Government by utilizing the Parliament ushered in by the new Constitution. Such feelings are encouraged and fed not only by this government and the vested interests but even by the Right-wing Socialists, who preach that the very fact of a strong opposition party on the parliamentary floor will shake the government and make it topple down.

But hardly had the people started to believe in the efficacy

FROM: Policy Statement of the Communist Party of India (in *Cross Roads*, Bombay, June 8, 1951, pp. 3, 6).

of the new Constitution which they thought was the outcome of their antiimperialist struggles of the past, when even the fiction of the fundamental rights and guarantees is thrown out of that very Constitution and the freedom of person, the press, speech and assembly, which the masses wanted to use to shake up this anti-democratic Government, are subjected to the rule of the police baton and the bureaucrat.

Even the most hardened liberal would now feel ashamed to maintain, let alone the Communist Party and other democrats and revolutionaries, that this government and the classes that keep it in power will ever allow us to carry out a fundamental democratic transformation in the country by parliamentary methods alone.

Hence, the road that will lead us to freedom and peace, land and bread, as outlined in the programme of the party, has to be found elsewhere.

History, enlightened for us by Marx, Engels, Lenin and Stalin, places before us its vast experience, arising out of struggles which have led nearly half of humanity to socialism, freedom and real democracy, at the head of which stands the Soviet Union and in which the great Chinese and People's Democracies join hands.

Thus, our main road is already charted out for us. Even then, each country has to seek its own path also. What is the path for us? . . .

Controversies inside the C.P.I. . . .

For a time, it was advocated that the main weapon in our struggle would be the weapon of general strike of industrial workers followed by countrywide insurrection as in Russia.

Later, on the basis of a wrong understanding of the lessons of the Chinese Revolution, the thesis was put forward that since ours is a semi-colonial country like China, our revolution would develop in the same way as in China, with the partisan war of the peasantry as its main weapon.

Among comrades, who at different periods accepted the correctness of the one or the other of these views, there were differences of the estimate of the situation in the country, on the degree of isolation of the present government from the people, and on many other vital issues. It was clear that these differences had to be resolved in order that the party could lead the people to victory.

After long discussion, running for several months, the party has now arrived at a new understanding of the correct path for attaining the freedom of the country and the happiness of the people, a path which we do not and cannot name as either Russian or Chinese.

It should be, and is, one that conforms to the teachings of Marx, Engels, Lenin and Stalin, and that utilizes the lessons given by all the struggles of history, especially the Russian and Chinese, the Russian because it was the first Socialist Revolution in the world carried out by the working class, under the leadership of the Communist Party of Lenin and Stalin in a capitalist and imperialist country; and the Chinese because it was the first People's Democratic Revolution in a semi-colonial, dependent country, under the leadership of the Communist Party, in which even the national bourgeoisie took part.

AT THE SAME TIME, ONE HAS TO REMEMBER THAT EVERY COUNTRY HAS ITS OWN PECULIARITIES, NATURAL AND SOCIAL, WHICH CANNOT FAIL TO GOVERN ITS PATH TO LIBERATION.

In what way then shall our path be different from the Chinese path?

China & India

First, let us see where we are the same as the Chinese. It is in the character of our revolution. The thing of primary importance for the life of our country, same as it was in China, is agriculture and the peasant problem. We are essentially a colonial country, with a vast majority of our people living on agriculture. Most of our workers also are directly connected with the peasantry and interested in the problem of land.

OUR REAL FREEDOM TODAY MEANS TAKING THE LAND FROM THE FEUDAL LANDLORDS AND HANDING IT OVER WITHOUT PAYMENT TO THE PEASANT. THIS ANTI-FEUDAL TASK, WHEN FULFILLED, ALONE WILL MEAN THE REAL LIBERATION FOR OUR COUNTRY BECAUSE THE MAIN PROPS OF IMPERIALIST INTERESTS

IN OUR COUNTRY, AS THEY WERE IN CHINA, ARE THE FEUDALS, SO, LIKE THE CHINESE, WE HAVE TO FIGHT FEUDALISM AND IMPERIALISM. OUR REVOLUTION IS ANTI-FEUDAL, ANTI-IMPERIALIST.

That makes the struggles of the peasantry of prime importance. Drawing upon the fact that in China the liberation war was fought mainly on the basis of the partisan struggles of the peasantry, during which the peasants took land from the feudal landlords, and, in the process, created the Liberation Army, it was asserted that in India too, the path would be the same, that is, the path of partisan struggle of the peasantry would almost alone lead us to liberation.

The Central Committee finds that drawing upon the Chinese experience in this way and to come to such a conclusion would mean neglecting to look to other factors of the Chinese Revolution and also neglecting to look into our own specific conditions. For example:

We CANNOT fail to take note of the fact that when the Chinese Party began to lead the peasantry in the liberation struggle, it had already an army which it inherited from the split in the Revolution of 1925.

We CANNOT fail to note the fact that China had no unified and good communication system, which prevented the enemy from carrying out concentrated and swift attacks on the liberation forces. India is different in this respect from China, in that it has a comparatively more unified, well-organized and far-flung system of communications.

India has a far bigger working class than China had during her march to freedom.

Further, we cannot fail to note the fact that the Chinese Red Army was surrounded and threatened with annihilation again and again until it reached Manchuria. There, with the industrial base in hand, and the great friendly Soviet Union in the rear, the Chinese Liberation Army, free from the possibility of any attack in the rear, rebuilt itself and launched the final offensive which led it to victory.

The geographical situation in India in this respect is altogether different.

Points of Similarity

This does not mean that there is nothing in common between us and China excepting the stage of our revolution and its main task. On the contrary, like China, India is of vast expanses. Like China, India has a vast peasant population. Our Revolution, therefore will have many features in common with the Chinese Revolution. But, peasant struggles along the Chinese path alone cannot lead to victory in India.

Moreover, we must bear in mind that the Chinese party stuck to the peasant partisan war alone, not out of a principle, but out of sheer necessity. In their long-drawn struggles, the party and the peasant bases got more and more separated from the working class and its organisations, which prevented the party and the Liberation Army from calling into action the working class in factories, shipping and transport to help it against the enemy.

Because it happened so with the Chinese, why make their necessity into a binding principle for us and fail to bring the working class into practical leadership and action in our liberation struggle?

SUCH AN OUTLOOK IGNORES THE FACT THAT WE HAVE A BIG WORKING CLASS AND THAT IT HAS A ROLE TO PLAY, WHICH CAN BE DECISIVE IN OUR STRUGGLE FOR FREEDOM. THE GRAND ALLIANCE OF THE WORKING CLASS AND THE PEASANTRY, ACTING IN UNISON, THE COMBINATION OF WORKERS' AND PEASANTS' STRUGGLES, UNDER THE LEADERSHIP OF THE COMMUNIST PARTY, AND UTILISING ALL LESSONS OF HISTORY FOR THE CONDUCT OF THE STRUGGLES IS TO BE THE PATH FOR US.

It can thus be seen that while the previous line of reliance on the general strike in the cities neglected the role of the peasantry, the subsequent one of partisan struggle minimised the role of the working class, which in practice meant depriving the peasantry of its greatest friend and leader. The working class remained leader only "in theory," only through the party, because the party is defined as the party of the working class.

Both the lines in practice meant ignoring the task of building the alliance of the working class and the peasantry, as the basis of the United National Front, ignoring the task of building the United National Front, ignoring the task of putting the working class at the head of this Front in the liberation struggle. . . .

The main question is not, whether there is to be armed struggle or not, the main question is not whether to be non-violent or violent. It is our opponents who pose for us the question whether our creed is violence or non-violence. Such a poser is a poser of Gandhian ideology, which in practice, misleads the masses and is a poser of which we must steer clear.

MARXISM AND HISTORY HAVE ONCE FOR ALL DECIDED THE QUESTION FOR THE PARTY AND THE PEOPLE OF EVERY COUNTRY IN THE WORLD LONG AGO. ALL ACTION OF THE MASSES IN DEFENCE OF THEIR INTERESTS TO ACHIEVE THEIR LIBERATION IS SACROSANCT. HISTORY SANCTIONS ALL THAT THE PEOPLE DECIDE TO DO TO CLEAR THE LUMBER-LOAD OF DECADENCE AND REACTION IN THEIR PATH TO PROGRESS AND FREEDOM. . . .

BUT IT WOULD BE GROSS EXAGGERATION TO SAY THAT THE COUNTRY IS ALREADY ON THE EVE OF ARMED INSURRECTION OR REVOLUTION, OR THAT CIVIL WAR IS ALREADY RAGING IN THE COUNTRY. IF WE WERE TO READ THE SITUATION SO WRONGLY, IT WOULD LEAD US INTO ADVENTURISM AND GIVING SLOGANS TO THE MASSES OUT OF KEEPING WITH THE DEGREE OF THEIR UNDERSTANDING AND CONSCIOUSNESS AND THEIR PREPAREDNESS AND THE GOVERNMENT'S ISOLATION. SUCH SLOGANS WOULD ISOLATE US FROM THE PEOPLE AND HAND OVER THE MASSES TO REFORMIST DISRUPTORS.

Equally wrong are they who see only the disunity of the popular forces, only the offensive of reaction and advocate a policy of retreat in the name of regrouping of forces, of eschewing all militant actions on the plea that this will invite repression. Tactics based on such an understanding of the situation will lead to betrayal of the masses and surrender before the enemy. . . .

We have to realise that although the masses are getting fast radicalised and moving into action in many parts of the country, the growth of the mass movement has not kept pace with the growth of discontent against the present government and its policies and methods. To ascribe this to repression alone would be wrong. This weakness of the mass movement, is due, above all, to the weakness of our party and the division in the camp of progressive forces.

The party, therefore, must strive to overcome this division and must stress the supreme need for unity of all progressive forces, build this unity in action and itself grow into a mass party by drawing into its fold the best elements from the fighting masses. . . .

Indonesian Communism

The Indonesian Communists, like the Indians, experienced a series of changes in leadership and tactics until the gradualist position prevailed with the assumption of leadership by D. N. Aidit in 1954. Aidit adopted the Chinese model and emphasized a multi-class nationalistic revolutionary movement in conjunction with strict Communist Party discipline.

a) Role of the Party and Doctrine

Stalin constantly taught us that if we want to be victorious in the revolution, we must have a revolutionary Party of the Lenin type, or as Comrade Mao Tse-tung has said, a Party of the Lenin-Stalin type. Without such a revolutionary Party, built according to revolutionary theory and in the Marx–Engels–Lenin–Stalin style, which is free from opportunism, it is not possible to lead the working class and the broad masses of the people to eliminate imperialism and its lackeys from Indonesian soil. In other words, if we want to be victorious in the revolution, if we want to change the physiognomy of society from a semi-colonial into a completely independent Indonesia, if we want to take part in changing the physiognomy of the world, we must have a Party of the model of the Communist Party of the Soviet Union and of the model of the Communist Party of China.

FROM: Aidit, *The Road to People's Democracy for Indonesia* (Report to the Fifth National Congress of the Communist Party of Indonesia, March, 1954; English edition, Jakarta, Pembaruan, 1955, pp. 50-51).

Without the theory of Marxism-Leninism it is not possible to have such a Party. The Party can only play a leading role if it is led by advanced theory. Only a Party which has mastered the theory of Marxism-Leninism can be relied on to be the vanguard of and lead the working class and other masses of the people. In order that our Party should be capable of fully shouldering its great and heavy historic burden, and in order to be capable of leading the Indonesian people from one victory to another, it must first of all create Marxist-Leninist ideological unity within its own ranks, raise the Marxist-Leninist ideological level of the entire Party and consolidate the correct Marxist-Leninist leadership. . . .

Our Party will only be able to fulfil its great and heavy historic task if it carries out an incessant and merciless struggle against both the right and "left" opportunists within its own ranks, if the Party continuously purges itself of capitulators and traitors within its own ranks and if it constantly preserves unity and discipline within its own ranks. . . .

Indonesia is a petty bourgeois country, that is, a country in which small-scale enterprise is still very widespread, especially individual peasant undertakings which are not sufficiently productive. Our Party is surrounded by this very large petty bourgeois class and many members of our Party come from this class, and it is unavoidable that those of them who enter our Party bring with them, to a greater or lesser extent, the thoughts and habits of the petty bourgeoisie. It is this petty bourgeoisie which is the social basis of two kinds of subjectivist diseases in our Party: dogmatism and empiricism. These two kinds of subjectivism have been the ideological basis of those people guilty of right and "left" opportunism in the Party in the past. . . .

b) *Stages of the Indonesian Revolution*

The C[ommunist] P[arty of] I[ndonesia] Programme states that the task of the Indonesian revolution is to create a people's government which "*will carry out not only socialist*

FROM: Aidit, *Indonesian Society and the Indonesian Revolution* (English edition, Jakarta, Pembaruan, 1958, pp. 52-53, 64-65, 68-69).

changes but also democratic changes. It will be a government which is capable of uniting all anti-imperialist and anti-feudal forces, which will be capable of giving land free of charge to the peasants, which will be capable of guaranteeing democratic rights for the people; a government which will be capable of protecting national industry and commerce against foreign competition, which will be capable of raising the material living standards of the workers and of abolishing unemployment. In brief, it will be a people's government which is capable of guaranteeing national independence and its development through the path of democracy and progress."

It is clear that the most important tasks are to fight against two enemies, that is, to carry out the national revolution to overthrow the forces of imperialism, the enemy from without, and to carry out the democratic revolution to overthrow the forces of the feudal landlords at home. Of these two important tasks, the principal one is the national revolution to overthrow imperialism. . . .

On the Nature of the Indonesian Revolution the C.P.I. Programme has the following to say, among other things: "*Bearing in mind the backwardness of the economy of our country, the C.P.I. is of the opinion that this government (the People's Democratic government) is not a government of the dictatorship of the proletariat but a government of the dictatorship of the people. This government does not have to carry out socialist changes but democratic changes.*" In other words, the character of the Indonesian revolution at the present stage is not a proletarian-socialist revolution but a bourgeois democratic revolution.

We can determine the character of our revolution after we understand the specific conditions of Indonesian society which is still semi-colonial and semi-feudal, after knowing that the enemies of the Indonesian revolution at the present time are imperialism and the feudal forces, that the tasks of the Indonesian revolution are to complete the national revolution and the democratic revolution so as to overthrow the two basic enemies (imperialism and feudalism), that the national bourgeoisie can also take part in this revolution and that if the big bourgeoisie betray the revolution and become an enemy of the revolution, the direct blows of the revolution must continue to be aimed more at imperialism and feudalism than at capitalism and private ownership of the national capitalists in general.

But the Indonesian bourgeois-democratic revolution of today is no longer general in character, is no longer of the old, out-dated type, but is something special, a new type. This new-type bourgeois-democratic revolution is also called the new democratic revolution or the revolution of people's democracy. It is a part of the world proletarian revolution which firmly opposes imperialism, that is, international capitalism. In the present era it is no longer possible to have a bourgeois democratic revolution that does not harm the interests of the international capitalists and that does not benefit the world proletarian revolution which was begun with the Great October Russian Socialist Revolution of 1917. . . .

If we know that the perspective of the Indonesian revolution is socialism and communism, the task of our party at the present stage of the revolution and in the future becomes clear. Our party has a dual task in leading the Indonesian revolution. Firstly, under the slogan, "Fulfill the demands of the August Revolution* in their entirety," we carry out to their completion the tasks of the bourgeois-democratic revolution; secondly, after the first task has been carried out, we carry out to their completion the tasks of the revolution which is proletarian-socialist in nature. This is, in total, the task of the Indonesian revolution. Every member of the C.P.I. must be ready to carry out this complete task of the revolution and must unswervingly continue without stopping half-way. The Indonesian revolutionary movement led by the C.P.I. is not a half-hearted revolutionary movement but a complete revolutionary movement and that is why it embraces two revolutionary processes which differ in character but which are linked up with each other. The first stage is the preparation necessary for the second stage, and the second stage is impossible until the first stage has been completed.

In order to carry out these great and difficult yet glorious

* I.e., the nationalist independence movement launched in August, 1945—Ed.